Schweiz
DEUTSCHLAND
Rhein
Schaffhausen
Bodensee
Basel
Winterthur
Baden
Zürich
St. Gallen
Zürichsee
Aare
Solothurn
Biel
Bieler See
ÖSTERREICH
Vaduz
LIECHTENSTEIN
Walensee
Neuchâtel
Luzern
Schwyz
FRANKREICH
Lac de Neuchâtel
Bern
Vierwaldstätter See
Chur
Davos
Inn
Yverdon-les-Bains
Fribourg
Thun
Brienzer See
Rhein
Thuner See
Interlaken
N
Jungfrau 4,158 m
St. Gotthard-Tunnel
E
St. Moritz
Genfer See
Lausanne
P
Montreux
L
Rhône
Simplonpass
Genf
A
Locarno
Zermatt
Lago Maggiore
Lugano
Lago di Lugano
Matterhorn 4,478 m
Mont Blanc 4,807 m
ITALIEN
0 25 50 75 km
0 25 50 mi
DEUTSCHLAND
LIECHTENSTEIN
ÖSTERREICH
SCHWEIZ
Österreich
TSCHECHISCHE REPUBLIK
Donau
SLOWAKEI
NIEDERÖSTERREICH
Schärding
Krems
Donau
WIENERWALD
Linz
St. Pölten
Wien
Inn
Braunau
Melk
OBERÖSTERREICH
WIEN
Leitha
Steyr
Eisenstadt
DEUTSCHLAND
Wiener Neustadt
Neusiedler See
Salzburg
Bodensee
St. Wolfgang
Bad Ischl
Wolfgangsee
Bregenz
Kitzbühel
Enns
SCHWEIZ
Dornbirn
Zugspitze 2,963 m
Inn
Zell am See
SALZBURG
Dachstein 2,995 m
Leoben
Innsbruck
Salzach
Mur
STEIERMARK
Vaduz
VORARLBERG
Badgastein
L
P
E
BURGENLAND
TIROL
A
N
Graz
UNGARN
Großglockner 3,798 m
Tauern-Tunnel
Brenner-Paß
Gurk
TIROL
Lienz
Spittal
KÄRNTEN
Wolfsberg
LIECHTENSTEIN
Drau
Wörther See
Klagenfurt
Villach
Drau
Mur
ITALIEN
SLOWENIEN
0 50 100 km
0 25 50 mi
KROATIEN

VORSPRUNG

Updated Edition

An Introduction to the German Language and Culture for Communication

Thomas A. Lovik
Michigan State University

J. Douglas Guy
Beverly High School

Monika Chavez
University of Wisconsin, Madison

Houghton Mifflin Company
Boston New York

Director, World Languages: New Media and Modern Language Publishing: Beth Kramer
Development Editor: Angela Schoenherr
Associate Project Editor: Elisabeth Kehrer
Senior Production/Design Coordinator: Carol Merrigan
Senior Manufacturing Coordinator: Jane Spelman
Marketing Manager: Annamarie Rice

Cover Image: *Green Town* by Friedensreich Hundertwasser. Courtesy Landau Fine Art, Inc.

Printed in the U.S.A.

Library of Congress Control Number: 96-76927

Student's Edition ISBN: 0-618-14249-5

Instructor's Annotated Edition ISBN: 0-618-14250-9

3 4 5 6 7 8 9-DOW-05 04 03

Contents

■ KAPITEL VIER ■ Unterwegs 124 ■

■ KAPITEL FÜNF ■ Freundschaften 172 ■

■ KAPITEL SECHS ■ Willkommen in Tübingen 214 ■

■ KAPITEL SIEBEN ■ Man kann alles in der Stadt finden 264 ■

■ KAPITEL ELF ■ Geschichte und Geographie 468 ■

■ KAPITEL ZWÖLF ■ Das neue Europa 520 ■

Reference Section

Preface

Vorsprung is a complete first-year program designed for beginning students of German. It offers a communicative introduction to the German language and culture and provides beginning German students with the necessary skills for successful communication in today's rapidly changing world by exposing them to a wealth of spoken and written authentic textual materials. ***Vorsprung*** combines a focus on spoken and written texts with interactive, in-class activities that foster accuracy in the language and that give students ample opportunity to practice realistic German in authentic contexts.

Chapter organization

The Student Text is divided into twelve chapters, each focusing on a different aspect of German culture. Each chapter is divided into three main parts, which are organized around a spoken or written text (chapters 1 and 11 deviate slightly from this format). Extensive pre- and post-listening or reading work is provided. In addition, important structural and lexical aspects of German are systematically explored in the first two parts of each chapter.

Chapter opener

Each chapter begins with a photo focusing on the cultural themes of the chapter. A statement of the chapter's communicative, structural, lexical, and cultural goals is included to provide students with an overview of what they can expect to learn in the chapter.

Anlauftext *(Warm-up text)*

The first part of each chapter begins with the **Anlauftext,** an audio text in dialogue form, which can also be found recorded on the audio program. The **Anlauftext** section presents new grammatical structures and important vocabulary in context, as well as the cultural theme of the chapter. Chapter 1 has two **Anlauftext** sections.

Vorschau *(Preview activities).* The **Anlauftext** section begins with the **Vorschau** activities, pre-listening activities that function as advance organizers. There are a variety of activities used for pre-listening. The **Thematische Fragen** *(Thematic questions)* help students activate prior knowledge of themes, vocabulary, and structures before listening to the **Anlauftext.** The **Wortdetektiv** or **Satzdetektiv** activities *(Word- or sentence-detective activities)* help students focus on synonyms and build their active vocabulary base. Other predictive activities help students establish context before listening to the text. The **Vorschau** section further promotes awareness of the culture of German-speaking countries and highlights cross-cultural contrasts.

Anlauftext. The **Anlauftext** is recorded on the audio program and is represented by a storyboard in the textbook. To aid comprehension, students can listen to the **Anlauftext,** while following the visual cues of the storyboard in their texts. The storyboards are a unique feature of ***Vorsprung.*** In the **Anlauftexte,** students meet Anna Adler, an American studying for a year in Germany, along with Anna's German relatives, the Günthers, and her new friends at the university in Tübingen. All these frame the story line and unify the contents of chapters 1–12.

Rückblick *(Postviewing).* The activities in the **Rückblick** section guide students from initial comprehension of the text to personalization of the topics in the text. The **Stimmt das?** *(True or false?)* activity, the first activity in the section, provides a quick check of the content to determine how much of the text students understood. The second activity, **Ergänzen Sie** *(Fill-ins),* requires students to focus on new vocabulary in the context of the text. The third activity, **Kurz gefragt** *(Short-answer questions),* guides students to produce more complete statements about the text. Further activities encourage students to use the **Anlauftext** as a jumping-off point for giving more personal reactions to the text.

Strukturen und Vokabeln (Structures and vocabulary)

These sections appear after the **Rückblick** in the **Anlauftext** and **Absprungtext** sections. They are each organized around a selection of important language functions, such as describing yourself, asking for information, or expressing likes and dislikes. Each language function is identified with a roman numeral.

The grammar structures needed to perform each language function are clearly and concisely explained in English. Numerous easy-to-interpret charts and tables aid comprehension. In addition, the vocabulary needed to fulfill the language function is presented in sections called **Wissenswerte Vokabeln** *(Vocabulary worth knowing).* Groups of thematically related words and phrases are presented in a richly illustrated format. This contextual approach to vocabulary presentation coincides with the functional and thematic approach of the book. A wide variety of productive and receptive activities are interspersed throughout the **Strukturen und Vokabeln** sections to aid in language development.

Absprungtext (Take-off text)

The second section of each chapter revolves around the **Absprungtext,** an authentic written text produced originally for native speakers of German. (Note that there is no **Absprungtext** in Chapter 1 while there are two **Absprungtexte** in Chapter 11.) The **Absprungtext** section parallels the format of the **Anlauftext** section by beginning with pre-reading activities in a **Vorschau** section. Many of the same activity types are used here to activate prior knowledge and to prepare students for reading and understanding the text. The **Absprungtext** itself is reproduced in as authentic a format as possible. Text types offered in this section include advertisements, brochures, newspaper and magazine articles, letters, short stories, time lines, and fairy tales. All text types relate directly to the chapter theme and to the continuing story presented in the **Anlauftext** sections, and were selected for their high frequency of occurrence and usefulness to students.

The **Absprungtext** is followed by post-reading activities featured in a **Rückblick** section, which is very similar to the **Rückblick** section that follows the **Anlauftext.**

The **Absprungtext** section ends with another **Strukturen und Vokabeln** section, which parallels the **Strukturen und Vokabeln** section at the end of the **Anlauftext.** Additional high-frequency language functions and the grammar and vocabulary to perform them are also presented and practiced.

Zieltext (Target text)

The third and final part of the chapter centers on the **Zieltext,** a listening text recorded on the audio program. As its name implies, the **Zieltext** is the culminating point of the chapter (there is no **Zieltext** for Chapter 1). **Vorschau** activities, much like those in the **Anlauftext** section, prepare students to listen to and understand the **Zieltext.** The **Zieltexte** themselves incorporate the structures and vocabulary of the chapter in a free-flowing dialogue spoken at normal speed by native speakers of German. While listening to the **Zieltexte** on the audio program, students can look at art-based cues in the Student Text, which help their listening comprehension. After listening to the **Zieltext,** students do follow-up activities in the **Rückblick** section that foster both comprehension and expansion skills. By understanding these audio texts and doing their accompanying activities, students will fulfill the communicative goals listed in the chapter opener.

Wortschatz (Vocabulary list)

Each chapter ends with a **Wortschatz** section that lists all the active words and expressions taught in the chapter. The vocabulary has been categorized by semantic fields, which facilitates acquisition of new vocabulary by encouraging students to associate words and word families.

Other features of the chapter

Brennpunkt Kultur *(Focus on culture)* These cultural notes appear throughout the chapter, as appropriate. Each note provides background information and insightful commentaries in English on themes encountered in the chapter. They are rich in descriptive detail and include additional thematic German vocabulary. The ***Vorsprung*** Website provides Web addresses for additional information about the cultural notes.

Sprache im Alltag *(Everyday language usage)* These short descriptions of variations in spoken German highlight useful vocabulary and expressions.

Freie Kommunikation *(Free communication)* These featured activities appear at regular intervals in the chapter, especially as the culminating activities for the **Strukturen und Vokabeln** sections. They guide students in role-play situations, in which they practice the communicative functions that have been introduced.

Schreibecke *(Writing activities)* These special unnumbered activities accompany the **Freie Kommunikation** activities throughout the chapter. They provide students with authentic tasks and the opportunity to practice their written skills in short, manageable writing assignments.

Activity icons With the exception of the **Freie Kommunikation** and the **Schreibecke** activities, all activities are numbered consecutively throughout the chapter. Each activity is preceded by one of three icons:

RECEPTIVE

PRODUCTIVE

INTERACTIVE

Receptive activities require students to recognize printed utterances. Productive activities require them to produce their own utterances. Interactive activities are productive activities that involve two or more students working together.

The Web icon at the beginning of each chapter directs students to the Web search activities to reinforce the vocabulary and grammar for each chapter in a culturally authentic context.

■ *Deutsch im Beruf (Career German)* ■

These special enrichment sections appear after chapters 3, 6, 9, and 12 in the text. They highlight the practical advantages of learning German for use in the modern working environment. The sections provide specific career-oriented information about German-speaking countries, as well as skill-based activities that will enhance students' positions in today's highly competitive job market.

■ *Supplementary materials for students* ■

Arbeitsbuch

The **Arbeitsbuch** is a three-part volume combining the Workbook, Laboratory Manual, and Video Workbook for the ***Vorsprung*** program. Each of the three components is coordinated with the ***Vorsprung*** text.

The Workbook provides additional practice on structures, vocabulary, reading comprehension, culture, and writing skills, all designed to expand upon the work in the Student Text. The Laboratory Manual is designed to be used in conjunction with the audio program. The activities focus on developing aural comprehension of spoken German. The audio texts reflect the themes, structures, and vocabulary encountered in the Student Text. The Video Workbook is coordinated with the video program, ***Unterwegs!*** These activities guide students through their viewing of the video and assist them with comprehension of the language and structures encountered in the video.

Audio program

The audio program complements the twelve chapters of ***Vorsprung.*** Each chapter of the audio program includes the **Anlauftexte, Absprungtexte** (when appropriate), and the **Zieltexte** from the textbook chapters, as well as supplementary listening and pronunciation activities found in the Laboratory Manual. The audio program is available for student purchase on audio CDs and cassettes, and can be listened to at home, in a car, or at school.

Unterwegs! *videocassette*

This exciting new video program was shot on location in Tübingen, Germany. It includes twelve five- to seven-minute episodes featuring a continuing story line and cast of characters. The video is thematically linked to the ***Vorsprung*** Student Text and focuses on the communicative functions and vocabulary taught in the text. The video is intended to be used in conjunction with the Video Workbook portion of the **Arbeitsbuch.**

Computer Study Modules

An interactive computer program for review, drill, and practice is available in both Windows® and Macintosh® formats. All activities are self-correcting. Units corresponding to each chapter in the Student Text include both *Flash* modules, for vocabulary practice, and *Foundations* modules, offering review of grammatical structures and contextualized reading and response.

Acknowledgments

Vorsprung grew out of the conviction that learning German can be both an enjoyable journey toward understanding German language and culture, and a valuable tool in today's changing world. We are deeply grateful to the numerous people over the years who have provided enthusiasm, encouragement, advice, moral and financial support, and humor. We owe special thanks to Margret Rettich for the generous use of her illustrations for the **Aschenputtel** fairy tale.

We are greatly indebted to many people at Houghton Mifflin Company, especially Isabel Campoy, Diane Gifford, Susan Mraz, and E. Kristina Baer, whose combined leadership and guidance helped bring this project to fruition.

We also wish to thank our editors: Barbara Lasoff, for her work on the earliest phases of manuscript development; Amy Davidson, Susan Winer-Slavin, and Katherine Gilbert for their able, amiable, and resourceful project management; Cynthia Hall Kouré, for yeoman's duty in the spiritual, emotional, and pedagogical development of the manuscript in its most critical phases and for psychological support of the author team; Hildegunde Kaurisch, for superb copyediting of the manuscript; Linda Hadley, for her sharp wit and good eye for photos, realia, and line art; Timothy C. Jones, for his enthusiasm and resourcefulness in producing outstanding storyboards and line art; Harriet C. Dishman and her associates at Elm Street Publications, for their ever-reliable and effective production management; the video team; the audio team; and many others.

The authors would also like to thank the following people who assisted in the creation of the ***Vorsprung*** program materials. For their assistance with the recorded improvisations, the authors would like to thank the following individuals:

At Michigan State University:

Thomas Achternkamp, Olaf Böhlke, Cornelia Hädrich, Karin Heinze-Evans, Anke and Georg Hofstätter, Volker Langeheine, Bettina O'Kulich, Annette Steigerwald, and Jan Tillmanns.

Elsewhere:

Max Coqui (Neu-Biberg), Katja Günther (Concord, Mass. and Frankfurt/M), Françoise Knaack (Keltern), Christine Müller (Luzern), Silvia Solf (Stuttgart), and Florian Will (Berlin).

For their assistance in the acquisition of materials, the authors would like to acknowledge the following people:

Susan Adams (Concord, Mass.), Robert Asch (Tufts in Tübingen), Gabrielle Beck (Hamburg), Karen Clausen (Hamburg), Thomas Conrad (Philadelphia), Gerda Grimm (Hoisdorf), Monica Hrabowy (East Lansing), Hans Ilmberger (Ahrensburg), Kenneth Munn (Jena), M.C. Roth (Tübingen), Margita and Hans Schulz (Georgetown, Mass.), John Seufert (Byfield, Mass.), Thomas Spranz-Fogasy (Heidelberg/Mannheim), Dieter and Ingrid Winter (Bad Krozingen), as well as the German Information Center (New York), the German National Tourist Office (New York), the Goethe Institut (Boston), Martin Vogel and Bettina Blumer (Braunwald/Switzerland), and numerous tourist offices throughout Austria, Germany, and Switzerland.

We would also like to thank the students at Michigan State University, Portsmouth (N.H.) High School, and Newburyport (Mass.) High School for their involvement during the class testing of ***Vorsprung;*** the Department of Linguistics and Germanic, Slavic, Asian, and African Languages at Michigan State University, especially Professor George Peters; the Department of German at the University of Wisconsin in Madison; and also Concord Academy, Governor Dummer Academy, Portsmouth High School, and Newburyport High School for institutional support.

We would also like to thank the following people who reviewed portions of the manuscript at various stages of development:

John Austin, Georgia State University, Atlanta, GA
Sharon Bailey, Michigan State University, Lansing, MI
Dorothy Chun, University of California, Santa Barbara, CA
Jeanette Clausen, Indiana University-Purdue University, Fort Wayne, IN
Ellen Crocker, Massachusetts Institute of Technology, Cambridge, MA
William Collins Donahue, Rutgers University, New Brunswick, NJ
Catherine Fraser, Indiana University, Bloomington, IN
Helen Frink, Keene State College, Keene, NH
Ilse Hoyle, National University, Inglewood, CA
Brian Lewis, University of Colorado, Boulder, CO
Gundhild Lischke, Cornell University, Ithaca, NY
Elke Matijevich, Collin County Community College, Spring Creek Campus, Plano, TX
Ursula McCune, Tufts University, Medford, MA
Stephen Newton, University of California, Berkeley, CA
Stephanie Pafenberg, Queen's University, Kingston, Ontario, Canada
John Pizer, Louisiana State University, Baton Rouge, LA
Terry Reisch, Hillsdale College, Hillsdale, MI
Veronica Richel, University of Vermont, Burlington, VT
Michael Schultz, New York University, New York, NY
Elizabeth Thibault, University of Delaware, Newark, DE
Janet Van Valkenburg, University of Michigan, Ann Arbor, MI
David Weible, University of Illinois, Chicago, IL

We are especially indebted to the following people, who offered advice and constructive suggestions for improvement through the many phases of development. Our program was greatly enriched by their contributions.

Phillip Campana, Tennessee Technological University, Cookeville, TN
Franziska Lys, Northwestern University, Evanston, IL
Gisela Moffit, Central Michigan University, Mount Pleasant, MI
Manfred Prokop, University of Alberta, Edmonton, Alberta, Canada

Finally, to our spouses and children—Mary, Julianna, William, Kathy, Jonathan, Nicolas, and Gabe—who endured the late night and early morning phone calls, the requests for undisturbed worktime on the weekends, and our mental and physical absence, we express our love and appreciation for their understanding and commitment.

Thomas A. Lovik
J. Douglas Guy
Monika Chavez

▪ *To the Student* ▪

Vorsprung is a communicative introduction to the German language and culture that fosters active use of the German language. The ***Vorsprung*** materials are designed to provide ample opportunity for you to practice realistic German in authentic contexts. While the program emphasizes all four language skills—listening, speaking, reading, and writing—it places a special emphasis on the development of good listening skills as a foundation for the other skills.

Did you know ... ?

- that when children learn their own language, they develop their listening skills first?
- that you spend about 40% of your time each day listening in your own language?
- that listening skills do not erode as quickly as speaking skills?
- that good listening skills can prove valuable in the development of speaking and writing skills?

What does this mean for learning German?

- During listening activities you should concentrate initially on comprehension without being too anxious about speaking. You will be asked to speak and write more German gradually, as your listening skills develop.
- Listen carefully to your instructor. He or she along with the audio and video recordings will be your primary models for good German.
- Listen carefully to other students in the class. You can learn a lot from them. Pay close attention to the words they use, their pronunciation, and their partner's comprehension and reaction to what they say.
- Listen carefully to what you are saying. This may seem difficult at first, but as time progresses it will become easier.

What else is important when learning German?

- **Learn to focus** on what you do understand and rely on your own intuition to guess at the meanings of words. Don't become discouraged by what you don't understand.
- **Have realistic expectations.** Real fluency in another language can take years of study and may seem slow at first; you may only be able to produce a word or two. However, by the end of Chapter 6, you can fully expect to be speaking in sentences about your family, your possessions, and your likes and dislikes. After two years of study you will find yourself quite comfortable conversing in German.
- **Be realistic** in your expectations of your pronunciation of German. Nobody expects you to have perfect pronunciation right away. With practice and time, your pronunciation will improve. Remember, communication is the goal of ***Vorsprung.***

- **Challenge yourself.** Try to express yourself in novel ways and go beyond using language that you have rehearsed extensively.
- **Develop good study skills.** Set aside enough time each day to listen to the recordings or read the texts several times until you are comfortable with them. Let the accompanying activities guide you through different levels of comprehension. Ask your instructor for help when things are unclear.
- **Assume responsibility** for your own learning. Prepare before you come to class. For example, you are expected to read the grammar explanations on your own. Class time should be used for learning experiences you cannot get on your own, especially for communication and interaction with other students, as well as hearing authentic spoken German. Make an effort to use German whenever you can and to learn to say everyday phrases in German. Try to acquire vocabulary that is relevant to your own communicative needs.
- **Study the models** in ***Vorsprung*** and be sure that you understand the structures and vocabulary used in them.
- **Know your learning style.** Develop an approach to working with the information provided in ***Vorsprung*** that suits your particular learning style or needs. Try to assess how you learn best, for example, through visualizing concepts or associating them with each other, through listening to recordings or hearing yourself formulate statements aloud, or perhaps through writing things down and underlining them. Do whatever you find helpful for learning German.
- **Develop a vocabulary strategy.** When learning new vocabulary, practice writing new words on note cards or identifying objects in your environment with stick-on tags. You may also find it helpful to record new vocabulary onto a cassette and play it back to yourself. Try to organize words into small, manageable groups organized thematically, by gender, or by ranking, for example. Continually test your knowledge of these new words. Avoid memorizing lists of words. Learn to associate new words with the visual or linguistic context provided in ***Vorsprung.***
- **Learn to use a dictionary,** but don't let your dictionary become a substitute for effective reading strategies. This can undermine your own ability to associate meanings with new words and may inhibit your acquisition of German.
- **Keep an open mind** to new information. Much of what you learn about the German language and culture may seem different and strange at first. Maintaining an openness to new things is an important goal of learning about another language and culture.
- **Expect to make lots of errors** as you learn German. However, you will also be expected to learn from your mistakes and to make fewer and fewer errors as you progress. When you do make mistakes in class, listen carefully to what your instructor says. It should be your model for fashioning your own speech.

The authors and your instructor want to congratulate you for deciding to learn German. You have made a very critical and valuable educational choice.

Viel Spaß!

In this chapter you will learn to introduce yourself, ask for and spell names, identify common classroom objects, and identify and describe classmates.

Kommunikative Funktionen

- Understanding commands and requests
- Making polite requests with **bitte**
- Describing yourself and others
- Asking for someone's name
- Asking for information and clarification
- Identifying people and classroom objects

Strukturen

- The imperative
- The word **bitte**
- Subject pronouns
- The verb **sein**
- The pronoun *you*
- The verb **heißen**
- Question formation (including **wie bitte?**)
- Noun gender
- The nominative case: definite and indefinite articles
- Negation with **nicht** and **kein**
- Subject of a sentence
- Predicate nominative
- Pronoun substitution

Vokabeln

- The alphabet
- Numbers
- Adjectives for personal description
- Classroom objects
- Colors
- Country names and nationalities

Kulturelles

- Greetings and farewells
- Titles of address
- Where German is spoken

Die Studenten machen eine Pause im Uni-Café.

KAPITEL EINS

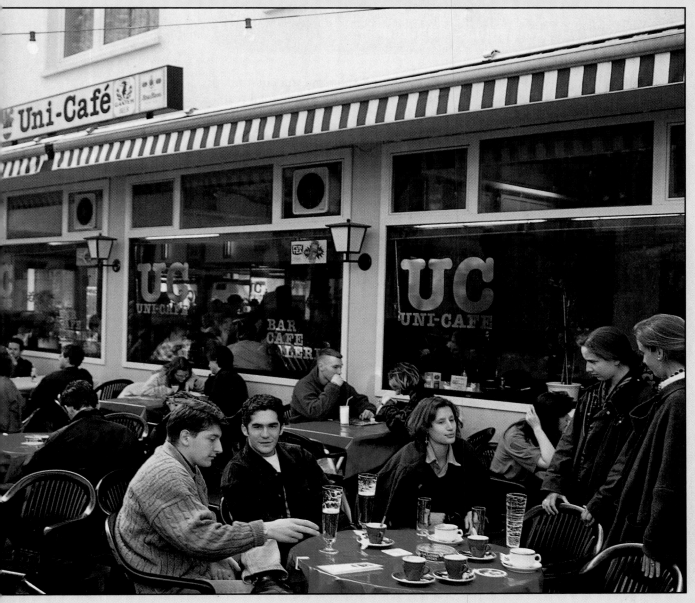

Fangen Sie bitte an.

Go to the ***Vorsprung*** Website at
www.hmco.com/college

ANLAUFTEXT I
Annas Albtraum°

nightmare

In the **Anlauftext** you are going to meet Anna Adler, an American student from Fort Wayne, Indiana, who is planning to study in Tübingen, Germany, for a year. Although excited about her year in Tübingen, Anna is also nervous and exhausted and falls asleep. In her dream, Anna works through her fears about being in a class in Germany and not being able to say what she wants.

This previewing section helps you establish the context of the text and understand important text vocabulary. Spend a few moments considering the questions you find here before you try to read the **Anlauftext.**

The icon for productive activities is [icon], and the one for receptive activities is [icon]. Interactive activities have the icon [icon]. Receptive activities require that students recognize a printed utterance. Productive activities require that students produce their own sentences. Interactive activities usually involve two or more students talking.

Vorschau°

Previewing activities

1 Deutschtest. *(German test.)* Find out how much German you already know. Match the following German and English words by drawing a line to connect the corresponding German and English equivalents.

Most German verbs in the infinitive (the equivalent of English *to + verb*, e.g., *to have*) end in **-en,** and all German nouns are capitalized while German verbs and adjectives use lower case letters.

Deutsch	*Englisch*
1. sprechen	a. to come
2. der Pass	b. German
3. kommen	c. to speak
4. Deutsch	d. the passport
5. Kanada	e. America
6. Deutschland	f. Germany
7. heißen	g. Canada
8. Amerika	h. to be called
9. haben	i. from *(a country)*
10. Willkommen!	j. car
11. aus	k. to have
12. Auto	l. Welcome!
13. fragen	m. to say
14. Mann	n. woman
15. Frau	o. to ask
16. sagen	p. man

2 **Thematische Fragen.** *(Topical questions.)* Discuss the following questions with your instructor or in pairs.

1. What feelings might you have if you were going to study abroad for a year in a German-speaking country? What things might excite you? What things might concern you?
2. How did you feel about coming to your first German class?

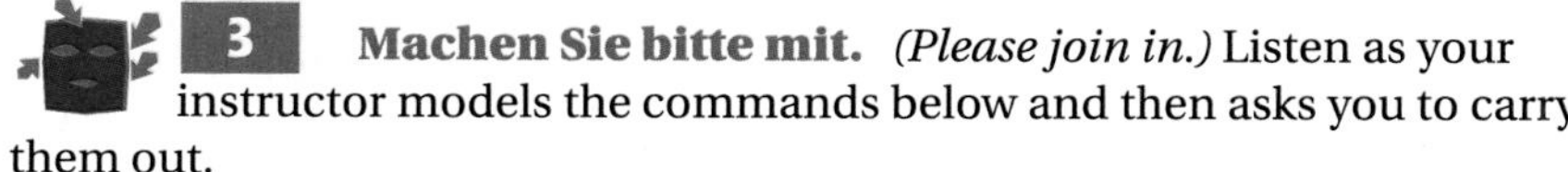

3 **Machen Sie bitte mit.** *(Please join in.)* Listen as your instructor models the commands below and then asks you to carry them out.

Stehen Sie auf.

Setzen Sie sich.

Drehen Sie sich um.

Gehen Sie an die Tafel.

Schreiben Sie.

Thematische Fragen. These questions are intended as a warm-up exercise before you read the German text. They activate ideas about the topic and prepare you for the reading. Starting in Chapter 4 these questions will be in German.

4 **Wortdetektiv.** *(Word detective.)* Which words convey approximately the same meaning? Draw a line from the German word to its logical English equivalent.

Deutsch	*Englisch*
1. grau	a. Excuse me!
2. Entschuldigung!	b. to ask
3. fragen	c. the dream
4. der Traum	d. nothing
5. nichts	e. gray
6. Gott sei Dank!	f. to seek, to look for
7. der Hörsaal	g. quickly
8. unpersönlich	h. the lecture hall
9. schnell	i. Thank God!
10. suchen	j. impersonal

Wortdetektiv. Intuition can be useful when it comes to deciphering new German words. You don't need to understand every word to get the gist of a text. Look for words that may be similar to English.

Annas Albtraum (p. 4). Study the pictures first, then listen to the text. You should not be reading along the first time you hear the text.

ANLAUFTEXT I

Now listen to the recording.

Annas Albtraum

Die Studentin sagt nichts.

Anna findet Hörsaal 20 und öffnet die Tür.

Aber die Tür knallt zu. Alle drehen sich um.

Rückblick°

Follow-up activities

Rückblick. This section guides you from understanding parts of the text to producing language based on the text.

Stimmt das? Do this exercise after reading the **Anlauftext** once to determine how much you understood.

5 **Stimmt das?** *(Is that correct?)* How much of the text can you remember without looking back at it? Look over the statements and mark the true statements as **Ja, das stimmt.** Mark the false statements as **Nein, das stimmt nicht.** Then, listen as your instructor reads the following statements and models their pronunciation. If the statement is true, say **Ja, das stimmt.** If the statement is not true, say **Nein, das stimmt nicht.**

	Ja, das stimmt.	*Nein, das stimmt nicht.*
1. Anna hat einen Albtraum.	___	___
2. Die Universität ist groß, grau und unpersönlich.	___	___

	Ja, das stimmt.	*Nein, das stimmt nicht.*
3. Anna fragt eine Studentin: „Bin ich hier richtig?"	—	—
4. Die Studentin sagt: „Ja."	—	—
5. Anna findet den Hörsaal und öffnet die Tür.	—	—
6. Die Studenten sagen: „Hallo, Anna! Willkommen in Tübingen!"	—	—
7. Der Professor fragt: „Was suchen Sie?"	—	—
8. Anna ist nervös und sagt nichts.	—	—
9. Der Professor fragt Anna: „Wie heißen Sie? Wie heißen Sie?"	—	—
10. Annas Mutter sagt: „Anna! Anna! Anna! Wach auf!"	—	—

6 **Ergänzen Sie.** *(Complete these sentences.)* Complete these questions and statements with words from the **Anlauftext.** Look back at the text as often as you would like to read the sentences and see the words in context.

1. Anna hat einen ____.
2. Da ist die ____ in Tübingen: ____ , grau und ____.
3. Der Professor sagt: „ ____ Sie sich! Aber schnell!"
4. Der Professor fragt: „Wie ____ Sie?"
5. Der Professor fragt: „ ____ Sie das nicht? Wie heißen Sie?"
6. Der Professor sagt: „ ____ Sie an die Tafel!"
7. Annas Mutter sagt: „Anna! Anna! Anna! ____ ____!"

7 **Kurz gefragt.** *(Brief questions.)* Now try using what you have already learned to answer some simple German questions about Anna's dream. The two question words that recur frequently are **wer** *(who)* and **was** *(what).* Try to be as complete in your answers as you can, but just a word or two may be enough.

1. Was sucht Anna?
2. Wer sagt: „Bin ich hier richtig?"
3. Was sagt die Studentin?
4. Wer sagt: „Setzen Sie sich!"?
5. Was fragt der Professor?
6. Wer sagt: „Anna! Anna! Anna! Wach auf!"?

„Heißen Sie zufällig° Ute?"

° *by chance*

Strukturen und Vokabeln

Strukturen und Vokabeln. This section guides you through many important features of German grammar necessary for communication. Annotations tell you which structures you are expected to produce and which ones you are expected to recognize only.

See the **Arbeitsbuch** for additional practice with structures and vocabulary.

I Understanding commands and requests

The imperative

A. Formation of the formal imperative

The infinitive **(der Infinitiv),** the basic form of all German verbs, consists of a stem plus either the ending **-n** or **-en.** The infinitive is the form listed in dictionaries and in the glossary at the end of this book.

Stem	+	Ending		Infinitive
geh	+	**en**	=	**gehen** *to go*
wander	+	**n**	=	**wandern** *to hike*

A formal command uses the infinitive form of the verb **(das Verb).** The formal imperative **(der Imperativ)** is formed by placing the infinitive at the beginning of the sentence followed by the pronoun **Sie** *(you).*

Schreiben Sie. *Write.*
Gehen Sie an die Tafel. ***Go** to the blackboard.*

The formal imperative for the verb **sein** *(to be)* is **seien.**

Seien Sie still. ***Be** quiet.*

In German, commands are sometimes written with an exclamation point **(!).** Speakers usually lower their pitch at the end of a command. The word **nicht** *(not)* is used to make a command negative. You will learn more about the position of **nicht** in Chapter 2.

Schreiben Sie **nicht!** *Don't write!*

Wissenswerte Vokabeln: Aktivitäten im Klassenzimmer

Understanding your instructor's requests

Stehen Sie still. Laufen Sie. Lachen Sie.

Machen Sie das Buch auf. Machen Sie das Buch zu. Lesen Sie das Buch.

B. The word bitte

The word **bitte** *(please)* softens commands and makes them into requests. **Bitte** can appear at the beginning, in the middle, or at the end of a request.

Bitte, gehen Sie an die Tafel.
Gehen Sie **bitte** an die Tafel.
Gehen Sie an die Tafel, **bitte.**

8 Bitte, stehen Sie auf. Listen as your instructor gives the following requests. You should only carry out requests given with **bitte.**

(Bitte) stehen Sie auf.

1. (Bitte) sagen Sie „Guten Tag".
2. (Bitte) setzen Sie sich (bitte).
3. (Bitte) gehen Sie (bitte) an die Tafel.
4. (Bitte) öffnen Sie die Tür.

ANLAUFTEXT II

Annas Traum°

dream

Now that she's awake, Anna realizes her fears were just a bad dream and that things in Tübingen will probably be a lot better. Her own experience learning German has actually been very good. In her daydream here, she knows that she will be able to say a lot in German, and she imagines how it will be studying in Germany and using the German language.

Vorschau

9 **Annas Albtraum.** Your instructor will read each question. Answer with a word or two in German.

1. Wer hat einen Albtraum?
2. Wo ist die Universität im Traum?
3. Ist die Universität persönlich° oder unpersönlich?
4. Was öffnet Anna?
5. Was fragt der Professor?
6. Was sagt Annas Mutter?

intimate

10 **Thematische Fragen.** Discuss the following questions with your instructor or in pairs.

1. What was causing Anna anxiety in her nightmare?
2. Now that she is awake, what kind of positive daydream images might she have concerning:
   a. studying German in the future?
   b. the professors and instructors she might have?
   c. the students in her classes?
   d. her own skill in understanding and speaking German?

11 **Wortmosaik.** *(Brainstorming words.)* Without looking at the **Anlauftext,** say as many German words and phrases as you remember that relate to **die Universität/der Hörsaal.**

12 **Wortdetektiv.** Which words convey approximately the same meaning? Draw a line from the German word to its logical English equivalent.

Wortdetektiv. Use your intuition to guide your choices. Look for similar patterns in the words, e.g., **freundlich** looks like *friendly.*

Deutsch	*Englisch*
1. hereinkommen	a. to answer
2. antworten	b. right
3. freundlich	c. to come in
4. richtig	d. in front
5. vorne	e. friendly
6. schön	f. to have a seat
7. hineingehen	g. to greet
8. Platz nehmen	h. beautiful
9. begrüßen	i. to walk in

ANLAUFTEXT II

Now listen to the recording.

Annas Traum

Anna sucht den Hörsaal und fragt eine Professorin:
Ich suche Hörsaal 20. Bin ich hier richtig?
Da ist die Universität in Tübingen: romantisch, historisch, schön.

Ja, Sie sind hier richtig. Hörsaal 20 ist gleich da vorne.

Die Professorin ist sehr freundlich und antwortet:

Anna öffnet die Tür und geht hinein.

Guten Morgen! Kommen Sie 'rein und nehmen Sie Platz. Setzen Sie sich, hier vorne.

Der Professor begrüßt Anna.

Annas Traum. Anna has some trouble understanding the professor because he speaks with an accent typical of the dialect in the Tübingen area. This dialect is called Swabian **(Schwäbisch).**

Rückblick

13 **Stimmt das?** How much of the text can you remember without looking back at it? Look over the statements and mark the true statements as **Ja, das stimmt.** Mark the false statements as **Nein, das stimmt nicht.** Then, listen as your instructor reads the following statements and models their pronunciation. If the statement is true, say **Ja, das stimmt.** If the statement is not true, say **Nein, das stimmt nicht.**

	Ja, das stimmt.	*Nein, das stimmt nicht.*
1. Die Universität Tübingen ist historisch.	___	___
2. Anna ist nervös. Anna kann nicht sprechen.	___	___
3. Anna fragt eine Professorin: „Bin ich hier richtig?“	___	___
4. Die Professorin antwortet: „Nein, Sie sind hier nicht richtig.“	___	___
5. Der Professor heißt Professor Fachmann.	___	___
6. Er fragt Anna: „Wie heißen Sie?“	___	___
7. Anna versteht nicht und sagt: „Entschuldigung.“	___	___
8. Der Professor fragt : „Wie heißen Sie? Wie ist Ihr Name?“	___	___
9. Anna antwortet: „Ich heiße Anna Adler.“	___	___
10. Anna sagt, sie kommt aus den USA.	___	___
11. Der Professor sagt: „Sie sprechen gut Japanisch!“	___	___

14 **Ergänzen Sie.** Complete these questions and statements with words from the **Absprungtext.** Look back at the text as often as you would like to read the sentences and see the words in context.

1. Da ist die Universität in Tübingen: historisch und ______.
2. Anna fragt eine ______.
3. Anna öffnet die ______.
4. Der Professor fragt: „Wie heißen ______?“
5. Anna versteht nicht und sagt: „Wie ______?“
6. Dann antwortet Anna: „Ich ______ Anna Adler.“
7. Der Professor fragt: „ ______ kommen Sie, Frau Adler?“
8. Anna antwortet: „Ich komme ______ Fort Wayne.“
9. Der Professor sagt: „Ach, sind Sie ______?“
10. Der Professor sagt: „Sie ______ sehr gut Deutsch.“
11. Anna sagt: „ ______ schön!“

15 **Kurz gefragt.** Now try using what you have already learned to answer some simple German questions about Anna's daydream. Try to be as complete as you can, but just a word or two may be enough.

1. Wie ist die Universität in Tübingen?
2. Wie ist die Professorin?
3. Was fragt der Professor?
4. Woher kommt Anna?
5. Wie spricht Anna Deutsch?

16 **Das bin ich.** Tell a partner three things about yourself using Anna's statements about herself as your model.

Ich bin | *Amerikaner(in).*
Student(in).
freundlich.
groß.

1. Ich bin ...
2. Ich heiße ...
3. Ich komme aus ...
4. Ich spreche ...

Das bin ich. Be careful to say only what you know how to say. Try to strike a balance between what you have already learned to say, and what you would like to express in the new language.

BRENNPUNKT KULTUR

Greetings and farewells

Greetings such as **Guten Morgen!** and **Guten Tag!** are used to initiate conversations and to acknowledge other people, even if just in passing. In the German-speaking countries people shake hands more often when they greet than in North America. Greetings differ according to geographic areas, time of day, and the social relationship of the people.

German has no single equivalent for the English greeting *hello!* Instead, German speakers use three different expressions depending on the time of day:

Guten Morgen!	*Good morning!*	Until about 11 A.M.
Guten Tag!	*Good day!*	From about 11 A.M. until sundown
Guten Abend!	*Good evening!*	After sundown

Speakers frequently shorten these greetings to **Morgen!, Tag!, Abend!** From approximately 11 A.M. through lunch time, co-workers sometimes greet each other in passing with **Mahlzeit!** (*Have a nice meal!*).

In addition to these general greetings, many others are regionally unique. Austrians and Bavarians say **Servus!** with their friends and **Grüß Gott!** generally, instead of **Guten Tag!** The Swiss, particularly those in the region of Zurich (**Zürich**), greet everybody with **Grüezi!**

Because of the growing influence of English throughout German-speaking countries, it is now quite common to hear **Hallo!** used as a friendly, neutral greeting by younger and middle-aged speakers.

To say good-bye, speakers use several different expressions, all meaning good-bye. **Tschüss** is more informal, although variations of it are heard by most speakers throughout Germany, Switzerland, and Austria.

Auf Wiedersehen! *Good-bye!*
Tschüss! *Bye!*
Gute Nacht! *Good night!*

Caution: Certain regional greetings sound out of place when used in a different part of the country, e.g., the southern **Grüß Gott** used in northern Germany. If you don't know the appropriate regional greeting, use a non-regional, time-specific greeting like **Guten Tag.**

Grüß Gott, Frau Hillgruber.

17 **Guten Morgen.** *(Good morning.)* Practice the following dialogues with a partner until you feel confident enough to perform one from memory for the class.

1. PROFESSOR KÜHLMANN: Guten Tag, meine Damen° und Herren°.
   STUDENTEN: Tag, Professor Kühlmann.
2. MUTTER: Morgen, Ulla. Kaffee?
   ULLA: Morgen, Mutter. Ja, bitte.
3. HERR LANGE *(in München)*: Grüß Gott.
   FRAU HILLGRUBER: Grüß Gott, Herr Lange.

ladies / gentlemen

18 **Grüß Gott.** Select an appropriate greeting based on the time of day, the region, and the person you are to greet. More than one answer may be possible.

Stuttgart

Berlin

Salzburg Innsbruck

Zürich

■ Strukturen und Vokabeln ■

II ▣ Describing yourself and others

See the **Arbeitsbuch** for additional practice with structures and vocabulary.

A. The verb sein; *subject pronouns*

A simple way to describe yourself or another person is to use a form of the verb **sein** *(to be).*

The verb *sein.* Sein is an infinitive.

Ich bin Amerikanerin. ***I am*** *(an) American.*
Sie sind freundlich. ***You are*** *friendly.*

In the examples above, the words **ich** and **Sie** are called subject pronouns. They refer to individual people or objects (singular pronouns) or groups of people or things (plural pronouns). Here are the present tense forms of **sein.**

		sein: *to be*		
Person	**Singular**		**Plural**	
1st	ich **bin**	*I am*	wir **sind**	*we are*
2nd, informal	du **bist**	*you are*	ihr **seid**	*you are*
2nd, formal	Sie **sind** (formal)	*you are*	Sie **sind** (formal)	*you are*
3rd	er/sie/es **ist**	*he/she/it is*	sie **sind**	*they are*

Ich bin Georg.
Sie sind Anna Adler, richtig?
Wir sind Studenten.
020
Du bist groß!
Er ist freundlich.
Sie ist freundlich.
Ihr seid hier richtig.
Sie sind freundlich.

19 **Kurze Gespräche.** *(Short conversations.)* Fill in the blanks with the correct form of the verb **sein.** With a partner, practice reading the dialogues.

1. ***Im Deutschunterricht°*** — *In German class*

DOKTOR LANGE: Guten Abend. Ich ______ Doktor Lange. Wer ______ Sie?
HERR ADJEMIAN: Ich ______ Herr Adjemian.
DOKTOR LANGE: ______ Sie Frau Nakasone?
FRAU TANAKA: Nein, ich ______ Frau Tanaka. Sie ______ Frau Nakasone.

2. ***An der Universität°*** — *At the university*

INGRID: ______ der Hörsaal da vorne?
KARL: Ja, da ______ er.
INGRID: Und der Professor?
KARL: Er ______ auch schon da.

3. ***Vor dem Hörsaal°*** — *In front of the lecture hall*

ANNA: Pardon, ______ ihr Studenten hier?
KARL UND ULI: Ja, wir ______ beide Studenten.
ANNA: ______ hier Hörsaal 20?
KARL UND ULI: Ja, gleich da vorne.

B. The pronoun *you*

The German language has three different words for *you*. **Du** is used when speaking to a friend, a family member, a child, a pet, or when praying to God.

Students, longtime colleagues, workers, and soldiers of equal rank typically also use **du** with each other.

Bist **du** Studentin? *Are you a student?*

The pronoun **ihr** is the plural form of **du.** Students, for example, use **ihr** when addressing more than one friend.

Ihr seid hier richtig. *You (guys) are in the right place.*

Sie is used with one or more adults when the speaker wants to show respect for them or does not know them well. When students are in about the eleventh grade, teachers begin to address them with **Sie.**

Wie heißen **Sie?** *What is your name?*

You will use the **Sie**-form exclusively in the early chapters. Using **du** instead of **Sie** may be considered offensive by an unfamiliar person. If you are unsure which form to use, it is always safest to use **Sie** until the person to whom you are talking suggests that you use **du.**

It is considered inappropriate and disrespectful to address a stranger with **du.** Some people feel insulted when not addressed properly.

20 **Du, ihr oder Sie?** Decide whether Anna should use **du, ihr,** or **Sie** with the following people.

	du	*ihr*	*Sie*
1. the professor she asks for directions	___	___	___
2. the student she sits next to	___	___	___
3. her dog	___	___	___
4. Professor Freund	___	___	___
5. her mother	___	___	___
6. some friends in a pub	___	___	___

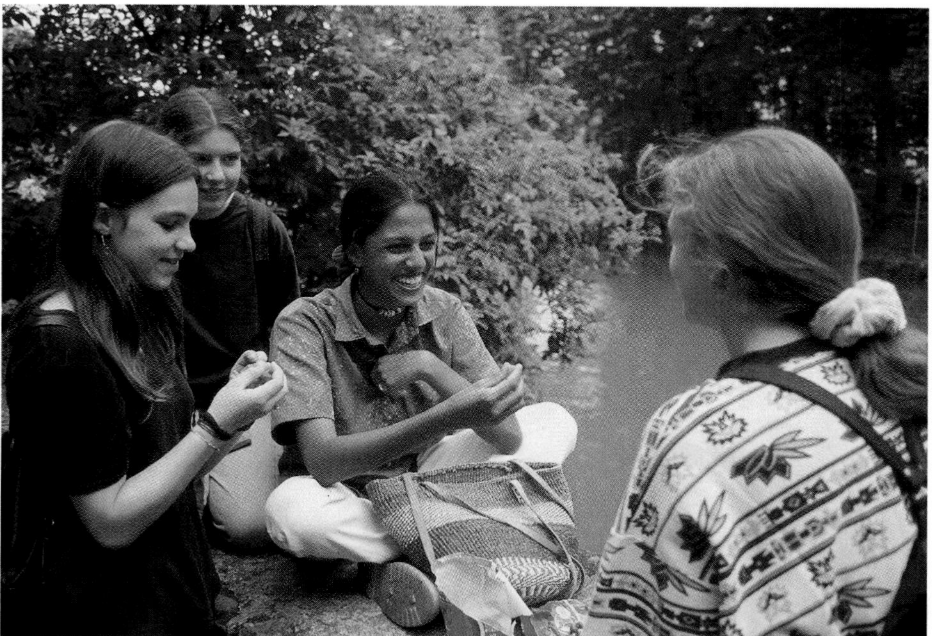

„du" oder „Sie"?

Titles of address

When addressing acquaintances, most German-speaking adults use a title before the person's last name. When talking to adults, it is better to err on the side of formality at first and use the title.

Herr *(for men):* **Herr Müller**	*Mr. Müller*
Frau *(for women):* **Frau Seifert**	*Mrs.* or *Ms. Seifert*
Fräulein *(for young girls):* **Fräulein Schmidt**	*Miss Schmidt*
Guten Morgen, Herr Müller.	*Good morning, Mr. Müller.*

Fräulein, when used with a last name, should not be used for adult women. It is outdated and carries negative connotations. In restaurants, **Frau Ober** is beginning to replace **Fräulein,** traditionally used to call the waitress.

In formal writing and speech and when talking about another person, German speakers also like to include the professional title of the person they are speaking with: **Guten Tag, Herr Professor Winkler.**

III Asking for someone's name

The verb **heißen**

Besides the verb **sein,** German speakers also use the verb **heißen** *(to be called)* to introduce themselves.

Ich **heiße** Barbara Müller.

These are the present tense forms of **heißen.**

	heißen: *to be called*			
Person	**Singular**		**Plural**	
1st	ich	heiße	wir	heißen
2nd, informal	du	heißt	ihr	heißt
2nd, formal	Sie	heißen	Sie	heißen
3rd	er/sie/es	heißt	sie	heißen

The verb *heißen.* Heißen is an infinitive.

The letter **ß** is used to represent the **s** sound after long vowels or diphthongs. The Swiss do not use **ß**, only **ss.**

21 **Wie heißen Sie?** You are at a formal reception. Go around and ask five students what their names are using the verb **heißen.** Below are some greetings and questions to help you. Try to remember the names of the students you meet so you can introduce them to the rest of the class.

S1: Guten Tag. Ich heiße Thomas Conrad. Wie heißen Sie?
S2: Ich heiße Clausen, Karen Clausen.
S1: Guten Tag, Frau Clausen. Sehr angenehm.
S2: Sehr angenehm, Herr Conrad.
S1 *(to S3):* Das ist Karen Clausen.

Guten Morgen. • Guten Tag. • Guten Abend. • Servus. • Grüezi.
Grüß Gott. • Hallo. • Wie heißen Sie? • Wer sind Sie? • Ich bin …

Wie heißen Sie? German speakers often give their family name, followed by their entire name when responding to the question **Wie heißen Sie?** or **Wer sind Sie?**

Wissenswerte Vokabeln: das Alphabet

Spelling names

a	ah	**h**	hah	**o**	oh	**u**	uh	**ß**	ess-tsett	**T**	großes „t“
b	beh	**i**	ih	**p**	peh	**v**	fau	**ä**	ah-Umlaut	**t**	kleines „t“
c	tseh	**j**	jot	**q**	kuh	**w**	weh	**ö**	oh-Umlaut	**tt**	Doppel „t“
d	deh	**k**	kah	**r**	err	**x**	iks	**ü**	uh-Umlaut		
e	eh	**l**	ell	**s**	ess	**y**	üppsilon				
f	eff	**m**	emm	**t**	teh	**z**	tsett				
g	geh	**n**	enn								

Wie schreiben Sie „Professor“? *P-r-o-f-e-ss-o-r.*
Wie schreiben Sie „Professorin“? *P-r-o-f-e-ss-o-r-i-n.*

22 **Das Alphabet.** Listen as your instructor models the sounds of the alphabet. Then repeat the sounds as instructed. Practice spelling the names of students in your class as well.

23 **Wie bitte?** *(Excuse me?)* You are working as a telemarketer in Vienna. Your job is to confirm the spelling of the names of people identified as winners of a trip to the United States of America. Choose a name from the telephone directory for Vienna and call that person to confirm the spelling of his/her name. Follow the model below.

Am Telefon

S1: Guten Morgen. Hier ist Herr (Frau) ______. Wie heißen Sie bitte?
S2: Jentschke.
S1: Wie bitte? Wie schreiben Sie das?
S2: J - e - n - t - s - c - h - k - e.
S1: Danke. Auf Wiederhören°.

Bleisch, Ute, 16, Effingerg.° 15, Stg.° 2	**456 45 32**
Jentschke, Hans, 22, Magdeburgerstr.° 63	**233 94 37**
Meißner, Günter, 13, Volkg. 7, Stg. 15	**812 69 54**
Schumm, Harry, 5, Marg. Gürtel° 126, Stg. 2	**45 41 47**
Wurmisch, Hedwig, 16, Speckbacherg. 8	**647 04 31**

Auf Wiederhören: *Good-bye (on the phone)*
Effingergasse: *Effinger Lane / **Stg.=Stiege:** stairway / Magdeburger Street*
Margareten Gürtel: *Margareten Loop*

Was ist die Adresse?

Wissenswerte Vokabeln: die Zahlen

Asking for personal information

0 = null			
1 = eins	11 = elf	21 = einundzwanzig	40 = vierzig
2 = zwei	12 = zwölf	22 = zweiundzwanzig	50 = fünfzig
3 = drei	13 = dreizehn	23 = dreiundzwanzig	60 = sechzig
4 = vier	14 = vierzehn	24 = vierundzwanzig	70 = siebzig
5 = fünf	15 = fünfzehn	25 = fünfundzwanzig	80 = achtzig
6 = sechs	16 = sechzehn	26 = sechsundzwanzig	90 = neunzig
7 = sieben	17 = siebzehn	27 = siebenundzwanzig	100 = hundert
8 = acht	18 = achtzehn	28 = achtundzwanzig	101 = hunderteins
9 = neun	19 = neunzehn	29 = neunundzwanzig	1000 = tausend
10 = zehn	20 = zwanzig	30 = dreißig	

Wie alt sind Sie? *Ich bin … Jahre alt.*

24 **Autogrammspiel.** *(Autograph game.)* Walk around and find a classmate for each age listed below. When you find someone who matches the age description, have that person sign his/her name.

S1: Sind Sie achtzehn Jahre alt?
S2: Nein, ich bin … *(oder°)*
Ja, ich bin achtzehn.

or

1. 18 Jahre alt ______
2. 19 Jahre alt ______
3. 20 Jahre alt ______
4. 21 Jahre alt ______
5. ? Jahre alt ______

Wie alt sind sie?

Wissenswerte Vokabeln: Aussehen

Describing physical characteristics

Ich habe … • Er hat … • Sie hat …

braune Augen

grüne Augen

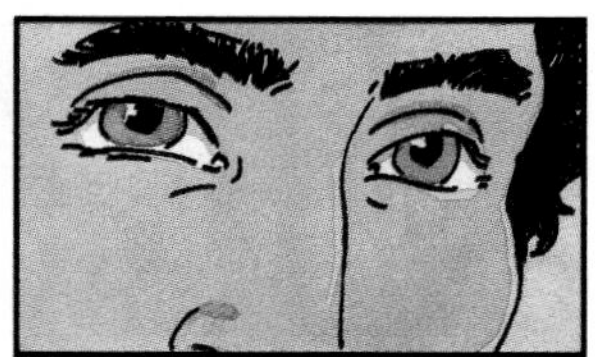
blaue Augen

langes Haar

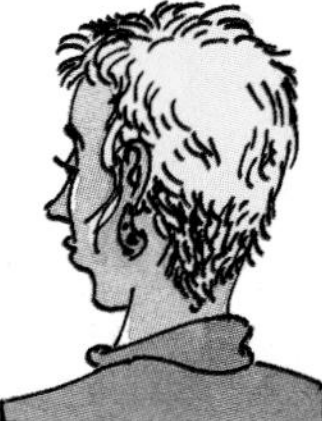
kurzes Haar

glattes Haar

krauses Haar

welliges Haar

blondes Haar

schwarzes Haar

braunes Haar

rotes Haar

graues Haar

die Brille: *glasses*

Ich bin …

schlank/mollig

groß/klein

alt/jung

hübsch/unattraktiv

Attraktiv is a synonym for **hübsch.**

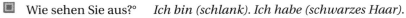

Wie sehen Sie aus?° *Ich bin (schlank). Ich habe (schwarzes Haar).*

What do you look like?

25 **Wer ist das?** *(Who is that?)* Match the descriptions below with the appropriate person in each photo.

1. Sie ist relativ jung und hübsch und hat braunes, welliges Haar.
2. Er ist sehr jung und klein.
3. Er ist schlank und hat kurzes, braunes Haar.
4. Sie ist 75 Jahre alt und mollig. Sie hat graues Haar.
5. Sie ist 28 Jahre alt und hat langes, rotes Haar.

Frau Winter Frau Becker

Frau Kinzelmann Herr Kinzelmann Fabian

26 **Anna ist jung.** *(Anna is young.)* Describe the following characters you have encountered so far, using words from **Wissenswerte Vokabeln.** Try to use at least three descriptive words for each picture.

■ Das ist Anna. Sie hat *(blondes Haar)*. Sie ist *(jung)*.

27 **Wie sehen sie aus?** *(What do they look like?)* As a class, generate a list of famous personalities that you all know. Describe one of these people to a partner and see if your partner can guess whom you are talking about.

■ S1: Er ist … Er hat …
Sie ist … Sie hat …

IV ■ Asking for information and clarification

Question formation

There are two types of questions in English and German: information questions and yes/no questions.

A. *Information questions*

Information questions **(Ergänzungsfragen)** are open-ended and require an answer that provides specific information. They begin with one of the following question words.

wann?	*when?*	**Wann** ist das?	***When*** *is that?*
was?	*what?*	**Was** sucht Anna?	***What*** *is Anna looking for?*
warum?	*why?*	**Warum** sagt Anna nichts?	***Why*** *doesn't Anna say anything?*
wer?	*who?*	**Wer** sind sie?	***Who*** *are they?*
wie?	*how?*	**Wie** heißen Sie?	***What*** *is your name?*
wie viel?	*how much?*	**Wie viel** ist das?	***How much*** *is that?*
wie viele?	*how many?*	**Wie viele** Studenten sind hier?	***How many*** *students are here?*
wo?	*where?*	**Wo** bin ich?	***Where*** *am I?*
woher?	*from where?*	**Woher** kommen Sie?	***Where*** *are you* ***from?***
wohin?	*where to?*	**Wohin** gehen Sie?	***Where*** *are you going* ***to?***

Was für? means *what kind of?*

Note that the question words **wo** and **wer** may confuse you at first, since they look like the English words *who* and *where.*

wo *where*
wer *who*

German does not always use the same question word as English in similar expressions.

Wie heißen Sie?	***What*** *is your name?*
Wie ist Ihr Name?	***What*** *is your name?*
Woher kommen Sie?	***Where*** *are you* ***from?***
	Where *do you come* ***from?***

Information questions are formed with one of the question words, followed by the verb, then the subject. The speaker lowers his/her pitch at the end of an information question.

Wo bin ich? *Where am I?*

Unlike English, German does not require a helping verb (e.g., *do/does*) to form questions.

Was sprechen Sie?	*What* ***do*** *you speak?*
Woher kommen Sie?	*Where* ***do*** *you come from?*

The question wie bitte?

Wie bitte? is commonly used when the listener does not understand and needs the speaker to repeat something for clarification.

WILLI: Ich heiße ...
JULIANNA: Wie bitte?

B. Yes/no questions

Yes/no questions **(Ja/Nein-Fragen** or **Entscheidungsfragen)** give information which the person answering is expected to negate or confirm. They always begin with the verb and the pitch rises at the end of the question.

Sind Sie Amerikanerin?	*Are you (an) American?*
Verstehen Sie Deutsch?	*Do you understand German?*

Note again that German does not require any helping verbs (e.g., *do/does*) to form questions.

28 **Drei Interviews.** Ask three different students the following questions.

▣ S1: Wie heißen Sie?
S2: Tom.

		1	2	3	
1. Wie heißen Sie?		_____	_____	_____	
2. Woher kommen Sie?	(aus ...)	_____	_____	_____	
3. Wo wohnen° Sie?	(in ...)	_____	_____	_____	
4. Wie alt sind Sie?		_____	_____	_____	(... Jahre)
5. Wie sehen Sie aus?	(Ich bin ...)	_____	_____	_____	

live

V ▣ Identifying people and classroom objects

A. *Noun gender*

All German nouns are capitalized, and every noun is categorized into one of three genders **(das Genus):** masculine, neuter, or feminine. Nouns often are accompanied by a definite article meaning *the.* The form this definite article takes **(der, das,** or **die)** depends on whether the noun is masculine, feminine, or neuter.

Masculine:	**der** Professor, **der** Hörsaal
Neuter:	**das** Buch, **das** Auto
Feminine:	**die** Professorin, **die** Mutter, **die** Tafel

In German both non-living things as well as living things are classified either as masculine (e.g., **der Hörsaal**), neuter (e.g., **das Zimmer**), or feminine (e.g., **die Tür, die Universität**). Some words for people are even categorized as neuter, e.g., **das Kind** *(the child),* **das Mädchen** *(the girl).* It is important to memorize the definite article (**der, das,** or **die**) that accompanies each new noun you learn.

Wissenswerte Vokabeln: der Hörsaal

Naming and identifying classroom objects

▣ Was ist das? *Das ist die Uhr.*

der Tisch: *table*

Another word for **Overheadprojektor** is **der Tageslichtprojektor**.

29 **Der Hörsaal.** Listen as your instructor models the commands below and then asks you to carry them out.

Zeigen Sie auf den Fernseher (den Overheadprojektor, den Papierkorb, den Schreibtisch, den Stift, den Stuhl).
Zeigen Sie auf die Kreide (die Lampe, die Landkarte, die Leinwand, die Steckdose, die Tafel, die Tür, die Uhr).
Zeigen Sie auf das Arbeitsbuch (das Buch, das Fenster).

You may have noticed your instructor saying **auf den Stuhl** instead of **der Stuhl.** The difference will be explained in a later chapter.

30 **Sie sind der Professor/die Professorin.** Ask your partner to identify as many classroom objects as possible.

S1: Ist das die Kreide?
S2: Ja, das ist die Kreide. *(oder)*
Nein, das ist nicht die Kreide.

Sie sind der Professor/die Professorin. If you do not know an answer, say **Ich weiß nicht.** *(I don't know.)*

B. The nominative case: definite articles der, das, die

As you learned above, the definite article **(der bestimmte Artikel)** identifies the gender of the noun: **der** for masculine nouns (e.g., **der Student, der Professor, der Stuhl**), **das** for neuter nouns (e.g., **das Kind, das Buch, das Fenster**), or **die** for feminine nouns (e.g., **die Studentin, die Professorin, die Lampe**). The nominative case definite article for all nouns in the plural, regardless of the gender, is **die.**

The definite article also identifies the grammatical function (or the case) of a noun in a sentence. You will learn about the grammatical functions of nouns later in this chapter. The following chart will help you remember the definite articles.

	Masculine	Neuter	Feminine	Plural
Nominative	der	das	die	die

31 **Ist das der Stuhl?** *(Is that the chair?)* Fill in the blanks with **der, das,** or **die.**

1. Wo ist _____ Schreibtisch?
2. Ist das _____ Stuhl?
3. Wo ist _____ Uhr?
4. Wo ist _____ Papierkorb?
5. Ist das _____ Fernseher?

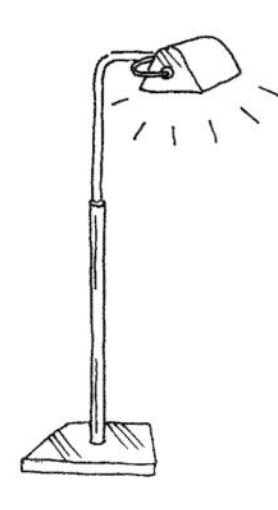

Wissenswerte Vokabeln: die Farben

Identifying objects by color

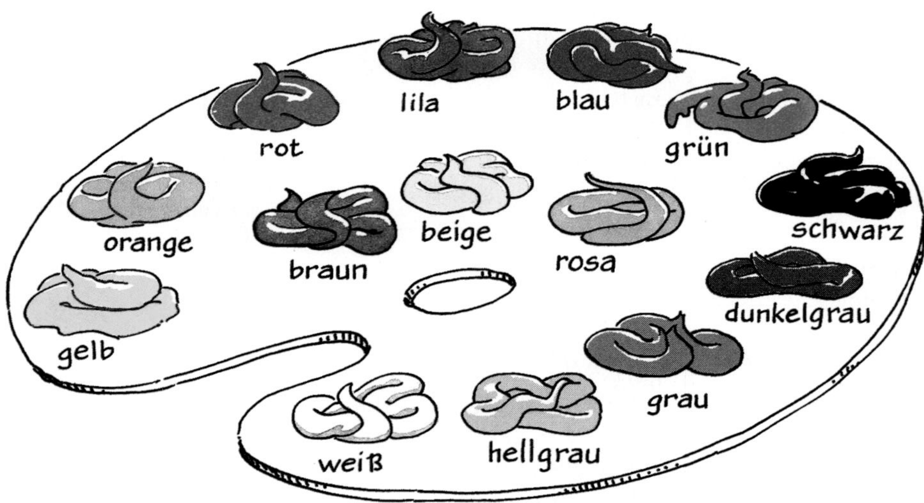

32 Welche Farbe hat ...? Work with a partner to describe the color of the classroom objects you now know.

die Tafel • die Tür • der Schreibtisch • die Wand • das Buch
das Arbeitsheft

S1: Welche Farbe hat der Stuhl?
S2: Der Stuhl ist schwarz.
S1: Richtig. *(oder)*
Nein, der Stuhl ist braun.

33 Annas Klassenzimmer. Complete the following description of Anna's classroom by providing **der, das,** or **die.**

Anna lernt Deutsch an der Universität. _____ Klassenzimmer ist relativ schön, aber auch sehr voll. Im Zimmer sind ein Schreibtisch, ein Papierkorb, ein Fernseher, eine Landkarte von Europa, ein Stuhl, eine Uhr, eine Professorin, zehn° Studenten und fünf° Studentinnen. _____ Schreibtisch ist hellbraun. _____ Papierkorb ist orange. _____ Fernseher ist relativ alt. _____ Landkarte zeigt° Europa. _____ Tafel ist nicht schwarz. Sie ist grün. _____ Uhr ist kaputt. _____ Professorin heißt Ziegler. Sie sagt: „Guten Morgen. Nehmen Sie bitte Platz." _____ Stühle stehen schon° im Halbkreis°. _____ Studenten sprechen sehr viel Deutsch miteinander°.

ten / five
shows
*already / **im Halbkreis:** in a semi-circle / with each other*

C. *The nominative case: indefinite articles* ein, eine

1. The indefinite article: ein

The indefinite article **(der unbestimmte Artikel)** identifies the typical rather than the particular.

Ein Klassenzimmer hat eine Tafel. *A classroom has a blackboard.*
Eine Tafel ist grün oder schwarz. *A blackboard is green or black.*

The indefinite articles in German are **ein** for masculine nouns, **ein** for neuter nouns, and **eine** for feminine nouns. All three correspond to *a* and *an* in English.

As with the definite article, the indefinite article signals the gender (masculine, neuter, or feminine) and the grammatical function (or the case, e.g., subject-nominative) of the noun in the sentence. Because **ein** literally means *one,* it cannot be used to refer to more than one item.

The following chart lists the nominative case indefinite articles.

	Masculine	Neuter	Feminine	Plural
Nominative	ein	ein	eine	–

34 **Das Klassenzimmer.** Professor Freund is talking about classroom objects with his German class. Fill in the following blanks with **ein** or **eine.**

PROFESSOR: Hier sind _____ Landkarte, _____ Leinwand und _____ Schreibtisch. Was ist das?
STUDENT: Das ist _____ Uhr.
PROFESSOR: Und was ist das?
STUDENT: Das ist _____ Stuhl.
PROFESSOR: Ist das _____ Fenster?
STUDENT: Nein, das ist _____ Fernseher.

2. Negating the indefinite article: kein

German has two ways of expressing negation. In the **Absprungtext,** you have already seen that speakers negate verbs with **nicht** *(not).*

Anna versteht **nicht.** *Anna does not understand.*

To negate a non-specific noun, German speakers use a form of the word **kein** (*not a/an, no* or *not any*).

Ist das ein Stuhl? *Is that a chair?*
Nein, das ist **kein** Stuhl. (Das ist ein Tisch.) *No, that is **not a** chair. (It is a table.)*

Ist das eine Tür? *Is that a door?*
Nein, das ist **keine** Tür. (Das ist ein Fenster.) *No, that is **not a** door. (It is a window.)*

Ist das ein Deutschbuch? *Is that a German book?*
Nein, das ist **kein** Deutschbuch. (Das ist ein Russischbuch.) *No, that is **not a** German book. (It is a Russian book.)*

The following chart lists the nominative case forms of **kein.**

	Masculine	Neuter	Feminine	Plural
Nominative	kein	kein	keine	keine

35 **Ein Marsmensch° im Klassenzimmer.** Find a partner and pretend one of you is a Martian who cannot get his/her "earth classroom" vocabulary right. The "Martian" asks whether various classroom objects are called by certain names. The "earthling" confirms what the Martian says or contradicts with the correct information.

Martian

S1 (MARTIAN): Ist das eine Tür?
S2 (EARTHLING): Ja, das ist eine Tür. *(oder)*
Nein, das ist keine Tür. Das ist eine Tafel.

Wissenswerte Vokabeln: Nationalitäten°

nationalities

Asking for personal information

Country	*Male citizen*	*Female citizen*
die USA/Amerika	der Amerikaner	die Amerikanerin
England	der Engländer	die Engländerin
Japan	der Japaner	die Japanerin
Kanada	der Kanadier	die Kanadierin
Mexiko	der Mexikaner	die Mexikanerin
Österreich	der Österreicher	die Österreicherin
die Schweiz	der Schweizer	die Schweizerin

Exceptions:

Deutschland	der (ein) Deutsche(r)	die Deutsche
Frankreich	der Franzose	die Französin

W. Vok.: Nationalitäten. The feminine designation is usually identified by the ending **-in** except for **die Deutsche.** Some terms for nationalities, among them those describing Germans, take different masculine endings, depending on whether they are used with a definite or with an indefinite article: **der Deutsche,** but **ein Deutscher.**

36 **Anna ist Amerikanerin.** Make statements about the nationalities of the following people.

Jennifer: aus den USA *Jennifer ist Amerikanerin.*

1. Helena: aus der Schweiz
2. Jean-Luc: aus Frankreich
3. Margaret: aus England

A few country names like **die Schweiz** require the article **die.** The **die** accompanying **die USA** is the plural article **die,** which refers to **die Staaten** *(the states).*

BRENNPUNKT KULTUR

Where German is spoken

German is the first language of an estimated 90–120 million speakers in Germany, Austria, Switzerland, and Liechtenstein. German is also spoken by substantial minorities in France (Alsace-Lorraine), Italy (Southern Tyrol), Luxemburg, the Czech Republic (Bohemia), Belgium, Russia (the former East Prussia, and other areas), and by immigrant populations throughout North and South America. For many former foreign workers who have returned to their native countries, e.g., Turkey, Greece, Italy, Spain, and the former Yugoslavia, German is a second language. Because of Germany's strong economic position, German vies with and even surpasses English as the preferred language of commerce for millions in Poland, Hungary, Russia, and the Czech and Slovak Republics. Since the unification of the two Germanys on October 3, 1990, interest in learning German has increased dramatically in Eastern Europe.

4. Franz: aus Österreich
5. Robert: aus den USA
6. Maria: aus Mexiko
7. Jill: aus Kanada
8. Klaus: aus Deutschland

37 **Nein, sie ist keine Deutsche.** Your partner has incorrect information about the nationalities of the people listed in the activity above. Respond to the questions with the correct information. Be sure to use **kein/keine** in your response.

Robert / Deutscher (aus den USA)

S1: Ist Robert Deutscher?
S2: Nein, er ist kein Deutscher. Er ist Amerikaner.

1. Franz / Deutscher (aus Österreich)
2. Helena / Amerikanerin (aus der Schweiz)
3. Klaus / Kanadier (aus Deutschland)
4. Jill / Mexikanerin (aus Kanada)
5. Margaret / Österreicherin (aus England)

38 **Auf einer Party.** *(At a party.)* Use the following cues to ask students about their nationalities.

USA / Schweiz

S1: Sind Sie Amerikaner(in)?
S2: Ja, ich bin Amerikaner(in). Und Sie?
S1: Ich bin Schweizer(in).

1. USA / Schweiz
2. Österreich / Japan
3. Kanada / Österreich
4. Deutschland / England
5. die Schweiz / Frankreich

6. Japan / Deutschland
7. Mexiko / Schweiz
8. England / Österreich

39 **Wer ist das?** Here are some famous personalities. Using the questions below to guide you, ask your partner as many questions as you can about each person.

S1: Wer ist das?
S2: Das ist … Er/Sie ist …

Wie heißt er/sie? • Woher kommt er/sie? • Ist das … ? • Ist er/sie Amerikaner/Amerikanerin? • Kommt er/sie aus Österreich?

D. The nominative case

1. Subject of a sentence

In German the subject of a sentence **(das Subjekt)** is in the nominative case. The subject is the person or thing that performs the action described by the verb. It answers the question **wer?** *(who?)* regarding people, and the question **was?** *(what?)* regarding inanimate objects.

subject **Wer** öffnet die Tür?	*Who is opening the door?*
subject **Der Professor** öffnet die Tür.	*The professor is opening the door.*
subject **Was** ist schwarz oder grün?	*What is black or green?*
subject **Eine Tafel** ist schwarz oder grün.	*A blackboard is black or green.*

In an English sentence the subject is often the first word or phrase. In a German sentence the subject is frequently not the first word or phrase. Nevertheless, the subject always determines the ending of the verb.

subject	*subject*
Da vorne ist **Hörsaal 20.**	***Lecture Hall 20*** *is up ahead.*

These are the nominative case definite articles, indefinite articles, and forms of **kein.**

	Masculine	Neuter	Feminine	Plural
Definite article	der	das	die	die
Indefinite article	ein	ein	eine	–
kein	kein	kein	keine	keine

2. Predicate nominative

The predicate nominative **(das Prädikatsnomen)** identifies (using **der, das, die**) or classifies (using a form of **ein**) people and inanimate objects. It restates the subject of the sentence and follows the verbs **sein** *(to be),* **heißen** *(to be called),* **werden** *(to become),* or **bleiben** *(to remain).*

Er ist **der Professor.**	*He is* ***the professor.***
Sie ist **die Studentin** aus Bonn.	*She is* ***the (female) student*** *from Bonn.*
Vorsprung ist **ein Deutschbuch.**	Vorsprung *is* ***a German textbook.***
Anna ist **Amerikanerin.**	*Anna is* ***(an) American.***
Das ist **eine Tafel.**	*That's* ***a blackboard.***

In the above sentences, **der Professor, die Studentin, das Deutschbuch,** and **Amerikanerin** are all predicate nouns. In German, the indefinite article is not used when stating a person's nationality, profession, or religion.

Er ist Amerikaner.	*He is (an) American.*
Sie ist Professorin.	*She is a professor.*

 **40** **Deutsche Prominente.** Match the prominent Germans on the left with their professions on the right.

 S1: Wer ist Gerhard Schröder?
S2: Er ist der Bundeskanzler.

1. Gerhard Schröder	a. der Chef von DaimlerChrysler
2. Steffi Graf	b. der Bundeskanzler
3. Johannes Rau	c. ein Formel-1-Autorennfahrer
4. Günter Grass	d. der Bundespräsident
5. Jürgen Schrempp	e. Autor und Nobelpreisträger° für Literatur
6. Michael Schumacher	f. Tennisspielerin

Nobel Prize winner

E. Pronoun substitution

The pronouns **er, sie,** and **es** are used to replace the nouns in a sentence. By referring back to nouns, pronouns unify sentences into a tight narrative thereby avoiding repetition and adding variety to sentences.

Hier ist **der Tisch. Er** ist braun.	*Here is **the table. It** is brown.*
Wo ist **das Buch?** Hier ist **es.**	*Where is **the book?** Here **it** is.*
Das ist **die Tafel. Sie** ist schwarz.	*That is **the board. It** is black.*
Wo sind **die Studenten?** Hier sind **sie.**	*Where are **the students?** Here **they** are.*

41 Wo ist der Tisch? – Hier ist er. Ask your partner questions about the location of various people and objects using the question word **wo?** *(where?).* Use the appropriate personal pronoun **(er, sie,** or **es)** in your response.

S1: Wo ist der Tisch?
S2: Hier/Da ist er.

das Fenster? • die Tafel? • die Mutter? • der Professor? • die Professorin? das Buch? • der Stuhl? • der Fernseher? • das Arbeitsbuch? • der Schreibtisch?

FREIE KOMMUNIKATION

Jeopardy. Form questions in German which accompany these statements from two categories: **Prominente Deutsche oder Österreicher** and **Prominente Amerikaner/Amerikanerinnen.** The monetary value of each item is listed.

Prominente Deutsche oder Österreicher

$ 10 1. Er ist der deutsche Bundeskanzler.
$ 20 2. Er kommt aus Österreich. Er ist stark°. Er lebt in Kalifornien. — *strong*
$ 30 3. Sie ist sehr attraktiv. Sie hat braunes Haar und ist Mannequin°. — *model*
$ 40 4. Er ist der deutsche Vize-Kanzler und Außenminister°. — *foreign minister*

Prominente Amerikaner/Amerikanerinnen

$ 10 1. Er ist der Präsident der USA.
$ 20 2. Er ist Tennisspieler und der Mann von Steffi Graf.
$ 30 3. Sie ist Japano-Amerikanerin. Sie ist Eiskunstläuferin°. — *figure skater*
$ 4C 4. Er ist Afro-Amerikaner. Er spielt Basketball für Los Angeles. Er spricht sehr gut Italienisch.

Schreibecke **Bitte schicken Sie ...** Look over the three forms below. Fill in the blank form with information about yourself.

Miele
Die Miele Küche
KÜCHEN INFO

Bitte senden Sie mir kostenlos Ihr umfangreiches Info-Material über 'Die Miele Küche' und Ihren Händlernachweis.

Name: Edith Müller
Straße: Albertstraße 30
Plz/Ort: 01097 Dresden

Miele & Cie.
Postfach, D-33325 Gütersloh, Tel. 05241/891902
Miele Ges.mbH.
Mielestraße 1, A-5071 Wals/Salzburg, Tel. 0662/850770-222

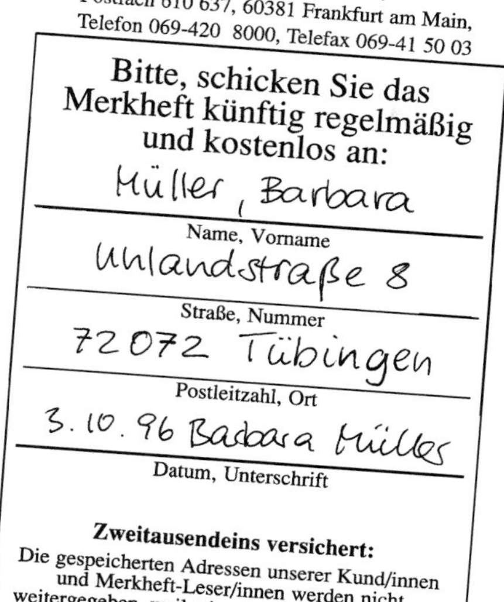

An Zweitausendeins:
Postfach 610 637, 60381 Frankfurt am Main,
Telefon 069-420 8000, Telefax 069-41 50 03

Bitte, schicken Sie das Merkheft künftig regelmäßig und kostenlos an:

Müller, Barbara
Name, Vorname

Uhlandstraße 8
Straße, Nummer

72072 Tübingen
Postleitzahl, Ort

3.10.96 Barbara Müller
Datum, Unterschrift

Zweitausendeins versichert:
Die gespeicherten Adressen unserer Kund/innen und Merkheft-Leser/innen werden nicht weitergegeben, weil wir mit Platten, Büchern und Videos handeln, aber nicht mit Adressen.

99913

The Euro, the new currency of the European Union, was introduced in 2000 for electronic transactions. Euro bills and coins went into circulation in early 2002 and could be used along with the D-Mark in Germany until June 2002, when the Euro completely replaced the national currency in all participating nations.

Ja, ich abonniere FOCUS
ab sofort zum Vorzugspreis von DM 3,60 statt DM 4,00 Normalpreis (nur im Ausland zzgl. Porto)
❑ für mich ❑ als Geschenk

Vorname, Name

Straße, Nr.

PLZ Ort

Telefon Fax

Ich bin damit einverstanden, daß Sie mich auch telefonisch oder per Fax ansprechen.

Focus Garantie: Als Dankeschön erhalte ich den FOCUS Füller. Das Abo kann ich nach Ablauf eines Jahres jederzeit wieder kündigen. Den FOCUS Füller darf ich in jedem Fall behalten.

✗
Datum, Unterschrift 611770 E

Das Geschenkabo geht an:
(Bei Geschenkabo bitte hier Namen und Adresse des Beschenkten eintragen.)

Vorname, Name

Straße, Nr.

PLZ Ort

Gewünschte Zahlungsweise bitte ankreuzen:
Bequem und bargeldlos durch Bankeinzug. Abbuchung vierteljährlich (nur im Inland möglich).
Gegen Rechnung (jährlich). Rechnung abwarten, keine Vorauszahlung leisten.

Bankleitzahl Kontonummer

Geldinstitut

Widerrufsgarantie: Diese Bestellung kann ich innerhalb von 10 Tagen nach Bestelldatum (rechtzeitige Absendung genügt) bei FOCUS Aboservice, Postfach 12 90, 77649 Offenburg, widerrufen.

✗
Datum, Unterschrift 611770 G

Einfach hier abtrennen!

Schicken Sie diese Karte sofort ab!

So sichern Sie sich noch heute den FOCUS Füller und erhalten FOCUS pünktlich jeden Montag frei Haus.

FOCUS
Abo-Service
Postfach 12 90
77649 Offenburg

Abo-Hotline

kostenlos ☎ 0130/4767

Fax: 07 81/84 69 53

Für den Abonnenten zum Verbleib. Widerrufsgarantie: Das FOCUS Abo (Berechnung vierteljährl. DM 46,80) kann innerhalb von 10 Tagen nach Bestelldatum (rechtzeitige Absendung genügt) durch eine kurze Mitteilung an FOCUS Abo-Service, Postfach 12 90, 77649 Offenburg, widerrufen werden. Den FOCUS Füller können Sie natürlich auch dann behalten.

■ Wortschatz ■

This vocabulary list represents words from Chapter 1 that you may want to use. The words have been categorized according to the thematic topics in this chapter. The sequence of words within each topic in the vocabulary list is always the same: nouns, verbs, adjectives and other words. The **Ausdrücke** will provide a list of useful expressions found in the chapter.

Personen *People*

der Amerikaner *(male) American*
die Amerikanerin[1] *(female) American*
der (ein) Deutsche(r) *(male) German*
die Deutsche *(female) German*
die Frau; Frau ... *woman; Mrs. ..., Ms. ...*
das Fräulein *Miss*
der Gott *God*
der Herr *man; Mr. ...*
der Kanadier *(male) Canadian*
die Kanadierin *(female) Canadian*
die Mutter *mother*
der Name *name*
der Österreicher *(male) Austrian*
die Österreicherin *(female) Austrian*
die Person *person*
der Professor *(male) professor*
die Professorin *(female) professor*
der Schweizer *(male) Swiss*
die Schweizerin *(female) Swiss*
der Student *(male) student*
die Studentin *(female) student*

Universität *University*

das Arbeitsbuch *workbook*
das Buch *textbook*
das Fenster *window*
der Fernseher *television set*
der Hörsaal *lecture hall*
das Klassenzimmer *classroom*
die Kreide *chalk*
die Lampe *lamp, light*
die Landkarte *map*
die Leinwand *projection screen*
der Overheadprojektor *overhead projector*
der Papierkorb *wastepaper basket*
der Schreibtisch *desk*
die Steckdose *electric socket*
der Stift *pen or pencil*
der Stuhl *chair*
die Tafel *blackboard*
die Tür *door*
die Uhr *clock*
die Universität *university*
die Wand *wall*

Länder *Countries*

das Land *country*
die Nationalität *nationality*
Amerika *America*
Deutschland *Germany*
England *England*
Frankreich *France*
Japan *Japan*
Kanada *Canada*
Mexiko *Mexico*
Österreich *Austria*
die Schweiz *Switzerland*
die USA *U.S.A.*

Verben *Verbs*

antworten *to answer*
auf·machen *to open*
auf·stehen *to get up*
auf·wachen *to wake up*
finden *to find*
fragen *to ask*
gehen *to go*
haben *to have*
heißen *to be called*
kommen (aus) *to come, be from*
lachen *to laugh*
laufen *to run; to walk (in So. Germany)*
lesen *to read*
machen *to make*
öffnen *to open*
nehmen *to take*
sagen *to say*
schreiben *to write*
sein *to be*
setzen (sich) *to sit (oneself) down*
sprechen *to speak*
stehen *to stand*
stimmen *to be correct*
suchen *to look for*
verstehen *to understand*
zeigen *to show, point*
zu·machen *to close*

Das Aussehen *Appearance*

alt old
attraktiv *attractive*
Augen eyes
  blaue (braune, grüne) Augen *blue (brown, green) eyes*
blond *blond*
das Haar *hair*
  blondes (braunes, rotes, schwarzes, graues) Haar *blond (brown, red, black, gray) hair*
langes (kurzes) Haar *long (short) hair*
glattes (krauses, welliges) Haar *straight (tightly curled, wavy) hair*
groß *tall; large, big*
hübsch *pretty*
jung *young*
klein *short*
kurz *short*
lang *long; tall*
mollig chubby, plump
schlank slim, slender
schön pretty, beautiful
unattraktiv unattractive

Farben

die Farbe *color*
beige *beige*
blau *blue*
braun *brown*
dunkel *dark*
  dunkelgrau *dark gray*
gelb *yellow*
grau *gray*
grün *green*
hell *light*
  hellgrau *light gray*
lila *purple*
orange *orange*
rosa *pink*
rot *red*
schwarz *black*
weiß *white*

Adjektive und Adverbien *Adjectives and adverbs*

angenehm *pleasant*
freundlich *friendly*
gut *good*
hier *here*
historisch *historic*

---

[1] The feminine form of many professions and nationalities is formed by adding the suffix **-in** to the masculine form.

richtig *right*
romantisch *romantic*
schnell *fast, quickly*
unpersönlich *impersonal*

Fragewörter *Question words*

wann? *when?*
was? *what?*
warum? *why?*
welche Farbe hat ...? *what color is . . . ?*
wer? *who?*
wie? *how? what?*
wie viel? *how much?*
wie viele? *how many?*
wo? *where?*
woher? *from where?*
wohin? *where to?*

Gruß- und Abschiedsformeln *Greetings and farewells*

Auf Wiedersehen! *Good-bye*
Grüß Gott! *Hello (in southern Germany)*
Grüezi! *Hello (in Switzerland)*
Gute Nacht! *Good night!*
Guten Abend! *Good evening!*
Guten Morgen! *Good morning!*
Guten Tag! *Good Day! Hello!*
Hallo! *Hello!*
Mahlzeit! *Have a nice lunch!*
Servus! *Hello! (in Austria)*
Tschüss! *Bye!*

Imperativ

Machen Sie das Buch zu. *Close the book.*
Nehmen Sie bitte Platz. *Have a seat.*
Öffnen Sie das Buch. *Open the book.*
Setzen Sie sich. *Sit down.*
Stehen Sie auf. *Stand up.*
Stehen Sie still. *Stand still.*

Ausdrücke *Expressions*

Bin ich hier richtig? *Am I in the right place?*
da vorne *over there in front*
Das stimmt (nicht). *That's (not) right.*
Gott sei Dank! *Thank God!*
Ich heiße Anna. *My name is Anna.*
Ich komme aus den USA. *I am from the U.S.A.*
Sehr angenehm! *Pleased to meet you.*
Wie bitte? *Please repeat that.*
Wie heißen Sie? *What's your name?*
Willkommen in Tübingen! *Welcome to Tübingen!*

Die Zahlen *Numbers*

null *zero*
eins *one*
zwei *two*
drei *three*
vier *four*
fünf *five*
sechs *six*
sieben *seven*
acht *eight*
neun *nine*
zehn *ten*
elf *eleven*
zwölf *twelve*
dreizehn *thirteen*
vierzehn *fourteen*
fünfzehn *fifteen*
sechzehn *sixteen*
siebzehn *seventeen*
achtzehn *eighteen*
neunzehn *nineteen*
zwanzig *twenty*
einundzwanzig *twenty-one*
dreißig *thirty*
vierzig *forty*
fünfzig *fifty*
sechzig *sixty*
siebzig *seventy*
achtzig *eighty*
neunzig *ninety*
hundert *hundred*
hunderteins *one hundred one*
tausend *thousand*

Andere Wörter *Other words*

aber *but*
alle *everybody*
aus *from*
bitte *please*
da *there*
danke *thanks*
dann *then*
du *you (informal singular)*
ein/eine *a, an*
Entschuldigung! *Pardon! Excuse me!*
er *he, it*
es *it*
ich *I*
ihr *you guys*
in *in*
ja *yes*
kein/keine *no, none*
nein *no*
nicht *not*
nichts *nothing*
nur *only*
oder *or*
schon *already*
sehr *very*
sie *she, it; they*
Sie *you (formal)*
und *and*
wir *we*

In this chapter you will learn how to talk about your family, your possessions, activities you like or routinely do, and when certain events occur.

Kommunikative Funktionen

- Indicating possession or ownership
- Expressing what you like and don't like
- Describing actions
- Talking about what you like and don't like to do
- Talking about what you have and don't have
- Creating variety and shifting emphasis
- Describing daily activities
- Expressing negation
- Talking about how much and how many

Strukturen

- The verb **haben**
- Verbs (including **haben**) + the adverb **gern**
- Present tense of regular verbs
- The accusative case
- Position of subject and verb
- Separable-prefix verbs
- Position of **nicht**
- Use of quantifiers

Vokabeln

- Die Familie und die Verwandten
- Studienfächer
- Die Monate
- Die Wochentage
- Zeitausdrücke
- Die Uhrzeit
- Der Alltag

Kulturelles

- German immigration to North America

Wohin fahren diese Leute?

KAPITEL · ZWEI

Familie und Freunde

Go to the *Vorsprung* Website at **www.hmco.com/college**

ANLAUFTEXT

Anna Adler stellt sich vor°

***stellt sich vor:** introduces herself*

Anna Adler, a German-American college student from Fort Wayne, Indiana, introduces herself and describes some of her favorite activities. She also introduces her immediate family — her father Bob Adler, her German-born mother Hannelore, and her teen-age brother Jeff. She talks about college, her German skills, and her anxieties and hopes as she looks ahead to a year abroad at the University of Tübingen.

Vorschau

1 Thematische Fragen. Discuss the following questions with your instructor or in pairs.

1. What do you already know about Anna Adler? Where does she come from? Where is she going to study? What is she going to study? How much German does she know?
2. If you were going to contact family friends or relatives who lived in a foreign country and whom you had never met before, what would you tell them about yourself?

Wissenswerte Vokabeln: Annas Familie

Identifying family relationships

Annas Familie: Note the absence of an apostrophe between the noun and the possessive **s.**

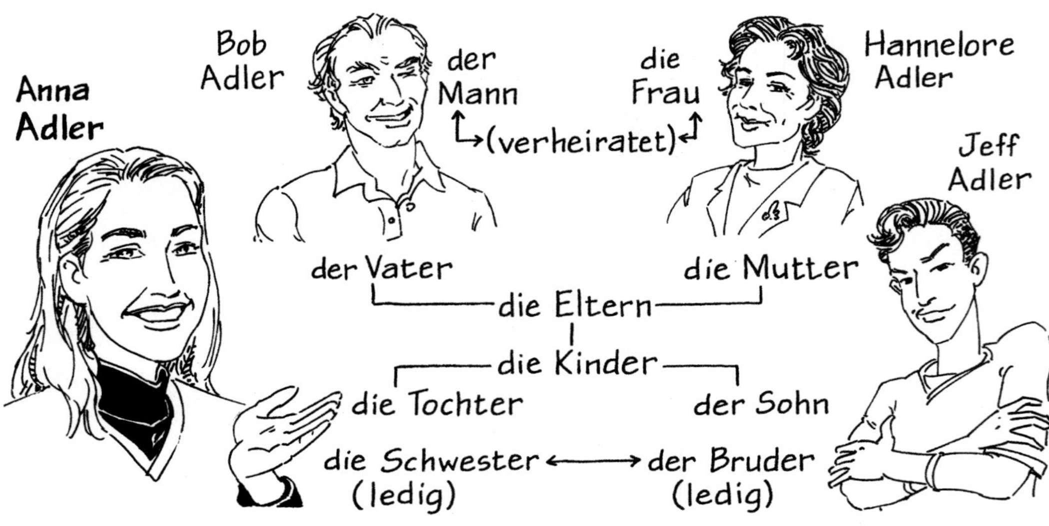

Annas Eltern heißen Bob und Hannelore Adler.
Hannelore Adler ist Annas Mutter.
Bob Adler ist Annas Vater.

Hannelore und Bob haben zwei Kinder, Anna und Jeff.
Der Sohn heißt Jeff.
Die Tochter heißt Anna.
Anna ist Jeffs Schwester. Jeff ist Annas Bruder.
Anna ist nicht verheiratet. Sie ist ledig.
Bob und Hannelore sind verheiratet. Sie sind Mann und Frau.

Sind Sie verheiratet? *Nein, ich bin ledig.*

2 **Wer ist wer in der Familie Adler?** *(Who's who in the Adler family?)* Complete these sentences with the correct term for each relationship.

1. Anna Adler ist die _____ von Bob und Hannelore Adler.
2. Bob und Hannelore haben zwei _____, Anna und Jeff.
3. Jeff ist der _____ von Bob und Hannelore.
4. Bob und Hannelore sind die _____ von Anna und Jeff.
5. Annas und Jeffs _____ heißt Bob Adler.
6. Annas und Jeffs _____ heißt Hannelore Adler.
7. Jeff ist Annas _____.
8. Anna ist Jeffs _____.
9. Bob und Hannelore Adler sind verheiratet. Sie sind Mann und _____.
10. Jeff und Anna sind nicht verheiratet. Sie sind _____.

3 **Wortdetektiv.** Which words convey approximately the same meaning? Draw a line from the German word to its logical English equivalent.

Deutsch	*Englisch*
1. meinen	a. to fly
2. klug	b. athletic
3. sportlich	c. smart, clever
4. fliegen	d. to think, mean
5. hören	e. history
6. zu Hause	f. to hear, listen
7. die Geschichte	g. I would like to
8. ich möchte	h. at home
9. verbringen	i. to make better, improve
10. lernen	j. to spend, pass time
11. die Angst	k. to learn
12. verbessern	l. fear
13. die Musik	m. young
14. ein bisschen	n. music
15. spielen	o. a little bit (of)
16. jung	p. to play

ANLAUFTEXT

Now listen to the recording.

Anna Adler stellt sich vor

Ich heiße Anna Adler. Ich bin 20 Jahre alt.

Ich fliege im August nach Deutschland.

Ich komme aus den USA, aus Fort Wayne. Ich bin Amerikanerin.

INDIANA

FORT WAYNE

INDIANAPOLIS

Lufthansa

Ich spiele gern Softball.

14

MOZART

Ich höre gern Musik, zum Beispiel Mozart.

Ich gehe auch gern wandern,

aber ich sehe nicht gern fern.

Mein Vater heißt Bob Adler. Er ist 48 Jahre alt.

Meine Mutter, Hannelore Adler, ist 46 Jahre alt. Sie kommt aus Deutschland, aber sie ist jetzt Amerikanerin.

Ich habe auch einen Bruder. Er heißt Jeff. Er ist 16. Er meint, er ist sehr klug und sehr sportlich. Naja ...

Ich habe keine Schwester.

Rückblick

4 **Stimmt das?** How much of the text can you remember without looking back at it? Look over the statements and mark the true statements as **Ja, das stimmt.** Mark the false statements as **Nein, das stimmt nicht.** Then, listen as your instructor reads the following statements and models their pronunciation. If the statement is true, say **Ja, das stimmt.** If the statement is not true, say **Nein, das stimmt nicht.**

	Ja, das stimmt.	Nein, das stimmt nicht.	
1. Anna Adler ist Deutsche.	—	—	
2. Anna kommt aus Fort Wayne, Indiana.	—	—	
3. Sie spielt gern Basketball.	—	—	
4. Sie hört gern Musik, Mozart zum Beispiel.	—	—	
5. Annas Vater Bob ist 48 Jahre alt.	—	—	
6. Annas Mutter Hannelore kommt aus Los Angeles.	—	—	
7. Annas Bruder Jeff ist 16.	—	—	
8. Anna möchte unbedingt ihr Deutsch verbessern.	—	—	
9. Anna verbringt ein Semester in Zürich.	—	—	
10. Anna hat etwas° Angst.	—	—	*a little*

5 **Ergänzen Sie.** Complete these statements with words from the **Anlauftext.**

1. Ist Anna Deutsche? Nein, sie ist ______.
2. Anna kommt ______ den USA.
3. Anna sagt: „Ich spiele ______ Softball."
4. Anna sagt: „Ich ______ gern Musik, zum ______ Mozart."
5. Annas Vater, Bob Adler, ist 48 ______ alt.
6. Annas Bruder ______ Jeff.
7. Anna ist Studentin. Sie studiert ______ und ______.
8. Anna sagt: „Ich ______ ein bisschen Deutsch von zu Hause."
9. Anna sagt: „Dieses Jahr ______ ich zwei Semester an der ______ in Tübingen."
10. Anna sagt: „Ich möchte so viel sehen und auch so viel ______."

6 **Kurz gefragt.** Answer the questions with just a word or two. Review the question words before you begin.

was?	= *what?*	**wo?**	= *where?*
wann?	= *when?*	**woher?**	= *where . . . from?*
wie?	= *how?*	**wohin?**	= *where . . . to?*

1. Woher kommt Anna?
2. Wann fliegt Anna?
3. Wohin fliegt Anna?
4. Was macht Anna gern? Was sind ihre Hobbys?
5. Wie alt ist Annas Vater?
6. Woher kommt Annas Mutter?
7. Was ist Annas Mutter: Deutsche oder Amerikanerin?
8. Ist Annas Bruder sportlich?
9. Was studiert Anna?
10. Wo verbringt Anna dieses Jahr zwei Semester?

7 **Jetzt sind Sie dran.** You are introducing yourself to a German class in Germany. Complete the statements below, then read them to your partner.

1. Ich heiße ______.
2. Ich komme aus ______.

3. Ich bin _____ Jahre alt.
4. Meine Mutter heißt _____.
5. Sie ist _____ Jahre alt.
6. Sie kommt aus _____.
7. Mein Vater heißt _____.
8. Er ist _____ Jahre alt.
9. Er kommt aus _____.
10. Ich bin Student(in).

BRENNPUNKT KULTUR

German immigration to North America

Anna, like approximately 20% of all Americans, is of German background. Germany's first immigrants to the new world, natives of the Lower Rhine city of Krefeld, settled in Philadelphia in 1683, establishing a German-speaking community called Germantown. This was the first of many waves of central European immigration to North America that continued well into the 20th century, with post-World War II immigrants coming to Canada and the U.S. These new German, Swiss, and Austrian immigrants brought their German language and customs with them as they moved to places as diverse as southern Ontario, New York, Wisconsin, Indiana, California, Missouri, and Texas. With over 57 million Americans claiming German heritage, Germans are the largest single ethnic group in the U.S. Since 1983, German-Americans celebrate their ethnic heritage every year on October 6, German-American Day.

Many German-Americans take great pride in the continued use of the German language. In some smaller towns and rural areas, you can still hear German as their language of choice. The Amish, for example, worship in High German, but in daily conversation they use the Swiss German dialect their ancestors brought with them over 200 years ago. Cities such as New York, Chicago, and Los Angeles used to have large German-speaking communities, which have, with time, blended into the larger society. But you can still find German restaurants, bakeries, bookstores, German-speaking churches or newspapers in German, and sometimes even radio stations with a German-language program.

George Herman (Babe) Ruth ist ein berühmter Deutsch-Amerikaner.

WILHELM TELL
FESTIVAL

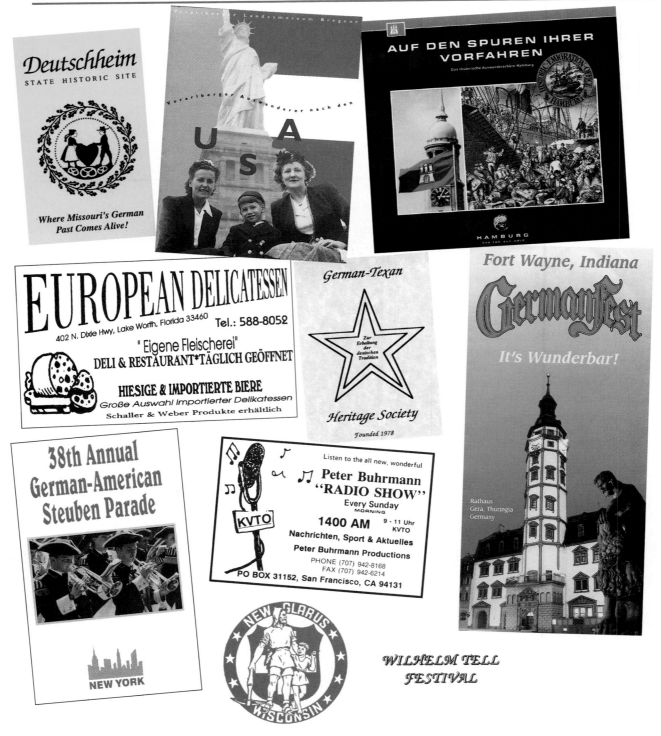

8 **Auf der Suche nach Deutsch-Amerikanern.** *(Searching for German-Americans.)* Look through your local telephone book and see how many German last names you can identify. Look in the yellow pages: Do any businesses emphasize their German background? Can you identify any German-speaking businesses?

■ Strukturen und Vokabeln ■

See the **Arbeitsbuch** for additional practice with structures and vocabulary.

Wissenswerte Vokabeln: die Familie und die Verwandten

Identifying family relationships

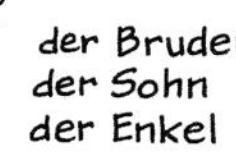

W. Vok. The first name of Anna's aunt is **Ursula.** However, family members and friends call her **Uschi,** which is a standard shortened version of the name.

The name **Johannes** is frequently abbreviated to **Hannes,** the name **Johann** to **Hans.**

der Mann, die Männer
die Frau, die Frauen
die Eltern *(pl.)*
die Mutter, die Mütter
der Vater, die Väter
das Kind, die Kinder
die Tochter, die Töchter
der Sohn, die Söhne
die Schwester, die Schwestern
der Bruder, die Brüder

die Großeltern *(pl.)*
die Großmutter, die Großmütter
die Oma, die Omas
der Großvater, die Großväter
der Opa, die Opas
das Enkelkind, die Enkelkinder
die Enkelin, die Enkelinnen
der Enkel, die Enkel

die Tante, die Tanten
der Onkel, die Onkel
die Nichte, die Nichten
der Neffe, die Neffen
der Cousin, die Cousins
die Kusine, die Kusinen
der Vetter, die Vetter

Relationships created by remarriage of a parent (e.g., stepfather, stepsister) are indicated by the prefix **Stief-: Stiefvater, Stiefmutter, Stiefkind, Stieftochter, Stiefschwester, Stiefsohn, Stiefbruder.** Relationships where siblings share only one biological parent are indicated by the prefix **Halb-: Halbbruder, Halbschwester.** Adoptive relationships are indicated by the prefix **Adoptiv-: Adoptivsohn, Adoptivtochter.**

Note that someone who has lost a spouse is **verwitwet** *(widowed).*

9 Die Familie. Complete the following sentences using the information provided in the family tree.

■ Anna ist die *Schwester* von Jeff.

1. Katja ist die _____ von Georg.
2. Annas _____ heißt Hannelore.
3. Katja ist Annas _____, und Georg ist Annas _____.

4. Onkel Hannes und _____ Ursula sind Katjas und Georgs _____.
5. Friedrich Kunz ist Katjas _____.
6. Bob und Hannelore Adler sind verheiratet: sie sind _____ und Frau.
7. Georg ist Katjas _____.
8. Bob Adler ist Katjas und Georgs _____.
9. Jeff ist Bobs und Hannelores _____.
10. Anna Adler ist Bobs und Hannelores _____.
11. Anna und Jeff sind die zwei _____ von Hannelore und Bob Adler.

I ▣ Indicating possession or ownership

The verb **haben**

The verb **haben** *(to have)* expresses possession or ownership.

Ich **habe** auch einen Bruder. *I also have a brother.*
Ich **habe** keine Schwester. *I don't have a sister.*

The form **einen** will be explained later in the chapter.

Haben is an irregular verb with the following present tense forms.

haben: *to have*				
Person	**Singular**		**Plural**	
1st	ich hab**e**	*I have; I am having*	wir hab**en**	*we have; we are having*
2nd, informal	du ha**st**	*you have; you are having*	ihr hab**t**	*you have; you are having*
2nd, formal	Sie hab**en**	*you have; you are having*	Sie hab**en**	*you have; you are having*
3rd	er/sie/es ha**t**	*he/she/it has; he/she/it is having*	sie hab**en**	*they have; they are having*

Although **haben** is considered an irregular verb (it drops the **b** in **du hast** and in **er/sie/es hat**), the highlighted endings are regular endings for all present tense verbs.

10 **Wer hat was?** *(Who has what?)* Put together meaningful sentences by matching the proper subjects from the left column with the correct forms of **haben** in the right column.

1. Ich ... a. haben eine intelligente Tochter.
2. Du ... b. habe keine Schwester.
3. Anna ... c. habt ein schönes Auto.
4. Herr Günther, Sie ... d. hat etwas Angst.
5. Ihr ... e. hast keine Verwandten in Deutschland.

Sprache im Alltag: Abbreviated ich-forms of verbs

In conversational German, speakers often drop the standard **-e** ending of the **ich**-form. These short forms are common in conversation, but they are considered non-standard in writing. When written, the deleted **-e** is sometimes indicated by the use of an apostrophe.

Ich **hab'** eine Frau und zwei Söhne. Ich **hab'** keine Töchter.
Ich **hör'** gern Musik. Und ich **spiel'** gern Softball.
Ich **hab'** Probleme mit …

11 **Ich habe Probleme mit …** Complete each sentence with the correct form of **haben.**

Der Patient *hat* Probleme mit der Religion.

1. Der Psychiater fragt: „_____ Sie Probleme?"
2. Der Patient _____ viele° Probleme. *a lot of*
3. Der Patient sagt: „Ich _____ Probleme mit meiner Identität."
4. Die Studenten sagen: „Wir _____ Probleme mit Professor Bauer."
5. _____ der Psychiater Geldprobleme°? *money problems*
6. Anna fragt Georg: „_____ du Geldprobleme?"
7. Georg sagt: „Nein, ich _____ keine Geldprobleme."
8. Anna fragt Katja und Georg: „_____ ihr Geldprobleme?"
9. Katja und Georg sagen: „Im Moment _____ wir keine Probleme."

Sprache im Alltag: Expressions with the verb haben

German uses the verb **haben** with specific nouns denoting a state of being to express a physical or emotional condition.

To negate these expressions, use **keine(n): Ich habe *keine* Angst. Ich habe *keinen* Hunger. Ich habe *keinen* Durst.**

Angst haben
Ich sehe einen Horrorfilm. Ich **habe Angst.** *to be afraid*

Hunger haben
Ich möchte essen°. Ich **habe Hunger.** *to be hungry*

Durst haben
Ich möchte trinken°. Ich **habe Durst.** *to be thirsty*

eat

drink

12 Interview. First, fill in the information about you and your family in the column with the head **Ich.** Then, ask your partner these questions and note his/her answers in the right column.

Interview. If you want to answer *a brother* or *a father,* say **einen Bruder** or **einen Vater.** You will learn why later in the chapter.

Remember to change questions 5, 6, 8, 9, and 13 if your partner indicates he or she has only one brother, sister, or child.

S1: Haben Sie Brüder?
S2: Ja, ich habe zwei Brüder (keine Brüder, einen Bruder).
S1: Wie heißen sie?
S2: Sie heißen Hans und Franz.

	Ich	*Mein Partner / Meine Partnerin*
1. Haben Sie Eltern?	______	______
2. Wie heißen sie?	______	______
3. Wie alt sind sie?	______	______
4. Haben Sie Brüder?	______	______
5. Wenn° ja, wie heißen sie?	______	______
6. Wie alt sind sie?	______	______
7. Haben Sie Schwestern?	______	______
8. Wenn ja, wie heißen sie?	______	______
9. Wie alt sind sie?	______	______
10. Sind Sie verheiratet?	______	______
11. Wenn ja, wie heißt Ihr Mann/ Ihre Frau?	______	______
12. Haben Sie Kinder?	______	______
13. Wenn ja, wie viele? Wie heißen sie?	______	______
14. Haben Sie Durst?	______	______
15. Haben Sie Hunger?	______	______
16. Haben Sie heute° Angst?	______	______

if, when

today

Wissenswerte Vokabeln: Studienfächer°

academic subjects

Identifying academic interests

W. Vok.: All sciences are feminine nouns. All languages are neuter.

Biologie • Chemie • Medizin • Musik • Mathematik • Philosophie • Physik • Psychologie • Soziologie • Deutsch • Englisch • Französisch • Russisch • Spanisch

Was studieren Sie? *Ich studiere Betriebswirtschaft.*

If your field of study is not listed here, ask your instructor for its German name.

1. Betriebswirtschaft
2. Geschichte
3. Informatik
4. Ingenieurwesen
5. Internationale Beziehungen
6. Kunst
7. Volkswirtschaft
8. Pädagogik
9. Politikwissenschaft

II ▣ Expressing what you like and don't like

The expression **gern haben**

When talking about what they like, German speakers use the verb **haben** with the adverb **gern. Gern** usually appears at the end of the sentence or clause.

Ich **habe** Deutsch **gern.**	*I like German.*
Meine Schwester **hat** Mozart **gern.**	*My sister likes Mozart.*
Haben Sie Mozart auch **gern?**	*Do you like Mozart, too?*

When talking about what they dislike, German speakers use the verb **haben** with **nicht gern,** which appears at the end of the sentence or clause.

Wir **haben** Musik **nicht gern.**	*We don't like music.*
Was? Ihr **habt** Musik **nicht gern?**	*What? Don't you (all) like music?*

Quantifiers such as **sehr** *(a lot)*, **nicht so** *(not so)*, and **nicht sehr** *(not much)* can be added to specify how much one likes or dislikes something.

Ich **habe** Biologie und Mathematik **sehr gern.**	*I like biology and math a lot.*
Geschichte **haben** wir **nicht so gern.**	*We don't like history so much.*

13 **Welche Studienfächer haben Sie gern?** Take a poll by asking the other students the following questions. Determine which subjects are studied, which are liked and which are disliked by at least three people.

Fragen	*Resultate*
1. Welche Fächer haben Sie dieses Semester?	Drei Leute haben ...
2. Welche Fächer haben Sie gern?	Drei Leute haben ... gern.
3. Welche Fächer haben Sie nicht so gern?	Drei Leute haben ... nicht so gern.

Schreibecke **Was wir gern haben**

In complete sentences describe which subjects you are studying this semester, which of these you like, and which ones you dislike. Based on interviews, describe which students in the class share your schedule, likes, and dislikes.

- Ich habe Deutsch, Mathematik und Chemie. Jenny hat auch Deutsch. Ben und Katie haben auch Mathematik. Ich habe Deutsch gern. Jenny hat ...

Schreibecke. To express the notion of *also*, insert **auch** after **haben.**

III Describing actions

Present tense of regular verbs

A. *Conjugation of regular verbs in the present tense*

When talking about the activities that we or other people do, a subject pronoun is used along with a conjugated verb. Often a word or phrase follows the verb. Different subject pronouns require different endings on the verbs. Here are the present tense endings of the verb **spielen** *(to play)* as an example.

spielen: *to play*				
Person	**Singular**		**Plural**	
1st	ich spiel**e**	*I play; I am playing*	wir spiel**en**	*we play; we are playing*
2nd, informal	du spiel**st**	*you play; you are playing*	ihr spiel**t**	*you play; you are playing*
2nd, formal	Sie spiel**en**	*you play; you are playing*	Sie spiel**en**	*you play; you are playing*
3rd	er/sie/es spiel**t**	*he/she/it plays; he/she/it is playing*	sie spiel**en**	*they play; they are playing*

Notice there are three forms that are always identical to the regular infinitive: **wir** *(we)*, **Sie** (*you*, formal), and **sie** *(they)*. As you learned in *Kapitel 1*, the infinitive is the form listed in the dictionary and is composed of two parts: the stem **(spiel-)**

and the ending **(-en).** The endings are attached to the verb stem. The verbs **tun** and **wandern** just add **-n** to the stem. Here are some other important verbs from the text.

Infinitive	**gehen**	**heißen**	**kommen**	**meinen**	**studieren**	**verstehen**
	to go	*to be called, named*	*to come*	*to think, mean*	*to study*	*to understand*
ich	geh**e**	heiß**e**	komm**e**	mein**e**	studier**e**	versteh**e**
du	geh**st**	heiß**t**	komm**st**	mein**st**	studier**st**	versteh**st**
Sie	geh**en**	heiß**en**	komm**en**	mein**en**	studier**en**	versteh**en**
er/sie/es	geh**t**	heiß**t**	komm**t**	mein**t**	studier**t**	versteh**t**
wir	geh**en**	heiß**en**	komm**en**	mein**en**	studier**en**	versteh**en**
ihr	geh**t**	heiß**t**	komm**t**	mein**t**	studier**t**	versteh**t**
Sie	geh**en**	heiß**en**	komm**en**	mein**en**	studier**en**	versteh**en**
sie	geh**en**	heiß**en**	komm**en**	mein**en**	studier**en**	versteh**en**

du heißt: Note that the typical **-st** ending for **du** is reduced to **-t** when it follows **ß, s,** or **sch.**

B. Present tense equivalents in English and German

English has three possible meanings for one present tense German form.

Er **spielt** Mozart. { *He **plays** Mozart.* / *He is **playing** Mozart.* / *He **does play** Mozart.* }

Wir **studieren** Kunst. { *We **study** art.* / *We **are studying** art.* / *We **do study** art.* }

The English use of *do* or *does* emphasizes the action expressed in the infinitive: *He does play Mozart.* There is no equivalent in standard German for this use of *do* or *does.* Instead, standard present tense is used, often in conjunction with the adverb **doch: Er spielt doch Mozart.**

C. Formulating yes/no questions in the present tense

A yes/no question is created by reversing the position of the conjugated verb and the subject.

Spielt er auch Bach? { ***Does** he **play** Bach, too?* / ***Is** he **playing** Bach, too?* }

Studierst du Chemie? { ***Are** you **studying** chemistry?* / ***Do** you **study** chemistry?* }

14 **Annas Familie.** In groups or pairs talk about Anna's family.

Anna: Ich heiße Anna.
Annas Eltern • Annas Bruder

S1: Annas Eltern heißen Hannelore und Bob Adler.
S2: Annas Bruder heißt Jeff.

1. Anna: Ich heiße Anna.
   Annas Eltern (Hannelore und Bob Adler) • Annas Bruder (Jeff) • Annas Großeltern (Friedrich und Elfriede Kunz) • Annas Kusine (Katja) • Annas Cousin (Georg)

2. Anna: Ich komme aus Fort Wayne.
   Katja und Georg (Weinheim) • Annas Großeltern (Bad Krozingen)
3. Anna: Ich spiele Softball.
   Jeff (Basketball) • Katja (Feldhockey) • Georg und Katja (Tennis) • Annas Mutter (Golf)
4. Anna: Ich höre gern Rockmusik.
   Katja (Oldies) • Annas Großeltern (klassische Musik) • Annas Eltern (Country) • Tante Uschi (Schlager°)
5. Anna: Ich verstehe etwas Deutsch.
   Katja (Englisch) • Georg (nur Fußball) • Annas Großeltern (kein Englisch)

easy listening hits

IV ▣ Talking about what you like and don't like to do

Verbs + the adverb gern

A. *Present tense of verbs with* gern

To talk about activities they like to do, German speakers use a verb that expresses the activity and add the adverb **gern** to the sentence.

Jeff **spielt gern** Basketball.	*Jeff likes to play basketball.*
Sind Sie **gern** in Deutschland?	*Do you like being in Germany?*

To talk about activities they dislike, German speakers add **nicht gern.**

Ich **fliege nicht gern.**	*I **don't like to fly.***
Hören Sie Rap-Musik **nicht gern?**	***Don't** you **like to listen** to rap music?*

B. *Position of* gern *and* nicht gern

Depending on the context of the sentence and the intention of the speaker, **gern** and **nicht gern** occur in different places. You will learn more about that later. For now, place **gern** and **nicht gern** as explained here. In statements, **gern** and **nicht gern** can be placed after the conjugated verb or at the end of the sentence. Placement after the conjugated verb is more common. In yes/no questions, **gern** and **nicht gern** are also placed after the conjugated verb or at the end of the sentence.

Statement	***Question***
Jeff **spielt gern** Basketball.	**Spielt** Jeff **gern** Basketball?
Jeff **spielt** Basketball **gern.**	**Spielt** Jeff Basketball **gern?**
Jeff **spielt nicht gern** Softball.	**Spielt** Jeff **nicht gern** Softball?
Jeff **spielt** Softball **nicht gern.**	**Spielt** Jeff Softball **nicht gern?**

Jeff spielt gern Basketball.
Jeff spielt nicht gern Softball.

15 **Autogrammspiel.** Walk around and find a classmate for each activity listed below. When you find someone who likes to do the activity, have that person sign his/her name.

▣ S1: Spielen Sie gern Tennis?
S2: Nein, ich spiele nicht gern Tennis. *(oder)*
Ja, ich spiele gern Tennis. *John*

1. Spielen Sie gern Tennis? ____________
2. Sprechen Sie gern Deutsch? ____________

3. Trinken Sie gern Bier? ____________
4. Gehen Sie gern einkaufen°? ____________
5. Hören Sie gern Rockmusik? ____________
6. Fliegen Sie gern? ____________

shopping

16 **Was meinen Sie?** Check all of the following phrases that apply to you. Then follow these steps.

Step 1: Tell the class in complete sentences which descriptions apply to you.

S1: Ich höre gern klassische Musik.

Step 2: Remember how other students describe themselves. After all students have described themselves, repeat what they said and ask them to confirm your statement for accuracy.

S2: Jenny hört gern klassische Musik. Stimmt das?
S1: Ja, das stimmt.
S3: Jenny, Eric und Tom verbringen die Semesterferien° in Florida.

semester break

Step 3: Find other students who share your interests. Together, tell the class what these interests are.

Jenny und ich hören gern klassische Musik. Wir hören gern klassische Musik.

	Ich	*Andere°*
1. gern klassische Musik hören	___	___
2. aus den USA kommen	___	___
3. gern einkaufen gehen	___	___
4. Deutsch interessant finden	___	___
5. die Semesterferien in Florida verbringen	___	___
6. dieses Jahr nach Deutschland fliegen	___	___
7. eine Schwester haben	___	___
8. gern Tennis spielen	___	___

others

Schreibecke. Use Katja's description of her own family as a model to write about your family.

Meine Familie wohnt in Weinheim.
Mein Vater heißt Johannes Günther. Er ist 45 Jahre alt. Er ist nicht sehr alt. Er kommt aus Paderborn. Er spielt gern Tischtennis.
Meine Mutter heißt Ursula Günther. Sie ist 48 Jahre alt. Sie ist sehr klug. Sie kommt aus Bad Krozingen. Sie spielt nicht gern Tischtennis.
Mein Bruder heißt Georg. Er ist 16 Jahre alt. Er kommt aus Weinheim. Er meint, er ist sehr klug. Er hört gern Rockmusik. Er lernt nicht gern Englisch.
Herzliche Grüße,
Katja

V ▣ Talking about what you have and don't have

The accusative case

A. *Definite and indefinite articles*

The subject of a sentence which performs the action described by the verb is in the nominative case **(der Nominativ),** and answers the questions **wer?** *(who?)* and **was?** *(what ?).* The accusative case **(der Akkusativ)** is used to designate the direct object **(das direkte Objekt).** The direct object is the recipient or target of the action expressed by the verb and answers the questions **wen?** *(whom?)* and **was?** *(what?).*

Was hat Anna?	*What is Anna having?*
Anna hat **einen Traum.**	*Anna is having a dream.*
Was sucht Anna?	*What is Anna looking for?*
Anna sucht **den Hörsaal.**	*Anna is looking for the lecture hall.*
Wen fragt Anna?	*Whom does Anna ask?*
Anna fragt **eine Studentin.**	*Anna asks a (female) student .*
Was schreibt Anna?	*What is Anna writing?*
Anna schreibt **ein Fax.**	*Anna is writing a fax.*

You can identify the accusative case by looking at the ending on the article. The ending denotes both the gender (masculine, feminine, neuter) and the number (singular or plural) of the noun, as well as its function (direct object as opposed to subject, etc.) The following chart shows all the forms of the definite and indefinite articles, plus **kein** in the nominative and accusative case.

Case	Singular						Plural	
	Masculine		Neuter		Feminine		All Genders	
	Definite	Indefinite	Definite	Indefinite	Definite	Indefinite	Definite	Indefinite
Nominative	der	ein kein	das	ein kein	die	eine keine	die	— keine
Accusative	den	einen keinen	das	ein kein	die	eine keine	die	— keine

Note that only the singular masculine forms are different in the accusative **(den, einen, keinen)** and in the nominative **(der, ein, kein).** Singular feminine and neuter forms as well as plural forms are identical in the nominative and in the accusative. Please also note that **kein** has the same endings as **ein.**

B. *Masculine N-nouns*

N-nouns are discussed mainly for recognition.

A small group of masculine nouns adds an **-n** or **-en** ending to the noun itself to signal the change in function from subject to direct object. Pay special attention to these nouns which include **der Herr** (→ **den Herrn), der Student** (→ **den Studenten),** and **der Junge** (→ **den Jungen).** The noun for a male German (**der Deutsche/ein Deutscher**) is not a masculine N-noun. It is a noun formed from an adjective. You will learn more about the endings on adjectives in Chapter 10. In vocabulary sections, the extra accusative case ending will be noted in brackets. The second **-en** ending listed is the plural ending: **der Student, [-en], -en.**

Ich kenne **den Herrn.**	*I know the man.*
Ich kenne **den Studenten** nicht.	*I don't know the student.*

17 **Ich habe ... zu Hause.** *(I have . . . at home.)* Ask what your partner has at home. Report your findings to the class. As you listen to what other students say, write down their names next to what they have.

Ich habe ... zu Hause. Make sure to mention things you don't have as well as things you do have.

S1: Haben Sie einen Hund zu Hause?
S2: Ja, ich habe einen Hund. Ich habe keine Katze.

	Personen/Tiere/Objekte	*Mein Partner/Meine Partnerin*	*Andere Leute*
1.	einen Hund	_____	_____
2.	einen Vater	_____	_____
3.	einen Bruder	_____	_____
4.	zwei (drei, vier) Brüder	_____	_____
5.	eine Mutter	_____	_____
6.	eine Schwester	_____	_____
7.	zwei (drei, vier) Schwestern	_____	_____
8.	eine Katze	_____	_____
9.	einen Sohn	_____	_____
10.	einen Basketball	_____	_____
11.	eine Tochter	_____	_____
12.	einen Fernseher	_____	_____
13.	einen Schreibtisch	_____	_____
14.	ein Deutschbuch	_____	_____

Ich habe einen Porsche, einen Audi, einen BMW, einen Mercedes und einen Trabi zu Hause.

Sprache im Alltag: The expression überhaupt kein

German speakers add the word **überhaupt** to a form of the negative article **kein** to signify intense negation and to express the total absence of an entity.

Haben Sie Verwandte in Deutschland?	*Do you have any relatives in Germany?*
Nein, ich habe **überhaupt keine** Verwandten.	*No, I don't have any relatives at all.*

18 **Meine° Familie.** Answer your partner's questions. Follow the model.

My

- Schwester in Mexiko
- S1: Haben Sie eine Schwester in Mexiko?
  S2: Nein, ich habe keine Schwester in Mexiko. Ich habe eine Schwester in Kanada, in Edmonton. *(oder)*
  Ich habe überhaupt keine Schwester.

1. Onkel in Österreich
2. Großvater in Kanada
3. Großmutter in Russland
4. Tante in China
5. Kinder in England
6. Vetter in Kalifornien
7. Sohn in Japan
8. Tochter in Australien

ABSPRUNGTEXT
Anna schreibt ein Fax

In preparation for her year in Germany, Anna Adler decides to contact her relatives in Germany. Her mother's sister, Ursula, lives with her family in Weinheim, not far from Frankfurt, where Anna's plane will land. Anna hopes to spend some time with them before her German course in Tübingen begins, but she is too unsure of her German to just call and talk on the phone. With a little help from her mother, Anna sends Tante Uschi a fax. Anna writes about her travel plans, her academic schedule in Germany, and her request to come for a visit. She asks Tante Uschi specifically to either write or fax back her answers. Anna clearly wants to avoid speaking German on the phone, at least for now.

Note again that the short version of **Ursula,** generally used by family and friends, is **Uschi.**

Vorschau

19 **Thematische Fragen.** Discuss the following questions with your instructor or in pairs.

1. If you were writing a letter or fax to relatives who lived in a foreign country and whom you'd never met, telling them that you wanted to come for a visit, what travel information would you include?
2. Pretend you wanted to visit these relatives before starting a study-abroad program in the country they live in. What would you tell them about yourself? What questions would you ask them?
3. Why might you prefer writing instead of calling someone abroad? Why would speaking a foreign language on the phone be more difficult than speaking it face to face with someone?

20 **Mein Tagtraum°.** Imagine that you are going to Germany. How do you see yourself?

daydream

1. das Alter
   a. Ich bin fünfzehn Jahre alt.
   b. Ich bin zwanzig Jahre alt.
   c. Ich bin fünfzig Jahre alt.
2. der Beruf°
   a. Ich bin Schüler(in).
   b. Ich bin Student(in).
   c. Ich habe einen Beruf.

occupation

3. die Personen
   a. Ich fahre allein.
   b. Ich fahre mit° Freunden.
   c. Ich fahre mit meiner Familie.

with

4. in Deutschland
   a. Ich gehe einkaufen.
   b. Ich studiere an der Universität.
   c. Ich besuche° meine Verwandten.

am visiting

5. die Zeit
   a. Ich bleibe° eine Woche.
   b. Ich bleibe einen Monat.
   c. Ich bleibe ein Jahr.

stay

6. die Sprache
   a. Ich spreche perfekt Deutsch.
   b. Ich spreche ein bisschen Deutsch.
   c. Ich spreche perfekt Englisch.

Mein Tagtraum. While **Student** and **Studentin** denote students at the university level, **Schüler** and **Schülerin** refer to students at the elementary and secondary school levels.

21 **Wortdetektiv.** Which words convey approximately the same meaning? Draw a line from the German word to its logical English equivalent.

Deutsch	*Englisch*
1. schicken	a. to arrive
2. beginnen	b. to send
3. ankommen	c. to begin
4. Verwandte	d. to get to know
5. kennen lernen	e. to spend two semesters
6. zwei Semester verbringen	f. relatives
7. allein	g. immediately
8. gleich	h. alone
9. die Frage	i. request
10. die Zeit	j. time
11. die Bitte	k. question

22 **Scanning.** Scanning is a reading technique used to identify specific information, without reading every word of the text. It also helps the reader to locate the features that are typical of a certain text type.

1. When composing a letter, formal or informal, the writer generally observes certain conventions. Scan Anna's letter for these customary elements.
   a. a return address
   b. a date
   c. an opening greeting
   d. a closing
2. Look over Anna's fax for answers to these questions.
   a. When is she arriving in Germany, and where?
   b. When does her German course begin?
   c. When does the actual fall semester begin?
   d. How does she express her wish to come for a visit? How does she repeat it?

ABSPRUNGTEXT

Anna schreibt ein Fax

Now read the text.

1835 Indian Village Blvd.
Fort Wayne
Indiana 46809
USA
Fax: 219/555-7890

den 5.Juli

Liebe Tante Uschi,

ich fliege in einem Monat nach Deutschland. Ich komme am 17. August um 8.15 Uhr in Frankfurt an. Ich verbringe zwei Semester an der Universität Tübingen. Mein Deutschkurs an der Universität Tübingen beginnt gleich am Montag, dem 27. August. Das Semester beginnt aber erst° im Oktober. Ich habe ein bisschen Zeit, und ich möchte° nach Weinheim kommen und meine Verwandten in Deutschland endlich besser kennen lernen. Ein Jahr in Deutschland finde ich wunderbar, aber ich habe auch ein bisschen Angst. Es ist meine erste Reise nach Deutschland, und ich komme ganz allein. Ich habe so viele Fragen. Ist es teuer in Europa? Wie sind die Leute in Deutschland? Gott sei Dank habe ich Verwandte in Deutschland.
Ich habe eine Bitte: Darf° ich nach Weinheim kommen? Schreib bitte bald zurück oder schick ein Fax.

Herzliche Grüße
deine Nichte

Anna

Absprungtext. In a German letter, a male is addressed with **Lieber ...** and a female with **Liebe ...** followed by that person's name (e.g., **Liebe Tante Uschi**).

German speakers conclude an informal letter with **dein/ deine ...** *(your . . .)* plus the name of a male/female writer.

not until

would like to

may

Rückblick

23 **Stimmt das?** How much of the text do you remember without looking back at it?

	Ja, das stimmt.	*Nein, das stimmt nicht.*
1. Anna fliegt im Juli nach Deutschland.	___	___
2. Anna kommt am 17. August in Frankfurt an.	___	___
3. Annas Deutschkurs beginnt am 27. August.	___	___
4. Anna möchte direkt nach Tübingen fahren.	___	___
5. Anna findet ein Jahr in Deutschland wunderbar.	___	___
6. Anna kommt allein.	___	___
7. Anna hat keine Angst; sie spricht perfekt Deutsch.	___	___
8. Gott sei Dank hat Anna Verwandte in Deutschland.	___	___
9. Tante Uschi soll° nicht zurückschreiben, sie soll anrufen°.	___	___

should / phone

24 **Ergänzen Sie.** Complete these questions and statements with words from the **Absprungtext.**

1. Ich _____ in einem Monat nach Deutschland.
2. Ich _____ am 17. August um 8 Uhr 15 in Frankfurt an.
3. Ich verbringe zwei _____ an der Universität in Tübingen.
4. Mein Deutschkurs _____ gleich am Montag, dem 27. August.
5. Ich möchte nach Weinheim kommen und meine Verwandten in Deutschland endlich besser _____ _____.
6. Ein Jahr in Deutschland ist wunderbar, aber ich habe auch ein bisschen _____.
7. Ich habe so viele _____.
8. Ist es _____ in Europa?
9. Wie sind die _____ in Deutschland?
10. Ich habe eine _____: Darf ich nach Weinheim kommen?

25 **Kurz gefragt.** Answer these questions with just a word or two.

S1: Wann kommt Anna nach Deutschland?
S2: In einem Monat. *(oder)*
Im August.

1. Wo kommt sie an?
2. Wo studiert sie?
3. Was studiert sie?
4. Wann beginnt das Semester?
5. Hat sie Angst?
6. Wo wohnen Annas Verwandte in Deutschland?

Jänner is used in Austria for **Januar.**

Wissenswerte Vokabeln: die Monate

Talking about birthdays

der Monat, -e

der Januar	... im Januar	am ersten Januar	am elften Januar
der Februar	... im Februar	am zweiten Februar	am zwölften ...
der März	... im März	am dritten März	am dreizehnten ...
der April	... im April	am vierten April	am vierzehnten ...
der Mai	... im Mai	am fünften Mai	am fünfzehnten ...

am dreiundzwanzigsten ... am dreißigsten ... am einunddreißigsten ... am vierzigsten ... am fünfzigsten ...

der Juni	... im Juni	am sechsten Juni	am sechzehnten ...
der Juli	... im Juli	am siebten Juli	am siebzehnten ...
der August	... im August	am achten August	am achtzehnten ...
der September	... im September	am neunten September	am neunzehnten ...
der Oktober	... im Oktober	am zehnten Oktober	am zwanzigsten ...
der November	... im November	am elften November	am einund-zwanzigsten ...
der Dezember	... im Dezember	am zwölften Dezember	am zweiund-zwanzigsten ...

Form the ordinal numbers for 2 and 4-19 by adding the ending **-ten** to the number. For numbers above 20, add **-sten**. The following ordinal numbers have individual forms: **ersten, dritten**, and **siebten**.

S1: Wann haben Sie Geburtstag?
S2: Im Januar.
S1: Wann haben Sie im Januar Geburtstag?
S2: Ich habe am fünfundzwanzigsten Januar Geburtstag.

26 **Wann haben Sie Geburtstag?** With a partner, state the date on which the following birthdays happen.

Wann? Ihr and **Ihre** are the formal equivalents of *your.* You will learn more about this form in Chapter 3.

S1: Wann haben Sie Geburtstag?
S2: Ich habe am dritten September Geburtstag.

	Ich	*Mein Partner/Meine Partnerin*
1. Wann haben Sie Geburtstag?	_____	_____
2. Wann hat Ihre Mutter Geburtstag?	_____	_____
3. Wann hat Ihr Vater Geburtstag?	_____	_____
4. Wann hat Ihre Schwester Geburtstag?	_____	_____
5. Wann hat Ihr Bruder Geburtstag?	_____	_____
6. Wann hat Ihr Freund/Ihre Freundin Geburtstag?	_____	_____

Strukturen und Vokabeln

VI Creating variety and shifting emphasis

Position of subject and verb

See the **Arbeitsbuch** for additional practice with structures and vocabulary.

In declarative sentences, the subject is generally the first element of the sentence, followed by the conjugated verb and the predicate (e.g., objects, prepositional phrases).

subject
Ich heiße Anna Adler. — *My name is Anna Adler.*

subject
Ich bin 20 Jahre alt. — *I am twenty years old.*

subject
Ich fliege im August nach Deutschland. — *I'm flying to Germany in August.*

However, it is also possible to begin a German sentence with something other than the subject. The first position can be occupied by a single word, a phrase, or an entire clause. The number of words in an element is not important. The purpose of placing an element other than the subject in first position is to emphasize this element. Regardless of the position of the subject, the position of the conjugated verb remains constant. It is always the second element of a sentence. Whenever an element other than the subject begins a sentence, the subject follows as the third element of the sentence.

	1	2 Verb	3 Subject
Time phrase:	Dieses Jahr	verbringe	**ich** zwei Semester in Deutschland.
Direct object:	Ein Jahr in Deutschland	finde	**ich** wunderbar.

Please note that words like **ja** or **nein** and the conjunctions **und, aber, oder** *(and, but, or)* do not affect the word order.

Ich heiße Anna, ***und*** *ich bin Amerikanerin.*

27 Annas Pläne. Match the following sentence parts so they accurately reflect Anna's plans.

1. In Fort Wayne ... a. beginnt das Semester.
2. In Frankfurt ... b. schreibe ich ein Fax.
3. Ein Jahr ... c. besuche ich Verwandte.
4. Im Oktober ... d. komme ich an.
5. In Weinheim ... e. studiere ich in Tübingen.

Wissenswerte Vokabeln: die Wochentage

Talking about weekly schedules

der Wochentag, -e

der Sonntag	... am Sonntag
der Montag	... am Montag
der Dienstag	... am Dienstag
der Mittwoch	... am Mittwoch
der Donnerstag	... am Donnerstag
der Freitag	... am Freitag
der Samstag *(in Süddeutschland)*	... am Samstag
der Sonnabend *(in Norddeutschland)*	... am Sonnabend
das Wochenende	... am Wochenende

Was ist heute?	*Heute ist Montag.*
Was haben wir heute?	*Heute haben wir Mittwoch.*
Wann spielt Anna Softball?	*Am Donnerstag.*

To find what day of the week it is, German speakers usually ask: **Was ist heute?**, or: **Was haben wir heute?** The answer states the day of the week without an article: **Heute ist Dienstag. Heute haben wir Sonnabend.**

28 Jetzt sind Sie dran. Restate these sentences by positioning the underlined words in the first position and making all the necessary changes.

1. Wir verbringen ein Semester an der Universität in Göttingen.
2. Wir haben so viele Fragen!
3. Wir fliegen in drei Tagen nach Frankfurt.
4. Wir verbringen das Wochenende in Frankfurt.
5. Wir fahren dann nach Göttingen weiter°.

fahren weiter: *go on to*

6. Wir kommen am Montag in Göttingen an.
7. Der Deutschkurs an der Universität beginnt gleich am Dienstag.
8. Wir spielen erst am Samstag ein bisschen Fußball.

29 **Was macht Katja heute?** Answer these questions about Katja's activities this week. You need not answer in complete sentences.

Montag	eine Postkarte schreiben
Dienstag	Tennis spielen
Mittwoch	mit Jutta Kaffee trinken
Donnerstag	einen Pullover kaufen
Freitag	tanzen gehen
Samstag	einen Spanischkurs haben
Sonntag	zu Hause bleiben
Notizen	

1. Was macht Katja am Mittwoch?
2. Wann bleibt Katja zu Hause?
3. Wann geht Katja tanzen?
4. Spielt Katja Tennis oder Fußball? Wann?
5. Was macht Katja am Montag?
6. Wann geht Katja einkaufen? Was kauft Katja?
7. Hat Katja Samstag frei?

Was macht Katja heute? When one takes brief notes in German and does not make complete sentences, the infinitive appears at the end.

Wissenswerte Vokabeln: Zeitausdrücke

Expressing repeated activities

sonntags
montags
dienstags
mittwochs
donnerstags
freitags
samstags, sonnabends
sonntags

Wann lernen Sie?

W. Vok.: To express that an activity repeatedly or habitually takes place on a certain day, German speakers use the adverbial forms of the days of the week. They are written small case with an **-s** at the end.

30 **Wann machen Sie das?** *(When are you doing that?)* Your partner will ask you about activities you do. Answer with **am** plus the particular day of the week if you will engage in the activity this week. Use the name of the day only plus an added **-s** if you do the activity regularly.

S1: Wann haben Sie Deutsch?
S2: Ich habe montags, mittwochs und freitags Deutsch.

1. Deutsch haben
2. einkaufen gehen
3. im Restaurant essen
4. Musik hören
5. Hausaufgaben° machen
6. zu Hause bleiben
7. tanzen° gehen
8. Bier trinken

homework

to dance, dancing

Wissenswerte Vokabeln: die Uhrzeit

Telling time

Es ist sieben Uhr morgens.

Es ist Viertel nach eins.
Es ist viertel zwei.

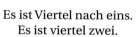

Es ist Viertel vor zwei.
Es ist drei viertel zwei.

Es ist halb sechs.

Es ist fünf Minuten vor sechs.

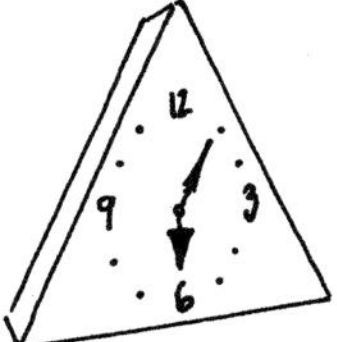

Es ist fünf Minuten nach sechs.

Es ist zehn Uhr abends.
Es ist zweiundzwanzig Uhr.

Wie viel Uhr ist es? *Es ist ...*

Expressing time periods

Wann kommt Anna in Frankfurt an?	Sie kommt um Viertel nach acht an. Sie kommt um viertel neun an. Sie kommt um acht Uhr fünfzehn an.
Wann haben Sie Deutsch?	Ich habe von acht (Uhr) bis acht Uhr fünfzig Deutsch.
Wann haben Sie Mathematik?	Ich habe von neun bis elf (Uhr) Mathematik.
Wie lange haben Sie Deutsch?	Ich habe fünfzig Minuten (lang) Deutsch.
Wie lange haben Sie Mathematik?	Ich habe zwei Stunden (lang) Mathematik.

A point in time is denoted by the use of **um,** followed by the time.

Especially for official purposes, the 24-hour clock is used. When using the 12-hour clock, **morgens** *(in the morning),* and **abends** *(in the evening)* may be added for further clarification.

31 **Georgs Stundenplan.** Georg is a student in the 11th grade at the **Johannes Kepler Gymnasium** in Weinheim. Complete the sentences below, referring to his weekly schedule for help.

	Mo.	Di.	Mi.	Do.	Fr.	Sa.
7.45	Mathe	—	Deutsch	—	Deutsch	—
8.35	Religion	Englisch	Mathe	—	Deutsch	Deutsch
9.25	Pause	Pause	Pause	Pause	Pause	Pause
9.45	Deutsch	Mathe	Englisch	Deutsch	Physik	Mathe
10.30	Englisch	Physik	Geschichte	Sport	Sport	—
11.15	Geschichte	Erdkunde	—	Englisch	Erdkunde	—
12.00	Geschichte	Religion	Physik	Englisch	Mathe	
12.55			Physik	Erdkunde		

▣ _____ hat Georg Mathe.
Montags um Viertel vor acht hat Georg Mathe.

1. Mittwochs beginnt er um _____.
2. _____ hat er Physik um 12.00 Uhr.
3. Er geht freitags um _____ nach Hause.
4. Religion hat er montags und _____.
5. Er hat Erdkunde freitags von _____ bis _____.
6. Samstags geht er um _____ nach Hause.
7. Samstags hat er Mathe um _____.
8. Mittwochs um _____ hat er frei.
9. Montags hat er um _____ frei.
10. Montags und dienstags geht er um _____ nach Hause°.

Fraction of hours may only be used for the 12-hour clock. **Viertel** *(quarter hour)* may be used in two ways: denoting a quarter of an hour beyond or before a full hour, or describing how much of the next full hour has passed. **Drei viertel zwei** is the same as **Viertel vor zwei. Viertel zwei** is identical to **Viertel nach eins.**

Halb means *half* and when used for telling time indicates that one half of the next full hour has passed. Thus, **halb zwei** means *one thirty.* Amounts of time which cannot be measured in halves or quarters are counted in minutes after **(nach),** or short of **(vor)** the full hour.

The beginning and end of an action is denoted by the use of **von** (starting point) and **bis** (end point).

geht nach Hause: *goes home*

32 **Mein Stundenplan für Montag.** Fill in your course schedule for Mondays in this **Stundenplan.** Then compare notes with a partner by asking each other the questions.

UNICUM DAS MONATSMAGAZIN VON UND FÜR STUDENTEN **STUNDENPLAN Sommersemester**

Zeit	Montag	Dienstag	Mittwoch	Donnerstag	Freitag	Wochenende
8-9						
9-10						
10-11						
11-12						
12-13						
13-14						
14-15						
15-16						
16-17						
17-18						
abends						

1. Um wie viel Uhr kommen Sie hier an?
2. Um wie viel Uhr gehen Sie nach Hause?
3. Wie lange sind Sie an der Uni?
4. Von wann bis wann haben wir Deutsch?
5. Wann und wie lange haben Sie Pause?
6. Was haben Sie um 10 Uhr? Um 11 Uhr? Um 3 Uhr?

The length of a period of time is asked with the question **wie lange?** The response may, but need not, include **lang: zwei Stunden,** or **zwei Stunden lang.**

33 **Wann senden sie?** *(When do they broadcast?)* Ask your partner about the radio stations shown.

WLVU-1470 AM
ZENTRAL FLORIDA
Deutsche Rundfunksendung
Samstags von 7:30 - 10:00 Uhr
Sonntags von 7:30 – 10:30 Uhr
Kurt Ortmann Stevie Anderson
PO Box 3877, Seminole, FL 34642

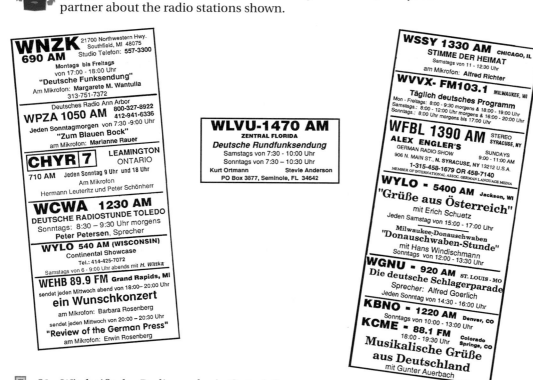

S1: Wie heißt der Radiosender in Ontario?
S2: *CHYR*
S1: Wann senden sie auf Deutsch?
S2: Sonntags um 9 Uhr und um 18 Uhr .

1. Ontario
2. Zentralflorida
3. St. Louis
4. Denver

Note that points in time are reported using the word **Uhr: Es ist drei Uhr.** Time periods, in contrast, are given using the word **Stunde,-n: Ich habe drei Stunden Deutsch.**

VII ■ Describing daily activities

Regular present-tense verbs with separable prefixes

Many German verbs that describe daily activities are composed of the verb stem and a prefix that is sometimes separated from the verb. Separable prefixes resemble independent words, such as prepositions, e.g., **an**kommen, **auf**stehen, **um**drehen, directions, e.g., **zurück**kommen *(to come back),* **fern**sehen *(to watch television),* or separate verbs, e.g., **kennen** lernen (*to get to know*),

English has similar verbs (e.g., *stand up, get up*), but unlike German the prefix is not always part of the infinitive (e.g., **upstand, *upget* do not exist but: *downplay, upgrade* are correct). Also, the placement of these prefixes within a sentence is different in English and German.

spazieren gehen *(to go for a walk).* In a sentence with a conjugated verb, the separable prefix occurs at the end of the clause. In speaking, separable prefixes are always stressed.

an•kommen:	Ich **komme** im August **an.**	*I arrive in August.*
auf•stehen:	**Stehen** Sie bitte **auf.**	*Get up, please.*
um•drehen:	Die Studenten **drehen** sich **um.**	*The students are turning around.*

Prefixes that do not resemble independent words (e.g., prepositions, verbs, or directions), such as **ver-** (**vergessen**: *to forget*) or **be-** (**besuchen**: *to visit*) are not separable.

Gern or **nicht gern,** when used with a separable prefix verb, occur right after the conjugated verb, or right before the separable prefix.

Separable prefix verbs that occur in vocabulary lists in this book are marked with a bullet between the prefix and verb stem (e.g., **auf•stehen, zurück•kommen**). In standard German, these infinitives are written as one word (e.g., **aufstehen, zurückkommen**).

Ich stehe samstags und sonntags **gern auf.**
Ich stehe **gern** samstags und sonntags **auf.**
I like to get up on Saturdays and Sundays.

Ich stehe montags bis freitags **nicht gern auf.**
Ich stehe **nicht gern** montags bis freitags **auf.**
I don't like getting up Monday through Friday.

Wissenswerte Vokabeln: Onkel Hannes' Alltag°

°*everyday life*

Talking about daily activities

1. Um halb sieben **wacht** Hannes Günther **auf.**

2. Um Viertel nach sieben **steht** Hannes **auf.**

3. Um zehn Minuten nach neun **kommt** er im Büro **an.**

4. Gegen zehn Uhr **ruft** er Tante Uschi **an.**

5. Um halb sechs **hört** die Arbeit **auf.**

6. Er **kommt** gegen sechs Uhr **zurück.**

7. Um Viertel nach sechs **geht** Hannes mit Uschi **spazieren.**

8. Um Viertel vor elf **gehen** sie **schlafen.**

■ Wann stehen Sie auf?

34 **Das Wochenende.** Ask your classmates whether they do the following activities on the weekend. Then determine the rank of these activities based on how many people in the class engage in them. Use the numbers 1 (most popular) to 6 (least popular).

Stehen Sie vor sieben Uhr auf?

	Person	*Rang°*
1. vor sieben Uhr aufstehen	_____	_____
2. nach zehn Uhr aufwachen	_____	_____
3. die Eltern anrufen	_____	_____
4. mit Freunden spazieren gehen	_____	_____
5. vor zehn Uhr abends zurückkommen	_____	_____
6. nach elf Uhr abends schlafen gehen	_____	_____

rank

VIII Expressing negation

Position of **nicht**

The following rules governing the placement of **nicht** may be helpful to you.

1. In very basic sentences, **nicht** follows the verb but precedes a separable prefix at the end of the sentence.

   Sie kommt **nicht** an.

2. In yes/no questions, **nicht** remains at the end of the sentence, even though the verb occurs at the beginning of the question.

   Kommen Sie **nicht?**

3. In statements and questions with a direct object, **nicht** usually occurs at the end of the sentence.

   Sie verstehen den Professor **nicht.**
   Verstehen Sie den Professor **nicht?**

4. **Nicht** precedes most adverbs, adjectives, and prepositional phrases.

Er spielt **nicht gern** Tennis.	*He doesn't like to play tennis.*
Sie kommt **nicht aus Deutschland**.	*She isn't from Germany.*
Wir haben **nicht so viel** Zeit.	*We don't have that much time.*
Der Professor ist **nicht freundlich.**	*The professor is not friendly.*

Remember to use a form of **kein** when you answer a question about the availability or existence of someone or something.

Hast du Zeit?	Nein, ich habe **keine** Zeit.
Haben Sie Verwandte in Frankfurt?	Nein, ich habe **keine** Verwandten in Frankfurt.

35 **Verstehen Sie den Professor?** Answer the following questions in the negative, using **nicht.**

S1: Verstehen Sie den Professor?
S2: Nein, ich verstehe den Professor nicht.

1. Verstehen Sie den Professor?
2. Sagen Sie gern „Guten Tag“?
3. Spielt er gern Fußball?

4. Haben Sie so viel Zeit?
5. Kommt Katja aus den USA?
6. Kommen Sie aus Deutschland?
7. Kommt Anna zurück?
8. Ist Anna sportlich?

36 **Nicht oder kein?** Decide whether to use **nicht** or a form of **kein** in your answers to these questions.

S1: Haben Sie einen Bruder in Sankt Petersburg?
S2: Nein, ich habe keinen Bruder in Sankt Petersburg.

1. Haben Sie einen Bruder in Sankt Petersburg?
2. Sprechen Sie perfekt Deutsch?
3. Haben Sie einen Cousin in Weinheim?
4. Haben Sie Zeit?
5. Fliegen Sie heute nach Berlin?
6. Verstehen Sie Finnisch°?
7. Beginnen Sie die Hausaufgaben um sechs Uhr?
8. Stehen Sie um halb zwölf auf?
9. Rufen Sie eine Tante in Istanbul an?
10. Schicken Sie Tante Ursula eine Postkarte?
11. Schreiben Sie ein Fax?

***das Finnische:** the Finnish language*

IX Talking about how much and how many

Use of quantifiers

You may have noticed that in her fax Anna uses two expressions to quantify her statements: **ein bisschen** and **(so) viele.** There are two groups of quantifiers: those that accompany countable nouns with plural endings and those that accompany nouns that can be measured but not counted. Below are two lists of commonly used quantifiers.

Countable quantifiers		***Non-countable quantifiers***	
viele	*many*	viel	*much*
wenige	*few*	wenig	*little*
ein paar	*a few*	ein bisschen, ein wenig, etwas	*a little*
wie viele?	*how many?*	wie viel?	*how much?*

When negating a certain quantity, **nicht** is placed immediately in front of the quantifier.

Haben Sie **viele** Freunde? — Nein, ich habe **nicht viele** Freunde.
Ich habe **wenige** Freunde.

37 **Wie viel? Wie viele?** Insert **wie viel** or **wie viele**.

1. _____ Kurse haben Sie dieses Semester? – Drei Kurse.
2. _____ Studenten sind im Deutschkurs? – Achtzehn Studenten.
3. _____ Angst hat Anna? – Ein bisschen.
4. _____ Fragen hat Anna? – Viele.
5. _____ Deutsch verstehen Sie? – Ein wenig.

38 **Ungefähre Daten.** *(Approximate data.)* Interview a partner on the following issues and check the appropriate response. Make sure to use the proper question words and take turns.

S1: Wie viel Sport treiben Sie°?
S2: Ich treibe viel Sport.

Sport … Sie: do you do sports

	Viel	*Viele*	*Wenige*	*Ein bisschen/Ein wenig*
1. Sport treiben	____	____	____	____
2. schlafen	____	____	____	____
3. Englisch verstehen	____	____	____	____
4. Verwandte haben	____	____	____	____
5. Milch trinken	____	____	____	____
6. Briefe° schreiben	____	____	____	____
7. spazieren gehen	____	____	____	____
8. Freunde an·rufen	____	____	____	____
9. Rockmusik hören	____	____	____	____
10. Pullover kaufen°	____	____	____	____

letters

to buy

ZIELTEXT

Ein Fax kommt an

The **Zieltext** in each chapter is a listening text. The text is intentionally not printed in your textbook in order to increase your understanding of spoken German. Listen carefully to the conversation. Expect to listen to the dialogue several times before you can comfortably understand it. However, remember that in order to understand a text you do not have to recognize every single word. You will be able to understand a lot of German in a fairly short time.

Anna's German relatives in Weinheim, Katja and Uschi Günther, receive her fax from America.

Vorschau

39 **Das wissen wir.** *(That's what we know.)* Please review what has happened so far by checking the correct statement.

1. a. Anna schreibt das Fax.
   b. Hannelore schreibt das Fax.
2. a. Das Fax ist auf Englisch.
   b. Das Fax ist auf Deutsch.
3. a. Anna kommt für ein Jahr nach Deutschland.
   b. Anna kommt für ein Semester nach Deutschland.
4. a. Annas Verwandte wohnen in Tübingen.
   b. Annas Verwandte wohnen in Weinheim.
5. a. Anna hat ein bisschen Angst.
   b. Anna hat viel Angst.
6. a. Die Günthers haben keinen Vater.
   b. Annas Onkel, Herr Günther, heißt Hannes.

40 **Thematische Fragen.** Discuss the following questions with your instructor or in pairs.

1. Who in the Günther family do you think receives the fax?
2. When the Günthers realize that the fax comes from the United States, who will they think wrote it?
3. How will the Günthers feel about Anna's impending visit?

41 **Erstes Zuhören.** *(First listening.)* Listen for the following information. You may want to listen to the text more than once.

1. Wen hören Sie?
   a. zwei Männer
   b. zwei Frauen
   c. einen Mann und eine Frau

2. Was fragt Tante Uschi?
   a. „Von wem ist das Fax?"
   b. „Ist das Fax auf Englisch oder auf Deutsch?"
   c. „Ist das Fax lang oder kurz?"

3. Was weiß° Katja *nicht?*
   a. Ein Fax kommt an.
   b. Das Fax kommt von Amerika.
   c. Anna schickt das Fax.

knows

4. Was fragt Katja?
   a. „Wo möchte Anna schlafen?"
   b. „Was möchte Anna essen und trinken?"
   c. „Was möchte Anna hier machen?"

5. Katjas und Tante Uschis Reaktion ist ...
   a. positiv.
   b. negativ.
   c. neutral.

ZIELTEXT

Ein Fax kommt an

Now listen to the recording.

Rückblick

42 Ordnung schaffen. *(Tidying up.)* Number these sentences from the text in the order in which you hear them.

___ Ich habe keine Ahnung.
___ Was? Wann denn? Warum denn?
___ Sie hat etwas Zeit.
_1_ Schau mal, Mutti!
___ Nein, Moment mal.
___ Das ist toll.

43 Austausch. *(Exchange.)* First, check the characteristics that apply to you. Then, check the characteristics that describe a person you would want to take in as an exchange student for a year if you were a German speaker. Finally, go around the class and ask as many students as possible about their characteristics and tell others about yours. The goal is for you to find an "exchange student" whom you would be comfortable with.

Austausch. The verb **spricht** is the third person singular form of **sprechen.** You will learn more about why the stem vowel changes in Chapter 3.

S1: Sprechen Sie viel Deutsch?
S2: Ja, ich spreche viel Deutsch.

Ich ...	*Der Austauschstudent/Die Austauschstudentin ...*
1. spreche ...	spricht° ...
a. ein bisschen Deutsch.	a. ein bisschen Deutsch.
b. viel Deutsch.	b. viel Deutsch.
2. spiele viel ...	spielt viel ...
a. Fußball.	a. Fußball.
b. Tennis.	b. Tennis.
c. Softball.	c. Softball.
3. höre gern ...	hört gern ...
a. klassische Musik.	a. klassische Musik.
b. Rockmusik.	b. Rockmusik.
c. Countrymusik.	c. Countrymusik.
4. gehe nicht gern ...	geht nicht gern ...
a. wandern.	a. wandern.
b. einkaufen.	b. einkaufen.
c. vor elf Uhr abends schlafen.	c. vor elf Uhr abends schlafen.
5. trinke wenig ...	trinkt wenig ...
a. Milch.	a. Milch.
b. Kaffee.	b. Kaffee.
c. Bier.	c. Bier.
6. stehe montags bis freitags ...	steht montags bis freitags ...
a. vor sieben Uhr auf.	a. vor sieben Uhr auf.
b. vor neun Uhr auf.	b. vor neun Uhr auf.
c. nach neun Uhr auf.	c. nach neun Uhr auf.
7. habe ...	hat ...
a. viele Verwandte.	a. viele Verwandte.
b. wenige Verwandte.	b. wenige Verwandte.

° *speaks*

8. bin ...	ist ...
a. ein Mann.	a. ein Mann.
b. eine Frau.	b. eine Frau.
9. bin ...	ist ...
a. freundlich.	a. freundlich.
b. intelligent.	b. intelligent.
c. jung.	c. jung.
10. studiere ...	studiert ...
a. Deutsch.	a. Deutsch.
b. Volkswirtschaft.	b. Volkswirtschaft.
c. ?	c. ?

■ **FREIE** ■ **KOMMUNIKATION** ■ **Das bin ich.** *(That's me.)* You have been asked to give a speech to an Austrian class that wants to know what American students are like. Describe yourself in as much detail as possible.

Das bin ich. Use items from the activity **Austausch,** but go into more detail.

Consider taping yourself as you speak. Submit the tape to your instructor, or to peers for feedback. You may also transcribe what you have said and rerecord yourself after you have corrected your mistakes.

Schreibecke **Einen Brief schreiben.** (*Writing a letter.*) You are planning to attend a summer course in Austria in July. Write a letter to your pen pal Annette announcing the date of your arrival in **Wien** *(Vienna).* Tell her when the course begins and that you have a little time prior to the beginning of the course to come visit her. Ask her if it is all right. Tell her that you are coming alone, and that you are a little concerned about your ability to speak German. Ask her questions about the weather and the people in Austria. Start some sentences with a grammatical element other than the subject and end your letter with a proper closing.

Einen Brief schreiben. Look back to the fax that Anna sends to her relatives in Germany for the typical format of a letter.

Die Familie

der Bruder, ¨ *brother*
der Cousin, -s *(male) cousin*
die Eltern *(pl.) parents*
der Enkel, - *grandson*
die Enkelin, -innen *granddaughter*
das Enkelkind, -er *grandchild*
die Familie, -n *family*
die Frau, -en *wife*
die Großeltern *(pl.) grandparents*
die Großmutter, ¨ *grandmother*
der Großvater, ¨ *grandfather*
das Kind, -er *child*
die Kusine, -n *(female) cousin*
der Mann, ¨er *husband*
die Mutter, ¨ *mother*
der Neffe, [-n], -n *nephew*
die Nichte, -n *niece*
die Oma, -s *grandma*
der Onkel, - *uncle*
der Opa, -s *grandpa*
die Schwester, -n *sister*
der Sohn, ¨e *son*
der Stiefbruder, ¨ *stepbrother*
die Stiefschwester, -n *stepsister*
die Tante, -n *aunt*
die Tochter, ¨ *daughter*
der Vater, ¨ *father*
die Verwandten *(pl.) relatives*
der Vetter, - *(male) cousin*

der Freund, -e *(male) friend, boyfriend*
die Freunde *(pl.) friends (a group of male and female)*
die Freundin, -nen *(female) friend, girlfriend*
die Leute *(pl.) people*

haben *to have*
gern haben *to like*
wohnen *to live*

geschieden *divorced*
ledig *single*
verheiratet *married*

Interessen und Aktivitäten

die Arbeit *work*
die Musik *music*
die Reise *trip, journey*

darf *may*
fern·sehen *to watch television*
finden *to find, consider*
fliegen *to fly*
gehen *to go*
gern + verb *to like to . . .*
hören *to hear, listen to*
kennen lernen *to meet, get to know*
möchte *would like to*
spielen *to play*
(sich) vor·stellen *to introduce (oneself)*
wandern *to hike*

doch *yes indeed*
klug *smart, intelligent*
nicht sehr *not very*
nicht so *not so*
sehr *very*
sportlich (unsportlich) *athletic (non-athletic)*

Kommunikation

das Fax *fax*
die Frage *question*

an·rufen *to phone, call up*
meinen *to think, have an opinion*
schicken *to send*
sehen *to see*

Ausdrücke

herzliche Grüße *sincerely yours*
Ich habe ein bisschen Angst. *I'm a little scared.*
Ich habe eine Bitte. *I have a request.*
Ich habe (keinen) Durst. *I'm (not) thirsty.*
Ich habe (keinen) Hunger. *I'm (not) hungry.*
Ich bin gespannt auf (das Jahr). *I'm excited about (the year).*
liebe/lieber *dear*
naja . . . *well . . . (as a hesitation marker)*
zum Beispiel *for example*

Die Studienfächer

die Betriebswirtschaft *business*
die Biologie *biology*
die Chemie *chemistry*
das Deutsch *German*
das Englisch *the English language*
das Französisch *French*
die Geschichte *history*
die Informatik *computer science*
das Ingenieurwesen *engineering*
Internationale Beziehungen *(pl.) international relations*
die Kunst *art*
die Mathematik *mathematics*
die Medizin *medicine*
die Musik *music*
die Pädagogik *education*
die Philosophie *philosophy*
die Physik *physics*
die Politik *politics*
die Politikwissenschaft *political science*
die Psychologie *psychology*
das Russisch *Russian*
die Soziologie *sociology*
das Spanisch *Spanish*
das Studienfach, ¨er *academic subject*
die Volkswirtschaft *economics*

Die Universität

der Deutschkurs, -e *German language course*
das Semester, - *semester*

der Student, [-en], -en *(male) student*
die Studentin, -innen *(female) student*
beginnen *to begin*
lernen *to learn; to engage in active study*
studieren *to study*
verbessern *to improve*

Ausdrücke

an der Universität *at the university, at college*

Die Zeit

das Jahr, -e *year*
der Monat, -e *month*
der Tag, -e *day*
die Zeit, -en *time*
verbringen *to spend (time)*

Ausdrücke

abends *in the evening*
am (17. August) *on the (17th of August)*
dieses Jahr *this year*
drei viertel zwei *quarter of two, quarter to two*
erst *not until; first*
gleich *right away*
halb *half way to the next hour*
  Es ist halb zwei. *It's half past 1 (1:30).*
Moment mal ... *wait a minute . . .*
morgens *in the morning*
nach *past, after*
um *at*
Viertel nach *quarter after, quarter past*
Viertel vor zwei *quarter to two*
von ... bis *from . . . until*
vor *to, of*
Wie viel Uhr ist es? *What time is it?*

Die Wochentage

der Sonntag *Sunday*
der Montag *Monday*
der Dienstag *Tuesday*
der Mittwoch *Wednesday*
der Donnerstag *Thursday*
der Freitag *Friday*
der Samstag *Saturday (southern German)*
der Sonnabend *Saturday (northern German)*
das Wochenende, -n *weekend*
der Wochentag, -e *day of the week, weekday*

Die Monate

der Januar *January*
der Februar *February*
der März *March*
der April *April*
der Mai *May*
der Juni *June*
der Juli *July*
der August *August*
der September *September*
der Oktober *October*
der November *November*
der Dezember *December*

Ausdrücke

heute *today*
montags *on Mondays*
am Montag *on Monday*
Wann haben Sie denn Geburtstag? *When's your birthday?*
im Januar *in January*

Der Alltag

der Alltag *everyday life*
an·kommen *to arrive*
auf·hören *to stop*
auf·stehen *to get up, get out of bed*
auf·wachen *to wake up*
ein·kaufen *to shop*
schlafen gehen *to go to sleep*
spazieren gehen *to go for a walk*
zurück·kommen *to come back, return*

Adjektive und Adverbien

allein *alone*
bald *soon*
besser *better*
ein bisschen *a little*
ein paar *a few*
ein wenig *a little*
endlich *finally*
etwas *some, somewhat*
ganz *all, entirely*
gern *gladly; (with any verb) like to*
jetzt *now*
teuer *expensive*
viel *a lot, much*
viele *many*
wenig *little*
wenige *a few*
wie viele? *how many?*
wunderbar *wonderful*

Andere Wörter

auch *also*
dein(e) *your*
ein– *a, an*
mein– *my*
mit *with*
nach *to (with countries, cities)*
nicht *not*
so *so*
überhaupt kein- *none at all*
unbedingt *absolutely, really*
von *from*
wen? *whom?*

Aus dem Zieltext

die Mutti, -s *mom, ma, mommy*

aus·sehen *to look*
besuchen *to visit*
schauen *to look*

bevor *before (conjunction)*
dass *that (conjunction)*
toll *great, neat, cool*
vielleicht *perhaps, maybe*
von wem? *from whom?*

Ausdrücke

Ich freue mich. *I'm pleased. I'm happy.*
Ich habe keine Ahnung. *I have no idea. I have no clue.*
Moment mal! *Wait a minute!*
Schau mal! *Look!*

In this chapter you will learn how to talk about the activities of others, what you like to do, and what you can do. You will begin using the informal form of *you* (du) with other students. You will also read about the German cities Heidelberg and Mannheim.

Kommunikative Funktionen

- Describing activities
- Expressing relationships or ownership
- Expressing additional and contrastive information and justifications
- Stating personal preferences
- Expressing what you would like to do
- Expressing possibilities
- Referring to people and things
- Talking about what you know as a fact and about people, places, and things
- Talking about more than one item

Strukturen

- Present tense of stem-changing verbs (including **wissen**)
- Nominative and accusative of possessive adjectives
- Coordinating conjunctions
- The particle **lieber**
- The modal verbs **möchte** and **können**
- Accusative pronouns
- The verb **kennen**
- Noun plurals

Vokabeln

- Lebensmittel
- Freizeitaktivitäten

Kulturelles

- Mealtimes in German-speaking countries
- The metric system
- Heidelberg and Mannheim
- The German language in the American tourist industry

Ist das typisch deutsch?

Was gibt es in Heidelberg und Mannheim zu tun?

WWW Go to the *Vorsprung* Website at **www.hmco.com/college**

ANLAUFTEXT

Was halten wir von Anna? Was hält sie von uns?

The Günthers are talking about their American relative, Anna Adler, and are making certain assumptions about her behavior and Americans in general, with whom they have had little direct contact. Anna, too, wonders about her German relatives. All of this talk reveals some glaring stereotypes about Americans and Germans.

Vorschau

1 Thematische Fragen. Discuss the following questions with your instructor or in pairs.

1. What are some of your assumptions about Germans and German culture?
2. Think about some German characters you have seen on TV or in a movie. How were they portrayed? What stereotypes do these characterizations of the Germans perpetuate?

2 Wortdetektiv. Which words convey approximately the same meaning? Draw a line from the German word to its logical English equivalent.

Wortdetektiv. To guess the meaning of the German words, look for similarities with English (cognates), determine which English and German words belong to the same categories (nouns, verbs, adjectives), and use a process of elimination.

Deutsch	*Englisch*
1. verstehen	a. to eat
2. das Gepäck	b. to bring along
3. mit·bringen	c. to understand
4. essen	d. luggage
5. wandern	e. to hike
6. trinken	f. pork
7. bleiben	g. to wear
8. der Bahnhof	h. to stay
9. das Schweinefleisch	i. to drink
10. tragen	j. train station

3 Kognate entdecken°.

°discover

Try to identify any of the following words in the **Anlauftext:**
1. Words borrowed from English, e.g., **Popmusik.**
2. Cognates or words with similar forms and meanings in English and German, e.g., **Mittag, gut.**
3. Direct translations from English, e.g., **Kaugummi.**

1. A cognate is a word that has a similar form in two different languages, like the German **Haus** and the English *house.* Scan the statements in the text below. Find six cognates in German and circle them.
2. Look at the statements and the drawings in the text and decide which daily habits or customs mentioned there lead to the creation of stereotypes about others.

Mit nur
einem Ticket
TICKET
24 PLUS
Sind Sie in ganz Mannheim mobil!

ANLAUFTEXT

Now listen to the recording.

Anlauftext. Try to identify the cultural stereotypes presented in the text.

Was halten wir von Anna? Was hält sie von uns?

Isst Anna vielleicht nur Hamburger? Trinkt sie nur Cola?

Willkommen, Anna!

Huh?

Anna spricht sicher nur Englisch.

Uschi

Lächelt sie immer, wie alle Amerikaner?

Versteht sie etwas von Politik? Von Fußball?

Wie alt bist du: 19 oder 20?

Ja!

Katja

Sie versteht sicher nur Bahnhof.

Sieht Anna wohl immer nur fern? Hat sie immer ein Stück Kaugummi im Mund?

CHIPS FRISCH

Hannes

Bringt Anna viel Gepäck mit? Sie trägt bestimmt immer Shorts und Tennisschuhe.

Georg

Bleibt sie lange bei uns?

Essen sie immer nur Schweinefleisch? Trinken sie immer nur Bier?

Wandern sie jedes Wochenende?

Es gibt wahrscheinlich keine gute Popmusik in Deutschland.

▣ Sprache im Alltag: Assumptions with **bestimmt, sicher, wohl**

A person who makes an assumption generally expects the listener to confirm a suspicion or thought. In German, the words **bestimmt** *(undoubtedly)*, **sicher** *(certainly, surely)*, and **wohl** *(in all likelihood, no doubt)* indicate that a statement is an assumption.

Anna spricht **sicher** nur Englisch.	*Anna certainly speaks only English.*
Sie versteht **bestimmt** wenig Deutsch.	*She undoubtedly understands little German.*
Anna sieht **wohl** immer nur fern.	*Anna no doubt watches TV all the time.*

Rückblick

4 **Stimmt das?** How much of the text can you remember without looking back at it? Look over the statements and mark the true statements as **Ja, das stimmt.** Mark the false statements as **Das stimmt nicht.** Then, listen as your instructor reads the following statements and models their pronunciation. If the statement is true, say **Ja, das stimmt.** If the statement is not true, say **Nein, das stimmt nicht.**

Stimmt das? Do this exercise after reading the text once to determine how much you understood and how much you missed. Then reread the text until you feel confident that you understand it.

	Ja, das stimmt.	*Nein, das stimmt nicht.*
1. Tante Uschi meint°, Anna isst nur Bratwurst.	____	____
2. Tante Uschi meint, Anna spricht nur Deutsch.	____	____
3. Tante Uschi meint, Anna lächelt immer, wie alle Amerikaner.	____	____
4. Katja meint, Anna versteht nicht viel Deutsch.	____	____
5. Onkel Hannes meint, Anna sieht immer fern.	____	____
6. Anna meint, die Günthers trinken nur Mineralwasser und essen vegetarisch.	____	____
7. Anna meint, die Günthers wandern jedes Wochenende.	____	____

° *thinks*

Nur Bahnhof verstehen is a German idiom that literally means *to understand only "train station."* It means *to not have a clue.* It is usually used in reference to not understanding a language and is not transferable to other contexts.

5 **Ergänzen Sie.** Complete these sentences with words from the **Anlauftext.**

Tante Uschi

1. Anna ____ nur Hamburger mit Ketchup.
2. Anna ____ sicher nur Englisch.

Katja

3. Anna ist so freundlich und optimistisch. Sie ____ immer, wie alle Amerikaner.
4. Anna ____ nicht viel Deutsch.

Onkel Hannes

5. Anna ____ wohl immer nur ____.
6. Anna hat immer ein ____ Kaugummi im Mund.

Georg

7. Vielleicht bringt Anna viel ____ mit.
8. Anna ____ bestimmt immer Shorts und Tennisschuhe.

Anna

9. Es ____ wahrscheinlich keine gute Popmusik in Deutschland.
10. Die Günthers ____ wahrscheinlich nur Schweinefleisch und trinken nur ____.

6 **Kurz gefragt.** Answer these questions. Try to create complete sentences.

Kurz gefragt. Respond with a word or phrase only.

Was, meinen die Günthers, ...

1. essen und trinken alle Amerikaner?
2. spricht Anna?
3. machen alle Amerikaner immer?
4. versteht Anna sicher nur? Was sagt Katja?

5. bringt Anna mit?
6. trägt Anna bestimmt?

Was, meint Anna, ...

7. essen und trinken die Günthers?
8. machen die Günthers jedes Wochenende?
9. gibt es wahrscheinlich nicht in Deutschland?

7 **Bin ich typisch?** Ask your classmates whether they are Americans. Every time a person indicates he/she is an American, confront him/her with one of the stereotypes listed below. Present these stereotypes in the form of assumptions, using **sicher, bestimmt,** and **wohl.** Your classmate says whether this stereotype applies to him/her.

S1: Sie kauen wohl gern Kaugummi.
S2: Nein, ich kaue nicht gern Kaugummi. *(oder)*
Ja, ich kaue gern Kaugummi.

1. gern Kaugummi kauen
2. gern Rockmusik hören
3. nur Hamburger essen
4. immer Cola trinken
5. nur Englisch sprechen
6. gern Shorts und Tennisschuhe tragen

BRENNPUNKT KULTUR

Mealtimes in German-speaking countries

Cultures are often defined by their cuisines. Since eating customs are often the most distinctive aspects of a culture, they are frequently the means by which others form stereotypes. For example, in Germany, Austria, and Switzerland, it is common to hold the knife in one hand and the fork in the other and rest the forearms on the edge of the table while eating. In the United States this may be considered rude mealtime behavior.

In German-speaking countries, three to five distinct mealtimes may be observed each day. Breakfast (**das Frühstück**) usually consists of coffee or tea and a crusty roll with butter, called **das Brötchen** in the north and **die Semmel** in southern areas. Most bakeries provide a variety of fresh-baked bread (**das Brot**) each morning. Fruit jam (**die Marmelade**), honey (**der Honig**), cheese (**der Käse**), or even cold cuts (**der Aufschnitt**) may be put on a roll or slice of bread. On occasion, a soft-boiled egg (**ein weichgekochtes Ei**), yogurt, or breakfast cereal, such as **(das) Müesli,** a Swiss whole grain, fruit-and-nut cereal, or the American-style **Choco Krispies** or **Cornflakes,** may round off a breakfast. While many foreign visitors find a German breakfast very filling, many Germans consider a nutritious breakfast the most important meal of the day.

Mid-morning, some people at work and at school break for a snack or second breakfast (**zweites Frühstück**), which may consist of a **Brötchen,** a cup of yogurt, or a piece of fruit.

Das Mittagessen is for many the main hot meal of the day. It often has three courses: an appetizer (**die Vorspeise**), most often soup (**die Suppe**); main course (**das Hauptgericht**) of meat or fish plus potatoes, noodles, or rice, plus vegetable; and a dessert (**die Nachspeise/der Nachtisch**) of pudding, fruit, or ice cream. On special occasions or on weekends, many people enjoy coffee and cake (**Kaffee und Kuchen**) around mid-afternoon.

The last meal of the day around 6 P.M. is called **das Abendbrot** or **das Abendessen.** Traditionally, it consists of cold cuts, cheese, breads, along with tomatoes, salad, and cucumbers. **Der Tee, das Mineralwasser, das Bier,** or **der Wein** complete the meal. In a growing number of working families, the main hot meal is now prepared in the evening.

Was isst man zum Frühstück?

Strukturen und Vokabeln

I Describing activities

Present tense of stem-changing verbs

Many of the most frequently occurring German verbs used to describe people and their activities have a stem-change in the **du-** and **er/sie/es**-forms. These verbs are called irregular or strong verbs **(starke Verben).** Compare how the verb stems change in the questions raised by the Günthers.

Anna	Familie Günther
Essen sie immer Schweinefleisch? *Do they always eat pork?*	**Isst** sie vielleicht nur Hamburger? *Does she perhaps only eat hamburgers?*
Sehen sie überhaupt fern? *Do they watch TV at all?*	**Sieht** Anna wohl immer nur fern? *Does Anna maybe always watch TV?*

With a few exceptions that will be noted later, the stem-changing verbs use the same present-tense endings as the other regular verbs **(schwache Verben)** that have been introduced so far. Here are the present tense forms of the stem-changing verb **sehen** *(to see)*.

Person	Singular	sehen: *to see*	Plural	
1st	ich **sehe**	*I see*	wir **sehen**	*we see*
2nd, informal	du **siehst**	*you see*	ihr **seht**	*you see*
2nd, formal	Sie **sehen**	*you see*	Sie **sehen**	*you see*
3rd	er/sie/es **sieht**	*he/she/it sees*	sie **sehen**	*they see*

The **ich**-form is included to show the vowel used in the forms other than the **du-** and **er/sie/es**-forms: **ich fahre, wir/Sie/sie fahren**, **ihr fahrt.**

There are four categories of verbs with distinct stem-vowel changes.

1. Stem-vowel change **a > ä**
   - **fahren** *(to drive)* — ich fahre, du f**ä**hrst, er/sie/es f**ä**hrt
   - **halten (von)** *(to stop; to think about)* — ich halte, du h**ä**ltst, er/sie/es h**ä**lt
   - **tragen** *(to wear)* — ich trage, du tr**ä**gst, er/sie/es tr**ä**gt

Other such verbs are **backen** *(to bake)*, **fallen** *(to fall)*, **fangen** *(to catch)*, **anfangen** *(to begin)*, **laden** *(to load)*, **einladen** *(to invite)*, **lassen** *(to let)*, **schlafen** *(to sleep)*, **waschen** *(to wash).*

2. Stem-vowel change **au > äu**
   - **laufen** *(to run, walk)* — ich laufe, du l**äu**fst, er/sie/es l**äu**ft

Another such verb is **saufen** *(to drink like an animal).* However, the common verb **kaufen** *(to buy)* is not irregular.

The **äu** is pronounced like the *'oy'* in *boy.*

3. Stem-vowel change **e > ie**
   - **sehen** *(to see)* — ich sehe, du s**ie**hst, er/sie/es s**ie**ht
   - **fern·sehen** *(to watch TV)* — ich sehe fern, du s**ie**hst fern, er/sie/es s**ie**ht fern
   - **lesen** *(to read)* — ich lese, du l**ie**st, er/sie/es l**ie**st

4. Stem-vowel change **e > i**
   - **essen** *(to eat)* — ich esse, du **i**sst, er/sie/es **i**sst
   - **geben** *(to give)* — ich gebe, du g**i**bst, er/sie/es g**i**bt
   - **nehmen** *(to take)* — ich nehme, du n**imm**st, er/sie/es n**imm**t
   - **sprechen** *(to speak)* — ich spreche, du spr**i**chst, er/sie/es spr**i**cht
   - **vergessen** *(to forget)* — ich vergesse, du verg**i**sst, er/sie/es verg**i**sst
   - **werden** *(to become)* — ich werde, du w**i**rst, er/sie/es w**i**rd

Other verbs are **fressen** *(to eat like an animal)* and **helfen** *(to help).*

Note the consonant change from **hm** to **mm** in the present tense **du-** and **er/sie/es**-forms of **nehmen.**

Another verb that changes its stem vowel is **wissen** *(to know as a fact).* Like the verbs listed above, **wissen** changes its stem vowel only in the singular (**i > ei**). The formal **Sie-** and the plural forms keep the original (infinitival) stem vowel. Moreover, **ich-** and **er/sie/es**-forms have no endings.

	wissen: *to know as a fact*			
Person	**Singular**		**Plural**	
1st	ich we**i**ß	*I know*	wir w**i**ssen	*we know*
2nd, informal	du we**i**ßt	*you know*	ihr w**i**sst	*you know*
2nd, formal	Sie w**i**ssen	*you know*	Sie w**i**ssen	*you know*
3rd	er/sie/es we**i**ß	*he/she/it knows*	sie w**i**ssen	*they know*

Note the change from **ss** to **ß** after **ei**, a diphthong.

The formal 2nd person singular **(Sie wissen)** shows a plural vowel because it is derived from the 3rd person plural.

Wissen generally refers to information that is expressed in a subordinate clause. The conjugated verb always occurs at the end of a subordinate clause. You will learn more about subordinate-clause word order in Chapter 5.

Weißt du, wo Anna wohnt? *Do you know where Anna lives?*
Ja, ich weiß, wo sie wohnt. *Yes, I know where she lives.*
Ja, ich weiß es. *Yes, I know it.*

You will encounter other verbs with vowel changes from singular to plural and zero endings in the 1st and 3rd person singular later in this chapter and in Chapter 4, namely with regard to modal verbs, e.g., **können** *(can).*

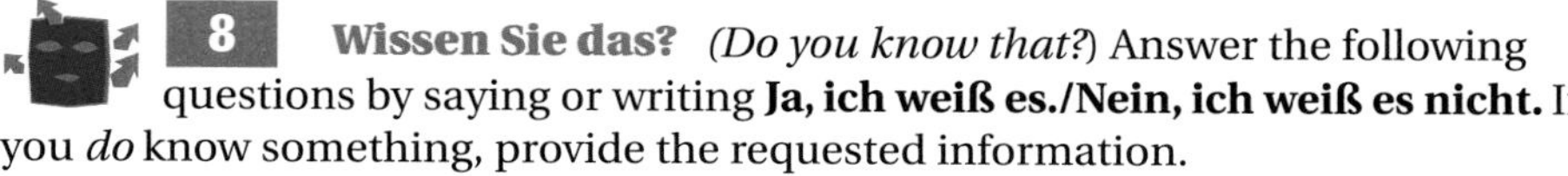

8 Wissen Sie das? *(Do you know that?)* Answer the following questions by saying or writing **Ja, ich weiß es./Nein, ich weiß es nicht.** If you *do* know something, provide the requested information.

Wissen Sie, wie alt Ihr Professor/Ihre Professorin ist?
Ja, ich weiß es. Er/Sie ist zweiundvierzig.

1. Wissen Sie, wie alt Ihr Professor/Ihre Professorin ist?
2. Wissen Sie, wie alt Sie sind?
3. Wissen Sie, wann Anna nach Deutschland fährt?
4. Wissen Sie, wo Annas Großeltern wohnen?
5. Wissen Sie, wie Annas Verwandten in Deutschland heißen?
6. Wissen Sie, wo in Deutschland Annas Flugzeug landet?
7. Wissen Sie, wer Georg ist?

9 Die Günthers. Choose a partner and one of the following two **Tabellen** about the Günthers. Your partner should refer to the other **Tabelle.** Note that **Tabelle B** is printed upside down. Ask each other what the Günthers like to do.

S1: Was macht Hannes gern?
S2: Er läuft gern Ski.
S1: Was macht er gern im Sommer?
S2: Er fährt gern Wasserski.

Ski is also spelled **Schi.** Either way, the pronunciation is ***Schi.***

Tabelle A (S1):

	Hobby	**Essen/Trinken**	**im Sommer**
Hannes	?	trinkt gern Weißwein	?
Ursula	liest gern Romane	?	trägt gern Shorts
Georg	fährt gern Rad°	?	fährt nach Italien
Katja	?	trinkt gern Cola	?

fährt ... Rad: *likes to go bicycling*

Tabelle B (S2):

	Hobby	Essen/Trinken	im Sommer
Hannes	läuft gern Ski	?	fährt gern Wasserski
Ursula	?	isst gern Hamburger	?
Georg	?	isst gern vegetarisch	?
Katja	spricht gern Französisch	?	fährt nach England

In information-gap activities, the second chart is always printed upside down to enhance communication.

10 **Autogrammspiel.** Walk around and find a classmate for each activity listed below. When you find someone who likes to do the activity, have that person sign his/her name.

S1: Trägst du gern Shorts?
S2: Nein, ich trage nicht gern Shorts. *(oder)*
Ja, ich trage gern Shorts.
S1: Unterschreib hier bitte. ____________________

Autogrammspiel. From this point on you will be expected to use the informal **du** when speaking with another student.

1. Trägst du gern Tennisschuhe? ____________________
2. Liest du gern Zeitung°? ____________________
3. Siehst du gern fern? ____________________
4. Sprichst du gern Deutsch? ____________________
5. Isst du gern Fleisch? ____________________
6. Trinkst du gern Bier? ____________________

° *the newspaper*

11 **Das Interview.** You are writing an article for the student newspaper. Interview a partner who plays an Austrian exchange student. Ask the following questions about his/her habits. Circle the response that comes closest to your partner's answer or have him/her supply one.

S1: Was isst du gern?
S2: Ich esse gern Hamburger.

	Fragen	*Antworten*			
1.	Was isst du gern?	Hamburger	Steak	Schokolade	?
2.	Was sprichst du gern?	Deutsch	Englisch	Französisch	?
3.	Was liest du gern?	Deutsch	Englisch	Französisch	?
4.	Was trägst du gern?	Shorts	Tennisschuhe	Lederhosen°	?
5.	Was trinkst du?	Kaffee	Milch	Cola	?
6.	Siehst du oft fern?	Ja, oft.	Nein, nicht oft.	Nein, überhaupt nicht.	?
7.	Was machst du gern?	Auto fahren	Ski laufen	einkaufen gehen	?

leather pants

12 **(Stereo)typisch.** The list below reflects stereotypical images of Americans and Germans. Determine to whom these stereotypes refer by creating 10 complete sentences.

Eine typische Amerikanerin lächelt immer.

Ein typischer Amerikaner/Deutscher	spricht	eine Zigarette im Mund.
Eine typische Amerikanerin/Deutsche	trinkt	jedes Wochenende.
	isst	nur Englisch.
	versteht	immer fern.
	hat	immer Kaugummi im Mund.
	trägt	etwas von Softball.
	wandert	Cola mit viel Eis.
	sieht	etwas von Fußball.
	lächelt	Schweinefleisch.
		Deutsch und eine Fremdsprache°.
		nur Bier.
		Tennisschuhe und Shorts.
		immer.

foreign language

Sprache im Alltag: Phrases with es gibt, was gibt es?, and was gibt's?

Es gibt is a useful phrase, meaning *there is, there are.*

Es gibt keine gute Popmusik in Deutschland.	*There's no good pop music in Germany.*
Gibt es frische Brötchen?	*Are there any fresh rolls?*

The phrase **was gibt es ... ?** means *what is there . . . ?*

Was gibt es in Heidelberg zu tun?	*What is there to do in Heidelberg?*
Was gibt es Neues?	*What's new?*

The expression **was gibt's?** is used informally to ask *what's up?, what's going on?*

II Expressing relationships or ownership

Nominative of possessive adjectives

German speakers use possessive adjectives (**Possessivpronomen**) to express ownership or a relationship.

Das ist **mein** Freund. Er heißt Jürgen.	*That's my friend. His name is Jürgen.*
Meine Freundin läuft gern Ski.	*My girlfriend likes to ski.*
Warum trägst du **meine** Shorts?	*Why are you wearing my shorts?*

Possessive adjectives are commonly referred to as ***ein-words*** because they take the same endings as the forms of the indefinite article **ein.** This is true for all possessive adjectives, not just for those that rhyme with **ein (mein, dein, sein).**

	Singular		**Plural**	
Person	**Subject pronoun**	**Possessive adjective**	**Subject pronoun**	**Possessive adjective**
1st	ich *I*	mein *my*	wir *we*	unser *our*
2nd, informal	du *you*	dein *your*	ihr *you*	euer *your*
2nd, formal	Sie *you*	Ihr *your*	Sie *you*	Ihr *your*
3rd	er *he* es *it* sie *she*	sein *his* sein *its* ihr *her*	sie *they*	ihr *their*

The ending of a possessive adjective denotes the case (e.g., nominative, accusative), gender (masculine, feminine, neuter), and number (singular or plural) of the noun that follows.

Here are the nominative endings for the possessive adjectives and **ein/kein:**

	Masculine	**Neuter**	**Feminine**	**Plural**
	ein/kein	ein/kein	eine/keine	—/keine
	Possessive adjectives:			
ich	mein Vater	mein Kind	meine Mutter	meine Kinder
du	dein Vater	dein Kind	deine Mutter	deine Kinder
Sie (Sg. & Pl.)	Ihr Vater	Ihr Kind	Ihre Mutter	Ihre Kinder
er	sein Vater	sein Kind	seine Mutter	seine Kinder
es	sein Vater	sein Kind	seine Mutter	seine Kinder
sie	ihr Vater	ihr Kind	ihre Mutter	ihre Kinder
wir	unser Vater	unser Kind	unsere Mutter	unsere Kinder
ihr	euer Vater	euer Kind	eu(e)re Mutter	eu(e)re Kinder
sie	ihr Vater	ihr Kind	ihre Mutter	ihre Kinder

Note that possessive adjectives for singular masculine and singular neuter nouns are identical as are the possessive adjectives for singular feminine nouns and plurals.

The **-er** on **unser** and **euer** is not an ending but part of the stem. **Unser** frequently and **euer** always loses the internal **-e-** when an ending is added.

unser: unsere Schwester
un**sr**e Schwester
euer: eu**re** Schwester

13 Meine Freunde. Create interesting descriptions of your friends and relatives by combining the subjects in the left column with an appropriate verb from the middle, and an item from the right column. Make up a few of your own, too.

Mein Freund	isst	kein Schweinefleisch.
Meine Freundin	trägt	immer fern.
Mein Vater	läuft	Spanisch, Deutsch und Englisch.
Meine Mutter	fährt	nicht.
Mein Bruder	sieht	sehr schnell°.
Meine Schwester	liest	gern Pizza.
Mein Deutschlehrer	spricht	keine Lederhosen.
Meine Deutschlehrerin		gern Bücher.
		einen VW.
		viel.
		wenig.

° *fast*

III ▣ Expressing additional and contrastive information and justifications

Coordinating conjunctions

German speakers use coordinating conjunctions **(nebenordnende Konjunktionen)** to provide additional information **(und),** justification **(denn),** or contrast (**sondern**, **aber**, **oder**). There are five frequently used coordinating conjunctions.

aber	*but*
denn	*for, because*
oder	*or*
sondern	*but rather*
und	*and*

All coordinating conjunctions provide some type of additional information. They may conjoin words, phrases, or clauses.

Meine Mutter spielt Tennis, **und** mein Vater spielt Golf. — *My mother plays tennis **and** my father plays golf.*

Aber is commonly used in conversation to present an idea that contrasts what has been stated or implied so far.

Anna ist gespannt auf das Jahr in Deutschland, **aber** ihre Mutter macht sich Sorgen. — *Anna is excited about the year in Germany, **but** her mother is worried.*

Denn is used to provide a reason or justification.

Mein Freund kommt nicht, **denn** er fährt nach Hause. — *My friend isn't coming **because** he's going home.*

Do not confuse the conjunction **denn** with **denn** as used in questions like: **Woher kommen Sie *denn?*** It is used to show personal interest and elicit further information. This **denn** does not join two clauses.

Oder is used to provide alternative information.

Geht Hannes nach Hause, **oder** geht er zu Uschi? — *Is Hannes going home **or** is he going to Uschi's?*

Sondern introduces a clause that contradicts a preceding negative statement which usually contains **nicht.**

Anna kommt **nicht** am Montag, **sondern** am Dienstag. — *Anna isn't coming on Monday, **but (rather)** on Tuesday.*

14 Warum machen sie das? Match the statements in the left column with the appropriate justifications in the right column.

1. Mein Bruder isst oft Fleisch,
2. Meine Tante isst gar kein Fleisch,
3. Meine Familie hört gern Musik,
4. Meine Schwester trägt heute Shorts und Sandalen,
5. Mein Bruder lächelt,
6. Unsere Großeltern sehen nie fern,
7. Mein Deutschlehrer trägt keine Lederhosen,
8. Ihre Mutter spricht Deutsch,

a. denn wir sind sehr musikalisch.
b. denn sie kommt aus Deutschland.
c. denn er kommt aus Norddeutschland.
d. denn es ist sehr warm.
e. denn er ist sehr glücklich°.
f. denn sie hat Fleisch nicht gern.
g. denn sie haben keinen Fernseher°.
h. denn er hat Fleisch gern.

glücklich° *happy*
Fernseher° *TV*

15 **Sie ist Amerikanerin, aber ...** Match the statements in the left column with the appropriate contrasting information in the right column.

1. Anna kommt aus den USA,
2. Anna wohnt in Fort Wayne,
3. Herr Günther isst oft bei McDonalds,
4. Katja liest Shakespeare,
5. Georg kommt aus Deutschland,
6. Frau Adler ist gut organisiert,
7. Es regnet° heute,
8. Es ist kalt heute,

a. aber Jeff trägt keinen Pullover.
b. aber Herr Adler nimmt seinen Regenschirm° nicht mit.
c. aber sie vergisst oft ihren Autoschlüssel°.
d. aber sie spricht etwas Deutsch.
e. aber er trinkt nicht gern Bier.
f. aber ihr Buch ist auf Deutsch.
g. aber sie hat Verwandte in Deutschland.
h. aber er wohnt in Frankfurt.

umbrella

car key

is raining

IV ▣ Stating personal preferences

The particle **lieber**

You have already learned how to talk about activities that you like to do using **gern.**

Ich spiele **gern** Tennis. *I **like to** play tennis.*

To express a preference for one of two options, use **lieber** with a verb.

Spielst du **lieber** Tennis oder Fußball? *Do you **prefer to** play tennis or soccer?*

Ich spiele **lieber** Fußball. *I **prefer to** play soccer./I **like to** play soccer **more.***

The word **als** *(rather than)* is used with **lieber** when stating a preference for one thing over another.

Ich spiele **lieber** Fußball **als** Tennis. *I prefer to play soccer **rather than** tennis.*

Was trägst du lieber, Lederhosen oder Shorts?

16 **Das mache ich lieber.** Ask each other about your personal preferences, using the appropriate verb. After you have finished, report back to the class.

▣ Lederhosen/Shorts tragen

S1: Trägst du lieber Lederhosen, oder trägst du lieber Shorts? *(oder)* Was trägst du lieber: Lederhosen oder Shorts?
S2: Ich trage lieber Shorts. Was trägst du lieber?
S1: Ich trage auch° lieber Shorts.

also

S1: (Lori) sagt, sie trägt lieber Shorts.
S2: (Raoul) sagt, er trägt lieber Shorts.

1. Hamburger/Bratwurst essen
2. Englisch/Deutsch sprechen
3. Cola/Bier trinken
4. klassische Musik/Rockmusik hören
5. Softball/Fußball spielen

6. Birkenstock-Sandalen/Tennisschuhe tragen
7. Mathematik/Literatur lesen
8. Auto/Fahrrad° fahren

bicycle

V Expressing what you would like to do

The modal verb möchte

German speakers use **möchte** *(would like to)* to express what they or somebody else would like to do. **Möchte** belongs to a group of helping verbs called *modal verbs* **(das Modalverb).** It is a special form of the verb **mögen.** You will be learning more about modal verbs in Chapter 4. Modal verbs express under which conditions an action takes place. **Möchte** implies that the action is desired by someone. The verb that expresses this action is an infinitive. In simple declarative sentences with a modal verb the infinitive occurs at the end of the sentence.

Ich **möchte** meine Verwandten in Deutschland **kennen lernen.** — *I would like to get to know my relatives in Germany.*

The present tense endings of **möchte** are slightly different from the verbs you have encountered so far. The **du-** and **ihr**-forms require an additional **e** before their verb endings and the third person singular ending looks like that of the **ich**-form: **-e.**

In general, verbs which have a **t** before the ending insert an **e** between this **t** and the **du-** and **ihr**-form endings, e.g., **arbeiten** *(to work):* **du arbeitest.**

möchte: *would like to*		
Person	**Singular**	**Plural**
1st	ich möchte *I would like (to)*	wir möchten *we would like (to)*
2nd, informal	du möchtest *you would like (to)*	ihr möchtet *you would like (to)*
2nd, formal	Sie möchten *you would like (to)*	Sie möchten *you would like (to)*
3rd	er/sie/es möchte *he/she/it would like (to)*	sie möchten *they would like (to)*

When using **möchte,** the infinitive can be omitted if it is clear from the context that an infinitive is implied. Infinitives which are commonly omitted are: **essen, trinken, fahren, gehen,** and **haben.**

Ich **möchte** eine Cola (haben), bitte. — *I would like (to have) a cola, please.*
Er **möchte** nach Heidelberg (fahren). — *He would like to go to Heidelberg.*

17 **Was möchtest du lieber?** Ask your partner questions about what he/she would prefer to do.

Was möchtest du lieber? Practice answering the questions with the book closed.

Cola/Kaffee trinken

S1: Möchtest du lieber Cola oder Kaffee (trinken)?
S2: Ich möchte lieber Kaffee (trinken), und du?

1. Cola/Kaffee (trinken)
2. fernsehen/einen Film sehen
3. Tennisschuhe/Bergschuhe° tragen — *hiking boots*
4. Deutsch/Englisch sprechen
5. früh°/spät° aufstehen — *early / late*
6. schwimmen/reiten° (gehen) — *(to go) horseback riding*
7. Hamburger/Bratwurst (essen)
8. nach Heidelberg/nach München (fahren)
9. ins Museum/ins Restaurant (gehen)
10. ...

Wissenswerte Vokabeln: Lebensmittel

Talking about foods that we like

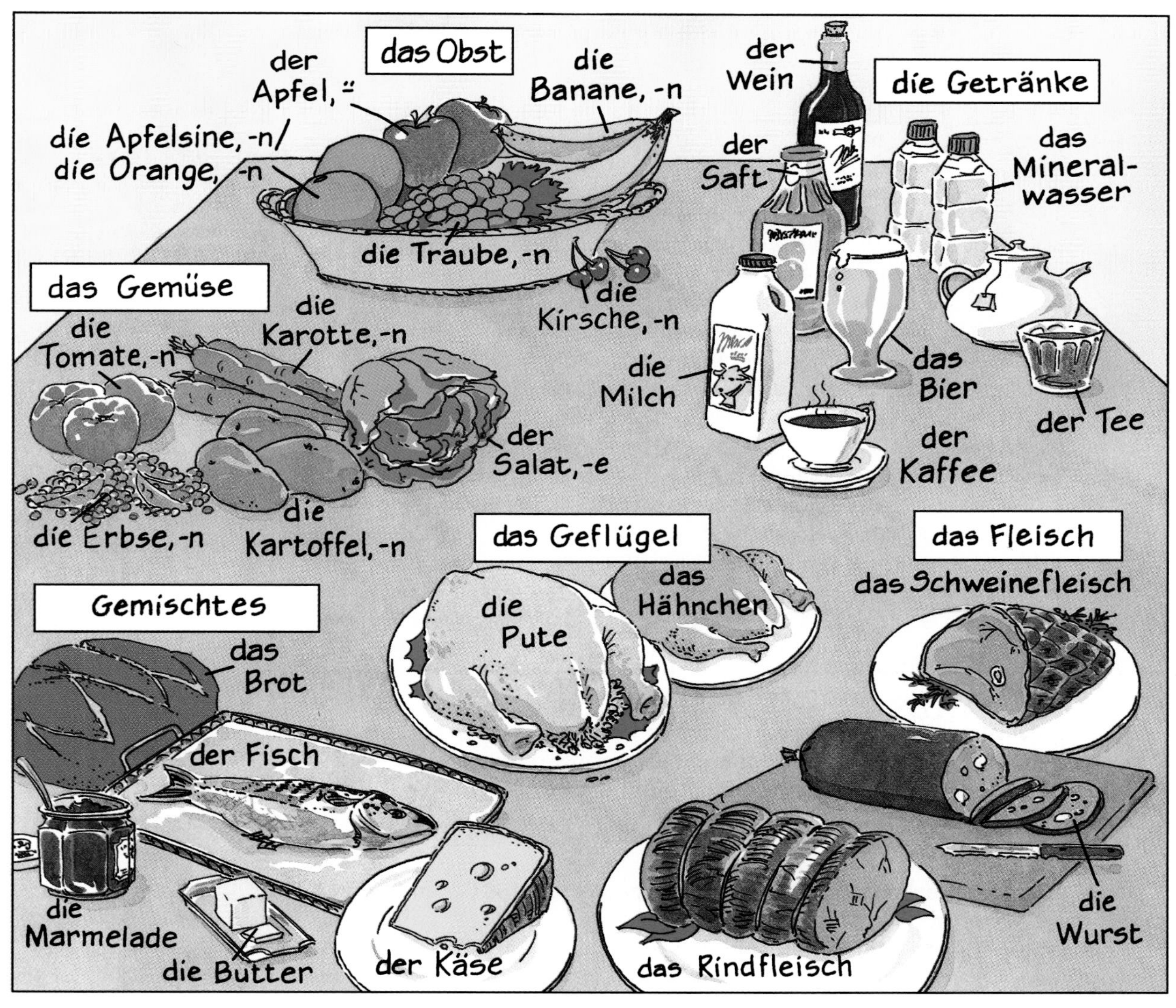

Was isst du gern? *Ich esse gern Salat.*

Wie viele Kilometer sind das?

BRENNPUNKT KULTUR

The metric system

The metric system is used in Europe and much of the world outside the United States. Liquids are measured in liters (**der Liter** = 1.05 liquid quarts); lengths in meters (**der Meter** = 1.094 yards); and solids in grams (**das Gramm** = .03527 ounces), or pounds (**das Pfund** = 500 grams).

Germans, Austrians, and the Swiss use the metric system when shopping. Gas, for example, is sold in liters (abbreviated as **l.**), and some drinks are sold in centiliters (**cl.**). In a bar, wine may be ordered by the quarter liter (**Ein Viertel Weißwein, bitte.**) and beer may be sold by the half liter (**ein Halbes**), or full liter (in Bavaria called **eine Maß**). Meats and breads are sold by the **Kilo,** which contains two pounds (**zwei Pfund**) or 1,000 grams (**tausend Gramm**). Two pounds of hamburger may be ordered as **ein Kilo** (**1 K.**), **zwei Pfund** (**2 Pf.**) or **1 000 Gramm** (**1 000 g.**) **Hackfleisch**. Amounts smaller than a pound are expressed as fractions of a pound (**ein halbes Pfund, ein Viertel Pfund**) or more frequently in specific **Gramm** (**g.**) amounts (e.g., **125 Gramm**).

Multiples of these base measurements are indicated by the prefixes **Deka:** = × 10, **Hekto:** = × 100, and **Kilo:** = × 1000. Fractional parts of these base measurements are expressed by the prefixes **Dezi:** = ⅒, **Zenti:** = 1/100, and **Milli:** = 1/1000. To specify a plural quantity, Germans say **500 Gramm Käse** or **zwei Pfund Äpfel** and do not use the plural form as in English, e.g., *grams* or *pounds.*

Distance between cities is measured in **Kilometer** (0.62 miles). Body weight is measured in **Kilogramm (kg),** height in **Meter** and **Zentimeter,** e.g., **einen Meter (und) siebzig Zentimeter.**

Sprache im Alltag: Use of the metric system

German speakers usually purchase small amounts of fresh cold cuts, cheese, meat, fruit and vegetables each day for immediate consumption. Shoppers **(Kunden)** therefore often request very small amounts and salespeople **(Verkäufer),** ask for approval if the amount on the scale is a little above or below the desired weight.

KUNDE/KUNDIN: Geben Sie mir 200 Gramm Leberwurst und 150 Gramm Gouda, bitte.

VERKÄUFER(IN): Darf° es etwas mehr° sein? *(oder)*
Darf es etwas weniger° sein?

may / more
less

18 **Was isst und trinkst du lieber?** Interview your partner about his/her preferences in food and drinks. After you have finished, report back to the class.

- Schweinefleisch/Rindfleisch

- S1: Was isst du lieber: Schweinefleisch oder Rindfleisch?
  S2: Ich esse lieber Rindfleisch.

  S1: (Karen) isst lieber ...
  S2: (Eric) isst lieber ...

1. Schweinefleisch/Rindfleisch
2. Fisch/Fleisch
3. Gemüse/Obst
4. Wurst/Käse
5. Hähnchen/Fisch
6. Bier/Milch
7. Kaffee/Tee
8. Butter/Marmelade

19 **In der Bäckerei°.** Listen to the following dialogue, then practice it with a partner.

° *bakery*

BÄCKER: Guten Tag. Bitte schön?
KUNDIN: Ich möchte ein Weißbrot und vier Brötchen.
BÄCKER: Sonst noch 'was°?
KUNDIN: Das war's.
BÄCKER: Das macht vier Mark neunzig.
KUNDIN: Bitte schön.
BÄCKER: Danke. Und zehn Pfennig zurück.
KUNDIN: Auf Wiedersehen.
BÄCKER: Wiedersehen.

° *(Would you like) anything else?*

Schreibecke **Der Wochenkauf.** Make up your family's weekly food shopping list; write the amounts in **Gramm.** Use the items you have learned in the chapter and the ad from **Interspar** for ideas.

ABSPRUNGTEXT

Heidelberg und Mannheim

In anticipation of Anna's arrival, the Günthers, who live in Weinheim just north of Heidelberg, send her tourist brochures on Heidelberg and Mannheim.

Heidelberg is famous for its "typical German" attractions—the historic university, the old castle, and the scenic location on the Neckar river with vineyards nearby. Heidelberg's neighbor to the west on the Rhine, Mannheim, is known less for its tourist attractions and more for its industrial significance.

Friedrichsplatz

Jesuitenkirche

Rosengarten

Vorschau

20 Thematische Fragen. Discuss the following questions with your instructor or in pairs.

1. What cities do you associate with Germany? Why?
2. What do you already know about Heidelberg? Where are you likely to get information about Heidelberg?
3. Heidelberg is considered one of Germany's most romantic cities. What makes a city romantic? What sort of buildings and other tourist attractions might you find in Heidelberg that make it a "romantic city"?
4. Do you know anything about Mannheim?

21 Wortdetektiv. Which words convey approximately the same meaning? Draw a line from the German word to its logical English equivalent.

	Deutsch		*Englisch*
1.	das Schloss	a.	bicycle
2.	die Stadt (e.g., Berlin)	b.	bridge
3.	das Fahrrad	c.	to sail
4.	segeln	d.	castle, palace
5.	die Brücke	e.	city, town
6.	die Bibliothek	f.	to fish
7.	reiten	g.	swimming pool
8.	die Kirche	h.	to ride horseback
9.	das Schwimmbad	i.	church
10.	angeln	j.	library
11.	die Jugendherberge	k.	old city hall
12.	Trimm-dich-Pfade	l.	art museum
13.	Wasserturm	m.	youth hostel
14.	Kunsthalle	n.	water tower
15.	Altes Rathaus	o.	fitness trails

22 Zum Text. Tourist brochures often list facts and figures to provide a quick overview of a city and its attractions. The following ads contain information on Heidelberg and Mannheim. Scan the texts to find . . .

1. the phone number of the tourist information offices.
2. the number of hotel beds in Heidelberg and Mannheim.
3. the year the university in Heidelberg was founded.
4. examples for how Heidelberg markets itself. (Scan the text for adjectives.)
5. the larger city: Is it Heidelberg or Mannheim?

ABSPRUNGTEXT

Heidelberg und Mannheim

Now read the text.

Der Zoo Heidelberg

Heidelberg

Das Heidelberger Schloß

Das Große Faß

Universitätsstadt am Neckar, 134 000 Einwohner, 3 600 Betten (davon 3 300 in Hotels, 300 in Gasthöfen und Pensionen)

Freizeit: Freischwimmbad°, Hallenschwimmbad°, Reiten, Tennis, Angeln, Segeln, Großgolf, Kleingolf, Fahrradverleih°, Neckarschiffahrt, Zoo, Kinderparadies

i Verkehrsverein Heidelberg e.V.
Tourist-Information am Hauptbahnhof
Telefon (0 62 21) 1 08 21 und 2 13 41

Sehenswürdigkeiten: Heidelberger Schloß – das Große Faß – das Deutsche Apothekenmuseum, historische, romantische Altstadt am Neckar, älteste Universität Deutschlands (1386), Universitätsbibliothek, Alte Brücke, Heiliggeistkirche, Kurpfälzisches Museum, historische Studentenlokale.

Die älteste Universität Deutschlands means *Germany's oldest university.*

outdoor pool
indoor pool

bicycle rental

Die Universität

Mannheim

Stadt der Quadrate° an Rhein und Neckar im Herzen der ehemaligen° Kurpfalz, 316000 Einwohner, 2095 Zimmer (davon 1830 in Hotels, 220 in Gasthöfen, 45 in Pensionen), 120 Betten in der Jugendherberge, Kongreßzentrum „Rosengarten"

Freizeit: Campingplätze an Rhein und Neckar, beheizte Freischwimmbäder, Hallenbäder, Tennis, Squash, Angeln, Reiten, Segeln, Kleingolf, Trimm-Dich-Pfade

i Tourist-Information Mannheim
Kaiserring 10/16
Telefon: (06 21) 10 10 11
Telefax: (06 21) 2 41 41

Sehenswürdigkeiten: Friedrichsplatz (Jugendstil°) mit Wasserturm (Wahrzeichen), Wasserspielen°, Kurfürstliches Residenzschloß (größtes Barock°schloß Deutschlands), Jesuitenkirche, Reiß-Museum, Kunsthalle, Nationaltheater, Kinder- und Jugendtheater im Kulturzentrum, Kunstverein, Altes Rathaus und Untere Pfarrkirchen (Glockenspiel°) am Marktplatz, Hafen°

Stadt der Quadrate means *city of squares* (like in a grid). Like all plurals, **Quadrate** takes the article **die** in the nominative. The reason why **die** appears as **der** is that it is a genitive. The genitive is the case expressing possession *(of)*. You will learn more about it in Chapter 10.

square blocks
former / Art Nouveau
fountains
Baroque
chimes
port

Größtes Barockschloss means *the largest baroque palace.* It is similar to **die älteste Universität.** Both are superlative forms *(the most).*

Rückblick

23 **Stimmt das?** How much of the text do you remember without looking back at it?

	Ja, das stimmt.	*Nein, das stimmt nicht.*
1. Heidelberg ist eine Industriestadt.	___	___
2. Heidelberg liegt am° Rhein.	___	___
3. Heidelberg hat 316.000 Einwohner.	___	___
4. In Heidelberg gibt es keinen Wassersport.	___	___
5. Für Kinder gibt es in Heidelberg den Zoo und das Kinderparadies.	___	___
6. Mannheim hat kein Schloss.	___	___
7. Heidelbergs Altstadt ist alt, kaputt und hässlich°.	___	___

***liegt am:** is situated on*

ugly

	Ja, das stimmt.	*Nein, das stimmt nicht.*
8. Mannheim hat die älteste Universität Deutschlands.	___	___
9. Die Alte Brücke führt über° den Neckar.	___	___
10. Die Tourist-Information in Heidelberg findet man in historischen Studentenlokalen.	___	___

***führt über:** goes across*

24 Was gibt's in Mannheim oder Heidelberg? Compare Mannheim's attractions to those of Heidelberg. Which of the following attractions and facilities do both cities offer and which are unique to Mannheim or Heidelberg?

Theater • Squash • Schloss • Segeln • Tennis • Kirche • Kleingolf • Museum • Kunsthalle • Wasserspiele • Hallenschwimmbad • Reiten • Universität • Motor- und Segelflugplatz • Rathaus • Trimm-dich-Pfade • Fahrradverleih • Studentenlokale • Neckar • das Große Fass • Hafen

Mannheim	*Heidelberg*	*Mannheim und Heidelberg*
______	______	______
______	______	______
______	______	______
______	______	______
______	______	______
______	______	______

25 Wo findet man diese Leute? With a partner, determine where in Heidelberg or Mannheim you would most likely find these people.

1. Studentinnen	in der Bibliothek
2. Amerikaner	an der Universität
3. Deutsche	im Schloss
4. Touristen	auf dem Tennisplatz
5. Boris Becker	in der Kirche
6. Professoren	im Schwimmbad
7. Pastoren	im Museum
8. Sportler	im Lokal

Boris Becker is a retired professional tennis player from Leimen, a suburb of Heidelberg, who won the Wimbledon Men's Tennis Singles 3 times (1985, 1986, 1989).

26 Ergänzen Sie. Complete these statements with words from the **Absprungtext.**

1. Heidelberg hat 134.000 _____.
2. Es gibt in Heidelberg über 3.600 Betten in _____, in Gasthöfen und in _____.
3. Es gibt in Mannheim 120 Betten für junge Leute in der _____.
4. Reiten, Tennis, Angeln und Segeln sind Aktivitäten für die _____ in Heidelberg.
5. Man kann Heidelberg vom Wasser sehen, wenn man eine _____ macht.
6. Das Heidelberger _____ ist das Wahrzeichen (Symbol) von Heidelberg.
7. Der _____ ist das Wahrzeichen (Symbol) von Mannheim.
8. Heidelberg hat eine historische, romantische _____ am Neckar.

9. Heidelberger Studenten gehen in historische _____ und trinken dort Wein und Bier.
10. Heidelbergs Altstadt ist historisch und _____.
11. Heidelbergs _____ ist die älteste in Deutschland (1386).
12. Heidelberger Studenten leihen Bücher für ihre Kurse aus der _____ aus°.
13. Sonntags gehen einige° Studenten in die Heiliggeist_____.
14. Man lernt viel über die kurpfälzische Geschichte, wenn man in das Kurpfälzische _____ geht.

***leihen aus:** check out*

a few

Ergänzen Sie. Kurpfalz: The prince of the Palatinate region **(Pfalz)** participated in the selection **(Kur)** of the German emperors until 1806.

27 Kurz gefragt. Answer these questions with just a word or two, or a short phrase.

1. Welche Stadt hat mehr Betten für Touristen?
2. Wie viele Heidelberger° gibt es?
3. Welche Freizeitaktivitäten in Heidelberg und Mannheim haben mit Wasser zu tun°?
4. Welche Freizeitaktivitäten in Heidelberg haben mit Tieren zu tun?
5. Für welche Sportarten braucht° man einen Ball?
6. Was sind zwei Sehenswürdigkeiten in der Nähe° vom Heidelberger Schloss?
7. Wo ist die Heidelberger Altstadt? Und wie ist sie?
8. Wie kommt man über den Neckar? Man geht über …
9. Wo bekommen Touristen Information über Heidelberg? Und wie?

inhabitants of Heidelberg

***haben zu tun:** have to do with*

need

near

BRENNPUNKT KULTUR

Heidelberg and Mannheim

Heidelberg and Mannheim are a study in contrasts. Whereas Heidelberg was spared the devastation of aerial bombing in WWII, Mannheim was badly damaged. After the war the downtown section was rebuilt as a square grid **(Quadrat)**, which resembles many American cities. Heidelberg's romantic and bustling **Hauptstraße** meanders for over a mile from the **Bismarckplatz** past the **Theaterplatz** and the **Universitätsplatz.** The many small streets and alleys make up the **Altstadt.**

Heidelberg's reputation is built on its proud academic tradition and its prominent role in German history. The **Heidelberger Schloss** is one of the most popular tourist attractions in Europe. The skull of *Homo Heidelbergensis,* the earliest human remains in Europe, is over 500,000 years old. Heidelberg's most famous export today is Boris Becker, the world champion tennis player.

Mannheim's reputation is built on its past and current industrial innovations. In 1885, Carl Friedrich Benz invented the first automobile in Mannheim, which later evolved to become the first **Mercedes** automobile. Today, Mannheim continues to be the home of mechanical and electrical engineering firms as well as car makers. Mannheim's sister city across the Rhein, Ludwigshafen, is home to BASF (Badische Anilin- und Soda-Fabrik), one of the largest chemical companies in the world.

28 **Was möchtest du in Heidelberg sehen?** Using the brochure of Heidelberg on page 99 and the map below as a visual guide, ask your partner what he/she would like to see in Heidelberg. Use the cues to the right.

S1: Möchtest du das Schloss sehen?
S2: Ja, ich möchte das Schloss sehen, und du?
S1: Ja, ich auch. *(oder)*
Nein, ich nicht.

S1: Möchtest du das Rathaus sehen?
S2: Nein, ich möchte das Rathaus nicht sehen, und du?
S1: Nein, ich auch nicht. *(oder)*
Ja, ich möchte das Rathaus sehen.

1. das Schloss
2. die Universität
3. die Alte Brücke
4. das Museum
5. den Neckar
6. die Heiliggeistkirche
7. den Zoo
8. das Große Fass

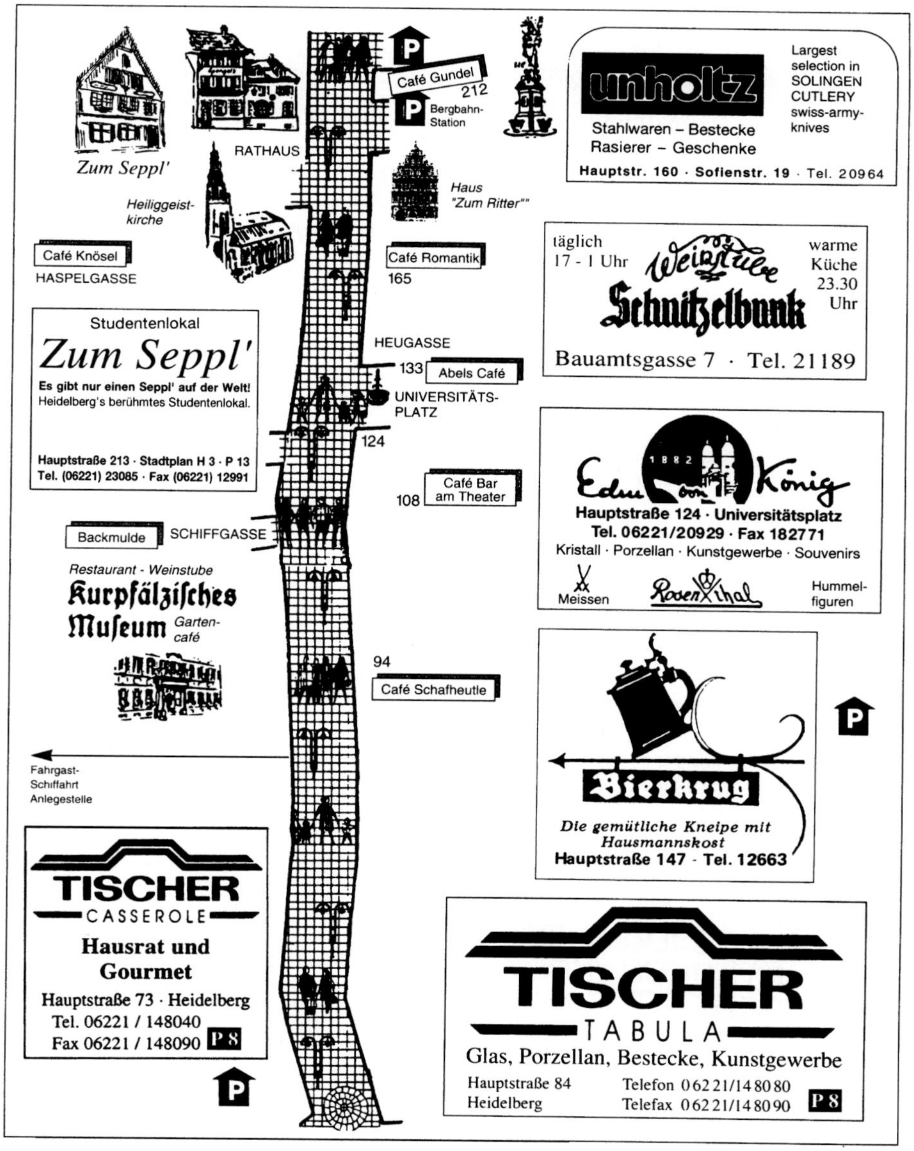

Zum Seppl'
RATHAUS
Café Gundel
212
Bergbahn-Station
unholtz
Stahlwaren – Bestecke
Rasierer – Geschenke
Largest selection in SOLINGEN CUTLERY swiss-army-knives
Hauptstr. 160 · Sofienstr. 19 · Tel. 20964
Heiliggeist-kirche
Haus "Zum Ritter"
Café Knösel
HASPELGASSE
Café Romantik
165
täglich 17 - 1 Uhr
Weinstube Schnitzelbank
warme Küche 23.30 Uhr
Bauamtsgasse 7 · Tel. 21189
Studentenlokal
Zum Seppl'
Es gibt nur einen Seppl' auf der Welt!
Heidelberg's berühmtes Studentenlokal.
Hauptstraße 213 · Stadtplan H 3 · P 13
Tel. (06221) 23085 · Fax (06221) 12991
HEUGASSE
133 Abels Café
UNIVERSITÄTS-PLATZ
124
Café Bar am Theater
108
Edm. von König
1882
Hauptstraße 124 · Universitätsplatz
Tel. 06221/20929 · Fax 182771
Kristall · Porzellan · Kunstgewerbe · Souvenirs
Meissen
Rosenthal
Hummel-figuren
Backmulde
SCHIFFGASSE
Restaurant - Weinstube
Kurpfälzisches Museum
Garten-café
94
Café Schafheutle
Fahrgast-Schiffahrt Anlegestelle
Bierkrug
Die gemütliche Kneipe mit Hausmannskost
Hauptstraße 147 · Tel. 12663
TISCHER
CASSEROLE
Hausrat und Gourmet
Hauptstraße 73 · Heidelberg
Tel. 06221 / 148040
Fax 06221 / 148090 P 8
TISCHER
TABULA
Glas, Porzellan, Bestecke, Kunstgewerbe
Hauptstraße 84
Heidelberg
Telefon 06221/148080
Telefax 06221/148090 P 8

■ Strukturen und Vokabeln ■

VI ■ Expressing possibilities

The modal verb **können**

The modal verb **können** *(to be able to)* is used to express what a person can or cannot do or knows how to do.

Ich kann Deutsch sprechen. *I can (know how to) speak German.*

Like **möchte, können** may occur without an infinitive, when the implied infinitive is clear from the context. This happens particularly often in the context of languages and musical instruments.

Angelika kann Deutsch (sprechen). *Angelika can speak German.*
Angelika kann Gitarre (spielen). *Angelika can play the guitar.*

Like other modals, **können** has stem vowels that are different in the singular and in the plural. Also, the 1st and 3rd person singular forms have no endings. You will learn more about these modal verbs in Chapter 4.

können: *to be able to*

Person	Singular		Plural	
1st	ich k**a**nn	*I can*	wir k**ö**nnen	*we can*
2nd, informal	du k**a**nnst	*you can*	ihr k**ö**nnt	*you can*
2nd, formal	Sie k**ö**nnen	*you can*	Sie k**ö**nnen	*you can*
3rd	er/sie/es k**a**nn	*he/she/it can*	sie k**ö**nnen	*they can*

The pronoun **man** is often used with **kann** to express what options are available.

In Heidelberg **kann man** segeln und Tennis spielen. ***You (one) can** sail and play tennis in Heidelberg.*

Heidelberger Schloß

Führungen
von 9.00 – 17.00 Uhr laufend nach Bedarf, auch in Englisch, Französisch, andere Sprachen (ca. 1. Std.). Auf Vereinbarung auch Kasemattenführungen

Festliche Veranstaltungen
im Königssaal und im Faßkeller

Ausstellungen
im Ottheinrichbau. Die Räumlichkeiten können von Privat angemietet werden.

Das Deutsche Apothekenmuseum
ist von April bis Oktober täglich geöffnet. Von November bis März am Samstag und Sonntag.

Auskünfte:
Telefon: Schloßverwaltung
Heidelberg 0 62 21/2 05 54

Mannheimer Schloß

Führungen
in den Repräsentationsräumen des Mittelbaues von April bis Oktober täglich außer Montag von 10.00 – 12.00 Uhr und von 15.00 – 17.00 Uhr. Von November bis März an Samstagen und Sonntagen zu den gleichen Zeiten.

STAATLICHE SCHLÖSSER UND GÄRTEN

Auskünfte:
Telefon: Schloßverwaltung
Mannheim 06 21/2 92 28 90
oder 0 62 02/81-4 71

Schwetzinger Schloß und Schloßgarten

Führungen im Schloß
April–Oktober 9.30–16.30 Uhr
November–März 11.00–15.00 Uhr
außer Montag

Schloßgarten
ganzjährig geöffnet
Gartenführungen für Gruppen nach telef. Vereinbarung
Bühnendemonstrationen des Rokokotheaters von Juli bis September 4 mal täglich.

Festliche Veranstaltungen
in den Zirkelsälen und im Rokokotheater

Auskünfte:
Telefon: Schloßverwaltung
Schwetzingen 0 62 02/81-482
oder 81-4 81 (Schloßkasse)

Wissenswerte Vokabeln: Freizeitaktivitäten

Talking about what you can do and like to do

Karten spielen, Fußball spielen, Klavier spielen, ins Kino gehen, tanzen, Ski laufen, wandern, reiten, kochen, lesen, Rad fahren, spazieren gehen

Was spielst du gern? *Ich spiele gern Tennis.*
Was kann man in Heidelberg machen? *Man kann Rad fahren.*

29 Das Interview. Find out as much as you can about your partner's leisure time activities. Write **ja,** if you or your partner like to do the activity, and **nein,** if you do not.

S1: Spielst du gern Karten?
S2: Ja, und du?

	Ich	*Mein Partner/Meine Partnerin*
Karten spielen	___	___
Tennis spielen	___	___
Klavier spielen	___	___
Gitarre spielen	___	___
ins Kino gehen	___	___
ins Konzert gehen	___	___
reiten	___	___
kochen	___	___
lesen	___	___
Rad fahren	___	___
spazieren gehen	___	___

Similar to **Fußball spielen,** you can say **Basketball spielen, Golf spielen, Tennis spielen,** and **Volleyball spielen.**

Similar to **Klavier spielen,** you can also say **Flöte** *(flute)* **spielen** and **Gitarre** *(guitar)* **spielen.**

Similar to **ins Kino gehen,** you can say **ins Konzert gehen** and **ins Theater gehen.**

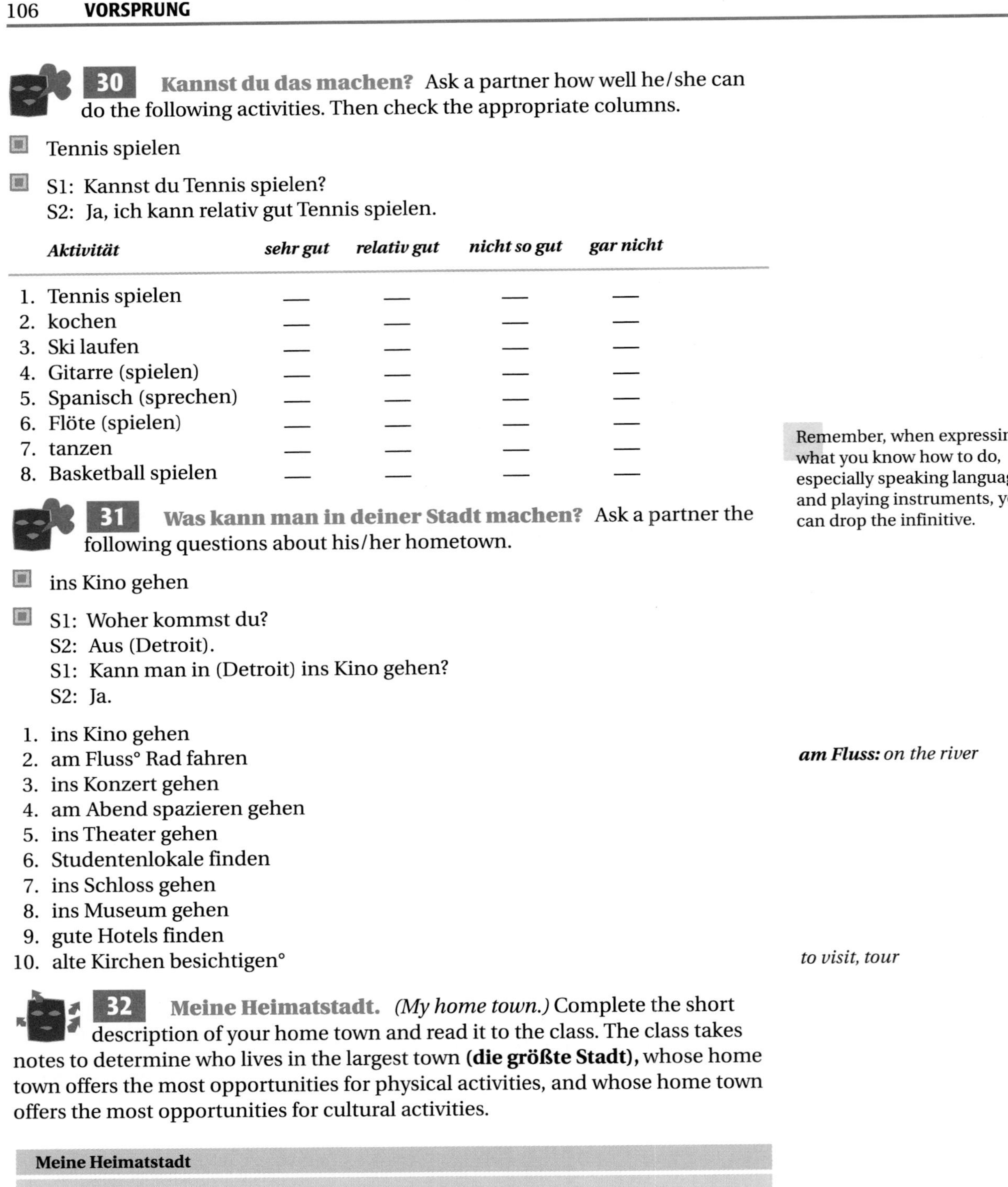

30 **Kannst du das machen?** Ask a partner how well he/she can do the following activities. Then check the appropriate columns.

Tennis spielen

S1: Kannst du Tennis spielen?
S2: Ja, ich kann relativ gut Tennis spielen.

Aktivität	*sehr gut*	*relativ gut*	*nicht so gut*	*gar nicht*
1. Tennis spielen	___	___	___	___
2. kochen	___	___	___	___
3. Ski laufen	___	___	___	___
4. Gitarre (spielen)	___	___	___	___
5. Spanisch (sprechen)	___	___	___	___
6. Flöte (spielen)	___	___	___	___
7. tanzen	___	___	___	___
8. Basketball spielen	___	___	___	___

Remember, when expressing what you know how to do, especially speaking languages and playing instruments, you can drop the infinitive.

31 **Was kann man in deiner Stadt machen?** Ask a partner the following questions about his/her hometown.

ins Kino gehen

S1: Woher kommst du?
S2: Aus (Detroit).
S1: Kann man in (Detroit) ins Kino gehen?
S2: Ja.

1. ins Kino gehen
2. am Fluss° Rad fahren
3. ins Konzert gehen
4. am Abend spazieren gehen
5. ins Theater gehen
6. Studentenlokale finden
7. ins Schloss gehen
8. ins Museum gehen
9. gute Hotels finden
10. alte Kirchen besichtigen°

am Fluss: *on the river*

to visit, tour

32 **Meine Heimatstadt.** *(My home town.)* Complete the short description of your home town and read it to the class. The class takes notes to determine who lives in the largest town **(die größte Stadt),** whose home town offers the most opportunities for physical activities, and whose home town offers the most opportunities for cultural activities.

Meine Heimatstadt

1. Meine Stadt heißt ______. Sie hat ______ Einwohner.
2. Es gibt ______ ein Theater, zwei Kinos, viele Hotels usw°.
3. Man kann ______.

etc.

Resultate:

1. ______ ist die größte Stadt. ______ *(name)* wohnt° da.

lives

2. In _____ kann man viel Sport machen. _____ *(name)* wohnt da.
3. In _____ gibt es viel Kultur. _____ *(name)* wohnt da.

VII Referring to people and things

Accusative pronouns

In Chapter 1 you learned that pronouns must reflect the gender and number of the nouns they replace.

> Hier ist **ein Tisch. Er** ist neu.
> **Meine Mutter** heißt Helga. **Sie** spricht am Telefon.
> Das ist **mein Deutschbuch. Es** hat sehr schöne Photos.

In each of the examples above, the highlighted pronoun in the second sentence is the subject of that sentence. The subject is always in the nominative case. Now look at the pronouns highlighted in the examples below. In each case the pronoun completes the action of the verb. These pronouns are direct objects and are in the accusative case. They are called **Akkusativpronomen.** A direct object answers the question **wen?** *(whom?)* or **was?** *(what?)*.

Klaus, ruf **mich** bitte zu Hause an.	*Klaus, call* ***me*** *at home, please.*
Hallo? Hallo? Hallo? Ich höre **dich** nicht.	*Hello? Hello? Hello? I can't hear* ***you.***
Wo ist mein Vater? Ich sehe **ihn** nicht.	*Where is my father? I don't see* ***him.***
Das ist meine Schwester. Möchtest du **sie** kennen lernen?	*That is my sister. Would you like to meet* ***her****?*
Hier ist mein Deutschbuch. Möchtest du **es** lesen?	*Here is my German book. Would you like to read* ***it****?*

Here are the nominative and accusative forms of the personal pronouns:

Person	Singular Nominative		Accusative		Plural Nominative		Accusative	
1st	ich	*I*	mich	*me*	wir	*we*	uns	*us*
2nd, informal	du	*you*	dich	*you*	ihr	*you*	euch	*you*
2nd, formal	Sie	*you*	Sie	*you*	Sie	*you*	Sie	*you*
3rd	er/sie/es	*he/she/it*	ihn/sie/es	*him/her/it*	sie	*they*	sie	*them*

33 **Kombinieren Sie.** Select a response from the column on the right that best complements each statement in the left column.

1. Ich liebe° dich, Annette!
2. Professor Bauer spricht sehr schnell, nicht?
3. Wo ist Frau Günther?
4. Anna trägt heute Shorts.
5. Wer hat meine Zeitung?

a. Ich weiß nicht. Ich sehe sie nicht.
b. Katja trägt sie auch.
c. Ich habe dich auch sehr gern, Hannes.
d. Claudia liest sie gerade°.
e. Ja, ich verstehe ihn auch nicht so gut.

love

right now

34 **Kurze Dialoge.** Supply the appropriate accusative pronouns (**mich, dich, euch, Sie,** or **uns**) in the dialogues below.

1. PROFESSOR: Sprechen Sie Deutsch? Verstehen Sie ______?
   STUDENTEN: Ja, wir verstehen ______.
2. GEORG *(am Telefon):* Meine Kusine aus Amerika …
   FRANK: Wie bitte? Ich höre ______ nicht so gut.
   GEORG: Meine Kusine besucht uns.
   FRANK: Ja? Wann besucht sie ______?
3. KATJA GÜNTHER: Besuchst du ______ bald, Anna?
   ANNA: Ja, ich besuche ______ im August.
4. SOHN: Papa, siehst du ______ nicht?
   VATER: Nein, wo bist du denn?
5. ENKEL: Opa, hörst du ______?
   OPA: Ja ich höre ______, Kleiner°.

little one

35 **Interview.** With a partner, create short dialogues about what you like to do. Use pronouns in your answers to the questions. Try to expand your answers by using **sondern** when you answer in the negative.

S1: Liest du gern Zeitung?
S2: Ja, ich lese sie gern. *(oder)*
Nein, ich lese Zeitung nicht gern, sondern Bücher.

1. Verstehst du die Professoren?
2. Sprichst du gern Deutsch?
3. Liest du das Buch *Vorsprung* gern?
4. Möchtest du Anna Adler kennen lernen?
5. Möchtest du die Stadt Heidelberg besichtigen?
6. Isst du gern Schweinefleisch?
7. Trägst du gern Tennisschuhe?
8. Spielst du gern Fußball?
9. Hast du den Deutschprofessor/die Deutschprofessorin gern?

VIII Talking about people and things that you know

The verb **kennen**

To express that they know people, places, films, and books, German speakers use the verb **kennen** *(to know, to be acquainted with)*. Unlike **wissen** *(to know as a fact)*, which refers to information described in a clause, **kennen** generally refers to information contained in a direct object. The present tense endings of **kennen** are like those of regular verbs.

Kennt er Heidelberg? Ja, er kennt es.	*Does he know Heidelberg?* *Yes, he knows it.*
Kennst du den Film von Spielberg? Nein, ich kenne ihn nicht.	*Do you know the movie by Spielberg?* *No, I don't know it.*

IX ▣ Expressing relationships or ownership

Accusative of possessive adjectives

Earlier in this chapter, you learned about the possessive adjectives in the nominative case. Here are the accusative endings for the possessive adjectives and **ein/kein:**

	Masculine	**Neuter**	**Feminine**	**Plural**
	einen/keinen	ein/kein	eine/keine	—/keine
	Possessive adjectives:			
ich	meinen Vater	mein Kind	meine Mutter	meine Kinder
du	deinen Vater	dein Kind	deine Mutter	deine Kinder
Sie (Sg. & Pl.)	Ihren Vater	Ihr Kind	Ihre Mutter	Ihre Kinder
er	seinen Vater	sein Kind	seine Mutter	seine Kinder
es	seinen Vater	sein Kind	seine Mutter	seine Kinder
sie	ihren Vater	ihr Kind	ihre Mutter	ihre Kinder
wir	uns(e)ren Vater	unser Kind	unsere Mutter	unsere Kinder
ihr	eu(e)ren Vater	euer Kind	eu(e)re Mutter	eu(e)re Kinder
sie	ihren Vater	ihr Kind	ihre Mutter	ihre Kinder

As in the nominative, the internal **e** is always dropped when adding an ending to **euer (eure, euren)** and occasionally dropped when adding one to **unser (unsre, unsren).**

36 **Freunde und Familie.** Ask your partner these questions about friends and family members.

▣ S1: Hier ist mein Freund Hans. Kennst du ihn?
S2: Ja, ich kenne deinen Freund Hans. *(oder)* Nein, ich kenne deinen Freund Hans nicht.

1. mein Freund Hans
2. meine Tochter Anna
3. mein Bruder Karl
4. meine Freunde Volker und Katharina
5. meine Freundin Barbara
6. mein Partner Robert
7. meine Kinder Fabian und Helena
8. meine Eltern

X ▣ Talking about more than one item

Noun plurals

In Chapter 2 you already encountered many plural forms like these family terms.

die Väter	*fathers*
die Mütter	*mothers*
die Brüder	*brothers*
die Schwestern	*sisters*
die Tanten	*aunts*

In Chapter 1 you learned that every German noun is accompanied by **der, das,** or **die,** depending on the gender of the noun. There is only one definite article for the plural: **die,** in both the nominative and accusative cases.

Gender	Singular	Plural
Masculine	der Student	**die** Studenten
Feminine	die Schwester	**die** Schwestern
Neuter	das Buch	**die** Bücher

The following lists provide an overview of the different plural endings for masculine/neuter and feminine nouns.

Good dictionaries list the plural changes of nouns. If two endings are listed, the second one is the plural ending. (The first ending denotes the genitive, a case which you will encounter in Chapter 10.) The symbol - indicates no ending, ¨ indicates an umlaut, and **-s, -n, -en, -er** indicate the ending.

1. Masculine nouns (der-words) and neuter nouns (das-words)

a. **-e**

der Tag	die Tag**e**	*days*
das Lokal	die Lokal**e**	*pubs*
der Freund	die Freund**e**	*friends*

b. **-s**

der Chef	die Chef**s**	*bosses*
das Hotel	die Hotel**s**	*hotels*
das Café	die Café**s**	*cafés*

Most nouns that add **-s** derive from a foreign language, mostly English. However, **der Computer** does not add any ending because it ends in **-er.**

c. **-er**

das Kind	die Kind**er**	*children*

Note the plurals **Väter, Brüder,** and **Lehrer** on one hand, and **Kinder** on the other. The **-er** ending in **Väter, Brüder,** and **Lehrer** is not a plural ending, while the ending **-er** in **Kinder** is.

d. no ending, with or without umlaut

Masculine and some neuter nouns ending in **-er** in the singular do not have any additional endings in the plural. An umlaut is often added to the following vowels in the plural: **a→ä, o→ö, u→ü.**

der Lehrer	die Lehrer	*teachers*
der Computer	die Computer	*computers*
der Amerikaner	die Amerikaner	*Americans*
das Fenster	die Fenster	*windows*
der Vater	die V**ä**ter	*fathers*
der Bruder	die Br**ü**der	*brothers*

While **Vater** and **Bruder** add an umlaut in the plural, **Lehrer** (plural: **Lehrer**) does not. There is no "e-umlaut." However, because masculine nouns have a different article in the plural (**die** instead of singular **der**), singular and plural nouns are clearly distinguishable.

Most masculine nouns ending in **-el** in the singular have no additional endings in the plural. The most frequently used noun in this category is **Onkel:**

der Onkel	die Onkel	*uncles*

The neuter suffix **-chen** remains the same in the plural.

das Mädchen	die Mädchen	*girls*

e. Some masculine and neuter nouns add an umlaut **(a→ä, o→ö, u→ü)** as well as the ending **-er** in the plural.

der Mann	die M**ä**nn**er**	*men*
das Schloss	die Schl**ö**ss**er**	*castles*
das Buch	die B**ü**ch**er**	*books*
das Fahrrad	die Fahrr**ä**d**er**	*bicycles*

Each of these nouns has two plural markers where one would suffice. This is the consequence of historical developments in the language.

f. **- (e)n**

Masculine nouns that derive from a foreign language (mostly Greek or Latin) and end in **-or, -ph (-f),** or **-t** add **-en** in the plural.

der Professor	die Professor**en**	*professors*
der Fotograf	die Fotograf**en**	*photographers*
der Pilot	die Pilot**en**	*pilots*

Such Greek or Latinate words often describe professions and look very similar to English.

Masculine N-nouns add **-(e)n** in the plural.

der Herr	die Herr**en**	*(gentle)men*
der Neffe	die Neffe**n**	*nephews*

Nouns of Latin origin ending in **-um**, form the plural by replacing the **-um** ending with **-en: das Museum, die Museen, das Studium, die Studien**.

2. Feminine nouns (die-words)

a. **-(e)n**

Feminine nouns ending in **-e** in the singular, add **-n** in the plural.

die Brücke	die Brücke**n**	*bridges*
die Tante	die Tante**n**	*aunts*

Feminine nouns ending in **-keit, -heit, -tät,** or **-ung** add **-en** in the plural.

die Möglichkeit	die Möglichkeit**en**	*possibilities*
die Universität	die Universität**en**	*universities*
die Zeitung	die Zeitung**en**	*newspapers*
die Schönheit	die Schönheit**en**	*beauties*

Feminine nouns ending in **-in** in the singular add an additional **n** before the ending **-en** in the plural.

die Professorin	die Professorin**nen**	*(female) professors*

Unlike their masculine counterparts, feminine nouns ending in **-el** typically add the ending **-n** in the plural.

die Semmel	die Semmel**n**	*crusty rolls*

b. umlaut or **-n**

Feminine nouns ending in **-er** change a vowel that occurs in the singular to an umlaut in the plural. Feminine nouns with the vowels **i, ie,** or **e,** which have no umlaut form, add **-n** in the plural.

die Mutter	die M**ü**tter	*mothers*
die Schwester	die Schwester**n**	*sisters*

Feminine nouns like **Schwester** that end in **-er** cannot take an umlaut in the plural and need to add an ending (**-n**) because they have the same article in the singular and in the plural **(die).**

37 **Wo ist der Plural?** Circle all the features that indicate that the following words are plurals. If there are no features because a plural word looks the same as its singular form, underline the word.

Väter • Lehrer • Schwestern • Professoren • Studenten • Freunde • Hamburger • Türen • Kinder • Betten • Einwohner • Menschen • Straßen • Plätze • Fahrräder • Suppen • Colas

Schreibecke **Was kann man hier sehen?** You are anticipating a phone call from a young person from a small Swiss village who is coming to your town for a one-year exchange. You will be speaking in German. International phone calls are expensive, so make some notes to yourself and write down at least five things in each category **(Unsere Stadt, Meine Universität)** that a person can see there. Think of all the things that might be different for your visitor.

Hier kann man viele ... sehen.

Unsere Stadt		***Meine Universität***	
___________	___________	___________	___________
___________	___________	___________	___________
___________		___________	

FREIE KOMMUNIKATION **Rollenspiel: Ein Telefongespräch.** The Swiss exchange person calls you to get an understanding of life in your town. She/he is especially interested in getting a sense for the things she/he will see and need for a one-year exchange. Discuss the items you listed in the activity above. International phone calls are expensive, so keep the call short. Here are some useful expressions:

Hallo
Hier ist ... ,
Ich möchte wissen ...
Was kann man dort sehen?
Gibt es viele ... ?

ZIELTEXT
Fahren wir nach Heidelberg oder nach Mannheim?

Georg is talking to his parents, Uschi and Hannes, about what to show Anna during her first weekend in Germany. They are discussing whether to take her to Heidelberg or Mannheim and what each city has to offer.

Vorschau

38 **Thematische Fragen.** Discuss the following questions with your instructor or in pairs.

1. When you expect visitors from out of town, what activities are you likely to do with them?
2. What kind of place do you prefer to visit—a historic city with many sights and tourist attractions, or a modern town that offers many sports and leisure-time activities?

39 **Wortdetektiv.** Which words convey approximately the same meaning? Draw a line from the German word to its logical English equivalent.

Deutsch	*Englisch*
1. die Fußgängerzone	a. record store
2. das Rathaus	b. market square
3. der Marktplatz	c. pedestrian zone
4. das Plattengeschäft	d. city (town) hall
5. die Aussicht	e. boring
6. langweilig	f. in the vicinity
7. in der Nähe	g. idea
8. die Idee	h. view
9. die Zeit	i. to be right
10. zuerst	j. to wait
11. warten	k. first
12. Recht haben	l. time
13. dann	m. main street
14. danach	n. afterwards
15. die Hauptstraße	o. people
16. Menschen	p. then

40 **Eine deutsche Stadt – eine amerikanische Stadt.** Which of these places and public and commercial buildings would you expect to find in a North American city and which in a German city? Write the locations in the appropriate categories. Then ask your partner about them.

S1: Wo findet man ein Schloss?
S2: Man findet ein Schloss in einer deutschen Stadt.

ein Schloss • ein Museum • ein China-Restaurant • eine Fußgängerzone • Cafés • einen Marktplatz • ein Theater • eine Universität • eine Disko • ein Rathaus • ein Plattengeschäft • eine Bibliothek • eine Altstadt • eine Kirche • einen Fahrradverleih • einen McDonald's • ein historisches Studentenlokal • ein Hallenschwimmbad

In einer amerikanischen Stadt findet man ...	*In einer deutschen Stadt findet man ...*
______________	______________
______________	______________
______________	______________
______________	______________

41 **Erstes Zuhören.** Focus on the following aspects as you listen to the text.

1. Who are the speakers?
2. Who suggests going to see Mannheim and why?
3. Who prefers Heidelberg and why?
4. Where do they intend to eat and when?

ZIELTEXT

Fahren wir nach Mannheim oder nach Heidelberg?

Now listen to the recording

Rückblick

42 **Ist das in Heidelberg oder in Mannheim?** Indicate where you can find these items mentioned in the dialogue. Check **Heidelberg** or **Mannheim.**

	Heidelberg	*Mannheim*
1. das Schloss	—	—
2. das Museum	—	—
3. das Rathaus	—	—
4. der Marktplatz	—	—
5. die Fußgängerzone	—	—
6. Plattengeschäfte	—	—
7. die Universität (Uni)	—	—
8. viele Menschen	—	—
9. die Hauptstraße	—	—
10. eine Disko	—	—

43 **Stimmt das?** How much of the text can you remember?

	Ja, das stimmt.	*Nein, das stimmt nicht.*
Georg meint, …		
1. Anna kommt am Samstag aus Amerika.	___	___
2. in Mannheim gibt es tolle Schuhgeschäfte.	___	___
3. sie sollen zuerst ins Schloss gehen und danach ins Restaurant gehen.	___	___
Hannes meint, …		
4. sie sollen lieber nach Mannheim fahren.	___	___
5. Heidelberg ist wahrscheinlich besser als Mannheim.	___	___
6. er isst lieber im Café am Theater als im Restaurant.	___	___
7. er fährt lieber am Sonntag nach Heidelberg, denn samstags sind zu viele Menschen da.	___	___
Uschi meint, …		
8. in Heidelberg gibt es viel zu sehen: das Schloss, die Universität, das Museum und das Große Fass.	___	___
9. sie isst lieber im Restaurant in der Nähe vom Schloss, denn da hat man eine schöne Aussicht auf den Neckar.	___	___
10. sie gehen zuerst in den Supermarkt, dann ins Schloss und zuletzt essen.	___	___

44 **Ergänzen Sie: Diktat.** Complete these sentences with words from the **Zieltext.**

1. HANNES: Warum fahren wir nicht nach Mannheim? Das ist sehr schön und _____ _____ dort viel zu sehen.
2. USCHI: Ich habe gedacht, wir _____ nach Heidelberg.
3. HANNES: Aber es gibt nicht viel zu _____ in Heidelberg. Das Schloss vielleicht und die Uni.
4. USCHI: _____! Es gibt viel zu sehen in Heidelberg: das Schloss, das Museum, und dann …
5. GEORG: Das Museum ist _____.
6. HANNES: Du _____ das Museum in Heidelberg doch _____ nicht.
7. HANNES: Heidelberg ist _____, wahrscheinlich besser als Mannheim. Wir _____ doch einfach ein bisschen spazieren gehen in der _____.
8. USCHI: Und ich _____ ein sehr gutes kleines Restaurant in der Nähe vom Heidelberger _____. Man hat eine schöne _____ auf den Neckar. Das ist eine gute _____.
9. HANNES: Gehen wir doch _____ ins Café am Theater.
10. USCHI: Das stimmt, und es ist auch in der Nähe von der _____.

45 **Kurz gefragt.** Answer these questions with just a few words, a phrase, or a complete sentence.

1. Wer sagt zuerst, die Günthers sollen Pläne für Anna machen?
2. Warum fährt Hannes lieber nach Mannheim als nach Heidelberg?

3. Was gibt es in Heidelberg zu sehen?
4. Was kennt Georg in Heidelberg gar nicht?
5. Was wollen sie zuerst in Heidelberg machen?
6. Was sind die zwei Möglichkeiten zum Essen?
7. Warum geht Hannes lieber ins Café in der Hauptstraße?
8. Warum geht Uschi lieber ins Restaurant in der Nähe vom Heidelberger Schloss?
9. Fährt Hannes lieber am Samstag oder am Sonntag nach Heidelberg? Warum?
10. Wann möchte Georg mit Anna in die Disko gehen?

46 **Was machen wir zuerst?** You will be accompanying the Günthers on their excursion with Anna. With a group of three to four students, decide in which order you will do the following activities.

Was machen wir zuerst? Remember that whenever the subject is not the first element in the sentence, it is repositioned immediately after the verb as the third element in the sentence.

a. das Schloss ansehen

b. das Museum besuchen

c. im Restaurant essen

d. in der Fußgängerzone spazieren gehen

e. in der Disko tanzen

Zuerst besuchen wir das Museum.
Dann ...

1. Zuerst ...
2. Dann ...
3. Danach ...
4. Später° ...
5. Zuletzt° ...

° *later*
° *last*

Die Universitätsstadt Heidelberg

Nicht weit von Heidelberg ist Mannheim. (Der Wasserturm)

■ FREIE ■ KOMMUNIKATION ■ **Der neue Zimmerkamerad.** Your German roommate has just told you that one of his/her friends is coming to live with you. Since you feel your apartment is quite small and you know nothing about this person, ask your roommate questions about the new roommate's eating and drinking preferences, TV viewing habits, free-time activities, and any other personal traits. Discuss these issues in German.

Schreibecke **Meine Stadt: Information für Touristen.** Write a description of your home town or college/university town that you would like to send to some German friends. Include all the information that is relevant to tourists, e.g., about sports facilities, cultural events, historic sights, restaurants, number of inhabitants.

Wortschatz

Das Essen

die Lebensmittel *(pl.) groceries*
der Apfel, ¨ *apple*
die Apfelsine, -n *orange*
die Banane, -n *banana*
das Brot, -e *bread*
das Brötchen, - *hard roll*
die Butter *butter*
die Erbse, -n *pea*
das Fleisch *meat*
das Geflügel *poultry, fowl*
das Gemüse *vegetable, vegetables*
das Hähnchen, - *chicken*
der Hamburger, - *hamburger*
die Karotte, -n *carrot*
die Kartoffel, -n *potato*
der Käse *cheese*
der Kaugummi, -s *chewing gum*
die Kirsche, -n *cherry*
die Marmelade, -n *fruit jam, preserves*
das Obst *fruit, fruits*
die Orange, -n *orange*
die Pute, -n *turkey*
das Rindfleisch *beef*
der Salat, -e *salad, lettuce*
das Schweinefleisch *pork*
die Semmel, -n *hard roll (in so. Germany & Austria)*
die Suppe, -n *soup*
die Tomate, -n *tomato*
die Traube, -n *grape*
die Wurst, ¨e *sausage*

das Getränk, -e *beverage, drink*
das Bier, -e *beer*
die Cola, -s *cola*
der Kaffee *coffee*
die Milch *milk*
das Mineralwasser *mineral water*
der Saft, ¨e *juice*
der Tee *tea*
der Wein, -e *wine*

das Abendbrot *light evening meal, supper*
das Abendessen *evening meal, supper*
das Frühstück *breakfast*
das Hauptgericht, -e *main course, entree*
das Mittagessen *lunch*
der Mund, ¨er *mouth*
die Nachspeise, -n *dessert*
der Nachtisch, -e *dessert*
die Vorspeise, -n *appetizer*

das Gramm *gram*
das Kilogramm *kilogram*
der Liter *liter*
der Meter *meter*
das Pfund *pound*
das Stück, -e *piece*

essen (er isst) *to eat*
trinken *to drink*

Freizeitaktivitäten

das Fahrrad, *pl.* **Fahrräder** *bicycle*
die Freizeit *leisure time*
der Fußball *soccer*
die Politik *politics*
die Popmusik *popular music*
der Trimm-dich-Pfad, -e *exercise course, trail*

angeln *to fish*
ins Kino gehen *to go to the movies*
kochen *to cook*
können *to be able to (can)*
lesen (er liest) *to read*
möchte *would like to*
Rad fahren (er fährt Rad) *to ride bikes*
reiten *to ride horseback*
segeln *to sail*
Ski laufen *to ski*
spazieren gehen *to go for a walk*
spielen *to play*
Fußball (Golf, Karten, Klavier, Tennis) spielen *to play soccer (golf, cards, piano, tennis)*
tanzen *to dance*
tun *to do*
wandern *to hike, go hiking*

Über Heidelberg und Mannheim

der Bahnhof, ¨e *train station*
der Hauptbahnhof *main train station*
das Bett, -en *bed*
der Campingplatz, ¨e *camp ground*
der Einwohner, - *inhabitant*
der Gasthof, ¨e *inn*
das Gepäck *luggage*
das Hotel, -s *hotel*
die Jugendherberge, -n *youth hostel*
die Information, -en *information*
die Pension, -en *guesthouse*
die Stadt, ¨e *city*
das Telefon, -e *telephone*
das Zimmer, - *room*

mit·bringen *to take along, bring along*

Die Sehenswürdigkeiten

die Altstadt *old town, historic district*
die Bibliothek, -en *library*
die Brücke, -n *bridge*
die Fahrt, -en *trip*
die Schiffahrt, -en *boat trip*
das Fass, *pl.* **Fässer** *barrel*
der Hafen, ¨ *harbor*
die Kirche, -n *church*
die Kunsthalle, -n *art museum*
das Kongresszentrum, *pl.* **Kongresszentren** *convention center*
das Kulturzentrum, *pl.* **Kulturzentren** *arts center, cultural center*
das Lokal, -e *pub*
der Marktplatz, *pl.* **Marktplätze** *market place*
das Museum, *pl.* **Museen** *museum*
der Platz, ¨e *plaza, square*
das Rathaus, *pl.* **Rathäuser** *city hall*
das Schloss, *pl.* **Schlösser** *castle, palace*
das Schwimmbad, ¨er *swimming pool*
die Sehenswürdigkeit, -en *sight-seeing attraction*

die Stadt, *pl.* **Städte** *city*
das Theater, - *theater*
der Verein, -e *association, organization, club*
der Verkehrsverein, -e *tourist office*
der Kunstverein, -e *art association*
der Wasserturm, ⸚e *water tower*
das Wahrzeichen, - *emblem, symbol, trademark*
der Zoo, -s *zoo*

kennen *to know (a city, person)*

Ausdrücke

im Herzen *in the heart*

Verben

bleiben *to stay*
fern·sehen (er sieht fern) *to watch television*
geben (er gibt) *to give*
es gibt *there is, there are*
halten (du hältst, er hält) von *to think of*
lächeln *to smile*
laufen (er läuft) *to run*
nehmen (er nimmt) *to take*
sprechen (er spricht) *to speak*
tragen (er trägt) *to wear*
vergessen (er vergisst) *to forget*
etwas verstehen von *to know something (anything) about*
werden (ich werde, du wirst, er wird) *to become*
wissen (ich weiß, du weißt, er weiß) *to know (a fact)*

Adjektive und Adverbien

bestimmt *undoubtedly*
einfach *simple, simply*
immer *always*
lange *for a long time*
schwach *weak*
stark *strong*
sicher *certainly, surely*
vielleicht *maybe, perhaps*
wahrscheinlich *probably*
wohl *in all likelihood, no doubt*

Andere Wörter

dein *your (singular familiar)*
euer *your (plural familiar)*
ihr *her; their*
Ihr *your (formal)*
man *one; you*
mein *my*
nur *only*
oder *or*
sein *his; its*
sondern *but, rather*
und *and*
unser *our*

Ausdrücke

in der Nähe von *in the vicinity of, near*
Sie versteht sicher nur „Bahnhof". *She probably doesn't know much German.*
Was gibt's? *What's up?*

Akkusativpronomen

dich *you (informal, singular, accusative)*
es *it (accusative)*
euch *you (informal, plural, accusative)*
ihn *him; it (accusative)*
mich *me (accusative)*
Sie *you (formal, singular and plural, accusative)*
sie *her; it; them (accusative)*
uns *us (accusative)*

Aus dem Zieltext

die Aussicht, -en *view*
das Café, -s *café*
die Diskothek, -en *discotheque*
die Fußgängerzone, -n *pedestrian zone*
die Hauptstraße, -n *main street*
die Idee, -n *idea*
der Mensch, [-en], -en *person*
das Plattengeschäft, -e *record store*
das Restaurant, -s *restaurant*
der Vati, -s *dad*

muss *have to, must*
warten *to wait*

besser *better*
doch *oh yes it is (response to negative statement)*
gar nicht *not at all*
langweilig *boring*
lieber (+ verb) *preferably; (I would) rather . . .*
lieber als *rather than*
zuerst *first of all*
zu viele *too many*

Ausdrücke

Das ist eine gute Idee! *That's a good idea!*
Du hast schon Recht. *You're right.*
Warte erst mal ab. *Wait awhile.*

Deutsch im Beruf 1

Employment in the tourist industry

Many tourists who visit the United States are German speakers who love to come especially when a weak dollar makes food, housing, and transportation a bargain. In addition to the major cities, e.g., New York, Boston, San Francisco, and Los Angeles, tourists from Germany, Austria, and Switzerland flock to the sunny beaches of Florida and California. Knowledge of German is often useful in the tourist industry for writing brochures, such as the one you will read here, as well as interpreting for and assisting travelers whose command of English may be limited.

The **Deutsch im Beruf** section will provide you with specific information about jobs in which you can use your language skills and will help develop language skills that are important on the job. In **Deutsch im Beruf 1,** you will read about employment opportunities in the tourist industry in the United States and as office support in the German-speaking countries. The skills you will practice are: identifying places of interest and taking a telephone message.

1 **Wo sind die Touristen?** Have you heard anyone speak German where you live? The following list names places where you might encounter German-speaking tourists. Check the places where you have heard German spoken.

___ am Flughafen
___ am Bahnhof
___ auf der Autobahn
___ auf dem Campingplatz
___ im Reisebus
___ auf dem Oktoberfest
___ im Hotel
___ im Restaurant
___ in einer Bank
___ im Bus

2 **San Diego: Auskunft über die Stadt auf Deutsch.** Look over the information about San Diego and match the titles with the appropriate paragraph.

a. Sehenswürdigkeiten b. Restaurants c. Klima

___ 1. In San Diego sind Restaurants, die mexikanische Küche, Fischgerichte, Rippchen, Steaks, Roast und Brathähnchen bieten, vorherrschend. Besucher können aber auch unter japanischen, chinesischen, französischen, deutschen sowie anderen ausländischen Gerichten europäischer und nahöstlicher Länder wählen. Eine vollständige Restaurantliste können Sie vom San Diego Convention and Visitors Bureau erhalten.

___ 2. San Diego ist für sein mildes Klima bekannt. Während des wärmsten Monats (August) ist die Durchschnittstemperatur 24° C. Im kühlsten Monat (Januar) durchschnittlich 18° C. Abends ist es meistens angenehm kühl. (Sweater empfohlen.)

Durchschnittstemperaturen

JAN	FEB	MÄR	APR	MAI	JUN
18.1	18.7	18.9	19.8	20.8	21.7
7.7	8.8	10.1	12.1	14.0	15.5

JUL	AUG	SEP	OKT	NOV	DEZ
24.1	25.2	24.7	23.2	21.2	18.9
17.7	18.6	17.3	14.7	10.8	8.4

___ 3. San Diego Zoo – Ein subtropischer Garten ...
Sea World – Ein Ozeanarium und Vergnügungspark in Mission Bay.

3 **Sprechen Sie das deutlich aus.** One important skill you must develop in order to use your German successfully on the job is clear pronunciation of the language. This skill is especially important when speaking to groups of people as a **Reiseleiter/ Reiseleiterin.** Practice the following phrases from the text.

1. Die Restaurants bieten mexikanische Küche und Fischgerichte.
2. Die Restaurants haben japanische, chinesische, französische, deutsche sowie andere ausländische Gerichte.
3. San Diego ist für sein mildes Klima bekannt.
4. Der Zoo ist ein subtropischer Garten.

4 **Sie sind Reiseleiter/Reiseleiterin.** Look at the map below. Introduce yourself to a partner and point out to him/her where the interesting sights are.

Guten Tag! Ich heiße (Jane). Ich bin Ihre Reiseleiterin für heute.
Links gibt es ...
Rechts haben wir ...
Links sehen wir ...
usw.

° *tourist information office*

If you are not a citizen of one of the member countries of the European Union, it may be difficult for you to work in Germany or Austria. Some countries will issue a work permit **(Arbeitserlaubnis),** if you are registered at a university as a full-time student. Companies that do trade with English-speaking countries or that represent the business interests of clients often require their support staff to know English.

5 **Lesen Sie die Annoncen.** Read the following job ads from the *Süddeutsche Zeitung* and answer the questions below.

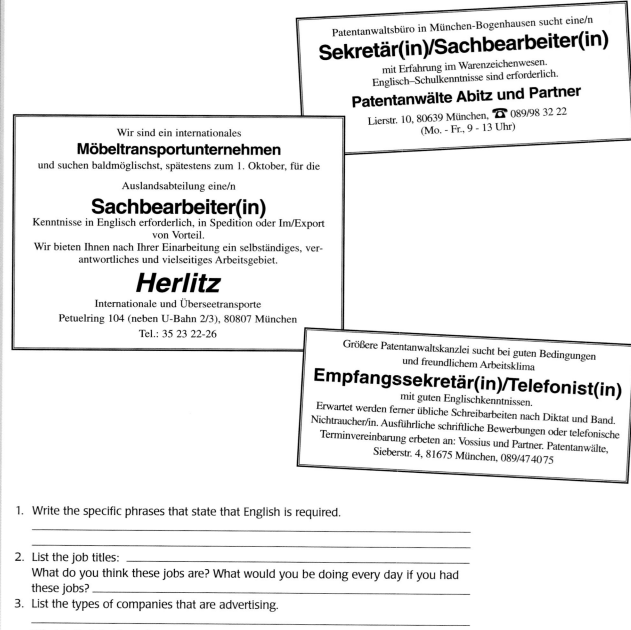

Patentanwaltsbüro in München-Bogenhausen sucht eine/n

Sekretär(in)/Sachbearbeiter(in)

mit Erfahrung im Warenzeichenwesen.
Englisch–Schulkenntnisse sind erforderlich.

Patentanwälte Abitz und Partner

Lierstr. 10, 80639 München, ☎ 089/98 32 22
(Mo. - Fr., 9 - 13 Uhr)

Wir sind ein internationales

Möbeltransportunternehmen

und suchen baldmöglischst, spätestens zum 1. Oktober, für die

Auslandsabteilung eine/n

Sachbearbeiter(in)

Kenntnisse in Englisch erforderlich, in Spedition oder Im/Export von Vorteil.
Wir bieten Ihnen nach Ihrer Einarbeitung ein selbständiges, verantwortliches und vielseitiges Arbeitsgebiet.

Herlitz

Internationale und Überseetransporte
Petuelring 104 (neben U-Bahn 2/3), 80807 München
Tel.: 35 23 22-26

Größere Patentanwaltskanzlei sucht bei guten Bedingungen und freundlichem Arbeitsklima

Empfangssekretär(in)/Telefonist(in)

mit guten Englischkenntnissen.
Erwartet werden ferner übliche Schreibarbeiten nach Diktat und Band. Nichtraucher/in. Ausführliche schriftliche Bewerbungen oder telefonische Terminvereinbarung erbeten an: Vossius und Partner. Patentanwälte, Sieberstr. 4, 81675 München, 089/474075

1. Write the specific phrases that state that English is required.
   ____
   ____
2. List the job titles: ________________________
   What do you think these jobs are? What would you be doing every day if you had these jobs? ____________________
3. List the types of companies that are advertising.
   ____
   What is their business? ____________________
4. In what city are these companies? ____________________

6 **Schreiben Sie das auf.** Look at the job ads again and fill out the envelopes with the names and addresses to which you will be sending your résumé.

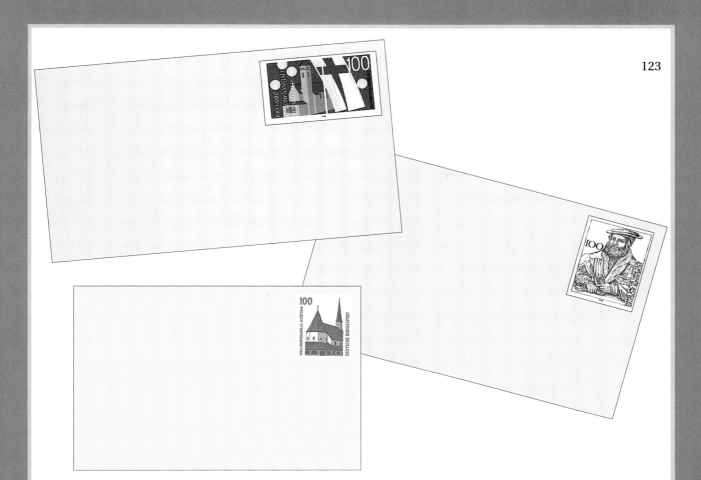

7 **Sie sind Telefonist/Telefonistin.** Answer the telephone calls that come into the office of Vossius & Partner. A client (S2) calls, asking for **Herr Vossius.** He is not in right now so you (S1) take a message.

S1: Guten Tag, Vossius und Partner.
S2: Ich möchte bitte Herrn Vossius sprechen.
S1: Er ist leider nicht da. Kann ich Herrn Vossius etwas ausrichten°?
S2: Ich habe heute einen Termin. Aber ich kann leider nicht kommen.
S1: Wie heißen Sie bitte?
S2: ...
S1: Wie schreiben Sie das?
S2: ...
S1: Was ist Ihre Telefonnummer, bitte?
S2: ...
S1: Vielen Dank, Herr (Frau) ... Auf Wiederhören!
S2: Auf Wiederhören!

° *give a message*

In this chapter you will learn how to make informal requests and express what you can, must, want to, should, and may do.

Kommunikative Funktionen

- Telling friends or relatives to do something
- Making inclusive suggestions
- Expressing ability, fondness, expected obligation, permission, prohibition, necessity, and strong desire
- Denoting the recipient of something

Strukturen

- The informal **(du-, ihr-)** imperative
- Particles with the imperative
- Inclusive suggestions (**wir-** imperative)
- Modal verbs **(können, mögen/möchte, sollen, dürfen, müssen, wollen)**
- Accusative prepositions

Vokabeln

- Das Gepäck
- Eigenschaften

Kulturelles

- Studienmöglichkeiten in Deutschland
- Fahrschule und Fahrrad fahren
- Mit der Bahn fahren
- Frankfurt am Main

Wohin fährst du?

KAPITEL VIER

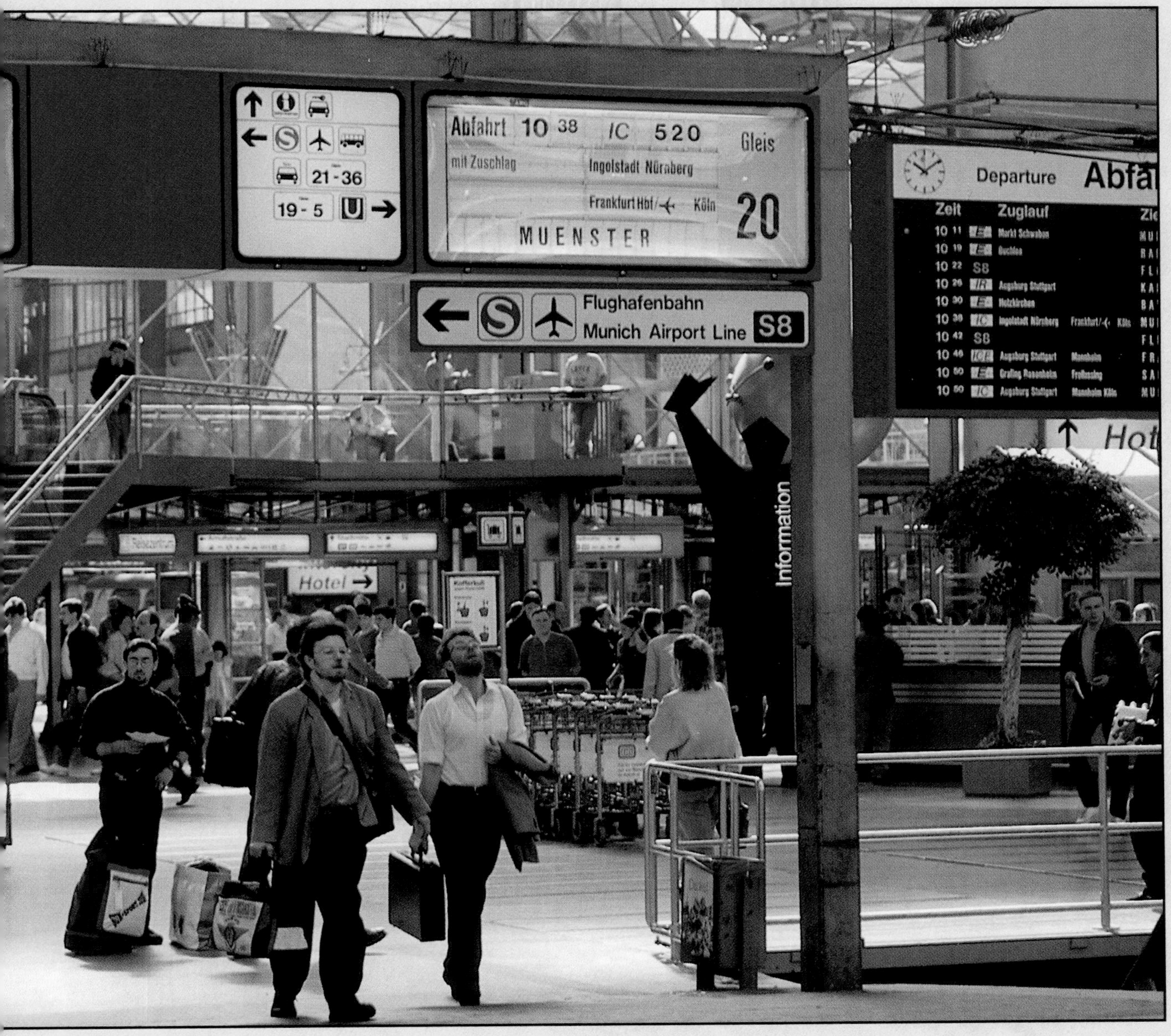

Unterwegs

ANLAUFTEXT

Mutters Ratschläge

Anna packt die Koffer für ihre Reise nach Deutschland. Sie ist gespannt auf das Jahr in Deutschland, aber ihre Mutter macht sich Sorgen wegen° Anna und der Reise. Sie gibt Anna Ratschläge°. Tante Uschi hat auch ein paar Ratschläge für Katja und Georg.

macht ... wegen: *is worried about / advice*

Vorschau

1 Thematische Fragen. Beantworten° Sie die folgenden° Fragen auf Deutsch.

answer / following

A. Anna ist noch° zu Hause in Indiana. Sie packt für zwei Semester in Tübingen. Was kommt mit nach Deutschland? Was bleibt zu Hause? Kreuzen Sie eine passende° Kategorie an° und bilden Sie dann Sätze.

still

appropriate / ***kreuzen Sie an:*** *check*

▣ Der warme Pullover kommt mit nach Deutschland.
Der Familienhund bleibt zu Hause.

	Nach Deutschland	*Bleibt zu Hause*
1. der warme Pullover	___	___
2. die Kamera	___	___
3. die Kreditkarte	___	___
4. der Reisepass°	___	___
5. das Auto	___	___
6. der Fernseher	___	___
7. der Familienhund°	___	___
8. die Reiseschecks	___	___
9. die Familienfotos	___	___
10. das Adressbuch	___	___

passport

family dog

B. Eine Mutter wie Hannelore Adler macht sich oft Sorgen, wenn die Kinder verreisen° – besonders° für ein Jahr. Sind die Sorgen realistisch oder unrealistisch? Kreuzen Sie an, was stimmt.

take a trip / especially

	Realistisch	*Unrealistisch*
1. Probleme mit der Sprache	___	___
2. Probleme mit Alkohol oder Drogen	___	___
3. Kriminalität	___	___
4. Fremdenhass°	___	___
5. Freunde im Ausland°	___	___
6. Liebe° im Ausland	___	___
7. nicht genug Geld haben	___	___
8. politische Revolutionen	___	___
9. Terrorismus	___	___

xenophobia
abroad
love

2 Für die Reise. Was ist wichtig für Sie, wenn Sie eine Reise machen? Kreuzen Sie an, was für Sie stimmt.

	Wichtig	*Nicht wichtig*
1. Verwandte besuchen	___	___
2. Geld ausgeben	___	___
3. Andenken° kaufen	___	___
4. Sehenswürdigkeiten (z.B.° Schlösser) sehen	___	___
5. Ansichtskarten° schreiben	___	___
6. Alkohol trinken	___	___
7. zu Hause anrufen	___	___
8. Fotos machen	___	___
9. schönes Wetter° haben	___	___
10. Freunde besuchen	___	___
11. neue Leute kennen lernen	___	___
12. tanzen gehen	___	___

souvenirs
z. B. (zum Beispiel): *for example / post cards*
good weather

3 Wortdetektiv. Welche Wörter und Ausdrücke° bedeuten° ungefähr° das Gleiche?

expressions / mean
approximately

Deutsch	*Englisch*
1. mit·nehmen	a. carefully
2. die Kleidung	b. clothing
3. vergessen	c. to take along
4. vorsichtig	d. to forget
5. sich Sorgen machen	e. to hitchhike
6. per Anhalter fahren	f. to worry
7. Andenken kaufen	g. glove
8. der Handschuh	h. to buy souvenirs
9. Geld ausgeben	i. to help
10. anrufen	j. surrounding area
11. helfen	k. to call up (on the phone)
12. die Umgebung	l. to spend money

ANLAUFTEXT

Hören Sie gut zu.° *Listen carefully.*

Mutters Ratschläge

Hannelore Adler hat viele Ratschläge für Anna, aber Anna interpretiert sie anders.

Frau Adler sagt:

Trink nicht so viel Cola!

Anna denkt:

Dann muss ich wohl Bier trinken, aber ich mag das nicht.

Nimm genug warme Kleidung mit!

Ich darf meine Handschuhe nicht vergessen.

Gib nicht zu viel Geld für Andenken aus!

Ich will aber Andenken kaufen.

Fahr nie per Anhalter!

Dann muss ich wohl ein Fahrrad haben.

Vergiss deine Eltern nicht!
Ich soll sie hin und wieder mal anrufen.

Sei immer vorsichtig!
Mutti, mach dir keine Sorgen!

Tante Uschi hat auch viele Ratschläge für ihre Familie. Die Günthers haben auch Missverständnisse

Helft Anna mit der Sprache.
Katja, bitte!
Anna kann ja ein bisschen Deutsch.

Zeigen wir Anna doch die Umgebung.
Dann müssen wir wohl mindestens 100 Schlösser besuchen.

Georg, sei nett zu Anna.
Anna will wohl mein Zimmer haben!

Rückblick

4 **Stimmt das?** Stimmen diese Aussagen° zum Text oder nicht? Wenn nicht, was stimmt?

°*statements*

Stimmt das? You may want to look at the explanation of the modal verbs later in the chapter before completing this activity.

	Ja, das stimmt.	*Nein, das stimmt nicht.*
1. Annas Mutter sagt, Anna soll Bier trinken.	___	___
2. Anna denkt, sie darf ihre Schuhe nicht vergessen.	___	___
3. Anna denkt, sie will Andenken kaufen.	___	___
4. Anna denkt, sie muss ein Auto kaufen.	___	___
5. Anna denkt, sie soll hin und wieder eine Postkarte schreiben.	___	___
6. Annas Mutter sagt, Anna soll in Deutschland vorsichtig sein.	___	___
7. Katja denkt, Anna kann kein Deutsch.	___	___
8. Onkel Hannes möchte gern viele Schlösser besuchen.	___	___
9. Georg möchte Anna sein Zimmer geben.	___	___

5 **Ergänzen Sie.** Ergänzen Sie diese Sätze mit Wörtern aus dem **Anlauftext.**

1. Frau Adler hat viele _____ für Anna.
2. Anna soll genug warme _____ mitnehmen.
3. Aber Anna meint, sie darf ihre _____ nicht vergessen.
4. Annas Mutter sagt, sie soll nicht zu viel _____ für Andenken ausgeben.
5. Anna will viele Andenken _____.
6. Annas Mutter sagt, sie soll nie per Anhalter _____.
7. Annas Mutter sagt: „_____ deine Eltern nicht!"
8. Anna meint, sie soll hin und wieder mal _____.
9. Onkel Hannes meint, sie müssen wohl 100 _____ besuchen.

6 **Kurz gefragt.** Beantworten Sie diese Fragen auf Deutsch.

Kurz gefragt. Try to answer these questions in complete sentences.

1. Was soll Anna mitnehmen?
2. Warum soll Anna nicht so viele Andenken kaufen?
3. Muss Anna ein Fahrrad haben? Warum? Warum nicht?
4. Wen soll Anna nicht vergessen?
5. Wie soll Anna mit den Eltern in Kontakt bleiben?
6. Was sollen die Günthers mit Anna besuchen?

7 **Interview.** Stellen Sie einem Partner/einer Partnerin die folgenden Fragen.

1. Du machst eine Reise. Welches Transportmittel benutzt° du?
   - a. ein Auto
   - b. einen Autobus
   - c. ein Flugzeug°
   - d. einen Zug°

°*use* °*airplane* °*train*

2. Wie bleibst du mit deinen Eltern in Kontakt?
   - a. Ich wohne zu Hause.
   - b. Ich rufe sie oft an.
   - c. Ich besuche sie oft.
   - d. Ich schreibe viele Briefe° und E-Mails.

°*letters*

3. Was möchtest du in Deutschland sehen?
   a. eine Stadt
   b. ein Schloss
   c. die Natur
   d. typische Deutsche

4. Was machst du, wenn Besucher° kommen? *visitors*
   a. Wir gehen ins Kino.
   b. Wir besuchen die Stadt.
   c. Wir besuchen Freunde oder Familie.
   d. Wir treiben Sport.

5. Du fährst nächste Woche nach Europa: Was vergisst du sicher nicht?
   a. mein Wörterbuch° *dictionary*
   b. mein Adressbuch
   c. warme Kleidung
   d. ein Familienfoto

BRENNPUNKT KULTUR

Studienmöglichkeiten in Deutschland

Germans, along with Austrian and Swiss people, place great importance on the study of the German language and culture. The German government supports numerous offices of the **Goethe-Institut** as part of its permanent foreign policy. Named for Germany's most famous poet, novelist, and dramatist—Johann Wolfgang von Goethe (1749–1832)—the **Goethe-Institut** promotes the study of the German language and culture in Germany and abroad and encourages international cultural cooperation. Its 143 offices in Germany and worldwide offer language courses, libraries of German literature and periodicals, film series, concerts and other cultural events, and support services for students and teachers of German. At its 15 sites within Germany, the **Goethe-Institut** offers intensive language training on all levels from beginning to advanced. There are three **Goethe-Institute** in Canada and 7 in the U.S. The Austrian Cultural Institute in New York City organizes cultural exhibitions, film festivals, lectures and panels; facilitates study exchanges to Austria; and maintains a lending library of educational materials on Austria.

Many institutions of higher learning in Germany, Austria, and Switzerland maintain cooperative relationships with colleges and universities in North America to facilitate the exchange of students and faculty. Many American and Canadian universities offer undergraduates a "year abroad" experience at a German-speaking university, while graduate students may receive research or teaching fellowships. The **Deutscher Akademischer Austauschdienst (DAAD),** with offices in Bonn and New York, provides study and research grants for students and scholars wishing to go to Germany. The **Congress-Bundestag** program provides year-long homestays to American high school students. College-aged students on the program work as interns in the German parliament **(Bundestag).** Many engineering and business programs facilitate internships with German firms for American students of German.

Strukturen und Vokabeln

Wissenswerte Vokabeln: das Gepäck

Identifying personal items

Im is a contraction of **in** *(in)* + **dem** *(the)*. The definite article **dem** appears in the dative case (see Chapter 6).

Im Kulturbeutel hat Anna:

Im Rucksack hat Anna:

Im Koffer hat Anna:

Some additional articles of clothing are: **die Jacke, -n:** *jacket,* **die Krawatte -n:** *necktie,* **der/das Sakko, -s:** *sportcoat,* **die Socken:** *socks.* You previously learned: **Shorts, Tennisschuhe.**

In der Handtasche hat Anna:

Die Geldbörse is also used for **das Portmonee.**

Was hat Anna im Rucksack?

8 **Was trägt man wahrscheinlich?** Wählen° Sie das beste Wort.

° *choose*

1. Karl geht ins Theater. Er trägt:
   a. ein Kleid b. einen Sakko c. einen Rock
2. Barbara geht Ski laufen. Sie trägt:
   a. Sandalen b. Tennisschuhe c. Skistiefel
3. Anna geht zur Universität. Sie trägt:
   a. Jeans b. ein Kleid c. einen Rock
4. Das ist mein Freund Stefan. Er trägt:
   a. ein Hemd b. eine Bluse c. eine Strumpfhose
5. Herr Professor Schmidt ist konservativ. Er trägt:
   a. ein T-Shirt und Shorts b. einen Pullover und Jeans c. ein Hemd, eine Krawatte und eine Hose

9 **Wer trägt das heute?** Wer in der Klasse trägt heute die folgenden Kleidungsstücke°?

° *clothes*

Wer trägt das heute? niemand: *nobody*

Wer trägt heute:

1. einen blauen Pullover
2. eine Krawatte
3. Jeans
4. Sandalen
5. eine weiße Bluse
6. einen Rock
7. ein gelbes Hemd
8. braune Schuhe
9. schwarze Stiefel
10. ein Kleid

10 **Interview: Was trägst du gern?** Stellen Sie einem Partner/einer Partnerin die folgenden Fragen.

S1: Was trägst du, wenn es kalt ist?
S2: Ich trage einen Mantel.

1. Was trägst du, wenn es kalt ist?
2. Was trägst du gern?
3. Was trägst du nicht so gern?
4. Was trägst du heute?
5. Was trägst du sehr oft?
6. Was trägst du nie?

Aber Mama! The verbs **brauchen** *(to need)* and **mitnehmen** *(to take along)* are followed by the accusative case.

11 **Aber Mama!** Frau Adler denkt, dass Anna bestimmte Gegenstände° in Deutschland unbedingt braucht. Wie so oft, denkt Anna anders. Spielen Sie mit einer Partnerin/mit einem Partner Mutter und Tochter.

° *objects*

- das Telefonbuch + das Wörterbuch

S1 (FRAU ADLER): Anna, nimm doch das Telefonbuch mit!
S2 (ANNA): Aber Mama. Ich brauche doch kein Telefonbuch. Ich brauche ein Wörterbuch.

Use the indefinite article to refer to an indefinite item and the definite article to refer to a specific item: **Nimm doch das Telefonbuch.**

	- Frau Adler:	*+ Anna:*
1.	das Telefonbuch	das Wörterbuch
2.	das Familienfoto	der Fotoapparat
3.	das Parfüm	das Deospray
4.	das Kleid	die Jeanshose
5.	das Scheckbuch	die Kreditkarte
6.	die Haarbürste	die Zahnbürste
7.	der Kassettenrecorder	der CD-Spieler
8.	der Führerschein°	der Pass
9.	die Handschuhe	der Lippenstift
10.	der Rock	das T-Shirt

7. Europe has 220 volt circuits instead of 120 volts as in the U.S. The plugs are also shaped differently. American appliances require a voltage converter and a plug adaptor.

driver's license

CD-Player is rapidly replacing **CD-Spieler** in Germany.

I ▣ Telling friends or relatives to do something

The informal imperative

A. The du*-imperative*

In Chapter 1, you learned how the formal imperative is formed for commands **(Befehlsformen)** and polite requests by placing the verb first and using the pronoun **Sie.**

Stehen Sie auf.
Setzen Sie sich bitte.

In this chapter you find that the characters use the informal **du**-imperative **(der informelle Imperativ).**

Mrs. Adler gives advice to Anna:
Trink nicht so viel Cola. — *Don't drink so much cola.*
Anna tells her mother:
Mach dir keine Sorgen. — *Don't worry.*

German speakers use the **du**-imperative whenever the situation requires the use of **du.**

1. when speaking to a family member, a friend, any child up to adolescence or when talking to their peers (e.g., students, athletes, workers, soldiers):

   Vergiss deine Eltern nicht. — *Don't forget your parents.*
   Gib mir den Ball. — *Give me the ball.*

2. when praying to God:

   Komm, Herr Jesu! — *Come, Lord Jesus!*

3. when intentionally showing disrespect or insulting someone:

   Geh weg! — *Scram!*

4. when speaking to animals, e.g., to a dog:

   Rollo, komm' her! — *Rollo, come here!*

For most verbs (all but the stem-changing verbs with an **a** or **au** in the infinitive), the **du**-imperative is formed by dropping the **st**-ending and the personal pronoun **du** from the **du**-form of the present tense of the verb.

Infinitive	Present tense	du-imperative
machen	du machst	**Mach** dir keine Sorgen.
trinken	du trinkst	**Trink** nicht so viel Cola.

In the present tense of many verbs, the stem vowel changes in the **du**-form. Note how the **du**-imperatives are formed for the following stem-vowel changing verbs.

Verbs whose stem vowel changes from **a** to **ä** in the present tense **du**-form retain the **a** from the infinitive in the **du**-imperative.

Infinitive	Present tense	du-imperative	
fahren	du fährst	**Fahr** nie per Anhalter.	*Don't ever hitchhike.*
tragen	du trägst	**Trag** warme Kleidung.	*Wear warm clothes.*

Also: **halten: du hältst, halt!, schlafen: du schläfst, schlaf!, waschen: du wäschst, wasch!**

Verbs whose stem vowel changes from **au** to **äu** retain the **au** from the infinitive.

laufen	du läufst	**Lauf** schnell.	*Run fast.*

Verbs whose stem vowel changes from **e** to **ie** form the **du**-imperative from the present tense **du**-form.

lesen	du liest	**Lies** das Deutschbuch.	*Read the German book.*
sehen	du siehst	**Sieh** Mannheim.	*Check out Mannheim.*

Also: **fernsehen: du siehst fern, sieh fern!**

Verbs whose stem vowel changes from **e** to **i** form the **du**-imperative from the present tense **du**-form.

essen	du isst	**Iss** keinen Hamburger.	*Don't eat a hamburger.*
geben	du gibst	**Gib** mir ein paar Ratschläge.	*Give me some tips.*
helfen	du hilfst	**Hilf** Anna mit der Sprache!	*Help Anna with the language!*
nehmen	du nimmst	**Nimm** das Auto.	*Take the car.*
vergessen	du vergisst	**Vergiss** deine Eltern nicht.	*Don't forget your parents.*

Also: **sprechen: du sprichst, sprich!**

Verbs whose stems end in **t-, d-,** or **-fn** have the ending **-e** in the **du**-imperative forms. The **e** is added to these verbs in their **du**-forms **(du antwortest)** and is retained when the **st** is dropped to form the **du**-imperatives.

Infinitive	Present tense	du-imperative	
antworten	du antwort**e**st	**Antworte** auf Deutsch.	*Answer in German.*
finden	du find**e**st	**Finde** meine Kreditkarte.	*Find my credit card.*
öffnen	du öffn**e**st	**Öffne** die Tür.	*Open the door.*

Verbs like **ändern** *(to change)* and **lächeln** *(to smile)* whose stems end in **-el** or **-er** also have an **e**-ending in the imperative, but drop the internal **e** in the **ich**-forms and in the **du**-imperative: **ich änd(e)re, änd(e)re!, ich läch(e)le, läch(e)le!**

These are the **du**-imperative forms of the verbs **sein** *(to be)* and **haben** *(to have)*.

Infinitive	du-imperative	
sein	**Sei** immer vorsichtig!	*Always be careful!*
haben	**Hab** keine Angst!	*Don't be afraid!*

Remember the **Sie**-imperative forms of **sein** and **haben: Seien Sie pünktlich!** *(Please be punctual!)* or **Haben Sie keine Angst!** *(Don't be afraid!)*

Verbs with separable prefixes (e.g., **an·rufen, auf·stehen, auf·wachen, mit·nehmen**) have the prefix at the end of the **du**-imperative phrase.

Ruf doch mal **an!**	*Give a call!*
Anna, **wach auf!**	*Anna, wake up!*
Gib nicht zuviel Geld **aus!**	*Don't spend too much money!*
Nimm genug warme Kleidung **mit!**	*Take enough warm clothes along!*

German speakers use **nicht** or **kein,** when telling somebody what not to do.

Vergiss bitte deine Eltern **nicht!**	*Please don't forget your parents!*
Mach dir **keine** Sorgen!	*Don't worry!*

12 Was sagt man zu Karl? Ein Student/eine Studentin spielt die Rolle von Karl. Karl hat Probleme im Deutschkurs. Ein anderer Student/eine andere Studentin gibt Rat. Wählen Sie die passende Antwort.

S1 (KARL): Ich komme immer zu spät.
S2 (SIE): Steh früh auf!

Karl	*Sie*
1. Ich komme immer zu spät.	a. Steh früh auf. b. Bleib bis mittags im Bett.
2. Ich bin so nervös.	a. Trink drei Glas Bier. b. Mach dir keine Sorgen.
3. Ich habe morgen um acht Uhr Deutsch.	a. Bring dein Buch nicht mit. b. Vergiss dein Buch nicht.
4. Ich schreibe morgen einen Test.	a. Lies heute Abend dein Buch. b. Fahr heute Abend nach Deutschland.
5. Ich bin heute krank°.	a. Geh in eine Bar. b. Ruf den Professor an.

° *sick*

13 Hast du einen Ratschlag für mich? Was sagen Sie in diesen Situationen? Formen Sie passende **du**-Imperative.

Hast du einen Ratschlag für mich? Note that some of these verbs contain separable prefixes.

S1: Es ist kalt heute.
S2: Trag warme Kleidung.

1. Es ist kalt heute.
2. Ich fahre dein Auto.
3. Es ist spät. Der Deutschkurs beginnt bald.
4. Meine Eltern sind traurig.
5. Ich gehe heute Abend auf eine elegante Party.
6. Morgen habe ich eine Deutschprüfung.
7. Ich habe Hunger.
8. Ich kaufe ein schönes Geschenk.

a. schnell zur Uni fahren
b. eine Pizza essen
c. heute Abend dein Deutschbuch lesen
d. deine Eltern (sie) doch mal anrufen
e. ein Kleid/ein Sakko und eine Krawatte tragen
f. warme Kleidung tragen
g. vorsichtig fahren
h. nicht zu viel Geld ausgeben

B. The ihr-imperative

When speaking informally with more than one person, German speakers use the **ihr**-imperative. The **ihr**-imperative forms are identical to the present tense **ihr**-forms of all verbs. As in the **du**-imperative, the personal pronoun **(ihr)** is dropped.

Infinitive	Present tense	ihr-imperative	
machen	ihr macht	**Macht** euch keine Sorgen.	*Don't (you, pl. inf.) worry.*
fahren	ihr fahrt	**Fahrt** nie per Anhalter!	*Don't ever hitchhike!*
essen	ihr esst	**Esst** kein Fleisch.	*Don't eat any meat.*

Verbs with stems ending in **-t, -d,** or **-fn** add the ending **-et** in the **ihr**-imperative forms.

Infinitive	Present tense	ihr-imperative	
antworten	ihr antwortet	**Antwortet** auf Deutsch.	*Answer in German.*
finden	ihr findet	**Findet** meine Kreditkarte.	*Find my credit card.*
öffnen	ihr öffnet	**Öffnet** die Tür!	*Open the door!*

These are the **ihr**-imperative forms of the verbs **sein** and **haben**.

Infinitive	Present tense	ihr-imperative	
sein	ihr seid	**Seid** immer vorsichtig!	*Always be careful!*
haben	ihr habt	**Habt** keine Angst.	*Don't (you all) be afraid.*

Verbs with a separable prefix place the prefix at the end of the **ihr**-imperative phrase.

Ruft doch mal **an.** — *Give a call.*
Anna und Katja, **wacht auf.** — *Anna and Katja, wake up.*
Gebt nicht zu viel Geld **aus.** — *Don't spend too much money.*
Nehmt genug warme Kleidung **mit.** — *Take enough warm clothes along.*

German speakers use **nicht** or **kein** when telling somebody what not to do.

Vergesst eure Eltern **nicht.** — *Don't forget your parents.*
Macht euch **keine** Sorgen. — *Don't (you all) worry.*

14 Was sagt Herr Günther zu Katja und Georg? Die Günthers holen Anna heute vom Flughafen ab°. Es ist früh morgens. Was sagt Herr Günther in diesen Situationen zu Katja und Georg?

holen ab: *pick up*

1. Wir holen Anna in einer Stunde ab.
   a. Wacht auf.
   b. Schlaft gut.
2. Ich räume auf°.
   a. Nehmt die Brötchen bitte.
   b. Esst das Schnitzel.

räume auf: *am cleaning up*

3. Kommt, wir müssen los°!
   a. Seid bitte langsam.
   b. Trinkt euren Tee aus.

***müssen los:** have to leave*

4. Es regnet heute.
   a. Vergesst den Regenmantel°.
   b. Nehmt einen Schirm° mit.

rain coat
umbrella

5. Wann kommt Anna an?
   a. Gebt mir bitte ihren Brief.
   b. Schreibt mir einen Brief.

15 **Reisetipps.** Diese Personen machen eine Reise. Was sollen° sie machen/nicht machen? Geben Sie diesen Personen Ratschläge und verwenden Sie **du-, ihr-** oder **Sie**-imperative**.**

should

- das Wasser nicht trinken (Dieter und Ingrid)
  Trinkt das Wasser nicht.
- dort keine Andenken kaufen (Herr und Frau Mertens)
  Kaufen Sie dort keine Andenken.

Reisetipps. Remember to use the **du-** or **ihr**-imperative forms when first names are provided and the **Sie**-imperative forms when last names are provided.

1. das Wasser nicht trinken (Dieter und Ingrid)
2. den Fisch nicht essen (Heiner und Beate)
3. die Andenken nicht vergessen (Claus)
4. kein Deutsch sprechen (Sigrid und Mario)
5. den Pass nicht vergessen (Professor Steinhuber)
6. nicht im billigen Hotel schlafen (Herr und Frau Günther)
7. den Kölner Dom° besuchen (Monika und Gabriel)
8. die Kreditkarte nicht mitnehmen (Martina)
9. Helga und Wilhelm in Bonn anrufen (Greta und Thomas)
10. nicht so viel Geld für Hummel-Figuren ausgeben (Tante Frieda)
11. nicht so viel Gepäck mitnehmen (Katja und Georg)
12. Dieter eine Postkarte schreiben (Onkel Fritz)

***Kölner Dom:** cathedral in Cologne*

C. Particles with the imperative

German speakers frequently use the words **bitte, doch,** or **mal** to modify a request. Only **bitte** has a direct English translation: *please.* It ensures that a request is expressed in a polite manner.

Mach dir **bitte** keine Sorgen. *Please don't worry.*

The word **doch** makes a request more persuasive. It indicates that the speaker may be anticipating opposition from the listener.

Zeigen wir Anna **doch** die Umgebung. *Let's show Anna the area.*

The word **mal** makes a request more emphatic. **Mal** is related to **ein mal** *(one time)* and leaves the time of when to carry out the request vague.

Schau **mal!** *Look!*

In combination with **doch, mal** adds great urgency to a request.

Ruf **doch mal** an! *Call sometime!*

16 **Lest bitte das Buch.** Kennen Sie das Spiel „Simon sagt ...“? Nun spielen wir eine deutsche Version. Ein Student/ Eine Studentin gibt die Befehle. Die anderen machen mit, solange er/sie **bitte** sagt. Wer etwas tut, ohne **bitte** zu hören, muss sich setzen. Der Gewinner/Die Gewinnerin gibt dann die Befehle in der nächsten Runde.

aufstehen S1: Steht auf! *(oder)*
Steht **bitte** auf!

1. die Tür öffnen
2. den Stift nehmen
3. zur Tür gehen
4. die Hand zeigen
5. das Buch lesen
6. die Nummer aufschreiben
7. den Lehrer/die Lehrerin anrufen
8. schnell laufen

D. *Inclusive suggestions: the wir-imperative*

German speakers form inclusive suggestions, also called **wir**-imperatives, by placing the **wir**-form of a verb followed by the pronoun **wir** at the beginning of the sentence. The word order is identical to that of a yes/no question, but the speaker's voice drops instead of rises at the end. The **wir**-imperative corresponds to the *let's* construction in English.

Zeigen wir Anna doch die Umgebung. *Let's show Anna the area.*

17 **Gute Idee! Machen wir das.** Machen Sie mit einem Partner/ einer Partnerin Pläne für heute Abend. Benutzen° Sie den **wir**-Imperativ.

use

heute Abend ins Kino/Theater gehen

S1: Gehen wir heute Abend ins Kino oder ins Theater?
S2: Gehen wir doch ins Kino.

Gute Idee! Machen wir das. Try to use the particle **doch** in your responses. Place it right after **wir.**

1. heute Abend in die Disko/Oper gehen
2. Klaus/Franz anrufen
3. Cornelia/Jürgen mitnehmen
4. mit dem Bus/Auto fahren
5. vorher° Karl/Professor Steinhuber besuchen
6. nachher° eine Pizza/einen Hamburger essen
7. nachher im Ratskeller einen Wein/eine Cola trinken
8. nachher die Hausaufgaben machen/fernsehen

beforehand
afterwards

„Trinken wir einen Kaffee zusammen."

18 **Eine Reise organisieren.** Planen Sie mit einem Partner/einer Partnerin eine Reise nach Österreich. Ihre Reise hat nur sieben Aktivitäten.

Eine Reise organisieren. Mozart was born Jan. 27, 1756, in Salzburg and died Dec. 5, 1791, in Vienna.

Sachertorte is an exquisite chocolate cake that is baked at Vienna's most famous hotel, the Hotel Sacher, and is shipped worldwide.

nach Wien fahren *Fahren wir nach Wien!*

- nach Wien fahren
- Mozarts Geburtshaus in Salzburg besuchen
- im Kaffeehaus einen Mokka trinken
- das Kunsthistorische Museum besuchen
- nach Innsbruck fahren
- in den Alpen wandern
- in Graz viele Andenken kaufen
- ein Drama im Wiener Burgtheater sehen
- ins Theater gehen
- Sachertorte im Hotel Sacher essen
- ein Konzert mit den Wiener Sängerknaben° hören
- die Lippizzaner in der Spanischen Reitschule° fotografieren

Vienna Boys Choir

riding school

II Expressing ability, fondness, and expected obligation

Modal verbs (I)

You already learned in Chapter 3 about the modal verbs **können** and **möchten**. Modal verbs in German, as in English, modify the meaning of the main verb by indicating ability **(können)**, fondness **(mögen)**, obligation **(sollen)**, permission **(dürfen)**, necessity **(müssen)**, or desire **(wollen)** to carry out the action. In German the main verb appears in its infinitive form at the end of the sentence.

Ich **kann** Deutsch **sprechen.** *I can (am able to) speak German.*
Ich **möchte** so viel **lernen.** *I would like to learn so much.*

Here are the modal verbs that you have encountered so far in this chapter:

Was muß ich hören?
88,8
BERLIN
Das Stadtradio
SFB

dürfen: Ich **darf** meine Handschuhe nicht vergessen.
I must not forget my gloves.
können: Anna **kann** ja ein bisschen Deutsch.
Anna can speak a little German.
mögen: Ich **mag** das nicht.
I don't like that.
müssen: Dann **müssen** wir wohl mindestens 100 Schlösser besuchen.
Then we probably have to visit at least a hundred castles.
sollen: Ich **soll** sie hin und wieder mal **anrufen.**
I should call them now and then.
wollen: Ich **will** aber Andenken **kaufen.**
But I want to buy souvenirs.

The use of **mögen** without an infinitive will be explained later in this chapter.

Modal verbs may occur without the infinitive of the main verb when the meaning of the missing infinitive is clear from the context.

Anna kann ein bisschen Deutsch (sprechen). *Anna can speak a bit of German.*

Robert kann nicht so gut Gitarre (spielen). *Robert can't play the guitar so well.*

These are three important facts about the forms of the modals:

1. Modals have no endings in the **ich-** and **er/sie/es**-forms. The **ich-** and **er/sie/es**-forms are identical: **ich (er/sie/es) darf, kann, mag, muss, soll, will.**
2. The stem vowel of the singular forms is different from the stem vowel of the infinitive for all modal verbs except for **sollen.**

   d**ü**rfen: ich d**a**rf, du d**a**rfst, er/sie/es d**a**rf
   s**o**llen: ich s**o**ll, du s**o**llst, er/sie/es s**o**ll

3. **Möchte** *(would like to)*, which you encountered in Chapter 3, is a special form of the modal **mögen. Mögen** and **möchte** are discussed in more detail below.

A. *Expressing ability:* können

In order to make the practice of modal verbs easier, we will start with the review of the modal verb **können** *(can, to be able to)* which you already encountered in Chapter 3.

		können: *can, to be able to*				
Person	**Singular**			**Plural**		
1st	ich	**kann**	*I can*	wir	**können**	*we can*
2nd, informal	du	**kannst**	*you can*	ihr	**könnt**	*you can*
2nd, formal	Sie	**können**	*you can*	Sie	**können**	*you can*
3rd	er/sie/es	**kann**	*he/she/it can*	sie	**können**	*they can*

19 **Anna kann nicht Ski laufen.** Was können diese Personen machen/nicht machen? Was können *Sie* machen/nicht machen? Diskutieren Sie die Aktivitäten mit einem Partner/einer Partnerin.

S1: Wer kann Ski laufen? Wer kann nicht Ski laufen?
S2: Katja und Georg können Ski laufen, aber Anna kann nicht Ski laufen.

				ich
	–	+	+	
	+	–	–	
	+	+	+	
	–	–	+	
 ¡Hola! ¿Qué pasa?	+	–	–	
	+	+	+	
	+	–	+	
	+	+	+	

20 Was können Sie tun? Was können Sie gut? Was können Sie nicht so gut? Schreiben Sie zehn Sätze.

+	+/–	–
sehr gut	ziemlich gut	nicht (so) gut
ausgezeichnet°	relativ gut	gar nicht
fantastisch	ein bisschen	überhaupt nicht

excellent(ly)

▣ Ich kann sehr gut Englisch sprechen.

Englisch (Deutsch, Japanisch) sprechen
Deutsch schreiben
Gitarre (Fußball, Golf, Karten, Klavier) spielen
Spanisch (Jiddisch, Chinesisch) verstehen
Auto fahren
kochen
tanzen
reiten
schwimmen
Ski laufen
fotografieren
?

21 Was kann man nicht machen? Welche Aktivitäten können diese Personen nicht machen?

▣ Ingrid hat ihre Kontaktlinsen nicht. *Ingrid kann nicht sehen.*

1. Ingrid hat ihre Kontaktlinsen nicht. — anrufen
2. Dieter hat keine Gitarre. — einkaufen° (*to shop*)
3. Roland hat die Telefonnummer nicht. — fahren
4. Jörg und Thomas haben kein Auto. — zur Party kommen
5. Oskar hat kein Geld. — schwimmen
6. Marion und Angelika haben keine Zeit. — Musik machen
7. Die Studentin ist heute krank°. — in den Deutschkurs kommen (*sick*)
8. Sophie hat Angst vor dem Wasser. — sehen

B. *Expressing fondness and desire:* mögen *and* möchte

The modal verb **mögen** expresses general liking, **möchte** expresses an immediate desire and specific preference.

In standard German, **mögen** generally occurs with a noun and **möchte** can be used with or without an infinitive (see Chapter 3).

Ich **mag** Bier.	*I (generally) like beer.*
Ich **möchte** ein Bier (haben).	*I would like to have a beer (right now).*
Ich **möchte** Deutsch sprechen.	*I would like to speak German.*

Möchten is used to express politeness when offering something to someone: **Möchten Sie ein Stück Kuchen?**

Remember to use the particle **gern** when talking about an activity you like in general (for which you would use a verb). When talking about an object you like (for which you would use a noun), use a form of **mögen.**

Ich **spreche gern** Deutsch.	*I (generally) enjoy speaking German.*
Sie **mag** klassische Musik.	*She likes classical music.*

		mögen: *to like*		
Person	**Singular**		**Plural**	
1st	ich **mag**	*I like*	wir **mögen**	*we like*
2nd, informal	du **magst**	*you like*	ihr **mögt**	*you like*
2nd, formal	Sie **mögen**	*you like*	Sie **mögen**	*you like*
3rd	er/sie/es **mag**	*he/she/it likes*	sie **mögen**	*they like*

22 **Was mögen Sie?** Kreuzen Sie Ihre Interessen mit +, +/– oder – an. Finden Sie dann einen Studenten/eine Studentin mit mindestens drei gleichen Interessen.

S1: Ich mag Deutsch, und du?
S2: Ich mag Deutsch ziemlich gut.

+	+/–	–
sehr	ziemlich nur ein bisschen	nicht (so) sehr überhaupt nicht

	Ich	*Mein(e) Partner(in)*
Deutsch	___	___
Tennis	___	___
Fußball	___	___
Golf	___	___
Shakespeare	___	___
Stephen King	___	___
Hermann Hesse	___	___
Spielberg-Filme	___	___
Theater	___	___
Jazzmusik	___	___
Brokkoli	___	___
Pizza	___	___
Bier	___	___
Wein	___	___

You already encountered **möchte** in Chapter 3. Here the present tense forms are presented again for review.

		möchte: *would like (to)*		
Person	**Singular**		**Plural**	
1st	ich **möchte**	*I would like (to)*	wir **möchten**	*we would like (to)*
2nd, informal	du **möchtest**	*you would like (to)*	ihr **möchtet**	*you would like (to)*
2nd, formal	Sie **möchten**	*you would like (to)*	Sie **möchten**	*you would like (to)*
3rd	er/sie/es **möchte**	*he/she/it would like (to)*	sie **möchten**	*they would like (to)*

German speakers use **möchte** to extend invitations and, often together with **lieber,** to inquire about or to express preferences.

Möchtest du nach Paris fahren? — *Would you like to go to Paris?*
Nein, ich **möchte** lieber nach Wien fahren. — *No, I would rather go to Vienna.*

23 Was möchten Sie tun? Sie reisen nach Deutschland. Geld ist kein Problem für Sie. Kreuzen Sie Ihre Wünsche° an. Planen Sie dann eine Reise zusammen mit einem Partner/einer Partnerin. *°wishes*

S1: Möchtest du nach Tübingen oder Berlin fahren?
S2: Ich möchte nach Tübingen fahren.
S1: Ich möchte auch nach Tübingen fahren. *(oder)*
Ich möchte lieber nach Berlin fahren.

	Ich	*Mein(e) Partner(in)*
1. nach Tübingen/Berlin fahren	___	___
2. Verwandte/Freunde besuchen	___	___
3. nicht viel Geld ausgeben/viele Andenken kaufen	___	___
4. viel essen/viel trinken	___	___
5. einen Mercedes/einen VW kaufen	___	___
6. viele Schlösser sehen/viele Menschen kennen lernen	___	___
7. in den Alpen wandern/in Mannheim einkaufen	___	___
8. München ansehen/in München wohnen	___	___

C. *Expressing expected obligation: sollen*

The modal verb **sollen** expresses an obligation that one has. Here are the present tense forms of the modal verb **sollen.**

sollen: *should; to be supposed to*				
Person	**Singular**		**Plural**	
1st	ich **soll**	*I should/am supposed to*	wir **sollen**	*we should/are supposed to*
2nd, informal	du **sollst**	*you should/are supposed to*	ihr **sollt**	*you should/are supposed to*
2nd, formal	Sie **sollen**	*you should/are supposed to*	Sie **sollen**	*you should/are supposed to*
3rd	er/sie/es **soll**	*he/she/it should/ is supposed to*	sie **sollen**	*they should/are supposed to*

24 Hausarbeit. Frau Günther hat eine Liste für Georg und Katja. Was sollen sie machen? Und was sollen *Sie* machen? Kreuzen Sie Ihre Aufgaben an. Fragen Sie dann einen Partner/eine Partnerin.

S1: Was soll Georg zu Hause machen?
S2: Georg soll das Zimmer aufräumen.
S1: Was sollst du zu Hause machen?
S2: Ich soll auch das Zimmer aufräumen.

	Georg	Katja	Ich
das Zimmer aufräumen	√		—
das Bett machen	√	√	—
das Essen kochen		√	—
Hausaufgaben machen	√	√	—
die Katze füttern°	√		—
die Wäsche° waschen		√	—
staubsaugen°	√		—

feed
laundry
vacuum

25 **Warum machst du das?** Fragen Sie einen Partner/eine Partnerin, warum er/sie das macht. Kann, soll, oder möchte er/sie das machen?

Warum machst du das? Remember to use **denn** *(for, because)* in your answers.

S1: Warum sprichst du Deutsch?
S2: Ich kann Deutsch sprechen. *(oder)*
Ich möchte Deutsch sprechen.

Deutsch sprechen • auf die Uni gehen • einen Film sehen • das Zimmer aufräumen • viel Geld ausgeben • Freunde besuchen • Stephen King lesen • Musik hören • laufen • Hausaufgaben machen • Brokkoli essen

■ FREIE ■ KOMMUNIKATION ■ **Rollenspiel: Die Einladung°.** Sie sind neu in Hannover. Frau Meyer ruft Sie an und lädt Sie zu Kaffee und Kuchen ein. Sie möchten kommen, aber Sie haben viel zu tun – die Kinder abholen, Essen kaufen und zur Bank gehen. Fragen Sie Frau Meyer, wann Sie kommen sollen und was Sie bringen können. Sagen Sie Frau Meyer, was Sie machen sollen und wann Sie kommen können.

invitation

Schreibecke Was können Sie in diesem Alter° machen? Was sollen Sie machen? Was möchten Sie machen?

in diesem Alter: at this age

1. Sie sind fünf Jahre alt.
2. Sie sind zehn Jahre alt.
3. Sie sind fünfzehn Jahre alt.

Absprungtext. Nr. is an abbreviation for **Nummer.**

ABSPRUNGTEXT

Sicherheitsinfo Nr. 8: Fahrrad fahren

In den USA fährt Anna sehr gern Rad. Sie möchte auch in Deutschland Fahrrad fahren. In Deutschland ist Radfahren auch sehr populär. Junge und alte Leute fahren oft Rad. Tante Uschi schickt Anna diese Broschüre über Radfahren in Deutschland.

Vorschau

26 **Thematische Fragen.** Beantworten Sie die folgenden Fragen auf Deutsch.

1. Haben Sie ein Fahrrad? Ist es ein Mountain Bike?
2. Wie oft fahren Sie Rad? Fahren Sie mit dem Fahrrad zur Uni?
3. Fahren viele Leute an Ihrer Uni Rad? Warum? Warum nicht?
4. Fahren Sie auch Auto? Welche Probleme gibt es für Radfahrer auf der Straße°?
5. Fahren viele junge und alte Menschen in Nordamerika Rad? Warum? Warum nicht?

street

27 **Satzdetektiv.** Welche Sätze bedeuten ungefähr das Gleiche? Wählen Sie für jeden Satz **a** oder **b.**

1. Radfahren ist gesund.
   a. Radfahren ist gut für den Körper°.
   b. Radfahren ist nicht gut für den Körper.

body

2. Die Kosten [für das Radfahren] sind vergleichsweise gering.
   a. Radfahren ist relativ teuer.
   b. Radfahren ist relativ billig.

3. Vieles spricht also für das Radfahren, das immer beliebter wird.
   a. Radfahren ist nicht populär.
   b. Radfahren ist populär.

4. Inzwischen dürfte es in Deutschland rund 50 Millionen Fahrräder geben.
   a. In Deutschland haben ungefähr° 50 Millionen Leute ein Auto.
   b. In Deutschland haben ungefähr 50 Millionen Leute ein Rad.

approximately

StadtAuto Bremen Car Sharing GmbH
Feldstraße 13 B • 28203 Bremen
Telefon 0421-77010 • Fax 0421-74465

ABSPRUNGTEXT

Sicherheitsinfo Nr. 8: Fahrrad fahren

Lesen Sie jetzt den Text.

Absprungtext. Many of the texts in ***Vorsprung*** were written for native speakers of German. This reading activity requires you to skim the text to locate enough information to answer the questions.

Radfahren ist gesund, es macht Spaß° und ist umweltfreundlich°. Wer mit dem Fahrrad fährt, verbraucht kein Öl und Benzin, die Kosten sind vergleichsweise° gering. Das Fahrrad kann man selbst warten und pflegen°. Ein Fahrrad braucht wenig Platz: Ein einziges Auto benötigt° mehr Fläche° als acht Fahrräder. Vieles spricht also für das Radfahren, das immer beliebter° wird. Inzwischen° dürfte es in Deutschland rund 50 Millionen Fahrräder geben.

es macht Spaß: *it's fun*
environmentally friendly
comparatively
warten und pflegen: *service*
requires
space
immer beliebter: *more and more popular / In the meantime*

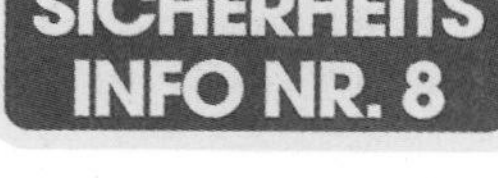

Es gibt viele Verkehrsregeln, die Radfahrer beachten müssen. Einige sind besonders wichtig. **Hier dürfen Radfahrer nicht fahren:**

Autobahn

Kraftfahrstraße

Fußgängerbereich

Verbot für Radfahrer

Verbot der Einfahrt

Verbot für Fahrzeuge aller Art

In Einbahnstraßen dürfen auch Radfahrer nur in vorgeschriebener° Richtung fahren.

prescribed

Einbahnstraße

Es gibt Ausnahmen. Dann steht folgendes Zeichen neben einem dieser Verkehrsschilder. In diesem Falle dürfen Radfahrer hier ausnahmsweise° doch fahren.

as an exception

Radfahrer frei

Es gibt aber auch Schilder, die dem Radfahrer anzeigen°, **wo er fahren muß:**

show, indicate

Getrennter Rad- und Fußweg

Gemeinsamer Fuß- und Radweg

Sonderweg Radfahrer

Rückblick

28 **Stimmt das?** Stimmen diese Aussagen zum Text oder nicht? Wenn nicht, was stimmt?

	Ja, das stimmt.	*Nein, das stimmt nicht.*
1. Radfahren macht Spaß.	___	___
2. Ein Fahrrad ist nicht leicht zu reparieren°.	___	___
3. Der Artikel hat gute Argumente für das Autofahren.	___	___
4. Fahrräder sind in Deutschland beliebt.	___	___
5. Auf der Autobahn ist Radfahren verboten.	___	___
6. Ein Fahrrad braucht so viel Platz wie 18 Autos.	___	___

repair

29 **Fahrrad oder Auto?** Das Fahrrad steht im Kontrast zum Auto. Füllen Sie die Liste mit Informationen über das Fahrrad aus°.

Füllen Sie aus: *Fill in (out)*

Auto	*Fahrrad*
verbraucht viel Öl und Benzin	______________
stinkt und ist schlecht für die Umwelt	______________
ist teuer	______________
braucht viel Platz	______________

Fahrrad oder Auto? Check the **Absprungtext** for helpful information.

30 **Ergänzen Sie.** Ergänzen Sie diese Sätze mit Wörtern aus dem **Absprungtext.**

1. Radfahren ist _____.
2. Radfahren _____ Spaß.
3. Radfahren ist _____.
4. Ein Fahrrad braucht wenig _____.
5. Vieles spricht also für das _____.
6. Es gibt viele _____, die Radfahrer beachten müssen.
7. Einige [Verkehrsregeln] sind besonders _____.
8. Es gibt aber auch _____, die dem Radfahrer anzeigen, wo er fahren muss.

31 **Kurz gefragt.** Beantworten Sie diese Fragen auf Deutsch.

1. Wer im Deutschkurs hat ein Fahrrad?
2. Welche Farbe hat es? Ist es schnell?
3. Wo kann man sicher° Rad fahren: in der Stadt, auf dem Campus, nur im Garten?
4. Ist Radfahren gesund oder gefährlich und ungesund? Warum?
5. Was sollen Radfahrer(innen) tragen?
   a. einen Hut° oder einen Helm°?
   b. Shorts oder Jeans?
   c. ein Kleid/einen Anzug oder Jeans?
   d. Sportschuhe oder Sandalen?

safely

hat / helmet

Junge und alte Menschen fahren gern Rad.

Fahrschule und Fahrrad fahren

Bicycling in Germany, as mentioned in the **Absprungtext,** is an inexpensive means of transportation. Indeed, the high expenses for automobile drivers in Germany begin with driver's training. To obtain a driver's license, Germans must take an extensive driver's education course at a private driving school **(die Fahrschule),** where tuition is high. Students have to be 18 years or older to receive the required 8 hours of classroom instruction and 35 hours of practice driving with an instructor. They must also be trained in night driving and driving on the **Autobahn.** After completing classroom instruction, practical instruction, a first aid course and an eye test, students take a written exam and the actual driver's test **(die Fahrprüfung),** which taken together can be very expensive. Only one in three people pass this test on the first try. The others need to complete more training classes before taking the test again. Upon passing the test, the student driver obtains a **Klasse III** license, which permits the owner to operate a passenger vehicle **(der Personenkraftwagen, der PKW)** for life. Expenses for car owners include insurance, a tax **(die Autosteuer),** and gasoline.

Young and old people alike enjoy riding bicycles, taking public transportation, or riding mopeds, for which they can obtain a license at age 16. Bicycles and public transportation are environmentally friendly **(umweltfreundlich)** ways to get around without the expense and environmental regulations that come with owning a car or moped. Too little parking space, traffic jams, and air pollution are common problems in German cities, making bicycling more convenient and socially acceptable than driving. Many families even do their grocery shopping by bicycle.

32 **Interview.** Stellen Sie einem Partner/einer Partnerin die folgenden Fragen.

1. Hast du ein Auto?
2. Hast du ein Fahrrad?
3. Wie viel kostet ein gutes Fahrrad?
4. Fährst du lieber per Anhalter oder mit dem Bus?
5. Fährst du gern Rad?
6. Wie viele Radfahrer kennst du? Wen? (deinen Vater? deine Mutter?)

■ Strukturen und Vokabeln ■

III Expressing permission, prohibition, necessity, and strong desire

Modal verbs (II)

D. Expressing permission: dürfen

The modal verb **dürfen** expresses that an action is permitted. These are the present tense forms of **dürfen.**

	dürfen: *may; to be permitted to*			
Person	**Singular**		**Plural**	
1st	ich **darf**	*I may*	wir **dürfen**	*we may*
2nd, informal	du **darfst**	*you may*	ihr **dürft**	*you may*
2nd, formal	Sie **dürfen**	*you may*	Sie **dürfen**	*you may*
3rd	er/sie/es **darf**	*he/she/it may*	sie **dürfen**	*they may*

German speakers use **darf** with **man** and **nicht** or **kein** to indicate that an action is not permitted.

Man darf keinen Alkohol trinken. *It is not permitted to drink any alcohol.*
Hier **darf man nicht** parken. *No parking allowed here.*

33 **Was bedeutet das Verkehrsschild?** Verbinden° Sie jeden Satz (links) mit einem Schild (rechts).

° *Connect*

1. Hier darf man nicht halten. ___
2. Hier beginnt die Autobahn. Hier darf man schnell fahren. ___
3. Hier dürfen keine Radfahrer fahren. ___
4. Hier darf man nicht hineinfahren. ___
5. Hier darf man parken. ___
6. Hier dürfen nur Autos fahren. ___
7. Hier dürfen Fahrräder fahren. ___

a. Autobahn

b. Kraftfahrstraße

c. Fußgängerzone

d. Parkplatz

e. Radfahrer frei

f. Verbot der Einfahrt (Einfahrtsverbot)

g. Halteverbot

34 Ist das erlaubt°? Die Klasse hat viele Ideen, wie man Deutschlernen leichter machen kann. Aber der Lehrer/die Lehrerin findet diese Ideen nicht immer gut. Spielen Sie Student/Studentin und Lehrer/Lehrerin.

permitted

▣ ich / die Hausaufgaben hin und wieder vergessen?
S1 (STUDENT/STUDENTIN): Darf ich die Hausaufgaben hin und wieder vergessen?
S2 (LEHRER/LEHRERIN): Nein, Sie dürfen die Hausaufgaben nicht vergessen.

1. die anderen Studenten / die Hausaufgaben später machen?
2. alle Studenten / im Deutschkurs Englisch sprechen?
3. die neue Studentin / die Prüfung zu Hause machen?
4. ich / ein Wörterbuch zur Prüfung mitbringen?
5. alle Studenten / heute früher nach Hause gehen?

35 Die Regeln° im Deutschunterricht. Schreiben Sie mit einem Partner/einer Partnerin eine Liste von zehn Regeln für den Deutschunterricht.

rules

▣ Wir dürfen nicht zu spät kommen.

zu spät kommen	im Klassenzimmer essen	die Hausaufgaben vergessen
Englisch sprechen	Cola trinken	Kaugummi kauen
zu dem Professor **du** sagen	eine Baseball-Mütze° tragen	?

cap

E. Expressing necessity: *müssen*

The modal verb **müssen** expresses necessity. Here are the present tense forms.

müssen: *must, to have to, need to*				
Person	**Singular**		**Plural**	
1st	ich **muss**	*I must*	wir **müssen**	*we must*
2nd, informal	du **musst**	*you must*	ihr **müsst**	*you must*
2nd, formal	Sie **müssen**	*you must*	Sie **müssen**	*you must*
3rd	er/sie/es **muss**	*he/she/it must*	sie **müssen**	*they must*

Note how the German translations vary greatly when *must, have to,* and *need to* are negated in English.

You **must not** do that. *Das **darfst** du **nicht.***
You **don't have to** do that. *Das **brauchst** du **nicht** zu tun.*
You **don't need to** do that. *Das **musst** du **nicht** tun.*

Unlike **muss nicht,** which states that something need not be done, **darf nicht** expresses a strong prohibition. Thus, *must not* and **muss nicht** have entirely different meanings and should not be confused.

36 **Was bedeutet das Verkehrsschild?** Verbinden Sie jeden Satz (links) mit einem Schild (rechts).

1. Hier muss man halten°. ___ — *stop*
2. Hier dürfen nur Radfahrer fahren. ___
3. Hier muss man langsam fahren. ___
4. Hier müssen Fahrräder links fahren und Fußgänger rechts gehen. ___

a. Kinder

b. Sonderweg Radfahrer

c. Getrennter Rad- und Fußweg

d. Stop

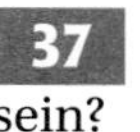

37 **Verkehrsregeln.** Was muss man beim Autofahren tun oder sein?

▣ bei rot/grün halten *Man muss bei rot halten.*

1. bei rot/bei grün fahren
2. bei gelb/blau aufpassen° — *pay attention*
3. im Schulbereich° langsam/schnell fahren — *in a school zone*
4. im Parkhaus schnell/langsam fahren
5. in der Stadt links/rechts überholen° — *pass*
6. im Nebel° schnell/vorsichtig° fahren — *fog / carefully*
7. mindestens° 16/18/21 Jahre alt sein — *at least*

38 **Darf ich nicht oder muss ich nicht?** Wählen Sie die beste Antwort.

1. Es ist warm heute.
   a. Du darfst keine Jacke tragen.
   b. Du musst keine Jacke tragen.
2. Darf ich hier rauchen°? — *smoke*
   a. Nein, das dürfen Sie nicht.
   b. Nein, das müssen Sie nicht.
3. Warum geht Jürgen zur Party?
   a. Er darf heute nicht lernen.
   b. Er muss heute nicht lernen.
4. Warum steht sie so spät auf?
   a. Sie muss heute nicht arbeiten.
   b. Sie darf heute nicht arbeiten.
5. Was bedeutet das Schild?
   a. Du musst nicht rauchen.
   b. Du darfst nicht rauchen.

F. Expressing strong desire: *wollen*

The modal verb **wollen** expresses a strong desire to do something. Here are the present tense forms.

		wollen: *to want to, wish*		
Person	**Singular**		**Plural**	
1st	ich **will**	*I want to*	wir **wollen**	*we want to*
2nd, informal	du **willst**	*you want to*	ihr **wollt**	*you want to*
2nd, formal	Sie **wollen**	*you want to*	Sie **wollen**	*you want to*
3rd	er/sie/es **will**	*he/she/it wants to*	sie **wollen**	*they want to*

39 Warum fahren Sie Rad? Was ist für Sie am wichtigsten°? Nummerieren° Sie diese Sätze von 1 (am wichtigsten) bis 6 (überhaupt nicht wichtig).

most important
number

___ Ich will gesund bleiben.
___ Ich will die Umwelt schonen°.
___ Ich will schnell zur Uni kommen.
___ Ich will nicht viel Geld ausgeben.
___ Ich will nicht per Anhalter fahren.
___ Ich will …

protect

40 Was wollen Barbara, Karl und Anna? Bilden Sie Sätze mit **will** oder **wollen.**

▣ Barbara hat Hunger. *Sie will essen.*

1. Barbara hat Hunger. — lesen
2. Karl hat Durst. — viel ausgeben
3. Anna hat ihren Tennisschläger°. — essen
4. Barbara und Karl haben ihre Fahrräder. — Tennis spielen
5. Anna hat eine englische Zeitung. — etwas trinken
6. Anna denkt an° ihre Familie in den USA. — anrufen
7. Karl nimmt viel Geld mit. — Rad fahren

tennis racket

denkt an: *thinks about*

Modal verbs summary chart		
Permission	**dürfen**	*may, to be permitted to*
Prohibition	**darf nicht**	*may not; must not*
Ability	**können**	*can, to be able to*
General fondness *(with nouns only)*	**mögen**	*to like*
Immediate desire *(with nouns and verbs)*	**möchte**	*would like*
Necessity	**müssen**	*must, to have to*
Expected obligation	**sollen**	*should; to be supposed to*
Strong desire	**wollen**	*to want to, wish*

41 Babysitten. Es ist 6 Uhr abends. Sie sind der Babysitter/die Babysitterin von drei Kindern. Die Kinder sind 3, 10 und 16 Jahre alt. Fragen Sie einen Partner/eine Partnerin, was die Kinder machen dürfen, können, möchten, müssen, sollen oder wollen.

▣ S1: Was darf die 3-jährige Tochter? — S2: Sie darf fernsehen.
S1: Was darfst du machen? — S2: Ich darf …

Tabelle A (S1):

	Die 3-jährige Tochter ...	Der 10-jährige Sohn ...	Der 16-jährige Bruder ...	Ich ...
darf	?	auf eine Party gehen	Auto fahren	______
muss	um 7 ins Bett gehen	?	Abendessen kochen	______
soll	?	Hausaufgaben machen	?	______
kann	gut sprechen	?	?	______
möchte	?	Freunde anrufen	ein Buch lesen	______
will	im Haus Rad fahren	?	?	______

Tabelle B (S2):

	Die 3-jährige Tochter ...	Der 10-jährige Sohn ...	Der 16-jährige Bruder ...	Ich ...
darf	fernsehen	?	?	______
muss	?	um 9 zu Hause sein	?	______
soll	etwas essen	?	sein Zimmer aufräumen	______
kann	?	gut schwimmen	gut kochen	______
möchte	um 9 ins Bett gehen	?	?	______
will	?	ins Kino gehen	fernsehen	______

In information-gap activities, the second chart is always printed upside down to enhance communication.

42 Was kann man in Amerika (in Deutschland) machen? Fragen Sie einen Partner/eine Partnerin nach Information aus der Tabelle.

S1: In Deutschland kann man Bratwurst essen. Kann man in Amerika Bratwurst essen?
S2: Ja, natürlich! In Milwaukee kann man Bratwurst essen.

Was kann man ... ? S1 bases his/her statements on items marked **Ja,** and his/her questions on items marked **?** in the table. S2 bases his/her responses on the information provided in parentheses.

Tabelle A (S1):

	In Amerika	In Deutschland
1. Bratwurst essen	?	Ja
2. Ski fahren	Ja	(in den Alpen)
3. Deutsch hören	?	Ja
4. Fußball spielen	(im Sommer)	Ja
5. das Oktoberfest besuchen	?	Ja
6. Spanisch hören	Ja	(nein, viel Türkisch)
7. gute Popmusik hören	Ja	?
8. campen gehen	Ja	(am Rhein)

Tabelle B (S2):

	In Amerika	In Deutschland
1. Bratwurst essen	(in Milwaukee)	Ja
2. Ski fahren	Ja	?
3. Deutsch hören	(in Indiana)	Ja
4. Fußball spielen	?	Ja
5. das Oktoberfest besuchen	(in San Diego)	Ja
6. Spanisch hören	Ja	?
7. gute Popmusik hören	Ja	(Die Prinzen)
8. campen gehen	Ja	?

43 **Regeln für den Deutschunterricht.** Lesen Sie die Regeln und diskutieren Sie sie mit der Klasse. Entscheiden Sie, ob° die Regeln gut oder nicht so gut sind.

entscheiden ... ob: *decide if*

▣ Man soll im Unterricht nur Deutsch sprechen.

▣ S1: Ja, das stimmt. Man soll im Unterricht nur Deutsch sprechen. *(oder)* Nein, das stimmt nicht. Man kann im Unterricht ein bisschen Englisch sprechen.

1. Man soll im Unterricht nur Deutsch sprechen.
2. Man darf nicht zum Unterricht kommen.
3. Man soll mit anderen Studenten nicht Deutsch sprechen.
4. Man soll nicht viele deutsche Bücher lesen.
5. Man darf jeden Tag Deutsch lernen.
6. Man muss die Grammatik nicht lernen.
7. Man soll alle neuen Wörter auswendig lernen°.
8. Man muss viele Fragen stellen.

auswendig lernen: *memorize*

44 **Anna macht sich Sorgen.** Bald fährt Anna nach Deutschland. Sie wird ein bisschen nervös. Können Sie Anna Rat geben? Spielen Sie Anna und Annas Freund/Freundin. Wählen Sie immer die beste Antwort.

▣ S1 (ANNA): Wie soll ich von Frankfurt nach Weinheim kommen?
S2 (FREUND/FREUNDIN): Fahr mit den Günthers im Auto.

1. von Frankfurt nach Weinheim kommen
   a. mit dem Zug fahren
   b. mit dem Taxi fahren
   c. mit den Günthers im Auto fahren
   d. ...

2. genug Geld für Andenken haben
   a. nichts essen
   b. einen Job finden
   c. bei Freunden und Verwandten essen
   d. ...

3. die acht Stunden im Flugzeug verbringen°
   a. Deutsch lernen
   b. ein Buch lesen
   c. schlafen
   d. ...

spend

Drehscheibe Frankfurt. Hier ballt sich der Verkehr.

4. die Verwandten anreden° — *address*
   a. „du" sagen
   b. „Sie" sagen
   c. einfach nichts sagen
   d. ?

5. mit Amerika in Kontakt bleiben
   a. oft anrufen
   b. viele Briefe schreiben
   c. Amerika vergessen
   d. ...

BRENNPUNKT KULTUR

Mit der Bahn fahren

Germany is much smaller in land area than the U.S. or Canada—it is roughly the size of Montana. For that reason many travelers prefer the convenience of taking a train **(Bahn fahren)** rather than travelling by plane. The German Federal Railway **(Deutsche Bahn AG = DB),** a private enterprise, maintains an extensive rail system, including direct train service to and from the Frankfurt airport. Young people, students, and retired persons are eligible for substantial discounts on the **Deutsche Bahn.** Non-Europeans can purchase a Eurail Pass, which allows for unlimited first- or second-class daily rail travel throughout Europe, or the Flexi-Pass, which is valid for a specified number of days over a longer time span.

Man kann mit der Bahn zum Flughafen fahren.

45 **Die BahnCard.** Wenn man eine BahnCard hat, kostet eine Fahrkarte nur die Hälfte vom normalen Preis. Lesen Sie die Informationen und füllen Sie dann die Tabelle aus. Was kostet eine BahnCard für Georg und Johannes Günther und Oma Kunz?

BahnCard

Ein Jahr Deutschland.
Für alle. Für die Hälfte.

Das ganze Angebot im Überblick:

BahnCard	Alter	Preis	Besonderheiten
Basiskarte	23–59	DM 260,–	
Für Senioren	ab 60	DM 130,–	Unter bestimmten Voraussetzungen auch für Schwerbehinderte, Frührentner und Pensionäre unter 60 Jahren.
Für Junioren	18–22	DM 130,–	Für Schüler und Studenten bis 22 Jahre gegen Berechtigungsnachweis
Zusatzkarte für Ehepartner	–	DM 130,–	Für Ehepartner von Inhabern einer Basiskarte, einer BahnCard für Senioren oder Junioren. Gleicher Gültigkeitszeitraum.
Für Teens	12–17	DM 65,–	
Für Kinder	4–11	DM 65,–	50 % Ermäßigung auf den Kindertarif.
Für Familien	–	DM 65,–	Nur gültig bei gemeinsamen Fahrten von mindestens einem Elternteil und einem Kind. Informationen und spezielle Anträge bei jeder Verkaufsstelle.

Reiseverbindungen

Deutsche Bahn

VON *Celle*
NACH *Chemnitz Hbf*
ÜBER

BAHNHOF		UHR	ZUG	
Celle	ab	12:26	E	3120
Hannover Hbf	an	12:59		
	ab	13:05	IC	604
Magdeburg Hbf	an	15:08		
	ab	15:48	D	2735
Leipzig Hbf	an	17:33		
	ab	17:51	RSB	4513
Chemnitz Hbf	an	19:13		

	Georg Günther	Johannes Günther	Elfriede Kunz (Oma)
Alter:	16	49	70+
Preis:	_____	_____	_____
Kategorie für:	*Teens*	_____	_____
Gültig° für:	*ein Jahr*	_____	_____

valid

46 **Reiseverbindungen.** Barbara Müller fährt von Celle in Niedersachsen zu Freunden in Chemnitz. Zeichnen° Sie ihre Reiseroute auf der Landkarte am Anfang des Buches. Stellen Sie dann einem Partner/einer Partnerin diese Fragen. *draw*

1. Wo muss sie einsteigen°? *get on*
2. Barbara muss dreimal umsteigen°, zuerst in Hannover. Wo muss sie noch umsteigen? *change trains*
3. Wo muss sie aussteigen°? *get off*

47 **Eine Reise planen.** Spielen Sie diese Situation mit einem Partner/einer Partnerin.

S1: Tourist(in)

Sie planen eine Reise im Sommer nach Spanien (Mexiko, Österreich usw.). Sie haben wenig Geld und viel Zeit, und Sie möchten viel sehen.

1. Ich möchte nach ... fahren.
2. Wann soll ich nach ... fahren?
3. Was kann ich in ... machen?
4. Was soll ich in ... sehen?
5. Was kann ich in ... essen?
6. Was soll ich in ... trinken?
7. Was muss ich in ... nicht machen?
8. Was darf ich in ... nicht machen?

S2: Experte (Expertin)

Sie kennen Spanien (Mexiko, Österreich usw.) gut. Geben Sie viele Reisetipps.

1. a. Das ist eine gute Idee!
   b. Das ist eine schlechte Idee! Fahr doch lieber nach ... !
2. Fahr doch im Januar.
3. am Strand° liegen (Sehenswürdigkeiten besuchen, Ski laufen, schwimmen, Rad fahren, Leute kennen lernen, tanzen usw.) — *on the beach*
4. das Museum (das Schloss, die Altstadt usw.)
5. das Brot (das Obst, den Kuchen usw.)
6. den Kaffee (den Wein, das Bier usw.)
7. dein Zimmer aufräumen (Hausaufgaben machen, Deutsch sprechen, zur Uni gehen, die Eltern anrufen, arbeiten usw.)
8. gefährliche° Wanderungen° machen (dich stressen, das Wasser trinken, viel Alkohol trinken, nach dem Essen schwimmen, mit Fremden° sprechen, zu lange in der Sonne° liegen, viel Geld ausgeben, schnell Auto fahren usw.) — *dangerous / hikes*; *strangers*; *sun*

Wissenswerte Vokabeln: Eigenschaften

Identifying personal characteristics

freundlich/unfreundlich

sportlich/unsportlich

locker/steif

offen (gesellig)/schüchtern

selbstsicher/unsicher (nervös)

ruhig/laut

kreativ / einfallslos

musikalisch / unmusikalisch

klug (intelligent) / dumm

heiter (lustig) / ernst

fleißig / faul

sympathisch / unsympathisch

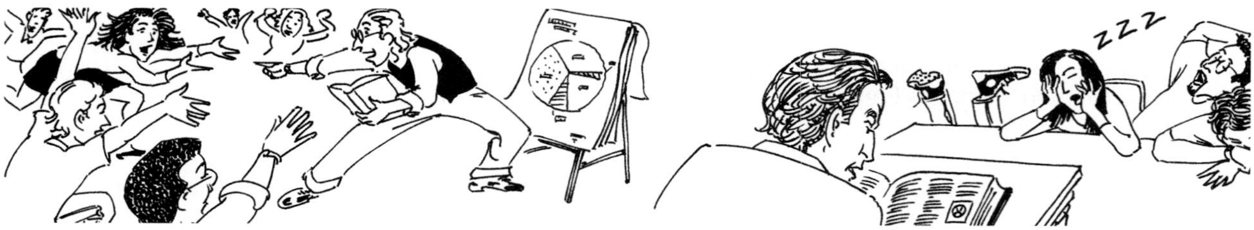

interessant / langweilig

- Ist Anna freundlich? *Ja, sie ist freundlich.*
  Ist Albert freundlich? *Nein, er ist unfreundlich.*

48 Katja ist freundlich. Welche Adjektive beschreiben° Katja, welche beschreiben Georg?

describe

- Katja mag andere Leute und hat viele Freunde. Sie ist freundlich.

Katja ...

1. mag andere Leute und hat viele Freunde. Sie ...
2. kann Klavier spielen. Sie ...
3. kann gut Tennis und Fußball spielen. Sie ...
4. geht gern auf Partys. Sie ...

Georg ...

5. kann Physik verstehen. Er ...
6. macht immer Hausaufgaben. Er ...
7. kann gut zeichnen°. Er ...
8. sieht nett aus°. Er ...

sketch
***sieht nett aus:** is handsome*

49 Georg ist nicht dumm! Beschreiben Sie, wie diese Personen wirklich sind. Benutzen Sie Argumente aus der Liste.

The word **doof** is often used for **dumm** to characterize a person as *goofy.*

S1: Katja denkt, Georg ist dumm.
S2: Georg ist nicht dumm, sondern klug. Er kann Mathematik verstehen und Spanisch sprechen.

kann gut Witze° erzählen° • kann 60 Meter in sieben Sekunden laufen • kann Spanisch sprechen • möchte oft allein sein • will immer lustige Filme sehen • will nie laut sprechen • muss oft lachen • möchte immer Hausaufgaben machen • kann fantastisch Klavier spielen • möchte jeden Tag schwimmen • kann Mathematik verstehen • will immer nur arbeiten

jokes / tell

1. KATJA: Georg ist dumm.
2. GEORG: Anna ist faul.
3. ANNA: Onkel Hannes ist ernst.
4. ANNA: Jeff ist unsportlich.
5. HANNES: Uschi ist laut.
6. HANNELORE: Bob ist unmusikalisch.

50 **Zwanzig Fragen: Wie heißt er/sie?** Bilden Sie Gruppen von vier bis fünf Personen. Ein Student/Eine Studentin denkt an eine prominente Person. Die anderen Studenten/Studentinnen stellen maximal zwanzig Fragen. Hier sind einige Fragen:

Ist es eine Frau?	Ist sie tot?
Ist sie kreativ?	Kann sie Klavier spielen?

S1: Ich denke an eine Person. Der Name beginnt mit B.
S2: Ist es ein Mann?

IV Expressing spatial movement, the recipient of something, opposition, and omission

Prepositions with the accusative

German has a group of five prepositions that are always followed by the accusative case.

Accusative prepositions

durch	*through*
für	*for*
gegen	*against*
ohne	*without*
um	*around*

1. durch, um

Spatial movement is expressed in German with the prepositions **durch** and **um.**

Anna geht **durch** das Zimmer.	*Anna is walking through the room.*
Anna geht **um** den Tisch.	*Anna is walking around the table.*

As you learned in Chapter 3, **um** is also used in time expressions, e.g., **um drei Uhr.**

2. für

German speakers use the preposition **für** to denote the recipient of an action.

To review the accusative case, go back to Chapter 2.

Anna bringt ein Geschenk **für** die Günthers. *Anna is bringing a present for the Günthers.*

3. gegen

Opposition to an action or an object is expressed with the preposition **gegen.**

Papa hat nichts **gegen** meine Reise. *Papa has nothing against my trip.*

Gegen is also used in time expressions to express approximate time.

gegen drei Uhr *around three o'clock*

4. ohne

Omission is expressed with the preposition **ohne.**

Anna kommt **ohne** ihr Fahrrad. *Anna is coming without her bicycle.*

51 Geschenke. Für wen bringt Anna die Geschenke? Für ihre Kusine, ihren Vetter, ihren Onkel oder ihre Tante? Was sagt Anna?

▣ Katja liest gern. Das Buch ist für meine Kusine.

1. Katja liest gern.
2. Georg kann gut zeichnen.
3. Tante Uschi mag Musik.
4. Onkel Hannes will Spanisch lernen.
5. Katja kann gut Tennis.

a. die Tennisbälle
b. das spanisch-deutsche Wörterbuch
c. der Zeichenblock° — *drawing pad*
d. die CDs
e. das Buch

52 Mutters Hilfe. Annas Mutter hilft Anna beim Packen. Im Flugzeug hat Anna aber nicht viel Platz. Ohne welche Sachen kann Anna nicht fahren und welche Sachen kann sie zu Hause lassen°? Bilden Sie Sätze mit **ohne.**

leave

▣ S1: Hier sind deine Reiseschecks, Anna.
S2: Danke, Mutti, ich kann ohne meine Reiseschecks nicht fahren.
S1: Hier ist dein Computer, Anna.
S2: Ach, Mutti, ich kann ohne meinen Computer fahren.

1. deine Reiseschecks
2. dein Computer
3. dein Pass
4. deine Bordkarte
5. deine Rollerblades
6. dein Fotoapparat
7. deine Zahnbürste
8. dein Fahrrad
9. deine Deutschbücher

53 Was passiert in Annas Leben? Schreiben Sie eine passende Präposition **(durch, für, gegen, ohne, um)** in die Lücke.

1. Anna fliegt _____ ihre Eltern nach Deutschland.
2. Hannelore hat viele Ratschläge _____ Anna.
3. Hannelore ist _____ Cola und Geldausgeben.
4. In Deutschland muss Anna _____ den Zoll°.

customs

5. Anna gibt gern Geld _____ Andenken aus.
6. Anna kommt _____ die Tür.

FREIE KOMMUNIKATION **Rollenspiel: Eine Abschiedsparty°.** Annas Deutschklasse in Indiana plant eine Abschiedsparty für Anna. Diskutieren Sie die Details für die Party (Essen, Trinken, Aktivitäten usw.) in kleinen Gruppen. Benutzen Sie diese Ausdrücke:

bon voyage party

Wer kann ...? • Wer soll ...? • Wer möchte ...? • Wer will ...?

Schreibecke **Das Fotoalbum.** Die Günthers sehen sich Annas Familienfotos im Fotoalbum an. Hier spricht Frau Günther über ihre Schwester Hannelore in Indiana. Lesen Sie, was Tante Uschi sagt, und schreiben Sie dann etwas über Ihre Schwester (Ihren Bruder, einen Cousin/eine Kusine, einen Freund/eine Freundin). Benutzen Sie Tante Uschis Aussagen als Beispiele.

In mancher Hinsicht° sind meine Schwester und ich gleich:

in mancher Hinsicht: *in some ways*

Ich bin groß und schlank und sie auch.
Ich habe braune Augen und braunes Haar und sie auch.
Ich habe einen Mann und eine Familie und sie auch.
Ich habe einen Sohn und eine Tochter und sie auch.
Ich bin relativ ruhig und sie auch.

Und in mancher Hinsicht sind meine Schwester und ich verschieden°: *different*

> Ich mag klassische Musik, aber sie nicht.
> Ich bin unsportlich, aber sie ist sehr sportlich.
> Ich bin relativ unsicher, aber sie ist sehr selbstsicher.
> Sie ist sehr lustig und locker, aber ich bin relativ steif und ernst.
> Sie ist sehr offen und gesellig, aber ich bin schüchtern.

Schreibecke **Eine Zeitungsannonce.** Suchen Sie einen Freund/eine Freundin durch die Zeitung. Schreiben Sie eine Anzeige° und sagen Sie, wie diese ideale Person sein soll. *ad*

Ich suche einen Freund/eine Freundin. Er/Sie muss intelligent sein. Er/Sie soll viel Kaffee trinken. Er/Sie soll kein Bier trinken. Er/Sie soll nur vegetarisch essen, usw.

ZIELTEXT

Endlich unterwegs!°

Finally, on the way!

Anna ist endlich unterwegs nach Deutschland. Hier kommt sie am Flughafen in Frankfurt an. Die Günthers holen Anna ab. In dem Dialog sprechen die Günthers zuerst über Anna. Anna trifft die Günthers. Sie sprechen kurz miteinander° und dann fahren sie alle nach Hause. *with each other*

Vorschau

54 **Thematische Fragen.** Beantworten Sie die folgenden Fragen.

1. Wo kommen Passagiere im Flughafen an?
   a. in Halle A
   b. beim Abflug
   c. an der Ankunft

2. Welche Kontrolle müssen ankommende Auslands-Passagiere *nicht* passieren?
   a. Passkontrolle
   b. Bordkartenkontrolle
   c. Zollkontrolle
3. Passagiere müssen ihre Koffer selbst ______.
   a. holen
   b. kaufen
   c. vergessen
4. Was kann man als Geschenk für einen Gast zum Flughafen bringen?
   a. einen Computer
   b. eine Hose
   c. Blumen
5. Was kann man für einen Gast im Flughafen machen, wenn man helfen will?
   a. Koffer tragen
   b. ein Taxi rufen
   c. das Flugticket bezahlen
6. Wo parkt man Autos am Flughafen?
   a. im Park
   b. im Parkhaus
   c. auf der Straße

55 **Zur Orientierung.** Schauen Sie sich die Zeichnung° zum Zieltext an und beantworten Sie diese Fragen. *sketch*

1. Wie viele Personen sind da? Wer sind diese Personen?
2. Wo sind die Personen: auf der Uni? auf einem Bahnhof? auf einem Flughafen?
3. Was machen sie: essen, warten, schlafen?

56 **Satzdetektiv.** Welche Sätze bedeuten ungefähr das Gleiche?

1. Wie können wir sie denn **erkennen?**
2. Das kann nicht mehr so lange **dauern.**
3. Anna muss durch den **Zoll.**
4. Gib ihr doch die **Blumen!**
5. Wie war dein **Flug?**

a. Anna muss durch die Kontrolle gehen.
b. Das kann nicht so lange sein.
c. Gib ihr die Rosen!
d. Wie war deine Reise?
e. Woher wissen wir, wer Anna ist?

---

6. Ich bin jetzt **todmüde.**
7. Du **siehst wirklich aus wie** Hannelore.
8. Tu die Koffer da in den **Kofferraum.**
9. Wir müssen erst die **Parkgebühr bezahlen.**

f. Stell die Taschen und Koffer hinten° ins Auto. *in the rear*
g. Ich bin extrem müde.
h. Man muss für das Parken Geld ausgeben.
i. Du und Hannelore sehen sehr ähnlich° aus. *similar*

57 Erstes Zuhören. Hören Sie sich den Dialog an und beantworten Sie diese Fragen.

1. Wie sollen die Günthers Anna erkennen? Was hat sie?
2. Was sagen die Günthers, wenn Anna endlich ankommt?
3. Wie geht es Anna? Was will sie jetzt machen?

ZIELTEXT

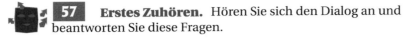

Endlich unterwegs!

Hören Sie gut zu.

Rückblick

58 Was hören Sie wann? Bringen Sie diese Sätze aus dem Text in die richtige Reihenfolge°. *order*

___ Georg, gib ihr doch die Blumen!
___ Hat sie nicht so einen lila Rucksack?
_1_ Da vorne steht's: Ankunft.
___ Hier, links, gehen wir zum Parkhaus.
___ Da kommen die ersten Leute raus.

59 Stimmt das? Stimmen diese Aussagen zum Text oder nicht? Wenn nicht, was stimmt?

	Ja, das stimmt.	*Nein, das stimmt nicht.*
1. Katja sieht das Schild „Ankunft".	___	___
2. Anna soll einen lila Rucksack tragen.	___	___
3. Anna soll lange braune Haare haben.	___	___
4. Anna muss durch den Zoo.	___	___
5. Georg hat Blumen für Anna.	___	___
6. Anna ist todmüde nach dem Flug.	___	___
7. Anna trägt die Koffer zum Parkhaus.	___	___
8. Anna soll vorne im Auto sitzen; da hat sie mehr Platz.	___	___

60 Ergänzen Sie: Diktat. Ergänzen Sie diese Sätze mit Wörtern aus dem **Zieltext.**

1. Georg, hier! Da vorne steht's: ______. Kannst du das Schild nicht sehen?
2. Mutti, wie können wir sie denn ______, unsere Kusine Anna?
3. Hat sie nicht so einen lila ______?
4. Dann kann es nicht so ______ sein, sie zu erkennen.
5. Wann kommt sie denn ______ raus?
6. Das kann nicht mehr so lange ______.
7. Sie muss noch ihr Gepäck ______ und dann noch durch den ______.
8. Georg, gib ihr doch die ______!
9 Wie war dein ______?
10. Und du ______ wirklich ______ wie Hannelore.
11. Ah, warte! Wir müssen erst die Parkgebühr ______.
12. Komm, Anna. Setz dich nach vorne. Da hast du mehr ______.

61 Wer muss/will/soll was? Hören Sie sich den Dialog noch einmal an und bilden Sie dann Sätze über die Situation am Flughafen.

▣ Die Günthers können Anna erkennen.

Die Günthers	sollen (müssen, können)	Anna erkennen.
Anna	soll (muss, kann)	das Gepäck holen.
Onkel Hannes		durch den Zoll gehen.
Tante Uschi		Annas Koffer tragen.
Katja		die Parkgebühr bezahlen.
Georg		Anna Blumen geben.
		die Koffer in den Kofferraum legen.
		warten.
		das Schild sehen.

62 Kurz gefragt. Beantworten Sie diese Fragen auf Deutsch.

1. Warum müssen die Günthers lange auf Anna warten?
2. Wie fühlt sich° Anna nach° dem Flug?
3. Wie fahren die Günthers nach Weinheim zurück?
4. Wo sitzt Anna im Wagen? Warum?
5. Wer hat ein Geschenk für wen?

fühlt sich: *feels / after*

BRENNPUNKT KULTUR

Frankfurt am Main

Frankfurt am Main, located in the heart of Germany, on the banks of the Main River in the state of Hesse **(Hessen)**, is both the geographic crossroads of the country and one of its key economic centers. As the major gateway to Germany and the nation's most important transportation center, Frankfurt is home to Europe's busiest international airport, the **Frankfurter Flughafen**, and to the German international airline **Deutsche Lufthansa**, as well as to the German Federal Railway, the **Deutsche Bahn**. Frankfurt is also the hub of the German business community: the German federal bank **(die Bundesbank)**, the national stock market **(die Börse)**, and many large publishing houses. In recognition of the city's important role in international finance, the Monetary Institute of the European Community **(Europäisches Währungsinstitut)** and the new central bank of the European Community **(die Europäische Zentralbank-EZB)** are situated in Frankfurt.

Frankfurt is also a center of German culture and history. Johann Wolfgang von Goethe was born in Frankfurt am Main. In 1848 Frankfurt was the site of the first attempt to establish a united German nation through a representative assembly. Frankfurt's university has become associated with some of Western philosophy's most progressive thinkers, reflecting a long liberal tradition in **Hessen.**

The people of Frankfurt enjoy a lively theater, opera, and music season, along with some of the best jazz in Germany. They relax by visiting the numerous museums located along the Main River, taking their children to the world-class **Frankfurter Zoo**, spending a day in the glass-enclosed **Palmengarten** terrarium, and sipping the popular local apple wine **(Äppelwoi)** in the cozy pubs of Sachsenhausen, the part of Frankfurt which is most famous for its ambience.

Um den historischen Römerberg in Frankfurt sieht man moderne Hochhäuser.

FREIE KOMMUNIKATION

1. Mutter/Vater und Tochter/Sohn. Machen Sie dieses Rollenspiel mit einem Partner/einer Partnerin: Ihr Sohn/Ihre Tochter fährt bald nach Deutschland. Welche Ratschläge haben Sie für ihn/sie? Wie reagiert Ihr Sohn/Ihre Tochter auf die Ratschläge?

S1 (MUTTER/VATER): Sprich nicht mit Fremden!
S2 (SOHN/TOCHTER): Was? Ich soll nicht mit Fremden sprechen? Wie kann ich neue Leute kennen lernen?
S1 (MUTTER/VATER): Geh auf die Uni und sprich nur mit den Professoren und mit Studenten.

2. In Frankfurt.

1. Was kann man in Frankfurt machen?
2. Sie sind in Frankfurt und heute ist Samstag. Was machen Sie?
3. Sie sind Anna Adler. Was sagen Sie zu den Günthers am Flughafen? Was sagen Sie im Auto auf der Fahrt nach Weinheim?

Schreibecke **Anna im Flugzeug.** Sie sind Anna im Flugzeug nach Frankfurt. Das Flugzeug landet in einer Stunde. Sie wissen, Sie treffen bald Ihre Verwandten und müssen dann Deutsch sprechen. Sie sind ein bisschen nervös. Was können Sie wohl sagen? Machen Sie sich zu den folgenden Fragen Notizen°.

° *notes*

1. Was sollen Sie in Deutschland machen? Was denken Sie? Was denken Ihre Eltern?
2. Was dürfen Sie in Deutschland nicht machen? Was denken Sie? Und Ihre Eltern?
3. Wie fühlen Sie sich jetzt?
4. Was wollen Sie machen, sobald° Sie in Weinheim sind?

° *as soon as*

Wortschatz

Die Reise

das Adressbuch, ⸚er *address book*
das Andenken, - *souvenir*
die Bordkarte, -n *boarding pass*
der Flugschein, -e *airline ticket*
das Geld, -er *money*
die Kreditkarte, -n *credit card*
das Missverständnis, -se *misunderstanding*
der Pass, *pl.* **Pässe** *passport*
das Portmonee, -s *wallet*
der Ratschlag, ⸚e *advice*
die Reise, -n *trip, journey*
der Reisescheck, -s *traveller's check*
die Sprache, -n *language*
die Umgebung *surroundings, area*

aus·geben (er gibt aus) *to spend money*
denken *to think*
denken an (+ *acc.*) *to think of*
fahren (er fährt) *to drive, ride*
helfen (er hilft) *to help*
kaufen *to buy, purchase*
mit·nehmen (er nimmt mit) *to take along*
vergessen (er vergisst) *to forget*

genug *enough*
hin und wieder *now and then*
immer *always*
mindestens *at least*
nie *never*
vorsichtig *careful, cautious*
warm *warm*
wohl *probably*

Ausdrücke

etwas anderes *something else*
Mach dir keine Sorgen! *Don't worry!*
per Anhalter fahren (er fährt per Anhalter) *to hitchhike*

Das Gepäck

das Blitzlicht, -er *flash (for a camera)*
die CD, -s *compact disc*
der CD-Player, - *CD player*
der Fotoapparat, -e *camera*
das Geschenk, -e *gift, present*
die Handtasche, -n *handbag, purse*
der Koffer, - *suitcase*
der Kulturbeutel, - *shaving kit/cosmetic kit*
der Rucksack, ¨-e *backpack*
das Wörterbuch, ¨-er *dictionary*

Die Kleidung

die Bluse, -n *blouse*
der Handschuh, -e *glove*
das Hemd, -en *shirt*
die Hose, -n *pants*
die Jacke, -n *jacket*
das Kleid, -er *dress*
die Kleidung, -en *clothing, clothes*
die Krawatte, -n *necktie*
der Mantel, ¨- *coat*
der Pullover, -s *pullover, sweater*
der Rock, ¨-e *skirt*
der/das Sakko, -s *sport coat*
der Schuh, -e *shoe*
die Socke, -n *sock*
die Strumpfhose, -n *panty hose*
der Stiefel, - *boot*
die Unterwäsche *underwear*

packen *to pack*
tragen (er trägt) *to wear*

Die Toilettenartikel

das Deospray, -s *deodorant spray*
der Lippenstift, -e *lipstick*
der Toilettenartikel, - *toiletry*
die Zahnbürste, -n *toothbrush*
die Zahnpasta, -pasten *toothpaste*

Die Eigenschaften

die Eigenschaft, -en *personal trait, quality*
dumm *dumb, stupid*
einfallslos *uncreative*
ernst *serious*
faul *lazy*
fleißig *industrious, busy*
gesellig *gregarious, sociable*
heiter *funny, cheerful*
intelligent *intelligent*
interessant *interesting*
kreativ *creative*
laut *loud*
locker *relaxed, cool*
lustig *funny, jovial*
musikalisch *musical*
offen *open*
nervös *nervous*
ruhig *quiet, peaceful*
selbstsicher *self-assured, self-confident*
schüchtern *shy*
sportlich *athletic*
steif *stiff, ill-at-ease*
sympathisch *likeable, pleasant, nice*
unfreundlich *unfriendly*
unmusikalisch *unmusical*
unsicher *unsure, insecure*
unsportlich *unathletic*
unsympathisch *unlikeable, disagreeable*

Der Verkehr

die Ausnahme, -n *exception*
die Autobahn, -en *autobahn, superhighway*
das Benzin *gasoline*
die Einbahnstraße, -n *one-way street*
das Fahrzeug, -e *vehicle*
der Fußgänger, - *pedestrian*
der Fußgängerbereich, -e *pedestrian zone*
die Info, -s *information*
die Kosten *(pl.)* *expenses, costs*
das Öl *oil*
der Platz, ¨-e *space, room; seat*
der Radfahrer, - *cyclist, bicycle rider*
die Regel, -n *rule, regulation*
die Richtung, -en *direction*
das Schild, -er *sign*
die Sicherheit *safety, security*
die Straße, -n *street*
der Verkehr *traffic*
das Verbot, -e *ban, prohibition*
das Verkehrszeichen, - *traffic sign*
der Weg, -e *path*
das Zeichen, - *sign, marker*

man *a person, anybody, you*

beliebt *popular*
besonders *especially*
einige *a few, several*
einzig *single*
frei *free, open; allowed*
gering *low, small, limited*
gesund *healthy*
rund *approximately, roughly*
selbst *self, by oneself*
umweltfreundlich *environmentally friendly*
wichtig *important*

beachten *to observe, obey, pay attention to*
brauchen *to need*
sprechen für (er spricht für) *to speak for, speak well of; to indicate*
verbrauchen *to consume, use*

Modalverben

dürfen (ich/er darf, du darfst) *may; to be allowed to, permitted to*
können (ich/er kann, du kannst) *can; to be able to*
möchten (ich/er möchte, du möchtest) *to like (immediate relevance)*
mögen (ich/er mag, du magst) *to like (generally)*
müssen (ich/er muss, du musst) *to have to, must; to be required to*
sollen (ich/er soll, du sollst) *should, ought to; to be supposed to*
wollen (ich/er will, du willst) *to want to*

bitte *please*
doch *go ahead and … (persuasive particle)*
mal *once (emphatic particle)*

Akkusativpräpositionen

durch *through*
für *for*
gegen *against; around (time)*
ohne *without*
um *around; at (time)*

Ausdrücke

aller Art *all kinds of*
es macht Spaß *it's fun*
immer (beliebter) *more and more (popular)*
in diesem Falle *in this case, in this situation*

Aus dem Zieltext

die Ankunft, ⁻̈e *arrival*
das Auto, -s *automobile, car*
die Blume, - n *flower*
der Flug, ⁻̈e *flight*
der Kofferraum *trunk (of a car)*
die Parkgebühr, -en *parking fee*
das Parkhaus, ⁻̈er *parking garage*
der Parkschein, -e *parking stub, ticket*
der Rucksack, ⁻̈e *backpack*
der Zoll *customs*
aus·sehen wie (er sieht aus wie) *to look like*
bezahlen *to pay*
dauern *to last*
erkennen *to recognize*
glauben *to believe, think*
holen *to go get, fetch*
los·fahren (er fährt los) *to take off, leave, drive away*
raus·kommen *to come out*
schauen *to look*
tun *to do; to put*
warten *to wait*

da *there*
genau *exactly*
links *left, on the left*
mehr *more*
rechts *right, on the right*
schwer *difficult*
todmüde *dead tired*
unterwegs *en route, underway*
vorne *up front*
wirklich *really*

Ausdrücke

also *well, all right, OK (conversation starter)*
durch den Zoll *through customs*
herzlich willkommen in … ! *welcome to . . . !*

In this chapter you will learn how to talk about events in the past, about personal relationships, the weather, and the seasons.

Kommunikative Funktionen

- Talking about past events
- Describing personal relationships
- Expressing what you know and don't know
- Giving reasons
- Positioning information in a German sentence
- Talking about activities that continue from the past into the present

Strukturen

- The conversational past
- Subordinate clauses with **ob, dass,** and **weil**
- Word order: subject-verb inversion, two-part verbs, and verb forms in subordinate clauses
- Present tense verbs with **schon, seit,** and **erst**

Vokabeln

- Das Wetter
- Die Jahreszeiten
- Freundschaft und Liebe

Kulturelles

- **Hansestadt Hamburg**
- **Bekannte** versus **Freunde**

Wo habt ihr euch kennen gelernt?

KAPITEL FÜNF

Freundschaften

Go to the *Vorsprung* Website at **www.hmco.com/college**

ANLAUFTEXT

Die Geschichte von Tante Uschi und Onkel Hannes

Onkel Hannes und Tante Uschi sitzen mit Anna an einem Abend zu Hause in Weinheim und sprechen über ihre Studienzeit in Hamburg. Hier erzählen sie Anna, wie sie sich kennen gelernt haben.

Vorschau

1 Thematische Fragen: Was sind Studentenjobs? Viele Studenten müssen arbeiten und ihr Studium selbst° finanzieren. Kreuzen Sie die passenden Kategorien an.

themselves

	Studentenjobs	*Meine Jobs*	*Jobs mit interessanten Leuten*
1. als Professor(in) an der Uni arbeiten	—	—	—
2. in einer Kneipe° als Kellner(in)° arbeiten	—	—	—
3. in der Bibliothek arbeiten	—	—	—
4. in einem Geschäft° arbeiten	—	—	—
5. als Arzt (Ärztin)° in einem Krankenhaus arbeiten	—	—	—
6. Taxi fahren	—	—	—
7. babysitten	—	—	—
8. im Restaurant oder in der Mensa° kochen	—	—	—
9. Nachhilfestunden geben°	—	—	—
10. Karten spielen und Geld gewinnen	—	—	—
11. Pizza ausfahren°	—	—	—
12. Zeitungen austragen°	—	—	—

pub
waiter (waitress)
store
doctor
dining hall
***Nachhilfestunden geben:** to tutor*
deliver
deliver

2 Kennen lernen. Sie finden jemanden attraktiv. Was machen Sie?

	Das mache ich.	*Das mache ich nicht.*
1. etwas fallen lassen°	—	—
2. viel Bier trinken	—	—
3. tolle Kleider tragen	—	—
4. freundlich sein	—	—
5. die Person direkt ansprechen	—	—
6. wild tanzen	—	—
7. viel Geld ausgeben	—	—
8. etwas Intelligentes sagen	—	—
9. Komplimente machen	—	—
10. anstarren° und warten	—	—

***fallen lassen:** to drop*
stare

3 **Zeitdetektiv.** Hier sind sechs Sätze im Präsens. Welche Sätze im Perfekt° bedeuten ungefähr das gleiche?

conversational past

Präsens	*Perfekt*
1. Du hast eine Erkältung°.	a. Er hat nie Trinkgeld gegeben.
2. Du tust mir Leid.	b. Er hat mich geküsst.
3. Er gibt nie Trinkgeld°.	c. Du hast eine Erkältung gehabt.
4. Danach heiraten° wir.	d. Ich war in Tante Uschi verliebt.
5. Ich bin in Tante Uschi verliebt°.	e. Du hast mir Leid getan.
6. Er küsst° mich.	f. Danach haben wir geheiratet.

cold
tips
marry
in love
kisses

Zeitdetektiv. You will learn how to form the conversational past later in this chapter. For now, recognizing it is sufficient.

War-*was* is frequently used in speech.

Note the meaning of **zum ersten Mal:** *for the first time;* **trotzdem:** *nevertheless;* **danach, nachher:** *after that, afterwards;* **Na, wie auch immer.** *Well, whatever;* **wenigstens:** at least.

ANLAUFTEXT

Hören Sie gut zu.

Die Geschichte von Tante Uschi und Onkel Hannes

Onkel Hannes und Tante Uschi erzählen Anna, wie sie sich kennen gelernt haben.
Uschi hat in Hamburg Pharmazie studiert und als Kellnerin in einer Studentenkneipe gearbeitet. Sie hat Geld fürs Studium verdient.
Ich bin oft in die Kneipe gegangen, weil mir die Uschi gut gefallen hat.
Ja, und er hat nie Trinkgeld gegeben. Wenigstens hat er gut ausgesehen ...

Und dann habe ich sie eines Tages ins Theater eingeladen, und nachher haben wir zusammen ein Bier getrunken. Wir haben leidenschaftlich diskutiert ...
Ja, aber nach dem zweiten Bier war ich etwas mutiger.
Leidenschaftlich diskutiert? Du warst so nervös, du hast keine drei Worte gesagt.

Und später haben wir einen romantischen Spaziergang an der Alster gemacht. Dort haben wir einander zum ersten Mal geküsst.
Romantisch, sagst du? Es hat die ganze Zeit geregnet, und du hast eine ganz schlimme Erkältung gehabt.

Aber du hast mich trotzdem geküsst!
Ich habe dich nur geküsst, weil du mir so Leid getan hast.

Na, trotzdem ... Von da an haben wir viel Zeit miteinander verbracht. Wir haben oft zusammen gekocht und gegessen und sind auch abends ausgegangen.
Ja, wir haben tolle Nächte in St. Pauli durchgemacht. Getanzt, getrunken und so weiter ...
Und sonntags sind wir immer zum Fischmarkt gegangen ...

... und an der Elbe spazieren gegangen.

Rückblick

Sprache im Alltag: Article with first names

German speakers frequently use a definite article with first names to signal familiarity.

Die Uschi hat als Kellnerin gearbeitet.
Der Hannes war nervös.

4 **Stimmt das?** Stimmen diese Aussagen zum Text oder nicht? Wenn nicht, was stimmt?

	Ja, das stimmt.	*Nein, das stimmt nicht.*
1. Tante Uschi hat in Heidelberg studiert.	___	___
2. Onkel Hannes hat Tante Uschi sehr viel Trinkgeld gegeben.	___	___
3. Onkel Hannes und Tante Uschi sind zusammen ins Kino gegangen.	___	___
4. Nachher haben Onkel Hannes und Tante Uschi einen Spaziergang gemacht.	___	___
5. Onkel Hannes hat Tante Uschi im Regen zum ersten Mal geküsst.	___	___

	Ja, das stimmt.	*Nein, das stimmt nicht.*
6. Tante Uschi war krank und sie hat Hannes Leid getan.	___	___
7. Tante Uschi und Onkel Hannes haben viel Zeit zusammen verbracht.	___	___
8. Tante Uschi hat ein Gedicht für Onkel Hannes geschrieben.	___	___
9. Tante Uschi und Onkel Hannes haben geheiratet.	___	___
10. Onkel Hannes war in Tante Uschi verliebt.	___	___

5 **Gut organisiert.** Was ist die korrekte Reihenfolge°? *sequence*

___ haben in St. Pauli Musik gehört, getanzt, getrunken
___ sind in die Kneipe gegangen
_1_ hat in der Kneipe gearbeitet
___ haben einen romantischen Spaziergang an der Alster gemacht
___ haben einander zum ersten Mal geküsst
___ haben geheiratet
___ hat Tante Uschi ins Theater eingeladen
___ haben viel Zeit miteinander verbracht

6 **Ergänzen Sie.** Ergänzen Sie diese Sätze mit Wörtern aus dem **Anlauftext.**

1. Tante Uschi hat in Hamburg als _____ in einer Studentenkneipe gearbeitet.
2. Onkel Hannes ist oft in die Kneipe gegangen, weil Uschi ihm gut _____ hat.
3. Onkel Hannes hat Tante Uschi nie _____ gegeben.
4. Eines Tages hat er Uschi ins Theater _____.
5. Nachher haben sie zusammen ein Bier _____.
6. Später haben sie einen romantischen _____ an der Alster gemacht.
7. Für Hannes war das nicht romantisch. Es hat die ganze Zeit _____ und Uschi hat eine ganz schlimme _____ gehabt.
8. Von da an haben sie viel Zeit miteinander _____.
9. Onkel Hannes war bis über beide Ohren in Tante Uschi _____.
10. Bald danach haben sie _____.

7 **Kurz gefragt.** Beantworten Sie diese Fragen auf Deutsch.

1. Was hat Tante Uschi in Hamburg gemacht?
2. Wie hat Onkel Hannes Tante Uschi kennen gelernt?
3. Was war ihre erste Verabredung°? Wer hat wen eingeladen? *date*
4. Was haben sie nachher zusammen gemacht?
5. Wo haben sie einander zum ersten Mal geküsst? Wer hat wen geküsst?
6. Was haben sie von da an gemacht?
7. Was hat Onkel Hannes für Tante Uschi geschrieben?

8 Romantisch? Welche Aktivitäten, die Tante Uschi und Onkel Hannes zusammen gemacht haben, finden Sie romantisch? Welche langweilig? Kreuzen Sie **Romantisch** oder **Langweilig** an. Dann fragen Sie einen Partner/eine Partnerin.

Finden Sie/Findest du ... ? is used to ask for a person's opinion.

ins Theater gehen

S1: Ins Theater gehen: Findest du das romantisch oder langweilig?
S2: Das finde ich romantisch (langweilig).

	Romantisch		*Langweilig*	
	Ich	*Partner(in)*	*Ich*	*Partner(in)*
1. ins Theater gehen	___	___	___	___
2. zusammen ein Bier trinken	___	___	___	___
3. einen Spaziergang im Regen machen	___	___	___	___
4. eine Person küssen	___	___	___	___
5. ein Liebesgedicht schreiben	___	___	___	___
6. tanzen gehen	___	___	___	___
7. auf einen Fischmarkt gehen	___	___	___	___
8. zusammen kochen und essen	___	___	___	___

9 Eine Verabredung. Was kann man zusammen machen? Schreiben Sie drei bis vier Aktivitäten auf. Ihr Partner/Ihre Partnerin schreibt auch drei bis vier Aktivitäten auf. Planen Sie dann eine interessante Verabredung miteinander. Beginnen Sie mit der Einladung: „Möchtest du ...?" Ihr Partner/Ihre Partnerin akzeptiert die Einladung und macht einen zweiten Vorschlag. Wechseln Sie sich ab°.

Wechseln ... ab: *Switch roles*

S1: Möchtest du ins Theater gehen?
S2: Gerne. Ich möchte auch ein Bier trinken.
S1: Gut. Zuerst können wir ins Theater gehen und nachher können wir ein Bier trinken.

S1:	*S2:*
ins Theater gehen	ein Bier trinken
______________	______________
______________	______________
______________	______________
______________	______________

BRENNPUNKT

Hansestadt Hamburg

Hamburg **(die Freie und Hansestadt Hamburg)**, Germany's largest seaport and second largest city (1.7 million inhabitants) constitutes one of the 16 states **(Länder)** of the Federal Republic of Germany. Hamburg, as well as Bremen, is a city-state, with an independent status which it owes to its history as a Hanseatic city.

The Hanseatic League **(die Hanse)** originated in the 13th century, when Hamburg and Lübeck agreed to reduce the trade barriers between them in order to foster trade in the North Sea and throughout the Baltic region. **Die Hanse** actively promoted trade, international contacts, and the accumulation of wealth, along with the relative independence that such economic wealth provided in a feudal society. Eventually over 200 cities, including Bergen

BRENNPUNKT KULTUR

(Norway), Novgorod (Russia), London (England), Bruges (Belgium), and Gdansk [Danzig] (Poland) joined the league and profited from the trade network. Strategically located on the Elbe River between the North and Baltic Seas, Hamburg became a hub of Hanseatic trade and has proudly maintained its role as a center of international trade into the 21st century.

From its center along the banks of the Alster, a river that forms large lakes in the center of the city, Hamburg revels in its maritime history and its position as Germany's window on the world. Being a port city has fostered a cosmopolitan image and a tolerant tradition for which Hamburg is famous. The copper-roofed, neo-renaissance city hall **(das Rathaus)** serves as the seat of city-state government and dominates the skyline from the Alster. The **Jungfernstieg** is home to Hamburg's most exclusive shops and hotels. It passes over the canals **(Fleete)** that crisscross Hamburg and leads to the main shopping street, **Mönckebergstraße. St. Pauli,** the harbor section, is home to the **St. Michaeliskirche (der Michel),** Hamburg's symbol **(das Wahrzeichen)** and largest Baroque church, as well as to **die Reeperbahn,** northern Europe's largest entertainment and red light district. The St. Pauli Fish Market **(der Fischmarkt)** is held every Sunday morning from six to ten o'clock. Hamburg was the birthplace of the composer Johannes Brahms and home of the author Gotthold Ephraim Lessing. Today, it enjoys a lively arts scene with over 20 theaters, the oldest opera house in Germany, three symphony orchestras, a ballet company, and numerous art museums and galleries. In addition, Hamburg is also home to one of Germany's largest urban universities **(die Universität Hamburg).** And not to be forgotten, Hamburg is the birthplace of the **Hamburger Steak,** chopped beef topped with a fried egg, which travelled to America, where it abandoned the egg but added a bun, mustard, and ketchup to become an American staple: the hamburger.

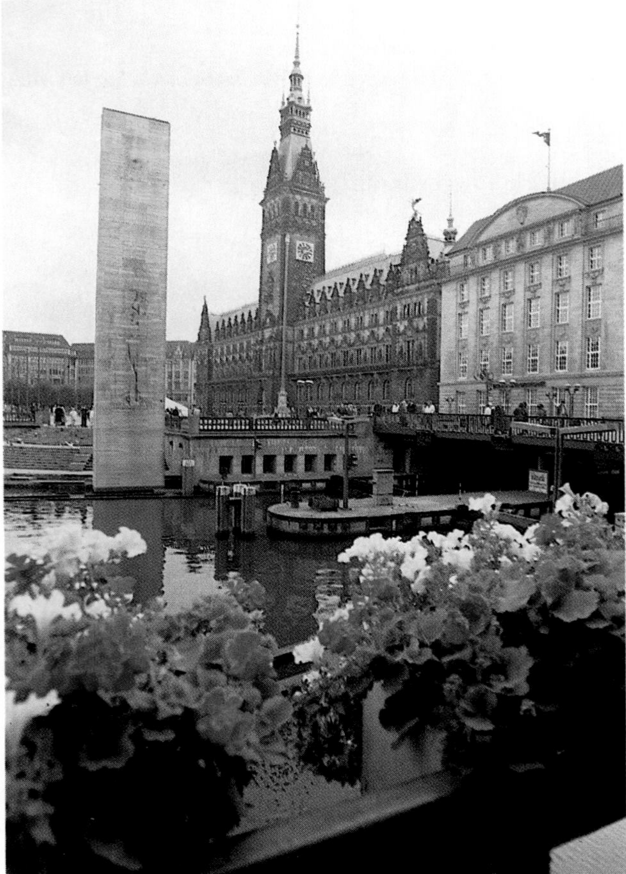

Das Hamburger Rathaus dominiert das Stadtbild von der Alster her.

Strukturen und Vokabeln

I Talking about past events

The conversational past

When speaking or writing informally about past events, German speakers often use the conversational past, which is also known as the present perfect tense **(das Perfekt).** The conversational past is formed with a present tense form of the auxiliary verb **haben** or **sein** and the past participle of the verb **(das Partizip).** The past participle is frequently, although not always, identifiable by a **ge-** prefix and either a **-t** or **-en** ending.

The formation of regular and irregular past participles is explained in section B below.

In general, the simple past is used more frequently (even in speaking) in northern regions, while the conversational past is used more frequently (even in writing) in southern regions.

Onkel Hannes **ist** in die Kneipe **gegangen.**	*Uncle Hannes went to the pub.*
Onkel Hannes **hat** Tante Uschi **geküsst.**	*Uncle Hannes kissed Aunt Uschi.*

The German conversational past (e.g., **hat geschrieben**) looks like the English present perfect *(has written),* but it does not have the same meaning. It is most commonly used for actions completed in the past. In contrast, the English present perfect expresses uncompleted actions that continue into the present.

The English term *present perfect* refers to the use of the present tense (auxiliary verb) and the perfect (past participle) verb forms (e.g., *I have eaten*).

German conversational past

Ich **habe** einen Brief **geschrieben.** — *I* ***wrote*** *a letter.*

English present perfect

I ***have known*** *him for three years.* — Ich **kenne** ihn seit drei Jahren.

For a discussion of the German form for the English present perfect, look up the paragraph *Talking about activities that continue from the past into the present* on p. 207 later in this chapter.

A few common verbs, such as **sein** *(to be)* and **haben** *(to have),* do not always occur in their conversational past forms, even in informal language. Instead, they frequently appear in the simple past forms: **war** *(was)* and **hatte** *(had).* You will learn more about the simple past in Chapter 10.

A. *The auxiliaries* haben *and* sein

German speakers use the two auxiliaries **haben** and **sein** with the conversational past. **Haben** is used most frequently. It is always used with any verb that takes a direct object.

The form of the past participle in no way affects whether one uses **haben** or **sein** as the auxiliary of the conversational past.

Tante Uschi **hat** in Hamburg studiert.	*Aunt Uschi went to college in Hamburg.*
Tante Uschi und Onkel Hannes **haben** Bier getrunken.	*Aunt Uschi and Uncle Hannes drank beer.*

Verbs that express a change of location require the auxiliary **sein.**

UNIVERSITÄT HAMBURG SEIT 1919 IN DER STADT

Infinitive		Conversational past	
fahren	*to drive; to go*	Ich bin gefahren.	*I drove; I went.*
fliegen	*to fly*	Ich bin geflogen.	*I flew.*
gehen	*to walk; to go*	Ich bin gegangen.	*I walked; I went.*
kommen	*to come*	Ich bin gekommen.	*I came.*
laufen	*to run*	Ich bin gelaufen.	*I ran.*
schwimmen	*to swim*	Ich bin geschwommen.	*I swam.*

When the verbs **fahren, fliegen,** and **schwimmen** are used with a direct object, they require **haben: Ich bin nach Hause gefahren** vs. **ich habe dein Auto gefahren.**

Verbs that express a change of condition also require **sein.** The verb **bleiben** *(to remain)* also uses **sein** even though it does not show a change of location, but instead the absence of a change of location.

Infinitive		Conversational past	
auf•stehen	*to get up*	Ich bin früh aufgestanden.	*I got up early.*
auf•wachen	*to wake up*	Ich bin aufgewacht.	*I woke up.*
bleiben	*to stay*	Wir sind zu Hause geblieben.	*We stayed home.*
ein•schlafen	*to fall asleep*	Ich bin eingeschlafen.	*I fell asleep.*
sterben	*to die*	Sie ist gestorben.	*She died.*
werden	*to become*	Sie ist böse geworden.	*She became angry.*

Formation of past participles of verbs with separable prefixes is explained in section C below.

Verbs requiring **sein** appear in the vocabulary lists with the auxiliary verb **ist,** e.g., **bleiben (ist geblieben):** *to stay, remain.*

The auxiliaries **haben** and **sein** are always conjugated to agree with the subject of the sentence. The past participle (e.g., **gegangen, eingeschlafen**) occurs at the end of the clause or sentence. The past participle never changes to agree with the subject or any other noun.

In standard German all verbs expressing non-motion, e.g., **stehen** *(to stand),* **sitzen** *(to sit),* **liegen** *(to lie, recline),* and **hängen** *(to hang),* use the auxiliary **haben.** However, in the southern regions these verbs use the auxiliary **sein.**

Tante Uschi und Onkel Hannes **sind** sonntags auf den Fischmarkt **gegangen.** — *Aunt Uschi and Uncle Hannes went to the fish market on Sundays.*

Georg **ist** vor dem Fernseher **eingeschlafen.** — *George fell asleep in front of the TV.*

Like all conjugated verbs, the forms of **haben** and **sein** occur in the second position in statements and in the first position in questions. The position of the subject has no influence on the position of the auxiliary verb. You will read more about German word order later in this chapter.

Statement	***Question***
Onkel Hannes (*subject*) **hat** Tante Uschi geküsst.	**Hat** Onkel Hannes (*subject*) Tante Uschi geküsst?
Bald danach **haben** sie (*subject*) geheiratet.	**Haben** sie (*subject*) bald danach geheiratet?
Tante Uschi (*subject*) **hat** als Kellnerin gearbeitet.	**Hat** Tante Uschi (*subject*) als Kellnerin gearbeitet?

10 **Was ist passiert°?** Verbinden Sie einen Satz in der linken Spalte° mit einem Satz in der rechten Spalte.

happened
column

1. Die Kellnerin ist heute Morgen sehr müde.
2. Tante Uschi ist heute Apothekerin° in Weinheim.
3. Hannelore Adler hat einen Brief von Anna.
4. Anna kann nicht schlafen.
5. Barbara und Anna finden den Film sehr gut.
6. Tante Uschi liebt Onkel Hannes.

pharmacist

a. Anna hat letzte Woche einen Brief geschrieben.
b. Onkel Hannes hat Tante Uschi geküsst.
c. Sie hat gestern Abend bis spät in der Kneipe gearbeitet.
d. Sie hat in Hamburg Pharmazie studiert.
e. Sie hat zu viel Kaffee getrunken.
f. Sie sind gestern ins Kino gegangen.

11 **Wo hast du studiert?** Ergänzen Sie diese Sätze mit den passenden Formen von **haben** und **sein.**

1. KARL: Wo _____ deine Eltern studiert?
2. BEATE: Mein Vater _____ in Heilbronn zur Schule gegangen, aber er _____ in München studiert.
3. KARL: Aber du _____ doch hier zur Schule gegangen, nicht?
4. BEATE: Eigentlich _____ ich in Amerika in den Kindergarten gegangen. Mein Vater _____ dort zwei Semester gearbeitet.
5. KARL: Wirklich? Was _____ er dort gemacht?
6. BEATE: Er _____ seine Dissertation geschrieben. Wir _____ ein Jahr in Cambridge in Massachusetts gelebt. Dort _____ ich Englisch gelernt.

B. *Past participles*

All verbs can be classified as regular (weak—**schwach**), irregular (strong—**stark**), or mixed (combining characteristics of weak and strong verbs—**gemischt**). Whether a verb is regular, irregular, or mixed affects the form of the past participle, particularly its stem and its ending.

1. Regular (weak) verbs

Regular (weak) verbs keep the unchanged present tense stem and add the **ge-** prefix and the ending **-t** to form the past participle. Verbs whose stem ends in **-t, -d, -gn,** or **-fn,** require the ending **-et** to form the past participle. All verbs ending in **-ieren** are regular (e.g., **studieren**) but do not add the prefix **ge-.** Verbs that have been recently incorporated into the German language are also regular (e.g., **faxen**).

Infinitive	Conversational past	
spielen	hat ge + spiel + **t**	Die Kinder haben gespielt.
arbeiten	hat ge + arbeit + **et**	Ich habe gearbeitet.
studieren	hat studier + **t**	Sie haben studiert.
faxen	hat ge + fax + **t**	Sie hat einen Brief gefaxt.
flirten	hat ge + flirt + **et**	Tante Uschi und Onkel Hannes haben geflirtet.
wandern	ist ge + wander + **t**	Anna ist viel gewandert.

12 **Katjas Freund Roland.** Hier erzählt Katja Anna, wie sie ihren Freund Roland kennen gelernt hat. Schreiben Sie das richtige Partizip.

arbeiten • kaufen • lernen • machen • öffnen • regnen • spielen

Ich habe Roland im Jugendklub kennen gelernt. Er hat dort als Kellner _____. Es war im September. Das Wetter draußen war miserabel. Es hat nämlich _____, und ich war total nass. Er hat mir die Tür _____, denn ich habe gerade im Kaufhaus viele Sachen _____ und ich hatte keine freie Hand. Er war ein richtiger Gentleman!

Danach haben wir viel zusammen _____. Für die Schule haben wir beide zusammen Mathe _____. Am Wochenende haben wir oft Tennis _____.

13 **Gestern Abend.** Was haben Barbara, Karl, Anna und Stefan gestern Abend gemacht? Fragen Sie einen Partner/eine Partnerin nach° einer Aktivität mit einem Fragezeichen. Beantworten Sie dann eine Frage von Ihrem Partner/Ihrer Partnerin.

about

S1: Was hat Barbara gestern Abend gemacht?
S2: Sie hat Spaghetti gekocht.
Und was hat Stefan gemacht?
S1: Er hat gebadet.

Partner(in) 1:

	Gespielt	Gemacht	Gelernt
Barbara	Billard gespielt	?	Mathe gelernt
Stefan	?	gebadet	?
Karl	Karten gespielt	?	Physik gelernt
Anna	?	zu Hause gearbeitet	?

Partner(in) 2:

	Gespielt	Gemacht	Gelernt
Barbara	?	Spaghetti gekocht	?
Stefan	Tischtennis gespielt	?	nichts gelernt
Karl	?	ein Buch gekauft	?
Anna	Gitarre gespielt	?	Deutsch gelernt

2. Irregular (strong) and mixed verbs

Irregular (also called strong) verbs generally include the **ge-** prefix and always have the ending **-en** in the past participle. The vowel in the present tense stem may or may not change. There is no way to recognize which verbs change the stem vowel in the past participle. They must be memorized.

Infinitive	*Conversational past*
g**e**ben	hat geg**eben**
l**e**sen	hat gel**esen**
g**e**hen	ist geg**angen**
tr**i**nken	hat getr**unken**

You will need to memorize the stem changes of irregular and mixed verbs. Some English verbs can help you remember the German verb forms (e.g., *speak, spoken:* **sprechen, gesprochen**). Irregular and mixed verbs undergo the same stem changes when they appear with or without prefixes, e.g., **nehmen** *(to take):* **genommen; annehmen** *(to assume):* **angenommen.** There are approximately 35 high-frequency irregular and mixed verbs.

Mixed verbs combine features of both regular and irregular verbs to form their past participles. Like regular verbs they add a **-t** and like some irregular verbs they change the stem vowel in the past participle.

Infinitive	*Conversational past*
d**e**nken	hat ged**acht**

The following list shows irregular and mixed verbs with their stem changes. You will find the complete list of irregular and mixed verbs in the Appendix.

	Infinitive	**Conversational past**	
No stem-vowel change	**e**ssen	hat geg**e**ssen	Hast du gegessen?
	f**a**hren	ist gef**a**hren	Sie ist gefahren.
	g**e**ben	hat geg**e**ben	Ich habe Frau Lange nichts gegeben.
	l**au**fen	ist gel**au**fen	Klaus ist gelaufen.
	l**e**sen	hat gel**e**sen	Haben Sie das Buch gelesen?
ei > ie	schr**ei**ben	hat geschr**ie**ben	Anna hat einen Brief geschrieben.
e > a	g**e**hen	ist geg**a**ngen	Er ist nach Hause gegangen.
	d**e**nken	hat ged**a**cht *(mixed)*	Was hat sie gedacht?
	k**e**nnen	hat gek**a**nnt *(mixed)*	Hat er dich gekannt?
	st**e**hen	hat gest**a**nden	Wir haben hier gestanden.
e > o	n**e**hmen	hat gen**o**mmen	Petra hat es genommen.
	spr**e**chen	hat gespr**o**chen	Die Studenten haben Deutsch gesprochen.
i > o	beg**i**nnen	hat beg**o**nnen	Der Kurs hat schon begonnen.
i > u	f**i**nden	hat gef**u**nden	Herr Meyer hat sein Auto gefunden.
	tr**i**nken	hat getr**u**nken	Habt ihr alles getrunken?
	w**i**ssen	hat gew**u**sst *(mixed)*	Ich habe das nicht gewusst.

nehmen: Note the change in consonant spelling in the past participle: **mm.**

14 **Eine Zeittafel°.** Lesen Sie Annas Zeittafel und schreiben Sie dann Ihre eigene Zeittafel. Erzählen Sie einem Partner/einer Partnerin von Ihrem Leben.

time line

S1: Anna ist 1982 geboren. Ich bin ... geboren.
S2: Annas Bruder ist 1986 geboren. Meine Schwester ist ... geboren.

	Anna Adler	*Ich*
1982	ist geboren	______
1986	Jeff (Bruder) ist geboren	______
1987	hat die Schule begonnen	______
1992	hat eine Reise nach Florida gemacht	______
1999	ist nach Kanada gefahren	______
1996	hat im Softballtournier° in Kalifornien gespielt	______
2000	ist zur Uni gegangen	______
2001	ist nach Deutschland geflogen	______

Note that past participles can be used as adjectives. **Ist geboren** (infinitive: **gebären**) is not a conversational past form, but the verb **sein** + a past participle **(geboren)** used as an adjective. **Gebären** is a verb that takes **haben** as its present perfect auxiliary.

Tournier: *tournament*

15 **Autogrammspiel: Was hast du heute gemacht?** Finden Sie für jede° Frage eine Person, die mit **Ja** antwortet. Bitten Sie jede Person um ihre Unterschrift.

each

S1: Hast du heute Kaffee getrunken?
S2: Ja.
S1: Unterschreib hier bitte. ____________________

1. Kaffee getrunken ____________________
2. Hausaufgaben gemacht ____________________
3. eine Pizza gegessen ____________________
4. zur Universität gefahren ____________________
5. das Bett gemacht ____________________
6. Musik gehört ____________________
7. eine Zeitung gekauft ____________________
8. Vokabeln gelernt ____________________
9. gut geschlafen ____________________
10. Deutsch gesprochen ____________________

16 **Übertreibungen°.** Ein alter Freund beschreibt seine Kindheit°, aber er übertreibt auch gern. Sie müssen ihn oft an die Realität erinnern.

exaggerations
childhood

perfekt Deutsch sprechen / ein bisschen Deutsch sprechen

S1 (DER FREUND): Ich habe perfekt Deutsch gesprochen.
S2 (SIE): Nein, du hast ein bisschen Deutsch gesprochen.

1. ein Auto kaufen/ein Fahrrad kaufen
2. viele Bücher lesen/Comichefte lesen
3. jeden Abend ein Bier trinken/jeden Morgen Orangensaft trinken
4. gesund° essen/ungesund essen
5. immer zur Schule laufen/immer zur Schule fahren
6. nie am Wochenende zu Hause bleiben/oft am Wochenende zu Hause fernsehen
7. das Abendessen immer kochen/das Abendessen nie kochen
8. viele Briefe schreiben/keine Briefe schreiben

healthy

C. *Prefixes of past participles*

Most verbs add the prefix **ge-** to form the past participle.

Onkel Hannes hat nie Trinkgeld **ge**geben. — *Uncle Hannes never gave tips.*
Sie haben zusammen ein Bier **ge**trunken. — *They drank a beer together.*

Verbs with separable prefixes insert **-ge-** between the prefix and the verb stem (e.g., **einladen, hat eingeladen**). Two types of verbs do not use **ge-** to form their past participles—verbs that end in **-ieren** (e.g., **studieren, hat studiert**) and verbs with inseparable prefixes such as **be-** (e.g., **besuchen, hat besucht**), **ent-** (e.g., **entscheiden, hat entschieden**), **er-** (e.g., **erkennen, hat erkannt**), **ge-** (e.g., **gefallen, hat gefallen**), **ver-** (e.g., **vergessen, hat vergessen**), and **zer-** (e.g., **zerstören** *[to destroy]*, **hat zerstört**).

The most common separable prefixes are: **ab, an, auf, aus, ein, mit, um, zu, zurück.**

1. Separable-prefix verbs

Verbs with separable prefixes insert **ge-** between the prefix and the stem.

Onkel Hannes hat Tante Uschi ins Theater ein**ge**laden. — *Uncle Hannes invited Aunt Uschi to the theater.*

Here is a list of past participles of common verbs with separable prefixes. The stress is always on the prefix in the infinitive, as well as in the past participle forms.

Infinitive	Conversational past	
an·fangen	hat an + **ge** + fangen	Der Film hat schon angefangen.
an·kommen	ist an + **ge** + kommen	Magda ist schon angekommen.
an·rufen	hat an + **ge** + rufen	Anna hat uns angerufen.
auf·hören	hat auf + **ge** + hört	Der Professor hat gerade aufgehört.
auf·stehen	ist auf + **ge** + standen	Wann bist du aufgestanden?
aus·geben	hat aus + **ge** + geben	Hast du viel Geld ausgegeben?
aus·gehen	ist aus + **ge** + gangen	Claudia ist mit Karl ausgegangen.
aus·sehen	hat aus + **ge** + sehen	Ihr habt gut ausgesehen.
durch·machen	hat durch + **ge** + macht	Sie haben die Nacht durchgemacht.
ein·kaufen	hat ein + **ge** + kauft	Katja hat viel eingekauft.
ein·laden	hat ein + **ge** + laden	Wen hast du zur Party eingeladen?
fern·sehen	hat fern + **ge** + sehen	Wir haben ferngesehen.
kennen lernen	hat kennen **ge** + lernt	Ich habe ihn in Tübingen kennen gelernt.
mit·bringen	hat mit + **ge** + bracht	Sie haben nichts mitgebracht.
spazieren gehen	ist spazieren **ge** + gangen	Wir sind spazieren gegangen.
zurück·kommen	ist zurück + **ge** + kommen	Franz ist schon zurückgekommen.

17 **Ein Einkaufsbummel° in Hamburg.** Es ist Abend. Onkel Hannes und Tante Uschi besuchen Hamburg. Katja ist zu Hause in Weinheim. Katja spricht am Telefon mit ihrer Mutter. Ein Student/Eine Studentin spielt Katja, ein Partner/eine Partnerin spielt ihre Mutter. Was sagt Katja? Was sagt Tante Uschi?

shopping spree

S1 (KATJA): Was hast du heute gemacht, Mama?
S2 (TANTE USCHI): Ich bin früh aufgestanden. Und was hast du gemacht, Katja?
S1 (KATJA): Ich habe lange geschlafen. Und was hast du noch° gemacht, Mama?

***was noch:** what else*

Partner(in) 1 (Katja):

Katja	Tante Uschi
ausgeschlafen	?
zur Schule losgefahren	?
heimgekommen	?
mit Claudia ferngesehen	?

Partner(in) 2 (Tante Uschi):

Katja	Tante Uschi
?	früh aufgestanden
?	an der Elbe spazieren gegangen
?	viele Sachen eingekauft
?	viel Geld ausgegeben
?	mit Papa ausgegangen

18 **Interview.** Stellen Sie einem Partner/einer Partnerin die folgenden Fragen.

S1: Hast du heute gut geschlafen?
S2: Nein, ich bin früh aufgestanden.

1. Hast du heute gut geschlafen?
2. Wann bist du aufgestanden?
3. Wann bist du zur Uni losgefahren?
4. Wann bist du gestern zurückgekommen?
5. Hast du heute oder gestern eingekauft?
6. Wie viel Geld hast du gestern ausgegeben?
7. Hast du gestern Abend ferngesehen oder bist du ausgegangen?
8. Wann hast du zuletzt deine Eltern angerufen?

2. Inseparable-prefix and -ieren verbs

Here is a list of past participles of common verbs with inseparable prefixes and verbs ending in **-ieren.** The stress is not on the inseparable prefix but rather on the stem vowel, as in **verstéhen.**

-ieren/-iert is always stressed.

Infinitive	Conversational past	
bedeuten	hat bedeutet	Das hat nichts bedeutet.
besuchen	hat besucht	Er hat uns besucht.
gefallen	hat gefallen	Der Film hat Anna gefallen.
verbringen	hat verbracht	Sie hat ein Jahr in Afrika verbracht.
verdienen	hat verdient	Uschi hat viel Geld verdient.
vergessen	hat vergessen	Monika hat Annas Geburtstag vergessen.
verlieben	hat verliebt	Sie hat sich in ihn verliebt.
verloben	hat verlobt	Sie haben sich verlobt.
versöhnen°	hat versöhnt	Klaus und Marga haben sich versöhnt.
buchstabieren°	hat buchstabiert	Fabian hat das Wort richtig buchstabiert.
diskutieren	hat diskutiert	Sie haben Politik diskutiert.
irritieren	hat irritiert	Die Kinder haben uns irritiert.
studieren	hat studiert	Wo hat Franz in den USA studiert?

to reconcile
to spell

19 **Das Happy-End: Ein Rätsel°.** Onkel Hannes und Tante Uschi haben einander in Hamburg kennen gelernt. Sie sind jetzt 25 Jahre verheiratet. Zum 25. Hochzeitstag° besuchen sie die Stadt wieder. Rekonstruieren Sie mit einem Partner/einer Partnerin die korrekte Reihenfolge der Geschichte von Uschi Kunz und Hannes Günther in Hamburg.

riddle
wedding anniversary

Vor 25 Jahren

___ Hannes Günther und Uschi Kunz haben sich verliebt.
___ Sie haben sich verlobt.
_1_ Uschi hat in Hamburg Pharmazie studiert.
___ Uschi hat als Kellnerin wenig Geld verdient.
___ Sie sind im Regen spazieren gegangen.
___ Hannes hat Uschi ins Theater eingeladen.

Gestern

___ Am Abend haben sie das Hamburger Ballett besucht.
___ Onkel Hannes hat die Karten im Hotel vergessen und Tante Uschi war irritiert.
___ Sie haben das Ballett nicht verstanden.
___ Onkel Hannes hat die Karten wieder gefunden und sie haben sich versöhnt.
_1_ Sie haben den Tag an der Alster verbracht.
___ Sie haben in einer Kneipe etwas getrunken und über Ballett diskutiert.

D. Past participles of sein *and* haben

The past participle of **sein** is **gewesen.** The past participle of **haben** is **gehabt.**

Tante Uschi **ist** in Hamburg Studentin **gewesen.**	*Aunt Uschi was a student in Hamburg.*
Du **hast** eine ganz schlimme Erkältung **gehabt.**	*You had a really bad cold.*

The simple past tense forms of **sein (war)** and **haben (hatte),** discussed in Chapter 10, are also frequently used to express the past tense in speaking.

Er **hat** Geburtstag **gehabt.** Er **hatte** Geburtstag.	*He had a birthday.*
Sie **ist** krank **gewesen.** Sie **war** krank.	*She was sick.*

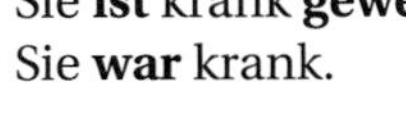

Meine Kindheit. Bilden Sie Sätze über Ihre Kindheit.

Als Kind bin ich selten krank° gewesen. — *sick*
Als Kind habe ich viele Erkältungen gehabt.

Mit sein	*Mit haben*	
1. oft/selten krank	6. wenige/viele Erkältungen	
2. in Europa (Mexiko, Kanada usw.)	7. Masern°, Windpocken°	*measles / chicken pox*
3. sehr aktiv/sehr ruhig	8. viele/wenige Spielsachen°	*toys*
4. sehr sportlich/nicht sehr sportlich	9. viele/ein paar Spielkameraden°	*playmates*
5. oft im Kino/selten im Kino	10. viele/wenige Regeln°	*rules*

21 Herr Günthers Geschäftsreise°. Ergänzen Sie diese Sätze mit der korrekten Partizipform.

business trip

Herr Günther war letzte Woche auf Geschäftsreise in München. Dort hat er die letzten fünf Tage _____ (verbringen). Er ist gestern Abend aus München _____ (zurückkommen). Er ist um 21.15 Uhr am Bahnhof in Weinheim _____ (ankommen). In München hat er mit Kollegen an einem Projekt _____ (arbeiten). Das Projekt haben sie vor einem Jahr _____ (anfangen). Die beiden Kollegen haben viel _____ (diskutieren). Aber zum Schluss haben beide sehr gut an dem Projekt _____ (verdienen).

In München hat Herr Günther auch etwas Zeit für die Sehenswürdigkeiten _____ (haben). Am Samstag hat er das BMW-Museum _____ (besuchen). Dort hat er viele alte Autos und Flugzeuge _____ (sehen). Er ist sehr lange im Museum _____ (bleiben). Für seine Kinder hat er auch Andenken _____ (kaufen). Für Georg hat er ein Buch über den BMW Autokonzern _____ (finden). Für Katja hat er eine CD mit südamerikanischer Flötenmusik _____ (mitbringen). Seine Frau hat er auch nicht _____ (vergessen). Für sie hat er einen Schal° _____ (kaufen). Er hat relativ viel Geld _____ (ausgeben).

scarf

Wissenswerte Vokabeln: das Wetter

Describing weather conditions

☼	sonnig
☼☁	heiter

Heute ist es | sonnig.
heiter.

Die Sonne scheint.

Es wird heiß und schwül. Die Temperatur liegt um vierundreißig Grad Celsius.

W. Vok. Use this formula to convert Fahrenheit temperatures to centigrade **(Celsius):** F – 32 × 5/9. Use this formula to convert centigrade to Fahrenheit: C × 9/5 + 32.

Heute ist es | wolkig.
bedeckt.
windig.

Es gibt | viele Wolken.
Nebel.

Es wird kühl. Die Temperatur liegt um zehn Grad Celsius.

Die Sonne hat gestern geschienen.

Es hat gestern viele Wolken gegeben.

Heute regnet es.
Wir haben Regen.
Es gibt | Schauer.
Gewitter.
Es donnert und blitzt.

Es ist | ganz nass.
wirklich mies.

Es wird aber warm. Die Temperatur liegt um zwanzig Grad Celsius.

Gestern hat es geregnet, gedonnert und geblitzt.

Heute schneit es.
Wir haben Schnee.
Es wird kalt. Die Temperatur liegt um null Grad Celsius (um den Gefrierpunkt).
Morgen soll es sonnig, aber kalt sein.
Wie ist das Wetter heute?

Gestern hat es viel geschneit.

22 **Wie ist das Wetter in Oslo?** Das Wetter in Tübingen ist momentan nicht so gut. Anna sucht schönes Wetter! Sie liest die *Frankfurter Allgemeine Zeitung* und findet den Wetterbericht für Europa. Beantworten Sie die Fragen.

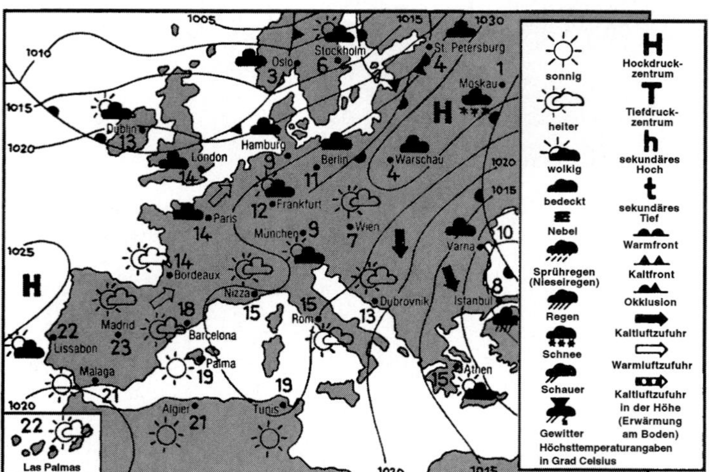

S1: Wie ist das Wetter in Oslo?
S2: In Oslo ist es bedeckt. Die Temperatur liegt um drei Grad.

1. Wien
2. Dublin
3. Bordeaux
4. Moskau
5. Rom
6. Istanbul
7. Athen
8. Madrid
9. München
10. Berlin
11. Nizza

23 **Das Wetter hier.** Beantworten Sie die Fragen.

1. Wie ist das Wetter heute?
2. Wie ist das Wetter gestern gewesen?
3. Wann hat es zuletzt° geregnet?
4. Wann hat es zuletzt geschneit?
5. Haben wir heute Morgen Nebel gehabt?
6. Wie soll das Wetter morgen (und übermorgen) sein?

°*last*

Wissenswerte Vokabeln: die Jahreszeiten

Talking about the seasons

der Frühling

der Sommer

der Herbst

der Winter

Wie ist das Wetter im Winter?

24 **Fragen zum Wetter.** Stellen Sie einem Partner/einer Partnerin diese Fragen über das Wetter.

1. Wie ist das Wetter heute?
2. Was ist die Temperatur heute in Fahrenheit? In Celsius?
3. Wie ist das Wetter im Winter?
4. Wann regnet es hier am meisten?
5. Ist es heute bedeckt oder heiter?
6. Wann haben wir das beste Wetter? Warum meinst du das?
7. Wann regnet es oft in Seattle?
8. Wie ist es im Sommer in Atlanta?
9. Wie ist das Wetter im Herbst im Mittelwesten?
10. Wann ist das Wetter hier sehr schlecht?

Vocabulary that might be important for your region: **der Sturm** *(storm)*, **der Orkan** *(hurricane)*, **der Tornado** *(tornado)*, **der Wirbelsturm** *(whirlwind)*.

Weather in Seattle is similar to that in Hamburg — lots of rain. Germany does not usually experience extreme cold or hot weather.

FREIE KOMMUNIKATION **Rollenspiel: Gestern Abend.** Sie treffen einen Freund/eine Freundin an der Uni. Der Freund/die Freundin sieht sehr müde aus°. Beginnen Sie die Konversation mit „Guten Tag". Stellen Sie dann die Frage: „Wie geht's?" Der Freund/Die Freundin erzählt, was er/sie gestern Abend gemacht hat. Hier sind einige Ideen.

looks

Freie Kommunikation. Remember to use the informal **du-** and **ihr-**forms of the verbs when talking to one another.

nicht so gut geschlafen	bis spät gearbeitet
für eine Prüfung gelernt	Basketball gespielt
in die Kneipe gegangen	Hausaufgaben gemacht
eine Party besucht	die ganze Nacht mit Freunden telefoniert

Rollenspiel: Letzten Sommer. Sie treffen einen Freund/eine Freundin und sprechen über letzten Sommer. Beginnen Sie die Konversation mit: „Hallo." Hier sind einige Ideen.

im Sommer gemacht	zum Strand° gefahren
fast immer geregnet	die Sonne hat geschienen
Wasserski gefahren	Baseball gespielt
eine Reise gemacht	mit Freunden ausgegangen
nichts Interessantes gemacht	viel gearbeitet und wenig verdient

beach

Ein Pechtag°. Beschreiben Sie einen Tag, an dem nichts gut gegangen ist. Hier sind einige Ideen.

unlucky, bad day

zu spät aufgestanden	kein Buch gehabt
Wasser nur kalt gewesen	Geld vergessen
kein Brot im Haus gehabt	Freunde nicht gekommen
keinen freien Platz gefunden	usw.

Schreibecke **Einen Brief schreiben.** Sie sind heute nicht in den Deutschkurs gekommen. Schreiben Sie Ihrem Lehrer/Ihrer Lehrerin einen kurzen Brief. Erklären Sie, warum Sie nicht da waren. Was haben Sie gemacht?

zu lange schlafen° • Auto kaputt • das Buch vergessen • Hausaufgaben nicht machen • krank sein

zu ... schlafen: oversleep

Lieber Herr ... (Liebe Frau ...)

Later in this chapter you will learn more about *subordinate word order.* Certain conjunctions, such as **was** *(which, that)* trigger this word order pattern and the conjugated verb occurs at the end of the clause. However, in colloquial German, the conjugated verb frequently does not occur in the last position, as in this **Absprungtext.**

ABSPRUNGTEXT
„Ein Freund, ein guter Freund ... das ist das Schönste, was es gibt auf der Welt"

Anna liest einen Artikel über Freunde im *Jugendmagazin.* Sie ist daran interessiert, denn sie hat auch neue Freunde kennen gelernt.

Vorschau

25 Thematische Fragen: Eigenschaften eines Freundes/einer Freundin. Welche Dinge finden Sie gut, welche schlecht für Freundschaften, und welche sind nicht wichtig?

	Gut	*Schlecht*	*Nicht wichtig*
1. Vertrauen° haben	___	___	___
2. über alles reden können	___	___	___
3. eifersüchtig° sein	___	___	___
4. gleiche Interessen haben	___	___	___
5. treu° sein	___	___	___
6. ehrlich° sein	___	___	___
7. oft zusammen sein	___	___	___
8. spontan sein	___	___	___
9. nie Krach° haben	___	___	___
10. alles besser wissen	___	___	___
11. immer die gleiche Meinung° haben	___	___	___
12. tolerant und offen sein	___	___	___
13. viel Geld haben	___	___	___

trust

jealous

faithful

honest

quarrel

***gleiche Meinung:** same opinion*

26 Satzdetektiv. Welche Sätze bedeuten ungefähr das Gleiche?

Satzdetektiv. Look for similarities in meaning between two German sentences. Guessing at the meaning of words from the context of other words is an essential reading skill. These sentences feature important words.

1. Welche **Eigenschaften** müssen Freunde haben?
2. Dirk ist mit Michaela **verlobt.**
3. Außerdem sind die drei Freunde in einer **Clique.**
4. Ich habe **Vertrauen** zu ihm.

a. Ich sage ihm alles.
b. Welche Qualitäten müssen Freunde haben?
c. Dirk und Michaela möchten heiraten.
d. Die drei Freunde sind zusammen in einer Gruppe.

---

5. Sie hat **hinter meinem Rücken** über mich geredet.
6. Ein guter Freund muss **zu mir stehen** und mit mir **durch dick und dünn** gehen.
7. So ein Gespräch kommt meistens ganz **spontan.**
8. Einer fängt an, dann erzählen die anderen von ihren **Erfahrungen.**

e. Ein guter Freund ist immer treu und für mich da.
f. Sie hat schlechte Dinge über mich gesagt.
g. Jemand beginnt, und dann sprechen die Freunde über ihr Leben.
h. Wir reden° automatisch und natürlich miteinander.

talk

---

9. Als ich mich von meiner ersten Freundin **getrennt habe,** haben sie mir sehr geholfen.
10. Es gibt auch schon mal **Krach.**
11. Wir sind jetzt in dem Alter, in dem wir **vernünftig** miteinander reden können.

i. Wir können über alles sprechen.
j. Das Mädchen ist nicht mehr meine Freundin, aber meine Freunde sind immer für mich da.
k. Es gibt auch Streit.

ABSPRUNGTEXT

„Ein Freund, ein guter Freund … das ist das Schönste, was es gibt auf der Welt"

Lesen Sie jetzt den Text.

„Ein Freund, ein guter Freund, das ist das Schönste, was es gibt auf der Welt!" So heißt es jedenfalls in einem alten deutschen Schlager°. Stimmt das? Was bedeuten Euch Freunde? Welche Eigenschaften müssen sie haben? ... Nils, Lars und Dirk aus Brühl/Deutschland kennen sich schon seit Jahren. Dirk ist mit Michaela verlobt. Außerdem sind die drei in einer Clique: gute Freunde, mit denen sie fast ihre ganze Freizeit verbringen. *JUMA* hat sie zum Thema „Freundschaft" gefragt.

der Song, das Lied

Michaela, 18 Jahre

„Für mich ist mein Freund [=Dirk] wichtiger als meine beste Freundin. Ich habe Vertrauen zu ihm. Man kann über alles reden°, immer zu ihm kommen. Dirk habe ich in der Disko kennengelernt. Er hat mich angesprochen. Wir kennen uns seit drei Jahren. Seit $1^1/_2$ Jahren sind wir verlobt. Als ich Dirk kennengelernt habe, bekam° ich Probleme mit meiner Freundin. Die war enttäuscht, daß ich keine Zeit mehr für sie hatte. Sie hat hinter meinem Rücken über mich geredet. Dirk und ich haben gleiche Interessen, machen alles zusammen. Auch die Clique ist sehr wichtig. Man braucht Freunde. Wir sind fast jeden Abend zusammen."

sprechen

habe bekommen

Nils, 19 Jahre

„Ein guter Freund muß zu mir stehen, mit mir durch dick und dünn gehen. Mit einem Mädchen geht das nicht so gut. Mit meinen Freunden kann ich über alles reden, mit meiner Freundin nicht. Sie verstehen meine Probleme. Ich glaube, es ist leichter, eine Freundin zu finden als einen guten Freund."

Dirk, 20 Jahre
„Mit Nils und Lars kann ich über alles reden. Auch, wenn ich Probleme mit meiner Freundin Michaela habe. So ein Gespräch kommt meistens ganz spontan. Einer fängt an°, dann erzählen die anderen von ihren Erfahrungen, und so geht das weiter. Ich glaube, die besten Freunde findet man in der Schulzeit. Danach habe ich kaum noch jemanden° kennengelernt."

fängt an: beginnt

anybody

Lars, 19 Jahre
„Nils und Dirk sind meine besten Freunde. Wir kennen uns schon seit der Schulzeit. Wir können über alles reden. Meine Freunde sind für alles da. Als ich mich von meiner ersten Freundin getrennt habe, haben sie mir sehr geholfen. Wir sind fast wie Brüder. Man sieht uns immer zusammen. Es gibt auch schon mal Krach. Wir sind aber jetzt in dem Alter, in dem wir vernünftig miteinander reden können."

Rückblick

27 **Stimmt das?** Stimmen diese Aussagen zum Text oder nicht? Wenn nicht, was stimmt?

	Ja, das stimmt.	*Nein, das stimmt nicht.*
Michaela		
1. Sie hat Dirk in der Schule kennen gelernt.	___	___
2. Für Michaela ist Dirk wichtiger als ihre beste Freundin.	___	___
3. Michaela hat Dirk zuerst angesprochen.	___	___
4. Sie wollen heiraten.	___	___
5. Michaelas beste Freundin mag Dirk und hat nie Probleme gehabt.	___	___
6. Michaela und Dirk haben die gleichen Interessen und machen alles zusammen.	___	___

	Ja, das stimmt.	*Nein, das stimmt nicht.*
Nils, Dirk, Lars		
7. Für Nils ist eine Freundin wichtiger als ein Freund.	___	___
8. Ein guter Freund muss zu Nils stehen, durch dick und dünn gehen.	___	___
9. Nils meint, seine Freunde verstehen seine Probleme besser als seine Freundin.	___	___
10. Für Nils und Lars sind viele Themen tabu.	___	___
11. Dirk meint, auch nach der Schulzeit kann man viele gute Freunde finden.	___	___
12. Lars, Dirk und Nils sind die besten Freunde und kennen einander seit der Schulzeit.	___	___
13. Die drei jungen Männer verstehen einander nicht immer – es gibt manchmal° Krach.	___	___

sometimes

28 Ergänzen Sie. Ergänzen Sie diese Sätze mit Wörtern aus dem **Absprungtext.**

Ergänzen Sie. Unlike previous **Ergänzen Sie** activities, many of these sentences are paraphrases of sentences from the text.

1. „Ein Freund, ein guter Freund, das ist das Schönste, was es gibt auf der ______."
2. Dirk, Nils und Lars kennen sich ______ seit Jahren.
3. Sie sind zusammen in einer ______ und verbringen fast ihre ganze Freizeit zusammen.
4. Für Michaela ist Dirk ______ als ihre beste Freundin.
5. Ihre beste Freundin war ______, dass Michaela keine Zeit mehr für sie hatte.
6. Dirk und Michaela haben gleiche ______ und machen alles ______.
7. Nils meint, ein guter Freund muss zu ihm stehen, durch dick und ______ gehen.
8. Dirk kann mit seinen Freunden über alles ______, auch über Michaela.
9. So ein ______ kommt meistens ganz spontan.
10. Nils und Dirk haben Lars geholfen, als er sich von seiner ersten Freundin ______ hat.
11. Lars sagt, es gibt schon mal ______.
12. Aber sie sind jetzt in dem Alter, in dem sie ______ miteinander reden können.

29 Interview: Der beste Freund/Die beste Freundin. Stellen Sie einem Partner/einer Partnerin die folgenden Fragen.

1. Wie heißt dein bester Freund/deine beste Freundin?
2. Wie lange kennt ihr einander?
3. Wo habt ihr einander kennen gelernt?
4. Welche Eigenschaften an dieser Person findest du am besten°?
5. Habt ihr gleiche oder andere Interessen?
6. Könnt ihr miteinander über Gefühle° reden?
7. Was macht ihr am liebsten miteinander?
8. Was macht ihr nie miteinander?

***am besten:** the best*

feelings

BRENNPUNKT KULTUR

Bekannte versus Freunde

In North America the formality of relationships between adults is not as clearly indicated with language as in German. In America, colleagues usually address each other by their first names, and even doctors sometimes call their patients by their first names. This seems quite forward to German speakers who often work together for long periods of time without calling each other by their first names or switching to the familiar **du.**

In North America it is also common to call most of the people you know reasonably well your "friends." German speakers distinguish between two types of "friends." **Bekannte** *(acquaintances)* may be people you know quite well or those you have seen only once in your life: classmates, co-workers, members of a club, or people you know only superficially. Even when the first name is used, a **Bekanntschaft** *(acquaintance relationship)* of this type maintains a certain emotional distance as indicated by the continued use of **Sie.** While German speakers may have many **Bekannte,** they have only a few **Freunde.** A **Freund** or **Freundin** is an intimate friend or a person with whom one shares a very special, permanent bond that is rare and treasured.

In the relatively stable, less mobile cultures of central Europe, students often go through school with the same classmates, growing up together and evolving into a close circle of friends **(der Freundeskreis, eine Clique).** Whether they are of the same sex or opposite sex, such **Freunde** acquired in school often become close friends for life. When a **Bekanntschaft** among adults evolves into a **Freundschaft,** the new friends may acknowledge their special relationship with a ceremonial drink **(Brüderschaft trinken).** This also indicates they will now use **du** with each other. Close friends of this type are usually referred to as **ein Freund von mir/eine Freundin von mir.** When German speakers refer to **mein Freund** or **meine Freundin,** they are talking about the person with whom they have a more intimate, even romantic relationship.

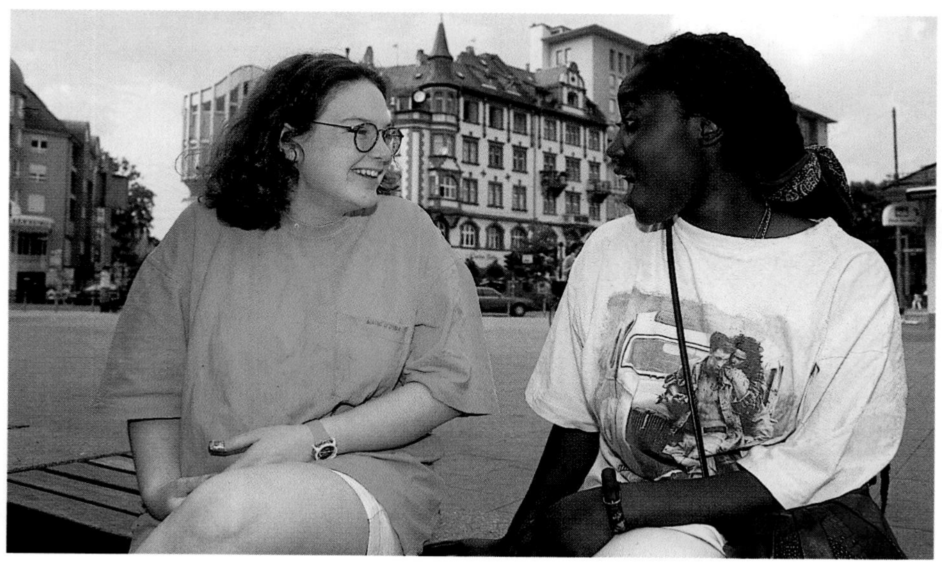

Meine Freundin heißt Annette.

30 Diskussion zu dritt: Zusammen ausgehen. In Europa geht man oft mit einer Gruppe aus. Bilden Sie eine Gruppe von drei Personen. Diskutieren Sie, welche Dinge man besser zu zweit° macht und welche man in der Gruppe machen kann. Welche Dinge machen Sie alle lieber zu zweit, welche lieber in der Gruppe?

***zu zweit:** as a couple*

S1: Gehst du lieber zu zweit oder in einer Gruppe ins Kino?
S2: Ich gehe lieber zu zweit ins Kino. Und du?
S3: Ich gehe auch lieber zu zweit ins Kino. *(oder)*
Ich gehe lieber in einer Gruppe ins Kino.

	Aktivität	*Zu zweit*	*In der Gruppe*
1.	ins Kino gehen	—	—
2.	tanzen	—	—
3.	in ein Restaurant gehen	—	—
4.	spazieren gehen	—	—
5.	fernsehen	—	—
6.	für eine Vorlesung lernen	—	—
7.	...	—	—

Wissenswerte Vokabeln: Freundschaft und Liebe

Describing personal relationships

Sie sieht gut aus.
Er findet sie attraktiv.

Sie spricht ihn an.
Sie flirtet mit ihm.

Sie umarmt ihn.
Er küsst sie. Sie küsst ihn.
Sie schmusen.

Sie mögen einander. Sie haben einander gern. Er hat sie gern. Sie hat ihn gern.

Sie verlieben sich ineinander. Es wird ernst. Er zieht ein. Sie leben zusammen.

Sie haben Krach miteinander.

Er hat Liebeskummer.

Sie versöhnen sich.

Sie verloben sich.

Sie lernen die Verwandten kennen.

Sie heiraten: Sie werden Mann und Frau.

Wie findest du sie/ihn?

W. Vok. Although the German reference to one's husband or wife as **mein Mann** or **meine Frau** may strike you as odd, it is in fact correct German.

Additional vocabulary: schwul *(gay)*, **lesbisch** *(lesbian)*

Sprache im Alltag: Expressing fondness or love

German speakers use three expressions to describe fondness or love for a person. Expressions with **mögen** or **gern haben** indicate fondness, those with **lieben** mostly romantic love.

Ich hab' dich gern.	*I like you.*
Ich mag dich.	*I like you.*
Ich liebe dich.	*I love you.*

31 Ein Liebesgedicht. Schreiben Sie ein Liebesgedicht mit sechs Zeilen und lesen Sie dann das Gedicht der Klasse vor. Bilden Sie Sätze mit den folgenden Verben.

geheiratet	schön ausgesehen	angesprochen
ernst geworden	geküsst	attraktiv gefunden
gut ausgesehen	geschmust	sich verliebt
Liebeskummer gehabt	sich verlobt	angesehen

Er hat gut ausgesehen.

32 Aktivitäten mit Freunden. Kreuzen Sie an, wie oft Sie die folgenden Aktivitäten mit einem (Ihrem) Freund/mit einer (Ihrer) Freundin im letzten Jahr gemacht haben. Dann fragen Sie einen Partner/eine Partnerin.

Aktivitäten mit Freunden. Remember that **ein Freund/eine Freundin** generally refer to good friends while **mein Freund/meine Freundin** mostly refer to a romantic relationship.

S1: Wie oft bist du mit deinem Freund (deiner Freundin) Rad gefahren?
S2: Wir sind selten miteinander Rad gefahren. Und du?
S1: Wir sind oft miteinander Rad gefahren.

	Nie 0%	*Selten 20%*	*Oft 60%*	*Sehr oft 80%*	*Immer 100%*
1. Rad gefahren	___	___	___	___	___
2. ins Kino gegangen	___	___	___	___	___
3. ins Restaurant gegangen	___	___	___	___	___
4. zusammen ein Bier getrunken	___	___	___	___	___
5. Hausaufgaben gemacht	___	___	___	___	___
6. ein Buch gelesen	___	___	___	___	___

	Nie 0%	Selten 20%	Oft 60%	Sehr oft 80%	Immer 100%
7. ein Theaterstück gesehen	___	___	___	___	___
8. Verwandte besucht	___	___	___	___	___
9. über andere Leute gesprochen	___	___	___	___	___
10. Pläne für die Zukunft diskutiert	___	___	___	___	___

■ FREIE ■ KOMMUNIKATION ■ **Eine romantische Verabredung°.** Beschreiben Sie einen romantischen oder humorvollen Abend, den Sie verbracht haben.

date

Schreibecke **Eine Seifenoper° schreiben.** Schreiben Sie eine kurze Seifenoper (fünf bis acht Sätze). Benutzen Sie die Schreibhilfe unten. Erfinden Sie einen Titel, nennen Sie die Namen der Hauptpersonen (so viele Sie wollen) und beschreiben Sie ihre Eigenschaften. Beschreiben Sie dann, was vorher passiert ist, und sagen Sie etwas über die momentanen Beziehungen°. Benutzen Sie Wörter und Ausdrücke aus **Wissenswerte Vokabeln: Freundschaft und Liebe.** Viel Spaß!

soap opera

relationships

Schreibhilfe

1. Titel der Seifenoper: ______
2. Die Personen heißen: ______

■ *Beate, Torsten, Hanno, Sabine ...*

3. Eigenschaften: ______

■ *Beate sieht gut aus. Hanno findet viele Frauen attraktiv.*

4. Was vorher passiert ist: ______

■ *Beate ist in Hanno verliebt gewesen, aber Hanno hat Sabine geküsst.*

5. Momentane Beziehungen: ______

■ *Beate ist jetzt böse auf Hanno. Sie ist in Torsten verliebt.*

II ■ Expressing what you know and don't know

The verbs **kennen** and **wissen**

You learned in Chapter 3 that German uses two separate verbs meaning *to know.* **Kennen** is used when referring to "knowing" people or places and occurs with a direct object.

Kennst du meinen Freund Lars?	*Do you **know** my friend Lars?*
Ja, ich **kenne** ihn.	*Yes, I **know** him.*

In contrast, German speakers use the verb **wissen** to express factual knowledge.

Es ist kalt heute. **Weißt** du das nicht?	*It's cold today. Don't you know that?*

Both **wissen** and **kennen** are mixed verbs. Their past participles are **gewusst** and **gekannt.**

The expressions **Wissen Sie ...** or **Weißt du ...** (often pronounced **weißte** in northern Germany) may be used in a narrative description to hold the listener's attention, much in the same way that English speakers use *you know . . . :* **Und dann, weißt du, haben wir uns geküsst.**

Subordinate clauses with **ob** and **dass**

A. *The subordinating conjunction* dass

Frequently the factual knowledge expressed by speakers with the verb **wissen** is in the form of an entire sentence or clause. Speakers use the verb **wissen** and the subordinating conjunction **dass** *(that)* followed by the clause.

Ich **weiß, dass** es heute kalt ist. *I know that it's cold today.*

A clause usually has a subject and verb. When a clause stands by itself it is known as a sentence or main clause **(Hauptsatz).** A clause that depends upon a main clause is known as a dependent or subordinate clause **(Nebensatz).** Subordinate clauses are always introduced by a subordinating conjunction, e.g., **dass** *(that),* and the conjugated verb always comes at the end of the subordinate clause. A comma always separates the main clause from the dependent clause. Separable prefixes are reunited with the conjugated verb and auxiliary verbs follow past participles at the end of the clause.

Ich weiß, **dass** er gut **aussieht.** *I know **that** he is good looking.*
Weißt du, **dass** ich ein neues Auto **gekauft habe?** *Do you know **that** I bought a new car?*

Speakers also often use a **dass**-clause to express that something is good **(gut),** interesting **(interessant),** important **(wichtig),** etc., or that a person is disappointed **(enttäuscht),** happy **(froh),** sad **(traurig),** etc.

Es ist wichtig, **dass** wir Deutsch sprechen. *It is important **that** we speak German.*

Sie war enttäuscht, **dass** ich keine Zeit für sie hatte. *She was disappointed **that** I didn't have any time for her.*

B. *The subordinating conjunction* ob

To express that they do *not* know something, German speakers use a negated form of the verb **wissen** with the subordinating conjunction **ob** *(if, whether),* followed by a reference to the missing information.

Ich **weiß nicht, ob** sie heute kommt. *I don't know whether she is coming today.*

In addition to using **ob** with the expression **weiß nicht,** speakers also use **ob** with the positive expressions **fragen** and **will wissen** to obtain more information.

Er **fragt, ob** sie ihn heiraten will. *He asks **whether** she wants to marry him.*
Sie **will wissen, ob** er sie wirklich geliebt hat. *She wants to know **whether** he really loved her.*

Ob is also used to ask about yes/no questions.

Liebst du mich? *Do you love me?*
Ich möchte wissen, **ob** du mich liebst. *I would like to know **if** you love me.*
Ich weiß nicht, **ob** du mich liebst. *I don't know **if** you love me.*

33 **Traumpartner(in).** Welche Eigenschaften hat Ihr Traumpartner/Ihre Traumpartnerin? Wie wichtig sind diese Eigenschaften für Sie? Kreuzen Sie sie **Gar nicht wichtig/Wichtig/Sehr wichtig** an. Fragen Sie dann einen Partner/eine Partnerin.

S1: Ist es wichtig, dass dein Traumpartner sportlich ist?
S2: Nein, das ist gar nicht wichtig. Ist es wichtig, dass deine Traumpartnerin viel Geld hat?
S1: Nein, das ist nicht wichtig. Ist es wichtig, dass ...?

	Gar nicht wichtig	*Wichtig*	*Sehr wichtig*
1. Er/Sie ist sportlich.	___	___	___
2. Er/Sie hat viel Geld.	___	___	___
3. Er/Sie ist unternehmungslustig°.	___	___	___
4. Er/Sie sieht gut aus.	___	___	___
5. Meine Eltern mögen ihn/sie.	___	___	___
6. Meine Katze (Mein Hund) mag ihn/sie.	___	___	___
7. Er/Sie mag die Natur.	___	___	___
8. Er/Sie ist ehrlich°.	___	___	___
9. Er/Sie liest viel.	___	___	___
10. Er/Sie trinkt keinen Alkohol.	___	___	___
11. Er/Sie spricht Deutsch und Englisch.	___	___	___
12. Er/Sie ist romantisch.	___	___	___
13. Er/Sie hat viel Humor.	___	___	___
14. Er/Sie wohnt in meiner Stadt.	___	___	___

likes to do things

honest

Schreibecke **Freund(in) oder Traumpartner(in)?** Gute Freunde sind nicht unbedingt Traumpartner. Beschreiben Sie in zehn Sätzen einen guten Freund/eine gute Freundin mit dem Vokabular aus der Aktivität „Traumpartner(in)".

III Giving reasons

Subordinate clauses with weil

To state a reason or a justification, German speakers use the subordinating conjunction **weil** *(because)*. The verb in the subordinate clause occurs at the end of the clause.

Ich habe dich geküsst, **weil** du mir Leid getan hast.	*I kissed you because I felt sorry for you.*
Onkel Hannes hat ein Bier getrunken, **weil** er Durst hatte.	*Uncle Hannes drank a beer because he was thirsty.*

You learned about the coordinating conjunction **denn** *(because, for)* earlier.

Other subordinating conjunctions are **bevor** *(before)*, **nachdem** *(after)*, and **obwohl** *(although)*

34 **Warum machen sie das?** Geben Sie einen Grund für die folgenden Handlungen°.

actions

Uschi und Hannes sind nach Hamburg gefahren, weil sie ihren Hochzeitstag haben.

1. Uschi und Hannes sind nach Hamburg gefahren,	a. er hat sein Geld im Hotelzimmer vergessen.

2. Hannes ist zum Hotel zurückgegangen,
3. Uschi hat an der Alster einen Spaziergang gemacht,
4. Uschi hat eine Cola bestellt°,
5. Uschi ruft das Deutsche Schauspielhaus an,
6. Uschi und Hannes müssen um 17.00 Uhr zurück sein,

b. das Wetter heute ist so schön.
c. Katja ruft heute Nachmittag an.
d. sie haben ihren Hochzeitstag.
e. sie hat Durst.
f. sie möchte für heute Abend Karten bestellen.

ordered

35 **Warum lernst du Deutsch?** Stellen Sie einem Partner/einer Partnerin die folgenden Fragen. Er/Sie gibt als Antwort einen Grund an.

S1: Warum lernst du Deutsch?
S2: Ich lerne Deutsch, weil ...

1. Warum lernst du Deutsch?
   a. Ich möchte Deutschland besuchen.
   b. Ich habe deutsche Verwandte.
   c. Ich möchte gut Deutsch sprechen.
   d. Ich möchte Deutschlehrer(in) sein.
   e. Ich muss es für Chemie (Musik, Geschichte usw.) haben.
2. Warum ist Deutsch wichtig?
   a. Meine Eltern (Großeltern) sprechen Deutsch.
   b. Über 90 Millionen Europäer sprechen Deutsch.
   c. Mein Freund/Meine Freundin spricht Deutsch.
   d. Die deutsche Industrie ist sehr stark.
   e. ...
3. Warum besuchen viele Deutsche die USA?
   a. Sie haben Verwandte in den USA.
   b. Sie möchten die Nationalparks besuchen.
   c. Die USA haben viele Attraktionen.
   d. Sie wollen Englisch sprechen.
   e. ...

IV Positioning information in a German sentence

Features of German word order

You have learned three important features of German word order **(Wortstellung).**

A. Subject-verb inversion

In Chapter 2 you learned that in a main clause the conjugated verb always comes in the second position.

Hannes **liebt** Uschi. *Hannes loves Uschi.*

The subject may appear *after* the verb when the sentence begins with other elements.

subject Für mich **ist** mein Freund wichtiger als meine Freundin.	*My friend is more important to me than my girlfriend.*
subject Dirk **habe** ich in der Disko kennen gelernt.	*I met Dirk at the disco.*

B. Two-part placement of German verbs

Some verb forms occur at the end of the main clause. In Chapter 4 you learned that the infinitives which accompany modal verbs are placed at the end of a main clause.

Man **kann** über alles **reden.**	*You can talk about everything.*

Earlier in this chapter you learned that in the conversational past the past participle is placed at the end of a main clause.

Er **hat** mich **angesprochen.**	*He started a conversation (with me).*

C. Verb forms at the end of a subordinate clause

You learned earlier in this chapter that in German the conjugated verb is placed at the end of a subordinate clause.

Sie war enttäuscht, dass ich keine Zeit für sie **hatte.**	*She was disappointed that I didn't have time for her.*
Sie will wissen, ob er sie wirklich geliebt **hat.**	*She wants to know whether he really loved her.*

A subordinate clause may begin with a subordinating conjunction (e.g., **dass, ob, weil**) as well as the question words **wann, warum, was, wie,** or **wo.**

ANNA: Weißt du, **wo** sie wohnt?	*Do you know where she lives?*
KATJA: Nein. Ich weiß auch nicht, **wie** sie heißt.	*No. I don't know her name either.*

The separable prefix appears joined with the verb at the end of a subordinate clause.

USCHI: Weißt du, wann Anna **ankommt?**	*Do you know, when Anna is arriving?*
KATJA: Nein, nur, daß sie vorher **anruft.**	*No, only that she will call first.*

36 **Ob sie mich liebt?** Karl und Inge sind Studenten an der Universität in Tübingen. Karl hat Inge kennen gelernt und jetzt hat er Liebeskummer. Stellen Sie einem Partner/einer Partnerin Fragen.

S1: Was weiß Karl über Inge?
S2: Er weiß, dass sie aus Ulm kommt. Und was weiß er nicht?
S1: Er weiß nicht, wie alt sie ist. Und was möchte er wissen?
S2: Er möchte wissen, ob sie gern italienisch isst.

Karl weiß	*Karl weiß nicht*	*Karl möchte wissen*
1. Sie kommt aus Ulm.	Wie alt ist sie?	Isst sie gern italienisch?
2. Sie studiert Betriebswirtschaft.	Ist sie romantisch?	Geht sie gern spazieren?
3. Sie hat viel Humor.	Ist sie sportlich?	Tanzt sie gern?
4. Sie sieht gut aus.	Wohnt sie schon lange hier?	Mag sie die Natur?

V Talking about activities that continue from the past into the present

Present tense verbs with **schon, seit,** and **erst**

English and German speakers express past activities that still have relevance in the present differently. Where English speakers use the present perfect (e.g., *have known*), German speakers use the present tense (e.g., **kennen**) together with the adverb **schon** *(already)* and an accusative time expression (e.g., **drei Jahre**).

Wir kennen uns **schon drei Jahre.** — *We have (already) known each other for three years.*

The preposition **seit** *(since, for)* used with the present tense also corresponds to the English present perfect. Note that **schon** *(already)* adds emphasis to the word **seit,** indicating that the speaker perceives the stated duration to be long. If the speaker perceives the duration to be short, he/she uses the word **erst** *(only)*.

The preposition **seit** requires the dative case. The dative case and dative endings of words will be explained in Chapter 6.

Wir kennen uns **schon seit drei Jahren.** / **schon drei Jahre.** — *We've already known each other for three years.*
Wir kennen uns **erst seit drei Jahren.** / **erst drei Jahre.** — *We've only known each other for three years.*

Because of the dative with **seit, Jahren** ends in an **-n.** The accusative expression does not: **Jahre.**

English verbs such as *to learn, to live, to eat, to smoke, to write, etc.,* express activities that may have started in the past and continue into the present. The idea of duration in English is expressed with the present perfect continuous form *(have been learning,* etc.). German does not have an equivalent verbal form for the English continuous *-ing* form.

Present perfect continuous

I ***have been learning*** *German for two years.*

Present tense + [schon/erst + accusative / seit + dative]

Ich **lerne seit zwei Jahren** Deutsch.
schon zwei Jahre

You will learn about the dative case in Chapter 6.

37 **Wie lange machst du das schon?** Sie möchten Ihren Partner/Ihre Partnerin besser kennen lernen. Stellen Sie einander die folgenden Fragen.

S1: Wie lange lernst du schon Deutsch?
S2: Ich lerne (erst) seit vier Monaten Deutsch.

Wie lange machst du das schon? This question requires **schon.** However, you can answer with **schon** or **erst,** depending on whether you feel the duration is long or short.

Was?

1. Deutsch lernen
2. (nicht) rauchen°
3. im Studentenwohnheim wohnen
4. an dieser Uni studieren
5. mit dem Computer schreiben
6. keinen Alkohol trinken
7. Auto fahren

Wie lange?

schon/erst seit ____ Jahren/Monaten/Tagen
schon/erst ____ Jahre/Monate/Tage
schon/erst seit ____ Minuten/Stunden
schon/erst ____ Minuten/Stunden

smoke

The time expression usually follows the conjugated verb unless the sentence contains a personal pronoun or a possessive (**mein, dein,** etc.). In that case, the time expression follows the pronoun or the possessive.

FREIE KOMMUNIKATION **Stolze° Eltern.** Sie sind eine stolze Mutter (ein stolzer Vater). Ihr Partner/Ihre Partnerin ist auch eine stolze Mutter (ein stolzer Vater). Vergleichen Sie Ihre tollen Kinder. Was hat Ihr Sohn (Ihre Tochter) schon gemacht?

proud

S1: Ich bin stolz darauf, dass mein Sohn schon drei Jahre Deutsch lernt.
S2: Und meine Tochter hat schon vier Bücher auf Deutsch, Englisch, Französisch und Chinesisch geschrieben.

Schreibecke Reisetagebuch. Sie sind in Deutschland. Schreiben Sie in ein Reisetagebuch, was Sie schon gemacht, gesehen und gelernt haben. Schreiben Sie auch auf, was Sie noch wissen oder sehen wollen. Verwenden Sie Konjunktionen wie **dass, ob** und **weil** und die Fragewörter als Konjunktionen.

Ich habe schon gesehen, wie freundlich die Leute sind. Ich habe schon viele nette Leute getroffen. Ich möchte aber auch wissen, ob ...

ZIELTEXT

Ein Gespräch mit Opa und Oma Kunz

Anna ist inzwischen° nach Bad Krozingen zu ihren Großeltern gefahren. Alle drei sind froh, dass sie einander endlich sehen. Anna hört, wie ihre Eltern einander in Heidelberg kennen gelernt haben. Sie will auch wissen, warum Oma und Opa Kunz noch nie nach Amerika gekommen sind.

in the meantime

Vorschau

38 Thematische Fragen: Deine Großeltern. Beantworten Sie die folgenden Fragen mit einem Partner/mit einer Partnerin auf Deutsch.

S1: Leben deine Großeltern noch?
S2: Ja, sie leben noch. *(oder)*
Nein, sie sind gestorben.

1. Leben deine Großeltern noch?
2. Wo wohnen deine Großeltern?
3. Wie oft sprichst du mit deinen Großeltern?
4. Besuchst du deine Großeltern oft? Wie oft?

Thematische Fragen. If your grandparents have passed away, answer these questions in the conversational past (e.g., **Meine Großeltern haben in Iowa gewohnt**).

5. Hast du mal mit deinen Großeltern über deine Eltern gesprochen?
6. Hast du Fotos von deinen Eltern als Kinder gesehen? Wie haben sie ausgesehen?
7. Hast du eine gute Beziehung zu anderen älteren Menschen? Welche Rolle spielen sie in deinem Leben?

39 **Annas Familienstammbaum°.** Können Sie sich noch an Annas Familie erinnern°? Füllen Sie den Stammbaum aus.

family tree
remember

 ________________  ________________

 ________________  ________________  ________________  ________________  ________________

  ________________  ________________  ________________

40 **Ein Gespräch mit Oma und Opa Kunz.** Wie wahrscheinlich ist es, dass Oma und Opa mit Anna über folgende Themen sprechen?

	Sehr unwahrscheinlich	*Vielleicht*	*Sehr wahrscheinlich*
1. Annas Mutter und Vater	___	___	___
2. Annas Freund in den USA	___	___	___
3. Rockmusik	___	___	___
4. die USA	___	___	___
5. die deutsche Sprache	___	___	___
6. das Wetter	___	___	___
7. junge Leute	___	___	___
8. Opas Gesundheit	___	___	___
9. Omas Freundin	___	___	___
10. Annas Studium	___	___	___
11. Geld	___	___	___
12. Annas Probleme	___	___	___

41 **Satzdetektiv.** Welche Sätze bedeuten ungefähr das Gleiche?

1. Mit dem Flugzeug **dauert** es nur sieben Stunden.
2. Das war keine leichte **Entscheidung.**
3. Wir waren eigentlich **dagegen.**
4. Nachher **schwätzen** deine Kinder dann nur Englisch.

a. Das war nicht einfach zu tun.
b. Mit Lufthansa fliegt man sieben Stunden von den USA nach Deutschland.
c. Später sprechen deine Kinder kein Deutsch.
d. Oma und Opa haben es nicht gut gefunden, dass Hannelore einen Amerikaner geheiratet hat.

---

5. Der Opa war überhaupt **nicht begeistert** von der Idee.
6. Ich habe ihm dann **zugeredet.**
7. Wir müssen schließlich **damit fertig werden.**
8. Warum kommt ihr uns nicht **besuchen** in Amerika?

e. Opa hat nicht gedacht, dass das eine gute Idee war.
f. Oma hat Opa gezeigt, dass das auch gut sein kann.
g. Opa und Oma müssen das eben akzeptieren.
h. Warum besucht ihr uns nicht?

ZIELTEXT

Ein Gespräch mit Opa und Oma Kunz

Anna besucht ihre Großeltern in Bad Krozingen. Sie sprechen über Annas Mutter Hannelore.

The **Zieltext** contains two simple past tense verb forms that will be explained in more detail in Chapter 10: **war** *(was)*, **wollten** *(wanted)*.

Hören Sie gut zu.

Rückblick

42 **Gemischte Sätze.** Bringen Sie diese Sätze aus dem Dialog in die richtige Reihenfolge.

___ Wir wollten° unsere Kinder eben hier behalten°. *wanted / keep*
___ Mit dem Flugzeug dauert es nur sieben Stunden.
_1_ Ach, Anna, es ist schön, dass du da bist.
___ Wie hat Mama Papa überhaupt kennen gelernt?
___ Ja, wir bekommen so viel aus Amerika.
___ Was habt ihr gedacht?

43 **Stimmt das?** Stimmen diese Aussagen zum Text oder nicht? Wenn nicht, was stimmt?

	Ja, das stimmt.	*Nein, das stimmt nicht.*
1. Oma findet, Amerika ist nicht sehr weit weg.	___	___
2. Oma und Opa Kunz mögen Bob nicht.	___	___
3. Hannelore und Bob haben einander in Berlin kennen gelernt.	___	___
4. Oma und Opa Kunz wollen bald nach Denver oder Dallas fahren.	___	___
5. Oma und Opa Kunz sind noch nie in Amerika gewesen.	___	___
6. Oma und Opa Kunz haben Amerika schon oft im Fernsehen gesehen.	___	___
7. Sie mögen Amerika nicht – da gibt es zu viel Gewalt und Hektik.	___	___

44 **Ergänzen Sie: Diktat.** Ergänzen Sie diese Sätze mit Wörtern aus dem **Zieltext.**

1. Anna sagt: „Ich bin auch _____, dass ich hier bin."
2. Ihr seid ja so weit _____ in den USA.
3. Ach Oma! ... Mit dem _____ dauert es nur sieben _____.
4. Was habt ihr eigentlich _____, als sie einen Amerikaner _____ hat?
5. Ach, Anna, weißt du, das war keine leichte _____ damals°.
6. Ja, ja, der Opa war _____ nicht begeistert von der Idee.
7. Sie [Hannelore] ist nach Heidelberg _____, hat da studiert, und da hat sie eben den Bob _____.
8. Wir sehen Amerika lieber im _____.

at that time

45 **Kurz gefragt.** Beantworten Sie diese Fragen auf Deutsch.

1. Warum sind Anna und ihre Großeltern froh?
2. Warum finden die Großeltern es nicht so gut, dass ihre Tochter Hannelore jetzt in den USA wohnt? Welche Probleme nennen sie?
3. Welches Kommunikationsproblem erwähnen° die Großeltern?
4. Warum kommen sie nicht nach Amerika?
5. Warum haben Oma und Opa die amerikanischen Städte Denver, Dallas, San Franzisko und Miami im Fernsehen gesehen?
6. Welche Vorstellungen° haben die Großeltern von Amerika?

mention

ideas

■ FREIE ■ KOMMUNIKATION ■

Rollenspiel: Das junge Ehepaar. Sie sind jung verheiratet und wohnen in Luzern in der Schweiz. Sie vermissen ihre Heimat und haben Heimweh°. Erzählen Sie Ihrem Mann/Ihrer Frau über Ihre Heimat und Ihre Familie zu Hause. Was haben Sie zu Hause alles gemacht? Was haben Sie im Frühling, Sommer, Herbst und Winter gemacht? Der Partner/Die Partnerin stellt viele Fragen.

***haben Heimweh:** you're homesick*

Schreibecke **Wir sind verliebt!** Sie studieren in Berlin und haben dort eine sehr nette Person kennen gelernt. Sie verbringen schon viel Zeit miteinander und Sie möchten bei dieser Person einziehen und zusammenleben. Schreiben Sie einen Brief an Ihre Eltern. Informieren Sie Ihre Eltern über die Fragen:

- Wie und wo haben Sie sich kennen gelernt?
- Was haben Sie zusammen gemacht?

Fragen Sie Ihre Eltern, ob sie dafür oder dagegen sind.

Wortschatz

Studium in Hamburg

die Erkältung, -en *common cold*
der Fischmarkt, ¨-e *fish market*
das Gedicht, -e *poem*
die Geschichte, -n *story; history*
das Gespräch, -e *conversation*
der Kellner, -/die Kellnerin, -nen *waiter/waitress*
die Kneipe, -n *bar, pub*
die Studentenkneipe, -n *student bar, pub*
die Nacht, ¨-e *night*
die Pharmazie *pharmaceutics*
die Schulzeit, -en *school days*
der Spaziergang, ¨-e *walk, stroll*
das Studium, *pl.* **Studien** *studies at college*
das Trinkgeld, -er *tip, gratuity*
das Wort, -e *or* **¨-er** *word*

arbeiten (hat gearbeitet) *to work*
buchstabieren (hat buchstabiert) *to spell*
durch·machen (hat durchgemacht) *to stay up, get through*
ein·kaufen (hat eingekauft) *to shop*
ein·schlafen (schläft ein, ist eingeschlafen) *to fall asleep*
irritieren (hat irritiert) *to irritate*
laufen (läuft, ist gelaufen) *to run*
schwimmen (ist geschwommen) *to swim*
sterben (stirbt, ist gestorben) *to die*
verdienen (hat verdient) *to earn*

Freundschaft und Liebe

das Alter *age*
die Clique, -n *circle of friends, clique*
die Eigenschaft, -en *characteristic*
die Erfahrung, -en *experience*
die Freizeit *free time*
die Freundschaft, -en *friendship*
der Krach *argument, quarrel, noise*
die Liebe, -n *love*
das Liebesgedicht, -e *love poem*
der Liebeskummer *lovesickness*
das Mädchen, - *girl*
das Problem, -e *problem*
das Thema, *pl.* **Themen** *topic, theme*
das Vertrauen *trust*
die Welt, -en *world*

an·fangen (fängt an, hat angefangen) *to start, begin*
an·sprechen (spricht an, hat angesprochen) *to initiate a conversation with someone*
aus·gehen (ist ausgegangen) *to go out*
bedeuten (hat bedeutet) *to mean*
brauchen (hat gebraucht) *to need*
denken (hat gedacht) an + *acc. to think of*
diskutieren (hat diskutiert) über + *acc. to discuss*
ein·laden (lädt ein, hat eingeladen) *to invite; to take out*
ein·ziehen (ist eingezogen) *to move in*
flirten (hat geflirtet) *to flirt*
gefallen (gefällt, hat gefallen) + *dat. to please; to like*
heiraten (hat geheiratet) *to get married*
helfen (hilft, hat geholfen) + *dat. to help*
küssen (hat geküsst) *to kiss*
Leid tun (hat Leid getan) + *dat. to feel sorry for*
reden (hat geredet) über + *acc. to talk about*
schmusen (hat geschmust) *to cuddle, make out*
umarmen (hat umarmt) *to embrace*
weiter·gehen (ist weitergegangen) *to continue*
zusammen·leben (hat zusammengelebt) *to live together*

sich trennen (hat sich getrennt) von + *dat. to break up, separate*
sich verlieben (hat sich verliebt) in + *acc. to fall in love with somebody*
verliebt sein (ist verliebt gewesen) in + *acc. to be in love with*
sich verloben (hat sich verlobt) *to get engaged*
sich versöhnen (hat sich versöhnt) *to make up, reconcile*

einander *each other*
enttäuscht *disappointed*
leidenschaftlich *passionately*
miteinander *with each other*
mutig *brave, courageous*
spontan *spontaneous*
verlobt *engaged*
vernünftig *reasonable, logical*
zusammen *together*

Ausdrücke

bis über beide Ohren verliebt in + *acc.* *head over heels in love*
durch dick und dünn *through thick and thin*
hinter meinem Rücken *behind my back*
Ich habe Vertrauen zu + *dat.* *I trust (someone)*

Das Wetter

Celsius *centigrade*
der Gefrierpunkt *freezing point*
das Gewitter *thunderstorm*
der Grad *degree*
der Nebel *fog*
der Regen *rain*
der Schauer, - *rain shower*
der Schnee *snow*
die Sonne, -n *sun*
die Temperatur, -en *temperature*
das Wetter *weather*
die Wolke, -n *cloud*

blitzen (es hat geblitzt) *there is lightning*
donnern (es hat gedonnert) *to thunder*
regnen (es hat geregnet) *to rain*
scheinen (es hat geschienen) *to shine*
schneien (es hat geschneit) *to snow*

bedeckt *overcast*
heiß *hot*
heiter *clear*
kalt *cold*
kühl *cool*
mies *rotten, lousy*
nass *wet, damp*
schwül *humid*
sonnig *sunny*
trocken *dry*
warm *warm*
windig *windy*
wolkig *cloudy*

Ausdrücke

Die Temperatur liegt um 15 Grad. *The temperature is 15°.*

Die Jahreszeiten

der Frühling *spring*
der Herbst *autumn, fall*
die Jahreszeit, -en *season*
der Sommer *summer*
der Winter *winter*

Zeitausdrücke

danach *afterwards*
die ganze Zeit *the whole time*
eines Tages *one day*
gestern *yesterday*
meistens *usually*
nachher *(adverb)* *afterwards*
schon, schon seit *since, for* (+ time phrase)
seit *since, for* (+ time phrase)
später *later*

Ausdrücke

von da an *from that point on*
zum ersten Mal *for the first time*
erst (seit) *just since*
schon (seit) Jahren *for years*

Andere Wörter

als *as, when*
an *along, by*
außerdem *besides, by the way*
dass *that*
deshalb *that's the reason why*
fast *almost, practically*
ganz [schlimm] *really [bad], very*
hinter *behind*
jedenfalls *anyway*
kaum *hardly*
kein ... mehr *no more ...*
leicht *easy*
na ... *well ...*
na, wie auch immer ... *yeah, whatever ...*
nämlich *namely*
noch *still*
ob *whether, if*
oje! *geez! oh boy!*
schlimm *bad, nasty*
trotzdem *nevertheless*
und so weiter (usw.) *etcetera (etc.)*
weil *because*
wenigstens *at least*
zu zweit *as a couple*

Aus dem Zieltext

die Entscheidung, -en *decision*
der Filmstar, -s *movie star*
das Flugzeug, -e *airplane*
die Gewalt *violence*
die Großstadt, *pl.* **Großstädte** *big city*
die Hektik *frenzy, fast pace*
die Stunde, -n *hour*

fertig werden (wird, ist geworden) mit + *dat.* *to come to grips with, accept*
schwätzen (hat geschwätzt) *(dialect)* *to talk, blab*
zu·reden (redet zu, hat zugeredet) + *dat.* *to talk to*

damals *back then*
dort drüben *over there*
eigentlich *actually*
froh *happy*
nachdem *(conjunction)* *after*
so war das *that's the way it was*
weit weg *far away*

In this chapter you will learn to express giving or lending to others, talk about the location of things, express when something happens, make compliments, and talk about ailments.

Kommunikative Funktionen

- Expressing the beneficiary or recipient of an action
- Indicating location
- Expressing when we do things
- Expressing temporal and spatial relationships with dative prepositions
- Expressing gratitude, pleasure, ownership, need for assistance, sorrow, and discomfort
- Specifying what you are talking about

Strukturen

- The dative case
- The subordinating conjunction **wenn**
- **Der-**words

Vokabeln

- Das Studentenzimmer
- Ein Einfamilienhaus
- Körperteile

Kulturelles

- Wo Studenten wohnen
- Tübingen
- Ausländer in Deutschland

Tübingen bietet viele Sehenswürdigkeiten.

KAPITEL SECHS

Willkommen in Tübingen

Go to the ***Vorsprung*** Website at
www.hmco.com/college

ANLAUFTEXT

Anna zieht im Wohnheim ein

Anna zieht in einem Tübinger Studentenwohnheim ein. Es heißt Waldhäuser-Ost. Barbara, eine Studentin im ersten Semester aus Dresden, hat das Zimmer neben Anna. Sie hilft Anna beim Einzug°.

hilft ... Einzug: *helps Anna with moving in*

Vorschau

Wissenswerte Vokabeln: das Studentenzimmer

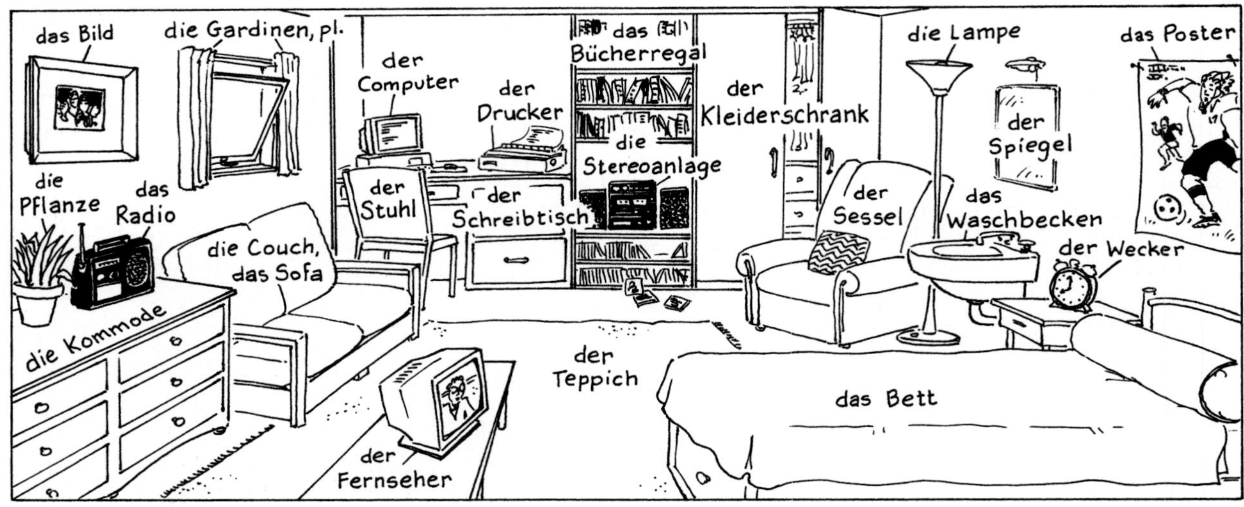

Identifying objects

Die Möbel

▣ Was für Möbel hast du im Zimmer? *Ich habe ...*
Hast du eine Stereoanlage im Zimmer? *Ja, ... (oder) Nein, ...*

W. Vok. In the northern dialects of German, **der Stuhl** (a regular chair) and **der Sessel** (an armchair) refer to different types of chairs. In Austria **der Stuhl** is rarely used at all.

1 Hast du das im Zimmer? Fragen Sie einen Partner/eine Partnerin, was er/sie im Zimmer hat.

▣ S1: Hast du eine Stereoanlage im Zimmer?
S2: Ja, ich habe eine Stereoanlage. Und du? *(oder)*
Nein, ich habe keine Stereoanlage. Und du?

Hast du das im Zimmer? Remember to use the accusative case forms of **ein** and **kein: eine/keine, einen/keinen.**

Ask your partner whether he/she has these additional items: **das Wasserbett, der Farbfernseher, das Telefon, der Mikrowellenherd, das Handy.**

2 Thematische Fragen. Beantworten Sie die folgenden Fragen auf Deutsch.

1. Was brauchen Studenten für die Universität? Machen Sie eine Liste.
2. Wohnen Sie mit anderen Studenten in einem Studentenwohnheim? Wie finden Sie das? Was können Sie da alles machen? Was ist verboten°?
3. Wohnen Sie zu Hause? Was können Sie machen? Was ist verboten?

forbidden

3 **Satzdetektiv.** Welche Sätze bedeuten ungefähr das Gleiche?

1. Anna **zieht** im Wohnheim **ein.**
2. Ich bin selber **erst vor einer Woche** hier **eingezogen.**
3. Ich **krieg'** die Tür nicht **auf.**
4. Gib mir deinen Schlüssel. Ich **schließ'** dir die Tür **auf.**
5. Hier, **guck mal,** Anna!
6. **Gefällt dir** dein Zimmer denn nicht?

a. Von jetzt an wohnt Anna im Studentenwohnheim.
b. Ich kann die Tür nicht öffnen.
c. Ich wohne erst seit einer Woche im Wohnheim.
d. Schau mal, Anna!
e. Findest du dein Zimmer nicht schön?
f. Gib mir den Schlüssel. Ich öffne die Tür.

---

7. Du hast einen Schrank für deine **Klamotten.**
8. Also, jetzt zeig' ich dir das Badezimmer, **wenn es dir recht ist.**
9. Du hast wirklich **Schwein gehabt.**
10. Du hast ein **Privatbad** bekommen: Klo, Dusche und Waschbecken.
11. Du, ich **danke dir** echt für die Hilfe!
12. Kannst du mir einen Stift **leihen?**

g. Das Badezimmer hast du für dich allein: Toilette, Dusche und Waschbecken.
h. Du hast einen Schrank für deine Kleidung.
i. Du hast Glück gehabt.
j. Ich zeige dir das Badezimmer, wenn das O.K. ist.
k. Kannst du mir einen Stift geben?
l. Vielen Dank für deine Hilfe.

In German-speaking countries, floors are counted as follows: **das Erdgeschoss** *(first floor)*, **erster Stock** *(second floor)*, **zweiter Stock,** etc.

German door locks often include a deadbolt which must be turned twice to lock the door.

Der Hölderlinturm in Tübingen

Zum + verb in the infinitive **(ein Bett zum Schlafen)** is the equivalent of *for* + *-ing* verb *(a bed for sleeping).*

ANLAUFTEXT

Hören Sie gut zu.

Anna zieht im Wohnheim ein

Vielen Dank, Barbara. Das ist wirklich nett von dir, dass du mir hilfst.
Das mach' ich doch gern. Ich bin selber erst vor einer Woche hier eingezogen.

Komm', ich zeig' dir dein Zimmer. Es ist gleich neben meinem, Zimmer 317.

So, Anna, hier sind wir schon, auf dem zweiten Stock.

Ich krieg' die Tür nicht auf. Kannst du mir bitte helfen?
Gib mir deinen Schlüssel. Ich schließ' dir die Tür auf. Hier, guck mal, Anna.

Aha, na ja ...
Was denn? Gefällt dir dein Zimmer denn nicht?
Also, eine Luxusbude ist es zwar nicht, aber du hast alles, was du brauchst: ein Bett zum Schlafen, einen Schreibtisch zum Lernen, einen Stuhl für den Schreibtisch, ein Regal für die Bücher und einen Schrank für deine Klamotten.

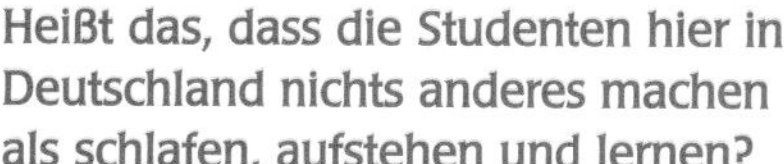
Heißt das, dass die Studenten hier in Deutschland nichts anderes machen als schlafen, aufstehen und lernen?

Na so ziemlich. Nur die Reihenfolge stimmt nicht so ganz.
Also, wir stehen so gegen Mittag auf, dann schlafen wir in den Vorlesungen – na, und abends lernen wir, in den Studentenkneipen.

Also, jetzt zeig' ich dir dein Badezimmer, wenn es dir recht ist.
Mein Badezimmer? Ich habe ein eigenes Badezimmer?
Klein aber fein! Du hast wirklich Schwein gehabt! Meistens gibt es nur ein Gemeinschaftsbad oder einen Duschraum auf dem Gang, aber du hast ein Privatbad bekommen: Klo, Dusche und Waschbecken.
Vielleicht ist es doch eine Luxusbude.

Was soll ich dir noch schnell sagen? Also, Cola- und Bierautomaten gibt's unten im Keller, und die Telefonzellen, das schwarze Brett und dein Postfach findest du im Erdgeschoss. Die Küche ist am Ende vom Korridor.

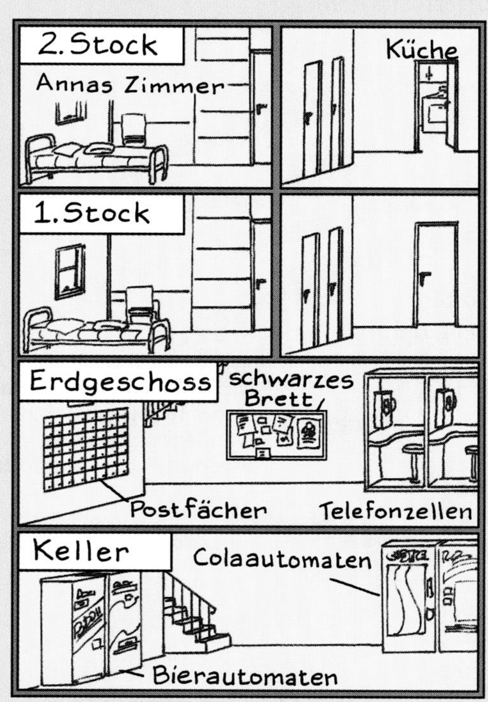
2. Stock
Annas Zimmer
Küche
1. Stock
Erdgeschoss
schwarzes Brett
Postfächer
Telefonzellen
Keller
Colaautomaten
Bierautomaten

Alles klar.
Du, ich muss zu einem Freund, aber ich komme später bei dir vorbei.
Danke, Barbara.
Gut. Kannst du mir einen Stift leihen? Ich schreibe dir die Zimmernummer von dem Freund aus Dresden auf. Er wohnt einen Stock tiefer.
Gut. Du, ich danke dir echt für die Hilfe!
Ja, bis gleich. Tschüss.

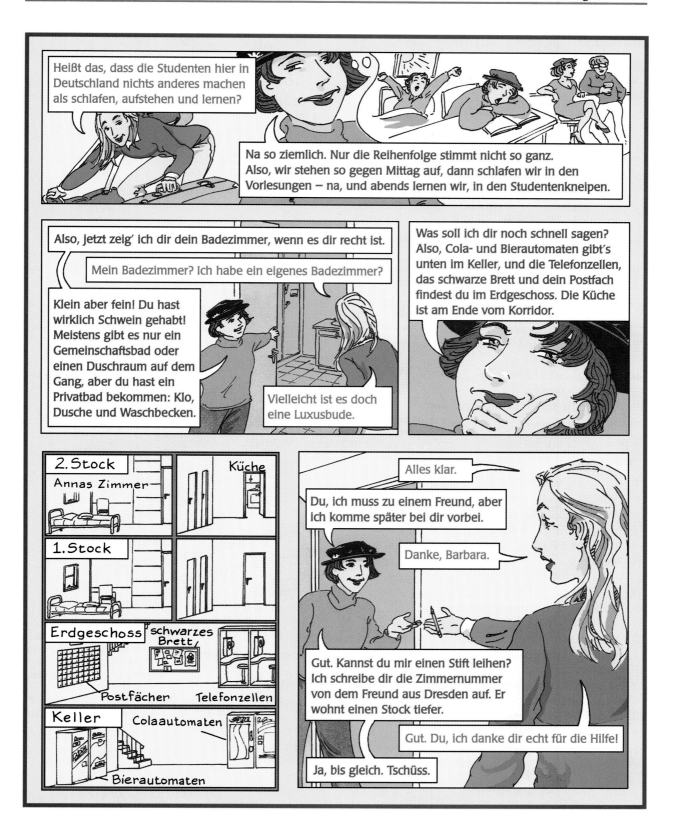

Rückblick

4 **Stimmt das?** Stimmen diese Aussagen zum Text oder nicht? Wenn nicht, was stimmt?

	Ja, das stimmt.	*Nein, das stimmt nicht.*
1. Anna muss den Weg zu ihrem Zimmer alleine finden.	___	___
2. Barbara studiert schon lange in Tübingen.	___	___
3. Annas Zimmer ist gleich neben Barbaras Zimmer im zweiten Stock.	___	___
4. Anna kann die Tür nicht aufschließen. Barbara nimmt den Schlüssel und hilft.	___	___
5. Anna und Barbara finden, sie haben Luxusbuden im Heim.	___	___
6. Barbara meint es ironisch, wenn sie sagt, deutsche Studenten stehen erst gegen Mittag auf und schlafen in den Vorlesungen.	___	___
7. In diesem Wohnheim haben alle Zimmer ein Privatbad.	___	___
8. Es gibt Milch- und Zigarettenautomaten im Erdgeschoss.	___	___
9. Die Studenten können am Ende vom Korridor selber kochen.	___	___
10. Anna leiht Barbara eine Zigarette.	___	___

5 **Ergänzen Sie.** Ergänzen Sie diese Sätze mit Wörtern aus dem **Anlauftext.**

1. Anna und Barbara sind neue Studentinnen im ______.
2. Barbara ist selber erst vor einer Woche hier ______.
3. Barbara ______ Anna ihr Zimmer.
4. Annas Zimmer ist gleich ______ Barbaras Zimmer.
5. Annas und Barbaras Zimmer sind auf dem zweiten ______.
6. Barbara nimmt Annas Schlüssel und ______ die Tür ______.
7. Annas Zimmer ist keine ______, aber es hat alles, was sie ______.
8. Es gibt ein ______ für die Bücher und einen ______ für die Klamotten.
9. Barbara erzählt, deutsche Studenten ______ erst gegen Mittag auf, dann schlafen sie in den ______.
10. Anna hat wirklich ______ gehabt: sie hat ein eigenes ______.
11. Meistens gibt es nur ein Gemeinschaftsbad oder einen Duschraum auf dem ______.
12. Cola- und Bierautomaten sind im ______, aber die Telefonzellen, das schwarze Brett° und Annas Postfach° sind im ______.
13. Sie haben auch eine ______ am Ende vom Korridor.
14. Anna ______ Barbara für ihre Hilfe.
15. Anna leiht Barbara einen ______, denn sie will etwas aufschreiben.

Because the legal drinking age in Germany for beer and wine is 16, it is quite common to find machines that dispense beer in dormitories.

das … Brett: *bulletin board* (lit. *black board*) / *mailbox*

Sprache im Alltag: Expressions with animals

German speakers like to use colorful expressions involving animals.

Schwein haben — *to be lucky*
Du hast **Schwein gehabt.**

einen Bärenhunger haben — *to be hungry as a bear*
Er **hat einen Bärenhunger.**

einen Vogel haben — *to be crazy*
Er **hat einen Vogel.**

(einen) Kater haben — *to have a hangover*
Wir **haben heute einen Kater.**

hundemüde sein — *to be dog-tired*
Ich **bin hundemüde.**

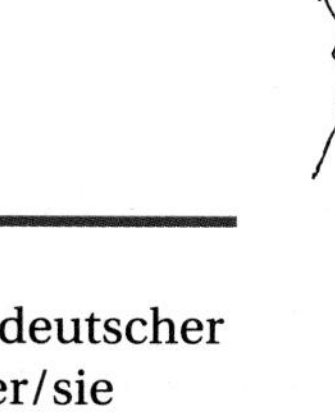

6 Sie/Er weiß (nicht), dass ... Welche Dinge weiß ein deutscher Student/eine deutsche Studentin wahrscheinlich nicht, wenn er/sie zuerst in ein amerikanisches Studentenwohnheim kommt? Welche Dinge weiß er/sie?

S1: Weiß ein deutscher Student (eine deutsche Studentin), dass es keine Bierautomaten gibt?
S2: Nein, er (sie) weiß nicht, dass es keine Bierautomaten gibt. *(oder)* Ja, er (sie) weiß, dass es keine Bierautomaten gibt.

1. Es gibt keine Bierautomaten.
2. Man schläft in einem Bett.
3. *First floor* ist das Erdgeschoss.
4. Man kann Türen ohne Schlüssel abschließen.
5. Das Zimmer hat meistens ein Telefon.
6. Das Badezimmer hat ein Klo.
7. Alle Studenten essen zusammen in der *cafeteria.*
8. Man darf oft nicht rauchen.

7 Deutsche Studenten – amerikanische Studenten. Barbara hat den Alltag der deutschen Studenten ironisch beschrieben. Was machen Sie als amerikanischer Student/amerikanische Studentin jeden Tag? Kreuzen Sie zuerst an, was Sie jeden Tag machen. Notieren Sie dann die Reihenfolge (zuerst ... , dann ... , später ...). Fragen Sie dann einen Partner/eine Partnerin.

S1: Was machst du zuerst?
S2: Zuerst stehe ich auf. Dann ...

Was?	*Jeden Tag?*	*In welcher Reihenfolge?*
1. frühstücken	___	_____
2. Kaffee trinken	___	_____
3. duschen°	___	_____
4. weggehen	___	_____
5. Radio hören	___	_____
6. aufstehen	___	_____
7. den Wecker abstellen°	___	_____
8. Deutsch lernen	___	_____

°*to shower*
°*turn off*

8 **Unser Traumzimmer.** Sprechen Sie in einer Gruppe von drei Personen über Ihr Traumzimmer. Was haben Sie alles im Zimmer? Schreiben Sie eine Liste. Machen Sie dann eine Skizze° des Zimmers. *sketch*

In unserem Traumzimmer gibt es ein Wasserbett, eine …
Das Zimmer ist …
Das Zimmer hat …

■ FREIE ■ KOMMUNIKATION ■ **Interview.** Stellen Sie einem Partner/einer Partnerin die folgenden Fragen.

1. Hast du eine Luxusbude? Wenn ja (nein), warum kann man das sagen?
2. Hat man hier im Wohnheim eine Küche auf dem Gang?
3. Gibt es Bierautomaten an unserer Uni? Kann man an der Uni überhaupt Bier kaufen oder trinken?
4. Kann man an der Uni Zigaretten kaufen?
5. Was hast du alles in deinem Zimmer?

Rollenspiel: Neu im Wohnheim. S1 ist neu im Wohnheim und sucht sein/ihr Zimmer. S2 wohnt schon im Wohnheim und hilft S1, das Zimmer zu finden. Was sagen Sie? Hier sind einige Ausdrücke.

Kannst du mir bitte helfen? • Das ist nett von dir. • Ich zeige dir … • Gib mir …

Schreibecke **Ein Brief an Katja.** Anna schreibt Katja Günther einen Brief. Sie will über ihren ersten Tag im Studentenwohnheim, über Barbara, ihr Zimmer und die Dinge im Keller und im Erdgeschoss schreiben. Aber Anna wird müde. Schreiben Sie Annas Brief fertig.

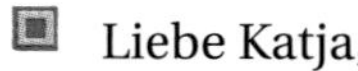

Liebe Katja,

heute bin ich im Studentenheim Waldhäuser-Ost angekommen. Ich habe eine nette Studentin kennen gelernt. Sie heißt Barbara Müller und kommt aus Dresden. Sie hat mir geholfen. Sie hat …

BRENNPUNKT KULTUR

Wo Studenten wohnen

Most universities in German-speaking countries are located in the center of town, surrounded by unrelated buildings, and are rarely arranged in an insular, campus-like setting. Because the universities do not assume responsibility for housing all students, students must compete for a limited number of subsidized dorm rooms or find their own housing on the more expensive open market **(der Wohnungsmarkt).** The shortage of space in town near the classroom buildings has resulted in the construction of many residence halls **(Studentenwohnheime),** as well as many research buildings, on the outskirts of town. Most dormitories consist primarily of single rooms **(Einzelzimmer),** which contain a bed, a desk, a bookcase, and a small table and chair. Separate from the sleeping quarters is a small entry way, which contains closet space or a freestanding wardrobe and a small sink. In older residence halls everyone living on the floor typically has to share the toilets **(die Toiletten/die WCs)** and the shower room **(der Duschraum).** Each floor is also equipped with a communal kitchen **(die Gemeinschaftsküche)** where students can store food and cooking utensils and cook their own meals. In general, student dormitories do not provide warm meals; instead, **die Mensa,** located at or near the university, serves both students and faculty.

In Tübingen, dormitories can house only 17% of the student body. The majority of the student body must look for other accommodations. Many universities offer a placement service for rooms and apartments in town **(Zimmer- und Wohnungsvermittlung)** free of charge and often have a special placement office for foreign students. Nonetheless, many students still have to find creative solutions to their housing problems. Roughly 15% of all students live at home with their parents or relatives. 20% rent rooms in private homes or apartments **(in Untermiete wohnen),** which often excludes cooking privileges and allows for little privacy. Another 20% of the student body shares apartments or private houses in residential cooperatives **(Wohngemeinschaften** or **WGs),** in which the housemates share costs and often the cooking, shopping, and cleaning responsibilities. Nearly 30% start out by simply renting their own apartment their first year away from home, near the university. Students have often staged demonstrations to focus government attention on the housing shortage, which has worsened since unification in 1990.

„... und wenn, liebe Eltern, mein Vermieter° mit dem Auto unterwegs ist, dann ist es sogar richtig gemütlich° hier..." Zeichnung: Buchegger

landlord
cozy

Brennpunkt Kultur. Students' expenses vary from city to city. In Freiburg, for example, dormitory rooms cost between 355 and 400 DM/month. A room in a private home usually costs much less. Real estate agencies **(Immobilienmakler)** require a 1–2 month rent fee. A meal in the **Mensa** costs 3,90 DM in Freiburg.

Strukturen und Vokabeln

I Expressing the beneficiary or recipient of an action

The dative case

To indicate the beneficiary of an action, German speakers use the dative case **(der Dativ).** The dative identifies the indirect object (e.g., **mir**). The indirect object is usually a person or animal. In English, it is often accompanied by a preposition (e.g., *for me, to me*).

Komm, ich zeig' **dir** dein Zimmer.	*Come on, I'll show **you** your room.* *Come on, I'll show the room **to you.***
Gib' **mir** deinen Schlüssel.	*Give **me** your key.* *Give your key **to me.***
Ich schließ' **dir** die Tür auf.	*I'll open the door **for you.***

The direct objects in these sentences are inanimate objects **(dein Zimmer, deinen Schlüssel, einen Stift)** and appear in the accusative case.

The German dative case, when used with people (e.g., **dir**), replaces the English prepositions, especially *to* and *for: to (for) you.*

A. The dative case: personal pronouns

The indirect object in the dative case is often a personal pronoun.

Kannst du **mir** einen Stift leihen? *Can you lend **me** a pen?*

When the direct object is a pronoun, it precedes the indirect object.

Kannst du **ihn** mir leihen? *Can you lend it to me?*

Here are the nominative and dative forms of the personal pronouns.

	Singular Nominative	**Dative**	**Plural Nominative**	**Dative**
1st	ich *I*	**mir** *(to/for) me*	wir *we*	**uns** *(to/for) us*
2nd, informal	du *you*	**dir** *(to/for) you*	ihr *you*	**euch** *(to/for) you*
2nd, formal	Sie *you*	**Ihnen** *(to/for) you*	Sie *you*	**Ihnen** *(to/for) you*
3rd	er *he* es *it* sie *she*	**ihm** *(to/for) him* **ihm** *(to/for) it* **ihr** *(to/for) her*	sie *they*	**ihnen** *(to/for) them*

Note: the sound similarities between the **-r** ending on **mir, dir,** and **ihr. Ihnen/ihnen** is a dative form but **ihn** is the singular masculine accusative form, related to **er** *(he)*. The dative forms of **er** and **es** are identical: **ihm.**

Note that the dative forms **ihm** and **ihr** resemble their English counterparts *him* and *her.* However, remember that the English forms *him* and *her* also correspond to the German accusative forms **ihn** and **sie.**

9 Was leihen sie einander? Was leihen die folgenden Studenten/Studentinnen einander? Unterhalten Sie sich mit einem Partner/einer Partnerin und benutzen Sie Personalpronomen in den Antworten.

S1: Was leiht Rolf Barbara?
S2: Er leiht ihr seinen Computer.

Partner(in) 1:

	Rolf	Barbara	Carlos	Torsten	Anna
Rolf		?	seine Sporttasche	?	5 DM
Barbara	nichts		?	ihre Zeitung	?
Carlos	?	seine Gitarre		sein Radio	?
Torsten	sein Heft	?	?		sein Wörterbuch
Anna	?	ihre Haarbürste°	ihr Shampoo	?	

hairbrush

Partner(in) 2:

	Rolf	Barbara	Carlos	Torsten	Anna
Rolf		seinen Computer	?	sein Auto	?
Barbara	?		ihre Karten	?	ihren Schlüssel
Carlos	20 DM	?		?	sein Fahrrad
Torsten	?	seinen Fernseher	seine Kassetten		?
Anna	ihr Auto	?	?	ihr Modem	

10 **Leihst du mir das?** Leihen Sie Freunden oft etwas? Ein Partner/Eine Partnerin fragt, ob er/sie sich die folgenden Gegenstände von Ihnen leihen kann. Was antworten Sie?

S1: Leihst du mir bitte dein Deutschbuch?
S2: Na klar! Ich leihe dir mein Deutschbuch. *(oder)*
Nein. Mein Deutschbuch leihe ich dir nicht.

1. dein neues Auto
2. dein Fahrrad
3. deine Zahnbürste
4. deine Haarbürste
5. dein Shampoo
6. zehn Dollar
7. 1000 Dollar
8. deinen Pullover
9. deine Schuhe

B. *The dative case: the question word* wem

German-speakers use **wem** when asking about the beneficiary of an action. The people or animals may be masculine **(ihm),** feminine **(ihr),** singular or plural **(ihnen).**

Wem leiht Anna einen Stift?	*To whom is Anna lending a pen?*
Sie leiht **Barbara** einen Stift.	*She is lending Barbara a pen.*
Sie leiht **ihr** einen Stift.	*She is lending her a pen.*

11 **Geburtstagsgeschenke.** Wem schenken Sie die folgenden Gegenstände zum Geburtstag? Besprechen Sie mit einem Partner/einer Partnerin, welche Leute welche Geschenke bekommen sollen. Besprechen Sie auch, warum.

Geburtstagsgeschenke. Remember that **weil** is a subordinate conjunction and requires the conjugated verb to be placed at the end of the clause.

S1: Wem schenkst du ein Auto zum Geburtstag?
S2: Ich schenke Mary ein Auto.

S1: Warum schenkst du ihr ein Auto?
S2: Weil ihr Auto kaputt ist.

Note that **ihr Auto** means *her car:* Remember that **ihr** is a possessive pronoun as well as a dative personal pronoun, (e.g., **Ich gebe ihr das Auto)** *(I give her the car).*

1. ein Flugticket nach Frankreich
2. Pokémon-Karten
3. ein Auto
4. ein Fahrrad
5. einen Computer
6. Blumen°
7. einen Fernseher
8. ein Buch über Deutschland
9. einen Reisekoffer

a. Marys Auto ist kaputt.
b. James studiert Französisch.
c. Sabine ist Hobbygärtnerin.
d. Bastian ist ein Internet-Fan.
e. Holger sieht gern Seifenopern.
f. Elke fliegt nach Spanien.
g. Stefan studiert Deutsch.
h. Luise ist sehr sportlich.
i. Frankie wird fünf Jahre alt.

° *flowers*

C. *The dative case: definite and indefinite articles, and possessive adjectives*

Here are the definite and indefinite articles and possessive adjectives in the dative case. Their endings look very similar to the endings on the personal pronouns in the dative case: **ihm, ihr, ihnen.**

	Masculine	Neuter	Feminine	Plural
Nominative	der Mann	das Kind	die Frau	die Freunde
Dative	de**m** Mann	de**m** Kind	de**r** Frau	de**n** Freunde**n**
	ein**em** Mann	ein**em** Kind	ein**er** Frau	kein**en** Freunde**n**
	mein**em** Mann	mein**em** Kind	mein**er** Frau	mein**en** Freunde**n**
	dein**em** Mann	dein**em** Kind	dein**er** Frau	dein**en** Freunde**n**
	Ihr**em** Mann	Ihr**em** Kind	Ihr**er** Frau	Ihr**en** Freunde**n**
	sein**em** Mann	sein**em** Kind	sein**er** Frau	sein**en** Freunde**n**
	ihr**em** Mann	ihr**em** Kind	ihr**er** Frau	ihr**en** Freunde**n**
	unser**em** Mann	unser**em** Kind	unser**er** Frau	unser**en** Freunde**n**
	eur**em** Mann	eur**em** Kind	eur**er** Frau	eur**en** Freunde**n**

Don't let identical endings confuse you: (1) Masculine and neuter singular forms are identical in the dative: **dem.** (2) The dative feminine singular form of the definite article and the nominative masculine singular form are identical: **der.** (3) The dative plural of the definite article and the accusative masculine singular form are identical: **den.**

Note that the nouns in the dative plural add the ending **-n** (e.g., **die Freunde > den Freunden**) unless the regular plural is formed by adding **-s** (e.g., **die Autos > den Autos**) or the plural already ends in **-n** (e.g., **die Tanten > den Tanten**).

Masculine N-nouns (e.g., **der Herr, Neffe, Student**) add **-(e)n** in the dative singular (e.g., **dem Herrn, Neffen, Studenten**) and dative plural (e.g., **den Herren, Neffen, Studenten**) as they do in the accusative singular and nominative and accusative plural.

12 Wem gibt Stefan den Schlüssel? Was ist die logische Antwort? Fragen Sie einen Partner/eine Partnerin.

S1: Wem gibt Stefan die Seminararbeit?
S2: Er gibt der Professorin die Seminararbeit.

1. Stefan / die Seminararbeit geben
   a. seinen Eltern b. der Professorin c. einer Studentin
2. Barbara / ihre Haarbürste leihen
   a. der neuen Studentin b. ihrer Katze c. dem Professor

3. Anna / ein Kleid schenken
   a. ihrem Freund Karl b. ihrer Freundin c. ihrer Professorin
4. Karl / einen CD-Player kaufen
   a. einem Schwerhörigen° b. seinem Bruder c. seinem Hund

   ° *a hearing-impaired man*
5. Barbara / einen Computer schenken
   a. ihrer Nachbarin b. ihrer Katze c. ihrem Vater
6. Anna / ein Poster von einer Rockgruppe schenken
   a. einer Freundin b. ihrer Mutter c. ihrem Physikprofessor
7. der Professor / die Prüfungen zurückgeben
   a. den Eltern b. den Studenten c. der Reinemachefrau°

   ° *cleaning lady*
8. Barbara / die Postkarte aus Italien schreiben
   a. der Bank in Tübingen b. dem Bundeskanzler° c. den Eltern in Dresden

   ° *chancellor*
9. Karl / das Bier bringen
   a. den Studenten b. den Kindern c. dem Hund

II Indicating location (I)

Dative of location: in der, im/in dem, in den

To indicate the location of a person, animal, object, or action, German speakers use the preposition **in** with a definite article in the dative case. **In** belongs to a group of prepositions called *two-case prepositions* **(die Wechselpräpositionen)** that can occur with either the accusative or the dative case. Two-case prepositions will be explained in more detail in Chapter 7. The preposition **in** frequently appears in contracted form **im (in + dem).**

Die Studenten essen **in der** Küche. — *The students eat in the kitchen.*
Was hast du **im** Zimmer? — *What do you have in the room?*
Bierautomaten gibt's **im** Keller. — *There are beer machines in the basement.*

The definite article **dem** is used for singular masculine and neuter nouns in the prepositional phrase, and **der** is used for singular feminine nouns.

	Nominative	Dative
Masculine	der Keller	im (in **dem**) Keller
Neuter	das Zimmer	im (in **dem**) Zimmer
Feminine	die Küche	in **der** Küche
Plural	die Kneipen	in **den** Kneipen

When referring to countries, e.g., **Deutschland,** or cities, e.g., **Tübingen,** as locations, German speakers use the preposition **in** without the definite article. However, certain countries always occur with a definite article, e.g., **die Schweiz** *(fem.),* **die Türkei** *(fem.),* or **die Vereinigten Staaten** *(pl.).*

Tübingen: Anna ist **in** Tübingen.
Deutschland: Tübingen ist **in** Deutschland.

die Schweiz: Bern ist eine Stadt **in der** Schweiz.
die Türkei: Birsens Großeltern leben **in der** Türkei.
die Vereinigten Staaten: Annas Familie lebt **in den** Vereinigten Staaten.

Wissenswerte Vokabeln: ein Einfamilienhaus

Describing the features of a house

Die Stockwerke, der Stock

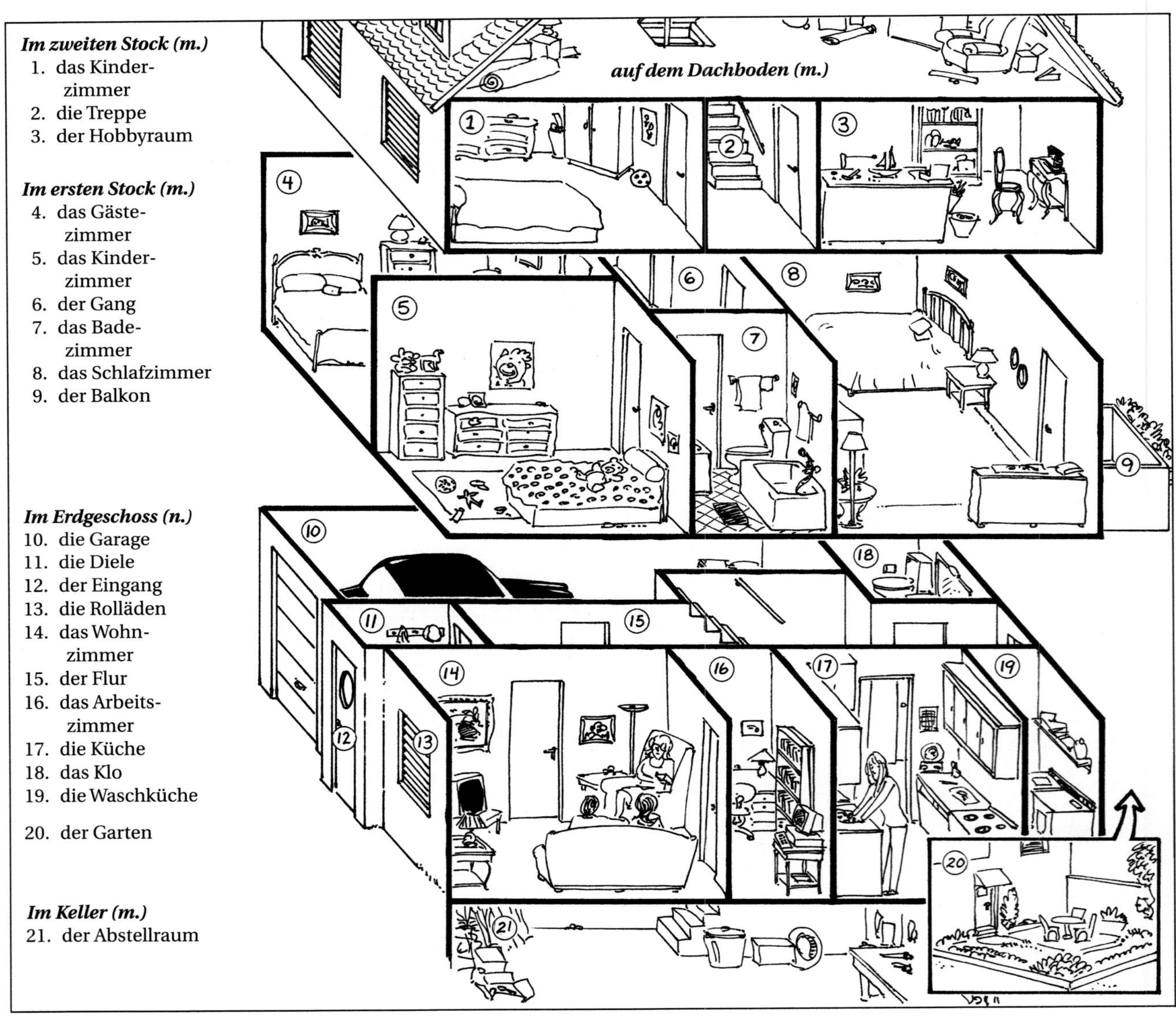

Was ist im Keller? *Im Keller ist der Abstellraum.*
Wo schläfst du? *Ich schlafe im Gästezimmer.*

13 Wo machst du das? Kreuzen Sie das Zimmer an, in dem Sie diese Aktivitäten machen.

S1: Wo schläfst du?
S2: Ich schlafe im Schlafzimmer.

	Im Schlafzimmer	*Im Badezimmer*	*In der Küche*
1. schlafen	___	___	___
2. Kaffee trinken	___	___	___
3. baden	___	___	___
4. fernsehen	___	___	___
5. die Zeitung lesen	___	___	___
6. frühstücken	___	___	___
7. aufstehen	___	___	___
8. duschen	___	___	___
9. die Hausaufgaben machen	___	___	___
10. die Kleidung aufhängen°	___	___	___

°*hang up*

14 Wo ist das Auto? Wo findet man normalerweise die folgenden Gegenstände?

S1: Wo ist das Auto?
S2: In der Garage.

das Auto • der Farbfernseher • die Waschmaschine • die Kaffeemaschine • der Rasierapparat • das Doppelbett • die Stereoanlage • der Mikrowellenherd • die Rolle Toilettenpapier • die Couch • das Waschbecken • das Bücherregal • die Rosen, Tulpen und Tomaten • die Zahnbürsten • die alten Klamotten • das Kinderbett • das Handy

15 Interview. Stellen Sie einem Partner/einer Partnerin die folgenden Fragen.

1. Wohnst du in einem Haus, in einer Wohnung oder in einem Studentenwohnheim?
2. Wie viele Schlafzimmer hat dein Haus, deine Wohnung, dein Studentenwohnheim?
3. Wie viele Badezimmer hat dein Haus, deine Wohnung, dein Studentenwohnheim?
4. Hast du eine Küche?
5. Wo isst du normalerweise?
6. Was hast du in deinem Zimmer?
7. Hast du eine Katze oder einen Hund?
8. Wo schläft die Katze (der Hund)?

BRENNPUNKT KULTUR

Tübingen

Located approximately 40 kilometers south of Stuttgart, Baden-Württemberg's urban capital and economic powerhouse, the old university city of Tübingen is distinguished by its historical town center **(die Altstadt)**. Straddling the Neckar and Ammer rivers, Tübingen contains a historic town hall **(das Rathaus)**, a castle **(Schloss Hohentübingen)**, and a myriad of half-timbered houses **(Fachwerkhäuser)** on narrow, winding streets. While the city boasts a population of 80,000 native inhabitants, it owes its fame to the 25,000 students at the **Eberhard-Karls-Universität**, who by its history and reputation are drawn to this dynamic educational institution. Founded in 1477 with only 300 students, the university quickly gained a reputation for outstanding scholarship and teaching. It has always attracted significant German intellectuals: the Renaissance astronomer and mathematician Johannes Kepler; the philosopher G.W.F. Hegel; the Romantic author Ludwig Uhland; the 20th century novelist, poet, and painter, Hermann Hesse; and the contemporary theologian Hans Küng. In the 18th century, the impassioned German poet Friedrich Hölderlin attended the university, but later descended into mental illness, spending his last 36 years in a tower on the banks of the Neckar, now known as the **Hölderlinturm.** Tübingen was the first German university to reopen its doors after the collapse of the Nazi government in 1945. Since then the university has aggressively pursued international cooperation and collaborative projects, establishing academic partnerships with numerous American universities. The city of Tübingen has a partnership with the city of Ann Arbor, Michigan.

(a)

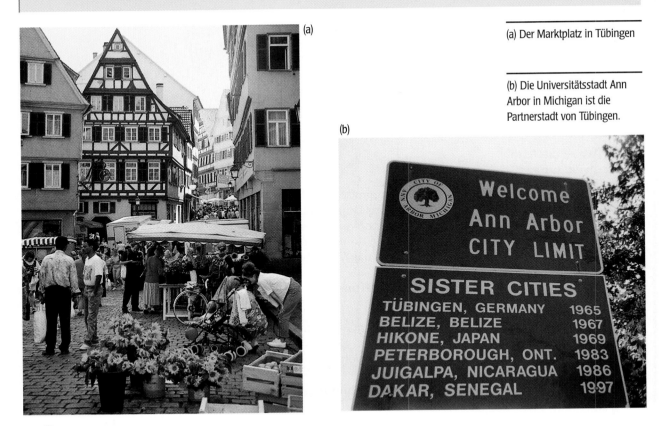

(a) Der Marktplatz in Tübingen

(b)

(b) Die Universitätsstadt Ann Arbor in Michigan ist die Partnerstadt von Tübingen.

16 Entschuldigung, können Sie mir sagen, wo der Hölderlinturm ist? Sie und ein Partner/eine Partnerin sind Touristen und fragen einige Tübinger nach Sehenswürdigkeiten in Tübingen. Benutzen Sie den Stadtplan von Tübingen.

Theater

1 Landestheater Württemberg-Hohenzollern, Eberhardtstr. 8
Theaterkasse Tel.: 9313149

2 Zimmertheater
Bursagasse 16
Tel.: 92730

Kinos

3 Kino Arsenal
Eine Institution. Programmkino. Anspruchsvolles Programm, Kinokneipe
Am Stadtgraben 33, Tel.: 51073

4 Kino Atelier
Das Programmkino und Café Haag, der American Diner
Am Haagtor, Tel.: 21225

5 Museum 1 + 2
Studio Museum Die Kino's mit Niveau Am Stadtgraben 2, Tel.: 23661

6 Blaue Brücke 1 - 3
Friedrichstr., Tel.: 23661

7 Kino Löwen
Kornhausstr., Tel.: 22410

Discotheken

8 Musicclub Patty
Di, Do + Sa. stimmungsvolle brasilianische Nächte.
Fr. Hits Hits Hits
Schlachthausstr. 9, Tel.: 51612

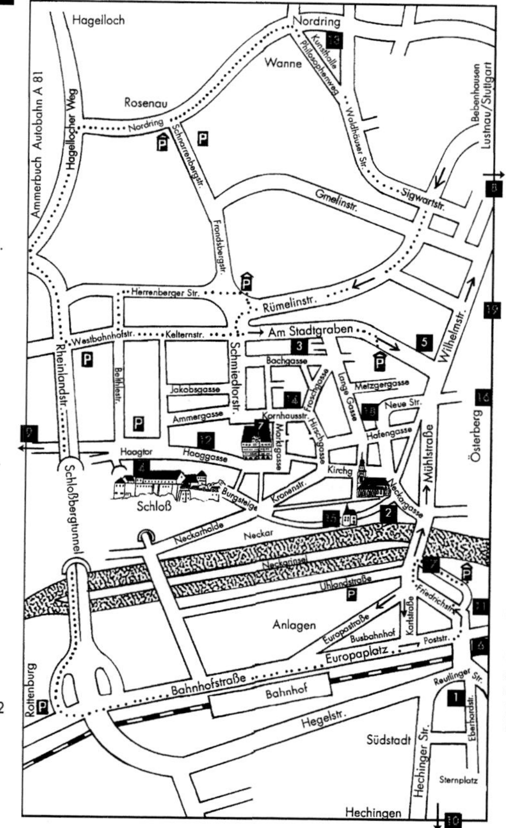

Veranstaltung/Konzert

9 Zentrum Zoo Diskothek, Kneipe, Konzerte. Schleifmühleweg 86. Tel: 40539

10 Sudhaus Veranstaltungen, Konzerte, Kabarett.
Hechinger Str. 203 Tel: 74696

11 Tübinger Matinee
Konzerte und Vorträge.
Casino, Wöhrdtstr. 25

12 Club Voltaire Kleinkunst, Konzerte. Haaggasse 26b, Tel.:51524

Ausstellungen

13 Kunsthalle Tübingen, Philosophenweg 76

14 Stadtmuseum Kornhaus, Kornhausstr. 10

15 Hölderlinturm, Bursagasse 6

16 Institut Culturel Franco-Allemand, Doblerstr. 25

17 Deutsch-Amerikanisches Institut, Karlstr. 3

18 Galerie im Alten Schlachthaus, Metzgergasse 3

19 Auto- und Spielzeugmuseum Boxenstop Autos, Motorräder, Puppen, (Blech) Eisenbahnen, Spielsachen - präsentiert in toller Atmosphäre Brunnenstr. 18, Tel.: 21996

S1: Entschuldigung, können Sie mir sagen, wo der Hölderlinturm ist?
S2: Der Hölderlinturm? Ja. In der Bursagasse 6.
S1: Danke schön.

Entschuldigung, ... Note: **die Gasse** *(lane)*, **die Straße** *(street)*, **der Weg** *(way, path)*.

1. das Zimmertheater
2. die Blaue Brücke
3. der Club Voltaire
4. die Kunsthalle Tübingen
5. das Deutsch-Amerikanische Institut
6. das Stadtmuseum Kornhaus

17 Fragen über Tübingen. Benutzen Sie den Stadtplan und beantworten Sie die Fragen über Tübingen.

S1: Wo kann man ein anspruchsvolles° Kinoprogramm finden?
S2: Im Kino Arsenal.

° *sophisticated*

1. Wo kann man Motorräder, Puppen und Spielsachen finden?
2. Wo kann man zwei Kinos mit Niveau finden?
3. Wo kann man Konzerte hören?
4. Wo kann man Kleinkunst finden?
5. Wo kann man amerikanisches Essen finden?
6. Was möchten Sie in Tübingen sehen?

Fragen über Tübingen: das Kino, das Museum, das Theater, der Zoo, die Matinee, der Club, das Institut, das Stadtmuseum.

■ FREIE ■ KOMMUNIKATION ■ **Neu im Heim.** Florian ist neu im Studentenwohnheim. Er zieht gerade ein. Heribert wohnt schon seit zwei Jahren im Heim. Heribert gibt Florian viele Tipps. Spielen Sie die drei Dialoge zu Ende.

FLORIAN: Was kann man hier im Wohnheim machen?
HERIBERT: ...

FLORIAN: Mein Gepäck ist noch am Bahnhof. Ich brauche dringend ... Was soll ich machen?
HERIBERT: ...

FLORIAN: Mein Zimmer ist total leer°! *empty*
HERIBERT: Kein Problem, ...

Ein Telefongespräch. Sie haben eine neue Wohnung° in Frankfurt. Sie rufen zu Hause an und sprechen mit Ihrer Mutter. Erzählen Sie ihr von der neuen Wohnung. Ihre Mutter ist sehr neugierig und stellt viele Fragen. *apartment*

In unserer Stadt. Ein Student/Eine Studentin ist neu in Ihrer Stadt. Welche interessanten Dinge soll er/sie machen? Und wo?

Unsere Studentenwohnheime. Zeigen Sie dem neuen Studenten/der neuen Studentin die Studentenwohnheime auf Ihrem Campus. Wie alt sind sie? Wie viele Studenten wohnen dort? Was hat man im Studentenwohnheim?

Schreibecke **Mein Zimmer.** Beschreiben Sie Ihr Zimmer. Was haben Sie alles?

■ In meinem Zimmer habe ich ...

Ein Zimmer einrichten°. Sie sind neu in Tübingen und brauchen einige Sachen für Ihr Zimmer in einer Wohngemeinschaft. Neue Sachen sind aber zu teuer und Sie möchten gebrauchte° Sachen kaufen. Schreiben Sie einen Zettel° für das schwarze Brett. *furnish* *used / note*

■ Ich bin neu in Tübingen und habe ein Zimmer in einer Wohngemeinschaft. Ich suche ...

ABSPRUNGTEXT
Am Kopierer

Über 2 Millionen Türken leben und arbeiten in Deutschland. Viele türkische Kinder sind in Deutschland geboren, wachsen in Deutschland auf° und gehen dort zur Schule oder zur Universität. *grow up*

Schüler und Studenten türkischer Abstammung haben besondere Probleme: sie sprechen perfekt Deutsch und fühlen sich° in Deutschland zu Hause. Erst seit dem 1. Januar 2000 sind sie automatisch deutsche Staatsbürger. ***fühlen sich:** feel*

In dieser Geschichte lesen wir von zwei Studentinnen. Eine Studentin ist Deutsche. Die andere Studentin (die Autorin) ist 1971 in der Türkei geboren, aber sie wohnt mit ihrer Familie schon seit 1972 in Deutschland. Beide studieren an der Universität Hamburg. Sie macht Fotokopien. Die deutsche Studentin will mit ihr ins Gespräch kommen, aber es gibt Kommunikationsprobleme.

Ausländer generally means *foreigner(s)*. However, an accurate definition of the word is complex because there is no clear distinction between ethnicity and nationality. German citizenship is automatically bestowed by way of German parentage. Thus, children born to parents of German descent in Romania or Russia are recognized as German citizens. With the introduction of liberalized citizenship laws on Jan. 1, 2000, children born in Germany to foreign-born parents also automatically become German citizens.

Vorschau

18 **Thematische Fragen.** Beantworten Sie die folgenden Fragen auf Deutsch.

1. Zu welcher Gruppe gehören Sie?
   a. Ich bin europäischer Abstammung.
   b. Ich bin asiatischer Abstammung.
   c. Ich bin afrikanischer Abstammung.
   d. Ich bin indianischer Abstammung.
   e. Ich bin hispanischer Abstammung.
   f. Ich bin gemischter Abstammung.
2. Haben Sie viele ausländische Studenten an Ihrer Universität? Woher kommen sie? Warum kommen sie an Ihre Uni?
3. Glauben Sie, dass es viele ausländische Studenten an deutschen Unis gibt? Warum? Warum nicht?
4. Sind die ausländischen Studenten an Ihrer Universität integriert und akzeptiert? Bleiben viele unter sich°? Warum? Warum nicht?
5. Wo findet man an der Uni am leichtesten mit anderen Studenten Kontakt? Im Kurs? Im Heim? Am Arbeitsplatz? Beim Sport? In Diskos und Bars?

unter sich: *to themselves*

19 **Satzdetektiv.** Welche Sätze bedeuten ungefähr das Gleiche?

1. Sie **erkennt** mich.
2. Ich **schaue** verwundert **hoch.**
3. Sie wird leicht **ungeduldig.**
4. Sie ist **nicht sehr zufrieden** mit der Antwort.

a. Ich sehe überrascht° weg vom Kopierer.
b. Sie findet meine Antwort nicht sehr gut.
c. Sie kennt mich, sie erinnert sich an mich.
d. Sie wartet nicht gern.

surprised

German has only one term for Native Americans: **Indianer (indianischer Abstammung.) Inder** refers to Asian Indians **(indischer Abstammung).**

5. Du siehst so **zerbrechlich** aus, so prinzeßhaft aus.
6. Ich bin **verblüfft.**
7. **Das scheint bei dir nicht so.**
8. Ich überlege, ob ich meinen 20-DM-Schein wechseln soll, oder ob mir meine Groschen **reichen** werden.
9. Unsere Mädchen **wachsen** wohlbehütet° **auf** in ihrer Familie.

e. Ich glaube, bei dir ist das anders.
f. Du bist so fragil wie eine Prinzessin.
g. Ich bin erstaunt.
h. Ich weiß nicht, ob ich mehr Kleingeld brauche.
i. Unsere Mädchen sind gut beschützt zu Hause.

Standard German requires that **auf** come at the end of the clause. In informal German, the placement of **in ihrer Familie** after **auf** gives this information special emphasis.

well-protected

10. Im Islam ist das ja anders. Da werden die Frauen ja **unterdrückt,** oder nicht?
11. Ich weiß ja nicht, wie das **bei euch** ist.
12. Sie [meine Groschen°] **reichen** nicht.
13. Ich sortiere **meine Blätter.**
14. Kannst du mir Geld **wechseln?**

j. Ich organisiere meine Papiere.
k. Ich denke, dass Frauen im Islam weniger wert sind als Männer.
l. Ich habe nicht genug [Groschen].
m. Kannst du mir Kleingeld für meine Geldscheine geben?
n. Ich habe keine Ahnung, wie das in der Türkei ist.

10-Pfennig-Stücke

ABSPRUNGTEXT

Am Kopierer

Lesen Sie jetzt den Text.

This story describes the thoughts of a Turkish student. Her thoughts reflect questions, comments, and actions by the German student she meets. Like the stereotypes about Germans and Americans found in Chap. 3, those expressed here may not necessarily be accurate nor reflective of the views of all people.

Ich stehe am Kopierer unserer Fachbereichsbibliothek. Am Kopierer nebendran steht eine Frau.

Hallo. Sie schaut auf, sagt auch: *Hallo.* Sie erkennt mich.

Warst du nicht auch gestern in diesem Seminar? Doch.

Ich überlege, wieviel Geld ich in diesen Automat stecken muß.

Sag mal, woher kommst du? Wie meinst du?

Ich schaue verwundert hoch. Sie wird leicht ungeduldig.

Na ja, dein Herkunftsland?

Ich blättere in meinem Buch. Aus der Türkei. *Aus der Türkei?*

Sie ist erstaunt, zieht die Augenbrauen hoch.

Und wie fühlst du dich hier? Ich schaue sie an.

Wie meinst du das? Sie wiederholt ihre Frage: *Na, wie fühlst du dich hier, in Deutschland?*

Ich ziehe die Schultern hoch°. Wie ich gerade drauf bin. Sie ist nicht zufrieden mit der Antwort.

ziehe ... hoch: *shrug*

Du siehst so zerbrechlich aus, so prinzeßhaft aus. Gar nicht wie die anderen Türken.

Ich schaue hoch, meine Stirn runzelt sich°.

Wie meinst du das? Sie hebt den Deckel° des Kopierers.

meine ... sich: *I frown*

cover

Na ja, die anderen Türken sehen halt anders aus. Ich bin verblüfft.

Wie sehen die denn aus? Keine Antwort, dafür ein kleiner Exkurs über den Islam.

Ich habe mal ein Buch darüber gelesen. Ein sehr positives, von ... , wirklich sehr positiv. Aber eigentlich weiß ich nichts darüber. Aber diese Selbstunterdrückung° der Frauen ... Sie schaut mich an.

self-oppression

Das scheint bei dir nicht so.

Ich überlege, ob ich meinen 20-DM-Schein wechseln soll, oder ob mir meine Groschen reichen werden. Was meinst du damit?

Na, unsere Mädchen wachsen wohlbehütet in ihrer Familie auf, bis sie in die weite Welt gehen.

Ich entscheide mich für die Groschen.

Im Islam ist das ja anders. Da werden sie ja unterdrückt, oder nicht. Ich weiß ja nicht, wie das bei euch ist.

Wie viele türkische Frauen kennst du?

Ich kenne niemanden. Ich weiß ja nicht, aber ich habe ein Buch darüber gelesen, ein sehr positives. Also wirklich sehr positiv. Dieselbe Autorin hatte auch eins über das Christentum geschrieben. Kennst du sie?

Sie reichen nicht.

Nein, ich kenne sie nicht. Ich sortiere meine Blätter.

Kannst du mir Geld wechseln?

Sie ist irritiert. Warum habe ich sie nicht gefragt, woher ihre Großmutter kommt.

BIRSEN KAHRAMAN

Rückblick

20 **Wer macht was?** Kreuzen Sie an, auf wen die folgenden Aussagen zu dieser Geschichte zutreffen°.

° *apply*

	Türkische Studentin	*Deutsche Studentin*	*Beide*
1. Sie macht Fotokopien in der Bibliothek.	___	___	___
2. Sie sagt zuerst: „Hallo."	___	___	___
3. Sie erkennt die andere Studentin.	___	___	___
4. Sie war gestern im Seminar.	___	___	___
5. Sie fragt, woher die andere kommt.	___	___	___
6. Sie sagt, sie kommt aus der Türkei.	___	___	___
7. Sie fragt, wie die andere sich hier fühlt.	___	___	___
8. Sie runzelt die Stirn und fragt: „Wie meinst du das?"	___	___	___
9. Sie sagt: „Die anderen Türken sehen halt anders aus."	___	___	___
10. Sie beantwortet die Frage nicht, sondern hält einen Diskurs über den Islam.	___	___	___
11. Sie meint, alle Frauen im Islam sind unterdrückt.	___	___	___
12. Sie hat nicht genug Groschen für den Kopierer und fragt, ob die andere Geld wechseln kann.	___	___	___
13. Sie zeigt, dass sie irritiert ist.	___	___	___
14. Sie zeigt nicht, dass sie irritiert ist.	___	___	___

21 **Ergänzen Sie.** Ergänzen Sie diese Sätze mit Wörtern aus dem **Absprungtext.**

1. Die türkische Studentin steht am ______ der Fachbereichsbibliothek.
2. Die deutsche Studentin ______ die türkische Studentin vom Seminar gestern.
3. Die türkische Studentin ______, wie viel Geld sie in diesen Automaten stecken muss.
4. Die deutsche Studentin fragt: „Sag mal, ______ kommst du?"
5. Die türkische Studentin ______ verwundert hoch.
6. Die türkische Studentin antwortet, sie kommt ______ der Türkei.
7. Die deutsche Studentin fragt: „Wie ______ du dich hier in Deutschland?"
8. Die deutsche Studentin ist nicht sehr ______ mit der Antwort.

9. Die deutsche Studentin sagt: „Du siehst so _____ aus, so prinzeßhaft aus. Gar nicht wie die anderen Türken."
10. Die türkische Studentin ist _____ und fragt: „Wie sehen die denn aus?"
11. Die türkische Studentin fragt sich, ob sie ihren 20-Mark-Schein _____ soll, oder ob ihr ihre Groschen _____ werden.
12. Die deutsche Studentin sagt: „Unsere Mädchen _____ wohlbehütet in ihrer Familie auf, bis sie in die weite Welt gehen."
13. Die deutsche Studentin hat ein Buch über den Islam gelesen und meint, alle Frauen im Islam werden _____.

22 Kurz gefragt – kurz interpretiert. Beantworten Sie die folgenden Fragen auf Deutsch.

1. Warum sind die zwei Studentinnen in der Fachbereichsbibliothek?
2. Welche Studentin spricht die andere an? Was sagt sie?
3. Welche Frage erstaunt die türkische Studentin?
4. Wie reagiert die deutsche Studentin, als die andere Studentin antwortet: „aus der Türkei"?
5. Was kritisiert die deutsche Studentin am Islam? Woher hat sie ihre Informationen?
6. Was wollte die türkische Studentin eigentlich die deutsche Studentin noch fragen? War die Frage ernst oder sarkastisch?
7. Die türkische Studentin sagt: „Ich komme aus der Türkei." Was meint sie wohl damit? Ist sie dort geboren? Aufgewachsen? Nur auf Besuch gewesen? Was meinen Sie und warum?

Ausländer in Deutschland

Over the last 50 years, Germany has become a multicultural society that includes a variety of ethnic groups, races, and religions. About 2 million people of Turkish descent (**die Türken**) live and work in Germany. In addition, thousands of people from Italy, the former Yugoslavia, Greece, Poland, Spain, Romania, and Portugal call Germany their home.

In the 1950s and 1960s, the German economy experienced unparalleled economic growth **(das Wirtschaftswunder)**. Recruited by German businesses, many so-called "guest workers" (**Gastarbeiter**) from poorer southern European countries came to Germany as a temporary work force to replace those German workers killed in the war. By the 1970s the children of the workers, particularly those from Turkey **(die Türkei)**, found it difficult to return to a country they hardly knew. At the same time, the Turks, more than any other ethnic group, maintained their identity through language, the Islamic religion (**der Islam**), and their customs. For many younger Turkish people the conflict between their ethnic background and where they lived was heightened by laws that prevented them until Jan. 1, 2000 from obtaining full German citizenship. The struggles of ethnic minorities are reflected in the literature of immigrant authors writing in German, such as the Turkish author Ermine Özdamar or the **Afro-Deutsche** author May Opitz.

Bolstered by the former West Germany's liberal asylum policy, the number of foreigners living in Germany swelled in the 1970s with political asylum-seekers from Iran and the Soviet Union. By 1992, nearly 80% of all immigrants seeking asylum in European countries were coming to Germany. Before long, the drain on government resources was straining German good will. Following German unification in 1990, the ethnic diversity of Germany had expanded to include communities of Russians, Poles, Chinese, Vietnamese, Africans, and Arabs from the former

German Democratic Republic (**die Deutsche Demokratische Republik**). Shelters where these people were housed soon became targets of right-wing extremist attacks. In 1991 a young African was murdered in the East German town of Hoyerswerda. In 1992 a shelter for asylum seekers in Rostock in the east was firebombed, and members of a family of Turks living in an apartment building in Mölln in western Germany were attacked and killed by arsonists. Following the beating death of an African immigrant in the eastern German city of Dessau by three Neo-Nazis in June 2000, a German court sentenced the ringleader to the maximum sentence of life in prison and the underage accomplices to nine years each. The current German government is attempting to crack down on right-wing extremism in Germany.

Etwa zwei Millionen Türken wohnen in Deutschland.

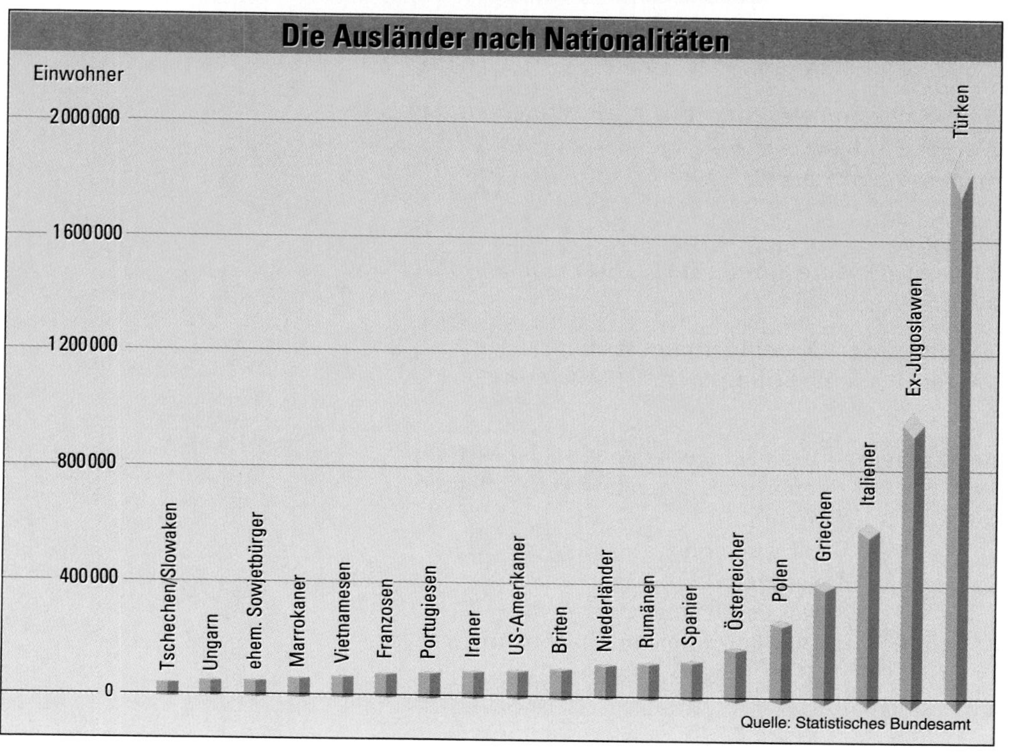

Strukturen und Vokabeln

III Expressing when we do things

The subordinating conjunction wenn

German speakers use the subordinating conjunction **wenn** *(when, whenever, if, as soon as)* to express when they do things. In Chapter 12 you will learn to use **wenn** *(if)* for unreal conditional statements. Like all subordinating conjunctions, **wenn** requires the conjugated verb to come at the end of the clause.

Wir fahren nach Hause, **wenn** er zurückkommt.	*We'll drive home when (as soon as) he returns.*
Jetzt zeig' ich dir das Badezimmer, **wenn** es dir recht ist.	*Now I'll show you your bathroom, if it's all right with you.*

23 Was passiert, wenn ... ? Die türkische Studentin in der Geschichte erzählt, wie sie und deutsche Studenten oft miteinander sprechen. Bilden Sie Sätze nach dem Beispiel.

Ich treffe andere Studenten am Kopierer. Ich sage immer „Hallo".
Wenn ich andere Studenten am Kopierer treffe, sage ich immer „Hallo".

Be sure to place the conjugated verb (e.g., **treffe**) at the end of a **wenn**-clause and to begin the main clause with the conjugated verb (e.g., **sage**).

1. Ich treffe andere Studenten am Kopierer. Ich sage immer „Hallo".
2. Deutsche Studenten fragen mich: „Woher kommst du?" Ich schaue oft verwundert hoch.
3. Ich sage: „Aus der Türkei." Deutsche Studenten sind oft erstaunt.
4. Deutsche Studenten fragen mich: „Wie fühlst du dich hier in Deutschland?" Ich frage oft: „Wie meinst du das?"
5. Deutsche Studenten sagen: „Du siehst gar nicht wie die anderen Türken aus." Ich bin oft verblüfft.
6. Ich frage: „Wie viele türkische Frauen kennst du?" Viele Studenten sagen, sie kennen niemanden.
7. Ich habe solche Konversationen. Ich werde oft irritiert.

24 Wann? Sie spielen ein zwölfjähriges Kind. Ein Partner/Eine Partnerin spielt Ihren Vater/Ihre Mutter. Stellen Sie einander Fragen und geben Sie passende Antworten.

S1 (VATER/MUTTER): Wann machst du dein Zimmer sauber?
S2 (KIND): Wenn ich meinen Computer nicht mehr finden kann.

Vater (Mutter):	
1. Wann machst du dein Zimmer sauber?	Mein Lehrer versteht mich besser.
2. Wann machst du deine Hausaufgaben?	Ich kann meinen Computer nicht mehr finden.
3. Wann bekommst du eine gute Note?	Wir haben den Videofilm zu Ende gesehen.
4. Wann gehen deine Freunde nach Hause?	Das Essen ist fertig.
5. Wann wäschst du dir endlich die Hände?	Die Hausaufgaben machen mehr Spaß.

Wann machst du dein Zimmer sauber?

Kind:

1. Wann darf ich bis drei Uhr morgens aufbleiben°?
2. Wann darf ich Auto fahren?
3. Wann bekomme ich mehr Taschengeld°?
4. Wann darf ich ins Kino gehen?
5. Wann muss ich nicht in die Schule gehen?

Du bist sechzehn.
Du hast deine Hausaufgaben gemacht.
Du bist dreißig.
Du bist sehr krank.
Du bekommst nur gute Noten.

stay up

allowance

IV ▣ Expressing temporal and spatial relationships

Dative prepositions

There are eight prepositions that are always used with the dative case **(die Dativpräpositionen).** You already encountered some in earlier chapters.

The translations of these prepositions are only approximate. The scope of their meanings generally varies depending on the context.

1. Expressing origin: **aus** *(from, out of)*

Anna kommt **aus** den USA.	*Anna is **from** the U.S.A.*
Anna kommt **aus** dem Zimmer.	*Anna is coming **out of** the room.*

As with the preposition **in,** be sure to alter the endings of articles that accompany country names (e.g., **aus den USA/Vereinigten Staaten, aus der Türkei, aus der Schweiz.).**

2. Expressing exclusion: **außer** *(except for)*

Außer ihm sprechen alle Studenten Deutsch.	***Except for** him all the students speak German.*

When **außer** occurs in the same sentence with **auch** *(also)*, it means *in addition to:* **Außer ihm sind auch Anna und Barbara hier.** *(In addition to him, Anna and Barbara are also here.)*

3. Expressing location: **bei** *(at, near, with)*

Karl war heute **bei** der Post.	*Karl was **at** the post office today.*
Das Studentenwohnheim ist **bei** der Autobahn.	*The dorm is **near** the freeway.*
Das scheint **bei** dir nicht so.	*That doesn't seem to be the case **with** you.*
Barbara hat **bei** einer Frau in Moskau gewohnt.	*Barbara lived **with** a woman in Moscow.*

There are two translations of *to live with:* **leben/wohnen bei** and **leben/wohnen mit.** The first **(bei)** indicates a relationship of dependency, as in **Jeff lebt/wohnt bei seinen Eltern.** The second **(mit)** implies a relationship of shared responsibilities: **Franz lebt/wohnt mit seiner Freundin (zusammen).**

Some common verbs used with **bei** are **arbeiten, essen, vorbeikommen** *(to stop by),* and **wohnen.**

Wir essen **bei** Stefanie.	*We're eating **at** Stefanie's.*
Werner arbeitet **bei** der Bank.	*Werner works **at** the bank.*
Karl kommt morgen **bei** uns vorbei.	*Karl is stopping by (**at** our place) tomorrow.*

Wir essen bei Stefanie. *(We're eating at Stefanie's.):* Note that German does not add a possessive *s* to the nouns or names describing a location. The same applies to destinations: **Wir gehen zu Karl.** *(We're going to Karl's place.).*

4. Expressing accompaniment: **mit** *(with)*

Mit meinen Freunden kann ich über alles reden.	*I can talk about everything **with** my friends.*

5. Expressing time: **nach** *(after, past)*

Es ist fünf **nach** drei.	*It's five after (past) three.*
Nach der Vorlesung gehen wir nach Hause.	*After the lecture we'll go home.*

6. Expressing destination: **zu, nach** *(to)*

People and institutions

Wir gehen **zu** Karl.	*We're going **to** Karl's (place).*
Anna geht **zur** Universität.	*Anna is going **to** the university.*

Cities, countries, and home

Ich fliege **nach** Deutschland.	*I'm flying **to** Germany.*
Ich gehe **nach** Hause.	*I'm going home.*

The dative case—not **zu**—is used for the recipient of an action.

The expression **zu Hause** means *at home.*

The preposition **in** is used with countries like **die USA, die Schweiz,** and **die Türkei,** e.g., **ich fahre in die Schweiz.**

7. Expressing duration: **seit** *(since, for)*

Wir kennen uns schon **seit** der Schulzeit.	*We have known each other **since** school.*
Ich rauche **seit** einem Jahr nicht mehr.	*I haven't smoked **for** a year.*

Remember that **ein** *(a)* when used as a number *(one)* takes endings. No other number takes endings, e.g., **seit einem Jahr.**

8. Expressing possession, association, or connection: **von** *(of, by, from)*

Der Bruder **von** Barbara wohnt noch zu Hause.	*Barbara's brother still lives at home.*
Das ist nett **von** dir.	*That's nice **of** you.*
Das Lied ist **von** der Gruppe „Die Prinzen".	*The song is **by** the group "Die Prinzen."*
Von da an ...	***From** that time on . . .*

In colloquial German, speakers often use **von** to indicate possession. Standard German uses the possessive *s*: **Barbaras Bruder wohnt noch zu Hause.**

The prepositions **von, zu,** and **bei** frequently form contractions with the definite article.

von + dem = vom	am Ende **vom** Korridor	*at the end of the hall*
zu + dem = zum	ein Bett **zum** Schlafen	*a bed for sleeping*
zu + der = zur	Sie geht **zur** Universität.	*She's going to the university.*
bei + dem = beim	Karl war **beim** Arzt.	*Karl was at the doctor's.*

When **beim** is used with an infinitive, it means *while.*

beim Essen	*while eating*
beim Lesen	*while reading*

Sprache im Alltag: Emphasizing one's opinion

German speakers frequently use expressions with dative prepositions to express or emphasize an opinion.

meiner Meinung nach	*in my opinion*
mit anderen Worten	*in other words*
von mir aus	*as far as I am concerned*
von daher	*therefore*
aus diesem Grund	*therefore, that's the reason why*

Note that in the expression **meiner Meinung nach** the preposition **nach** occurs at the end of the prepositional phrase.

25 Anna spricht mit Oma und Opa. Wählen Sie die richtige Dativpräposition.

1. Anna spricht (aus/seit/mit) ihren Großeltern.
2. OMA: Wir sind so froh, dass du (nach/zu/aus) uns gekommen bist, Anna.

3. OPA: Wir haben auch so gern die Briefe (aus/mit/von) dir und deiner Mutter gelesen. Wir sind wirklich froh, dass du da bist. Es ist nur schade, dass deine Mutter nicht auch gekommen ist.
4. OMA: Ja, die Hannelore haben wir (seit/von/außer) fünf Jahren nicht mehr gesehen.
5. ANNA: Meiner Meinung nach wollte Mama im Dezember (zu/mit/bei) Papa (zu/aus/nach) Deutschland kommen, aber er muss Mitte Dezember für zwei Wochen nach Florida fahren, und sie weiß nicht, wann sie endlich kommen können.
6. OMA: Also, von mir aus kommen sie hoffentlich bald. Wie lange dauert der Flug (außer/von/zu) Amerika?
7. ANNA: (Bei/Nach/Mit) dem Flugzeug dauert es sieben Stunden. Also nicht so lange.
8. OPA: Sieben Stunden! Meine Güte!

26 **Wie ich wohne und lebe.** Bilden Sie Sätze mit den folgenden Elementen.

1. Ich wohne
   a. bei meinen Eltern zu Hause.
   b. mit Freunden zusammen.
   c. alleine
2. Ich wohne … hier.
   a. seit wenigen Wochen
   b. seit vielen Monaten
   c. seit einigen Jahren
3. Ich arbeite
   a. bei (McDonald's).
   b. in der Mensa°.
   c. zu Hause.
4. Ich esse oft
   a. mit meinem Zimmerkollegen.
   b. mit meiner Zimmerkollegin.
   c. allein.
5. Ich fahre … zur Uni.
   a. mit dem Rad
   b. mit dem Bus
   c. mit dem Auto

° *cafeteria*

27 **Neue Leute kennen lernen.** Kreuzen Sie die beste Antwort an.

S1: Wann lernst du neue Leute kennen?
S2: Beim Essen.

	Beim Lernen	*Beim Schlafen*	*Beim Spielen*	*Beim Essen*
1. neue Leute kennen lernen	___	___	___	___
2. vom Sommer träumen	___	___	___	___
3. Kollegen aus Kursen erkennen	___	___	___	___
4. Kleingeld brauchen	___	___	___	___
5. ungeduldig werden	___	___	___	___
6. über Physik und Deutsch lesen	___	___	___	___
7. mit Ausländern sprechen	___	___	___	___
8. einem Partner den Ball geben	___	___	___	___

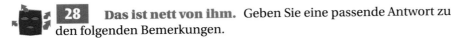

28 **Das ist nett von ihm.** Geben Sie eine passende Antwort zu den folgenden Bemerkungen.

Karl hilft Anna mit den Hausaufgaben.
Das ist nett von ihm.

Das ist	nett	von ...
	freundlich	
	nicht nett	
	unfair	

1. Karl hilft Anna mit den Hausaufgaben.
2. Barbara hilft Anna beim Einzug.
3. Inge leiht sich immer das Fahrrad von Barbara.
4. Wir leihen unseren Freunden gern Geld.
5. Karl gibt Carlos seine 20 Mark nicht zurück.
6. Die Studenten haben den Test vor der Prüfung gesehen.
7. Ich habe meiner Freundin Blumen geschenkt.
8. Der Professor gibt gar keine Prüfungen!

29 **Mein Tagesablauf.** Denken Sie an einen ganz normalen Tag. Schreiben Sie sechs Aktivitäten oder Termine° auf sechs Karten auf, z.B. (das) Aufstehen, die Vorlesung. Geben Sie dann einem Partner/einer Partnerin die gemischten Karten. Der Partner/Die Partnerin versucht, mit Fragen die richtige Reihenfolge der Aktivitäten und Termine festzustellen°. Benutzen Sie immer die Präposition **nach.**

appointments

determine

S1: Was machst du nach der Vorlesung?
S2: Nach der Vorlesung esse ich.
S1: Was machst du nach ...?

30 **Interview.** Stellen Sie einem Partner/einer Partnerin die folgenden Fragen.

Interview. German speakers use the question word **wohin** to ask for destinations (e.g., **Wohin fährst du?**). They use **wo** to ask for locations (e.g., **Wo wohnst du?**).

1. Bei wem wohnst du oder mit wem wohnst du zusammen?
2. Wie lange wohnst du schon in dieser Stadt?
3. Hast du einen Job? Wo arbeitest du?
4. Mit wem lernst du oft?
5. Wohin gehst du nach dem Unterricht?
6. Zu wem fährst du gern?
7. Wohin möchtest du fahren, wenn du Geld hast?
8. Aus welchem Land kommst du? Deine Eltern? Deine Großeltern?
9. Von wem bekommst du jedes Jahr ein Geschenk zum Geburtstag?
10. Zu wem gehst du, wenn du persönliche Probleme hast?

Ehrlich, ich bin mir da ganz sicher – die eine ist für Frauen mit Hosen und die andere für Frauen mit Rock.
TOILETTEN
© E. HAUSCHENBACH

V Expressing attitudes and conditions such as gratitude, pleasure, ownership, and need for assistance

Dative verbs and expressions

A. Dative verbs

There are five common verbs in German that always occur with the dative **(Dativverben).**

1. Expressing gratitude: **danken** *(to thank)*

   Ich **danke dir** für die Hilfe! *Thanks for your help!*

2. Expressing pleasure: **gefallen** *(to be appealing, pleasing)*

   Gefällt dir dein Zimmer denn nicht? *Don't you like your room?*

3. Expressing like and dislike for food: **schmecken** *(to taste good, bad)*

   Schokolade **schmeckt mir** immer. *Chocolate always tastes good to me.*
   Milch **schmeckt mir** nicht. *Milk doesn't taste good to me.*

4. Expressing ownership: **gehören** *(to belong)*

   Der Bleistift **gehört ihr.** *The pencil belongs to her.*

5. Expressing the need for assistance: **helfen** *(to help)*

   Kannst du mir bitte **helfen?** *Can you help me, please?*

German speakers often use expressions with **gefallen** or **schmecken** to compliment another person. The other person then responds with a comment or detail, or sometimes downplays the compliment.

KARL: Dein Pullover gefällt mir echt.
BARBARA: Danke. Er ist aus Norwegen. *(oder)*
Danke. Aber er ist schon alt.

BARBARA: Deine Spaghettisauce schmeckt mir wirklich gut.
KARL: Danke. Ich habe sie speziell für dich gemacht. *(oder)*
Danke. Aber ich hab' sie nur im Supermarkt gekauft.

31 **Komplimente machen.** Machen Sie Komplimente. Verwenden Sie **gefallen** oder **schmecken.**

S1: Dein Pullover gefällt mir gut.
S2: Danke. Ich habe ihn erst vor ein paar Tagen gekauft. *(oder)*
Ich danke dir, aber er ist schon alt.

1. dein Pullover
2. deine Schuhe
3. dein Kuchen
4. deine Freunde
5. dein Poster
6. dein Haus
7. dieser Wein
8. diese Tomaten

32 Ein Ratespiel. Bilden Sie Gruppen von vier bis sechs Leuten. Eine Person ist der Gruppenleiter/die Gruppenleiterin. Jede Person in der Gruppe gibt dem Leiter/der Leiterin ein oder zwei Gegenstände. Dann zeigt der Leiter/die Leiterin der Gruppe jeden Gegenstand und fragt: „Wem gehört das?" Die anderen Leute in der Gruppe beschreiben den Besitzer°/die Besitzerin. Nennen Sie keine Namen!

Ein Ratespiel. The noun **der Student** adds **-en** in all cases but the nominative singular.

owner

S1: Wem gehört das Buch?
S2: Das gehört einem Studenten mit schwarzen Haaren.
S3: Gehört das Buch einem Studenten mit einer Brille?
S1: Ja.
S4: Ist es Jeremy?
S1: Ja.

ein Student (eine Studentin) mit	schwarzen (blonden, roten, braunen, weißen) Haaren blauen (braunen, grünen, grauen) Augen einer Brille

B. *Adjectives with the dative case*

Some adjectives appear in conjunction with the dative in order to indicate a temporary condition rather than a permanent quality. When used with the dative case, these adjectives always refer to people. They are **warm, heiß, kalt, peinlich°, schlecht,** and **langweilig.**

embarrassing

It is important to use the dative with these adjectives. Incorrect use with **heiß, kalt,** and **warm** may lead to unintended meanings.

Temporary condition

Mir ist langweilig. — *I am bored.*
Ihr ist schlecht. — *She feels ill (nauseous).*
Mir ist kalt. — *I'm cold.*

Permanent quality

Ich bin langweilig. — *I am a boring person.*
Sie ist schlecht. — *She is a bad person.*
Es ist kalt heute. — *It's cold today.*

33 So fühle ich mich jetzt. Beschreiben Sie, wie Sie sich in dieser Situation fühlen.

Kannst du bitte das Fenster aufmachen?
Mir ist heiß.

1. Kannst du bitte das Fenster zumachen?
2. Kannst du bitte die Heizung° anmachen?
3. Ich möchte etwas Interessantes machen.
4. Ich kann jetzt nichts essen.

heat

C. *Idiomatic expressions with the dative case*

Here are some common idiomatic expressions that require the dative case.

Wie geht es Ihnen/dir? — *How are you?*
Das tut mir Leid. — *I'm sorry.*

Der Arm tut mir weh. *My arm hurts.*
Die frische Luft tut ihm gut. *Fresh air is good for him.*

Wissenswerte Vokabeln: Körperteile

Describing your body; talking about physical discomfort

■ Was tut dir weh?
Mir tun die Füße (die Augen) weh. (oder)
Ich habe mir das Bein gebrochen.

34 **Ursache° und Wirkung°: Mir tut der Arm weh.** Verbinden Sie eine Ursache mit einer Wirkung. *cause / effect*

■ Karl hat sich das Bein gebrochen.
Ihm tut das Bein weh.

1. Karl hat sich das Bein gebrochen.
2. Die Studenten haben heute sehr viel gelesen.
3. Frau Müller war heute Morgen beim Zahnarzt°. *dentist*
4. Ich habe ein Aspirin eingenommen.

a. Mir tut der Kopf weh.
b. Ihm tut das Bein weh.
c. Ihnen tun die Augen weh.
d. Ihr tun die Zähne weh.

5. Monika ist vom Fahrrad gefallen.
6. Stefan hat seine Wohnung eingerichtet und viele Möbel getragen.
7. Wir haben viel zu viel gegessen.
8. Anna und Barbara sind heute sehr weit gelaufen.
9. Die Musik im Konzert war zu laut.

e. Ihr tun die Knie weh.
f. Den Zuhörern tun die Ohren weh.
g. Ihm tun die Schultern und die Arme weh.
h. Ihnen tun die Füße weh.
i. Uns tut der Bauch weh.

35 **Mein Bauch tut mir weh.** Ihr Zimmerkollege°/Ihre Zimmerkollegin hat Pläne für den Abend. Sie haben aber gar keine Lust mitzumachen. Beantworten Sie die Fragen mit einer Ausrede° und sagen Sie, was Ihnen weh tut.

roommate

excuse

Mein Bauch tut mir weh. Select these situations at random and take turns.

S1: Ich gehe heute Abend essen. Hast du auch Lust?
S2: Nein, danke. Mein Bauch tut mir weh.

1. heute Abend essen gehen
2. mit Freunden Basketball spielen
3. einer Freundin beim Einziehen im Heim helfen
4. um acht Uhr ins Hard-Rock-Konzert gehen
5. in einer Stunde eine Fahrradtour machen
6. am Samstag wandern gehen
7. Karten spielen
8. Bier trinken gehen

VI Indicating location (II)

Dative of location: an der, am/an dem, an den

Earlier in this chapter you learned that German speakers use **in** with a definite article in the dative case (e.g., **in der, in dem, in den**) to indicate location. **An** is another two-case preposition that is used with a definite article in the dative case (e.g., **an der, an dem, an den**) to indicate location.

Ich stehe **an der** Tür. — *I'm standing at (near) the door.*
Viele Ausländer studieren **an den** Universitäten in Deutschland. — *Many foreigners study at the universities in Germany.*

Instead of **an dem,** German speakers generally use the contraction **am.**

Ich stehe **am** Kopierer. — *I'm standing at the copy machine.*

36 **Wo macht man das?** Verbinden Sie eine Handlung mit einem Platz.

Die Studentin macht Fotokopien.
Sie steht am Kopierer.

1. Die Studentin macht Fotokopien.
2. Der Türke fährt mit dem Zug nach Istanbul.
3. Die Studenten sprechen mit ihrem Professor.

a. Er ist am Bahnhof.
b. Er ist am Flughafen.
c. Er steht am Auto.

4. Die Studentin möchte ins Zimmer gehen.
5. Herr Müller will zur Arbeit fahren.
6. Der Gastprofessor aus China fliegt in 30 Minuten ab.

d. Sie sind an der Uni.
e. Sie steht am Kopierer.
f. Sie steht an der Tür.

37 **Wo ist ...?** Diese Leute sind an ihrem Arbeitsplatz. Wo ist das genau? Fragen Sie einen Partner/eine Partnerin.

S1: Wo ist Erika?
S2: Sie ist an der Uni.

Personen und ihre Berufe	***Arbeitsplätze***
1. Erika ist Studentin.	a. der Flughafen
2. Herr Meyer ist Pilot.	b. der Kopierer
3. Frau Wallner arbeitet bei der Bahn.	c. die Tür zum Kino
4. Hermann kontrolliert° Kinokarten.	d. der Bahnhof
5. Bettina arbeitet in einem Kopierladen.	e. die Uni

° *is checking*

VII Specifying what you are talking about

Der-words

You have already encountered examples of the **der**-words **dieser/dieses/diese** *(this, that)* in the directions for activities as well as in the **Absprungtext** of this chapter. German speakers use forms of **dieser/dieses/diese** when they want to point to something specific.

> The literal translation of *that* is **jener/jenes/jene** (e.g., **jener Mann, jenes Kind, jene Frau, jene Leute**). It is almost entirely used in written German only. Generally, **dieser/dieses/diese** stands for both *this* and *that.*

Ergänzen Sie **diese** Sätze mit Wörtern aus dem **Absprungtext.**
Complete these sentences with words from the **Absprungtext.**
Warst du nicht auch gestern in **diesem** Seminar?
Weren't you in this seminar yesterday too?

Dieser/dieses/diese are classified as **der-** words because they exhibit endings similar to **der/das/die.**

dieser/dieses/diese	*this, that*
Ich kenne **diese Frau.**	*I know this woman.*
Kannst du **dieser Studentin** helfen?	*Can you help this student?*
jeder/jedes/jede	*each, every*
Jeden Tag stehe ich um sechs Uhr auf.	*Every day I get up at six o'clock.*
Jeder Student in diesem Seminar muss ein Referat schreiben.	*Every student in this seminar must write a paper.*

The plural of **jeder/jedes/jede** is **alle** *(all)* in the nominative and accusative cases and **allen** *(all)* in the dative.

Alle Studenten müssen ein Referat schreiben.	*All students have to write a paper.*
Welcher/welches/welche	*which*
Welche Sätze bedeuten ungefähr das Gleiche?	*Which sentences have approximately the same meaning?*
Welcher Student kommt aus der Türkei?	*Which student is from Turkey?*

Here are the nominative, accusative, and dative endings for **der**-words:

	Masculine	Neuter	Feminine	Plural
Nominative	dies**er** Mann jed**er** Mann welch**er** Mann	dies**es** Kind jed**es** Kind welch**es** Kind	dies**e** Frau jed**e** Frau welch**e** Frau	dies**e** Freunde all**e** Männer welch**e** Freunde
Accusative	dies**en** Mann jed**en** Mann welch**en** Mann	dies**es** Kind jed**es** Kind welch**es** Kind	dies**e** Frau jed**e** Frau welch**e** Frau	dies**e** Freunde all**e** Frauen welch**e** Freunde
Dative	dies**em** Mann jed**em** Mann welch**em** Mann	dies**em** Kind jed**em** Kind welch**em** Kind	dies**er** Frau jed**er** Frau welch**er** Frau	dies**en** Freunde**n** all**en** Kinder**n** welch**en** Freunde**n**

Remember that plural nouns add an **-n** in the dative plural unless they already end in **-n**, **dieser Freund, diese Freunde, mit diesen Freunden.**

38 **Nimm diesen hier!** Fragen Sie einen Freund/eine Freundin, ob er/sie Ihnen diese Gegenstände leihen oder geben kann.

einen Stift leihen

S1: Kannst du mir einen Stift leihen/geben?
S2: Ja, nimm diesen Stift hier.

1. einen Stift
2. eine Lampe
3. ein Radio
4. ein Fahrrad
5. ein Poster
6. eine Cola
7. einen 20-Mark-Schein
8. ein Buch über Deutschland

39 **Entscheidungen° am Bahnhof.** Barbara ist am Bahnhof. Sie hat aber noch keine konkreten Reisepläne. Karl hilft ihr. Finden Sie einen Partner/eine Partnerin und spielen Sie Barbara und Karl. Setzen Sie auch eine richtige Form von **welcher/welches/welche** in Barbaras Fragen ein.

decisions

Entscheidungen am Bahnhof. Der Lokalzug stops in every train station. **Der Eilzug** is a faster train with stops in larger towns and cities only. In addition, there are **Intercity-Züge,** which stop only in very large cities. They require an extra fee **(der Zuschlag)** of 10 DM.

S1 (BARBARA): Um welche Zeit soll ich nur abfahren: um vier Uhr oder um vier Uhr dreißig?
S2 (KARL): Fahr um vier Uhr ab.

1. Um ______ Zeit soll ich nur abfahren: um vier Uhr oder um vier Uhr dreißig?
2. Mit ______ Zug soll ich nur fahren: mit einem Eilzug oder mit einem Lokalzug?
3. ______ Stadt soll ich nur besuchen: Bonn oder Hamburg?
4. ______ Buch soll ich im Zug lesen: mein Deutschbuch oder einen Roman?
5. ______ CDs soll ich für die Reise mitbringen: Jazz oder Rock?
6. ______ Freund oder ______ Freundin soll ich auf der Reise ein Souvenir kaufen: dir oder Anna?
7. Mit ______ Leuten soll ich nur im Abteil° sitzen: mit jungen oder mit alten?

compartment

40 **Übertreibungen.** Barbara beschreibt das deutsche Studentenleben. Sie übertreibt ein bisschen. Setzen Sie eine richtige Form von **jeder/jedes/jede** und **alle** ein. Benutzen Sie **alle** für Nominativ und Akkusativ Plural und **allen** für Dativ Plural.

1. _____ Tag müssen die Studenten um fünf Uhr morgens aufstehen.
2. Dann lernen _____ Studenten zwei bis drei Stunden.
3. Danach isst _____ Student und _____ Studentin nur ein Stück Brot mit Käse.
4. Dann gehen die Studenten zur Uni: sie gehen zu _____ Vorlesung.
5. Die Studenten stellen viele Fragen und _____ Frage ist intelligent und wichtig.
6. _____ Professoren freuen sich über die Fragen. Sie helfen _____ Studenten gern.
7. _____ Abend arbeiten die Studenten schwer.
8. Und _____ Wochenende lernen oder arbeiten sie auch. Sie haben keine Freizeit.

FREIE KOMMUNIKATION

Rollenspiel: Am Automaten. Sie stehen am Automaten und möchten etwas kaufen (z.B. eine Cola, Zigaretten, etwas zu essen). Sie haben aber nicht das richtige Kleingeld. Sie haben nur Geldscheine. Sie brauchen ein 50-Pfennig-Stück. Neben Ihnen steht ein Ausländer/eine Ausländerin. Fragen Sie, ob er/sie Ihnen Geld wechseln kann. Fragen Sie, woher er/sie kommt, wo er/sie wohnt, was er/sie hier macht usw.

Rollenspiel: Ausländer. Sie treffen in der Küche im Studentenwohnheim einen Ausländer/eine Ausländerin. Er/Sie ist neu. Er/Sie möchte wissen, wo man einkaufen kann, wo man telefonieren kann, wie man in die Stadt kommt usw. Helfen Sie ihm/ihr. Sagen Sie, dass Sie auch ein Ausländer/eine Ausländerin sind.

Rollenspiel: Beim Arzt. Patient(in): Sie sind ein Hypochonder. Sie gehen zum Arzt, denn Sie fühlen sich schon wieder nicht sehr wohl. Beschreiben Sie dem Arzt Ihre Symptome. Arzt (Ärztin): Sie kennen diesen Patienten/diese Patientin sehr gut. Er/Sie ist ein Hypochonder. Sie wissen, dass die beste Lösung° ist, wenn Sie gut zuhören und viele Fragen über die Probleme stellen.

°solution

ARZT (ÄRZTIN): Wie fühlen Sie sich heute?
PATIENT(IN): Mir tut der Bauch weh.
(oder)
PATIENT(IN): Können Sie mir helfen?
ARZT (ÄRZTIN): Wo tut es Ihnen weh?

Ärzte

Dr. med. T. Thongbhoubesra, Basler Straße 54, Tel. 15 03 30	nach Vereinbarung
Dr. med. Neels Wallgrün, Schlatter Straße 15, Tel. 35 26	Mo - Fr 10 - 12 Uhr, Mo u. Fr 15 - 17 Uhr, Mi 15 - 18 Uhr

Schreibecke **Rundherum in dieser Stadt: eine Werbebroschüre.**

Sie haben einen neuen Job bei einer Werbeagentur° in Frankfurt und müssen für Ihre Chefin° eine Broschüre für eine kleine Fantasiestadt in Deutschland schreiben. Die Stadt heißt Neuheim am Main. In der Broschüre sollen Sie viele Informationen über Neuheim am Main geben. Geben Sie an,

ad agency
boss

Rundherum in dieser Stadt. Helpful words: **die Gasse, die Straße, der Weg, das Schloss, die Schule, die Wiese, das Café, der Wald, das Kino, das Theater, der Zoo, der Club, das Stadtmuseum, das Institut.**

- wo man gut essen kann
- wo man Musik hören kann
- wo man einen Spaziergang machen kann
- wo man gut trinken kann usw.

Beschreiben Sie detailliert, wo man diese Aktivitäten machen kann, z.B.: Man kann in der Beethovenstraße viel Jazzmusik hören. Benutzen Sie auch den Imperativ, z.B.: Besuchen Sie mit Ihrer Familie unsere Stadt am Main! Beginnen Sie die Broschüre mit dem folgenden Satz.

Neuheim am Main bietet dem Besucher viele Attraktionen und Sehenswürdigkeiten.

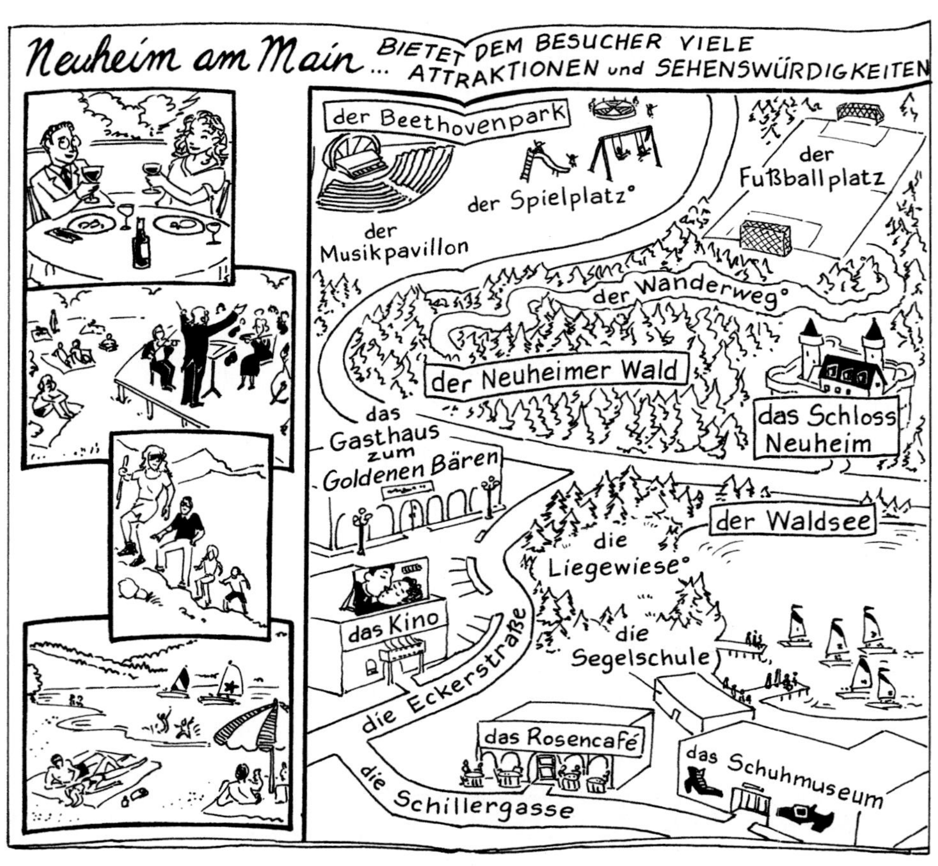

playground

hiking path

meadow

ZIELTEXT

Gespräch in der Gemeinschaftsküche

Anna hat inzwischen ihr Zimmer eingerichtet° und hat jetzt Hunger. Sie geht mit Barbara in die Gemeinschaftsküche. In der Küche lernen sie Karl und Inge kennen. Barbara möchte etwas zu essen machen, aber sie weiß nicht so genau, wo alles ist. Karl und Inge geben Anna und Barbara viele Tipps über die Küche und das Wohnheim. Aber zuerst trinken sie zusammen einen Tee.

° *furnished*

Vorschau

41 **Thematische Fragen: Ein Gespräch mit Karl und Inge.** Kreuzen Sie an, wie wahrscheinlich es ist, dass Karl und Inge mit Anna und Barbara über die folgenden Themen sprechen.

	Sehr unwahrscheinlich	*Vielleicht*	*Sehr wahrscheinlich*
1. Tübingen	___	___	___
2. die Sachen in der Küche	___	___	___
3. Ausländer im Heim	___	___	___
4. den Islam	___	___	___
5. Hunger haben	___	___	___
6. die Organisation in der Küche	___	___	___
7. Annas Kochen	___	___	___
8. das Essen in der Mensa°	___	___	___

° *cafeteria*

42 **Satzdetektiv.** Welche Sätze bedeuten ungefähr das Gleiche?

1. Hier wohnen eigentlich viele **Ausländer** im Haus.
2. Ich weiß nicht, wo die **Töpfe** sind.
3. Es gibt zwei **Kühlschränke** hier.
4. Ich hoffe, dass dir der Hauswart einen Schlüssel **mitgegeben** hat.

a. Du kannst das Essen in diesen beiden Schränken kühl halten.
b. Hoffentlich hast du vom Hausmeister einen Schlüssel bekommen.
c. Studenten aus vielen Ländern wohnen im Studentenheim.
d. Wo sind die Pfannen und anderen Sachen in der Küche?

---

5. Also du kannst nur **das Notwendigste reinstellen.**
6. Das ist dein **Fach** für Brot und Reis und so.
7. Die Küche ist immer offen, deswegen musst du eben dein Fach immer **unter Verschluss halten.**
8. Sonst kommen die Leute rein und **nehmen** dir einfach **das Zeug weg.**

e. Das ist dein Platz im Schrank für Brot und Reis und andere Sachen.
f. Du hast nur Platz für die wichtigsten Sachen.
g. Schließ dein Fach immer ab, weil jeder in die Küche gehen kann.
h. Wenn du das nicht machst, kommen andere Studenten und essen deine Sachen.

ZIELTEXT

Gespräch in der Gemeinschaftsküche

Hören Sie gut zu.

Rückblick

43 **Gemischte Sätze.** Bringen Sie diese Sätze aus dem Dialog in die richtige Reihenfolge.

___ Also, ich muss mal etwas Essen kaufen.
___ Anna hat ein bisschen Hunger, wir wollen uns eigentlich 'was zu essen machen.
___ Guten Appetit!
___ Ich hab' mir gerade einen Tee gekocht.
_1_ Ich glaube, ich habe euch auch schon mal gesehen.
___ Und ich hoffe, dass dir der Hauswart einen Schlüssel mitgegeben hat.
___ Wir sind am Ende vom Gang.

44 **Stimmt das?** Stimmen diese Aussagen zum Text oder nicht? Wenn nicht, was stimmt?

	Ja, das stimmt.	*Nein, das stimmt nicht.*
1. Anna weiß, wo die Küche im Studentenheim ist.	___	___
2. Barbara hat Karl und Inge noch nie vorher im Leben gesehen.	___	___
3. Karl und Inge wohnen beide am Ende vom Flur.	___	___
4. Im Studentenwohnheim gibt es viele Ausländer.	___	___
5. Karl lädt Anna und Barbara zu einem Kaffee ein.	___	___
6. In der Gemeinschaftsküche gibt es zwei Kühlschränke mit einem Fach für jeden Studenten.	___	___
7. Alle Studenten im Heim müssen sich diese Küche teilen.	___	___
8. Die Küche ist nur für wenige Stunden am Tag offen.	___	___
9. Man muss sein Essen unter Verschluss halten, sonst nehmen es die anderen weg.	___	___

45 **Der aktive Zuhörer.** Hören Sie sich den Text noch einmal an und ergänzen Sie die Sätze mit Wörtern aus dem **Zieltext.**

1. ANNA: Barbara, ich habe Hunger. Weißt du, _____ ich essen kann?
2. BARBARA: Wir können _____ hier etwas zu essen machen.
3. INGE: Du bist da _____, ja?
4. KARL: Hier wohnen eigentlich viele _____ im Haus.
5. KARL: Dann können wir _____ das erklären.
6. KARL: Und _____ du die Tür aufmachst, hat _____ sein Fach.
7. KARL: Ich hoffe, dass _____ der Hauswart einen Schlüssel mitgegeben hat.
8. BARBARA: Sonst kommen die Leute rein und nehmen _____ einfach das Zeug weg.

In der Gemeinschaftsküche darf man jederzeit kochen.

46 **Ergänzen Sie.** Ergänzen Sie diese Sätze mit Wörtern aus dem **Zieltext.**

1. Anna hat nichts gegessen. Sie hat _____ und will etwas essen.
2. Man kann in der _____ Essen machen.
3. „Essen machen" heißt auch _____.
4. Anna und Barbara möchten etwas zu essen machen, aber sie wissen nicht, wo die _____ sind.
5. Karl hat gerade einen _____ gekocht und lädt sie alle ein.
6. Niemand im Wohnheim hat eine Privatküche, alle Studenten müssen sich eine Küche _____.
7. In der Küche im Studentenwohnheim hat jeder sein eigenes _____ für Trockenprodukte wie Brot und _____.

8. Die Fächer sind ziemlich klein; deswegen kann man nur das Notwendigste _____.
9. Man soll sein Fach unter Verschluss _____, denn die Küche ist immer offen.
10. Sonst kommen die Leute rein und nehmen einfach das _____.

■ FREIE ■ KOMMUNIKATION ■

Rollenspiel: In der Küche. Sie sind mit einem Freund/einer Freundin in der Küche und möchten eine Pizza für eine Party machen. Ihr Freund/Ihre Freundin hilft Ihnen und gibt Ihnen, was Sie brauchen. Hier sind einige Ausdrücke.

das Brot • dieser Topf da • Salz und Pfeffer • der Löffel • das Messer • die Gabel • der Teller • das Mehl° • die Tomaten • der Käse • die Wurst • die Pilze° • die Oliven • das Öl • das Wasser

flour
mushrooms

S1: Kannst du mir helfen?
Wo ist/sind ...?
Wem gehört/gehören ...?
Gefällt/Gefallen dir ...?
Kannst du mir ... geben?
Kannst du ... | finden? / waschen? / schneiden°?

S2: Ich helfe dir gern.
Leider haben wir das nicht.
im Kühlschrank.
Ich weiß nicht.
Ich kann den Käse nicht finden.

cut

Rollenspiel: Im Leihhaus°. Sie brauchen dringend Möbel für ein Studentenzimmer, aber Sie haben kein Geld. Sie gehen ins Leihhaus und versuchen dort, die folgenden Gegenstände gegen Möbel einzutauschen°. Spielen Sie die Situation.

pawn shop
exchange

Sie haben ...
eine Kamera • eine Gitarre • einen Ring • viele CDs • einen Tennisschläger • einen Golfschläger

Sie brauchen ...
einen Stuhl • ein Sofa • eine Lampe • einen Farbfernseher • einen Schreibtisch

Ich habe eine Kamera. Können Sie mir einen Tisch für die Kamera geben?
(oder)
Ich brauche ein Bett. Wollen Sie meine Gitarre?

Rollenspiel: Beim Skilaufen. Sie sind mit Freunden Skilaufen in den Alpen. Leider haben Sie viele Skisachen im Zug vergessen. Zum Glück haben Ihre Freunde vieles doppelt. Versuchen Sie, die Skisachen von Ihren Freunden zu leihen.

diese Skier • der Skianorak° • die Skistiefel • diese Skistöcke° • die Skimaske • die Handschuhe • der Pullover • die Sonnenbrille • die Sonnenschutzcreme°

ski jacket / ski poles
suntan lotion

Welche Größe° ist das (brauchst du)?
Wem gehören (diese Skier)?
Was gefällt dir besser?

size

Schreibecke **Die Skihütte° in Zermatt.** Sie haben eine Luxusskihütte in Zermatt für eine Woche. Schreiben Sie einen Brief an Karl in Tübingen. Wie viele Zimmer hat die Skihütte? Wo ist sie? Was gefällt Ihnen? Was gefällt Ihnen nicht so gut? Was haben Sie im Zug vergessen? Wer hat sich beim Skilaufen verletzt°?

ski lodge

injured

Lesen Sie die Legende und schreiben Sie dann den Brief zu Ende.

Lieber Karl,
unsere Skihütte in Zermatt ist ganz toll! Sie ist sogar eine Luxusskihütte! …

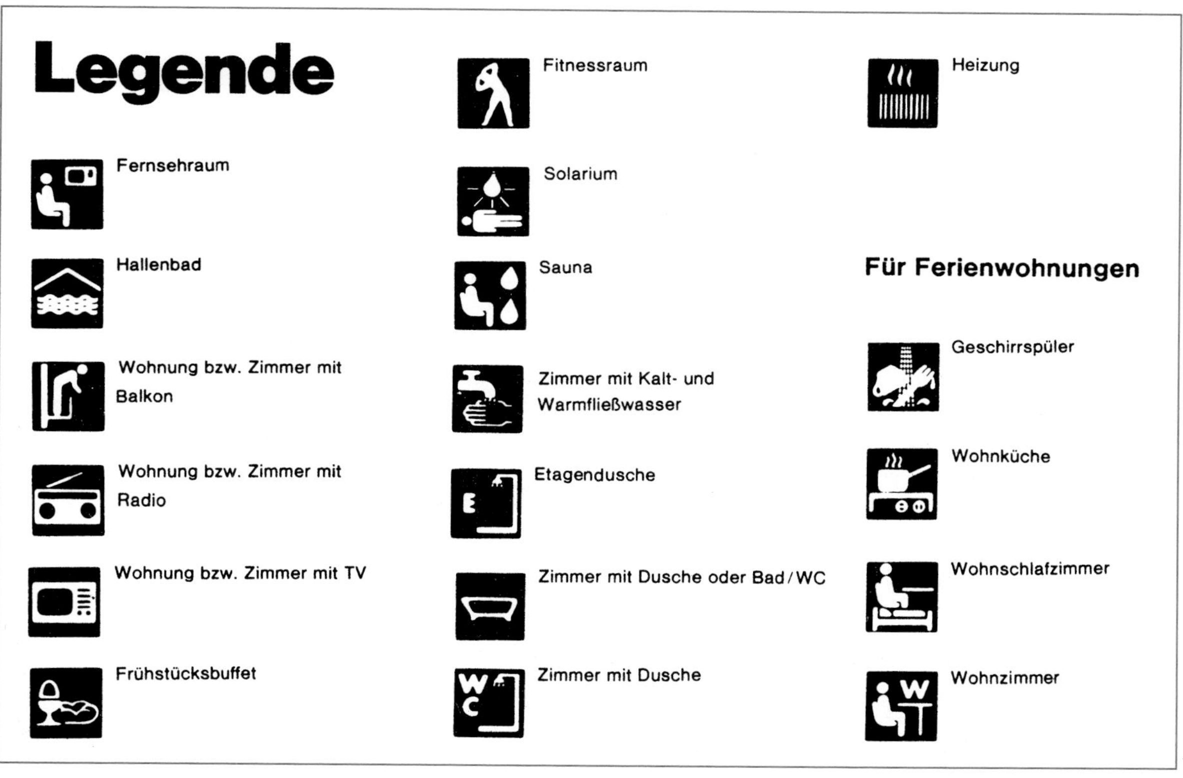

Wie heißt mein Studentenwohnheim? Beschreiben Sie Ihr Studentenwohnheim in zehn Sätzen, aber nennen Sie nicht den Namen des Wohnheims! In welchem Stock wohnen Sie? Seit wann wohnen Sie dort? Was haben Sie alles? Welche Zimmernummer haben Sie? Was gefällt Ihnen gut/nicht gut? Dann geben Sie die Beschreibung einem Partner/einer Partnerin und er/sie soll erraten, in welchem Wohnheim Sie wohnen.

Die Küche. In der Küche fehlen° viele Sachen. Der Hausmeister will wissen, was die Studenten in der Küche haben und was sie brauchen. Anna, Barbara, Karl und Inge schreiben eine Liste für den Hausmeister.

are missing

ein Herd • ein Fernseher • Töpfe • eine Faxmaschine • ein Bett • ein Mikrowellenherd • Kochbücher • Fächer für Brot und Reis • ein Kühlschrank • eine Geschirrspülmaschine° • eine Kaffeemaschine • Tee und Kaffee • ein Spiegel° • ein Spülbecken° • ein Teppich • eine Brot- und Wurstschneidemaschine°

dishwasher
mirror / sink
bread and meat slicer

An den Hausmeister:

betreff°: Küche im Studentenheim

Regarding

Es gibt: einen Herd: ______________________ ,
______________________ , ______________________ ,
______________________ , ______________________ ,
______________________ , ______________________ ,
______________________ , ______________________ ,
______________________ , ______________________ ,

Wir brauchen: ______________________ ,
______________________ , ______________________ ,
______________________ , ______________________ ,
______________________ , ______________________ ,
______________________ , ______________________ ,
______________________ , ______________________ ,

■ Wortschatz ■

Das Studentenzimmer

das Bett, -en *bed*
das Bild, -er *picture*
das Bücherregal, -e *book case*
der Computer, -s *computer*
die Couch *couch*
der Drucker, - *printer*
die Gardine, -n *curtain(s)*
die Klamotten *(pl.) things to wear, duds*
der Kleiderschrank, ¨-e *wardrobe, armoire*
die Kommode, -n *chest of drawers*
die Möbel *furniture*
die Pflanze, -n *green plant*
das Poster, - *poster*
das Radio, -s *radio*
das Regal, -e *shelves*
der Schrank, ¨-e *closet, wardrobe*
der Sessel, - *armchair (North), chair (South)*
das Sofa, -s *sofa*
der Spiegel, - *mirror*
die Stereoanlage, -n *stereo set*
der Teppich, -e *carpet*
das Waschbecken, - *sink*
der Wecker, - *alarm clock*

Das Studenten(wohn)heim, -e

der Automat, [-en], -en *vending machine*
das Badezimmer, - *bathroom*
das Brett, -er *board*
  das schwarze Brett *bulletin board*
die Bude, -n *student room*
  die Luxusbude, -n *luxury student room*

die Dusche, -n *shower*
der Duschraum, ¨-e *shower room*
der Einzug *moving into (an apartment)*
das Ende, -n *end*
das Erdgeschoss, *pl.* **Erdgeschosse** *ground floor*
der Gang, ¨-e *hallway, corridor*
das Gemeinschaftsbad, ¨-er *shared bathroom, floor bathroom*
die Hilfe, -n *help, aid*
der Keller, - *basement, cellar*
das Klo, -s (das Klosett) *toilet (colloq.)*
der Korridor, -e *hall, corridor*
die Küche, -n *kitchen*
das Postfach, ¨-er *mailbox*
das Privatbad, ¨-er *private bath*
die Reihenfolge, -n *order, sequence*
der Schlüssel, - *key*
der Stock, *pl.* **Stockwerke** *floor, story*
  der erste Stock (die erste Etage) *second floor*
  der zweite Stock (die zweite Etage) *third floor*
die Telefonzelle, -n *telephone booth*
die Vorlesung, -en *lecture*
die Zimmernummer, -n *room number*

Wo?

am Ende vom Korridor *at the end of the hall*
auf dem zweiten Stock *on the third floor*
einen Stock höher *one floor up*
einen Stock tiefer *one floor down*
im Erdgeschoss *on the first (ground) floor*

an·halten (hält an, hat angehalten) *to stop*
auf·kriegen (hat aufgekriegt) *to get open (slang)*
auf·schließen (hat aufgeschlossen) *to unlock*
auf·schreiben (hat aufgeschrieben) *to write down*
bekommen (hat bekommen) *to get, receive*
danken (hat gedankt) + *dat. to thank*
ein·ziehen (ist eingezogen) *to move in*
gefallen (gefällt, hat gefallen) + *dat. to please (to like)*
gucken (hat geguckt) *to look*
leihen (hat geliehen) *to lend; borrow*
recht sein + *dat. to be all right with someone*
schlafen (schläft, hat geschlafen) *to sleep*
  ein Bett zum Schlafen *a bed for sleeping*
wohnen (hat gewohnt) *to live*

Andere Wörter

also ... *well . . . , so . . . (for stalling)*
du, ... *hey . . . (for introducing an utterance in an informal but friendly manner)*
echt *authentic, genuine, real(ly)*
eigen *own*
fein *fine*
na ... *well . . . (for stalling)*
neben *next to, beside*
nett *nice*
richtig *authentic, real(ly)*
schnell *fast, quickly*
selber *self (my/your/his/herself, etc.)*
unten *downstairs*
vor + *dat. ago*
ziemlich *rather*
zwar nicht *certainly isn't*

Ausdrücke

alles, was du brauchst *everything you need*
Alles klar! *O.K.! Great!*
Bis gleich! *See you soon!*
Du hast wirklich Schwein gehabt! *You were really lucky!*
Du, ich danke dir echt für die Hilfe! *Hey, thanks a lot for the help!*
Er hat einen Vogel. *He's crazy; he's nuts.*
Ich bin hundemüde *I'm dog-tired.*
nett von dir *nice of you*
so gegen Mittag *sometime around noon*
tschüss! *bye!*
vielen Dank *thanks a lot*
vor einer Woche *a week ago*
wenn es dir recht ist *if it's all right with you*

Das Einfamilienhaus, ¨-er

der Abstellraum, ¨-e *storage room*
das Arbeitszimmer, - *work room, study*
der Balkon, -s *balcony*
der Dachboden, ¨ *attic*
die Diele, -n *entrance hallway*
der Eingang, ¨-e *entrance, front door*
die Etage, -n *floor, story*
der Flur, -e *hall, corridor*
der Gang, ¨-e *hall, hallway*
die Garage, -n *garage*
der Garten, ¨ *garden*
das Gästezimmer, - *guest room*
der Hobbyraum, ¨-e *hobby room*
das Kinderzimmer, - *children's room*
der Rolladen, ¨ *roll-top shutter(s)*
das Schlafzimmer, - *bedroom*
die Toilette, -n *toilet*
die Treppe (das Treppenhaus) *stairway*
die Waschküche, -n *laundry room*
das WC, -s *toilet*
das Wohnzimmer, - *living room*

Wo?

auf dem Dachboden *in the attic*
im Erdgeschoss *on the ground floor*
im Keller *in the basement*

im ersten Stock (auf der ersten Etage) *on the second floor*
im zweiten Stock (auf der zweiten Etage) *on the third floor*

„Am Kopierer"

die Antwort, -en *answer*
der Autor, -en/die Autorin, -nen *author*
das Blatt, ¨er *page, sheet*
das Christentum *Christianity*
der Diskurs, -e *discourse*
das Geld, -er *money*
der Groschen, - *10-Pfennig coin*
der Islam *Islam*
der Kopierer, - *photocopier*
der Schein, -e *paper money, bill*
der Türke, [-n], -n/die Türkin, -nen *Turk*
die Türkei *Turkey*
die Unterdrückung *oppression, repression*
die Welt, -en *world*
niemand *no one, nobody*

an·schauen (hat angeschaut) *to look at*
auf·schauen (hat aufgeschaut) *to look up*
auf·wachsen (wächst auf, ist aufgewachsen) *to grow up*
aus·sehen (sieht aus, hat ausgesehen) *to appear, look (like)*
blättern (hat geblättert) in + *dat.* *to leaf through*
sich entscheiden (hat sich entschieden) *to decide*
sich entscheiden für + *acc.* *to decide on, in favor of*
erkennen (hat erkannt) *to recognize*
sich fühlen (hat sich gefühlt) *to feel*
heben (hat gehoben) *to lift*
reichen (hat gereicht) *to be enough, suffice, last*
schauen (hat geschaut) *to look*
scheinen (hat geschienen) *to appear to be*
sortieren (hat sortiert) *to sort*
stecken (hat gesteckt) *to stick*
überlegen (hat überlegt) *to consider, think about*
unterdrücken (hat unterdrückt) *to oppress, repress*
wechseln (hat gewechselt) *to change money*
wiederholen (hat wiederholt) *to repeat*
ziehen (hat gezogen) *to pull, raise*

eigentlich *actually*
erstaunt *astonished*
hoch *high, up*
irritiert *irritated*
nebendran *adjacent, next to*
positiv *positive*
prinzeßhaft *princess-like*
selbst *self*
ungeduldig *impatient*
verblüfft *stunned*
verwundert *amazed*
wenn *if, when, as soon as*
wohlbehütet *well-protected, sheltered*
zerbrechlich *fragile, breakable*
zufrieden *satisfied*

Ausdrücke

bei euch *where you live, in your house/country*
wie ich gerade drauf bin *however I feel at the moment*

Dativpräpositionen

aus *from; out of*
außer *except for*
bei *at, by, near, with*
mit *with*
nach *to; after*
seit *since, for*
von *from, by*
zu *to*

Dativverben

danken (hat gedankt) + *dat.* *to thank*
gefallen (gefällt, hat gefallen) + *dat.* *to please; to like*
gehören (hat gehört) + *dat.* *to belong to*
helfen (hilft, hat geholfen) + *dat.* *to help*
schmecken (hat geschmeckt) + *dat.* *to taste good to*

Ausdrücke

Das tut mir Leid. *I am sorry.*
meiner Meinung nach *in my opinion*
Mir ist warm (heiß/kalt/schlecht/langweilig). *I'm warm (hot/cold/sick/bored).*
mit anderen Worten *in other words*
von mir aus *as far as I'm concerned*
Wie geht es Ihnen/dir? *How are you? How's it going?*

Die Körperteile

der Arm, -e *arm*
das Auge, -n *eye*
die Augenbraue, -n *eyebrow*
der Bauch, ⸚e *stomach*
das Bein, -e *leg*
die Brust, ⸚e *breast, chest*
der Ellenbogen, - *elbow*
der Finger, - *finger*
der Fuß, ⸚e *foot*
das Gesicht, -er *face*
das Haar, -e *hair*
der Hals, ⸚e *throat*
die Hand, ⸚e *hand*
der Hintern *rear*
das Kinn, -e *chin*
das Knie, - *knee*
der Kopf, ⸚e *head*
die Lippe, -n *lip*
der Mund, ⸚er *mouth*
die Nase, -n *nose*
das Ohr, -en *ear*
der Rücken, - *back*
die Schulter, -n *shoulder*
die Stirn, -en *forehead*
der Zahn, ⸚e *tooth*
der Zeh, -en *toe*

Ausdrücke

Was tut dir weh? *Where do you hurt?*
Mir tut das Auge weh. *My eye hurts.*
Mir tun die Füße weh. *My feet hurt.*
Ich habe mir das Bein gebrochen. *I broke my leg.*

Der-Wörter

dieser, diese, dieses; diese *this, that; these, those*
jeder, jede, jedes; alle *each, every; all*
welcher, welche, welches, welche *which*

Aus dem Zieltext

der Ausländer, -/die Ausländerin, -nen *foreigner*
das Fach, ⸚er *compartment*
die Gemeinschaftsküche, -n *shared kitchen*
der Hauswart, -e *custodian, janitor*
der Kühlschrank, ⸚e *refrigerator*
das Notwendigste *bare necessities*
der Reis *rice*
der Tee, -s *tea*
der Topf, ⸚e *pot*
der Verschluss, ⸚e *lock, clasp*
das Zeug *stuff, things*
erklären (erklärt, hat erklärt) *to explain*
unter Verschluss halten (hält, hat gehalten) *to keep under lock and key*
hoffen (hat gehofft) *to hope*
Tee kochen (hat gekocht) *to make tea*
rein·stellen (hat reingestellt) *to put in*
sich teilen (hat sich geteilt) *to share*

Ausdrücke

Gern geschehen! *Glad to help! My pleasure!*
Grüßt euch! *Hi, you guys!*
Guten Appetit! *Bon appetit! (Have a nice meal!)*
jederzeit *anytime*

Andere Wörter

deswegen *therefore, for that reason*
eigentlich *actually*
klar *sure, all clear*
kompliziert *complicated*
sonst *otherwise*
ziemlich [klein] *kind of, pretty, quite*

Deutsch im Beruf 2

Identifying job interests

Choosing an occupation **(der Beruf)** or even a temporary job is an important and often difficult choice **(die Berufswahl)** for many people. The first step to finding an occupation is determining your interests **(Interessen)** and abilities **(Fähigkeiten)** as well as describing personal characteristics **(persönliche Eigenschaften).**

1 **Berufswahl-„Steckbrief": Was ist wichtig?** Lesen Sie die Grafik und entscheiden Sie, welche Faktoren für die Berufswahl wichtig sind.

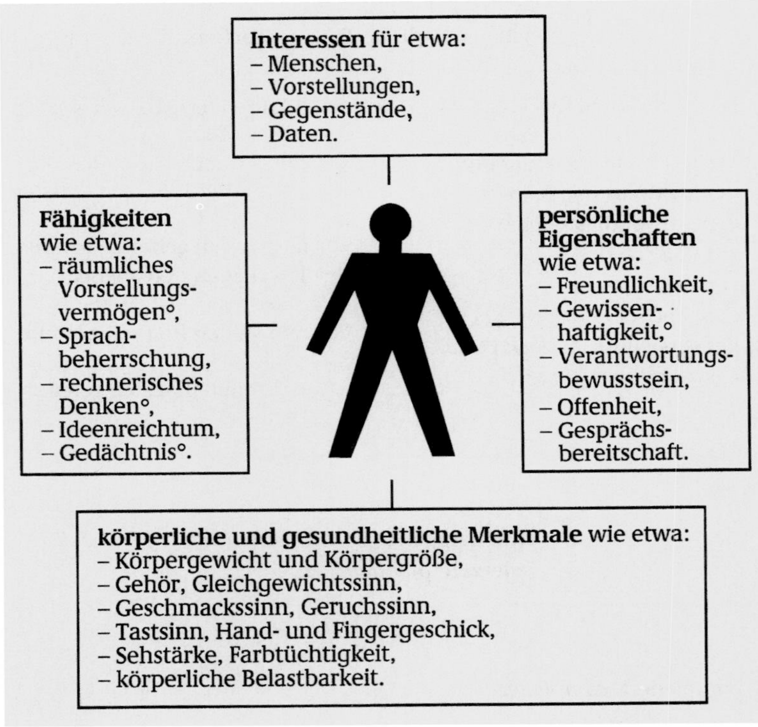

Interessen für etwa:
– Menschen,
– Vorstellungen,
– Gegenstände,
– Daten.
Fähigkeiten wie etwa:
– räumliches Vorstellungsvermögen°,
– Sprachbeherrschung,
– rechnerisches Denken°,
– Ideenreichtum,
– Gedächtnis°.
persönliche Eigenschaften wie etwa:
– Freundlichkeit,
– Gewissenhaftigkeit,°
– Verantwortungsbewusstsein,
– Offenheit,
– Gesprächsbereitschaft.
körperliche und gesundheitliche Merkmale wie etwa:
– Körpergewicht und Körpergröße,
– Gehör, Gleichgewichtssinn,
– Geschmackssinn, Geruchssinn,
– Tastsinn, Hand- und Fingergeschick,
– Sehstärke, Farbtüchtigkeit,
– körperliche Belastbarkeit.

räumliches Vorstellungsvermögen: *spatial sense*
conscientiousness
rechnerisches Denken: *quantitative thinking*
memory

Interesse für …

1. Menschen.	a. Zahlen und Nummern interessieren mich.
2. Vorstellungen und Ideen.	b. Arbeit mit Personen interessiert mich.
3. Gegenstände.	c. Ich bin kreativ. Ich habe viele Ideen.
4. Daten.	d. Objekte interessieren mich.

Persönliche Eigenschaften wie …

5. Freundlichkeit.	e. Ich bin offen.
6. Verantwortungsbewusstsein.	f. Ich spreche gern mit anderen Menschen.
7. Offenheit.	g. Ich bin freundlich.
8. Gesprächsbereitschaft.	h. Ich bin zuverlässig°.

reliable

Fähigkeiten wie ...

9. Sprachbeherrschung.
10. rechnerisches Denken.
11. Ideenreichtum.
12. Gedächtnis.

i. Ich rechne gern. Ich finde Mathematik interessant.
j. Ich vergesse wichtige Dinge nicht.
k. Ich habe immer viele und gute Ideen.
l. Ich kenne meine Muttersprache gut.

2 **Der Berufswahl-„Steckbrief"° von Oliver.** Lesen Sie die Informationen über Oliver, und füllen Sie dann die Liste aus.

°"wanted poster" but here personal description

Fangen wir mit der Schule an: Meine besten Fächer sind Deutsch und die Fremdsprachen. Alles, was mit Sprache zu tun hat, beherrsche° ich, glaube ich, ziemlich gut, ich lese auch sehr viel in meiner Freizeit. Fürs Lesen brauche ich übrigens eine Brille. In den anderen Fächern schlage ich mich auch ganz gut. Nur mit Mathe stehe ich auf Kriegsfuß°, rechnen kann ich einfach nicht so gut.

In meiner Freizeit spiele ich Handball. Dafür trainiere ich ziemlich hart und mit Ausdauer, obwohl ich „nur" im Tor stehe. Aber in meiner Mannschaft habe ich mit das beste Reaktionsvermögen. Unsere Mannschaft ist ganz gut, und meist gewinnen wir. Wenn wir mal verlieren, ist für mich vor allem wichtig, dass wir wenigstens gekämpft und eine gute Leistung gezeigt haben. Wenn's dann in einem Spiel mal nicht gereicht hat, kratzt das mein Selbstbewusstsein nicht allzusehr an.

Zu fremden Menschen finde ich schnell und problemlos Kontakt. Deswegen habe ich mir auch schon mal überlegt, ob ich das beruflich nutzen soll. Für Tätigkeiten°, die etwas mit Kaufen und Handeln zu tun haben, interessiere ich mich nämlich, mir fällt's auch nicht schwer°, andere im Gespräch zu überzeugen°. In eine andere Richtung geht mein Interesse für gestalterische Arbeiten. Ich sollte vielleicht noch ergänzen, dass mir Zeichnen° in der Schule am meisten Spaß macht und dass mir zu einem Thema, das der Lehrer stellt, oft mehrere Ideen einfallen°.

Gesundheitlich fühle ich mich ausgesprochen fit, klar, durch das Handballtraining. Nur habe ich seit etwa drei Jahren im Sommer mit einem Heuschnupfen° zu tun.

°master, have control of

°Nur ... Kriegsfuß: Ich habe große Probleme mit Mathemathik

°Aktivitäten

°mir ... schwer: Ich finde etwas nicht schwierig

°convince / drawing

°Ideen einfallen: Ideen haben

°eine Allergie gegen Pollen

	Oliver	*Ich*
Schule		
die besten Fächer:	________	________
Lesen:	________	________
Mathe:	________	________
macht am meisten Spaß:	________	________
Freizeit		
spielt:	________	________
Reaktionen:	________	________
Kontakt mit anderen		
Wie?	________	________
Gesundheit		
Allergien?	________	________

3 **Wo können Sie arbeiten?** Sie suchen Arbeit und haben ein Interview mit dem Personalchef/der Personalchefin. Beantworten Sie die Fragen und fragen Sie dann, welche Stelle Sie bekommen. Der/Die Personalchef(in) schreibt auf, welche Fähigkeiten für welche Stelle wichtig sind.

S1 (PERSONALCHEF/IN): Können Sie Deutsch sprechen?
S2: Ja, ich kann …
S1: Gut, bei McDonald's (im Hotel, im Sportclub) müssen Sie Deutsch sprechen.

	Im Hotel	*Bei McDonald's*	*Im Sportclub*
Deutsch sprechen	_____	_____	_____
früh anfangen	_____	_____	_____
bis spät arbeiten	_____	_____	_____
schnell arbeiten	_____	_____	_____
gut Tennis spielen	_____	_____	_____
gut rechnen°	_____	_____	_____
freundlich sein	_____	_____	_____
pünktlich° sein	_____	_____	_____
gut tippen°	_____	_____	_____
Volleyball spielen	_____	_____	_____

gut rechnen: gut in Mathe

punctual

type

4 **Vorteile und Nachteile von Berufen.** Hier sind sechs Berufe. In einer Gruppe von drei Personen wählen Sie drei Berufe und geben Sie drei Vorteile° und drei Nachteile° für jeden Beruf. Hier sind einige Ideen:

advantages
disadvantages

Man muss …

Geduld, Talent, gute Augen usw. haben
stark, intelligent, freundlich, gut organisiert usw. sein

Dieser Beruf ist …

leicht, hart, gefährlich, stressig usw.

Ein(e) Lehrer/in muss …
Ein(e) Hausfrau/Hausmann hat …

Lehrer/in	Hausfrau/Hausmann	Polizist/in°
Profi-Tennisspieler/in	Pilot/in	Briefträger/in°

police(wo)man
letter carrier

FREIE KOMMUNIKATION **Interview.** Lesen Sie den Dialog mit dem Personalchef und Barbara Müller. Spielen Sie dann mit einem Partner/einer Partnerin eine ähnliche° Situation: Sie suchen eine Stelle in einem Restaurant, in einem Museum oder in einer Jugendherberge.

similar

BARBARA: Guten Tag.
PERSONALCHEF: Guten Tag. Wie heißen Sie?
BARBARA: Ich heiße Barbara Müller.
PERSONALCHEF: Sie sind hier für die Stelle im Musikgeschäft, ja?
BARBARA: Ja.
PERSONALCHEF: Haben Sie Erfahrung als Verkäuferin?
BARBARA: Ja, ich habe im Lebensmittelgeschäft gearbeitet.
PERSONALCHEF: Wo war das?
BARBARA: Das war in Dresden.
PERSONALCHEF: Was sind Ihre besten Eigenschaften?
BARBARA: Ich bin sehr pünktlich, sehr freundlich und arbeite gern mit Menschen.
PERSONALCHEF: Sind Sie gut in Mathematik?
BARBARA: Ja. Rechnen kann ich sehr gut.
PERSONALCHEF: Danke schön, Frau Müller.

Schreibecke **Schreiben Sie Ihren persönlichen „Steckbrief".** Benutzen Sie Olivers Steckbrief als Beispiel und schreiben Sie Ihren persönlichen Steckbrief. Benutzen Sie die folgenden Wörter und Ausdrücke.

Fangen wir mit der Schule an: …
Meine besten Fächer …
Ich … sehr gern.
… kann ich nicht so gut.
In meiner Freizeit …
Zu fremden Menschen finde …
… macht mir Spaß.
Gesundheitlich fühle ich mich …

In this chapter you will learn where to do errands and where to spend free time in a city, how to ask for and give directions, and how to talk about travel and transportation.

Kommunikative Funktionen

- Expressing location and destination
- Talking about when events happen
- Talking about means of travel
- Expressing time, manner, and place
- Giving directions
- Expressing the purpose for an action

Strukturen

- Two-case prepositions
- **Wo?** and **wohin?**
- The verbs **hängen/hängen, legen/liegen, setzen/sitzen,** and **stellen/stehen**
- Time expressions in the dative and accusative
- The preposition **mit** with the dative case
- Word order: time, manner, place
- Prepositional phrases
- The prefixes **hin** and **her**
- The subordinating conjunction **damit**

Vokabeln

- Wo gehst du gern hin?
- Wo macht man das in der Stadt?
- Wie kommt man dahin?
- Literatur und Film

Kulturelles

- Studentenermäßigungen
- Einkaufen
- Stuttgart
- Der Holocaust
- Politischer Extremismus und politische Parteien

Was muss die Frau in der Stadt kaufen?

KAPITEL SIEBEN

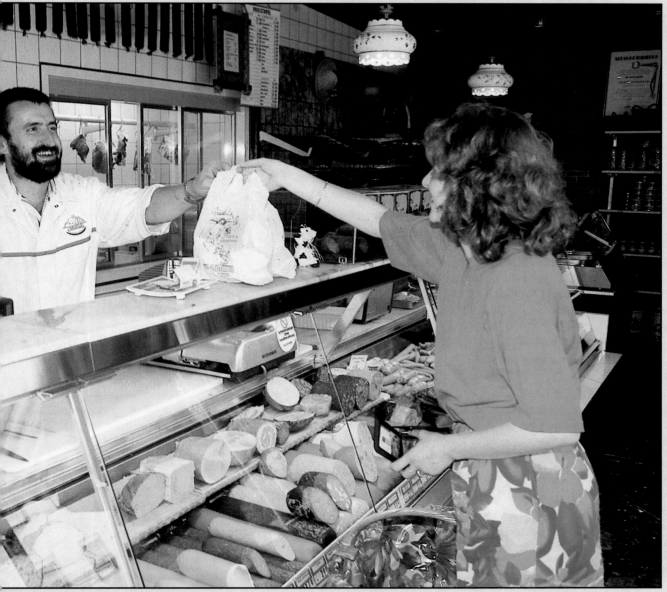

Man kann alles in der Stadt finden

Go to the ***Vorsprung*** Website at
www.hmco.com/college

ANLAUFTEXT

Barbara muss ein Konto eröffnen

Barbara, die neue Studentin aus Dresden, sucht eine Bank, denn sie will ein Konto eröffnen. Auf dem Weg zur Bushaltestelle trifft sie Stefan und Karl. Zusammen fahren sie mit dem Bus in die Stadt. Karl und Stefan geben Barbara ein paar gute Tipps, zum Beispiel, wo sie eine gute Buchhandlung finden kann und wo sie eine Semesterkarte für den Bus kaufen kann.

Vorschau

1 Thematische Fragen. Beantworten Sie die folgenden Fragen auf Deutsch.

1. Wie kommen Sie zur Universität: mit dem Auto, mit dem Rad, mit dem Bus oder zu Fuß?
2. Was gibt es in Ihrer Stadt – Busse, eine U-Bahn, Privatautos?
3. Wie kaufen Sie Ihre Bücher für die Uni: mit Bargeld°, mit einem Scheck, mit einer Kreditkarte?
4. Wie bekommen Sie Bargeld, wenn Sie es brauchen: von den Eltern, vom Bankautomaten, direkt von der Bank?
5. Wie viel Geld brauchen Sie pro Woche? Wie viel pro Monat?

cash

2 Satzdetektiv. Welche Sätze bedeuten ungefähr das Gleiche?

1. Karl will auf der Bank Geld **abheben.**
2. Barbara muss auf der Bank ein **Konto eröffnen.**
3. Könnt ihr mir eine Bank **empfehlen?**
4. Die Sparkasse hat eine **Filiale** ganz in der Nähe von der Uni.

a. Bei der Uni gibt es auch eine Sparkasse.
b. Karl möchte von der Bank Geld holen°.
c. Barbara braucht ein neues Bankkonto.
d. Kennt ihr eine gute Bank?

---

5. Ich hab' eine **Semesterkarte.**
6. Wo kann ich mir eine Semesterkarte **besorgen?**
7. Am **Kiosk** Schmid gibt es Semesterkarten.
8. Dann kann ich praktisch alles in der Stadt **erledigen.**

e. Alles, was ich brauche, kann ich in der Stadt machen.
f. Ich habe einen Buspass für Studenten.
g. Wo kann ich mir eine Semesterkarte für den Bus kaufen?
h. Semesterkarten kann man an einem Stand für Zigaretten, Zeitschriften usw. kaufen.

Satzdetektiv. A **Kiosk** offers a variety of items, such as stamps, magazines, newspapers, stationery, cigarettes, and lottery and bus tickets.

pick up

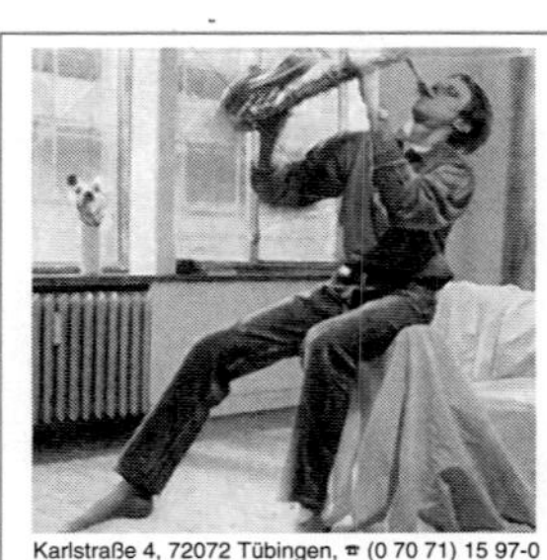

ANLAUFTEXT

Hören Sie gut zu.

Barbara muss ein Konto eröffnen

Grüß dich, Barbara!

Ah, grüßt euch! Was macht ihr denn hier? Wo geht ihr hin?

Wir fahren runter in die Stadt.

Ja, ich muss auf die Post und Karl will Geld abheben. Und du?

BRIEFMARKEN

Ich muss in die Buchhandlung und auch ein Konto eröffnen. Könnt ihr mir eine Bank empfehlen?

DEUTSCHE BANK

COMMERZBANK

DRESDNER BANK

Die Kreissparkasse. Die hat eine Filiale ganz in der Nähe von der Uni. Da hab' ich mein Konto.

Da fahren wir hin. Komm doch mit!

Na, gerne. Fahrt ihr immer mit dem Bus in die Stadt?

529

Ich nicht. Ich fahr' meistens mit dem Rad.

Ich schon. Ich hab' eine Semesterkarte.

Wo kann ich mir eine besorgen?

Am Kiosk Schmid am Hauptbahnhof oder in der Sparkasse.

HAUPTBAHNHOF TÜBINGEN

KREISSPARKASSE

Und gleich gegenüber von der Sparkasse gibt's eine gute Buchhandlung.

Na, fein. Dann kann ich praktisch alles in der Stadt erledigen.

KREISSPARKASSE

Rückblick

3 **Stimmt das?** Stimmen diese Aussagen zum Text oder nicht? Wenn nicht, was stimmt?

	Ja, das stimmt.	*Nein, das stimmt nicht.*
1. Stefan muss auf die Post.	___	___
2. Karl braucht Geld von seinem Bankkonto.	___	___
3. Barbara sucht ein Buch, und dann will sie auch ein Bankkonto eröffnen.	___	___
4. Stefan und Karl empfehlen Barbara die Kreissparkasse.	___	___
5. Die Kreissparkasse hat eine Filiale ganz in der Nähe von der Universität.	___	___
6. Karl und Stefan fahren immer mit dem Bus in die Stadt.	___	___
7. In der Kreissparkasse kann Barbara eine Semesterkarte für den Bus kaufen.	___	___
8. Gleich gegenüber von der Sparkasse ist der Hauptbahnhof.	___	___

Germans typically have a **Girokonto,** a debit account, from which money is electronically transferred (**Überweisung**). Cash (**Bargeld**) is more common than checks (**Schecks**) or credit cards (**Kreditkarten**).

4 **Ergänzen Sie.** Ergänzen Sie diese Sätze mit Wörtern aus dem **Anlauftext.**

1. Stefan muss auf die ____.
2. Barbara muss auf der Bank ein ____ eröffnen.
3. Barbara fragt Stefan und Karl: „Könnt ihr mir eine Bank ____?"
4. In der ____ von der Uni hat die Kreissparkasse eine Filiale.
5. Stefan fährt oft mit dem ____ in die Stadt.
6. Karl fährt aber meistens mit dem ____.
7. Barbara will sich auch eine Semesterkarte für den Bus ____.
8. Die Semesterkarte bekommt man am Kiosk Schmid am ____.
9. Eine gute ____ gibt es gleich gegenüber von der Sparkasse.
10. Barbara ist froh, dass sie praktisch alles in der Stadt ____ kann.

R EIN SEMESTER KASSEN-STER!

tudenten-Paß vom TÜbus von Anfang Oktober bis Ende Februar: lang fahren und sparen - mit einer einzigen Karte in Tübingen!

bei allen Kartenverkaufsstellen

 **5** **Kurz gefragt.** Beantworten Sie diese Fragen auf Deutsch.

m fahren Karl und Stefan in die Stadt?
vill Barbara alles in der Stadt erledigen?
m empfiehlt Karl die Kreissparkasse?
ährt Karl meistens in die Stadt?
m fährt Stefan meistens mit dem Bus?
ann Barbara einen Studentenpass kaufen?
bt es eine gute Buchhandlung?

Kurz gefragt. Review the subordinating conjunction **weil** *(because)* from *Kapitel 6* if necessary.

Studentenermäßigungen

In the German-speaking countries, all students receive a student identification card (**der Studentenausweis** for university students and **der Schülerausweis** for high school students and apprentices). With this ID, students are entitled to receive discounts for museums, theaters, movie theaters, ballet and music performances, but not popular music concerts. Students may also purchase a **Semesterkarte** (called a **Studentenpass** in Tübingen), which is a discounted ticket for use on public transportation such as subways (**die Untergrundbahn** or **U-Bahn**), trains, or busses during the semester. Students also pay low rates for rooms in university residence halls, and the mandatory usage fees for television and radio may be waived for financially-strapped students. The federal government subsidizes many of these benefits.

Brennpunkt Kultur. Remember that in German speakers distinguish between university students (**Studenten**) and all elementary and secondary school pupils (**Schüler**). Similarly, when a person says that he/she **zur Schule geht,** he/she refers to a primary or secondary school. Attending university is called **auf die Universität gehen** or simply **studieren.**

You will learn later that apprenticeship is an integral part of certain types of technical education. Students participating in apprenticeship programs are called **Auszubildende** (literally: *to-be-educated people*) or **Azubis** for short.

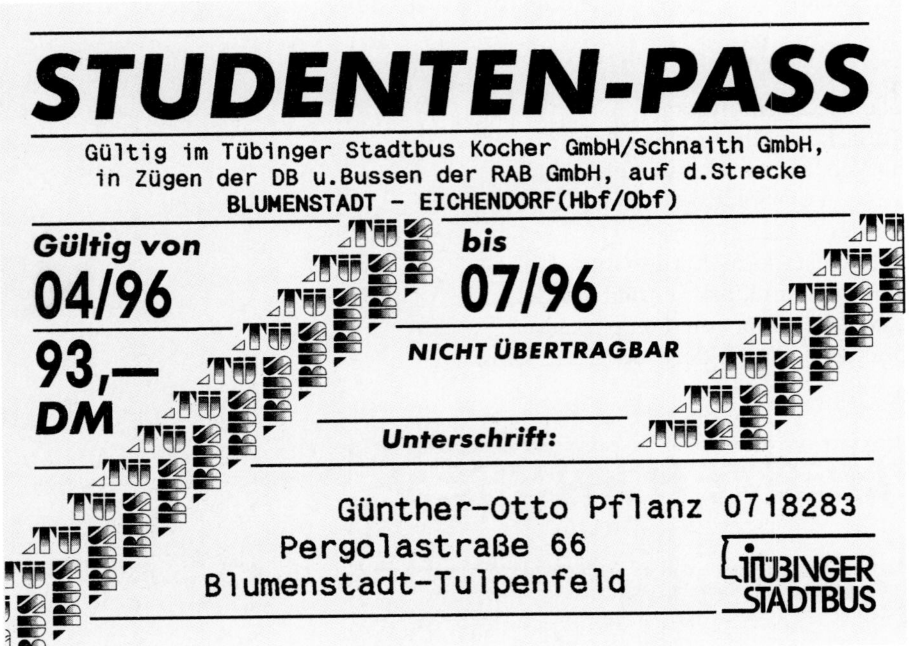

STUDENTEN-PASS

Gültig im Tübinger Stadtbus Kocher GmbH/Schnaith GmbH,
in Zügen der DB u.Bussen der RAB GmbH, auf d.Strecke
BLUMENSTADT - EICHENDORF(Hbf/Obf)

Gültig von
04/96

bis
07/96

93,— DM

NICHT ÜBERTRAGBAR

Unterschrift:

Günther-Otto Pflanz 0718283
Pergolastraße 66
Blumenstadt-Tulpenfeld

TÜBINGER STADTBUS

Non-students qualify for reduced fares by purchasing weekly or monthly passes which entitle passengers to unlimited use of any public transportation (varying by city: subway, bus, streetcar, or city trains). Tourists may consider the purchase of one-, two-, or three-day passes.

6 **Preisermäßigungen in Tübingen.** Lesen Sie zuerst die Informationen für Studenten/Studentinnen und beantworten Sie dann die folgenden Fragen.

Tübingen is environmentally conscious and offers students a transportation ID that supports a clean environment **(die Umwelt)** and is transferable **(übertragbar)** from one means of public transportation to another.

Preisermäßigungen

Die Möglichkeiten, Preisermäßigungen zu erhalten, werden zwar immer weniger - ab und zu lohnt es sich jedoch noch, einen Studentenausweis bei sich zu haben. Hier einige Tipps:

- Eintritte in Theater, Konzerte und Museen sind ermäßigt.
- Die Jahreskarte für die Hallenbäder und das Freibad der Stadt Tübingen kostet für Studierende 190 DM; die Saisonkarte 45 DM anstatt 65 DM.
- Die Tübinger Verkehrsbetriebe° geben eine übertragbare Umweltfahrkarte° heraus; für Studierende kostet diese 44,- DM pro Monat, eine nicht übertragbare Monatskarte kostet 37,- DM. Außerdem gibt es für Studierende Semesterkarten (Oktober bis Februar = 148 DM, April bis Juli = 111,- DM)

Übrigens: Im Zweifelsfall ist Fragen vor dem Bezahlen nie verkehrt!

transportation authority/ environmental transportation (pass)

1. Wofür bekommen Tübinger Studenten/Studentinnen Preisermäßigungen? Kreuzen Sie die richtige Antwort an.

	Ja	*Nein*		*Ja*	*Nein*
Bücher	___	___	Museen	___	___
Theater	___	___	Schwimmbäder	___	___
Konzerte	___	___	Computer	___	___
Wohnungen	___	___	Toiletten	___	___
Bier	___	___	Busse	___	___

Public toilets in Germany are frequently coin-operated or guarded by a person who cleans the facility and who charges a fee and/or expects a tip.

2. Wie viel kostet das? Füllen Sie die Tabelle aus.

Wo?	**Normalpreis**	**Studentenpreis**
Schwimmbäder	______ DM/Saison	______ DM/Saison
Verkehrsbetriebe	______ DM/Monat	______ DM/Monat

Strukturen und Vokabeln

I Expressing location and destination

Two-case prepositions: wo versus wohin

A. Two-case prepositions and their contractions

In Chapter 6 you learned that the two-case prepositions **(Wechselpräpositionen) in** and **an,** when used with the dative case, express location.

Sie steht **am** Kopierer. *She is standing at the copier.*

When used with the accusative case, these prepositions express destination.

Sie geht **an den** Kopierer. *She is going to the copier.*

The preposition itself does not indicate destination or location. The form of the article that follows the preposition does.

Stefan muss **auf die** Post. *Stefan has to go to the post office.*
Er kauft Briefmarken **auf der** Post. *He is buying stamps at the post office.*

Here are some examples of two-case prepositions from this chapter's **Anlauftext.**

Dative of location
Die hat eine Filiale ganz **in der** Nähe von der Uni. *It has a branch right near the university.*
Am Kiosk Schmid **am** Hauptbahnhof oder **in der** Sparkasse. *At Schmid's kiosk at the train station or at the bank.*
Dann kann ich praktisch alles **in der** Stadt erledigen. *Then I can take care of practically everything in town.*

Accusative of destination
Wir fahren runter **in die** Stadt. *We are going (in)to town.*
Ich muss **in die** Buchhandlung. *I have to go to the bookstore.*

To ask about the location German speakers use **wo** *(where).* A two-case preposition with the dative case is commonly part of the answer.

Wo stehen Karl und Stefan? *Where are Karl and Stefan standing?*
An der Haltestelle. *At the bus stop.*

To ask about the destination German speakers use **wohin** *(where . . . to).* A two-case preposition with the accusative case is commonly part of the answer.

Wohin fahren sie? *Where are they driving (going) to?*
In die Stadt. *(In)to town.*

Two-case prepositions are also known as two-way prepositions.

Remember that **am** is a contraction of **an + dem.**

In English, ***Where** are you going?* often replaces ***Where** are you going **to?*** In German, however, the distinction between **wo** and **wohin** must be strictly observed. An old English equivalent of German **wohin** is *whither.*

English has only two preposition pairs that are comparable to the German two-case prepositions: *in/into* and *on/onto.*

It is normal to split the interrogative **wohin: *Wo* fahren sie *hin?***

German has nine two-case prepositions. Here is a list of these prepositions used with the accusative **(wohin?)** and the dative **(wo?).**

In der Stadt

	Wohin?	*Wo?*

an *(at, to, on)*	Barbara geht **an die** Ampel. *Barbara walks up to the light.*	Das Auto steht **an der** Ampel. *The car is standing at the light.*

auf *(on, to, onto)*	Die Kinder laufen **auf den** Spielplatz. *The children are running (on)to the playground.*	Das Kind spielt **auf dem** Spielplatz. *The child is playing on the playground.*

hinter *(behind, to/in the back of)*	Der Tankwart fährt den Wagen **hinter die** Tankstelle. *The station attendant is driving the car to the back of the gas station.*	Der Tankwart wäscht den Wagen **hinter der** Tankstelle. *The station attendant is washing the car behind the gas station.*

in

(in, to, into)

Die Familie steigt **ins (in das)** Auto.
The family is getting into the car.

Die Familie sitzt **im (in dem)** Auto.
The family is in the car.

ins Kino / Konzert / Theater / Museum / Schloss gehen occurred in **Aktivität 31**, in **Kapitel 3**.

neben

(next to, beside)

Er hängt den Fahrplan **neben das** Poster.
He is hanging the train schedule next to the poster.

Der Fahrplan hängt **neben dem** Poster.
The train schedule is hanging next to the poster.

über

(above, over)

Der Bus fährt **über die** Brücke.
The bus is driving over the bridge.

Über der Bäckerei ist ein China-Restaurant.
There's a Chinese restaurant above the bakery.

unter

(under, underneath)

Der Ball rollt **unter das** Auto.
The ball is rolling underneath the car.

Der Ball ist **unter dem** Auto.
The ball is underneath the car.

vor	Der BMW fährt **vor den** Hoteleingang vor.	Der Mercedes steht **vor dem** Hoteleingang.
(in front of)	*The BMW is driving up to the hotel entrance.*	*The Mercedes is standing in front of the hotel entrance.*

zwischen	Der Ball rollt **zwischen die** Autos.	Der Kiosk steht **zwischen dem** Theater und **der** Bank.
(between)	*The ball is rolling between the cars.*	*The kiosk is between the theater and the bank.*

The following contractions are very common.

am = an dem
ans = an das
aufs = auf das
im = in dem
ins = in das

7 **Wo sind die Bücher?** Anna sucht ihre Bücher in ihrem Zimmer. Wo sind sie alle?

■ Ein Buch ist unter dem Bett.

Wo sind die Bücher? Useful words: **das Bett, der Schreibtisch, die Lampe, der Spiegel, der Schrank, der Computer, der Stuhl, die Tür, der Tennisschläger.**

8 Das ist mein Zimmer. Sie haben einen Gast, der für ein paar Tage in Ihrem Zimmer wohnt. Erklären Sie dem Gast, wo alles ist. Spielen Sie mit einem Partner/einer Partnerin Gastgeber/Gastgeberin° und Gast. Während der Gastgeber/die Gastgeberin alles erklärt, macht der Gast eine Skizze von allem, was er/sie hört. Der Gast kann auch Fragen stellen, wenn er etwas nicht genau versteht. Zum Schluss überprüft° der Gastgeber/die Gastgeberin, ob die Skizze stimmt. Wechseln Sie Ihre Rollen.

host
checks

S1 (GASTGEBER[IN]): Das Bett steht hinter der Tür.
S2 (GAST): Hinter der Tür?
S1: Ja, hinter der Tür.

Seinen Gästen darf man es nicht zu bequem...

...aber auch nicht zu unbequem machen.

B. *The two-case prepositions* an, auf, *and* in

An, auf, and **in,** the three most common German two-case prepositions, have a variety of meanings that often differ from the English words they may look like. German speakers use the preposition **an** with the dative case to describe the location of objects on vertical surfaces like a wall or a door. When used with the accusative, **an** means *to.*

Die Uhr hängt **an** der Wand. *The clock is hanging **on** the wall.*
Er geht **an** die Wand. *He is going **to** the wall.*

German speakers use the preposition **auf** with the dative case to refer to the location of objects on horizontal surfaces like a table, the floor, or a desk. It corresponds to English *on (top of).*

Das Buch ist **auf** dem Tisch. *The book is **on (top of)** the table.*
Er legt das Buch **auf** den Tisch. *He is placing the book **on(to)** the table.*

German speakers use the preposition **in** with the dative case to refer to an enclosed space like a room or a very defined space like a city. When used with the accusative case it expresses entrance into an enclosed space and means *into.*

Der Student ist **im** Klassenzimmer. *The student is **in** the classroom.*
Stefan fährt **in** die Stadt. *Stefan is driving **into** town.*

A common English equivalent for the prepositions **an, auf,** and **in** when used with the accusative case is *to.* When used with the dative case, the prepositions **an** and **auf** usually mean *at,* and the preposition **in** usually means *in,* although it occasionally means *at.*

Preposition	*Dative of location*	*Accusative of destination*
an	*at* Uwe sitzt **an** der Tür / **am** Fenster. *at the door/at the window*	*to* Er geht **an** die Tür / **ans** Fenster. *to the door/to the window*
auf	*at* Er arbeitet **auf** der Post. *at the post office*	*to* Er geht **auf** die Post. *to the post office*
in	*in* Er sitzt **in** der Küche. *in the kitchen* Er ist **in** der Metzgerei. *at the butcher's*	*to* Er geht **in** die Küche. *(in)to the kitchen.* Er geht **in** die Metzgerei. *to the butcher's*

The prepositions **an** and **auf** can also mean *on* when used with the dative case and *on(to)* when used with the accusative case.

Preposition	*Dative of location*	*Accusative of destination*
an	*on* Die Nummer ist **an** der Tür. *on the door*	*onto* Er schreibt die Nummer **an** die Tür. *(on)to the door*
auf	*on* Das Buch ist **auf** dem Tisch. *on the table*	*onto* Er legt das Buch **auf** den Tisch. *on(to) the table*

Wissenswerte Vokabeln: Wo gehst du gern hin?

Talking about where you like to go in your free time

in die Kirche (Synagoge, Moschee) gehen

ins Konzert gehen

ins Museum gehen

in den Jazzkeller gehen

in die Oper gehen

ins Theater gehen

ins Kino gehen

ins Schwimmbad gehen

ins Stadion gehen

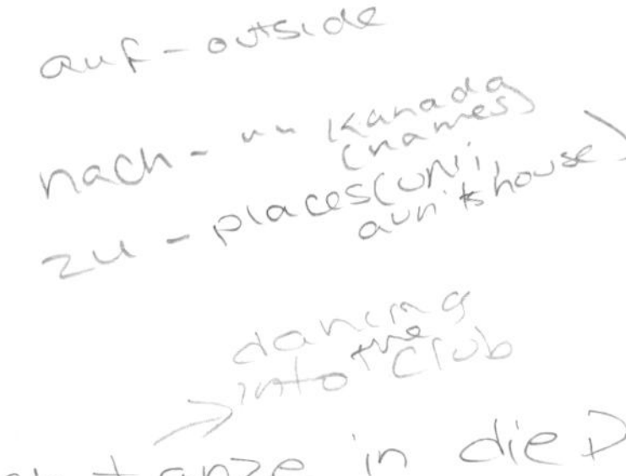

ins Fitnessstudio gehen

in die Disko(thek) gehen

in die Kneipe gehen

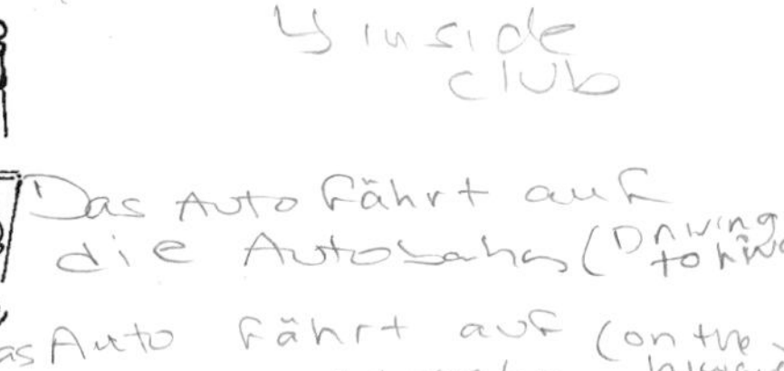

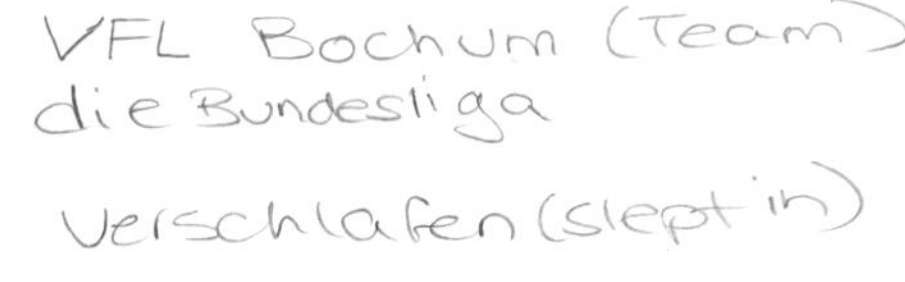

ins Restaurant gehen

auf eine Party (Fete) gehen

▣ Wohin gehst du (nicht) gern?

9 **Wohin gehen Karl und Stefan?** Finden Sie für jede Situation einen passenden Ort°.

° *place*

▣ Wenn sie Durst haben, gehen sie in die Kneipe.

1. Wenn sie Durst haben, gehen sie	auf den Fußballplatz.
2. Wenn sie billig essen wollen, gehen sie	in den Hörsaal.
3. Wenn sie gut essen wollen, gehen sie	in die Mensa.
4. Wenn sie einen Film sehen wollen, gehen sie	in die Oper.
5. Wenn sie ein Buch suchen müssen, gehen sie	in die Kneipe.
6. Wenn sie Fußball spielen wollen, gehen sie	in das Kino.
7. Wenn Karl kochen will, geht er	in das Restaurant.
8. Wenn Stefan Musik hören will, geht er	in die Bibliothek.
9. Wenn sie eine Vorlesung haben, gehen sie	in die Küche.
10. Wenn sie auf eine Hochzeit° gehen, gehen sie	in die Kirche.

° *wedding*

10 **Interview.** Stellen Sie einem Partner/einer Partnerin die folgenden Fragen.

1. Wohin gehst du, wenn du lernen willst?
2. Wohin gehst du, wenn du mit jemandem ausgehst?
3. Wohin gehst du am Sonntag?
4. Wohin gehst du, wenn es im Sommer sehr heiß ist?
5. Wohin gehst du, wenn du Sport treiben willst?
6. Wohin gehst du, wenn du einen Kurs oder ein Seminar hast?

Sprache im Alltag: Names of cities with an/am

A few prominent German cities indicate their location on a major river by using the preposition **an/am** and the name of the river in their name. The two Frankfurts rely on this designation to distinguish between them.

Frankfurt am Main	Fluss: der Main
Frankfurt an der Oder	Fluss: die Oder
Marburg an der Lahn	Fluss: die Lahn

Wissenswerte Vokabeln: Wo macht man das in der Stadt?

Talking about where to run errands

Am Bahnhof kauft man Fahrscheine.

An der Haltestelle wartet man auf den Bus.

Auf der Post kauft man Briefmarken und gibt Pakete auf.

Auf der Bank (Auf der Sparkasse) zahlt man Geld ein, oder man hebt es ab°.

hebt ab: holt

Am Kiosk (Am Zeitungsstand) kauft man Zeitungen und Zeitschriften.

In der Buchhandlung kauft man Bücher.

Im Reformhaus (Im Bioladen) bekommt man gesunde, natürliche Kost°.

In der Bäckerei kauft man Brot, Brötchen und Brezeln.

Essen

In der Konditorei kauft man Kuchen, Torten und Gebäck.

Im Supermarkt hat man eine große Auswahl.

In der Fleischerei (In der Metzgerei) bekommt man Fleisch, Wurst und Geflügel.

Auf dem Markt kauft man alles frisch vom Lande: Obst, Gemüse, Käse, Eier.

▣ Wo kauft man Bücher?

11 Wo treffen sie einander°? Lesen Sie die Liste von Stefan und die von Barbara und fragen Sie dann einen Partner/eine Partnerin, wo sie einander treffen. Wählen Sie Orte aus der **wo?**-Liste.

°each other

▣ S1: Stefan holt Briefmarken und Barbara muss ein Telegramm schicken. Wo treffen sie einander?
S2: Sie treffen einander auf der Post.

Stefans Liste

1. Briefmarken holen
2. Geld abheben
3. frische Landeier kaufen
4. eine Zeitung kaufen
5. Fleisch kaufen
6. Brot kaufen
7. einen Apfelkuchen kaufen

Barbaras Liste

1. ein Telegramm schicken
2. ein Konto eröffnen
3. ein Eis essen
4. einen Studentenpass kaufen
5. Wurst kaufen
6. Brötchen holen
7. ein Lotterielos kaufen

Wo?

auf ___ Markt	auf ___ Post	in ___ Konditorei	in ___ Bäckerei
in ___ Metzgerei	auf ___ Bank	an ___ Kiosk	

12 Wohin müssen sie gehen? Klaus, Barbara und Anna müssen vieles erledigen. Stellen Sie einem Partner/einer Partnerin Fragen über Klaus, Barbara und Anna.

Wohin müssen sie gehen? Note that you are talking about destinations. Therefore, the following two-case prepositions require the accusative case.

▣ S1: Klaus muss Briefmarken kaufen. Wohin muss er gehen?
S2: Er muss auf die Post (gehen).

Klaus muss	Briefmarken kaufen. Euroschecks holen. Medizin kaufen.
Barbara muss	Kaffee und Käse kaufen. Bücher zurückgeben. Wurst und Fleisch kaufen.
Anna muss	Kuchen holen. Brot kaufen. frische Eier kaufen.

Euroschecks are issued by banks throughout Europe. They come with a specific ID and owners can write them to purchase goods or to obtain cash throughout Europe, in any European currency.

Wohin müssen sie gehen?

in ______ Bäckerei	in ______ Bibliothek	auf ______ Post
in ______ Supermarkt	in ______ Konditorei	auf ______ Markt
auf ______ Bank	in ______ Metzgerei	in ______ Apotheke°

°*pharmacy*

BRENNPUNKT KULTUR

Einkaufen

While the **Supermarkt** has found its niche throughout German-speaking Europe for one-stop grocery shopping, many customers prefer the higher quality and personal service available in smaller specialty shops. Shoppers do not mind making frequent, often daily, trips for the sake of obtaining extremely fresh goods.

Since shops and residential housing are well integrated, many people walk to stores and carry the groceries home. Therefore the bags need to be sturdy and customers prefer to take their own bags (**die Tragetaschen**) or basket (**der Einkaufskorb**) with them. Because people shop so frequently, they don't need great quantities of groceries. Stores charge a small fee for plastic grocery bags (**die Einkaufstüten**) and customers expect to bag their own groceries. To ensure that customers promptly return shopping carts, some supermarkets require a deposit for them.

13 **Rätsel: Wo ist die Buchhandlung?** Lesen Sie die Sätze und bestimmen Sie, wo die Buchhandlung ist.

Die Buchhandlung ist zwischen dem Zeitungskiosk und der Drogerie.
Die Bank ist an der Ecke.
Rechts neben der Bäckerei ist die Metzgerei.
Direkt gegenüber von der Metzgerei ist die Konditorei.
Rechts von der Buchhandlung ist die Drogerie.
Die Buchhandlung ist nicht an der Ecke.
Die Post ist zwischen der Bank und der Bäckerei.
Quer gegenüber von° der Post ist der Zeitungskiosk.

***Quer … von:** diagonally across from*

BRENNPUNKT KULTUR

Stuttgart

Approximately one hour by train north of Tübingen lies Stuttgart, the capital **(die Landeshauptstadt)** of the federal state of Baden-Württemberg and the dialect region of **Schwaben.** With a population of 586,000, it ranks as Germany's eighth largest city. Stuttgart is home to two of the world's most famous car-makers: Daimler-Benz and Porsche. Largely destroyed in WW II, Stuttgart has emerged as a vibrant city offering wide-ranging cultural attractions like **die Staatsgalerie, das Mercedes-Benz-Museum, das Carl-Zeiss-Planetarium,** and **das Staatstheater Stuttgart** with its world-famous **Stuttgarter Ballett.**

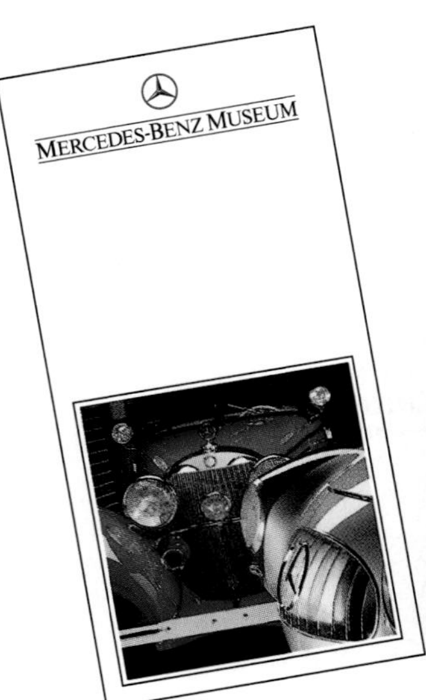

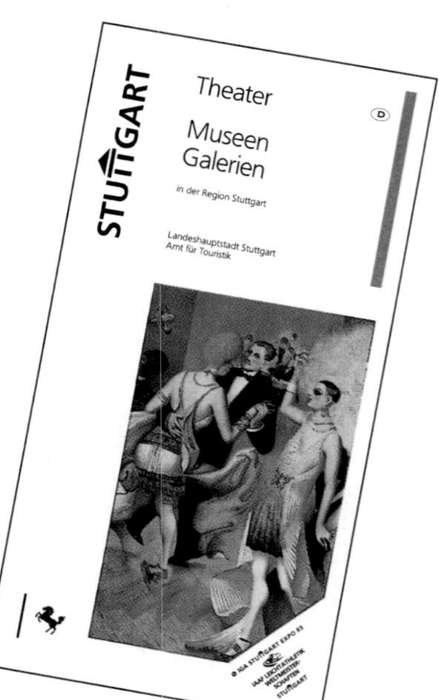

14 **Stuttgart.** Anna, Barbara, Karl und Stefan besuchen Stuttgart. Helfen Sie Anna und Barbara, die folgenden Sehenswürdigkeiten in Stuttgart zu finden.

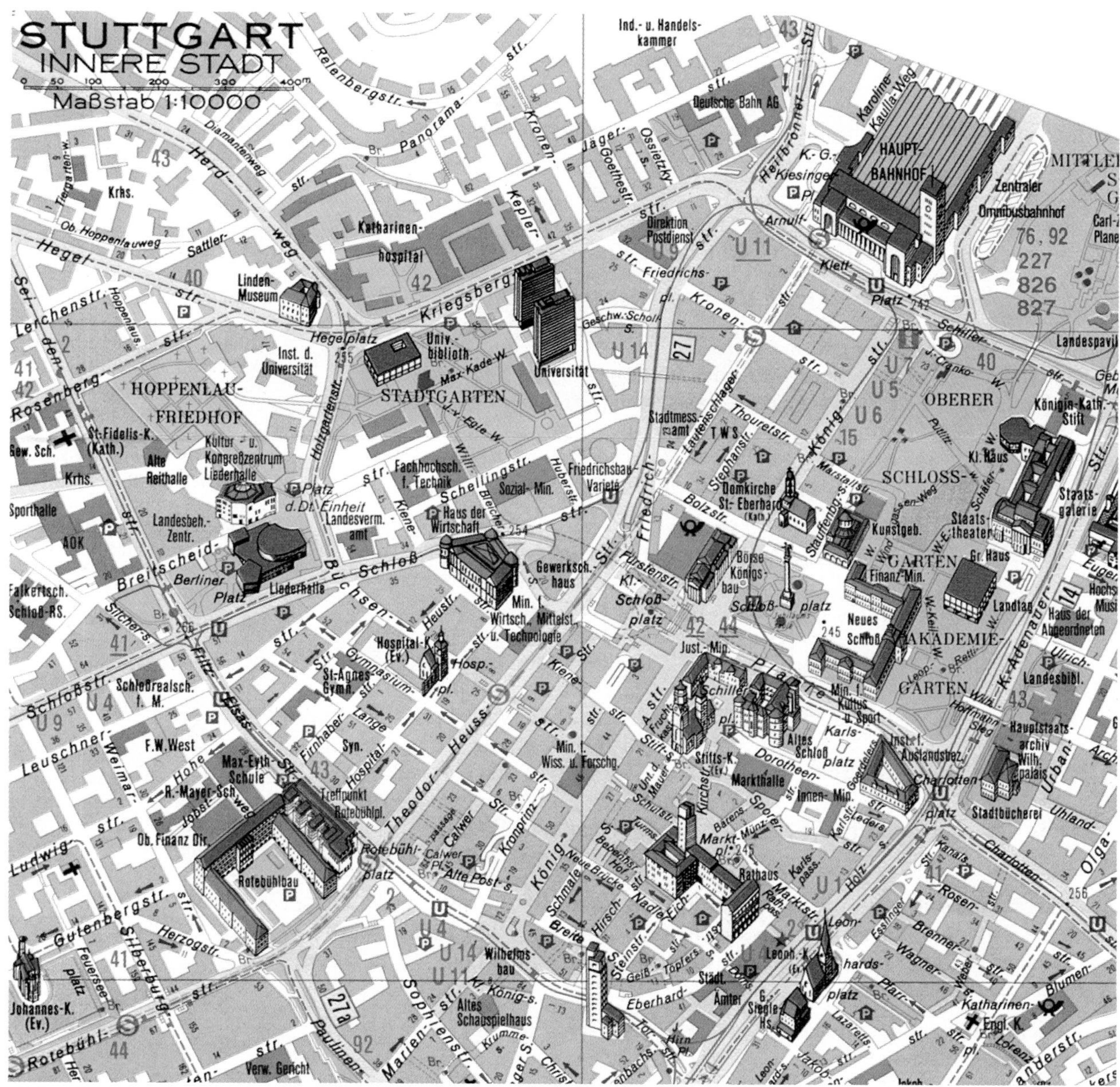

▣ Der mittlere Schlossgarten ist neben dem Hauptbahnhof.

1. Der mittlere Schlossgarten
2. Das Carl-Zeiss-Planetarium
3. Der Schlossplatz
4. Die Universitätsbibliothek
5. Das Alte Schloss
6. Das Rathaus
7. Die Markthalle
8. Die Staatsgalerie

a. am Karlsplatz.
b. am Marktplatz.
c. hinter dem Staatstheater.
d. im mittleren Schlossgarten.
e. im Stadtgarten.
f. neben dem Hauptbahnhof.
g. vor dem Postamt.
h. zwischen dem Alten Schloss und dem Rathaus.

15 **Wohin gehen sie in Stuttgart?** Barbara und die anderen machen Pläne. Hier sind ihre Interessen. Wohin gehen sie wahrscheinlich in Stuttgart?

S1: Anna findet Astronomie interessant. Wohin möchte sie gehen?
S2: Sie möchte ins Planetarium gehen.

Anna	*Barbara*	*Karl*	*Stefan*	*Du*
Astronomie	Picasso	Bücher	Schlösser	?
Theater	Briefmarken	Geschichte	Autos	?

C. Verbs commonly used with the two-case prepositions

1. Verbs with accusative prepositions

Verbs that express movement toward a destination occur with two-case prepositions followed by the accusative case. Such sentences always answer the question **wohin?** Some of the verbs that frequently trigger accusatives after two-case prepositions are: **gehen** *(to go)*, **fahren** *(to drive)*, **fallen** *(to fall)*, **fliegen** *(to fly)*, **laufen** *(to run, walk)*, and **springen** *(to jump)*.

Question	*Sentence*
Wohin gehen Stefan und Karl?	Sie gehen **auf die Bank.** *They are going to the bank.*
Wohin fahren sie?	Sie fahren **in die Stadt.** *They are driving to the city.*
Wohin fällt das Buch?	Das Buch fällt **auf den Boden.** *The book falls down on the floor.*
Wohin ist Anna gefahren?	Anna ist **in die Schweiz** gefahren. *Anna drove to Switzerland.*
Wohin läuft der Professor?	Der Professor läuft **in den Hörsaal.** *The professor is walking into the lecture hall.*
Wohin springt das Kind?	Das Kind springt **in das Wasser.** *The child is jumping into the water.*

Remember that the preposition assigns the case. Thus, any of these verbs may occur with prepositions other than two-case prepositions. The prepositions may be followed by a dative or an accusative, as appropriate, e.g., **Ich fliege über das Meer** (two-case preposition with the accusative), **ich fliege mit dem Flugzeug (mit** = dative preposition), **ich fliege ohne meinen Bruder (ohne** = accusative preposition).

While these verbs mostly occur with a two-case preposition followed by the accusative, a dative is appropriate if the movement is not directed towards a destination: **Stefan läuft im Park.** *(Stefan is running inside the park.)*

2. Expressions with two-case prepositions followed by the accusative

There are also idiomatic expressions that involve two-case prepositions. These expressions combine verbs and specific prepositions and are frequently followed by the accusative case.

Idiomatic expressions include two-case as well as dative and accusative prepositions.

Er **achtet** nie **auf** das Wetter.	*He never pays attention to the weather.*
Ich **denke** oft **an** dich.	*I think of you a lot.*
Er **erinnert** mich **an** meinen Vater.	*He reminds me of my father.*
Sie **schreibt an** ihren Freund.	*She's writing to her boyfriend.*
Ich bin **böse auf** meine Schwester.	*I'm mad at my sister.*
Wir **hoffen auf** eine Tochter.	*We're hoping for a daughter.*
Ich muss immer **auf** sie **warten.**	*I always have to wait for them.*
Sie **lachen über** ihn.	*They are laughing at him.*
Er **spricht über** das Problem.	*He's talking about the problem.*
Sie **bittet** uns **um** DM 10,-.	*She is asking us for 10 marks.*

3. Verbs with dative prepositions

Verbs that express location are used with two-case prepositions followed by the dative case. **Sein** and **wohnen** are among the verbs that frequently trigger datives after two-case prepositions.

Wo **wohnt** Cornelia?	Sie wohnt **in der** Stadt.
Where does Cornelia live?	*She lives in town.*

4. The verbs hängen/hängen; legen/liegen; setzen/sitzen; stellen/stehen
There are four verb pairs that demonstrate the difference between location and movement toward a destination. To show location, an irregular (strong) verb (e.g., **hängen—hat gehangen; liegen—hat gelegen; sitzen—hat gesessen; stehen—hat gestanden**) is used with the dative case. To show movement toward a destination, a regular (weak) verb (e.g., **hängen—hat gehängt; legen—hat gelegt; setzen—hat gesetzt; stellen—hat gestellt**) is used with the accusative case. In standard German, **haben** is used to form the conversational past of all these verbs, e.g., **ich habe gestanden.** In Southern German, however, verbs that express an action take **haben,** but verbs that express location take **sein,** e.g., **ich bin dort gestanden.** The verbs **stellen, legen,** and **setzen** may all be translated as *to put.*

Please note that even in colloquial German, speakers always distinguish between verbs that express actions and verbs that express results. Confusions such as the one between *to lie* (**liegen**) and *to lay* (**legen**) in colloquial English are not typical in German.

stellen to put something (e.g., a bottle or suitcase) in(to) an upright position
legen to lay or put something (e.g., a newspaper) in(to) a horizontal position
setzen to seat, set, or put something (e.g., a person, a child, a doll) down

One use of **stellen** is idiomatic, e.g., **Er stellt** (not **legt**) **den Teller auf den Tisch.**

Accusative of destination

Er **hängt** den Fahrplan an die Wand.

Er **legt** die Zeitung auf den Sitz.

Er **setzt** das Kind auf die Bank.

Dative of location

Der Fahrplan **hängt** an der Wand.

Die Zeitung **liegt** auf dem Sitz.

Das Kind **sitzt** auf der Bank.

Sie **stellt** den Koffer in den Bahnhof.

Der Koffer **steht** im Bahnhof.

16 **Mein Zimmer.** Machen Sie eine Zeichnung von Ihrem Zimmer und beschreiben Sie es dann für einen Partner/eine Partnerin. Der Partner/Die Partnerin soll Ihr Zimmer zeichnen. Stimmt die Zeichnung? Wechseln Sie die Rollen.

S1: Das Bett steht an der Wand.

Das	Bett	steht	in der	Ecke.
	Poster	liegt	auf dem	Tisch.
Der	Schreibtisch	hängt	am	Boden.
	Stuhl	ist	an der	Stuhl.
	Computer	sind		Fenster.
Die	Lampe			Wand.
	Stereoanlage			Tür.
	Bücher			

17 **Annas Zimmer.** Annas Zimmer ist durcheinander°. Was soll Anna machen? Helfen Sie Anna das Zimmer aufzuräumen.

messy

Die Papiere liegen auf dem Boden. Sie liegen nicht auf dem Tisch.
Sie soll die Papiere auf den Tisch legen.

1. Die Papiere liegen auf dem Boden. Sie liegen nicht auf dem Tisch.
2. Das Poster liegt auf dem Bett. Es hängt nicht an der Wand.
3. Die Zeitung liegt unter dem Stuhl. Sie ist nicht auf dem Stuhl.
4. Der Stuhl steht an der Tür. Er steht nicht am Tisch.
5. Das Radio steht neben dem Bett. Es steht nicht auf dem Nachttisch.
6. Die Uhr liegt auf dem Teppich. Sie hängt nicht über dem Bett.
7. Die Pflanze steht in der Ecke. Sie steht nicht am Fenster.
8. Die Flaschen liegen neben dem Stuhl. Sie stehen nicht im Schrank.
9. Mein Hund liegt unter dem Bett. Er sitzt nicht auf dem Bett.

FREIE KOMMUNIKATION

Rollenspiel: Bett frei. Sie haben ein Doppelzimmer im Studentenwohnheim und suchen einen Zimmerkameraden/eine Zimmerkameradin. Eine Person ruft an und möchte mehr über das Zimmer wissen. Beschreiben Sie der Person das Zimmer.

Schreibecke **An meinen Lehrer/meine Lehrerin.** Schreiben Sie eine Postkarte an Ihren Deutschlehrer/Ihre Deutschlehrerin. Beschreiben Sie, was Sie schon alles in Tübingen gemacht haben: Wo und was haben Sie eingekauft? Wie haben Sie Ihr Zimmer eingerichtet? Was haben Sie schon alles gesehen? Wen haben Sie schon kennen gelernt? Schreiben Sie in einem sehr positiven Ton.

ABSPRUNGTEXT

„Schindlers Liste" und „Die Abrechnung"

Die Abrechnung was published in English in 1996 (Random House) as *Führer-Ex*.

Anna hat Barbara von dem Film „Schindlers Liste" erzählt. In einem Katalog vom Bertelsmann Club liest Barbara über das Buch „Schindlers Liste" von Thomas Keneally. Sie liest auch über „Die Abrechnung°", ein Buch über Neonazis in Deutschland. Das eine oder das andere Buch will sie bestellen° oder sogar noch heute in der Stadt kaufen.

The Reckoning
order

Vorschau

18 **Thematische Fragen.** Beantworten Sie die folgenden Fragen auf Deutsch.

Thematische Fragen. This activity will help you establish the context for understanding the reading by asking you to answer short questions in German.

1. Kennen Sie „Schindlers Liste"? Woher?
   a. von einem Buch
   b. von der Uni
   c. vom Kino oder als Video
   d. von der Zeitung
2. Haben Sie den Film gesehen?
3. Ist der Film lustig oder ernst?
4. Kennen Sie andere Filme mit demselben Thema?
5. Wer hat den Film gemacht?
6. Hat der Filmemacher einen deutschen Namen?
7. Wissen Sie etwas über Neonazis? Wo haben Sie von ihnen gehört?
   a. im Fernsehen
   b. in der Zeitung
   c. an der Uni
   d. bei Freunden
   e. in Büchern
8. Welche Gruppen in Ihrem Land vertreten eine radikale oder extremistische Politik?

Spielberg is a German name. Many Jews with ancestors from Germany, Austria, Switzerland, Hungary, the Czech Republic, and France have German names because their heritage is German.

19 **Was wissen Sie?** Was wissen Sie über den Film „Schindlers Liste" und das Dritte Reich? Kreuzen Sie an, was stimmt.

	Das stimmt.	*Das stimmt nicht.*
1. Oskar Schindler war Jude°.	___	___
2. Der Film spielt in der Nazizeit.	___	___
3. Oskar Schindler war Nazi.	___	___
4. Die Nazis haben die Juden systematisch getötet°.	___	___
5. Oskar Schindler war Unternehmer° oder Geschäftsmann°.	___	___
6. Die Nazis waren antisemitisch und rassistisch.	___	___

Jew
killed
entrepreneur
businessman

	Das stimmt.	Das stimmt nicht.	
7. Die Nazis haben Polen, Frankreich und andere europäische Länder besetzt°.	___	___	*occupied*
8. Die Nazis haben Juden, Homosexuelle, Kranke, Kommunisten und Zigeuner° getötet.	___	___	*gypsies*
9. Auschwitz war ein Konzentrationslager in Polen.	___	___	

20 **Lesestrategien: „Schindlers Liste".** Benutzen Sie die folgenden Lesestrategien, um den Text „Schindlers Liste" zu verstehen.

Lesestrategien. This special section is introduced in English to provide you with general reading strategies which you will practice in German in subsequent reading texts.

Good readers do not necessarily know more words. They are, however, good at guessing the meaning of new words, and there are several skills that help make them successful readers.

1. **Den Kontext verstehen.** Understanding the context is an important first step in approaching a new text. Begin by finding answers in "Schindlers Liste" to the following questions:

Wer?	__________	Wann?	__________
Was?	__________	Sonstiges?°	__________
Wo?	__________	Kognate?	__________

Other information?

2. **Neue Wörter lernen: erster Versuch.** After you understand the context of a reading, it is easier to decode some of the new words. What do you think the following words from "Schindlers Liste" mean in English?

   Gaskammer Nazigrößen kriegswichtig

3. **Wichtige Wörter finden: Verben.** Focus your attention only on words that may convey important information. A good place to start is with verbs. Here are five verbs from "Schindlers Liste." How many of these verbs do you know? Can you guess their meaning, based on the other words in the sentence? Use associations to make a guess.

   a. … **drehte** Steven Spielberg … einen Film.
   b. Spielberg **bezeichnet** diesen Film … als sein wichtigstes Werk.
   c. … **rettet** … Oskar Schindler 1300 jüdische Arbeiter vor der Gaskammer.
   d. Er … **erklärt** ihre Arbeit für „kriegswichtig".
   e. Schindler **war** ein Besessener, der bereit war, alles zu riskieren.

4. **Neue Wörter lernen: Vier Strategien verwenden.** Listed here are four strategies that will sometimes enable you to determine the exact meaning and other times the approximate meaning of a word.

   Strategy 1: Background knowledge
   Guess at the meaning of unfamiliar words by using what you know about the world, e.g., history, human behavior, how things work.

   a. … **drehte** Steven Spielberg … einen Film.

   What do you know about Steven Spielberg? What is his profession? What do people in this profession do? The verb **drehen** here probably means __________________.

Strategy 2: Similar words
Guess at the meaning of unfamiliar words by using what you know about similar looking words.

a. … rettet … Oskar Schindler 1300 **jüdische** Arbeiter vor der **Gaskammer.**

What do you know about Oskar Schindler? What did he do? What associations do you have of Nazis and *gas?* What do the words **jüdische** and **Gaskammer** resemble? ____________________

Strategy 3: Context
Guess at the meaning of unfamiliar words by using your knowledge of other German words as clues.

a. … **rettet** … Oskar Schindler 1300 jüdische Arbeiter vor der Gaskammer.

The verb **retten** probably means ____________________.

b. … alles zu riskieren für eine … phantastische **Rettungsaktion.**

The verb **rettet** is related to **Rettungsaktion.** What do you think a **Rettungsaktion** means? ____________________

c. mit … **Verstand,** … rettet … Oskar Schindler 1300 jüdische Arbeiter vor der Gaskammer.

The noun **Verstand** looks like the past participle ____________________, which comes from the verb ____________________. **Verstand** probably means ____________________.

Oskar Schindler hat 1300 Juden vor der Gaskammer gerettet.

Strategy 4: Grammatical cues

Guess at the meaning of unfamiliar words by using your knowledge of grammatical cues. For example, try to identify the part of speech of the unfamiliar word. Recurring words often provide clues for comprehending unfamiliar structures. Look at the preposition **mit** in the following sentence.

mit List und Verstand, **mit** Bestechung und **mit** guten Beziehungen zu Nazigrößen ... rettet ... Oskar Schindler ...

The word **mit** explains where Oskar Schindler did something, why Oskar Schindler did something, and how Oskar Schindler did something. In order to guess at the meaning of the word **Beziehungen,** look at the words surrounding it, **guten** and **zu.** The word **zu** signals that Oskar Schindler had something with respect *to* the **Nazigrößen.** The phrase **mit guten Beziehungen zu Nazigrößen** probably means ____________________.

Even though there may still be some unfamiliar words, you should be able to understand and appreciate the text.

21 **Lesestrategien: „Die Abrechnung".** Benutzen Sie die Lesestrategien, um den Text „Die Abrechnung" zu verstehen.

1. **Den Kontext verstehen.** Finden Sie im Text Antworten auf diese Fragen.

Wer?	__________	Wann?	__________
Was?	__________	Sonstiges?	__________
Wo?	__________	Kognate?	__________

2. **Neue Wörter lernen: erster Versuch.** Was bedeuten diese Wörter auf Englisch?

   Rechtsradikalismus
   die ostdeutsche rechtsextremistische Szene
   die Strukturen und Planungen der Neonazis

3. **Wichtige Wörter finden.** Welche Wörter im Text sind besonders wichtig? Finden Sie mindestens fünf Verben. Erraten° Sie ihre Bedeutung aus dem Kontext. ____________________ — *guess*

4. **Neue Wörter lernen: vier Strategien.** Versuchen Sie, die fett gedruckten° Wörter zu erraten. Benutzen Sie die Strategien, die Sie für „Schindlers Liste" gelernt haben. — *boldfaced*

   a. Dieser aktuelle, authentische Bericht zum Thema Rechtsradikalismus bringt **Zündstoff** in die öffentliche Diskussion.

   Zündstoff beschreibt die Diskussion über Rechtsradikalismus. Wie ist die Diskussion über Rechtsradikalismus – ruhig und leise oder laut und kontrovers? **Zündstoff** bedeutet wahrscheinlich ____________________.

   b. ... eines der **dringlichsten** und **widersprüchlichsten** deutschen Themen.

   Ist das Thema Rechtsradikalismus kontrovers (widersprüchlich) in Deutschland oder nicht? Ist das Thema in Deutschland wichtig (dringlich) oder unwichtig? Das Adjektiv **dringlich** bedeutet wahrscheinlich auch ____________________. Das Adjektiv **widersprüchlich** bedeutet wahrscheinlich auch ____________________.

c. **Hintermänner** und **Anführer**

Beide Wörter bestehen aus° zwei Teilen. Was können Sie in diesen Wörtern identifizieren? **Hintermänner** bedeutet wahrscheinlich ______________________. **Anführer** bedeutet wahrscheinlich ______________________.

bestehen aus: *consist of*

d. ... wie eine Droge **wirkt**

Droge ist ein Kognat mit einem englischen Wort. Wissen Sie, was eine Droge ist? Was macht eine Droge? Ist Rechtsradikalismus eine richtige Droge? Das Verb **wirken** bedeutet wahrscheinlich ______________________.

e. ... schildert seinen **Ausstieg** aus der [neonazistischen] Szene.

Wenn man mit der Bahn fährt, hört man die Verben **aussteigen** und **einsteigen** sehr oft. Sie bedeuten wahrscheinlich ______________________, ______________________. Mit welchen von diesen Verben assoziieren Sie das Substantiv **der Ausstieg?** ______________________. Im Text hat das Wort eine metaphorische Bedeutung. **Der Ausstieg aus der Szene** bedeutet wahrscheinlich ______________________.

BRENNPUNKT KULTUR

Der Holocaust

The Holocaust (**der Holocaust**) was the worst case of genocide in the 20th century. Beginning with the Nazi rise to power in 1933, German Jews were forcibly removed from their homes, separated from their families, denied basic civil rights, and eventually sent to their deaths. The Nazis called this systematic murder of all "undesirable" groups, which they initiated in 1942, the final solution (**die Endlösung**). Over 6 million Jews in German-occupied territories were systematically killed primarily between 1939 and 1945. In addition to Jews, the Nazis also targeted gypsies, homosexuals, the mentally ill, and political opponents. The most notorious concentration camps (**das Konzentrationslager**) and death camps (**das Todeslager**), e.g., Auschwitz in Poland and Buchenwald, Bergen-Belsen, and Dachau in Germany, are now memorials to their victims and remain powerful reminders of the dangers of state-supported racism and ethnic intolerance.

Im Konzentrationslager

22 **Satzdetektiv.** Welche Sätze bedeuten ungefähr das Gleiche?

„Schindlers Liste"

1. An **Originalschauplätzen** in Polen drehte Steven Spielberg im Frühjahr 1993 einen Film über Oskar Schindler.
2. Spielberg **bezeichnet** diesen Film ... als sein wichtigstes Werk.
3. Oskar Schindler **lässt** die Juden für sich **arbeiten.**
4. Oskar Schindler **erklärt** die Arbeit **für** „kriegswichtig".
5. Schindler war ein **Besessener,** der bereit war, alles zu riskieren für eine **waghalsige,** phantastische Rettungsaktion.
6. ... mit **Bestechung** ... rettet ... Oskar Schindler 1300 jüdische Arbeiter.

a. Die Juden arbeiten für Schindler.
b. Oskar Schindler gibt den Nazis illegal Geld für jüdische Arbeiter und rettet 1300 Menschen.
c. Schindler hat nur eine riskante und phantastische Idee – vielen Juden zu helfen.
d. Schindler sagt, die Juden machen wichtige Produkte für den Krieg.
e. Spielberg hat den Film 1993 in Polen und nicht im Studio gemacht.
f. Spielberg sagt, „Schindlers Liste" bedeutet mehr als alle seine anderen Filme.

Spielberg bezeichnet „Schindlers Liste" als sein wichtigstes Werk.

„Die Abrechnung"

7. Dieser aktuelle, authentische **Bericht ...**
8. Der Rechtsradikalismus ist eines der **dringlichsten** und **widersprüchlichsten** deutschen Themen.
9. Ingo Hasselbach [war] noch vor einem Jahr **der führende Kopf** der ostdeutschen rechtsextremen Szene.
10. Hasselbach beschreibt die **Strukturen** und **Planungen** der Neonazis.
11. Hasselbach schildert seine Motive für den **Ausstieg aus der** [neonazistischen] **Szene.**

g. „Die Abrechnung" ist ein Report ...
h. Der Rechtsradikalismus ist ein großes Problem.
i. Hasselbach gibt Informationen über die Organisation und Pläne der Neonazis.
j. Hasselbach sagt, warum er kein Neonazi mehr ist.
k. Ingo Hasselbach war bis vor kurzer Zeit der Boss der Neonazis.

ABSPRUNGTEXT

„Schindlers Liste" und „Die Abrechnung"

Lesen Sie jetzt die zwei Texte.

DAS BUCH ZUM FILM

An Originalschauplätzen in Polen drehte Steven Spielberg im Frühjahr 1993 einen Film über Oskar Schindler. Spielberg bezeichnet diesen Film, der jetzt in den Kinos anläuft, als sein wichtigstes Werk.

Thomas Keneally · Schindlers Liste

Mit List und Verstand, mit Bestechung und mit guten Beziehungen zu Nazigrößen im besetzten Polen, rettet der deutsche Unternehmer Oskar Schindler 1300 jüdische Arbeiter vor der Gaskammer: Er läßt sie für sich arbeiten, erklärt ihre Arbeit für »kriegswichtig«. Schindler war ein Besessener, der bereit war, alles zu riskieren für eine waghalsige, phantastische Rettungsaktion.

Roman. 352 Seiten.
Gebunden mit Schutzumschlag. **02698 9 Club-Preis nur 22.90**

Dieser aktuelle, authentische Bericht zum Thema Rechtsradikalismus bringt Zündstoff in die öffentliche Diskussion über eines der dringlichsten und widersprüchlichsten deutschen Themen.

Ingo Hasselbach · Die Abrechnung · Ein Neonazi steigt aus

Ingo Hasselbach – noch vor einem Jahr der führende Kopf der ostdeutschen rechtsextremen Szene – gibt öffentlich seinen Austritt aus den neonazistischen Organisationen bekannt. Er beschreibt die Strukturen und Planungen der Neonazis, ihre europäischen Vernetzungen, Hintermänner und Anführer, schildert seine Motive für den Ausstieg aus einer Szene, die wie eine Droge wirkt ...

160 Seiten. Mit vielen
Abbildungen. Gebunden. **02603 9 Club-Preis nur 19.90**

Rückblick

23 Bücher beschreiben. Füllen Sie die Tabelle mit Informationen aus dem Text aus.

	„Schindlers Liste"	„Die Abrechnung"
der Autor	___________	Ingo Hasselbach
das Genre	___________	Bericht
das Thema	ein kluger Mann rettet Juden	___________
die Länge	352 Seiten	___________
der Preis	___________	___________

24 **Stimmt das?** Stimmen diese Aussagen zum Text? Wenn nicht, was stimmt?

	Ja, das stimmt.	*Nein, das stimmt nicht.*
1. „Schindlers Liste" ist ein Film von Steven Spielberg.	___	___
2. „Schindlers Liste" ist ein Roman von Thomas Keneally.	___	___
3. Spielberg meint, von allen Filmen ist dies sein wichtigstes Werk.	___	___
4. Spielberg hat seinen Film in Deutschland gedreht.	___	___
5. Spielberg hat den Film über einen Nazi namens° Oskar Schindler gedreht.	___	___
6. Schindler hat über 1300 Juden gerettet.	___	___
7. Die 1300 Juden haben für Schindlers Unternehmen gearbeitet.	___	___
8. Schindler hat nichts riskiert.	___	___

by the name of

25 **Ergänzen Sie.** Ergänzen Sie diese Sätze mit Wörtern aus dem **Absprungtext.**

1. „Schindlers Liste" war ursprünglich° ein _____ von Thomas Keneally.
2. Steven Spielberg hat einen _____ über Oskar Schindler gedreht.
3. Schindler _____ über 1300 jüdische Arbeiter vor der Gaskammer.
4. „Die Abrechnung" ist ein Bericht zum _____ Rechtsradikalismus.
5. Der Untertitel vom Buch ist: „Ein Neonazi _____ _____."
6. Die Diskussion zum Thema ist nicht privat, sondern _____.
7. Noch _____ einem Jahr war Hasselbach Rechtsextremist.
8. Er war der führende Kopf von der ostdeutschen Neonazi-_____.
9. Er _____ die Strukturen und Planungen der Neonazis.
10. Er schildert die _____ für seinen Ausstieg aus der Szene.

originally

26 **Kurz gefragt.** Beantworten Sie diese Fragen auf Deutsch.

1. Wo hat Steven Spielberg im Frühjahr 1993 gearbeitet?
2. Warum war Oskar Schindler wichtig?
3. Wer hat den Originalroman geschrieben?
4. Was hat Ingo Hasselbach früher gemacht?
5. Was gibt er in seinem Buch öffentlich bekannt?
6. Was beschreibt er in seinem Buch?

BRENNPUNKT KULTUR

Politischer Extremismus und politische Parteien

Recent German history has seen political extremism on the right and on the left. The legal election of Adolf Hitler as chancellor of Germany on January 30, 1933, and the ascent of the right-wing Nazi party in the 1930s and 1940s demonstrate the danger such extremist groups pose to political systems and human life. Political extremist movements exist both on the left, e.g., the Baader-Meinhof group in the 1970s, as well as on the right, with the recent emergence of the right-wing party **die Republikaner** and the different groups of **Skinheads.**

Fortunately, the democratic system, which dates from the founding of the Federal Republic of Germany **(Bundesrepublik Deutschland)** in 1949, is able to tolerate the small but visible extremist minority on the fringe of the political spectrum. Several political parties reflect the political spectrum in Germany today, beginning with the extremist anti-foreigner parties on the right, **die Deutsche Volksunion** and **die Republikaner,** which remain essentially outside the political establishment. Parties that have held power in recent years are the conservative Christian Democrats **(die Christlich Demokratische Union–CDU)** and its sister party in Bavaria **(die Christlich-Soziale Union–CSU),** the Social Democrats **(die Sozialdemokratische Partei Deutschlands–SPD),** and the environmental Green Party **(die Grünen),** which first entered the national scene in 1979. Following the unification of Germany in 1990, the Greens formed a coalition with other like-minded groups from former East Germany and became **Die Grünen/Bündnis 90.** Since October 1998, the Green Party has formed a coalition government with the SPD. The political force of the centrist Free Democrats **(die Freie Demokratische Partei–FDP),** is in question, due to its inability to obtain the minimum 5% of the popular vote needed in national elections. The former communist party of East Germany was re-organized as the **Partei des Demokratischen Sozialismus (PDS)** after the unification of the two Germanys in 1990 and seems to be gaining popularity, especially in former East Germany.

Das Politische Spektrum in Deutschland

Links						***Rechts***
PDS	Die Grünen/Bündnis 90	SPD	FDP	CDU/CSU	Republikaner	DVU

Strukturen und Vokabeln

The *D*eutsche *V*olks*u*nion is a far-right nationalist party.

Skinhead groups have openly demonstrated against foreigners in Germany and have claimed responsibility for the deaths of many foreigners in recent years.

II Talking about when events happen

Time expressions in the dative and accusative case

A. *Time expressions in the dative case*

German speakers use the two-case prepositions **in/im, am,** and **vor** frequently with the dative case to express a specific time when an event occurs. These expressions answer the question **wann?** *(when?).*

Wann kommen die Schmidts? – **In einer** Stunde.
When are the Schmidts coming? — In an hour.
Wann hast du Geburtstag? – **Im** Mai.
When is your birthday? — In May.
Wann hast du Geburtstag? – **Am** 11. (elften) Mai.
When is your birthday? — On the 11th of May.
Wann hast du in Zürich studiert? – **Vor einem** Jahr.
When did you study in Zurich? — A year ago.

The preposition **in/im** also defines the point in time of an event happening.

Ich bin **im Jahre 1964** geboren. — *I was born in the year 1964.*
Ich habe **im Juli** frei. — *I am off in July.*
Ich möchte dich **in der dritten Juniwoche** besuchen. — *I would like to visit you during the third week of June.*

German speakers use **am** to describe an event that happens on a specific day or date or on the weekend.

Am Freitag wollen wir ins Theater, nicht? — *We want to go to the theater on Friday, don't we?*
Weihnachten ist immer **am 25. (fünfundzwanzigsten) Dezember.** — *Christmas is always on the 25th of December.*
Am Wochenende spielen wir Fußball. — *We're going to play soccer on the weekend.*

Use **in/im** when referring to years, months, and weeks. Use **am** when referring to days and weekends. Remember to use the accusative preposition **um** when referring to hours and minutes: **um zwei Uhr; um drei Minuten nach zwei.**

The preposition **vor** expresses time in the past in the way that *ago* does in English.

Ich habe die Karten schon **vor einer Woche** abgeholt. — *I picked up the tickets a week ago.*
Vor einem Jahr bin ich nach Afrika geflogen. — *One year ago I flew to Africa.*

Note that **in/im** and **vor** have opposite meanings here. **Vor** refers to a point in time at which events took place while **in/im** refers to a point in time at which events *will take* place: **Jetzt bin ich 30 Jahre alt. Vor einem Jahr war ich 29 Jahre alt. In einem Jahr bin ich 31 Jahre alt.**

Sprache im Alltag: Expressing regularity

German speakers use the expressions **einmal** *(once)*, **zweimal** *(twice)*, **dreimal** *(three times)*, etc. before non-specific time expressions (e.g., **im Sommer, im Jahr, am Tag, am Wochenende, in der Woche)** to tell how often they do an activity.

Einmal im Sommer spielen wir Golf. — *We play golf once a summer.*
Karl wäscht sein Auto **einmal im Monat.** — *Karl washes his car once a month.*

For special emphasis or to express their exasperation speakers use the expressions **hundertmal** *(a hundred times)*, **zigmal,** or **x-mal** *(umpteen times)*.

Ich habe dir schon **x-mal** gesagt: Du musst um zehn Uhr zu Hause sein. — *I've told you umpteen times: You have to be home by ten.*

B. *Time expressions in the accusative case*

To express definite time, German speakers use a time expression in the accusative case without a preposition. When used with the conversational past, these time expressions often correspond to an expression with the preposition *for* in English.

Diesen Samstag fahren wir nach Stuttgart. — *We are driving to Stuttgart this Saturday.*
Ich habe **ein Jahr** in Heidelberg gewohnt. — *I lived in Heidelberg for one year.*
Er bleibt **eine Woche** bei uns. — *He's staying with us for one week.*

27 **Wann ist Barbara zu Hause gewesen?** Fragen Sie einen Partner/eine Partnerin nach einer Aktivität mit einem Fragezeichen. Beantworten Sie dann eine Frage von Ihrem Partner/Ihrer Partnerin.

S1: Wann ist Stefan zu Hause gewesen?
S2: Stefan ist vor einer Woche zu Hause gewesen.
S1: Wann bist du zu Hause gewesen?
S2: Ich bin am Wochenende zu Hause gewesen.

Partner(in) 1:

	Barbara	**Stefan**	**Partner(in) 2**
zu Hause gewesen	am Freitag	?	?
Freunde in Berlin besucht	?	vor einem Jahr	?
in die Stadt gefahren	?	vor einer Stunde	?
ein gutes Buch gelesen	vor einem Monat	?	?
ein Konto eröffnet	?	vor zwei Wochen	?
auf die Post gegangen	gestern	?	?
an der Uni gewesen	heute Morgen	?	?
einen Film gesehen	?	am Samstag	?
mit dem Rad gefahren	dieses Wochenende	?	?

Partner(in) 2:

	Barbara	**Stefan**	**Partner(in) 1**
zu Hause gewesen	?	vor einer Woche	(am Wochenende)
Freunde in Berlin besucht	im Sommer	?	?
in die Stadt gefahren	vor 25 Minuten	?	?
ein gutes Buch gelesen	?	am Wochenende	?
ein Konto eröffnet	gestern	?	?
auf die Post gegangen	?	vor zehn Minuten	?
an der Uni gewesen	?	um zehn Uhr	?
einen Film gesehen	gestern Abend	?	?
mit dem Rad gefahren	?	am Sonntag	?

28 **Oft oder nie?** Notieren Sie, wie oft Sie die folgenden Aktivitäten machen: **einmal (zweimal** usw.) **am Tag (in der Woche, im Monat, im Jahr)** oder **nie?** Fragen Sie dann einen Partner/eine Partnerin, wie oft er/sie das macht.

S1: Wie oft gehst du in eine Buchhandlung?
S2: Ich gehe (einmal in der Woche) in eine Buchhandlung.

Oft oder nie? Mention references to time *before* references to a place (e.g., **Ich fahre um sieben Uhr nach Hause.**) You will learn more about this later in this chapter.

	Ich	*Partner(in)*
1. in eine Buchhandlung gehen	________	________
2. ins Restaurant gehen	________	________
3. ins Kino gehen	________	________
4. zu Fuß zur Uni gehen	________	________
5. auf eine Party gehen	________	________
6. in die Kneipe gehen	________	________

	Ich	*Partner(in)*
7. ins Fitnessstudio gehen	________	________
8. auf die Bank gehen	________	________
9. in die Kirche (Synagoge, Moschee) gehen	________	________
10. in die Oper gehen	________	________

29 **Interview.** Stellen Sie einem Partner/einer Partnerin die folgenden Fragen.

Interview. Remember that **wenn** *(if)* is a subordinating conjunction in German. The verb always occurs at the end of the clause.

S1: Wohin gehst du am Montag?
S2: Ich gehe in die Bibliothek.

1. Wohin gehst du am Montag?
2. Wohin gehst du am Freitagabend?
3. Wohin gehst du, wenn du ein Theaterstück sehen willst?
4. Wohin gehst du, wenn du tanzen willst?
5. Wohin gehst du, wenn du ein Bier trinken willst?
6. Wohin gehst du, wenn du gute Musik hören willst?
7. Wohin gehst du, wenn du einen Film sehen willst?
8. Wohin gehst du, wenn du schwimmen willst?
9. Wohin gehst du, wenn du Bodybuilding machen willst?

III Talking about means of transportation

The preposition **mit** with the dative case

German speakers use the dative preposition **mit** *(with, by)* to talk about means of transportation.

Barbara fährt **mit dem Bus** in die Stadt.	*Barbara is taking the bus downtown.*
Stefan fährt **mit dem Auto.**	*Stefan is taking the car.*

To talk about travel on foot, speakers most commonly use the expression **zu Fuß** with the verb **gehen**.

Wir gehen **zu Fuß.** *We walk (are walking).*

To ask about means of transportation German speakers use the question words **wie?** *(how?)* or **womit?** *(with what?)*.

Wie kommst du nach Hause?	Mit dem Taxi.
Womit fährt Stefan in die Stadt?	Mit dem Fahrrad.

In answers to a question that contains a **mit** expression, speakers often use **da + mit: damit.**

Kannst du **mit deinem alten Fahrrad** noch fahren?
Klar. Ich fahre jeden Tag **damit.**

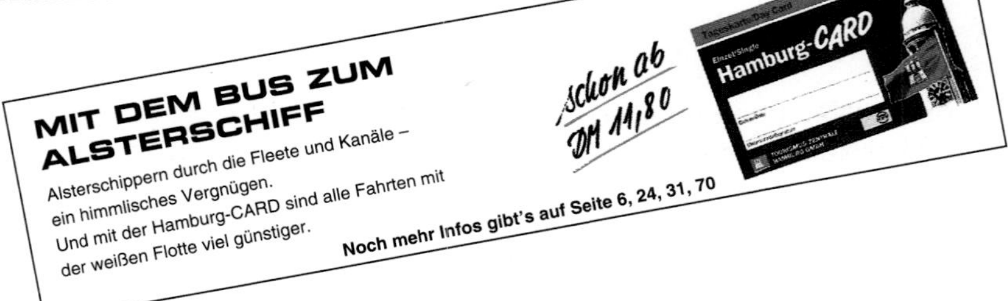

MIT DEM BUS ZUM ALSTERSCHIFF
Alsterschippern durch die Fleete und Kanäle –
ein himmlisches Vergnügen.
Und mit der Hamburg-CARD sind alle Fahrten mit
der weißen Flotte viel günstiger.
schon ab DM 11,80
Hamburg-CARD
Noch mehr Infos gibt's auf Seite 6, 24, 31, 70

Wissenswerte Vokabeln: Wie kommt man dahin?

Talking about means of transportation

mit dem Fahrrad (Rad)

mit dem Auto (Wagen, Pkw)

mit dem Bus

mit der Bahn (dem Zug)

mit der Straßenbahn

mit der U-Bahn (Untergrundbahn)

mit dem Schiff

mit dem Flugzeug

mit dem Taxi

zu Fuß

mit dem Motorrad

mit Rollerblades

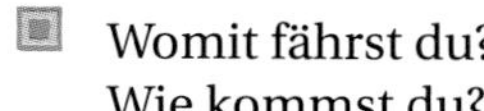

Womit fährst du? *Ich fahre mit dem Bus.*
Wie kommst du? *Ich komme mit dem Taxi.*

30 **Interview.** Stellen Sie einem Partner/einer Partnerin die folgenden Fragen.

S1: Womit fährst du meistens zur Uni?
S2: Ich fahre mit dem Rad. Und du?
S1: Ich fahre mit dem Bus.

	Ich	*Partner(in)*
1. Womit fährst du zur Uni?	________	________
2. Womit kommst du im Winter zur Uni?	________	________
3. Womit fährst du nach Hause?	________	________
4. Womit fährst du lieber: mit der Straßenbahn oder mit der U-Bahn?	________	________
5. Womit kommt man am besten° nach Europa?	________	________

***am besten:** the best way*

31 **Fahren Sie am besten mit dem Taxi.** Sie arbeiten in einem Luxushotel in Köln und geben den Hotelgästen Rat, womit sie fahren sollen.

S1: Wir müssen in fünf Minuten im Stadttheater sein. Aber das ist am anderen Stadtende. Wie kommen wir am schnellsten dahin?
S2: Dann fahren Sie am besten mit dem Taxi.

1. Wir wollen den Kölner Dom besuchen. Aber mit kleinen Kindern können wir nicht den ganzen Weg laufen. Wie kommen wir dahin?
2. Heute Nachmittag muss ich in Düsseldorf sein, aber ich habe kein Auto. Das ist aber nicht so weit – weniger als eine Stunde von hier. Wie fährt man dahin?
3. Ich möchte so gern die Schlösser und die Weinberge am Rhein sehen!
4. Wir suchen ein kleines Café oder eine Konditorei hier gleich in der Nähe.
5. Wie kommt man von Köln nach Bonn?
6. In zwei Stunden muss ich in London sein! Was soll ich machen?

IV Expressing time, manner, and place

The position of information regarding time, manner, and place

References to time in German often occur at the beginning of a main clause, followed by the conjugated verb and the subject.

time *verb* *subject*
Heute fahren wir in die Stadt. *We are going (driving) into town today.*

Such time references may also appear after the verb and within the sentence.

Wir fahren **heute** in die Stadt.

Information about how an action occurs (the manner) follows the time reference.

1 time *2 manner*
Wir fahren **heute mit dem Auto** in die Stadt.

Information about where an action occurs follows the references to time and manner. In sum, information in a German sentence follows the sequence: (1) time, (2) manner, (3) place.

1 time *2 manner* *3 place*
Wir fahren **heute mit dem Auto in die Stadt.**

The sequence of information in an English sentence is organized in the opposite order: (1) place, (2) manner, (3) time.

1 place *2 manner* *3 time*
We are driving **to town by car today**.

32 **Wann, wie und wo lesen Sie das?** Wählen Sie aus jeder Spalte ein Element und formulieren Sie eine passende Antwort.

S1: Liest du dein Deutschbuch?
S2: Ja, ich lese mein Deutschbuch so oft wie möglich laut vor dem Kamin°. *fireplace*

eine deutsche Zeitung • „Vorsprung" • eine Wirtschaftszeitung (z.B. „Money Magazine") • ein Mathematikbuch • eine Lokalzeitung • eine Frauenzeitschrift (z.B. „Cosmopolitan") • ein Automagazin • ein Physikbuch • einen Roman von Stephen King • einen Krimi von Agatha Christie • Gedichte von Goethe • einen Roman von Danielle Steele • eine Tratschzeitschrift (z.B. „People Magazine") • ein Nachrichtenmagazin (z.B. „Time Magazine")

Wann?	***Wie?***	***Wo?***	
jeden Abend	leise°	im Wohnzimmer	*quietly*
jeden Tag	laut	auf der Post	
am Morgen	im Kopf	im Bett	
selten	mit den Kindern	vor dem Fernseher	
einmal im Monat	allein	beim Friseur°	*hairdresser's*
nie	mit großem Interesse	in der Schlange° im Supermarkt	*line*
immer	ohne großes Interesse		
so oft wie möglich	mit dem Lehrer	in meinem Zimmer	
jede Woche	mit der Lehrerin	an der Uni	
einmal am Vormittag		im Schwimmbad	
einmal am Abend		im Café	
		vor dem Kamin	

Schreibecke **Eine Postkarte schreiben.** Sie sind in Stuttgart und vermissen Ihren Deutschlehrer/Ihre Deutschlehrerin sehr. Schreiben Sie ihm/ihr wieder eine Postkarte. Verwenden Sie die folgenden Vokabeln und Ausdrücke.

Gestern bin ich ...

Mein Freund	ist	mit dem	Bus	ins	Museum	gegangen.
Meine Freundin	sind	mit der	Auto		Theater	gefahren.
			Schiff	in die	Kneipe	
Meine Freunde			Taxi		Oper	
Meine Freundinnen			Straßenbahn	auf die	Uni	
			U-Bahn			
		zu Fuß				

V ▣ Giving directions

Prepositional phrases; **hin** and **her**

A. Prepositional phrases indicating location

When you visit an unfamiliar city in Germany you will need to ask for and understand directions. German speakers frequently use two-case prepositions with the accusative when giving directions.

Gehen Sie **über die Brücke in die Stadt.** *Go over the bridge into town.*

Other prepositions are common, too. Here are some useful prepositional phrases for asking for and giving directions.

Wie komme ich zur/zum ...?	*How do I get to . . . ?*
bis zur Kreuzung/Ampel	*as far as the intersection/traffic light*

links/rechts abbiegen	*turn left/right*
die Straße entlang	*down the street*
über die Straße	*across the street*
geradeaus	*straight ahead*
(gleich) um die Ecke	*(right) around the corner*
an der Ecke	*at the corner*

Note that the preposition **um** (e.g., **um die Ecke**) always occurs with the accusative, while the preposition **zu** (e.g., **bis zur Kreuzung**) always occurs with the dative.

33 Wie kommt Anna zur Staatsgalerie? Anna ist in Stuttgart und möchte vieles sehen. Welche Wegbeschreibung° ist richtig?

direction

Use the map on page 283.

Anna ist ...

1. am Bahnhof und möchte zur Staatsgalerie.
2. am Marktplatz und möchte zum Karlsplatz.
3. am Postgiroamt und möchte zum Bahnhof.
4. in der Staatsgalerie und möchte zum Staatstheater.
5. im neuen Schloss und möchte zum Königsbau.
6. am Marktplatz und möchte zum Rathaus.

Ein Stuttgarter/Eine Stuttgarterin sagt:

a. „Gehen Sie gleich um die Ecke."
b. „Gehen Sie über den Schlossplatz."
c. „Gehen Sie die Münzstraße entlang."
d. „Nehmen Sie die Boltzstraße bis zur Königstraße, biegen Sie links ab und gehen Sie dann geradeaus."
e. „Gehen Sie die Schillerstraße entlang bis zur Konrad-Adenauer-Straße und biegen Sie dann rechts ab."
f. „Gehen Sie über die Konrad-Adenauer-Straße."

34 Wie komme ich zum Bahnhof? Sie sind in Stuttgart am Schlossplatz. Ein Tourist/Eine Touristin fragt nach dem Weg. Beschreiben Sie, wie man dahin kommt. Benutzen Sie den Stadtplan von Stuttgart.

S1 (TOURIST/TOURISTIN): Entschuldigung, wie komme ich zum Bahnhof?
S2 (SIE): Fahren Sie geradeaus in die Königstraße. *(oder)* Gehen Sie die Königstraße entlang.

S1 (Tourist/Touristin):

zum Bahnhof	zum Königsbau
zum Neuen Schloss	zum Karlsplatz
zum Schillerplatz	zum Staatstheater
zum Postgiroamt	zur Markthalle

B. *The prefixes* hin *and* her

You have already encountered **hin** and **her** in the question words **wohin** *(where to)* and **woher** *(where from).*

Wo**her** kommst du?	Ich komme aus Berlin.
Wo**hin** fährst du?	Ich fahre in die Stadt.

Both prefixes also occur with verbs of motion to express the notion of origin, (e.g., **herkommen**) and destination (e.g., **hinfahren**).

Komm mal **her!**	*Come over here!*
Möchtest du dort **hin**fahren?	*Would you like to go (drive) there?*
Wo soll ich das Buch **hin**legen?	*Where should I put the book?*

35 **Der neugierige° Zimmernachbar.** Karls Nachbar im Studentenwohnheim ist sehr neugierig. Er möchte alles ganz genau wissen. Welche Fragen hat er gestellt und was hat Karl geantwortet? Verbinden Sie seine Fragen mit den passenden Antworten von Karl und lesen Sie sie dann laut mit einem Partner/einer Partnerin.

nosy

S1 (NACHBAR): Woher hast du deine Schecks?
S2 (KARL): Von der Sparkasse bei der Universität.

1. Woher hast du deine Schecks?
2. Woher hast du das gute Brot?
3. Wohin gehst du, wenn du eine Semesterkarte brauchst?
4. Woher hast du diese interessante Zeitschrift?
5. Wohin bringst du das Geld?
6. Wohin gehst du, wenn du schnell ein bisschen Milch brauchst?

a. Aus der Bäckerei gleich um die Ecke.
b. Vom Kiosk bei der Kreuzung.
c. Zum Kiosk bei der Kreuzung.
d. Auf die Sparkasse bei der Uni.
e. Von der Sparkasse bei der Uni.
f. In die Bäckerei, wo es auch das gute Brot gibt.

FREIE KOMMUNIKATION

So kommt man dahin. Ihr Partner/Ihre Partnerin ist ein Freund/eine Freundin aus einer anderen Stadt. Erklären Sie ihm/ihr, wie man von Ihrem Haus zu gewissen° Punkten in der Stadt kommt: der Universität, dem Flughafen, einem guten Restaurant usw. Ihr Partner/Ihre Partnerin zeichnet° einen Plan und wiederholt dann, was Sie gesagt haben. Stimmt alles?

certain
draws

Wissenswerte Vokabeln: Literatur und Film

Talking about literature and film

Other types of movies are: **der Actionfilm, die Komödie, der Kriegsfilm, der Liebesfilm, der Western, der Science fictionfilm.**

die Biographie, -n/ Autobiographie

das Drama, *(pl.)* Dramen

das Theaterstück, -e

die Erzählung, -en

der Film, -e

der Abenteuerfilm

der Dokumentar-film

der Horrorfilm

der Zeichentrick-film

das Gedicht, -e

die Kurz-geschichte, -n

das Märchen, -

der Roman, -e

der Kriminalroman (der Krimi, -s)

der Liebesroman

spannend

lustig

unterhaltend

Was liest du gern? *Ich lese gern Abenteuerromane.*
Siehst du gern Horrorfilme? *Nein, ich sehe lieber Dokumentarfilme.*

36 Fantasietitel. Der Titel von einem Buch oder Film sagt oft etwas über das Genre aus. Aus welchem Genre kommen die Filme und Bücher mit dem folgenden Titel?

Filmtitel	***Genre***
1. Die Nacht der Wer-Elefanten	a. der Zeichentrickfilm
2. 101 Elefanten	b. der Abenteuerfilm
3. Illinois Jones und der Elefant des Maharadschas	c. der Dokumentarfilm
	d. der Actionfilm
4. Die Elefanten Afrikas	e. der Horrorfilm
5. Ein Elefant sieht rot	

Buchtitel	
1. Der Elefantenprinz	a. ein Gedicht
2. Der Elefantenmord	b. ein Theaterstück
3. Ode an den Elefanten	c. ein Kriminalroman
4. Warten auf Elefanten	d. eine Autobiographie
5. Mein Leben als Elefant	e. ein Märchen

VI ■ Expressing the purpose for an action

The subordinating conjunction damit

A clause introduced by the subordinating conjunction **damit** *(so that)* expresses one's intent or purpose in carrying out an action. This contrasts with **weil** *(because)*, which provides a reason for the action.

> Barbara geht in die Buchhandlung, **damit** sie „Die Abrechnung" kaufen kann.
> *Barbara is going to the bookstore so that she can buy* Die Abrechnung.
> Barbara geht in die Buchhandlung, **weil** sie „Die Abrechnung" sucht.
> *Barbara is going to the bookstore because she is looking for* Die Abrechnung.

The subordinating conjunction **damit** must not be confused with the compound **damit,** which substitutes for **mit** + a noun and cannot join clauses.

> Hier sind die Papiere. Was soll ich **damit** machen?
> *Here are the papers. What should I do with them?*

37 Lesen nur zum Spaß? Warum lesen Sie das? Benutzen Sie **weil** oder **damit** in Ihrer Antwort.

■ Ich lese eine deutsche Zeitung, weil ich sie gern lese.

Ich lese ...

1. eine deutsche Zeitung,
2. mein Deutschbuch,
3. das Mathematikbuch,
4. die Lokalzeitung,
5. Frauenzeitschriften (z.B. „Cosmopolitan"),
6. ein Automagazin,
7. Wirtschaftszeitschriften (z.B. „Money Magazine"),
8. Romane von Stephen King (Danielle Steele usw.),
9. das Horoskop,
10. Gedichte von Goethe,
11. eine Geschichte von Agatha Christie,
12. Nachrichtenmagazine (z.B. „Time Magazine"),

damit ich gute Noten bekomme.
weil es mich interessiert.
weil ich (sie/es) gern lese.
weil ich neue Ideen suche.
damit ich neue Informationen finden kann.
damit ich etwas Neues lernen kann.
weil ich Stephen Kings (Danielle Steeles usw.) Romane liebe.
weil es lustig ist.
weil es mir gefällt.
weil ...
damit ...

■ FREIE ■ KOMMUNIKATION ■ **Rollenspiel: In die Stadt fahren.** Es ist Samstag. Sie müssen vieles erledigen (z.B. Bücher, Lebensmittel einkaufen, Geld abheben). Sie möchten aber nicht allein in die Stadt fahren. Ihr Partner/Ihre Partnerin möchte nicht mitkommen, denn es sind immer so viele Leute in der Stadt und es ist zu hektisch **(Ich will nicht kommen, weil ...).** Versuchen Sie, Ihren Partner/Ihre Partnerin zu überreden°, dass er/sie mitkommt. Erklären Sie, womit Sie fahren, wohin Sie in der Stadt gehen und wann Sie zurückkommen.

° *persuade*

Schreibecke **Meine Biographie/Autobiographie.** Beschreiben Sie Ihre Biographie/Autobiographie für einen Buchkatalog.

1. Was ist der Titel?
2. Was ist die Länge?
3. Wie heißt der Autor/die Autorin? (Schreiben Sie selbst? Wenn nicht, wer schreibt? Warum?)
4. Was ist der Preis?
5. Was steht in der Biographie/Autobiographie so im Allgemeinen?
6. Was ist passiert? Wann? Wie oft?
7. Wohin sind Sie (oft, selten) gefahren? Womit?

Schreibecke. Provide basic information such as where and when you were born, how and where you spent your early years, etc. Use the conversational past.

ZIELTEXT

In der Buchhandlung

Barbara hat im Bertelsmann Katalog über die Bücher „Schindlers Liste“ und „Die Abrechnung“ gelesen. Sie geht in eine Buchhandlung, denn sie möchte vielleicht die Bücher kaufen. Sie braucht auch ein Vorlesungsverzeichnis für die Uni. Ihr Freund Karl kommt mit und wartet draußen auf Barbara.

Vorschau

38 **Thematische Fragen.** Beantworten Sie die folgenden Fragen auf Deutsch.

1. Was lesen Sie gern?
2. Welche Autoren sind im Moment populär?
3. Wo finden Sie neue Bücher über aktuelle Themen, z. B. Bestseller?
4. Nennen Sie einige berühmte deutsche Autoren/Autorinnen.

39 **Satzdetektiv.** Welche Sätze bedeuten ungefähr das Gleiche?

1. Also, wir haben **momentan** „Die Abrechnung“ von Ingo Hasselbach.
2. Das Buch „Die Abrechnung“ ist **hochaktuell.**
3. „Die Abrechnung“ **handelt von** Ingo Hasselbach.
4. Ingo Hasselbach **schildert** die Vernetzungen nicht nur in Deutschland, sondern auch in den anderen europäischen Staaten.

a. Das Buch „Die Abrechnung“ ist sehr relevant und neu.
b. Ingo Hasselbach schreibt über das rechtsextremistische Netzwerk in Deutschland und in Europa.
c. „Die Abrechnung“ von Ingo Hasselbach ist im Moment neu im Buchhandel.
d. „Die Abrechnung“ ist die Geschichte von Ingo Hasselbach.

5. Kommen Sie bitte mit zur **Kasse.**
6. **Manche haben's im Kopf, andere in den Beinen.**
7. Ich brauch' noch ein **Vorlesungsverzeichnis.**
8. Möchten Sie eine **Tüte** oder geht's auch ohne?
9. **Die Quittung** liegt auf der ersten Seite.

e. Der Zettel° mit dem Preis darauf ist im Buch.
f. Ich möchte ein Buch über Universitätskurse kaufen.
g. Kommen Sie bitte mit. Sie können für das Buch dort bezahlen.
h. Manche Leute vergessen nichts und andere Leute vergessen alles.
i. Möchten Sie auch eine Plastiktasche haben?

° *slip of paper*

ZIELTEXT

In der Buchhandlung

Hören Sie gut zu.

Rückblick

40 **Stimmt das?** Stimmen diese Aussagen zum Text oder nicht? Wenn nicht, was stimmt?

	Ja, das stimmt.	*Nein, das stimmt nicht.*
1. Barbara sucht ein Buch in der Buchhandlung.	___	___
2. Barbara hat „Die Abrechnung" schon gelesen.	___	___
3. „Die Abrechnung" ist sehr alt.	___	___
4. Die Buchhandlung hat „Die Abrechnung" nicht.	___	___
5. Barbara kauft das Buch nicht.	___	___
6. Das Buch kostet 19,90 DM.	___	___
7. Karl geht mit in die Buchhandlung.	___	___
8. Barbara hat schon ein Vorlesungsverzeichnis.	___	___
9. Karl kauft das Vorlesungsverzeichnis für Barbara.	___	___
10. Barbara hat keinen Rucksack.	___	___

41 Ergänzen Sie: Diktat. Ergänzen Sie diese Sätze mit Wörtern aus dem **Zieltext.**

1. Guten Tag! Was kann ich für Sie _____?
2. Ich habe gestern von einem Buch über _____ gelesen.
3. Das soll ein Bestseller sein, eine _____.
4. Sie _____ da vorne aus.
5. Es _____ von Ingo Hasselbach.
6. Gut, da _____ ich mal dieses Buch.
7. Kommen Sie bitte mit zur _____.
8. Du wolltest doch dein _____ noch holen, oder?
9. Möchten Sie eine _____, oder geht's auch ohne?
10. Die _____ liegt auf der ersten Seite.

42 Wann sagt man das? Wann hört man diese Sätze aus dem **Zieltext?** Kreuzen Sie für jeden Satz eine passende Situation an.

Eine Person sagt:	*Man hört es,*
1. „Kommen Sie bitte mit zur Kasse."	___ a. wenn man für ein Buch bezahlen will. ___ b. wenn man ein Buch sucht.
2. „Sie bekommen 20 Pfennig zurück."	___ a. wenn ein Buch 19 Mark 80 kostet und man mit einem 20-Mark-Schein bezahlt. ___ b. wenn ein Buch 19 Mark 80 kostet und man mit einem 10-Mark-Schein bezahlt.
3. „Entschuldigen Sie bitte, ich muss Sie noch einmal stören."	___ a. wenn der Deutschlehrer/die Deutschlehrerin in das Klassenzimmer kommt. ___ b. wenn man aus einem Geschäft schon hinausgegangen ist, aber dann gleich wieder zurückkommt.
4. „Möchten Sie eine Tüte?"	___ a. wenn man Schokolade kauft. ___ b. wenn man einen Hund kauft.
5. „Die Quittung liegt auf der ersten Seite."	___ a. wenn ein Freund/eine Freundin Ihnen ein Buch leiht. ___ b. wenn man ein Buch in einer Buchhandlung kauft.

FREIE KOMMUNIKATION

Rollenspiel: In der Buchhandlung. Spielen Sie eine von diesen Situationen in einer Buchhandlung mit einem Partner/mit einer Partnerin. S1 ist der Kunde/die Kundin, S2 arbeitet in der Buchhandlung.

S1: Wählen Sie eine von diesen Personen und spielen Sie sie in der Buchhandlung.

1. Sie suchen ein Buch als ein Geschenk für einen Freund/eine Freundin. Der Freund/die Freundin ist sehr sportlich und reist gern. Sie wollen ein gutes Buch finden; der Preis ist nicht so wichtig.
2. Sie haben eine Einladung zu einer Party. Sie brauchen ein Geschenk für den Gastgeber/die Gastgeberin. Sie kennen ihn/sie nicht gut und suchen ein Buch, das teuer aussieht aber wirklich wenig kostet.
3. Sie machen bald eine lange Reise. Sie verbringen viel Zeit im Flugzeug (im Zug) und brauchen etwas zum Lesen, damit Ihnen nicht so langweilig wird.

The "clerks" may invent fictitious books (content and title) to recommend to their "customers."

A **Buchhändler** *(bookseller)* is a skilled occupation in Germany requiring 2–3 years of specialized education.

S2: Sie arbeiten in einer Buchhandlung. Wählen Sie eine von diesen Personen und spielen Sie sie.

1. Sie helfen dem Kunden/der Kundin gern, sind sehr freundlich und kennen sich gut mit Büchern aus.
2. Es ist spät am Nachmittag und Sie wollen lieber nach Hause gehen. Sie haben wenig Interesse an Ihrem Kunden/Ihrer Kundin und sind ziemlich unhöflich.
3. Sie arbeiten erst seit ein paar Stunden in der Buchhandlung. Sie wissen fast nichts von Büchern. Sie wollen helfen, können es aber nicht.

Schreibecke Touristenbroschüre. Viele deutsche Touristen wollen Ihre Stadt besuchen. Die Stadt braucht eine Broschüre, die auf Deutsch erklärt, wie man zu bestimmten Gebäuden, Geschäften usw. kommt. Wählen Sie einen zentralen Punkt in Ihrer Stadt. Erklären Sie, wie der Punkt heißt und wo er ist. Beschreiben Sie dann, wie man von diesem Punkt zu mindestens drei anderen wichtigen oder interessanten Punkten kommt.

Wortschatz

Einkaufen und Persönliches erledigen

die Bäckerei, -en *bakery*
die Bank, -en *bank*
der Bioladen, ¨e *health food store*
die Briefmarke, -n *stamp*
die Buchhandlung, -en *bookstore*
die Filiale, -n *branch office*
die Fleischerei, -en *butcher shop*
der Kiosk, -s *kiosk, stand*
die Konditorei, -en *pastry shop*
das Konto, *pl.* **Konten** *bank account*
der Markt, ¨e *farmer's market*
die Metzgerei, -en *butcher shop*
das Paket, -e *package*
die Post *post office*
der Preis, -e *price*
das Reformhaus, ¨er *health food store*
die Sparkasse, -n *savings bank*
der Supermarkt, ¨e *supermarket*
der Zeitungskiosk, -s *newspaper stand*
der Zeitungsstand, ¨e *newspaper stand*

Wo?

in der Bäckerei *at the bakery*
auf der Bank *at the bank*
in der Buchhandlung *at the bookstore*
in der Konditorei *at the pastry shop*
auf dem Markt *at the farmer's market*
in der Metzgerei *at the butcher shop*
in der Nähe *in the vicinity, nearby*
auf der Post *at the post office*
im Reformhaus *at the health food store*
auf der Sparkasse *at the savings bank*
im Supermarkt *at the supermarket*
am Zeitungsstand *at the newspaper stand*

Verben

ab·heben (hat abgehoben) *to withdraw money*
auf·geben (gibt auf, hat aufgegeben) *to drop off, post*
besorgen (hat besorgt) *to acquire, get*
bestellen (hat bestellt) *to order*
ein·zahlen (hat eingezahlt) *to deposit*
empfehlen (empfiehlt, hat empfohlen) *to recommend*
erledigen (hat erledigt) *to take care of, deal with*
eröffnen (hat eröffnet) *to open*
sparen (hat gespart) *to save*
treffen (trifft, hat getroffen) *to meet*
zurück·gehen (ist zurückgegangen) *to go back*

Freizeit und Unterhaltung

die Diskothek, -en *discotheque*
das Fitnessstudio, -s *health club*
der Jazzkeller, - *jazz club*
das Kino, -s *movies*
die Kirche, -n *church*
die Kneipe, -n *bar, pub*
das Konzert, -e *concert*
die Moschee, -n *mosque*
das Museum, *pl.* **Museen** *museum*
die Oper, -n *opera*
das Restaurant, -s *restaurant*
das Schwimmbad, ¨er *swimming pool*
das Stadion, *pl.* **Stadien** *stadium*
die Synagoge, -n *synagogue*
das Theater, - *theater*

Wohin?

auf eine Fete gehen *going to a party*
auf eine Party gehen *going to a party*
in die Kneipe gehen *going to the bar*
ins Kino gehen *going to the movies*

Geschichte und Politik

die Abrechnung, -en *reckoning, accounting*
der Anführer, - *ringleader*
der Arbeiter, - *worker*
der Ausstieg, -e *stepping down, resignation*
der Austritt, -e *withdrawal, resignation*
der Bericht, -e *report*
die Beziehung, -en *contact, relationship*
die Diskussion, -en *discussion*
die Droge, -n *drug*
die Gaskammer, -n *gas chamber*
die List *cunning*
die Liste, -n *list*
das Motiv, -e *motive*
die Nazigröße, -n *important Nazi figure*
die Organisation, -en *organization*
die Planung, -en *plan*
der Rechtsradikalismus *right-wing radicalism*
die Rettungsaktion, -en *rescue mission*
die Struktur, -en *structure*
die Szene, -n *scene*
das Thema, *pl.* **Themen** *topic, theme*
der Verstand *reason, logic*
der Zündstoff *explosive material*

Verben

bekannt geben (gibt bekannt, hat bekannt gegeben) *to announce*
beschreiben (hat beschrieben) *to describe*
bezeichnen (hat bezeichnet) als *to characterize, designate as*
erklären (hat erklärt) für + *acc. to declare; to describe*
retten (hat gerettet) vor + *dat. to rescue, save from*
riskieren (hat riskiert) *to risk*
wirken (hat gewirkt) *to effect, have an effect, impact*

Andere Wörter

aktuell *current, up-to-date*
authentisch *authentic*
bereit *ready*
damit *so that*
dringlich *urgent, pressing*
jüdisch *Jewish*
kriegswichtig *essential for the war effort*
öffentlich *public, publically*
ostdeutsch *East German*
rechtsextremistisch *right-wing extremist*
widersprüchlich *contradictory*

in einer Stunde *in an hour*
in einer Woche *in a week*
einmal im Jahr *once a year*
in den Ferien *during vacation*
im [Juli] *in [July]*
im Jahre 1964 *in 1964*
am 11. Mai *on May 11th*
am Wochenende *on the weekend*
am Freitag *on Friday*
vor einer Woche *a week ago*
vor einem Jahr *a year ago*

Ausdrücke

Er lässt sie für sich arbeiten. *He has them work for him.*

Verkehrsmittel

die Ampel, -n *traffic light*
die Bahn, -en *train*
der Bus, -se *bus*
die Bushaltestelle, -n *bus stop*
das Flugzeug, -e *airplane*
der Hauptbahnhof, ¨-e *main train station*
die Kreuzung, -en *intersection*
das Motorrad, ¨-er *motorcycle*
der Pkw, -s (der Personenkraftwagen, -) *car*
das Rad, ¨-er *bicycle*
die Rollerblades *(pl.) in-line skates*
das Schiff, -e *boat*
die Semesterkarte, -n *semester bus pass*
die Straßenbahn, -en *streetcar*
das Taxi, -s *taxi cab*
die U-Bahn, -en *subway*
der Wagen, - *car*
der Zug, ¨-e *train*

Wo?

an der Ecke *at the corner*
an der Haltestelle *at the bus stop*
am Hauptbahnhof *at the main train station*

Wechselpräpositionen

an *at, on, to*
auf *on, onto*
hinter *behind, in back of*
in *in, into*
neben *next to, beside*
über *above, over*
unter *under, underneath*
vor *in front of; ago*
zwischen *between*

Verben

fallen (fällt, ist gefallen) *to fall*
hängen (hat gehängt) *to hang up*
hängen (hat gehangen) *to be hanging*
laufen (läuft, ist gelaufen) *to run, walk*
legen (hat gelegt) *to lay down, put down*
liegen (hat gelegen) *to be lying down, lie*
setzen (hat gesetzt) *to set down, sit down*
sitzen (hat gesessen) *to be sitting, sit*
springen (ist gesprungen) *to jump*
stehen (hat gestanden) *to stand*
stellen (hat gestellt) *to put standing*

achten (hat geachtet) auf + *acc. to pay attention to*
bitten (hat gebeten) um + *acc. to ask for, request*

böse sein (ist gewesen) auf + *acc.* *to be upset with, mad at*
denken (hat gedacht) an + *acc.* *to think of*
erinnern (hat erinnert) an + *acc.* *to remind someone of/about*
hoffen (hat gehofft) auf + *acc.* *to hope for*
lachen (hat gelacht) über + *acc.* *to laugh about/at*
schreiben (hat geschrieben) an + *acc.* *to write to*
sprechen (spricht, hat gesprochen) über + *acc.* *to talk about*
warten (hat gewartet) auf + *acc.* *to wait for*

Anweisungen geben

links/rechts ab·biegen (ist abgebogen) *turn to the left/right*
an der Ecke *at the corner*
gleich um die Ecke *right around the corner*
geradeaus *straight ahead*
her *here [from point of origin]*
hin *there [point of destination]*
bis zur Kreuzung *up to the intersection*
die Straße entlang *down the street*
über die Straße *across the street*
woher? *from where?*
wohin? *where to?*

Verben

ab·biegen (ist abgebogen) *to turn*
aus·steigen (ist ausgestiegen) *to get out of a vehicle*
ein·steigen (ist eingestiegen) *to get into a vehicle*

Ausdrücke

Komm mal her! *Come over here!*
Wie komme ich zur/zum ...? *How do I get to . . . ?*
x-mal *umpteen times*
zigmal *umpteen times*
zu Fuß *on foot*

Literatur und Film

der Abenteuerfilm, -e *adventure film*
die Autobiographie, -n *autobiography*
der Bericht, -e *report*
der Bestseller, - *best seller*
die Biographie, -n *biography*
der Dokumentarfilm, -e *documentary film*
das Drama, *pl.* **Dramen** *drama, play*
die Erzählung, -en *story*
der Film, -e *movie, film*
der Filmemacher, - *filmmaker*
das Gedicht, -e *poem*
der Horrorfilm, -e *horror film*
der Kriminalroman, -e (der Krimi, -s) *detective story*
die Kurzgeschichte, -n *short story*
der Liebesroman, -e *romance novel*
die Literatur, -en *literature*
das Märchen, - *folk tale, fairy tale*
der Roman, -e *novel*
das Theaterstück, -e *play, drama*
der Zeichentrickfilm, -e *animation, cartoon*
die Zeitschrift, -en *magazine*

einen (Film) drehen (hat gedreht) über + *acc.* *to make a movie about*

spannend *exciting*
lustig *funny, comical*
unterhaltend *entertaining*

Aus dem Zieltext

die Kasse, -n *check-out counter, cash register*
der Katalog, -e *catalogue*
der Preis, -e *price*
die Quittung, -en *receipt*
die Tüte, -n *sack, bag*
der Verkäufer, - *salesman*
die Verkäuferin, -nen *saleslady*
die Vernetzung, -en *network, connection*
das Vorlesungsverzeichnis, -se *course catalogue*

genau *exactly*
hochaktuell *very current, very timely*
momentan *at the moment*

an·schauen (hat angeschaut) *to look at, take a look at*
aus·liegen (hat ausgelegen) *to be displayed*
handeln (hat gehandelt) von + *dat.* *to be about*
schildern (hat geschildert) *to portray, describe (action)*
stören (hat gestört) *to disturb*
tun (hat getan) *to do*

Ausdrücke: zum Einkaufen

Kommen Sie bitte mit zur Kasse. *Please come to the cash register.*
Könnten Sie mir vielleicht mal helfen? *Could you help me?*
Möchten Sie eine Tüte oder geht's auch ohne? *Would you like a bag or can you do without one?*
Was kann ich für Sie tun? *What can I do for you?*

In this chapter you will learn to talk about your daily routine, about issues of personal health, and what you will do in the future. You will also learn to talk about university-related activities.

Kommunikative Funktionen

- Talking about activities we do for ourselves
- Talking about daily hygiene routines
- Talking about future events
- Expressing probability
- Specifying additional information about actions

Strukturen

- Reflexive verbs; reflexive pronouns
- Future time and time expressions
- The verb **werden** + **wohl**
- Verbs with prepositional objects
- **Da-** and **wo-**compounds

Vokabeln

- Die tägliche Routine
- Im Badezimmer
- Krank sein

Kulturelles

- Universitätskurse
- Wie Studenten ihr Studium finanzieren
- Das deutsche Universitätssystem
- Das deutsche Schulsystem

Du, ich muss mich beeilen. Die Vorlesung fängt gleich an.

KAPITEL ACHT

An der Uni studieren

Go to the ***Vorsprung*** Website at
www.hmco.com/college

ANLAUFTEXT

Ein Gruppenreferat

Karl und Stefan sind Partner in einem Betriebswirtschaftsproseminar. Ihre Arbeitsgruppe soll nächste Woche ein Referat° halten; sie müssen im Proseminar über ihr gemeinsames° Projekt sprechen, aber sie haben noch gar nichts° geschrieben. Karl geht zu Frau Dr. Osswald in die Sprechstunde° und erfindet Ausreden°, warum er und Stefan noch nicht viel gemacht haben.

oral report
common/nothing, not anything at all
office hours
***erfindet Ausreden:** makes excuses*

Vorschau

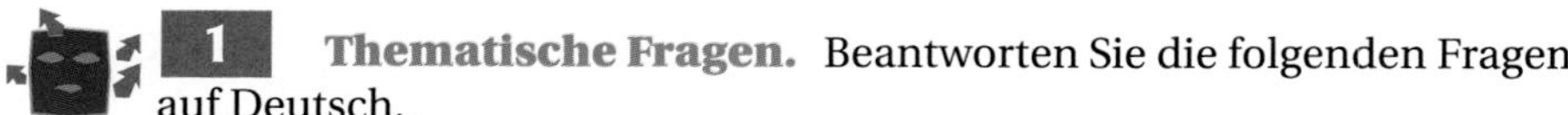

1 Thematische Fragen. Beantworten Sie die folgenden Fragen auf Deutsch.

1. Mit wem sprechen Sie zuerst, wenn Sie Probleme in einem Kurs haben?
   a. mit Freunden
   b. mit Kommilitonen° — *college classmates*
   c. mit dem Professor/der Professorin
   d. mit den Eltern
   e. mit dem Dekan° — *dean*
   f. mit dem/der Vorsitzenden° — *chairperson*
2. Besuchen Sie Professoren/Professorinnen in der Sprechstunde? Warum? Warum nicht? Wie oft haben Ihre Professoren/Professorinnen Sprechstunden?
3. Haben Sie schon mal ein Gruppenprojekt gemacht? Was ist passiert? Was war gut? Was war schlecht?
   a. Wir haben nicht genug Zeit für das Projekt gehabt.
   b. Manche Leute haben mehr gearbeitet als andere.
   c. Wir haben viele gute Ideen gehabt.
   d. Wir haben viele Talente in der Gruppe gehabt.
   e. Wir haben verschiedene Interessen gehabt.
   f. Wir haben Konflikte gehabt.

2 Die Seminararbeit°. Was muss man machen, wenn man eine gute Seminararbeit schreiben will? Ordnen Sie die Faktoren nach ihrer Wichtigkeit von 1 (sehr wichtig) bis 10 (unwichtig). — *term paper*

	Wichtigkeit	
Bücher aus der Bibliothek holen	1	
ein Thema wählen°	3	*select*
einen Partner/eine Partnerin finden	8	
Notizen machen	10	
in die Bibliothek gehen	4	
Bücher und Artikel lesen	2	
ein paar Versionen schreiben	9	
mit dem Professor/der Professorin sprechen	5	
Folien° und Handouts vorbereiten	6	*transparencies*
eine Tabelle° oder eine Grafik zeichnen	7	*table, chart*

3 **Satzdetektiv.** Welche Sätze bedeuten ungefähr das Gleiche?

1. Schön, dass Sie **sich** endlich **melden.**
2. Wie sieht es mit Ihrem **Referat** aus?
3. Ich habe **mich** schwer **erkältet.**
4. Sie haben wirklich **Pech gehabt!**

a. Es ist gut, dass Sie jetzt zu mir gekommen sind.
b. Ich bin krank – ich habe eine schlimme Erkältung.
c. Das ist wirklich eine schlechte Situation für Sie!
d. Wie weit sind Sie mit Ihrem Projekt?

---

5. Haben Sie **sich** überhaupt **für** ein Thema **entschieden?**
6. Wie lange wird das Referat **dauern?**
7. Ich **freue mich** schon **auf** Ihr **Referat.**
8. Wir müssen unser **Referat** schon nächste Woche **halten.**
9. Das werden wir bis nächste Woche nie **schaffen.**

e. Das können wir bis nächste Woche nicht zu Ende machen!
f. Nächste Woche müssen wir unsere Arbeit mündlich° präsentieren. *orally*
g. Wie viel Zeit werden Sie für das Referat brauchen?
h. Wissen Sie schon, über welches Thema Sie sprechen werden?
i. Ich bin auf Ihren Vortrag° gespannt. *presentation*

ANLAUFTEXT

Hören Sie gut zu.

Ein Gruppenreferat

Dr. L. Osswald

Ja, herein, bitte.

Guten Tag. Sie haben heute Sprechstunde, nicht?

Ja. Schön, dass Sie sich endlich melden. Wie sieht es mit Ihrem Referat aus? Kann Ihre Arbeitsgruppe nächste Woche das Referat halten?

Ja, deswegen bin ich da. Wir haben ein paar Probleme gehabt.

Ja?

Ja, ich habe mich schwer erkältet und habe drei Tage im Bett gelegen.

Ja, und Ihr Partner?

Tja, er hat sich das Bein gebrochen.

So, so. Sie haben wirklich Pech gehabt! Haben Sie sich überhaupt für ein Thema entschieden?
Ja. Haben wir das nicht angemeldet?

Ich kann mich jedenfalls nicht daran erinnern. Wie heißt Ihr Thema noch mal?

„Die Rolle der Industrie in der Europäischen Union".

Schön. Das ist ein wirklich aktuelles Thema. Wie lange wird das Referat dauern?
Das wissen wir noch nicht so genau.

Vergessen Sie nicht: Sie haben maximal fünfundvierzig Minuten. Konzentrieren Sie sich auf das Wichtigste.

Wird es einen Overheadprojektor im Seminarraum geben? Wir haben nämlich viele Folien.

Ich werde einen Overheadprojektor für Sie bestellen.
Und haben Sie zusätzlich auch Handouts?

Ja, natürlich, natürlich. Die haben wir schon vorbereitet und kopiert.

Fein. Ich freue mich schon auf Ihr Referat.
Ja, danke. Auf Wiedersehen, bis nächste Woche.

Na, Karl, wie war's? Was hast du ihr gesagt?
Ach, Stefan, wir müssen unser Referat schon nächste Woche halten. Das werden wir bis nächste Woche nie schaffen. Ich fühle mich jetzt schon krank. Ich muss mich unbedingt hinlegen.

Rückblick

4 **Stimmt das?** Stimmen diese Aussagen zum Text oder nicht? Wenn nicht, was stimmt?

	Ja, das stimmt.	*Nein, das stimmt nicht.*
1. Karl und Stefan sind Partner in einer Arbeitsgruppe.	___	___
2. Stefan sagt, er hat sich erkältet.	___	___
3. Karl und Stefan haben Glück gehabt.	___	___
4. Frau Dr. Osswald kann sich nicht an das Thema für Karls Arbeitsgruppe erinnern.	___	___
5. Das Thema für das Referat ist „Die Rolle der Industrie in der Europäischen Union".	___	___
6. Karl weiß noch nicht, wie lange das Referat dauern wird.	___	___
7. Die Arbeitsgruppe soll sich auf die Details konzentrieren.	___	___
8. Karl wird einen Overheadprojektor bestellen.	___	___
9. Dr. Osswald freut sich auf das Referat.	___	___
10. Stefan und Karl haben das Referat schon geschrieben.	___	___

5 **Ergänzen Sie.** Ergänzen Sie diese Sätze mit Wörtern aus dem **Anlauftext.**

1. Karl kommt zu Frau Dr. Osswald in die ______.
2. Frau Dr. Osswald ist froh, dass Karl sich endlich ______.
3. Sie fragt, ob Karls Arbeitsgruppe ihr Referat nächste Woche ______ kann.
4. Karl sagt, Stefan hat sich das Bein ______.
5. Karl und Stefan haben Schwierigkeiten gehabt; sie haben ______ gehabt.
6. Frau Dr. Osswald meint, Karls Arbeitsgruppe hat kein ______ für das Referat.
7. Frau Dr. Osswald kann sich nicht ______, wie es heißt.
8. Karls Gruppe hat sich für dieses Thema ______: „Die Rolle der Industrie in der Europäischen Union".
9. Karl weiß nicht so genau, wie lange das Referat ______ wird.
10. Karls Arbeitsgruppe soll sich auf das Wichtigste ______.
11. Frau Dr. Osswald wird einen Overheadprojektor für die Gruppe ______.
12. Karl ______ sich schon krank und meint, er muss sich hinlegen.

Kurz gefragt. A **Dozent/Dozentin** is a tenured university professor with a Ph.D. who is not yet a full professor **(Professor/Professorin).** The number of professors is limited in Germany to the number of positions determined for the country.

6 **Kurz gefragt.** Beantworten Sie die Fragen auf Deutsch.

1. Welche Probleme haben Karl und Stefan angeblich° gehabt?
2. Was ist das Thema von ihrem Gruppenreferat?
3. Warum gefällt das Thema der Dozentin?
4. Warum will die Dozentin wissen, wie lange das Referat dauern wird?
5. Warum will Karl wissen, ob es einen Overheadprojektor im Seminarraum gibt?
6. Wie wird die Dozentin Karls Arbeitsgruppe helfen?
7. Was haben Karl und Stefan angeblich für die ganze Klasse vorbereitet?
8. Warum fühlt sich Karl nach dem Gespräch krank?

° *supposedly*

7 Unsere Universität. Diskutieren Sie die folgenden Sätze in kleinen Gruppen, bis Sie alle dieselbe Meinung haben. Teilen° andere Gruppen Ihre Meinung? *share*

1. An dieser Universität muss man _____ schreiben.
   a. sehr viel b. viel c. nicht sehr viel
2. Dozenten/Dozentinnen auf dieser Universität verbringen viel Zeit _____.
   a. mit Studenten b. mit Forschen° c. im Unterricht *research*
3. Es ist _____, mit Lehrkräften° auf diesem Campus zu sprechen. *instructors*
   a. leicht b. schwierig c. undenkbar° *unthinkable*
4. Der beste Fachbereich° auf diesem Campus ist _____. *department*
5. In diesem Deutschkurs müssen wir viel _____.
   a. sprechen b. lesen c. schreiben
   d. zuhören e. Grammatik lernen
6. In diesem Kurs müssen wir zu viele _____.
   a. Hausaufgaben machen b. Prüfungen schreiben c. Referate halten
7. Unsere Bibliotheken sind _____.
   a. nicht besonders gut b. recht gut c. ausgezeichnet
8. Wer° hier abends im Studentenwohnheim lernen will, _____. *Whoever*
   a. muss sich sehr intensiv konzentrieren
   b. muss extrem unfreundlich sein
   c. wird keine Probleme haben
9. Assistenten (und nicht Professoren) unterrichten bei uns _____.
   a. nie b. nicht sehr oft c. oft
   d. viel zu oft
10. Wer hier Schwierigkeiten in einem Kurs hat, _____.
    a. hat einfach Pech
    b. muss selber Hilfe suchen
    c. kann ohne Probleme Hilfe bekommen
    d. hat viele Möglichkeiten, mit Dozenten, Tutoren und anderen Studenten zu arbeiten
11. Studenten hier meinen, Pflichtkurse° sind _____. *required courses*
    a. nervig b. akzeptabel c. wertvoll
    d. absolut notwendig° *necessary*

8 Ausreden bewerten°. Sie sind der Dozent/die Dozentin. Ein Student/Eine Studentin hat seine/ihre Hausaufgabe vergessen. Hier sind einige typische Ausreden. Bewerten Sie die Ausreden als **sehr glaubhaft, akzeptabel** oder **Unsinn.** *evaluate*

	Sehr glaubhaft	*Akzeptabel*	*Unsinn*	
1. Mein Hund hat mein Referat gefressen°.	___	___	___	*ate (for animals)*
2. Ich habe es zu Hause vergessen.	___	___	___	
3. Der Bus hat Verspätung° gehabt.	___	___	___	*late*
4. Ich habe verschlafen. Mein Wecker ist kaputt.	___	___	___	

	Sehr glaubhaft	*Akzeptabel*	*Unsinn*
5. Mein Auto ist kaputt.	___	___	___
6. Ich habe mir das Bein gebrochen.	___	___	___
7. Meine Mutter hat mich nicht geweckt.	___	___	___
8. Meine Oma ist gestorben.	___	___	___

FREIE KOMMUNIKATION

Rollenspiel: Ausreden. Spielen Sie diese Situation mit einem Partner/einer Partnerin.

S1: Sie sind in einer Arbeitsgruppe, aber Sie haben gar nichts getan. Sie müssen morgen mit dem Dozenten/der Dozentin sprechen. Geben Sie ihm/ihr so viele Ausreden wie möglich.

S2: Sie sind der Dozent/die Dozentin. Sie glauben nicht, was dieser Student/diese Studentin erzählt, aber Sie spielen mit. Stellen Sie viele Fragen über die Ausreden.

BRENNPUNKT KULTUR

Universitätskurse

A lecture course (**die Vorlesung**), literally "reading aloud," is open to the public and may have as many as 600 students — most of them beginning students. In a **Vorlesung** a professor lectures on a specific topic, with a question-answer section (**die Übung**) scheduled at a different time from the **Vorlesung.** In most **Vorlesungen** the professor reads aloud, either from notes or from books, and the students take notes or sometimes purchase the notes (**Skripten**) in a bookstore. There is little opportunity for interaction between students and teacher.

German students are introduced to the specifics of an academic discipline in an introductory seminar (**das Proseminar**), where they often form study groups (**Arbeitsgruppen**) and work together outside of class to prepare a group research paper for oral presentation in class (**das Gruppenreferat**). Completion of a **Vorlesung, Übung,** or a **Seminar** is verified by a graded certificate of completion (**der Schein**) and is recorded in a personal transcript book (**das Studienbuch**). After accumulating enough **Scheine** during their **Grundstudium,** students are admitted to the **Hauptstudium,** where they take advanced-level **Hauptseminare,** which concentrate on specific themes and topics. A seminar is intended for a small group of 15–25 students and allows for closer student-teacher interaction. However, in reality many seminars may have from 25 to 60 participants, more like a lecture.

NEUPHILOLOGISCHE FAKULTÄT / 09

Nordische Philologie

Vorlesung

Geschichte der altnordischen Literatur I: Dänemark und Schweden (mit Textlektüre): 2 st. — *Glauser*

Proseminare

Einführung in die Skandinavistik II: Methoden der Literaturwissenschaft: 2 st., Fr 14–16 — *Glauser*

Schwedische Lyrik – vom Expressionismus bis zum Ende des »femtiotalet«: 2 st., Di 18–20 — *Cienkowska-Schmidt*

Svenska serier: 2 st., Mi 16–18 — *Raab*

Hauptseminar

Ibsenes Gesellschaftsdramen: 2 st., Do 16–18 — *Glauser*

■ Strukturen und Vokabeln ■

I ▣ Talking about activities we do for ourselves

Reflexive verbs with accusative reflexive pronouns

A. Reflexive and non-reflexive usage of verbs

In both German and English, many active verbs may be followed by a direct object that refers to another person, animal, or object.

Ich wasche **das Kind.** *I wash/am washing the child.*

The direct object may also refer back to the subject of the sentence.

Ich wasche **mich.** *I wash/am washing myself.*

To describe activities people do for themselves, German speakers use a verb with a reflexive pronoun **(das Reflexivpronomen).** The reflexive pronoun refers back to the subject of the sentence, which is the person, animal, or object performing the action indicated by the verb. A verb that has a reflexive pronoun as the direct object is called a *reflexive verb* **(das Reflexivverb).** Many German verbs require a reflexive pronoun where in English the reflexive pronoun *self/selves* is never required.

Ich ziehe **mich** an.	*I get/am getting (myself) dressed.*
Karl rasiert **sich.**	*Karl shaves/is shaving (himself).*
Ich fühle **mich** jetzt schon krank.	*I feel/am feeling sick already.*

Here are some more reflexive verbs that you encountered in the previous **Anlauftext.**

sich erinnern an *(to remember)*
Ich kann **mich** nicht daran **erinnern.** — *I don't remember (anything).*

sich entscheiden für *(to decide on)*
Für welches Thema haben Sie **sich entschieden?** — *Which topic did you decide on?*

sich fühlen *(to feel)*
Ich **fühle mich** jetzt schon krank. — *I feel/am feeling sick already.*

sich hin·legen *(to lie down)*
Ich muss **mich** unbedingt **hinlegen.** — *I have to lie down.*

sich melden *(to report, get in touch)*
Schön, dass Sie **sich** endlich **melden.** — *I am glad that you're finally getting in touch.*

Haben Sie sich entschieden, niemals dick zu werden?

Dabei möchte LÄTTA Ihnen ein wenig helfen.
LÄTTA hat nur halb soviel Fett wie Butter oder Margarine.
Aber der volle Geschmack ist immer da.

Here are the accusative forms of the reflexive pronouns.

Person	Singular Nominative	Accusative		Plural Nominative	Accusative	
1st	ich	**mich**	*myself*	wir	**uns**	*ourselves*
2nd, informal	du	**dich**	*yourself*	ihr	**euch**	*yourselves*
2nd, formal	Sie	**sich**	*yourself*	Sie	**sich**	*yourselves*
3rd	er es sie	**sich** **sich** **sich**	*himself* *itself* *herself*	sie	**sich**	*themselves*

Note that the reflexive pronouns look like direct object pronouns **(mich, dich)** except in the singular and plural forms of the 3rd person, and the 2nd person formal **(sich).**

Note that the only new reflexive pronoun you need to learn is **sich.**

B. Verbs that always require a reflexive pronoun

At the beginning of this section you learned that some German verbs may or may not be used with a reflexive pronoun (e.g., **waschen** vs. **sich waschen**). Some German verbs and verb + preposition expressions always require a reflexive pronoun and cannot be used without one. You already know a few of these reflexive verbs from this and earlier chapters.

Verbs that require a reflexive pronoun appear in the *Vorsprung* vocabulary lists and glossary preceded by the reflexive pronoun **sich** (e.g., **sich beeilen**). In commercial dictionaries, these reflexive verbs are followed by the abbreviation *vr.*

sich beeilen	*to hurry*
sich freuen auf	*to look forward to*
sich freuen über	*to be happy about*
sich konzentrieren auf	*to concentrate on*
sich verlieben in	*to fall in love with*
sich verloben mit	*to get engaged to*
sich trennen von	*to break up with, separate from*
sich etwas teilen	*to share something*

C. Word order in sentences with reflexive pronouns

In main clauses, the reflexive pronoun always follows the conjugated verb, which occurs in the second position of the sentence.

The reflexive pronoun can also precede a subject noun in a main clause with transposed subject and verb, **Heute zieht sich Inge an.** and in a subordinate clause, **Ich glaube, dass sich Hans beeilt.**

Inge zieht **sich** an. *Inge is getting dressed.*
Wir müssen **uns** beeilen! *We have to hurry!*

In questions, the reflexive pronoun can precede a subject noun.

Zieht **sich** Inge an?
Zieht Inge **sich** an? } *Is Inge getting dressed?*

If the subject is a pronoun, the reflexive pronoun must follow it immediately.

Wann habt ihr **euch** erkältet? *When did you catch a cold?*
In wen hat sie **sich** verliebt? *Who did she fall in love with?*

9 **In der Sprechstunde.** Barbara spricht mit ihrem Professor in seiner Sprechstunde. Schreiben Sie die richtigen Reflexivpronomen in die Lücken°.

blanks

PROFESSOR: Guten Tag, Frau Müller. Setzen Sie ____!
BARBARA: Danke schön.
PROFESSOR: Was kann ich für Sie tun?
BARBARA: Ich habe ____ für das Examen im Dezember angemeldet und ich habe einige Fragen.
PROFESSOR: Dezember? Das überlegen° wir ____ besser. Warum beeilen Sie ____ so? Ist das nicht etwas früh?
BARBARA: Ich glaube nicht. Ich habe ____ schon für meine Schwerpunkte entschieden.
PROFESSOR: Ja, wenn Sie meinen. Aber ich rate Ihnen, konzentrieren Sie ____ auf das Wichtigste, ja?
BARBARA: Ja, natürlich. Ich freue ____ eigentlich schon auf das Examen.

consider

In der Sprechstunde. Students at German universities sign up for graduation exams in their majors once they feel they are fully prepared. Depending on the degree they take and on the individual professor, they are often allowed to choose the topic of the exams.

Wissenswerte Vokabeln: die tägliche Routine

Talking about your daily routine and personal hygiene

Volker bereitet sich auf den Tag vor.

Ich ziehe mich aus und dusche (mich).

Ich trockne mich ab.

Ich rasiere mich.

Ich ziehe mich an und beeile mich.

W. Vok. Remember that the reflexive form **(mich)** refers back to the subject **(ich)** of the verb.

Sabine bereitet sich auf den Abend vor.

Sie badet.

Sie wäscht sich.

Sie trocknet sich ab.

Sie zieht sich an.

Sie schminkt sich.

Remember that **waschen** is a stem-vowel changing verb.

■ Was machst du morgens?

10 **Am Morgen.** In welcher Reihenfolge machen Sie diese Aktivitäten? Benutzen Sie die Zahlen 1 bis 6.

___ Ich trockne mich ab.
___ Ich ziehe mich an.
___ Ich dusche mich.
___ Ich stehe auf.
___ Ich beeile mich.
___ Ich rasiere mich./Ich schminke mich.

11 **Was hast du heute schon gemacht?** Sagen Sie, was Sie heute schon gemacht haben, und fragen Sie dann einen Partner/eine Partnerin.

S1: Ich habe mich heute schon rasiert. Und du?
S2: Ich habe mich heute auch schon (noch nicht) rasiert.

angezogen • ausgezogen • gebadet • geduscht • geschminkt • gewaschen • abgetrocknet • rasiert • beeilt • hingelegt • gesetzt

12 **Minidialog.** Ingo wohnt in einer Wohngemeinschaft mit fünf anderen Studenten. Er ist gerade aufgestanden und ist jetzt im Badezimmer. Holger wohnt auch in der Wohngemeinschaft und möchte auch das Badezimmer benutzen. Schreiben Sie das richtige Reflexivpronomen **(dich, mich)** in die Lücken. Lesen Sie dann den Dialog mit einem Partner/einer Partnerin.

(Holger klopft an die Tür zum Badezimmer.)

HOLGER: Ingo, bist du's?
INGO: Ja.
HOLGER: Kannst du ___ beeilen? Ich muss ___ rasieren.
INGO: Du, zieh ___ erstmal an. Ich habe ___ gerade geduscht. Ich muss ___ noch abtrocknen.
HOLGER: Ich habe ___ schon angezogen. Ich muss ___ schnell waschen, denn ich muss in die Stadt.
INGO: Gut. Ich bin gleich fertig.

Wissenswerte Vokabeln: im Badezimmer

Talking about bathroom objects

W. Vok. If German speakers need to go to the bathroom, they say: **Ich muss auf die Toilette gehen.** In a very informal setting they may say: **Ich muss aufs Klo.**

Wo machst du das? *Ich trockne mich im Badezimmer ab.*
Womit° machst du das? *Ich trockne mich mit dem Badetuch ab.* — *with what*

13 Was wollen sie machen? Erklären Sie, was Karl und Inge mit diesen Gegenständen° im Badezimmer machen. — *objects*

S1: Was will Karl machen, wenn er den Rasierapparat hat?
S2: Er will sich rasieren.

Was will Karl machen,

1. wenn er den Rasierapparat hat?
2. wenn er das Badetuch nimmt?
3. wenn er die Seife hält?
4. wenn er unter die Dusche geht?

Was will Inge machen,

5. wenn sie in den Spiegel schaut?
6. wenn sie in die Badewanne steigt°? — *climbs*

14 Was hat er gerade° gemacht? Volker hat sich schon auf den Tag vorbereitet. Was hat er bereits gemacht? Bilden Sie Sätze im Perfekt. Verwenden Sie die Partizipien aus der Liste in Aktivität 11. — *just*

S1: Volker steigt aus der Badewanne.
S2: Er hat gerade gebadet.

1. Volker steigt aus der Badewanne.
2. Volker ist gerade aufgestanden. Er schläft in seinem Pyjama, aber jetzt steht er nackt° im Schlafzimmer. — *naked*
3. Volkers Gesicht ist glatt°. Er legt den Rasierapparat auf den Tisch. — *smooth*
4. Volker kommt gerade nass aus der Dusche.
5. Volker hat einen Pullover und Jeans an.
6. Volker kommt um neun Uhr pünktlich zu seiner ersten Klasse.

15 **Wo und womit macht man das?** Erklären Sie, wo oder mit welchem Gegenstand im Badezimmer man diese Aktivitäten machen kann.

S1: Wo kann man baden?
S2: In der Badewanne. Womit kann man sich waschen?
S1: Mit Seife.

1. Wo kann man baden?
2. Wo kann man sich duschen?
3. Wo kann man sich rasieren?
4. Wo kann man Wasser trinken?
5. Wo kann man sich abtrocknen?
6. Wo kann man sich die Haare trocknen?
7. Wo kann man sich waschen?

II Talking about daily hygiene routines

Reflexive verbs with dative reflexive pronouns

You have already learned some of the reflexive verbs that German speakers use to talk about personal hygiene activities (e.g., **sich waschen, sich duschen, sich rasieren, sich an·ziehen, sich aus·ziehen**). The sentences you encountered had accusative reflexive pronouns and expressed only general activities.

Ich rasiere mich.	*I am shaving.*
Hast du dich gewaschen?	*Did you wash (yourself)?*

To specify which part of the body is being groomed, you need to add more information.

	Dative	***Accusative***	
Ich rasiere	**mir**	die Beine.	*I shave/am shaving my legs.*
Hast du	**dir**	die Hände gewaschen?	*Did you wash your hands?*

When a part of the body or an article of clothing is specified, the reflexive pronoun is in the dative case and the direct object (the part of the body or clothing) is in the accusative.

New verbs in this chapter are: **sich kämmen, sich putzen, sich föhnen, sich bürsten.**

Wir putzen **uns** die Zähne.

Du rasierst **dir** die Beine.

Sie wäscht **sich** die Haare.

Er föhnt **sich** die Haare.

Kämmst du **dir** die Haare?

Habt ihr **euch** die Haare gebürstet?

English speakers say *I'm combing **my** hair.* German avoids using possessive pronouns. Instead it uses the definite article along with a dative reflexive object: **Ich kämme *mir die Haare.***

When talking about specific items of clothing that are being put on or taken off German speakers often use a dative case reflexive pronoun to designate the beneficiary of the action.

sich die Hose an·ziehen:	Ich ziehe **mir** die Hose an.	*I put/am putting my pants on.*
sich die Socken aus·ziehen:	Du hast **dir** die Socken ausgezogen.	*You took off your socks.*

A dative case reflexive pronoun may also designate the beneficiary of actions other than grooming.

Ich backe **mir** einen Kuchen.	*I bake/am baking a cake for myself.*
Er hat **sich** einen BMW gekauft.	*He bought himself a BMW.*
Schreib **dir** einen Zettel!	*Write yourself a note!*

Here are the dative forms of the reflexive pronouns.

Person	Singular Nominative	Accusative	Dative		Plural Nominative	Accusative	Dative	
1st	ich	mich	**mir**	*myself*	wir	uns	**uns**	*ourselves*
2nd, informal	du	dich	**dir**	*yourself*	ihr	euch	**euch**	*yourselves*
2nd, formal	Sie	sich	**sich**	*yourself*	Sie	sich	**sich**	*yourselves*
3rd	er es sie	sich sich sich	**sich** **sich** **sich**	*himself* *itself* *herself*	sie	sich	**sich**	*themselves*

Note that the only dative reflexive forms that are different from the accusative forms are those for **ich (mich** vs. **mir)** and **du (dich** vs. **dir).** All other reflexive pronouns are identical in the accusative and dative.

These reflexive pronouns look like dative pronouns, except in the singular and plural forms of the 3rd person, and the 2nd person formal, which again are all **sich.**

16 **Am Morgen.** In welcher Reihenfolge machen Sie diese Aktivitäten? Benutzen Sie die Zahlen 1 bis 10.

___ Ich kämme (bürste) mir die Haare.
___ Ich stehe auf.
___ Ich putze mir die Zähne.
___ Ich ziehe mich an.
___ Ich föhne mir die Haare.
___ Ich gehe aufs Klo.
___ Ich setze mich hin und frühstücke.

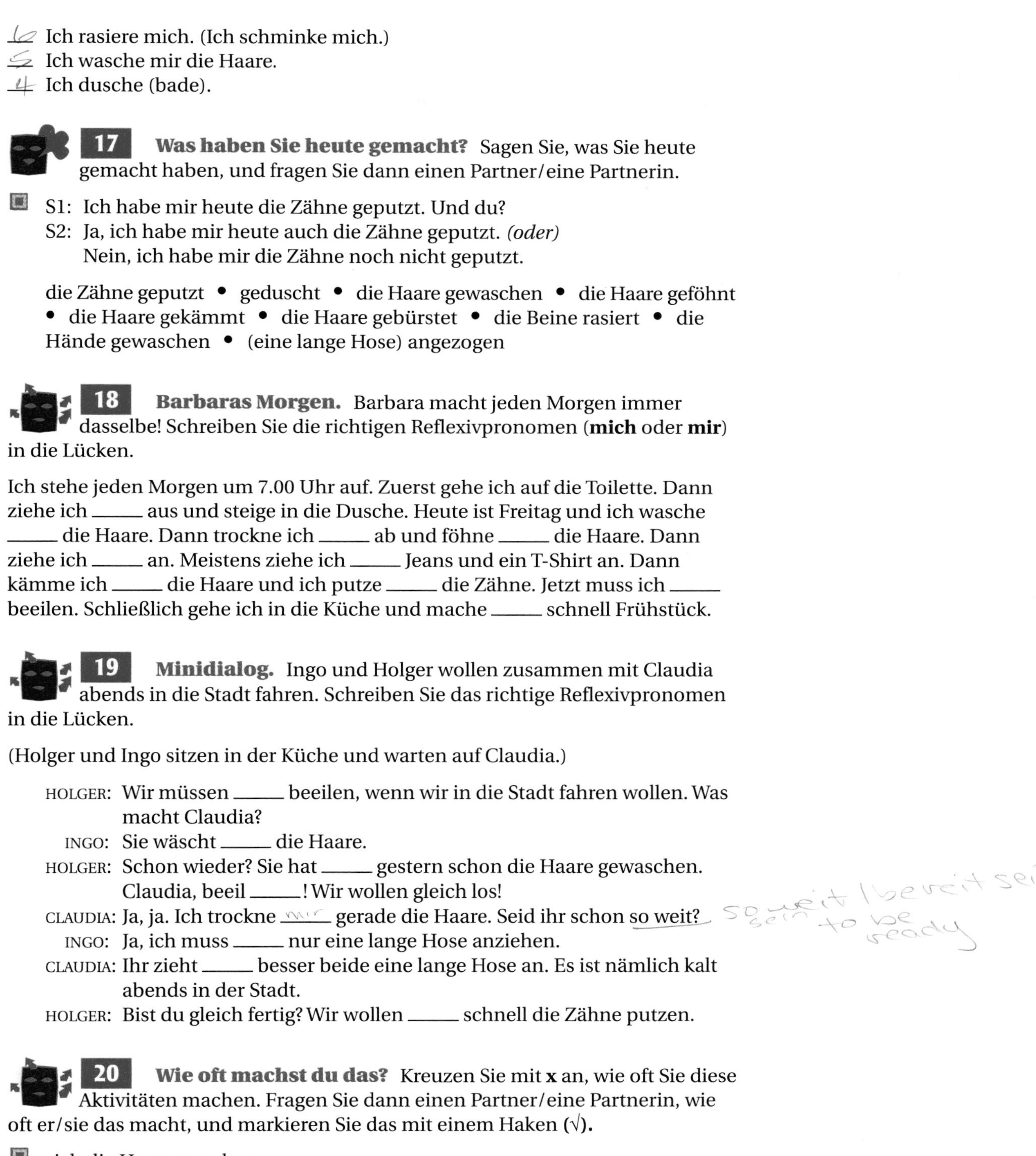

___ Ich rasiere mich. (Ich schminke mich.)
___ Ich wasche mir die Haare.
___ Ich dusche (bade).

17 **Was haben Sie heute gemacht?** Sagen Sie, was Sie heute gemacht haben, und fragen Sie dann einen Partner/eine Partnerin.

S1: Ich habe mir heute die Zähne geputzt. Und du?
S2: Ja, ich habe mir heute auch die Zähne geputzt. *(oder)*
Nein, ich habe mir die Zähne noch nicht geputzt.

die Zähne geputzt • geduscht • die Haare gewaschen • die Haare geföhnt • die Haare gekämmt • die Haare gebürstet • die Beine rasiert • die Hände gewaschen • (eine lange Hose) angezogen

18 **Barbaras Morgen.** Barbara macht jeden Morgen immer dasselbe! Schreiben Sie die richtigen Reflexivpronomen (**mich** oder **mir**) in die Lücken.

Ich stehe jeden Morgen um 7.00 Uhr auf. Zuerst gehe ich auf die Toilette. Dann ziehe ich ____ aus und steige in die Dusche. Heute ist Freitag und ich wasche ____ die Haare. Dann trockne ich ____ ab und föhne ____ die Haare. Dann ziehe ich ____ an. Meistens ziehe ich ____ Jeans und ein T-Shirt an. Dann kämme ich ____ die Haare und ich putze ____ die Zähne. Jetzt muss ich ____ beeilen. Schließlich gehe ich in die Küche und mache ____ schnell Frühstück.

19 **Minidialog.** Ingo und Holger wollen zusammen mit Claudia abends in die Stadt fahren. Schreiben Sie das richtige Reflexivpronomen in die Lücken.

(Holger und Ingo sitzen in der Küche und warten auf Claudia.)

HOLGER: Wir müssen ____ beeilen, wenn wir in die Stadt fahren wollen. Was macht Claudia?
INGO: Sie wäscht ____ die Haare.
HOLGER: Schon wieder? Sie hat ____ gestern schon die Haare gewaschen. Claudia, beeil ____! Wir wollen gleich los!
CLAUDIA: Ja, ja. Ich trockne ____ gerade die Haare. Seid ihr schon so weit?
INGO: Ja, ich muss ____ nur eine lange Hose anziehen.
CLAUDIA: Ihr zieht ____ besser beide eine lange Hose an. Es ist nämlich kalt abends in der Stadt.
HOLGER: Bist du gleich fertig? Wir wollen ____ schnell die Zähne putzen.

20 **Wie oft machst du das?** Kreuzen Sie mit **x** an, wie oft Sie diese Aktivitäten machen. Fragen Sie dann einen Partner/eine Partnerin, wie oft er/sie das macht, und markieren Sie das mit einem Haken (√).

sich die Haare waschen

S1: Wie oft wäschst du dir die Haare?
S2: Ich wasche mir jeden Tag die Haare.

	Zweimal am Tag	*Jeden Tag*	*Alle zwei Tage*	*Einmal die Woche*	*Nie*
1. sich die Haare waschen	___ ___	___ ___	___ ___	___ ___	___ ___
2. sich die Haare föhnen	___ ___	___ ___	___ ___	___ ___	___ ___
3. sich anziehen	___ ___	___ ___	___ ___	___ ___	___ ___
4. sich ausziehen	___ ___	___ ___	___ ___	___ ___	___ ___
5. sich die Zähne putzen	___ ___	___ ___	___ ___	___ ___	___ ___
6. sich duschen	___ ___	___ ___	___ ___	___ ___	___ ___
7. baden	___ ___	___ ___	___ ___	___ ___	___ ___
8. sich die Haare bürsten	___ ___	___ ___	___ ___	___ ___	___ ___
9. sich die Haare kämmen	___ ___	___ ___	___ ___	___ ___	___ ___
10. sich rasieren	___ ___	___ ___	___ ___	___ ___	___ ___
11. sich schminken	___ ___	___ ___	___ ___	___ ___	___ ___

21 **Ja, aber was brauche ich?** Sie sind im Badezimmer. Sie wissen, was Sie tun wollen, aber Sie haben nicht den Gegenstand, den Sie brauchen. Ihr Partner/Ihre Partnerin hilft Ihnen mit einer Frage.

sich das Gesicht waschen

S1: Ich will mir das Gesicht waschen.
S2: Brauchst du die Seife?

1. sich das Gesicht waschen
2. sich ins warme Wasser setzen
3. sich abtrocknen
4. sich die Haare trocknen
5. sich rasieren
6. sich die Hände waschen
7. sich die Zähne putzen
8. sich die Haare waschen
9. sich die Haare bürsten

Hair dryers and electric razors sold in North America may not work in Europe, where the plugs are different and the circuits are 220 volts and not 120 volts.

22 **Was wollen sie damit machen?** Bilden Sie Sätze mit einem Reflexivverb.

S1: Inge hält den Föhn in der Hand. Was will sie damit machen?
S2: Sie will sich die Haare föhnen.

1. Inge: den Föhn in der Hand halten
2. Oliver: den Kamm in der Hand halten
3. Annegret: die Zahnbürste haben
4. Michael: den Rasierapparat haben
5. Gudrun: das Shampoo haben
6. Werner: die Seife halten
7. Monika: den Rasierapparat haben
8. Torsten: das Badetuch haben
9. Liselotte: den Taschenspiegel in der Hand halten
10. Jens: die Haarbürste haben

23 **Womit tut man das?** Fragen Sie einen Partner/eine Partnerin, mit welchen Gegenständen er/sie diese Aktivitäten macht.

Inge: sich die Zähne putzen

S1: Womit putzt sich Inge die Zähne?
S2: Mit der Zahnbürste.

1. Inge: sich die Zähne putzen
2. Markus: sich die Haare waschen
3. Rainer: sich die Haare bürsten
4. Martina: sich die Haare kämmen
5. Christine: sich die Haare föhnen
6. Hans: sich die Hände waschen
7. Brigitte: sich die Beine rasieren
8. Norbert: sich die Hände abtrocknen

A useful reflexive verb for conversation is **sich etwas vor·stellen** *(to imagine something):* **Das kann ich mir nicht vorstellen.** *(I can't imagine that).* Don't confuse this with **sich vor·stellen** *(to introduce oneself):* **Darf ich mich vorstellen? Mein Name ist (Mueller).**

FREIE KOMMUNIKATION

Rollenspiel: Ein Badezimmer teilen. Sie wohnen mit vier Personen in einem Haus mit nur einem Badezimmer. Zu viele Leute wollen das Badezimmer zur gleichen Zeit° benutzen. Formulieren Sie einen Plan für die Benutzung des Badezimmers. Benutzen Sie Ausdrücke aus der Liste.

zur ... Zeit: *at the same time*

Um wie viel Uhr? • Wann? • Von wann bis wann? • Wie oft? • Wie lange? • baden • duschen • sich die Haare waschen • sich die Zähne putzen • sich rasieren • sich die Haare föhnen • sich schminken

Schreibecke **Studenten am Morgen.** Schreiben Sie mit den Informationen, die Sie in Aktivität 20 gesammelt haben, einen kurzen Absatz° über das Morgenritual von Ihrem Partner/Ihrer Partnerin. Benutzen Sie den Absatz in Aktivität 18 als Beispiel.

paragraph

Schreibecke. To prepare for this writing assignment, ask your partner about the daily habits and find out in what order your partner does them: **Was machst du zuerst? Und dann?**

Wissenswerte Vokabeln: krank sein

Talking about illnesses

Ich habe Fieber. Meine Temperatur ist über 38 Grad.

Ich habe mich in den Finger geschnitten. Ich brauche ein Heftpflaster.

Ich habe mir das Bein gebrochen. Ich habe einen Gips.

Ich lege mich hin. Ich liege im Bett. Ich ruhe mich aus. Ich erhole mich.

37°C is considered normal body temperature.

Ich fühle mich nicht wohl.

Ich muss mich übergeben.

Ich habe Durchfall.

Ich habe (einen) Muskelkater.

W. Vok. Ich muss kotzen. *(I have to throw up—vulgar.)*

Ich habe Zahnschmerzen. Mein Zahn tut mir weh.

Ich habe Halsschmerzen. Mein Hals tut mir weh.

Ich habe Kopfschmerzen. Mein Kopf tut mir weh.

Ich nehme Schmerztabletten.

Ich habe mich erkältet. Ich habe eine Erkältung.

Ich habe (einen) Schnupfen.

Wie geht's dir? – Mir geht es solala.
Wie fühlst du dich? –
Mir ist/geht es ziemlich schlecht.
– Gute Besserung!

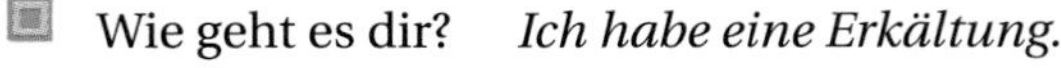
Wie geht es dir? *Ich habe eine Erkältung.*

24 **Ursache und Wirkung.** Bilden Sie Sätze, die Ursache und Wirkung beschreiben.

1. Wer zu viel Alkohol trinkt,
2. Wer Zahnschmerzen hat,
3. Wer Kopfschmerzen hat,
4. Wer zu viel Sport treibt,
5. Wer sich in den Finger schneidet,
6. Wer im Winter im Meer schwimmen geht,

a. bekommt am nächsten Tag einen Muskelkater.
b. braucht ein Heftpflaster.
c. muss sich übergeben.
d. soll eine Schmerztablette nehmen.
e. soll zum Zahnarzt° gehen. *dentist*
f. wird sich erkälten.

25 **Studentenkrankheiten.** Kann ein Deutschstudium krank machen? Diese Studenten/Studentinnen behaupten° es jedenfalls. Besprechen Sie mit einem Partner/einer Partnerin, wie sich die Kommilitonen/Kommilitoninnen fühlen und was sie jetzt machen.

claim

S1: John hat die ganze Nacht ohne viel Licht sein Deutschbuch gelesen.
S2: Und wie fühlt er sich jetzt?
S1: Er hat Augenschmerzen. Ihm tun die Augen weh. Jetzt legt er sich hin und ruht sich aus.

1. John hat die ganze Nacht ohne viel Licht sein Deutschbuch gelesen. Er hat ...
2. Susie hat das ganze Wochenende intensiv gelernt. Jetzt ist ihr ganz heiß und sie kann sich nicht konzentrieren. Sie nimmt Aspirin. Sie hat ...
3. Daniel war den ganzen Samstag im Sprachlabor und hat sich Deutschkassetten angehört, bis er nicht mehr konnte. Er hat ...
4. Philip hat morgen ein Referat und ist ziemlich nervös. Er kaut an seinen Fingernägeln, isst Chips, Salzstangen und Nüsse und trinkt viel. Er hat ...
5. Joan hat die Nacht beim Tippen° am Computer durchgemacht und hat gerade ihr Referat mit 30 Seiten abgegeben. Sie hat ...

a. Kopfschmerzen. Jetzt ...
b. Ohrenschmerzen. Jetzt ...
c. Augenschmerzen. Jetzt ...
d. Handgelenkschmerzen°. Jetzt ...
e. Bauchschmerzen. Jetzt ...

(das) Handgelenk: *wrist*

typing

26 **Was ist passiert?** Ein Freund/Eine Freundin beklagt sich°. Was ist wahrscheinlich passiert? Stellen Sie Fragen. Wechseln Sie sich ab.

beklagt sich: *is complaining*

S1: Ich nehme Schmerztabletten.
S2: Hast du Kopfschmerzen?

sich den Arm gebrochen • sich in den Finger geschnitten • Durchfall/einen Muskelkater/Schmerzen gehabt • sich übergeben/sich erkältet/sich ausgeruht

1. Ich nehme Schmerztabletten.
2. Ich habe jetzt einen Gips am Arm.
3. Ich trage jetzt ein Heftpflaster am Finger.
4. Ich komme von der Massage zurück und fühle mich nicht mehr so steif°.
5. Ich komme von der Toilette zurück, aber der Bauch tut mir noch weh.
6. Der Zahnarzt hat mir einen Weisheitszahn° gezogen.
7. Ich brauche ein Taschentuch°.
8. Ich bin nicht mehr müde.

stiff

wisdom tooth

tissue

27 **Wie fühlst du dich, wenn ...?** Kreuzen Sie zuerst an, was auf Sie zutrifft°. Fragen Sie dann einen Partner/eine Partnerin.

applies

S1: Ich fühle mich nicht wohl, wenn ich zu viel Alkohol trinke. Und du?
S2: Ich fühle mich auch nicht wohl, wenn ich zu viel Alkohol trinke. Ich fühle mich nicht wohl, wenn ich zu viel esse. Wie fühlst du dich, wenn du zu viel isst?

	Ich	*Partner(in)*
Ich fühle mich nicht wohl,		
1. wenn ich zu viel esse.	—	—
2. wenn ich eine Prüfung in Physik habe.	—	—
3. wenn ich sehr früh aufstehen muss.	—	—
4. wenn ich mit meinem Professor sprechen muss.	—	—
5. wenn ich am Telefon Deutsch sprechen muss.	—	—
6. wenn ich täglich das Essen in der Mensa essen muss.	—	—
7. wenn ich …	—	—

FREIE KOMMUNIKATION **Rollenspiel: Den Notarzt° anrufen.** Spielen Sie die folgende Situation mit einem Partner/einer Partnerin.

emergency room doctor

S1: Sie sind sehr krank. Es ist Samstag. Rufen Sie Dr. Meiser, den Notarzt/die Notärztin an und beschreiben Sie ihm/ihr Ihre Symptome. Sagen Sie auch, was Sie gemacht haben, bevor Sie diese Symptome bekommen haben.

S2: Sie sind Dr. Meiser. Ein Patient/Eine Patientin ruft an. Es ist Samstag und Sie wollen heute nicht ins Büro kommen. Er/Sie ist sehr krank. Fragen Sie, wie er/sie sich fühlt, was er/sie gemacht hat und warum er/sie diese Symptome hat. Geben Sie auch ein paar Tipps. Beginnen Sie das Telefongespräch wie folgt.

DR. MEISER: Dr. Meiser. Guten Tag.
PATIENT(IN): Guten Tag. Hier ist …

Schreibecke **Eine Entschuldigung.** Schreiben Sie eine Entschuldigung° an Ihren Dozenten/Ihre Dozentin. Sie sollen heute ein Referat halten, aber es ist noch nicht fertig. Schreiben Sie, dass Sie sehr krank sind und nicht kommen können. Beschreiben Sie drei Symptome und warum Sie diese Symptome haben.

excuse

ABSPRUNGTEXT

Welche Uni ist die Beste?

In einer Sonderausgabe° vom deutschen Nachrichtenmagazin „Der Spiegel" erzählen drei Studenten von ihren Universitäten in Dortmund, Mainz und Braunschweig und von dem Studentenleben dort.

special edition

Vorschau

28 **Thematische Fragen.** Beantworten Sie die folgenden Fragen auf Deutsch.

1. An wie vielen Universitäten (Colleges) haben Sie sich beworben°?
2. Warum studieren Sie an dieser Universität? Nennen Sie drei wichtige Faktoren.

applied

3. Wie viel muss man hier im Monat für Zimmer° und Verpflegung° im Wohnheim ausgeben? Für eine Wohnung in der Stadt? Für ein Zimmer in einer Wohngemeinschaft? *room / board*
4. Wie ist das Essen im Studentenwohnheim? Was ist für Sie wichtiger: der Preis oder die Qualität?
5. Wo können Studenten auf dem Campus oder in der Stadt jobben°? Was verdient man bei diesen Jobs pro Stunde? *work part-time*

29 Kriterien für die Uni-Wahl. Was waren Ihre Kriterien bei der Wahl einer Universität? Bewerten° Sie die Wichtigkeit von den Kriterien mit den Zahlen 1 (sehr unwichtig) bis 5 (wichtig). *evaluate*

	Unwichtig 1	2	3	4	*Sehr wichtig* 5
1. das Image	___	___	___	___	___
2. die Kosten	___	___	___	___	___
3. die Lage° *(location)*	___	___	___	___	___
4. die Klassengröße	___	___	___	___	___
5. die Wohnsituation	___	___	___	___	___
6. Jobs	___	___	___	___	___
7. Praktikantenstellen° *(internships)*	___	___	___	___	___
8. Freizeitmöglichkeiten	___	___	___	___	___
9. die Sportmannschaften	___	___	___	___	___
10. Multikulturalismus	___	___	___	___	___

Sind Sie mit Ihrer Universität zufrieden°? Warum? Warum nicht? *satisfied*

30 Lesestrategien: Welche Uni ist die Beste? Benutzen Sie die Lesestrategien aus Kapitel 7, um die Texte zu verstehen.

1. **Den Kontext verstehen.** Finden Sie in den Texten Antworten auf die folgenden Fragen.
   a. Wer sind die drei Studenten?
   b. Wo studieren sie?
   c. Was machen sie?
   d. Welche Themen besprechen° sie? *discuss*
   e. Welche Kognate erkennen Sie?
2. **Neue Wörter lernen: erster Versuch.** Was bedeuten diese Wörter? Lesen Sie die Erklärungen° und beantworten Sie die Fragen. *explanations*
   a. **Pendler-Universität:** Ein Pendler ist eine Person. Ein Pendler fährt (pendelt) jeden Tag zur Arbeit oder zur Universität und dann nach Hause zurück. Die Fahrt ist relativ lang. Wo wohnt ein Pendler? Warum studieren wohl einige Studenten an einer Pendler-Universität?
   b. **Neubau:** Man baut (konstruiert) Häuser und Gebäude. So ein neues Haus oder Gebäude ist ein Neubau. Was ist ein Altbau?
   c. **Ballungsraum Rhein-Main:** Der Rhein und der Main sind zwei Flüsse in Deutschland. Zwischen den zwei Flüssen wohnen sehr viele Menschen. Die starke Konzentration von Menschen ist ein Ballungsraum. Wo gibt es in den USA Ballungsräume?
   d. **Massen-Uni:** Ist das eine große oder eine kleine Uni?
   e. **Kommilitonen:** Am Arbeitsplatz nennt man die Leute Kollegen, aber Studenten auf der Universität nennen einander Kommilitonen. Nennen Studenten ihre Professoren Kommilitonen?

3. **Wichtige Wörter finden: Adjektive und Adverbien.** Erraten Sie die Bedeutung von den Adjektiven und Adverbien aus dem Kontext.
   a. Rund um den Campus gibt es **zahllose** Parkplätze.
      ☐ viele ☐ wenige
   b. Das Mensa-Essen ist **ausgesprochen lecker.**
      ☐ schmeckt sehr gut ☐ schmeckt sehr schlecht
   c. Die Studenten finden Wohnungen zu **erträglichen** Preisen. Ein Zimmer … kostet 200 Mark.
      ☐ akzeptablen ☐ hohen
   d. Man muss allerdings **knapp** ein Jahr warten.
      ☐ mehr als ☐ ungefähr
   e. … auf dem privaten Wohnungsmarkt sind die Zimmer **bezahlbar.**
      ☐ billig ☐ teuer
   f. Die Uni **wächst und wächst.**
      ☐ wird kleiner° ☐ wird größer *smaller*
   g. Der Fachbereich hat im letzten Semester einen **großzügigen** Neubau bezogen°. *moved into*
      ☐ voluminösen ☐ kleinen und unbequemen
   h. Die Bibliothek finde ich **vorbildlich.**
      ☐ fantastisch, erstklassig ☐ nicht sehr gut
   i. Zwei bis drei Semester Wartezeit sind **üblich.**
      ☐ nicht normal ☐ normal
   j. Die Zahl der Hiwi-Stellen° ist eher **begrenzt.** *research assistant jobs*
      ☐ limitiert ☐ nicht limitiert

4. **Neue Wörter lernen: zwei Strategien.** Erraten Sie die fett gedruckten Wörter mit Hilfe der zwei folgenden Strategien. Beantworten Sie die Fragen.

Strategie 1: Weltwissen

a. auf der grünen **Wiese:**

Wo sitzen/liegen/lesen Studenten im Sommer auf dem Campus?

b. Wer° nicht in einem Wohnheim **unterkommt,** muss mit 500 Mark **Miete rechnen.** *whoever*

Was macht man in einem Wohnheim? Wofür sind die 500 Mark? Was lernt man traditionell in der Schule? Lesen, Schreiben und …

c. Mit vielen **Dozenten** habe ich auch außerhalb der Sprechstunden Kontakt.

Wer hält Sprechstunden an der Uni? Studenten oder Dozenten?

Strategie 2: Wortformen

a. **Maschinenbau**-Student:

Was studiert man, wenn man den Bau einer Maschine studiert?

b. am Stadtrand **gebaut**

Wie heißt der Infinitiv von **gebaut**? Was ist ein Gebäude? Was ist ein Neubau?

c. in Uni-**Nähe**

Wenn ein Wohnheim in Uni-Nähe ist, ist es nah oder weit von der Uni?

d. Ein **Anglist** an der TU° Braunschweig ist ein **Exot.**

Technische Universität

Studiert ein Anglist Deutsch oder Englisch? Ist ein Anglist an einer Technischen Universität exotisch oder normal?

ABSPRUNGTEXT

Welche Uni ist die beste?

Lesen Sie jetzt die Texte.

Billig wohnen

können Studenten in Dortmund nach Erfahrung° von **Peter Ohm,** 25. Zum Nachtleben in der Umgebung der Universität fallen dem Maschinenbau-Studenten im 10. Semester allerdings nur zwei Worte ein°: „Tote Hose"°

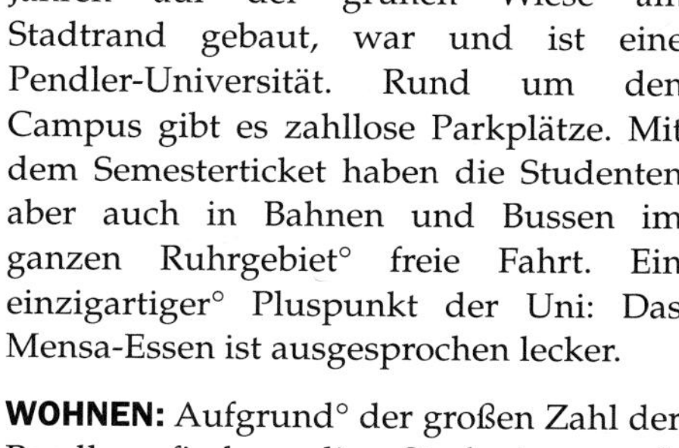

UNIVERSITÄT: Die Uni Dortmund, vor 25 Jahren auf der grünen Wiese am Stadtrand gebaut, war und ist eine Pendler-Universität. Rund um den Campus gibt es zahllose Parkplätze. Mit dem Semesterticket haben die Studenten aber auch in Bahnen und Bussen im ganzen Ruhrgebiet° freie Fahrt. Ein einzigartiger° Pluspunkt der Uni: Das Mensa-Essen ist ausgesprochen lecker.

Ruhr River region
unique

WOHNEN: Aufgrund° der großen Zahl der Pendler finden die Studenten noch Wohnungen zu erträglichen Preisen. Ein Zimmer im Studentenwohnheim in Uni-Nähe – darauf muß man allerdings knapp ein Jahr warten – kostet 200 Mark, und auch auf dem privaten Wohnungsmarkt sind die Zimmer bezahlbar.

Based on
experience
***fallen ein:** come to mind*
***„Tote Hose":** "completely dead"*

Der grüne Campus

lockte° **Werner Bendix,** 25, nach Mainz. Obwohl sich die Zahl seiner Kommilitonen mittlerweile° verdoppelt° hat, zieht der Betriebswirtschafts-Student (9. Semester) die Uni noch immer allen anderen vor°.

UNIVERSITÄT: Ich gehe gern hin, obwohl die Uni wächst und wächst. Nach zwei Jahren Provisorium° im Hörsaal-Zelt° (dem „Bierzelt") hat der Fachbereich im letzten Semester einen großzügigen Neubau bezogen. Die Räume sind hell, die Bibliothek finde ich vorbildlich. Nur die Mensa ist noch nicht auf den Ansturm° eingestellt°, wer billig essen will, braucht Geduld.

temporary quarters / tent
rush / prepared for

JOBS: Im Ballungsraum Rhein-Main kein Problem. Ich habe als Aushilfspfleger° in der Psychiatrie° 21 Mark pro Stunde verdient.

temporary orderly
psychiatric ward

WOHNEN: Zimmer sind rar und teuer. Plätze im Studentenwohnheim gibt es nur für jeden zehnten°, zwei bis drei Semester Wartezeit sind üblich. Wer nicht in einem Wohnheim unterkommt, muß mit 500 Mark Miete rechnen.

enticed
meanwhile
doubled
***zieht vor:** prefers / **für ... zehnten:** for one out of ten*

Ganz exotisch

findet **Lutz Harder,** 23, sein Anglistik-Studium an der Technischen Universität Braunschweig. Der Student im 5. Semester zieht persönliche Kontakte dem Lehrangebot° einer Massen-Uni vor.

UNIVERSITÄT: Ich will mir nichts vormachen°: Ein Anglist° an der TU Braunschweig ist ein Exot°. Mir gefällt indes gerade, daß unser Seminar so klein ist: Das Arbeiten hier macht Spaß. Anders als an einer Massen-Uni kenne ich meine Kommilitonen, mit vielen Dozenten habe ich auch außerhalb° der Sprechstunden persönlichen Kontakt.

JOBS: Wer seinem BAföG etwas auf die Sprünge helfen muß°, findet außerhalb° der Uni problemlos einen Job. Die Zahl der Hiwi-Stellen° ist eher begrenzt.

WOHNUNG: Die Wartezeit für Wohnheime liegt bei zwei bis drei Semestern, kann aber mit genug Druck reduziert werden°. Auf dem freien Markt gehört neben ein bißchen Kleingeld (Monatsmiete für ein Zimmer: 300 bis 500 Mark) eine Portion Glück dazu.

exotic person, "rare bird"

outside of

***auf ... muß:** needs to boost / outside*

research assistantships

***reduziert werden:** be reduced*

course selection

***Ich ... vormachen:** I don't want to kid myself / English major*

Rückblick

31 Informationen suchen. Lesen Sie die Interviews mit Peter Ohm, Werner Bendix und Lutz Harder noch einmal. Suchen Sie die folgenden Informationen und ergänzen Sie die Tabelle.

	Peter Ohm	Werner Bendix	Lutz Harder
Alter	______	25	______
Universität	______	Universität Mainz	______
Semester	______	______	im 5. Semester
Studienfach	Maschinenbau	______	______
etwas Interessantes über die Uni	______	Uni wächst	______
das Beste an der Uni	______	______	Arbeiten macht Spaß
Mensa/Essen	______	man braucht Geduld	(keine Information)
Wartezeit für ein Zimmer im Studentenwohnheim	knapp ein Jahr	______	______
Preis für ein Zimmer in der Stadt	______	500 Mark	______
Jobs für Studenten	(keine Information)	______	______

32 Ergänzen Sie. Ergänzen Sie diese Sätze mit Wörtern aus dem **Absprungtext.**

Peter Ohm

1. Die Universität Dortmund wurde vor 25 Jahren am Stadtrand ______.
2. So viele Studenten fahren nach Dortmund aber wohnen woanders, dass man die Universität Dortmund eine „______-Universität" nennt.
3. Parken ist nie ein Problem, weil es so viele ______ für Autos rund um den Campus gibt.

4. Dass das Mensa-Essen so lecker ist, ist ein einzigartiger _____ der Uni Dortmund.

Werner Bendix

5. Die Uni _____ so schnell, dass die Studentenzahl sich verdoppelt hat.
6. Weil er sich keine bessere Bibliothek vorstellen kann, nennt er sie _____.
7. Wer in der Mensa essen will, muss viel _____ haben.
8. Zwei bis drei Semester Wartezeit sind _____ für ein Zimmer im Studentenwohnheim.
9. In der Psychiatrie hat Werner 21 Mark pro Stunde _____.

Lutz Harder

10. Es gefällt Lutz, dass das _____ so klein ist.
11. Das Arbeiten macht ihm _____.
12. Anders als an einer Massen-Universität kennt er seine _____.
13. Er hat auch persönlichen _____ mit vielen Dozenten.
14. Auf dem freien Wohnungsmarkt ist die monatliche _____ für ein Zimmer 300 bis 500 Mark.

BRENNPUNKT KULTUR

Wie Studenten ihr Studium finanzieren

University study in Germany is tuition-free. However, students pay a modest registration fee of 60 marks or more per semester to the university. They pay for their own living expenses, books, and supplies. Residence halls and meals in the university cafeteria are subsidized by the government. Students can receive financial aid through a loan system known as **BAföG (Bundesausbildungsförderungsgesetz)**, named after the law that provides for it. The federal government provides this loan interest-free to students of families with low and middle incomes. The maximum amount allowed is 950 marks per month.

Because of the relatively low education costs and general affluence, German students do not usually hold part-time jobs during the academic year. Students typically work during the two semester breaks (**Semesterferien**) to finance a trip or a major purchase. However, student habits are changing. Whereas only six percent of German university students financed their education by working in 1985, now roughly 56 percent of students work while attending college.

In June 2000 the education ministers approved a non-binding recommendation that partial tuition be charged for students who exceed the allotted time to complete a degree (14 semesters) and for those in their second degree program. A nominal tuition fee of approximately 1,000 marks per semester for students varies from state to state.

33 **Kurz gefragt.** Beantworten Sie diese Fragen auf Deutsch.

Peter Ohm

1. Wo ist die Universität in Dortmund?
2. Warum gibt es so viele Parkplätze rund um den Campus?
3. Warum sind Zimmerpreise in Dortmund billig?
4. Was kostet ein Zimmer im Studentenwohnheim? Wie lange muss man darauf warten?

Werner Bendix

5. Er sagt, die Uni Mainz wächst und wächst. Wie ist die Situation jetzt in Mainz? Welche Probleme haben Studenten in Mainz?
6. Wie hat Werner mal gearbeitet? Was hat er pro Stunde verdient?

Lutz Harder

7. Was gefällt Lutz am Englischen Seminar?
8. Er sagt, man braucht Glück, wenn man ein Zimmer finden will. Warum ist das ein Problem in Braunschweig?
9. Wo findet man problemlos einen Job in Braunschweig?
10. Gibt es viele Hiwi-Stellen an der Uni?

Kurz gefragt. Adjectives for nationalities, such as **englisch,** are generally not capitalized. Because it is part of the name of a university department, it is capitalized here.

34 **Kurz interpretiert.** Beantworten Sie diese Fragen auf Deutsch.

1. Nennen Sie einen Unterschied zwischen der Universität Dortmund und einer traditionellen deutschen Universität.
2. Warum sind Zimmer in Dortmund billiger als in Mainz oder Braunschweig?
3. Warum ist ein Anglistikstudent wie Lutz Harder ein „Exot" an der TU Braunschweig?
4. Was sind die Nachteile von einer Massen-Universität für einen Anglistikstudenten wie Lutz? Was sind für Lutz die Vorteile von seinem kleinen Englischen Seminar?
5. Welche Probleme haben deutsche Studenten, die untypisch für Studenten in Nordamerika sind?

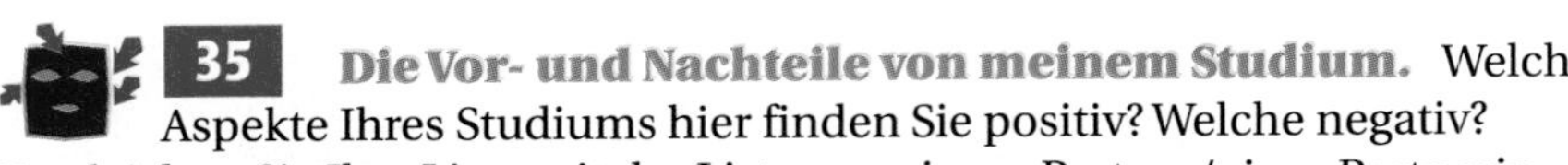

35 **Die Vor- und Nachteile von meinem Studium.** Welche Aspekte Ihres Studiums hier finden Sie positiv? Welche negativ? Vergleichen Sie Ihre Liste mit der Liste von einem Partner/einer Partnerin.

	Positiv	*Negativ*
1. die Dozenten und Professoren	___	___
2. die Kontaktmöglichkeiten	___	___
3. die Kurse	___	___
4. meine Kommilitonen/Kommilitoninnen	___	___
5. die Arbeitsatmosphäre	___	___
6. die Bibliothek	___	___
7. die Arbeitsmöglichkeiten	___	___
8. die Beratung°	___	___

Studienberatung: *academic advising*

36 **Interview: Mein Studentenleben.** Beantworten Sie die folgenden Fragen zuerst für sich. Stellen Sie sie dann einem Partner/einer Partnerin.

	Ich	*Partner(in)*
1. Was studierst du?	______	______
2. Welche Kurse belegst° du?	______	______
3. Wie viele Kurse hast du mit Lehrassistenten°?	______	______
4. Wo lernst du normalerweise? In der Bibliothek? Zu Hause?	______	______
5. Wie viele Stunden lernst du jeden Tag?	______	______
6. Wie viele Stunden verbringst du pro Woche in der Bibliothek?	______	______
7. Wie viele Referate schreibst du dieses Semester?	______	______
8. Wie oft schreibst du eine Prüfung?	______	______
9. Hast du einen Job?	______	______
10. Hast du noch Zeit für Sport oder andere Hobbys?	______	______

are taking
teaching assistants

SPIEGEL-RANGLISTE DER WEST-UNIVERSITÄTEN

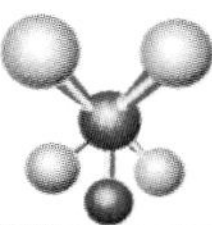

Rang	Universität	Prozent	POLITIK/ SOZIALWISS. Platz	MATHEMATIK Platz	ANGLISTIK Platz	BIOLOGIE Platz	PÄDAGOGIK Platz	ÖKONOMIE Platz	CHEMIE Platz
1	Uni Düsseldorf	95.5	▲	●	▲	▲	▲	▲	▲
2	UGH Duisburg	90.9	▲	▲	▲		▲	▲	●
3	Uni Konstanz	85.0	▲	●	●	▲		▲	▲
4	UGH Siegen	83.3	▲	●	▲			●	▲
5	Uni Bielefeld	81.8	▲	●	▲	●	▲	●	●
6	Uni Passau	78.6	▲	●				●	
6	Uni Trier	78.6	▲		●		●	▲	
8	Uni Mannheim	75.0	●	▲	●		▲	▲	
9	Uni Regensburg	72.7	▲	●	●	▲	▲	▲	●
10	Uni Bayreuth	71.4		●		▲		▲	●
11	FU Berlin	66.7	●	▲	▲	●	●	●	▲
12	Uni Kaiserslautern	64.3		▲		●			●
13	Uni Bamberg	58.3	●		●		▲	●	
14	Uni Ulm	57.1		●		●			▼
15	Uni Freiburg	54.5	●	●	●	●		●	●
16	Uni Kiel	54.2	●	●	●	●		●	●
16	Uni Mainz	54.2	●	▲	●	▼	●	●	●
18	Uni Saarbrücken	53.6	●	●	▼	●	●	●	▼
19	TH Aachen	50.0	▲	●	●	●		▼	▼
19	TU Braunschweig	50.0	●	▼	▲	●	▼		▲
19	Uni Dortmund	50.0		●	●		●	●	●
25	UGH Paderborn	45.5		▼	●		▼	▼	●
28	Uni Osnabrück	43.8	●	●		▼		●	
29	Uni Erlangen-Nürnberg	42.3	●	▼	▲	●		●	●
29	Uni Würzburg	42.3	●	●	●	●	▼	▲	●
31	Uni Göttingen	41.7	▼	●	▲	●	●	●	▼
31	Uni Marburg	41.7	●	●	●	●	●	▼	▲
31	Uni Stuttgart	41.7	▼	●	▼		●	●	●
34	UGH Essen	40.9		●	●	▼	▼	●	●
35	Uni Tübingen	38.5	●	▲	▼	●	●	▼	●

BRENNPUNKT KULTUR

Das deutsche Universitätssystem

The German system of higher education, respected and emulated around the world, is undergoing change as more and more **Gymnasium** graduates try to go on to study at universities. To limit the number of students, the universities have established maximum enrollments (**Numerus clausus**) in many subject areas. Students interested in these subjects submit credentials to a central clearing-house, **die Zentralstelle für die Vergabe von Studienplätzen (ZVS)** in Dortmund, which assesses the student's academic record and length of time spent waiting for admission, along with tests and interviews. The student then may get a "space" (**der Studienplatz**), that is, admission to study a particular subject at an institution chosen by **ZVS**, or the student is directed to another subject area. The requirements for getting a **Studienplatz** by the **ZVS** are particularly high for subjects such as medicine, economics, law, and computer science.

Once enrolled in a post-secondary program, students begin taking courses for their majors. Since there are no requirements outside of a student's major and no general distribution requirements, students can concentrate on their specialty. Once students have taken the required courses and feel fully prepared, they sign up for graduation exams in their subject areas, often collaborating with their instructors to determine the topics for the exams. The average German student spends fourteen semesters (seven years) at the university to earn a Master's degree (**Magister**), a **Diplom** in an area of specialization, or the **Staatsexamen**, which qualifies the graduate for employment in public service such as teaching or law practice. Thereafter, students may continue their studies through the doctoral level.

37 **Wie es bei uns ist.** Das Studium in den USA und in Kanada ist in vielen Aspekten ganz anders als das Studium in deutschsprachigen Ländern. Wie unterscheidet° sich Ihr Studium von einem mitteleuropäischen Studium? Besprechen Sie diese Fragen in einer kleinen Gruppe von drei bis fünf Personen. Berichten Sie dann der Klasse Ihre Ergebnisse.

differ

1. Besuchen die meisten Studenten hier im ersten Jahr Vorlesungen?
2. Gibt es auch hier wie in Deutschland keine Diskussionen und keine Prüfungen in Vorlesungen?
3. Was ist einem Proseminar äquivalent?
4. Haben Sie je in einer organisierten Arbeitsgruppe gearbeitet? Woran?
5. Halten Sie lieber ein Referat oder schreiben Sie lieber eine Prüfung? Warum?
6. Was sind die Vor- und Nachteile von Gruppenreferaten oder Einzelreferaten?
7. Ist es hier typisch, Dozenten/Dozentinnen in der Sprechstunde zu besuchen? Warum?
8. Kann man hier leicht ein Praktikum außerhalb der Uni machen? Ist das hier populär? Wollen Sie selbst ein Praktikum machen? Was für eins?
9. Was bekommen Studenten an Ihrer Uni anstelle von° Scheinen? Was finden Sie besser?

Due to several influences, e.g., the European Union, widespread use of the English language, and the growth of international business, Germany has seen an increase in prestigious private universities to about 30. Like American universities, they charge students tuition, sometimes 40,000 marks per year.

***anstelle von:** instead of*

Strukturen und Vokabeln

III Talking about future events

Future time

A. *The present tense with a time expression*

You have already learned that German speakers commonly express the future with a present tense verb and a future time expression, such as **morgen, nächste Woche, im Sommer.**

Morgen fliege ich nach Berlin. *I'm going to fly to Berlin tomorrow.*

Time expressions **(Zeitausdrücke)** frequently begin German sentences. This helps organize the sequence of events chronologically in a narrative. Once a future time expression establishes the time frame, other future time expressions are not necessary in subsequent sentences.

Morgen um 7.00 Uhr stehe ich auf.	*I'll get up at 7 A.M. tomorrow.*
(Morgen) Um 8.00 Uhr fahre ich zum Flughafen.	*I'll drive to the airport at 8 A.M. (tomorrow).*
(Morgen) Um 10.15 Uhr komme ich in Frankfurt an.	*I'll arrive in Frankfurt at 10:15 A.M. (tomorrow).*

Remember that expressions of time always precede expressions of place when they occur together after the verb.

Ich fliege (*verb*) morgen (*time*) nach Berlin (*place*). *I'm going to fly to Berlin tomorrow.*

Here are some time expressions German speakers frequently use when talking about the future. Some of them will already be familiar to you.

heute	*today*
heute Morgen	*this morning*
heute Nachmittag	*this afternoon*
heute Abend	*this evening, tonight*
morgen	*tomorrow*
morgen früh	*tomorrow morning*
morgen Nachmittag	*tomorrow afternoon*
morgen Abend	*tomorrow evening*
übermorgen	*the day after tomorrow*
in zwei Tagen (Wochen, Monaten)	*in two days (weeks, months)*
diese Woche	*this week*
nächste Woche	*next week*
dieses Wochenende	*this weekend*
am Wochenende	*on the weekend*
jeden Tag	*every day*
am Samstag	*on Saturday*
diesen Freitag	*this Friday*
nächsten Samstag	*next Saturday*
nächstes Jahr	*next year*
am Abend	*in the evening, at night*
im Sommer (Winter, Juli)	*in the summer (winter, July)*
später	*later*

Remember to use the accusative case to designate specific time periods (e.g., **nächstes Jahr, nächsten Sommer, nächste Woche**). The preposition **am** with the dative case designates a specific point in time (e.g., **am Wochenende, am Samstag, am Abend**).

38 **Wann machst du das?** Fragen Sie einen Partner/eine Partnerin, wann diese Situationen in der Zukunft stattfinden°. Benutzen Sie Zeitausdrücke aus der Liste oben.

°*take place*

S1: Wann bringst du die Bücher in die Bibliothek zurück?
S2: Morgen früh bringe ich die Bücher zurück.

1. Wann lernst du mit Freunden für die Prüfung?
2. Wann gehst du zu deinem Dozenten/deiner Dozentin in die Sprechstunde?
3. Wann triffst du Freunde in der Mensa?
4. Wann musst du zum Zahnarzt gehen?
5. Wann ist die nächste Deutschprüfung?
6. Wann fährst du nach Hause?
7. Wann treibst du Sport?
8. Wann gehst du in die Bibliothek?
9. Wann putzt du dir die Zähne?
10. Wann beginnen die Semesterferien?

B. *The future tense: werden + infinitive*

Besides using the present tense with a future time expression, German speakers also use the future tense **(das Futur)** to describe events in the future. The **Futur** consists of the auxiliary or helping verb **werden** with an infinitive at the end of the clause. The **Futur** may be used with or without a future time adverbial.

With a reflexive verb in the future tense, the reflexive pronoun occurs immediately after **werden** or after the subject if it is positioned mid-sentence: **Ich werde *mich* bald melden. Jetzt werde ich *mir* ganz schnell die Hände waschen.**

Wie lange **wird** das Referat **dauern?**	*How long is the presentation going to last?*
Wird es einen Overheadprojektor im Seminarraum **geben?**	*Will there be an overhead projector in the seminar room?*
Bei diesem Wetter **wirst** du dich **erkälten!**	*You are going to catch a cold in this weather!*

Note the spelling changes in the verb **werden: e>i** in the 2nd, informal, and 3rd person **(wirst, wird)** and the loss of **d** in the 2nd, informal person **(wirst).**

werden bauen: *will build, going to build*		
Person	**Singular**	**Plural**
1st	ich **werde** bauen *I will, am going to build*	wir **werden** bauen *we will, are going to build*
2nd, informal	du **wirst** bauen *you will, are going to build*	ihr **werdet** bauen *you will, are going to build*
2nd, formal	Sie **werden** bauen *you will, are going to build*	Sie **werden** bauen *you will, are going to build*
3rd	er/sie/es **wird** bauen *he/she/it will, is going to build*	sie **werden** bauen *they will, are going to build*

When used with the first person pronouns, the future tense with **werden** can express a mild promise if directed toward another person.

Ich **werde** einen Overheadprojektor für Sie **bestellen.**	*I will/am going to order an overhead projector for you.*

Be careful not to confuse the modal verb **wollen** *(to want to)* with English *will.*

Ich **will** nach Deutschland fliegen.	*I **want to** fly to Germany.*
Ich **werde** nach Deutschland fliegen.	*I **will** fly to Germany.*

39 Meine Pläne nach dem Studium. Kreuzen Sie zuerst an, was für Sie stimmt. Fragen Sie dann einen Partner/eine Partnerin.

S1: Ich werde mein Diplom mit Auszeichnung° bekommen. Wirst du auch dein Diplom mit Auszeichnung machen?

S2: Ja, ich werde auch mein Diplom mit Auszeichnung bekommen. *(oder)* Nein, ich werde es nicht mit Auszeichnung bekommen.

distinction

Ich werde:	*Ich*	*Partner(in)*
1. mein Diplom mit Auszeichnung bekommen.	—	—
2. andere Kontinente sehen, bevor ich meine erste Arbeitsstelle suche.	—	—
3. in einer neuen, unbekannten Großstadt leben.	—	—
4. in meine Heimatstadt zurückkehren°.	—	—
5. meinen Doktor machen.	—	—
6. ein Haus kaufen.	—	—
7. Präsident/Präsidentin von den USA werden.	—	—
8. eine Familie mit vielen Kindern haben.	—	—

in ... zurückkehren: *go back to my hometown*

	Ich	Partner(in)	
9. mich auf meine Karriere° konzentrieren und keine Kinder haben.	___	___	*career*
10. in einem Hollywoodfilm mitspielen.	___	___	
11. eine Firma gründen°.	___	___	*start*
12. ökologisch (politisch, sozial) aktiv sein.	___	___	

40 **Feste Termine machen.** Ein Freund/Eine Freundin fragt, ob Sie oder andere diese Dinge machen werden. Antworten Sie affirmativ mit **werden** und geben Sie eine Zeit an. Benutzen Sie Zeitausdrücke wie **heute, heute Abend, später, morgen, nächste Woche, nächstes Jahr** usw.

S1: Kannst du mir bei den Hausaufgaben helfen?
S2: Morgen werde ich dir bei den Hausaufgaben helfen.

1. Wird dein Freund meine Seminararbeit schreiben?
2. Kannst du mit mir in die Sprechstunde gehen?
3. Möchtest du meine Vorlesung in Betriebswirtschaft besuchen?
4. Kannst du mit uns ins Seminar gehen?
5. Wird der Professor uns die Folien geben?
6. Kannst du mir deinen Computer leihen?
7. Können deine Freunde mit in die Bibliothek gehen?
8. Möchtest du mit uns in einer Arbeitsgruppe sein?

41 **Ja, ich verspreche es°!** Bevor Sie nach Deutschland reisen, müssen Sie Ihren Eltern versprechen, dort verantwortungsvoll° zu handeln°. Sagen Sie, was Sie machen und was Sie nicht machen werden.

promise
responsibly
act

S1 (VATER/MUTTER): Wirst du immer in die Vorlesung gehen?
S2 (TOCHTER/SOHN): Ja, ich verspreche es, ich werde immer in die Vorlesung gehen. *(oder)*
Nein, ich werde nicht immer in die Vorlesung gehen.

1. immer in die Vorlesung gehen
2. viel Zeit in der Bibliothek verbringen
3. jeden Abend ausgehen
4. viele Parties besuchen
5. keinen Alkohol trinken
6. jedes Wochenende nach Paris fahren
7. einen deutschen Freund/eine deutsche Freundin finden und heiraten
8. ins Museum, ins Konzert und in die Oper gehen
9. am Schreibtisch sitzen und sich auf Seminare vorbereiten
10. nie kochen und immer in guten Restaurants essen

IV Expressing probability

The verb **werden** + **wohl**

When used with the word **wohl** *(probably)* and an infinitive, **werden** expresses probability.

Er **wird wohl** krank sein. *He is probably sick.*
Er **wird wohl** ein Motorrad kaufen. *He'll probably buy a motorcycle.*

You have now learned these three uses of the verb **werden:**

1. As a main verb, meaning *to become, get.*

   Ich **werde** müde. *I am getting tired.*

2. As an auxiliary verb that, together with an infinitive, designates future tense.

   Das Referat **wird** 45 Minuten **dauern.** *The presentation will last 45 minutes.*

3. As an auxiliary verb that, together with **wohl** and an infinitive, expresses probability in the present tense.

   Stefan **wird wohl** nach Moskau fahren. *Stefan is probably going to Moscow.*

42 **Pläne für nächstes Jahr.** Was werden Sie nächstes Jahr machen? Kreuzen Sie **werde, werde wohl** oder **werde nicht** an. Fragen Sie dann einen Partner/eine Partnerin, was er/sie nächstes Jahr bestimmt machen wird, was er/sie wohl machen wird und was er/sie bestimmt nicht machen wird.

S1: Wirst du nächstes Jahr eine Hiwi-Stelle suchen?
S2: Ja, ich werde wohl eine Hiwi-Stelle suchen. *(oder)*
Nein, ich werde keine Hiwi-Stelle suchen.

	Werde	*Werde wohl*	*Werde nicht*
1. eine Hiwi-Stelle suchen	___	___	___
2. viele Seminararbeiten schreiben	___	___	___
3. viel Zeit in der Bibliothek verbringen	___	___	___
4. jeden Abend ausgehen	___	___	___
5. oft in die Sprechstunde gehen	___	___	___
6. neue Freunde kennen lernen	___	___	___
7. ein Motorrad kaufen	___	___	___
8. jedes Wochenende intensiv lernen	___	___	___
9. mein Studium zu Ende machen	___	___	___
10. so weit wie möglich von hier weggehen	___	___	___

BRENNPUNKT KULTUR

Das deutsche Schulsystem

Germany and Switzerland have similar public school systems that are centrally administered, in Germany by each state Ministry of Education and the Arts **(das Kultusministerium)** and by the individual Cantonal Ministries in Switzerland. The Federal Ministry of Education in Austria oversees educational policy there. These ministries initiate the educational curricula that schools will follow. This guarantees greater educational uniformity.

In Germany eighty percent of all three- to six-year-olds attend a private pre-school **(der Kindergarten).** Thereafter, children enter the public school system (or a private school), where they attend primary school **(die Grundschule)** through the fourth grade. In the third and fourth grades teachers assess each pupil's abilities and then recommend that they attend **die Hauptschule, die Realschule,** or **das Gymnasium.** During the fifth and sixth grades, called **die Orientierungsstufe,** students can change their minds and switch to a more appropriate school. All German students are required by law to attend school at least on a part-time basis through the age of 18 **(die Schulpflicht).**

Roughly one-third of all German students are **Hauptschüler.** They attend school through the 9th grade, and thereafter enter the workforce as an apprentice (**der Lehrling** or **der/die Auszubildende [Azubi]**), continuing with part-time classroom work for three more years.

BRENNPUNKT KULTUR

Another one-third of all German students attend **die Realschule. Realschüler** follow a middle-track educational path with a more demanding academic program that concludes with examinations at the end of the 10th grade. An intermediate diploma **(die Mittlere Reife)** is awarded upon successful completion of their training. This diploma qualifies students to attend specialized training colleges (e.g., **die Fachschule** or **die Fachoberschule**) and receive training in areas such as engineering, administration, and business. In Austria, this type of school does not exist.

Gymnasiasten, making up the final third of German high school students, pursue the traditional college preparatory track that continues through the 13th grade. They usually take courses in German, math, chemistry, physics, biology, English, a second foreign language, social studies, sports, and the arts. In the 11th through 13th grades, students choose two major areas of academic specialization for their **Leistungskurse** and several minor subjects for their **Grundkurse.** Before graduating from a **Gymnasium,** students must have completed coursework in at least nine subjects. The two major subjects are tested in depth when students face the comprehensive exams required for graduation (**das Abitur,** called **die Matura** in Austria, and **die Reifeprüfung** in Switzerland). With this diploma **(der Abschluss),** the student is qualified to attend a university or any other post-secondary educational institution, such as a **Musikhochschule, Kunsthochschule,** or a **Fachhochschule** specializing in engineering or the sciences.

A fourth type of German school, **die Gesamtschule,** modeled on the comprehensive American high school, was a product of the reform movement of the 1960s. It incorporates the curricula of all three traditional German secondary schools, giving students a broad choice of programs and courses. While hailed by some as more progressive and democratic schools, **Gesamtschulen** have been criticized by others for lowering standards. They remain controversial but are growing in number.

The school system in the new federal states of the former East Germany **(die neuen Bundesländer)** is undergoing dramatic structural change as these **Länder** convert their 10-year polytechnic schools to the three-track school system used in western Germany. The transition has been complicated because under socialism many teachers were hired for political and ideological reasons, rather than for their academic and pedagogical qualifications. Since unification, many such teachers have been let go. Many others have undergone retraining while the **Kultusministerien** of the **neue Bundesländer** work out the details of institutional restructuring.

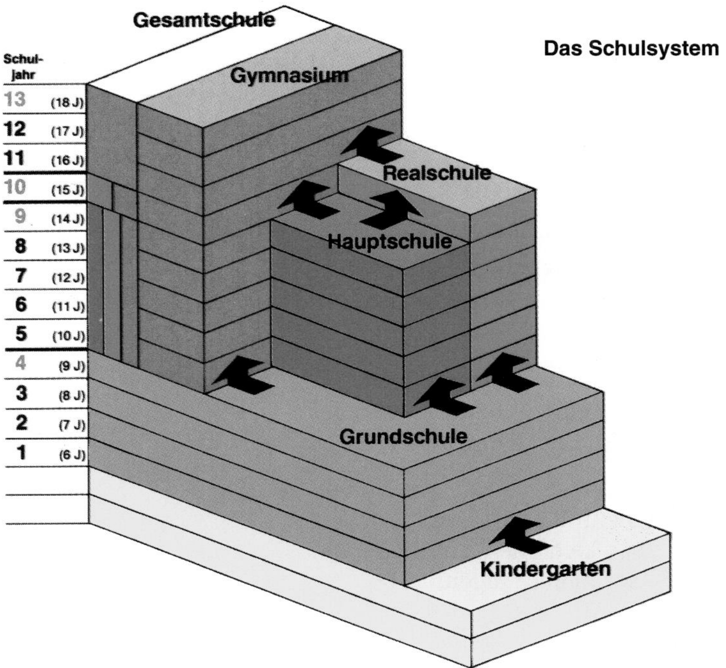

Das Schulsystem

43 **Interview: Pläne für die nähere Zukunft.** Stellen Sie einem Partner/einer Partnerin die folgenden Fragen.

S1: Was wirst du heute nach dem Deutschkurs machen?
S2: Ich werde wohl (in die Mensa gehen).

1. Was wirst du heute nach dem Deutschkurs machen?
2. Was wirst du heute Abend machen?
3. Was wirst du morgen früh machen?
4. Was wirst du übermorgen machen?
5. Wohin wirst du am Wochenende fahren?
6. Wann wirst du mit Freunden ausgehen?
7. Was wirst du im Sommer machen?
8. Wo wirst du nächstes Jahr wohnen?

44 **Julia wird wohl in den Kindergarten gehen.** Was werden diese Leute wohl nächstes Jahr machen?

Julia wird im Juli fünf Jahre alt.

S1: Sie wird wohl im September in den Kindergarten gehen.

1. Julia wird im Juli fünf Jahre alt.
2. Florian ist im Kindergarten.
3. Thomas ist in der vierten Klasse. Er will später nicht auf die Universität gehen. Er will eine Lehre machen.
4. Frank ist in der Hauptschule und möchte eine Kfz°-Mechaniker-Lehre machen.
5. Golo hat die Mittlere Reife gemacht.
6. Claudia ist in der sechsten Klasse und möchte auf die Universität gehen.
7. Gabriele ist Schülerin an einem Gymnasium in Wien.
8. Monika interessiert sich für Musik und möchte nach dem Gymnasium weiter studieren.

Kfz (Kraftfahrzeug): automotive

a. die Matura machen
b. aufs Gymnasium gehen
c. in den Kindergarten gehen
d. zur Fachschule gehen
e. zur Grundschule gehen
f. zur Hauptschule gehen
g. zur Musikhochschule gehen
h. zur Realschule gehen

▪ FREIE ▪ KOMMUNIKATION ▪

Rollenspiel: Das Gruppenreferat. Spielen Sie mit einem Partner/einer Partnerin die folgende Situation.

S1: Sie sind Professor/Professorin. Sie halten jetzt Ihre Sprechstunde und wollen mit Repräsentanten von jeder Arbeitsgruppe über das Gruppenreferat sprechen. Fragen Sie nach dem Thema, nach den Vorbereitungen und nach den anderen Studenten/Studentinnen in der Arbeitsgruppe.

S2: Sie sind Student/Studentin und gehen in die Sprechstunde von Ihrem Professor/Ihrer Professorin. Ihre Arbeitsgruppe hat noch kein Thema für das Referat, aber das dürfen Sie dem Professor/der Professorin nicht sagen.

Rollenspiel: Die Sommerreise. Spielen Sie mit einem Partner/einer Partnerin die folgende Situation.

S1: Sie sind der Sohn/die Tochter. Sie haben eine Sommerreise geplant und möchten mit einem Rucksack nach Europa fliegen. Sie haben nicht sehr viel Geld aber viele Ideen. Erklären Sie Ihren Eltern, was Sie machen möchten.

S2: Sie sind der Vater/die Mutter. Ihr Sohn/Ihre Tochter erzählt Ihnen, dass er/sie nach Europa fliegen möchte. Sie machen sich Sorgen, denn er/sie hat nicht viel Geld. Stellen Sie viele Fragen (z.B. **Wo wirst du schlafen? Was wirst du alles machen?**)

Schreibecke **Ein Brief an Lutz, Werner oder Peter.** Sie werden zwei Semester an der Universität in Mainz, Braunschweig oder Dortmund studieren. Sie haben den **Absprungtext** gelesen and wollen einen Brief an Lutz Harder, Werner Bendix oder Peter Ohm schreiben. Stellen Sie sich vor° und beschreiben Sie Ihre konkreten Pläne für das Jahr in Deutschland. Behandeln Sie auch die Themen Wohnen, Arbeiten und Studieren und stellen° Sie Lutz, Werner oder Peter ein paar Fragen.

Stellen vor: *Introduce*
stellen: *pose*

V Specifying additional information about actions

A. Using verbs with prepositional objects

Some German verbs may be accompanied by a preposition and its object that offers more specific information about the activity expressed by the verb.

Konzentrieren Sie **sich.**	*Concentrate.*
Konzentrieren Sie **sich auf** das Wichtigste.	***Concentrate on*** *the most important things.*

The meaning of a verb + prepositional object can change when the preposition changes.

Ich habe gestern **mit** Markus **gesprochen.**	*I* ***talked to*** *Markus yesterday.*
Wir haben **über** das Examen **gesprochen.**	*We* ***talked about*** *the exam.*

The German preposition does not necessarily have an obvious English equivalent. It needs to be learned together with the verb and the required case.

Here are some important verb-preposition combinations grouped according to case and preposition.

Da haben alle drauf gewartet.
Brigitte
YOUNG MISS

1. Preposition + accusative case

an + *accusative*

denken an (hat gedacht)	*to think of*
sich erinnern an (hat sich erinnert)	*to remember*
glauben an (hat geglaubt)	*to believe in*

auf + *accusative*

sich freuen auf (hat sich gefreut)	*to look forward to*
gespannt sein auf (ist gespannt gewesen)	*to be excited about*
sich konzentrieren auf (hat sich konzentriert)	*to concentrate on*
sich vor·bereiten auf (hat sich vorbereitet)	*to prepare for, get ready for*
warten auf (hat gewartet)	*to wait for*

für + *accusative*
danken für (hat gedankt) — *to thank for*
sich entscheiden für (hat sich entschieden) — *to decide on, in favor of*

sich entscheiden gegen: *to decide against*

in + *accusative*
sich verlieben in — *to fall in love with*
über + *accusative*
sich freuen über (hat sich gefreut) — *to be happy about*
reden/sprechen über (hat geredet/gesprochen) — *to talk about*
sich ärgern über (hat sich geärgert) — *to get angry about*
um + *accusative*
bitten um (hat gebeten) — *to ask for, request*

2. Preposition + dative case
nach + *dative*
fragen nach (hat gefragt) — *to ask about*
von + *dative*
erzählen von (hat erzählt) — *to tell a story about, talk about*
halten von (hat gehalten) — *to think of, about*
handeln von (hat gehandelt) — *to be about*
sich trennen von (hat sich getrennt) — *to break up with, separate from*
etwas verstehen von (hat verstanden) — *to know something about*
wissen von (hat gewusst) — *to know about*
vor + *dative*
Angst haben vor (hat Angst gehabt) — *to be afraid of*
retten vor (hat gerettet) — *to rescue from*

45 **Annas Jahr in Deutschland.** Ergänzen Sie die Sätze mit der richtigen Präposition **(an, auf, für, in, über, um, von, vor).**

Anna Adler verbringt jetzt das Jahr an der Universität in Tübingen. Am Anfang war sie sich nicht sicher, ob sie in Hamburg oder Tübingen studieren sollte°. Sie war natürlich gespannt _____ das Jahr in Deutschland.

Zuerst wollte° sie in Hamburg oder in Tübingen studieren. Sie hat mit ihren Eltern und mit ihrer Deutschlehrerin in Ft. Wayne _____ die Vorteile und die Nachteile von beiden Unis gesprochen. Ihre Eltern haben sehr viel Positives _____ Hamburg erzählt. Sie hat auch ihre Deutschlehrerin gefragt, was sie _____ Tübingen weiß. Dann hat sie sich _____ Tübingen entschieden.

Anna hat sich gut _____ das Jahr vorbereitet und profitiert sehr von der Erfahrung. Sie freut sich täglich _____ ihre Entscheidung, in Tübingen zu studieren, obwohl° sie sich deshalb° für eine Zeit lang _____ ihrer Familie und ihren Freunden trennen musste°. Bald ist das Jahr aber zu Ende und sie denkt wieder _____ ihre Freunde und Familie in den USA. Jetzt freut sie sich natürlich auch _____ ihre Heimkehr im Sommer.

should
wanted to
even though / for that reason
had to

B. Using da- and wo-compounds

When the object of the preposition in a sentence is a pronoun, German speakers attach **da** to the preposition to refer to the object. This **da**-compound only refers to objects that are things and not people.

Was verstehen Sie von diesem Thema? Ich verstehe nichts **davon.**	*What do you know about this topic? I don't know anything about it.*
Haben Sie etwas gegen dieses Thema? Nein, ich habe nichts **dagegen.**	*Do you object to this topic? No, I don't object to it.*
Haben Sie etwas gegen Carlos? Ich habe nichts **gegen ihn.**	*Do you have something against Carlos? No, I don't have anything against him.*

Prepositions beginning with a vowel require that an **r** be inserted between **da** and the preposition.

Ich kann mich nicht **daran** erinnern.	*I don't remember that.*
Er hat sich wochenlang **darauf** vorbereitet.	*He prepared himself for it for weeks.*
Ist schon Milch und Zucker **darin?**	*Is there already milk and sugar in it?*
Sie haben lange **darüber** geredet.	*They talked about it for a long time.*

To form a question that refers to the object of a preposition, German speakers attach **wo** to the preposition. Prepositions beginning with a vowel require that an **r** be inserted between **wo** and the preposition.

Wofür hat er sich entschieden?	*What did he decide on?*
Worauf freut ihr euch?	*What are you looking forward to?*

To refer to people, speakers use a preposition with **wen** for expressions with the accusative. For expressions with the dative, they use a preposition and **wem.**

Woran erinnern Sie sich?	*What do you remember?*
An wen erinnern Sie sich?	*Whom do you remember?*
Wovon handelt das Buch?	*What is the book about?*
Von wem handelt das Buch?	*Whom is the book about?*

AN WEN WENDEN SICH° STUDIERENDE?

wenden sich: *turn to*

Aufgabenbereich	Auskunftgebende Stelle
Anerkennung von Reifezeugnissen	Studentenabteilung Wilhelmstr. 11, T. 29-68 41
Anrechnung von Studienzeiten	zuständiges Prüfungsamt bzw. Prüfungsausschuß
Arbeitsvermittlung für Akademiker, Werk- und Gelegenheitsarbeit	Dienststelle Tübingen des Arbeitsamts Reutlingen und Außenstelle Universität Wilhelmstr. 26, T. 29-35 61
Auslandsstipendien/Auslandsstudium	Akademisches Auslandsamt Nauklerstr. 14, T. 29-64 48
BAföG	Studentenwerk Tübingen AöR Karlstr. 11, T. 29-38 52
Beglaubigung von Urkunden und Zeugnissen	Bürgermeisteramt Tübingen – Amt für öffentliche Ordnung –
Beratung in Fragen der Krankenversicherung	Studentenabteilung Wilhelmstr. 11, T. 29-25 19

Here are the most common **da-** and **wo-**compounds.

Accusative preposition	Da-compound	Wo-compound
durch	dadurch	wodurch
für	dafür	wofür
gegen	dagegen	wogegen
um	darum	worum
Dative preposition	**Da-compound**	**Wo-compound**
aus	daraus	woraus
bei	dabei	
mit	damit	womit
nach	danach	wonach
von	davon	wovon
zu	dazu	wozu
Two-case preposition	**Da-compound**	**Wo-compound**
an	daran	woran
auf	darauf	worauf
in	darin	worin
hinter	dahinter	wohinter
neben	daneben	
über	darüber	worüber
unter	darunter	worunter
vor	davor	wovor
zwischen	dazwischen	

Woran Konfitüren träumen!
SCHWARTAU MÖVENPICK

In speech **darum, daran,** and **darin** are contracted to **drum, dran,** and **drin.**

46 **Worauf wartet Anna?** Beantworten Sie die folgenden Fragen.

▣ Anna steht an der Bushaltestelle. Worauf wartet sie?
Sie wartet auf den Bus.

1. Anna steht an der Bushaltestelle. Worauf wartet sie?
2. Sie braucht Auskunft, wann der Bus abfährt. Worum bittet sie?
3. Im Bus muss sie eine dumme Hausaufgabe für Deutsch schreiben. Worüber ärgert sie sich?
4. Claudia will nächstes Jahr aufs Gymnasium gehen. Wofür hat sie sich entschieden?
5. Karl und Stefan haben heute eine Prüfung. Worauf bereiten sie sich vor?
6. Am Wochenende gibt Barbara eine Party. Worauf freut sie sich?
7. Karl hat seine Bücher vergessen. Woran hat er sich nicht erinnert?
8. Stefan versteht das Thema in Physik kaum. Wovon versteht er nicht viel?
9. Stefan muss einen Bericht für Physik schreiben. Wovor hat er Angst?
10. Nächste Woche hat Stefan zwei Prüfungen. Woran denkt er?

47 **Was macht Karl?** Stellen Sie einem Partner/einer Partnerin eine Frage mit **wo(r)-** oder **wen/wem.**

Karl hat sich in die Inge verliebt.

S1: In wen hat er sich verliebt?
S2: Er hat sich in die Inge verliebt.

1. Karl hat sich in die Inge verliebt.
2. Inge hat sich an Karls Geburtstag erinnert.
3. Karl ist gespannt auf die Party heute Abend.
4. Karl und Inge warten auf die Gäste.
5. Die Gäste reden über Karl.
6. Karl hält nicht viel von Rap-Musik.
7. Die Gäste freuen sich über das leckere Essen.
8. Inge hat auch an alkoholfreie Getränke gedacht.
9. Anna erzählt von ihrer Reise nach Mainz.

48 **Gespräch über das Studentenleben.** Stellen Sie einem Partner/einer Partnerin diese Fragen über das Studentenleben. Berichten Sie dann der Klasse von Ihrem Partner/Ihrer Partnerin.

1. Warum hast du dich für Deutsch als Fremdsprache entschieden?
2. Wie lange bereitest du dich auf Deutschprüfungen vor?
3. Worauf freust du dich am meisten im Herbst? Im Winter? Im Frühling?
4. Vor welchen Kursen (oder Professoren/Professorinnen) hast du Angst?
5. Auf welche Kurse (Professoren/Professorinnen) bist du gespannt?
6. Was hält man von den Professoren/Professorinnen und den Kursen in deinem Hauptfach?
7. Worüber hast du dich in der letzten Zeit geärgert?
8. Wovon verstehst du wirklich absolut nichts?
9. Wovon handelt das letzte Buch, das du in deiner Freizeit gelesen hast?
10. Über welche aktuellen Themen redet man auf diesem Campus?
11. In was für einen Mann/In was für eine Frau möchtest du dich verlieben? Beschreib ihn/sie.

FREIE KOMMUNIKATION

Rollenspiel: Gespräch mit dem Studienberater°. Spielen Sie die folgende Situation mit einem Partner/einer Partnerin.

academic advisor

S1: Sie sind Student/Studentin. Ihre Noten sind dieses Semester schrecklich schlecht, Sie haben Pech mit Ihrem Zimmerkameraden/Ihrer Zimmerkameradin und Sie haben Ihren Job verloren. Sie sind gerne an der Uni, aber dieses Semester klappt einfach nichts°, und Sie sind frustriert.

klappt ... nichts: nothing is working out

Sie überlegen sich, ob Sie mit dem Studium aufhören sollen. Sie melden sich bei Ihrem Berater und reden darüber.

S2: Sie sind Berater/Beraterin. Sie halten sehr viel von diesem Studenten/dieser Studentin, aber Sie verstehen auch die Frustration. Geben Sie ihm/ihr Rat. Stellen Sie Fragen, sagen Sie Ihre Meinung, machen Sie Vorschläge und helfen Sie dem Studenten/der Studentin, sich richtig zu entscheiden.

Schreibecke **Interviews mit Prominenten.** Sie schreiben einen Zeitungsartikel über eine prominente Person. Nächste Woche machen Sie ein Interview mit dieser Person. Überlegen Sie sich jetzt schon, welche Fragen Sie stellen möchten. Schreiben Sie sieben bis zehn Fragen auf. Benutzen Sie die Ausdrücke aus der Liste.

> Angst haben vor • glauben an • fragen nach • erzählen von • sich ärgern über • sich vor·bereiten auf • warten auf • sich erinnern an • sich freuen auf • halten von • bitten um

ZIELTEXT

Gespräch auf einer Party

Karl und Inge nehmen Anna und Barbara mit auf eine Party im Wohnheim. Bald sehen Inge und Karl eine Studentin aus einem Seminar, aber sie können sich nicht an ihren Namen erinnern. Die Studentin kommt vorbei, stellt sich als Sabine vor und lernt dabei Anna kennen. Sie kommen ins Gespräch und diskutieren die Probleme an der Universität.

Vorschau

 **49** **Partybenehmen.** Kreuzen Sie die richtige Kategorie an.

1. Wie oft machen Sie so etwas auf Partys?

	Nie 0%	*Selten 20%*	*Oft 60%*	*Sehr oft 80%*	*Immer 100%*
mit Freunden/Bekannten sprechen	___	___	___	___	___
neue Leute ansprechen	___	___	___	___	___
etwas essen	___	___	___	___	___
Alkohol trinken	___	___	___	___	___
alkoholfreie Getränke trinken	___	___	___	___	___
tanzen	___	___	___	___	___
Musik hören	___	___	___	___	___
Musik spielen	___	___	___	___	___
singen	___	___	___	___	___
zu viel Alkohol trinken	___	___	___	___	___

2. Mit wem sprechen Sie über diese Themen auf einer Party? Kreuzen Sie an, was stimmt.

	Mit dem Freund (der Freundin)	*Mit meinen Freunden*	*Mit Bekannten*
Liebesprobleme	___	___	___
Vorlesungen und Seminare	___	___	___
Dozenten und Professoren	___	___	___
Freunde	___	___	___
die Musik auf der Party	___	___	___
Politik	___	___	___

	Mit dem Freund (der Freundin)	*Mit meinen Freunden*	*Mit Bekannten*
das Essen auf der Party	___	___	___
die Getränke auf der Party	___	___	___
die Familie	___	___	___
Sport	___	___	___
Skandale	___	___	___
die Kleidung von Leuten auf der Party	___	___	___

50 **Satzdetektiv.** Welche Sätze bedeuten ungefähr das Gleiche?

1. Die Musik ist ein bisschen **lahm.** Die könnte ein bisschen **peppiger** sein.
2. Wollen wir einfach so 'ne Weile **plaudern?**
3. Ja, die [Studentin] **kommt** mir **bekannt vor.**
4. Mir gefällt der Kurs, weil die Dozentin so **gute Bücher ausgewählt hat.**
5. Der **Inhalt** ist gut.

a. Der Kurs ist gut. Die Dozentin hat interessante Bücher gefunden.
b. Ich denke, ich kenne die Studentin.
c. Die Musik ist etwas langsam und nicht so toll.
d. Sprechen wir ein bisschen?
e. Die Themen im Kurs sind interessant.

---

6. Zwanzig Leute stehen in der **Schlange.**
7. Habt ihr schon **probiert,** mit der Dozentin zu sprechen?
8. Das **passt** so gar nicht **zu ihr.**
9. Im Kurs **klingt** sie immer so **studentenfreundlich.**
10. Sie hat halt **wenig Zeit.**

f. Habt ihr schon versucht, mit der Dozentin zu sprechen?
g. Zwanzig Studenten warten auf die Dozentin.
h. Die Dozentin hat eben zu wenig Zeit.
i. Das ist untypisch für sie.
j. Wenn sie im Kurs spricht, hat man den Eindruck, dass sie Studenten mag.

ZIELTEXT

Gespräch auf einer Party

Hören Sie gut zu.

Rückblick

51 **Stimmt das?** Stimmen diese Aussagen zum Text oder nicht? Wenn nicht, was stimmt?

	Ja, das stimmt.	*Nein, das stimmt nicht.*
1. Karl findet die Musik auf der Party toll.	___	___
2. Karl und Inge treffen eine Studentin aus ihrem Seminar. Die Studentin heißt Martina.	___	___
3. Der Kurs soll ein Seminar sein, aber er ist mehr wie eine Vorlesung.	___	___
4. Dem Karl gefällt der Kurs nicht.	___	___
5. Es ist leicht, mit der Dozentin in ihrer Sprechstunde zu sprechen.	___	___
6. Die Dozentin scheint im Seminar studentenfreundlich zu sein.	___	___

52 **Ergänzen Sie.** Ergänzen Sie diese Sätze mit Wörtern aus dem **Zieltext.**

1. Karl fragt Anna und Barbara, ob sie lieber tanzen oder ___ möchten.
2. Karl sagt, dass Sabines Gesicht ihm ___ vorkommt.
3. Inge, Sabine und Karl sind zusammen in einem ___.
4. Inge meint, dass der Kurs kein ___ sondern mehr eine ___ ist.
5. Mit fünfzig Leuten oder so ist das Seminar wirklich ___.
6. Karl sagt, dass ihm der Kurs gefällt, weil die Dozentin gute Bücher ___ hat.
7. Inge fragt, ob die anderen schon mal ___ haben, mit der Dozentin zu sprechen.
8. Es ist schwierig, mit der Dozentin in ihrer ___ zu sprechen.
9. Zwanzig Leute stehen in der ___ und warten auf die Dozentin.
10. Inge sagt, dass das irgendwie nicht zu ihr ___, weil sie immer so studentenfreundlich klingt.

53 **Der Kurs ist gut.** Wie wichtig sind Ihnen diese Faktoren für einen guten Kurs? Kreuzen Sie eine passende Kategorie an.

	Nicht wichtig	*Wichtig*	*Sehr wichtig*
1. ein interessantes Thema			
2. ein netter Dozent/eine nette Dozentin	___	___	___
3. hochintelligente Professoren	___	___	___
4. motivierte Studenten	___	___	___

Der Kurs ist gut. Be prepared to state your opinion to the class: **Ich finde es wichtig, dass das Thema interessant ist. Ich meine, es ist nicht so wichtig, dass der Dozent/die Dozentin nett ist. Meiner Meinung nach soll es keine teuren Bücher geben.**

5. hohes akademisches Niveau° ___ ___ ___
6. viele Bücher ___ ___ ___
7. teure Bücher ___ ___ ___
8. Diskussionen im Kurs ___ ___ ___
9. Sprechstunden ___ ___ ___
10. andere Medien: Video, Computer, Kassetten ___ ___ ___
11. nicht zu früh am Tag ___ ___ ___
12. praktisch ___ ___ ___
13. wenige Studenten ___ ___ ___

level

54 **Probleme an der Uni.** Welche Probleme an einer Uni finden Sie besonders schlimm? Arbeiten Sie in einer Gruppe von drei Personen und ordnen Sie diese Probleme nach ihrer Wichtigkeit. Benutzen Sie die Zahlen 1 (am schlimmsten°) bis 10 (am wenigsten schlimm°).

***am schlimmsten:** the worst /* ***am ... schlimm:** the least bad*

___ Zu viele Studenten sind in einem Kurs.
___ Die Dozenten und Professoren haben zu wenige Sprechstunden.
___ Der Kurs ist zu schwierig.
___ Der Kurs ist nicht interessant.
___ Die Professoren sind zu konservativ.
___ Die Hörsäle sind schmutzig°.
___ Man muss im Kurs zu viel arbeiten.
___ Die Kommilitonen sind unfreundlich.
___ Das Studium kostet zu viel Geld.
___ Das Semester dauert zu lange.

dirty

Probleme an der Uni. Be prepared to state your opinion: **Ich meine, es ist wirklich schlimm, wenn zu viele Studenten in einem Kurs sind.**

FREIE KOMMUNIKATION

Rollenspiel: Wie sind die Dozenten bei euch? Spielen Sie die folgende Situation mit einem Partner/einer Partnerin.

S1: Sie sind Dozent/Dozentin. Sie sprechen mit einem Studenten/einer Studentin aus Österreich. Er/Sie hat gehört, dass die Dozenten in den USA sehr studentenunfreundlich sind. Was sagen Sie zu ihm/ihr?

S2: Sie sind der Student/die Studentin aus Österreich. Sie wollen wissen, ob amerikanische Dozenten/ Dozentinnen viele Aufgaben aufgeben, ob sie oft Sprechstunden haben, ob sie hilfreich oder distanziert sind usw.

Rollenspiel: Wie sind die Studenten bei euch? Spielen Sie die folgende Situation mit einem Partner/einer Partnerin.

S1: Sie sind Student/Studentin aus Zürich; Sie waren noch nie in Amerika. Sie sprechen mit einem Amerikaner/einer Amerikanerin auf einer Party und erzählen, was Sie so von amerikanischen Studenten hören: Sie lernen nicht viel, sie brauchen nicht viel zu arbeiten, sie haben am Ende keine Examen, aber viele Parties, und die Diplome sind wertlos. Sie fragen, ob das wirklich stimmt.

S2: Sie sind Amerikaner/Amerikanerin. Beantworten Sie die Fragen und beschreiben Sie das US-Bildungssystem und das Studentenleben.

Schreibecke **Der ideale Kurs im 21. Jahrhundert.** Wie wird wohl der ideale Universitätskurs im Jahre 2020 sein? Was wird wohl anders sein, was wird dasselbe sein? Besprechen Sie den Inhalt, die Prüfungen, die Lehrkräfte, die Medien usw. von einem solchen Kurs.

Ein Brief an die Günthers. Barbara hat Anna den folgenden Brief von ihrer Freundin aus Dresden gezeigt. Anna entscheidet sich, auch so einen Brief an die Günthers in Weinheim zu schreiben. Benutzen Sie den Brief von Barbaras Freundin Caroline als Beispiel für Annas Brief an die Günthers.

Meißener Straße 27
01069 Dresden
Dienstag, den 2. November

Liebe Barbara,

es tut mir Leid, dass ich nicht geschrieben habe. Ich habe mich erkältet und war eine Woche lang krank. Jetzt geht's mir besser.

Wie geht es dir an der Uni in Tübingen? Mir gefällt die Uni hier in Dresden sehr gut. Ich habe in diesem Semester einen Kurs in Biologie. Er gefällt mir sehr, denn der Professor ist ausgezeichnet. Er ist sehr studentenfreundlich. Nur sind seine Sprechstunden immer überfüllt. Ich habe mich auch entschieden Medizin zu studieren. Ich warte jetzt nur noch auf einen Studienplatz.

Mir gefallen auch meine Vorlesungen hier. Sie sind nicht so voll, und ich habe andere Studenten kennen gelernt.

Wie sind deine Kurse? Stimmt es, was man über Tübingen hört? Die Uni ist überfüllt und Kontakt mit Professoren hat man kaum. Schreib doch mal wieder!

Ich werde wohl nächste Woche mehr Zeit haben. Dann kann ich dich eventuell besuchen. Ich warte auf eine Antwort per E-Mail oder einen Anruf von dir.

Alles Liebe,
deine Caroline

Wortschatz

In der Sprechstunde

die Arbeitsgruppe, -n *study group*
der Dozent, [-en], -en *assistant professor, lecturer (male)*
die Dozentin, -nen *assistant professor, lecturer (female)*
die Folie, -n *overhead transparency*
das Handout, -s *handout*
die Industrie, -n *industry*
das Referat, -e *seminar paper, presentation*
der Seminarraum, ¨-e *seminar room*
die Sprechstunde, -n *office hour*
das Thema, *pl.* **Themen** *topic, theme*
die Europäische Union *European Union*
das Wichtigste *the most important thing*

Verben

an·melden (hat angemeldet) *to announce, register*
bestellen (hat bestellt) *to order, reserve*
dauern (hat gedauert) *to last*
sich entscheiden (hat sich entschieden) für/gegen + *acc. to decide on, against*
sich erinnern (hat sich erinnert) an + *acc. to remember*
sich freuen (hat sich gefreut) auf + *acc. to look forward to*
sich fühlen (hat sich gefühlt) *to feel*
sich hin·legen (hat sich hingelegt) *to lie down*
sich melden (hat sich gemeldet) *to report, show up; get in touch*
sich konzentrieren (hat sich konzentriert) auf + *acc. to concentrate on*
kopieren (hat kopiert) *to copy*
vor·bereiten (hat vorbereitet) *to prepare*
schaffen (hat geschafft) *to manage, get done; to "make it"*

ein Referat halten (hält; hat gehalten) *to make an oral presentation*
Pech haben (hat Pech gehabt) *to have bad luck*

fein *fine*
genau *exact, exactly*
jedenfalls *at any rate, in any case*
maximal *maximally*
nämlich *namely, that is*
zusätzlich *additionally*

Ausdrücke

auf Wiedersehen *good-bye*
bis *until*
bis nächste Woche! *see you next week!*
deswegen *that's why, that's the reason*
herein, bitte! *please come in!*

Das Studium und das Studentenleben

die Anglistik *English language and literature*
der Ansturm, ¨-e *onslaught, rush*
die Aushilfe, -n *temporary hire, part-time worker*
das BAföG *federal tuition assistance, financial aid*
der Ballungsraum, ¨-e *population center*
der Campus *campus*
der Druck *pressure*
der Fachbereich, -e *department; subject area*
die Geduld *patience*
das Glück *good luck*
der Job, -s *job*
das Kleingeld *pocket change*
der Kommilitone, [-n], -n *fellow student (male)*
die Kommilitonin, -nen *fellow student (female)*
der Kontakt, -e *contact*
der Maschinenbau *mechanical engineering*
die Massen-Uni, -s *mega-university*
die Mensa, *pl.* **Mensen** *student dining hall*
die Miete, -n *rent*
die Nähe *vicinity*
der Neubau, -ten *new building*
der Parkplatz, ¨-e *parking space, parking lot*
der Pendler, - *commuter*
der Pluspunkt, -e *advantage, plus*
die Portion, -en *portion*
das Seminar, -e *seminar; department*
der Stadtrand, ¨-er *outskirts of the city*
die Stelle, -n *position, job*
die Hiwi-Stelle, -n *research assistant position*
das Studentenleben *student life*
das Studium, *pl.* **Studien** *studies, attending college*
die Wartezeit, -en *waiting period*
die Wiese, -n *meadow*
der Wohnungsmarkt, ¨-e *real estate market*
das Zelt, -e *tent*

bauen (hat gebaut) *to construct, build*
beziehen (hat bezogen) *to move in*
rechnen (hat gerechnet) mit + *dat. to reckon with, expect*
unter·kommen (ist untergekommen) *to find lodging*
verdienen (hat verdient) *to earn*
wachsen (wächst, ist gewachsen) *to grow*
warten (hat gewartet) auf + *acc. to wait for*
werden (wird, ist geworden) *will, shall [future tense auxiliary]*

allerdings *nonetheless*
ausgesprochen *decidedly*
begrenzt *limited*
bezahlbar *payable*

eher *rather*
erträglich *tolerable, manageable*
exotisch *exotic*
großzügig *generous*
knapp *just barely, almost*
lecker *delicious*
problemlos *without a problem, hassle-free*
rar *rare*
üblich *usual, common*
vorbildlich *exemplary*
wohl *probably; well*
zahllos *innumerable*

Ausdrücke

eingestellt sein *to be geared for, ready for*
pro Stunde *per hour*
rund um *all around*
Spaß machen (hat Spaß gemacht) *to be fun*

Die tägliche Routine

die Routine, -n *routine*

sich ab·trocknen (hat sich abgetrocknet) *to dry off*
sich an·ziehen (hat sich angezogen) *to put on clothes, get dressed*
sich aus·ziehen (hat sich ausgezogen) *to get undressed*
baden (hat gebadet) *to bathe*
sich beeilen (hat sich beeilt) *to hurry*
bürsten: sich die Haare bürsten (hat sich gebürstet) *to brush one's hair*
(sich) duschen (hat [sich] geduscht) *to shower*
gehen: unter die Dusche gehen (ist gegangen) *to take a shower*
föhnen: sich die Haare föhnen (hat sich geföhnt) *to blow-dry one's hair*
kämmen: sich die Haare kämmen (hat sich gekämmt) *to comb one's hair*
putzen: sich die Zähne putzen (hat sich geputzt) *to brush one's teeth*
sich rasieren (hat sich rasiert) *to shave*
sich schminken (hat sich geschminkt) *to put on make-up*
waschen: sich die Haare waschen (wäscht sich, hat sich gewaschen) *to shampoo*

Im Badezimmer

das Badetuch, ¨er *bath towel*
die Badewanne, -n *bathtub*
der Becher, - *cup*
die Bürste, -n *hairbrush*
die Dusche, -n *shower*
der Föhn, -e *blow dryer*
das Haarwaschmittel, - *shampoo*
der Haken, - *hook*
der Kamm, ¨e *comb*
der Rasierapparat, -e *electric razor*
die Seife, -n *soap*
das Shampoo, -s *shampoo*
der Spiegel, - *mirror*
die Steckdose, -n *electric outlet*
das Waschbecken, - *sink*

Krank sein

der Durchfall *diarrhea*
das Fieber *fever, temperature*
der Gips *cast*
das Heftpflaster, - *Band-Aid*
der Muskelkater, - *sore muscle*
die Schmerztablette, -n *painkiller*
der Schmerz, -en *pain*
die Temperatur, -en *temperature*

sich aus·ruhen (hat sich ausgeruht) *to relax*
sich etwas brechen (bricht sich, hat sich gebrochen) *to break*
sich erholen (hat sich erholt) *to recuperate*
sich erkälten (hat sich erkältet) *to catch cold*
sich (krank) fühlen (hat sich gefühlt) *to feel (sick)*
sich hin·legen (hat sich hingelegt) *to lie down*
schneiden: sich in den Finger schneiden (hat sich geschnitten) *to cut one's finger*
sich weh tun (hat sich weh getan) + *dat.* *to hurt (oneself)*
sich übergeben (übergibt sich, hat sich übergeben) *to vomit*

Durchfall haben *to have diarrhea*
Fieber haben *to have a fever*
Gute Besserung! *Speedy recovery! Hope you feel better!*
Halsschmerzen haben *to have a sore throat*
Kopfschmerzen haben *to have a headache*
einen Schnupfen haben *to have a head cold*
Zahnschmerzen haben *to have a toothache*

Idiomatische Zeitausdrücke

heute Morgen *this morning*
heute Nachmittag *this afternoon*
heute Abend *this evening*
morgen *tomorrow*
morgen früh *tomorrow morning*
morgen Nachmittag *tomorrow afternoon*
morgen Abend *tomorrow evening*
übermorgen *the day after tomorrow*

diese Woche *this week*
nächste Woche *next week*
dieses Wochenende *this weekend*
jeden Tag *every day*
nächsten Samstag *next Saturday*
nächstes Jahr *next year*

Verben mit präpositionalem Objekt

Angst haben (hat gehabt) vor + *dat.* *to be afraid of*
sich ärgern (hat sich geärgert) über + *acc.* *to be angry about*
bitten (hat gebeten) um + *acc.* *to ask for, request*

danken (hat gedankt) für + *acc. to thank for*

denken (hat gedacht) an + *acc. to think of*

sich erinnern (hat sich erinnert) an + *acc. to remember*

erzählen (hat erzählt) von + *dat. to talk about, tell a story about*

fragen (hat gefragt) nach + *dat. to ask about*

sich freuen (hat sich gefreut) über + *acc. to be happy about*

gespannt sein auf + *acc. to be excited about*

glauben (hat geglaubt) an + *acc. to believe in*

halten (hält, hat gehalten) von + *dat. to think of, about*

handeln (hat gehandelt) von + *dat. to be about*

rechnen (hat gerechnet) mit + *dat. to reckon with, expect*

reden (hat geredet) über + *acc. to talk about, discuss*

retten (hat gerettet) vor + *dat. to save, rescue from*

sprechen (spricht, hat gesprochen) über + *acc. to talk about, discuss*

sich trennen (hat sich getrennt) von + *dat. to break up with, separate from*

sich verlieben (hat sich verliebt) in + *acc. to fall in love with*

sich vor·bereiten (hat sich vorbereitet) auf + *acc. to prepare for, get ready for*

verstehen (hat verstanden) von + *dat. to know about*

wissen (weiß, hat gewusst) von + *dat. to know about*

Aus dem Zieltext

der Inhalt, -e *content*

der Kurs, -e *course*

die Schlange, -n *waiting line; snake*

die Vorlesung, -en *lecture*

die Weile *awhile*

aus·wählen (hat ausgewählt) *to pick out, select*

klingen (hat geklungen) *to sound*

könnte *could*

passen (hat gepasst) zu + *dat. to suit, fit*

plaudern (hat geplaudert) *to chat*

probieren (hat probiert) *to try*

vor·kommen (ist vorgekommen) + *dat. to appear to be*

wieder·kommen (ist wiedergekommen) *to come back, return*

zu·hören (hat zugehört) + *dat. to listen*

bekannt *familiar*

halt *just*

lahm *weak, boring, lame*

peppig *peppy*

überfüllt *overfilled, oversubscribed*

verschieden *different*

Lust haben *to want, wish*

[in der] Schlange stehen (hat gestanden) *to stand/wait in line*

In this chapter you will continue to learn how to describe people, objects, and activities. You will talk and read about professions, job interviews, and job qualifications.

Kommunikative Funktionen

- Providing additional information about people and topics
- Describing people and things
- Preparing for a job interview
- Expressing the city of origin
- Comparing people and things

Strukturen

- Nominative, accusative, and dative case relative pronouns
- Endings on adjectives preceded by **ein**-words or a definite article
- Forming adjectives from city names
- Comparative and superlative forms of adjectives and adverbs

Vokabeln

- Berufe
- Eigenschaften von jungen Bewerbern

Kulturelles

- Freistaat Sachsen: Leipzig und Dresden
- Sozialleistungen in Deutschland
- Berufswahl und Berufsausbildung in den deutschsprachigen Ländern

Haben diese Leute eine interessante Arbeit?

KAPITEL NEUN

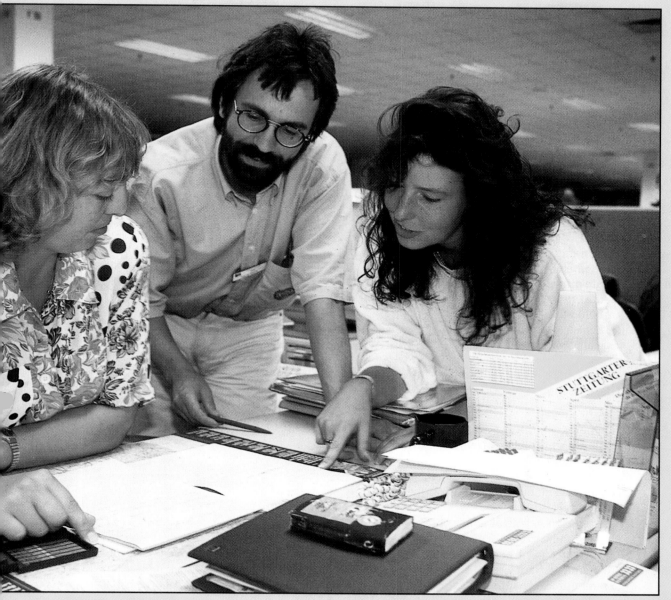

Arbeiten und Geld verdienen

Go to the ***Vorsprung*** Website at
www.hmco.com/college

ANLAUFTEXT

Ich habe morgen ein Vorstellungsgespräch

Barbara bekommt einen Telefonanruf von ihrer Mutter aus Dresden. Frau Müller, die früher als Bibliothekarin° in Chemnitz gearbeitet hat, möchte wieder in ihrem Beruf arbeiten. Sie hat Glück gehabt, denn morgen hat sie ein Interview für eine Stelle° als Bibliothekarin in Dresden. Barbara, die dringend° Geld für ihr Studium braucht, sucht einen Teilzeitjob° in Tübingen, aber sie hat weniger Glück.

librarian
position / urgently
part-time job

Vorschau

1 Thematische Fragen. Beantworten Sie die folgenden Fragen auf Deutsch.

1. Wer hat normalerweise keine Probleme, eine Arbeitsstelle zu finden?
   a. Hausfrauen und Mütter
   b. Studenten mit Diplom
   c. Leute mit viel Arbeitserfahrung° (*work experience*)
   d. Leute ohne Ausbildung° (*training*)
2. Wo arbeitet Ihre Mutter?
   a. zu Hause b. im Büro c. anderswo d. Sie lebt nicht mehr.
3. Hat sie an einer Universität studiert? Was?
4. Hat sie eine Berufsschule besucht?
5. Was sind typische Studentenjobs an Ihrer Uni? Kreuzen Sie für jeden Job die passende Kategorie an.

	Typisch	*Untypisch*	
a. Kellner/Kellnerin	___	___	
b. Tellerwäscher/Tellerwäscherin° im Restaurant/in der Mensa	___	___	*dishwasher*
c. Aushilfe° in einem Kopiergeschäft	___	___	*temporary help*
d. Aushilfe in einem Studentenwohnheim	___	___	
e. Babysitter/-sitterin	___	___	
f. Pizzazusteller/-zustellerin°	___	___	*pizza deliverer*
g. Büroaushilfe	___	___	
h. Mitarbeiter/Mitarbeiterin° in der Unibibliothek	___	___	*co-worker, employee*
i. Reinemachefrau°	___	___	*cleaning lady*
j. Fremdenführer/-führerin°	___	___	*tour guide*

An alle Studierenden:

Wir haben Arbeit nach Maß!

Aushilfskräfte

KARSTADT

Senden Sie uns jetzt Ihre Bewerbung:

KARSTADT AG
Personalabteilung,
Eppendorfer Landstraße 77
20249 Hamburg

2 Auf Jobsuche. Welches Bild passt zu welchem Wort? Schreiben Sie die Nummer von dem Bild in die Lücke.

Auf Jobsuche. The gender of a compound noun is determined by the last noun (e.g., **die Vorstellung** + **das Gespräch** = **das Vorstellungsgespräch**). Occasionally German adds a linking **s** when combining two or more nouns. Sometimes the meaning of a compound word is not clear from the individual parts, e.g., **Studentenarbeits-vermittlung** *(student job office)*, where **Vermittlung** means *facilitating* and not *office.*

___ der Fremdenführer
___ das Fremdenverkehrsbüro°
___ die Tellerwäscherin
___ die Lagerarbeiterin°
___ die Mitarbeiterin
___ die Reinemachefrau
___ der Telefonanruf
___ die Studentenarbeitsvermittlung°
___ das Vorstellungsgespräch

Germans also use the gender-neutral expression, **das Reinigungspersonal.**

tourist office
student job placement office
das Lager: *warehouse*

3 Autogrammspiel: Arbeiten und Geld verdienen. Finden Sie für jede Frage eine Person, die mit **Ja** antwortet. Bitten Sie die Person um ihre Unterschrift.

Wer arbeitet nur im Sommer?

S1: Arbeitest du nur im Sommer?
S2: Ja.
S1: Unterschreib hier bitte. ___________

1. Wer arbeitet nur im Sommer? ___________
2. Wer arbeitet während° des Semesters? ___________
3. Wer arbeitet nur abends? ___________
4. Wer arbeitet nur am Wochenende? ___________
5. Wer arbeitet das ganze Jahr durch? ___________
6. Wer muss gar nicht arbeiten? ___________

during

ANLAUFTEXT

Hören Sie gut zu.

Ich habe morgen ein Vorstellungsgespräch

Rückblick

4 Gesprächspuzzle. Welches von den zehn Bildern passt zu welchem Dialogteil? Schreiben Sie über jeden Dialogteil die passende Bildnummer. Lesen Sie dann die Dialogteile in der richtigen Reihenfolge.

Bild ___

MUTTER: Ist das etwas für dich? …

BARBARA: Ich glaube nicht. Aber ich habe einen Freund, der als Fremdenführer arbeitet.

Bild ___

MUTTER: Die Dresdner Stadtteilbibliothek sucht eine erfahrene Mitarbeiterin, die sich mit Kinderliteratur auskennt°. Das war ja früher mein Fach und so hab' ich mich eben gemeldet. Und jetzt haben sie mich zum Vorstellungsgespräch eingeladen. Toll, nicht?

° *is familiar with*

Bild ___

BARBARA: Müller.

MUTTER: Hallo, Barbara. Ich bin's, Mutti.

German speakers typically answer the phone by stating their last name. This is changing as more people choose to answer with **Hallo** to avoid giving their name over the phone.

Bild ___

BARBARA: Ach, Mutti! Ist zu Hause etwas passiert?

MUTTER: Ja, etwas Gutes. Ich habe morgen ein Vorstellungsgespräch für eine Stelle in einer neuen Stadtteilbibliothek.

BARBARA: Das ist ja fantastisch! Aber seit wann willst du denn wieder arbeiten?

Bild 6

MUTTER: Nee, nee, das hat keinen Zweck°. Du brauchst einen Job, der dir Spaß macht. Kennst du sonst niemanden, der einen guten Job hat?

There's no point to it.

Bild 3

MUTTER: Tja, das war eine ziemlich spontane Idee. Am Wochenende habe ich ein kleines Inserat in der Zeitung gelesen.

Bild 7

BARBARA: Ich habe eine Freundin, die an Wochenenden als Aushilfskellnerin jobbt.

Bild 10

MUTTER: Das klingt schon besser. Bewirb dich beim Fremdenverkehrsbüro – das kann nicht schaden°. Ich drücke dir ganz fest die Daumen°. Und melde° dich, wenn sich etwas ergibt°.

BARBARA: Klar. Tschüss, Mama!

hurt / ***Ich ... Daumen:*** *I'll keep my fingers crossed* / *get in touch* / ***sich ... ergibt:*** *something materializes*

Bild 9

MUTTER: Wer ist das?

BARBARA: Das ist der Karl-Heinz, ein ganz netter Typ. Er trifft die interessantesten Leute bei der Arbeit. Und das ist ein Job, in dem man viel Trinkgeld bekommt. Ein guter Fremdenführer verdient mehr als ein Kellner.

Bild 5

BARBARA: Mutti, das ist genau das Richtige für dich! Ich wünsch' dir alles Gute dabei!

MUTTER: Danke. Und was macht deine Suche nach einem Job?

BARBARA: Bisher nicht viel. Ich bin zur Studentenarbeitsvermittlung gegangen. Aber die Jobs, die sie dort anbieten, sind alle stinklangweilig und unterbezahlt: Reinemachefrau, Tellerwäscherin, Lagerarbeiterin ...

▣ Sprache im Alltag: Wishing someone luck

There are several expressions for wishing people luck in German:

Ich drücke dir die Daumen!	*I'm crossing my fingers for you!*
Hals- und Beinbruch!	*Break a leg!*
Ich wünsch' dir 'was!	*I'm hoping for you!*
Toi, toi, toi!	*Lots of luck!*

Instead of crossing one's fingers, German speakers make a clenched fist enclosing the thumb on the left hand to gesture that they're wishing someone good luck.

---

5 **Stimmt das?** Stimmen diese Aussagen zum Text oder nicht? Wenn nicht, was stimmt?

	Ja, das stimmt.	*Nein, das stimmt nicht.*
1. Frau Müller sucht eine Stelle als Bibliothekarin.	___	___
2. Frau Müller hat im Moment keine Arbeit.	___	___
3. Frau Müller hat von der Arbeitsvermittlung Auskunft° über die Stelle bekommen.	___	___

die Information

	Ja, das stimmt.	*Nein, das stimmt nicht.*
4. Die Bibliothek sucht eine Mitarbeiterin mit Erfahrung.	___	___
5. Barbara sucht einen Job, aber sie findet keine gute Stelle.	___	___
6. Frau Müller meint, Barbara soll Teller waschen.	___	___
7. Barbaras Freund arbeitet am Wochenende mit Touristen.	___	___
8. Karl Heinz verdient viel Geld.	___	___
9. Frau Müller sagt, Barbara soll einen Job beim Fremdenverkehrsbüro suchen.	___	___
10. Frau Müller wünscht Barbara viel Glück.	___	___

6 **Ergänzen Sie.** Ergänzen Sie diese Sätze mit Wörtern aus dem **Anlauftext.**

1. Ach, Mutti, ist zu Hause etwas _____?
2. Ich habe morgen ein _____ für eine Stelle in einer neuen Stadtteilbibliothek.
3. Am Wochenende habe ich ein kleines _____ in der Zeitung gelesen.
4. Die Stadtteilbibliothek sucht eine erfahrene Mitarbeiterin, die sich mit Kinderliteratur _____.
5. Was macht deine _____ nach einem Job?
6. Aber die Jobs, die sie dort anbieten, sind alle _____ und _____.
7. Nee, nee, das hat keinen _____.
8. Du brauchst einen _____, der dir Spaß macht.
9. Ich habe eine Freundin, die an Wochenenden als _____ jobbt.
10. Das ist ein Job, in dem man viel Trinkgeld _____.
11. Ein guter Fremdenführer _____ mehr als ein Kellner.

7 **Kurz gefragt.** Beantworten Sie diese Fragen auf Deutsch.

1. Wer ruft wen an? Warum?
2. Wo hat Frau Müller Auskunft über die Stelle gefunden?
3. Was für eine Stelle sucht Frau Müller?
4. Was für einen Job möchte Barbara in Tübingen finden?
5. Wie beschreibt Barbara die Jobs bei der Studentenarbeitsvermittlung?
6. Was für Jobs haben Barbaras Freunde?
7. Warum ist Karl-Heinz' Job angeblich° besser?
8. Warum soll Barbara zum Fremdenverkehrsbüro gehen?

Kurz gefragt. The apostrophe as indication of the possessive has become more common in German, especially when the noun ends in **s, x,** or **z.**

° *supposedly*

8 **Interview: Studentenjobs.** Stellen Sie einem Partner/einer Partnerin die folgenden Fragen.

1. Hast du einen Job? Ist er gut? Warum? Warum nicht?
2. Welche Studentenjobs sind gut? Welche sind nicht gut? Warum? Warum nicht?
3. Warum arbeiten so viele Studenten heute? Ist das gut? Schlecht?
4. Wie viele Stunden pro Woche sind zu viel für einen Studentenjob?
5. Wie kann man als Student sehr viel Geld verdienen?
6. In welchen Jobs verdient man sehr wenig Geld?

Interview. Jot down notes as your partner answers each of these questions and be prepared to report your findings to the class.

BRENNPUNKT KULTUR

Freistaat Sachsen: Leipzig und Dresden

Dresden, where Barbara's mother lives, is in the Free State of Saxony **(der Freistaat Sachsen),** which borders Poland and the Czech Republic. With a population of 4.5 million and a rapidly improving infrastructure, Saxony is well positioned to compete economically. It is also the home of two of the most important and vibrant cities in eastern Germany, Leipzig and Dresden.

Leipzig, with 457,000 inhabitants, is located at the intersection of two important medieval trade routes, making it a natural center for the exchange of ideas and for East-West trade. Leipzig is also home to Germany's second oldest university.

Johann Sebastian Bach served the city of Leipzig as choirmaster **(Kantor)** from 1723 until his death in 1750, directing the famous boys' choir, **der Thomanerchor,** at the **Thomaskirche,** and playing the organ at the Church of St. Nicholas **(die Nikolaikirche).** In 1989, the **Nikolaikirche** was the site of the "Monday demonstrations" which ultimately brought down the German Democratic Republic and led to unification with then West Germany.

Dresden, the capital of Saxony **(Sachsen),** is located on the banks of the Elbe River and is known as **das deutsche Florenz** for the beauty of its art collections and architectural treasures. On February 13–14, 1945, Dresden was the target of Allied fire bombing attacks. The bombing left more than 35,000 civilians dead and completely destroyed large parts of the city. In the decades after WWII, the East German government slowly reconstructed such architectural masterpieces as the Semper Opera House **(die Semperoper), die Brühlsche Terrasse** along the Elbe River, and **der Zwinger,** an elaborate complex of baroque pavilions, galleries, and gardens built by Saxony's ruler **August der Starke** (1670–1733). Today the Zwinger is home to many art treasures and exhibits of the world-famous **Meißner Porzellan.** The ruins of the **Frauenkirche** served as a reminder of WWII for many years. The church is now being reconstructed.

Companies such as Audi, Zeiss, and Melitta Coffee, and inventions such as the single-reflex camera, the washing machine, the tea bag, the coffee filter, and toothpaste all hail from Saxony.

Famous graduates of Leipzig's university include the philosopher and mathematician Baron Gottfried Wilhelm von Leibnitz, the writer Gotthold Ephraim Lessing, and the philosopher Friedrich Nietzsche.

Creative genius has always thrived in Dresden. The composers Carl Maria von Weber, Robert Schumann, and Richard Wagner were born there, as was the German Romantic painter Caspar David Friedrich. ***Die Brücke,*** the art movement (German Expressionist) was started here in 1905 by Ernst Ludwig Kirchner, Karl Schmidt-Rottluff, Fritz Bleyl, and Erich Heckel.

Der Zwinger in Dresden

Die Semperoper in Dresden beim Sonnenuntergang

Strukturen und Vokabeln

I Providing additional information about topics

A. *Nominative case relative pronouns*

A relative clause **(der Relativsatz)** provides additional information about topics mentioned in the main clause.

relative clause
Ich habe eine Freundin, die an Wochenenden als Aushilfskellnerin jobbt.
I have a girlfriend who works as a temporary waitress on weekends.

A relative clause always has a relative pronoun **(das Relativpronomen),** which comes at or near the very beginning of the relative clause. The relative pronoun (e.g., **die**) always refers back to a preceding noun in the sentence (e.g., **eine Freundin**). This noun is known as the antecedent **(das Bezugswort).** The gender and number of the relative pronoun are taken from the antecedent. A relative clause is formed from an independent sentence. Using a relative clause enables the writer or speaker to avoid unnecessary repetition of the noun substituted by the relative pronoun, and produces a more sophisticated style.

masculine, singular
Ich habe einen Freund. Mein Freund arbeitet als Fremdenführer.
I have a friend. My friend works as a tour guide.

Ich habe **einen Freund, der** als Fremdenführer arbeitet.
I have a friend who works as a tour guide.

When the relative pronoun is the subject of the relative clause, the relative pronoun appears in the nominative case. German uses three different relative pronouns in the nominative case, depending on the gender and number of the noun-antecedent: **der, das,** and **die**.

In English, relative clauses are formed with either *whom (who)* or *that.*

Masculine singular (e.g.,* der Job*)

Du brauchst einen Job, **der** dir Spaß macht.	*You need a job that is fun for you.*

Neuter singular (e.g.,* das Auto*)

Ich habe ein Auto gekauft, **das** gar nicht so teuer war.	*I bought a car that was not at all expensive.*

Feminine singular (e.g.,* die Mitarbeiterin*)

Die Bibliothek sucht eine erfahrene Mitarbeiterin, **die** sich mit Kinderliteratur auskennt.	*The library is looking for an experienced co-worker who is familiar with children's literature.*

Plural (e.g.,* die Jobs*)

Aber Jobs, **die** interessant sind, sind relativ selten.	*But jobs that are interesting are relatively rare.*

As with other subordinate clauses **(der Nebensatz),** German speakers place the conjugated verb at the end of the relative clause. In written German, a comma sets off the relative clause from the main clause.

Du brauchst einen Job**,** der dir Spaß **macht.**	*You need a job that is fun for you.*

All relative clauses in German are set off with commas. In English only non-restrictive relative clauses, e.g., those which can be eliminated, have commas: *Barbara, whom everybody knows, was elected president of the class.*

9 **Definitionen.** Definieren Sie die fett gedruckten Wörter. Verbinden Sie jeden Hauptsatz in der linken Spalte mit einem passenden Relativsatz in der rechten Spalte.

1. Eine **Stadtteilbibliothek** ist eine Bibliothek,	a. die mit anderen Menschen zusammenarbeitet.
2. Eine **Mitarbeiterin** ist eine Arbeiterin,	b. der ab und zu° als Kellner arbeitet.
3. **Kinderliteratur** ist Literatur,	c. die im Lager° arbeiten.
4. Ein **Fremdenführer** ist ein Mann,	d. die Häuser sauber machen.
5. Ein **Aushilfskellner** ist ein Kellner,	e. der Touristen die Stadt zeigt.
	f. die das Geschirr wäscht.
6. **Reinemachefrauen** sind Frauen,	g. die von der Stadt geleitet wird°.
7. Eine **Geschirrspülmaschine** ist eine Maschine,	h. die für Kinder geschrieben ist.
8. **Lagerarbeiter** sind Männer,	

ab … zu: *now and then*

warehouse

geleitet wird: *is run by*

10 **Was für ein Job ist das?** Beschreiben Sie die Jobs der folgenden Personen mit Hilfe der Informationen in der rechten Spalte.

1. Ich habe einen Job,	der/die mir/ihm/ihr Spaß macht.
2. Ich möchte eine Stelle haben,	der/die hart und langweilig ist.
3. Mein Freund hat einen Job,	der/die interessant ist.
4. Meine Freundin hat eine Arbeit,	der/die viel Kreativität verlangt°.
5. Mein Vater hat einen Job,	der/die ein gutes Gehalt° bietet°.
	der/die …

requires

wage / offers

Wissenswerte Vokabeln: Berufe

Talking about occupations

der Automechaniker/die Automechanikerin

der Koch/die Köchin

der Kellner/die Kellnerin

der Bäcker/die Bäckerin

der Fleischer, der Metzger/die Fleischerin, die Metzgerin

der Arzt/die Ärztin

der Zahnarzt/die Zahnärztin

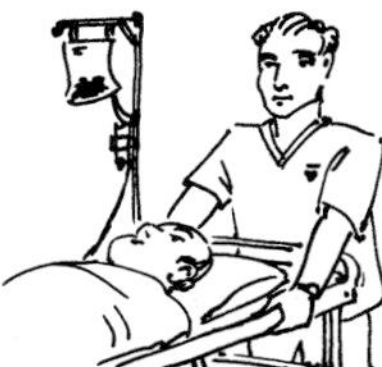
der Krankenpfleger/die Krankenschwester

der Apotheker/die Apothekerin

der Tierarzt/die Tierärztin

der Friseur/die Friseurin

der Lehrer/die Lehrerin

der Berater/die Beraterin

der Chef/die Chefin

der Geschäftsmann/die Geschäftsfrau

der Kaufmann/die Kauffrau

W. Vok. Additional professions include: **der Schauspieler/die Schauspielerin** *(actor/actress)*, **der Regisseur/die Regisseurin** *(film or play director)*, **der Politiker/die Politikerin** *(politician)*, **der Musiker/die Musikerin** *(musician)*, **der Sänger/die Sängerin** *(singer)*, **der Komponist/die Komponistin** *(composer)*, **der Dirigent/die Dirigentin** *(orchestra conductor)*, **der Künstler/die Künstlerin** *(artist)*, **der Wissenschaftler/die Wissenschaftlerin** *(scientist)*, **der Journalist/die Journalistin** *(journalist)*, **der Arbeiter/die Arbeiterin** *(worker)*, **der Schriftsteller/die Schriftstellerin** *(author)*, **der Dichter, Poet/die Dichterin** *(poet)*, **der Filmemacher/die Filmemacherin** *(filmmaker)*, **der Bauer/die Bäuerin,** *(farmer)*.

When naming a person's profession, German speakers omit the indefinite article **ein/eine,** e.g., **Er ist Arzt.** *(He's a doctor.)*. When describing specifics about a person's professional skills, they use an article before the adjective e.g., **Er ist mein neuer Arzt.** *(He's my new doctor.)*.

der Sekretär/die Sekretärin

der Verkäufer/die Verkäuferin

der Architekt/die Architektin

der Ingenieur/die Ingenieurin

An older term for **die Friseurin** is **die Friseuse**.

der Programmierer/die Programmiererin

der Makler/die Maklerin

der Rechtsanwalt/die Rechtsanwältin

der Beamte/die Beamtin

▣ Wer unterrichtet Deutsch? *Der Lehrer oder die Lehrerin.*

11 Berufe. Was ist z.B. ein Kellner? Geben Sie zusammen mit einem Partner/einer Partnerin Definitionen für diese Berufe.

▣ S1: Was ist ein Kellner?
S2: Ein Kellner ist ein Mann, der im Restaurant das Essen serviert.

1. Kellner
2. Lehrerin
3. Bäcker
4. Beraterin
5. Ärztin
6. Bibliothekarin
7. Taxifahrer
8. Architekt
9. Tierarzt
10. Verkäuferin

anderen Menschen Ratschläge geben
Brot und Brötchen backen
Bücher verleihen° (°loan out)
im Krankenhaus arbeiten
im Restaurant das Essen servieren
etwas im Geschäft verkaufen
in einer Schule unterrichten
Pläne für Häuser zeichnen
Leute in der Stadt herumfahren
kranke Tiere behandeln

12 Autogrammspiel: Was möchten Sie werden? Finden Sie für jede Frage eine Person, die mit **Ja** antwortet. Bitten Sie die Person um ihre Unterschrift.

▣ S1: Möchtest du Lehrer/Lehrerin werden?
S2: Ja.
S1: Unterschreib hier bitte. __________

1. Lehrer/Lehrerin __________
2. Architekt/Architektin __________
3. Arzt/Ärztin __________
4. Ingenieur/Ingenieurin __________
5. Geschäftsmann/Geschäftsfrau __________
6. Kaufmann/Kauffrau __________
7. Krankenpfleger/Krankenschwester __________
8. Rechtsanwalt/Rechtsanwältin __________
9. Programmierer/Programmiererin __________
10. Künstler/Künstlerin° __________

artist

B. Accusative case relative pronouns

In the preceding activities you practiced the use of the relative pronoun in the nominative case, when it functions as the subject of the relative clause.

Ein Mann, **der** Brot bäckt, ist ein Bäcker.

You should be able to recognize the use of relative pronouns in the accusative and dative cases.

When a relative pronoun functions as a direct object, it is in the accusative case.

Der Mann kommt aus Algerien. Barbara hat **den Mann** bei der Arbeit kennen gelernt.
The man is from Algeria. Barbara met the man at work.

Der Mann, **den** Barbara bei der Arbeit kennen gelernt hat, kommt aus Algerien.
The man, whom Barbara met at work, is from Algeria.

C. Dative case relative pronouns

A relative pronoun may also replace a noun in the dative case. Frequently the relative pronoun functions as the indirect object of the relative clause. Relative pronouns used with prepositions are explained below in section D.

Remember that the dative case is used with the prepositions **aus, außer, bei, mit, nach, seit, von, zu,** and **gegenüber.**

Der Mann ist Herr Kronemeyer. Wir geben **dem Mann** die Materialien.
The man is Mr. Kronemeyer. We are giving the materials to the man.

Der Mann, **dem** wir die Materialien geben, ist Herr Kronemeyer.
The man, who(m) we are giving the materials to, is Mr. Kronemeyer.

This is a summary chart of the relative pronouns.

	Masculine	Neuter	Feminine	Plural
Nominative	der	das	die	die
Accusative	den	das	die	die
Dative	dem	dem	der	denen

Note that most forms of the relative pronouns are identical to the forms of the definite articles. Like the definite articles, all relative pronouns begin with the letter **d.** The forms that differ are **denen** and the genitive forms, which are introduced in Chapter 10.

13 **Im Büro.** Verbinden Sie einen Hauptsatz in der linken Spalte mit einem passenden Relativsatz in der rechten Spalte.

Ist das der neue Kollege, den wir gestern in der Kantine getroffen haben?

1. Ist das der neue Kollege,
2. Wo ist der neue Computer,
3. Herr Diehl, haben Sie das Inserat geschrieben,
4. Frau Albrecht, hier sind die Formulare,
5. Frau Anders, geben Sie mir bitte den Brief für die Firma Stoll,
6. Ich suche das kurze Fax,
7. Ach, Herr Siegebert. Wie heißt denn dieser Mann in Bad Godesberg,

a. den Herr Tingelmann gestern bei Siemens gekauft hat?
b. das wir in die Zeitung setzen wollen?
c. die wir heute losschicken müssen.
d. das gerade aus New York angekommen ist.
e. den Sie gestern getippt haben.
f. dem wir den Auftrag° für die Fotokopierer gegeben haben?
g. den wir gestern in der Kantine getroffen haben?

contract, order

D. Relative pronouns after prepositions

You have learned that a relative pronoun can function as a subject, a direct object, or an indirect object in a relative clause. A relative pronoun can also replace a noun after a preposition and then appears in the case required by that preposition.

***Accusative prepositions* (durch, für, gegen, ohne, um):**

Das ist die Stelle, **für die** ich morgen ein Vorstellungsgespräch habe.
That's the position for which I have an interview tomorrow.

***Dative prepositions* (aus, außer, bei, mit, nach, seit, von, zu):**

Klein und Co. ist die Firma, **bei der** er früher gearbeitet hat.
Klein & Co. is the company that he used to work for.
Das sind die Produkte, **mit denen** wir den Preis gewinnen wollen.
Those are the products with which we want to win the prize.

***Two-case prepositions* (an, auf, hinter, in, neben, über, unter, vor, zwischen):**

Das ist ein Job, in **dem** man viel Trinkgeld bekommt.
That's a job in which one gets a lot of tips.
Das ist eine Karriere, **an die** ich gedacht habe.
That's a career (that) I've thought about.

Note that in German the preposition and the relative pronoun must always appear together at the beginning of the relative clause and can never be separated as in this English example: **Heidelberg ist eine Stadt, von der man viel hört.** (*Heidelberg is a city* that *one hears a lot* about.)

The interrogative **wo** often replaces the preposition **in** and the relative pronoun in spoken German.

Das ist ein Job, **in dem** man viel Trinkgeld bekommt.
Das ist ein Job, **wo** man viel Trinkgeld bekommt.

14 **Richtig bewerben.** Hier sind drei Anzeigen aus einem Magazin. Identifizieren Sie in jedem Satz das Relativpronomen und das Bezugswort.

Das ist ein Job, in dem man viel Trinkgeld bekommt.
Relativpronomen: *dem*
Bezugswort: *Job*

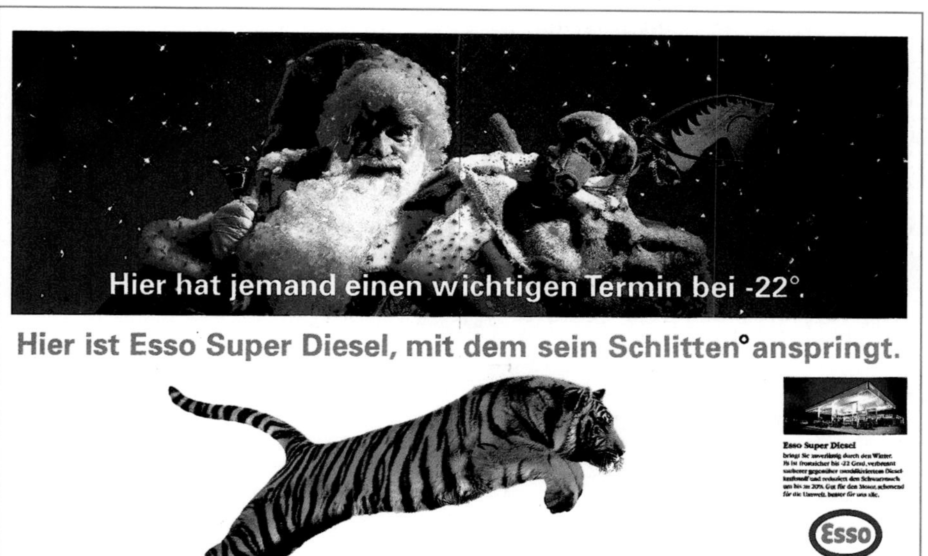

sled (informal for "car")

1.

Relativpronomen: ______
Bezugswort: ______

Die Weihnachtskarte, über die man sich ein ganzes Jahr lang freut.

Unternehmen Zukunft
Deutsche Bahn DB

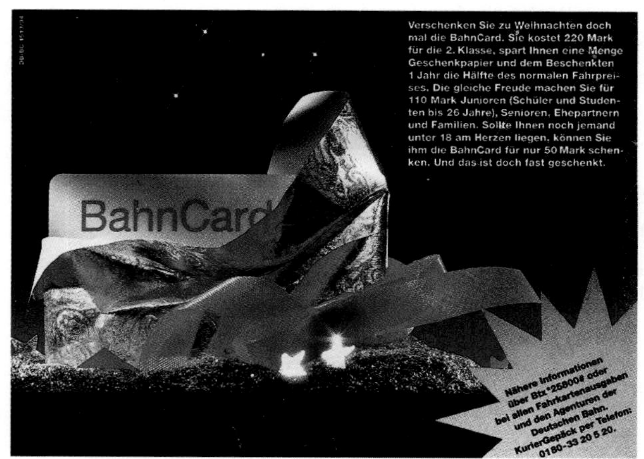

2.

Relativpronomen: ______
Bezugswort: ______

3.

Relativpronomen: ______
Bezugswort: ______

15 **Definitionen.** Definieren Sie die fett gedruckten Wörter. Verbinden Sie jeden Hauptsatz in der linken Spalte mit einem passenden Relativsatz in der rechten Spalte.

1. Ein **Teilzeitjob** ist ein Job,
2. Ein **Inserat** ist eine Annonce in der Zeitung,
3. Ein **Vorstellungsgespräch** ist ein Gespräch,
4. **Kinderliteratur** ist Literatur,
5. Eine **Bibliothek** ist ein Gebäude°, *building*
6. Die **Studentenarbeitsvermittlung** ist ein Amt°, *agency*
7. Ein **Mitarbeiter** ist ein Mann,
8. Eine **Chefin** ist eine Frau,

a. für die man arbeitet.
b. in der man Geschichten für und über Kinder finden kann.
c. aus der man Informationen über Stellen bekommt.
d. mit dem man arbeitet.
e. auf dem Studenten Informationen und Jobs finden können.
f. in dem man nicht die volle Arbeitswoche arbeitet.
g. in dem man Bücher ausleihen kann.
h. in dem man sich vorstellt.

FREIE KOMMUNIKATION

Jeopardy. Teilen Sie die Klasse in zwei Gruppen auf. Jede Person in der Gruppe spielt abwechselnd° für die Gruppe. Der Dozent/Die Dozentin sagt ein Kompositum und ein Spieler aus jeder Gruppe meldet sich, wenn er/sie das Kompositum mit einem Relativsatz definieren kann. Die richtige Antwort muss eine Frage sein. *alternatingly*

LEHRER(IN): Personenwagen
S1: Wie heißt ein Wagen, in dem Personen fahren?

Schreibecke **Die Übersetzung°.** Sie arbeiten als Englischübersetzer/-übersetzerin in einer Werbeagentur°. Ihr Kollege Herr Neumeier hat Sie gebeten, die folgenden englischen Ausdrücke auf Deutsch zu erklären. Schreiben Sie ihm eine Mitteilung°, in der Sie kurze, einfache Definitionen geben.

translation
advertising agency
memo

An: Herrn Neumeier
Anbei sind die Definitionen der englischen Ausdrücke, die Sie mir gestern geschickt haben.

desktop computer: Das ist ein Computer, der ...

desktop computer: (der Computer)	*high-speed modem:* (das Modem)
freeware: (die Software)	*computer nerd:* (die Person)
color monitor: (der Monitor)	*help line:* (die Telefonnummer)

BRENNPUNKT KULTUR

Sozialleistungen in Deutschland

Germany has a long tradition of social security dating back to the 1880s. Laws enacted at that time laid the foundation for today's federally mandated health insurance, accident insurance, disability insurance, old-age pension insurance, as well as unemployment benefits, child allowance, and rent subsidies.

Pension insurance **(die Rentenversicherung)** covers all wage and salary earners. The self-employed can join voluntarily. Male retirees **(die Rentner)**, and women, as of 1996, receive a pension at age 65, and in some cases at age 60. It amounts to 70% of their net salary. All citizens are covered by federal or privately purchased health insurance **(die Krankenversicherung)**, which pays for the costs of physician fees, some dentist fees, drugs, and hospitalization. Co-payments are considerably lower than in most health maintenance programs in the U.S.A. Unemployment insurance **(die Arbeitslosenversicherung)** is obligatory for all workers, except professional civil servants. Employers and employees split the premium equally. The benefit can be as much as 68% of the net pay and is paid for a maximum of one year. Thereafter, an unemployed person can receive unemployment support **(die Arbeitslosenunterstützung)**, which can amount to 58% of the net pay.

Additional benefits include subsidies for children **(das Kindergeld)**, which are paid monthly to parents, regardless of income level. As of 1998, parents receive 220 marks for the first child, 220 marks more for the second child, 300 marks more for the third child, and 350 marks more for the fourth and any additional children. Victims of the war — war-disabled veterans, their widows and orphans — as well as disabled **Bundeswehr** servicemen receive pensions, therapy, and occupational training support. In addition, all residents, native or foreign-born, who experience financial hardship, are entitled to welfare grants, most of which are provided by the state and local governments.

Diese deutschen Rentner und Rentnerinnen genießen einen hohen Lebensstandard.

ABSPRUNGTEXT

Richtig bewerben: Vorstellungsgespräch

Frau Müller will wieder arbeiten gehen und hat ein Vorstellungsgespräch für eine Stelle als Bibliothekarin in Dresden. Sie weiß, dass sie einen guten Eindruck machen muss, und bereitet sich auf das Gespräch gut vor°. Im folgenden Artikel für Auszubildende erfahren° Sie, wie man sich am besten in einem Interview präsentiert.

bereitet sich vor: *is preparing / find out*

Vorschau

16 Thematische Fragen. Beantworten Sie die folgenden Fragen auf Deutsch.

1. In welchen Situationen hat man ein Interview?
2. Erinnern Sie sich an Ihr letztes Interview. Wo waren Sie? Mit wem haben Sie gesprochen? Was war der Grund für das Interview? Wie lange hat es gedauert?
3. Wie kann man sich auf ein Vorstellungsgespräch für einen Job gut vorbereiten?

17 Wie soll ich mich vorbereiten? Sie haben morgen ein Vorstellungsgespräch. Was ist für Sie wichtig?

	Wichtig	*Unwichtig*
1. Ich muss mich gut vorbereiten.	___	___
2. Ich soll nicht zu viel daran denken.	___	___
3. Ich muss neue Kleidung kaufen.	___	___
4. Ich soll heute Abend früh ins Bett gehen.	___	___
5. Ich werde pünktlich in der Firma sein.	___	___
6. Ich werde mir zu Hause die Fragen überlegen, die ich stellen möchte.	___	___

	Wichtig	*Unwichtig*
7. Ich werde mich in der Bibliothek über die Firma informieren.	___	___
8. Ich werde mir zu Hause überlegen, warum ich mich für diese Stelle bewerben möchte. Ich werde auch meine Antwort zu Hause aufschreiben.	___	___
9. Ich werde Interesse an der Firma zeigen. Wenn ich eine Frage nicht verstehe, werde ich noch einmal fragen.	___	___
10. Wenn ich nervös bin, werde ich es zugeben°.	___	___

admit

18 Lesestrategien. Richtig bewerben: Vorstellungsgespräch. Benutzen Sie die Lesestrategien aus Kapitel 7, um den **Absprungtext** zu verstehen.

1. **Den Kontext verstehen.** Finden Sie im Text Antworten auf die folgenden Fragen.
   a. Wie heißt eine Person, die ein Vorstellungsgespräch führt?
   b. Wer ist Michael Schäfer? Wer ist Jochen Turbanski?
   c. Wo ist Michael Schäfer? Wo ist Jochen Turbanski?
   d. Was sind sie von Beruf?
   e. Warum geht man zu einem Berufsberater°?
   f. Welche Themen besprechen sie im Interview?

career counselor

2. **Neue Wörter lernen: erster Versuch.** Erraten Sie aus dem Kontext, was die fett gedruckten Wörter bedeuten.

   a. Wer kennt nicht dieses **Gefühl** – das Herz **pocht** etwas stärker.

   Im Interview wird man schnell nervös. Ist Nervosität ein Gefühl oder nur eine Idee? Assoziiert man das Herz oder den Kopf mit einem Gefühl? Was macht das Herz, wenn man nervös ist? **Gefühl** bedeutet wahrscheinlich ____; **pocht** bedeutet wahrscheinlich ____.

   b. Michael Schäfer ... weiß, wie man die **Aufregung** vor einem Vorstellungsgespräch **abbauen** kann.

   Aufregung ist Nervosität. Will man im Interview mehr oder weniger Aufregung haben? Das Verb **abbauen** bedeutet wahrscheinlich ____.

   c. Zunächst die Kleidung: Man muss sich nicht **übermäßig herausputzen.**

   Das Thema hier ist Kleidung. Was macht man normalerweise mit Kleidung? **Übermäßig herausputzen** bedeutet:
   □ sich zu schlecht anziehen □ sich zu gut anziehen

   d. Aber es müssen auch nicht die **abgetragenen** Jeans sein ...

   Jeans, die man jeden Tag trägt, werden mit der Zeit kaputt. Sind **abgetragene** Jeans schön? Das Adjektiv **abgetragen** bedeutet wahrscheinlich ____.

Die Jeans is plural here. It is also frequently used in the singular.

   e. Noch wichtiger als die Kleidung: dass man **hellwach** und in guter Verfassung ist. Also früh ins Bett ...

   Wenn man aufwacht, steht man auf. **Müde** und **verschlafen°** bedeuten das Gegenteil von **hellwach.** Wie fühlt man sich, wenn man lange und gut geschlafen hat? Das Adjektiv **hellwach** bedeutet wahrscheinlich ____.

sleepy

3. **Strategien verwenden.** Versuchen Sie, die fett gedruckten Wörter zu erraten. Benutzen Sie die Strategien, die Sie in Kapitel 7 gelernt haben, und wählen Sie die korrekte Antwort, oder beenden Sie den Satz mit der richtigen Wortform.

Strategie 1: Weltwissen

a. Aber es müssen auch nicht die abgetragenen Jeans sein, in denen man sich dem Personalchef oder dem **Ausbildungsleiter** eines Betriebes präsentiert.
   □ eine Person mit Autorität □ ein Mitarbeiter

Strategie 2: Kontext

a. Noch wichtiger als die Kleidung: dass man **hellwach und in guter Verfassung** ist.
   □ frisch und robust □ müde und verschlafen

b. Hat man sich vorher über den **Betrieb** informiert und fragt gezielt°, dann zeigt man Interesse: ein großes Plus. *specifically*
   □ das Essen in der Kantine □ die Firma

c. Wer den Grund für die Wahl des Ausbildungsberufs einmal aufgeschrieben hat, dem **fällt** im Bewerbungsgespräch mit Sicherheit etwas **ein.**
   □ hat eine Idee □ fällt hin oder stolpert° *stumbles*

d. Wichtig ist aber vor allem, dass ich mich mit dem Bewerber oder der Bewerberin **unterhalten** kann.
   □ wohnen □ sprechen

e. Wer Interesse hat, lernt in der Ausbildung und **schafft** später den Abschluss°. *degree, diploma*
   □ macht □ macht kaputt

f. Schlimm ist nur, wenn jemand **sich verschließt** und gar nichts mehr sagt.
   □ keine Reaktion hat □ offen bleibt

Strategie 3: Wortformen

a. Wer auf die letzte Minute **angerannt** kommt …
   Angerannt kommt von dem Verb _____ und bedeutet *schnell gelaufen.*

b. … dass ich mich mit dem **Bewerber** oder der **Bewerberin** unterhalten kann.
   Bewerber/Bewerberin kommt von dem Verb **sich** _____. Ein Bewerber/Eine Bewerberin ist eine Person, die sich für eine Arbeit _____.

c. Wer Interesse hat, lernt in der Ausbildung und schafft später den **Abschluss.**
   Abschluss kommt von dem Verb _____ und bedeutet, dass man etwas
   □ beginnt. □ beendet.

d. Dafür hat jeder **Verständnis.**
   Verständnis kommt von dem Verb _____. Wenn man etwas _____, hat man **Verständnis** dafür.

e. Man kann doch einfach sagen, dass man jetzt **aufgeregt** ist.
   Aufgeregt kommt von dem Verb **sich** _____ und bedeutet, dass man nervös ist.

ABSPRUNGTEXT

Richtig bewerben: Vorstellungsgespräch

Read through the entire text once without trying to figure out unfamiliar words.

Lesen Sie jetzt den Text.

Die Bewerbungen um eine Ausbildungsstelle sind verschickt – dann liegt die erste Einladung zu einem Vorstellungsgespräch im Briefkasten. Jetzt kommt's drauf an.

RICHTIG BEWERBEN

Vorstellungsgespräch

Wer kennt nicht dieses Gefühl – das Herz pocht etwas stärker, die Sätze gehen nicht ganz so flüssig über die Lippen, und am liebsten wäre man ganz woanders. Nur – bei einem Vorstellungsgespräch kann man nicht einfach aufstehen und „Bis dann!" sagen. Was tun?

Michael Schäfer, Berufsberater in Berlin, weiß, wie man die Aufregung vor einem Vorstellungsgespräch abbauen kann. Sein Rat: „Bereite Dich auf das Gespräch gut vor!"

Zunächst die Kleidung: Man muß sich nicht übermäßig herausputzen – dann fühlt man sich nicht wohl. Aber es müssen auch nicht die abgetragenen Jeans sein, in denen man sich dem Personalchef oder dem Ausbildungsleiter eines Betriebes präsentiert.

Gezielt vorbereiten

Noch wichtiger als die Kleidung: daß man hellwach und in guter Verfassung ist. Also früh ins Bett vor dem Vorstellungsgespräch und genügend Zeit für den Anfahrtsweg eingeplant. Wer auf die letzte Minute angerannt kommt, hat gute Chancen, einen konfusen Eindruck zu hinterlassen. Michael Schäfer: „Am besten ist man 15 Minuten vor der Zeit bei der Firma. Wer eine halbe Stunde vorher da ist, kann ja noch einen kurzen Spaziergang machen."

Eine gute Hilfe für das Bewerbungsgespräch: Zu Hause überlegen, welche Fragen man dem Personalchef zum Betrieb stellen möchte. Hat man sich vorher über den Betrieb informiert und fragt gezielt, dann zeigt man Interesse: ein großes Plus. Natürlich wird jeder Personalchef fragen, warum man sich für diese Ausbildung beworben hat. Vielleicht auch: Warum gerade bei diesem Betrieb? Darauf kann man sich schon zu Hause eine Antwort überlegen. Wer den Grund für die Wahl des Ausbildungsberufs einmal aufgeschrieben hat, dem fällt im Bewerbungsgespräch mit Sicherheit etwas ein.

Interesse zeigen

Was wird von einem Jugendlichen erwartet, der sich bei Ihnen bewirbt? Jochen Turbanski, Leiter der Aus- und Weiterbildung bei der STILL GmbH, lacht: „Ganz normale Jugendliche sollen es sein!"

„Wichtig ist aber vor allem, daß ich mich mit dem Bewerber oder der Bewerberin unterhalten kann. Fragt der Jugendliche nach, wenn er etwas nicht verstanden hat? Versucht er, Antworten auf meine Fragen zu finden?" So beschreibt Jochen Turbanski seine Erwartungen. Denn wer nachfragt, zeigt Interesse. Wer Interesse hat, lernt in der Ausbildung und schafft später den Abschluß. Natürlich sollte der Jugendliche auch sagen können, was er gerade an dem Ausbildungsberuf interessant findet, für den er sich bewirbt.

Was tun, wenn man nervös wird? „Ich war bei meinen eigenen Bewerbungen auch aufgeregt," erinnert sich der Ausbildungsleiter. „Man kann doch einfach sagen, daß man jetzt aufgeregt ist. Dafür hat jeder Verständnis. Schlimm ist nur, wenn jemand sich verschließt und gar nichts mehr sagt."

Rückblick

19 Inhaltsanalyse. Der Text besteht aus drei Teilen: aus einer Einführung und zwei weiteren Teilen mit Titeln. Die Titel sind gleichzeitig Tipps für Bewerber. Welchem Teil sind die folgenden Themen untergeordnet? Kreuzen Sie den richtigen Titel an.

	Einführung	*„Gezielt vorbereiten"*	*„Interesse zeigen"*
1. früh ins Bett gehen	___	___	___
2. gute Kleidung tragen	___	___	___
3. gute Fragen stellen	___	___	___
4. gute Antworten geben	___	___	___
5. über den Ausbildungsberuf sprechen	___	___	___
6. sich über den Betrieb informieren	___	___	___
7. früh zum Interview kommen	___	___	___

20 Stimmt das? Stimmen diese Aussagen zum Text oder nicht? Wenn nicht, was stimmt?

	Ja, das stimmt.	*Nein, das stimmt nicht.*	
1. Wenn man im Interview nervös ist, kann man nicht so fließend sprechen.	___	___	
2. Es ist erlaubt°, in einem Interview sehr informell zu sein.	___	___	*permitted*
3. Der beste Plan für ein Interview ist sich gut vorzubereiten.	___	___	
4. Man kann ruhig alte Jeans und ein T-Shirt zum Vorstellungsgespräch tragen.	___	___	
5. Man soll vor dem Vorstellungsgespräch genug schlafen.	___	___	
6. Wer nicht pünktlich zum Interview kommt, kann einen konfusen Eindruck machen.	___	___	
7. Es macht immer einen positiven Eindruck, wenn man ein paar intelligente, gut informierte Fragen stellen kann.	___	___	
8. Es ist eine gute Idee, die Antworten zu möglichen Interviewfragen zu Hause aufzuschreiben.	___	___	
9. Es ist vor allem wichtig, dass man im Interview nicht zu viele Fragen stellt.	___	___	
10. Wenn man im Interview aufgeregt und nervös wird, soll man das zugeben und sagen, dass man jetzt aufgeregt ist.	___	___	

21 Ergänzen Sie. Ergänzen Sie diese Sätze mit Wörtern aus dem **Absprungtext.**

1. Michael Schäfer ist ____ in Berlin.
2. Er weiß, wie man die ____ vor einem Vorstellungsgespräch abbaut.
3. Wenn man sich zu sehr herausputzt, fühlt man sich nicht ____.
4. In einem Interview spricht man mit dem Personalchef oder dem Ausbildungsleiter von dem ____.
5. Wer zu spät angerannt kommt, kann einen konfusen ____ hinterlassen.

6. Man soll sich zu Hause überlegen, welche Fragen man dem Personalchef _____ möchte.
7. Jeder Personalchef wird fragen, warum man sich für diese Stelle _____ hat.
8. Wer einmal den Grund für die Wahl aufgeschrieben hat, dem _____ im Interview gewiss etwas _____.
9. Wichtig ist vor allem, dass man sich mit dem Bewerber oder der Bewerberin _____ kann.
10. Wer sich über den Betrieb informiert hat und gezielt Fragen stellt, zeigt _____.

BRENNPUNKT KULTUR

Berufswahl und Berufsausbildung in deutschsprachigen Ländern

Students in Germany, Austria, and Switzerland are trained in a profession that they will most likely have for life. Occupational choices come early in school. During the third and fourth grades in Germany, parents and teachers decide if students will go to **die Hauptschule, die Realschule,** or **das Gymnasium.**

German businesses, government, and schools collaborate closely to provide thorough vocational and academic training for **Hauptschüler,** who will learn manual trades, or for **Realschüler,** who seek administrative positions. This close collaboration ensures a skilled workforce and streamlines the vocational education that students receive.

In an on-the-job apprenticeship (**die Lehre** or **die Ausbildung**) an apprentice from the **Hauptschule** (**der Lehrling** or **der/die Auszubildende, Azubi**) learns his or her trade in three years. Only about one-third of all apprentices get placed in their first choice of fields, while many others must pursue careers in new fields. During this time apprentices are paid a trainee wage that increases annually. They must also attend academic classes at a school **(die Berufsschule)** one or two days a week. There they take courses in their specialty along with courses in German, history, economics, and other subjects. The training ends when the apprentice passes an exam given by a board of teachers, employer-trainers, and representatives of the appropriate trade guild.

Students who are interested in technical professions or careers in business, administration, or civil service attend **die Realschule** for six years and participate in short-term internships (**die Praktikantenstellen** or **Praktika**). Upon passing **die Mittlere Reife** at the end of the 10th grade, these students may start an apprenticeship in areas such as banking, business, or office administration or attend a technical college **(die Fachschule)** or a special school (**die Fachoberschule**).

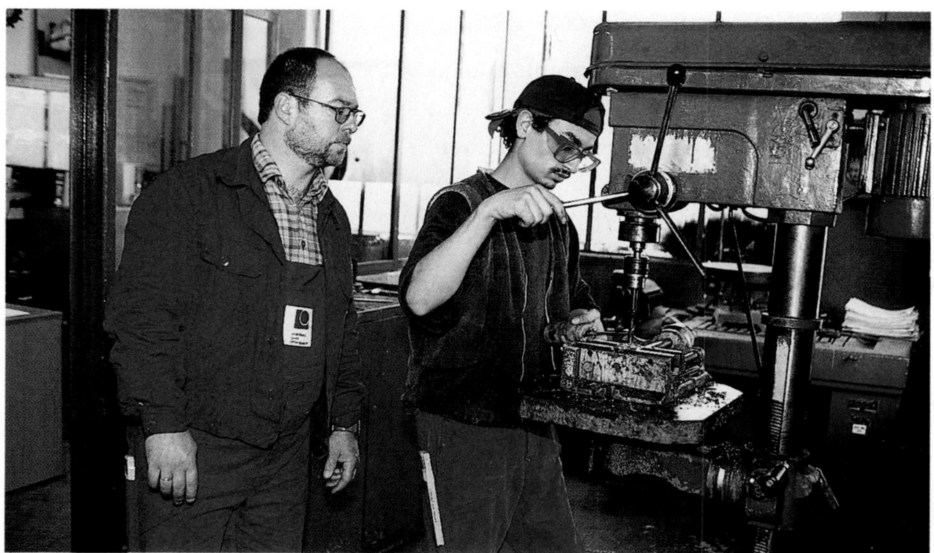

Ein Azubi bei der Ausbildung

22 **Kurz gefragt.** Beantworten Sie diese Fragen auf Deutsch.

1. Wie fühlen sich viele Menschen bei einem Vorstellungsgespräch?
2. Wie kann man die Aufregung vor einem Interview am besten abbauen?
3. Wie soll man sich nicht für das Vorstellungsgespräch anziehen?
4. Welche Frage stellt der Personalchef garantiert? Wie kann man sich auf diese Frage am besten vorbereiten?
5. Was für Kriterien sind für Jochen Turbanski vor allem wichtig?
6. Wie kann der Bewerber am besten Interesse zeigen?
7. Was ist wirklich schlimm in einem Vorstellungsgespräch?

23 **Ein Arbeitsinterview.** Stellen Sie einem Partner/einer Partnerin die folgenden Fragen.

1. Hast du mal ein Interview für eine Arbeitsstelle gehabt?
2. Was für eine Arbeit war das?
3. Wo war der Job?
4. Hast du den Job bekommen?
5. Hat dir der Job Spaß gemacht?
6. Wie hast du dich auf das Interview vorbereitet? Was hast du getragen? Was hast du dir zu Hause überlegt?
7. Welche Fragen haben dich überrascht°?
8. Wie war der Interviewer/die Interviewerin?

° *surprised*

■ *Strukturen und Vokabeln* ■

II Describing people and things (I)

Adjective endings with ein-words

A. Adjectives preceded by ein*-words: nominative case endings*

Adjectives are words that describe the nature or quality of nouns and occur in one of these two positions in a sentence.

1. as a predicative nominative after the verbs **sein, werden,** or **bleiben**

   Der Job ist **toll.** *The job is great.*

2. before a noun

   Ein **guter Job** für Studenten ist Fremdenführer. *A good job for students is that of a tour guide.*

In German, only adjectives that occur before a noun have an ending. The ending reflects the gender, the number, and the case of the noun that the adjective precedes.

masculine, singular, nominative
Er ist ein sehr **netter Typ.** — *He is a really nice guy.*

neuter, singular, nominative
Heute steht ein **kleines Inserat** in der Zeitung. — *There is a small ad in the newspaper today.*

feminine, singular, nominative
Das war eine **spontane Idee.** — *That was a spontaneous idea.*

In the nominative case the adjective following the **ein**-word has one of these endings, depending on the gender of the noun.

Gender		Adjective ending		
Masculine	der Typ	**-er**	ein nett**er** Typ	*a nice guy*
Neuter	das Inserat	**-es**	ein klein**es** Inserat	*a small ad*
Feminine	die Idee	**-e**	eine spontan**e** Idee	*a spontaneous idea*

Note that the ending on the definite article is the same as the ending on the adjective following **ein:** masculine de**r** → ein nett**er** Mann; neuter da**s** → ein klein**es** Auto; feminine di**e** → eine spontan**e** Idee.

Remember that the **ein**-words include the possessive adjectives **mein, dein, sein, ihr, unser, euer, ihr,** and **Ihr,** along with the negative article **kein.**

Ein *(a, an)* cannot be used with plural nouns.

Mein neu**er** Job ist ganz prima. — *My new job is great.*
Das ist **kein** alt**es** Auto. — *That is not an old car.*
Ihre neu**e** Stelle ist in der Stadtteilbibliothek. — *Her new position is at the public library branch.*

The plural ending on adjectives that follow these possessive adjectives and the negative article **kein** is **-en.**

Unsere neu**en** Azubis sind alle in der Kantine. — *Our new apprentices are all in the cafeteria.*
Das sind **keine** gut**en** Computer. — *Those are not good computers.*

These are the nominative adjective endings following an **ein**-word.

	Singular	Plural
Masculine	ein nett**er** Mann	keine nett**en** Männer
Neuter	ein neu**es** Inserat	keine neu**en** Inserate
Feminine	eine gut**e** Idee	keine gut**en** Ideen

Adjectives that end in **-el** or **-er** drop the internal **e** when an ending is added.

miserabel: Das ist ein **miserabler** Job. — *That is a miserable job.*
teuer: Ein **teures** Auto ist nicht unbedingt ein gutes Auto. — *An expensive car is not necessarily a good car.*
flexibel: Die **flexible** Arbeitszeit gefällt ihm sehr. — *He likes the flexible work hours.*
edel: Der 96-er ist ein **edler** Rotwein. — *The '96 is a fine red wine.*

The adjective **hoch** has a special form, **hoh-,** to which endings are added.

Das Gebäude ist **hoch.**
Das ist ein **hohes** Gebäude.

24 **Was ist das?** Erklären Sie einem Partner/einer Partnerin, was diese Begriffe° bedeuten.

terms

S1: Was ist die Volkswagen AG°?
S2: Das ist eine deutsche Autofirma.

Aktiengesellschaft: *corporation*

1. die Volkswagen AG
2. BMW
3. Dresden
4. der Neckar
5. Bayern
6. BASF
7. der Intercity

a. Das ist eine deutsche Chemiefirma.
b. Das ist eine deutsche Stadt.
c. Das ist ein deutsches Auto.
d. Das ist ein deutscher Zug.
e. Das ist ein deutscher Fluss.
f. Das ist ein deutsches Bundesland.
g. Das ist eine deutsche Autofirma.

25 **Was für eine Arbeit ist das?** Wählen sie für jeden Beruf ein passendes Adjektiv und schreiben Sie es auf. Geben Sie dann Ihre Meinung zu den folgenden Berufen.

Kellner/Kellnerin:
Das ist eine gute Arbeit (ein guter Beruf, ein gutes Leben).

+	+/–	–
gut	relativ gut	schlecht
fantastisch	ziemlich gut	blöd
interessant	anständig	langweilig
toll	mittelmäßig	mies
großartig		hart
fabelhaft		stressig
einmalig		dreckig

Was für eine Arbeit ist das? The words **relativ** and **ziemlich** are adverbs modifying **gut** and do not have adjective endings.

	Die Arbeit	*Der Beruf*	*Das Leben*
1. Kellner/Kellnerin	_____	_____	_____
2. Taxifahrer/Taxifahrerin	_____	_____	_____
3. Professor/Professorin	_____	_____	_____
4. Automechaniker/Automechanikerin	_____	_____	_____
5. Pilot/Pilotin	_____	_____	_____
6. Tellerwäscher/Tellerwäscherin	_____	_____	_____
7. Schauspieler°/Schauspielerin°	_____	_____	_____
8. Rechtsanwalt/Rechtsanwältin	_____	_____	_____

actor / actress

26 **Ein Spiel: Trivialwissen.** Was wissen Sie über Deutschland und Österreich? Bilden Sie zwei Teams und stellen Sie einander Fragen. Antworten Sie in ganzen Sätzen.

ein(e)- / österreichisch- / Stadt

S1 (TEAM 1): Nennen Sie eine österreichische Stadt.
S2 (TEAM 2): Salzburg ist eine österreichische Stadt.

Team 1

1. ein(e) / österreichisch- / Stadt
2. ein(e) / deutsch- / Basketballspieler in der NBA

3. ein(e) / deutsch- / Stadt im Osten Deutschlands
4. ein(e) / deutsch- / Bundesland im Norden
5. ein(e) / deutsch- / österreichisch- Schauspieler in den USA
6. ?

Team 2

1. ein(e) / deutsch- / Autofirma in München
2. ein(e) / österreichisch- / Musiker aus Salzburg
3. ein(e) / deutsch- / Komponist aus Bonn
4. ein(e) / deutsch- / Fluss in Bayern
5. ein(e) / deutsch- / Politiker
6. ?

Wissenswerte Vokabeln: Eigenschaften von Bewerbern

Talking about characteristics of job applicants

selbstständig — pünktlich — zuverlässig

dynamisch — kontaktfreudig — kollegial

analytisch — begabt — motiviert

diszipliniert

qualifiziert

gründlich

▣ Soll ein Bäcker analytisch sein? *Nein, er soll (zuverlässig) sein.*

27 Stellensuche: Beschreibung in einem Inserat. Wenn man eine Stelle sucht, liest man die Anzeigen in der Zeitung. Die Anzeigen beschreiben die gewünschte Person mit besonderen Adjektiven, wie „dynamisch". Welche von den folgenden Adjektiven findet man wahrscheinlich in einem Jobinserat, welche nicht?

kontaktfreudig • intelligent • dynamisch • faul • langsam • selbstständig • interessiert • unpünktlich • flexibel • passiv • zuverlässig • schüchtern • aggressiv • begabt • desorganisiert

In einem Inserat		*Nicht in einem Inserat*	
______	______	______	______
______	______	______	______
______	______	______	______
______	______	______	______
______	______	______	______
______	______	______	______

2. Einkommen:
Monatlich
ca. DM 1.600,–
durch seriöse
Nebentätigkeit (Büro).
Hervorragende
Zukunfts-Perspektiven.

28 Wie heißt eine Person, die ...? Stellen Sie einem Partner/einer Partnerin Fragen über die folgenden Personen und ihre Eigenschaften.

▣ Eine Person, die gern neue Leute kennen lernt, ist eine ...

▣ S1: Wie nennt man eine Person, die gern neue Leute kennen lernt?
S2: Eine Person, die gern neue Leute kennen lernt, ist eine kontaktfreudige Person.

1. Eine Person, die gern neue Leute kennen lernt, ist eine ...
2. Ein Arbeiter, der allein gut arbeiten kann, ist ein ...
3. Eine Ärztin, die nie zu spät kommt, ist eine ...
4. Ein Friseur, der gern mit Kollegen arbeitet, ist ein ...
5. Eine Lehrerin, die gute Qualifikationen hat, ist eine ...

a. selbstständig
b. pünktlich
c. kollegial
d. qualifiziert
e. kontaktfreudig

6. Ein Sekretär, der viel Talent hat, ist ein ...
7. Ein Kaufmann, der hohe Motivation hat, ist ein ...
8. Eine Architektin, die an alle Details denkt, ist eine ...
9. Ein Rechtsanwalt, der viel Energie hat, ist ein ...
10. Eine Person, die viel Disziplin bei der Arbeit zeigt, ist eine ...

f. gründlich
g. dynamisch
h. motiviert
i. diszipliniert
j. begabt

B. *Adjectives preceded by* ein-*words: accusative and dative case endings*

An adjective that describes a noun in the accusative or dative case has one of these endings.

	Accusative	Dative
Masculine	Ich habe einen neu**en** Job.	Sie ist glücklich mit ihrem neu**en** Job.
Neuter	Er verkauft sein alt**es** Auto.	Der Schreibtisch ist aus unserem alt**en** Büro.
Feminine	Sie liebt ihre neu**e** Stelle.	Er gibt seiner neu**en** Mitarbeiterin den Brief.
Plural	Wir haben keine frei**en** Stellen.	Sie spricht heute mit keinen neu**en** Bewerbern.

These are the nominative, accusative, and dative case adjective endings following an **ein**-word.

	Masculine	Neuter	Feminine	Plural
Nominative	ein nett**er** Mann	ein neu**es** Inserat	eine gut**e** Idee	keine gut**en** Ideen
Accusative	einen nett**en** Mann	ein neu**es** Inserat	eine gut**e** Idee	keine gut**en** Ideen
Dative	mit einem nett**en** Mann	in einem neu**en** Inserat	von einer gut**en** Idee	mit keinen gut**en** Ideen

29 Autogrammspiel. Finden Sie für jede Frage eine Person, die mit **Ja** antwortet. Bitten Sie die Person um ihre Unterschrift.

S1: Hast du einen guten Job?
S2: Ja.
S1: Unterschreib hier bitte. ________

1. Hast du einen guten Job? ________
2. Hast du von einem alten Freund Jobinformationen bekommen? ________
3. Kommst du aus einer kleinen Stadt? ________
4. Hast du einen teuren Computer? ________
5. Hast du einen festen Freund/eine feste° Freundin? ________ *°steady*
6. Arbeitet deine Mutter in einer großen Firma? ________
7. Arbeitest du mit einem guten Freund zusammen? ________
8. Hast du einen guten Deutschlehrer/eine gute Deutschlehrerin? ________

30 **Was für einen Job hast du?** Karl und Stefan haben beide einen neuen Job gefunden und sprechen jetzt über ihre neue Arbeit. Karl ist immer sehr positiv, aber Stefans Situation ist nicht so rosig.

S1 (KARL): Ich habe einen guten Job. Und du?
S2 (STEFAN): Ich habe einen schlechten Job.

		Karl	*Stefan*
1.	einen ... Job	gut	schlecht
2.	von meinem ... Chef viel gelernt	neu	alt
3.	heute eine ... Aufgabe gehabt	interessant	langweilig
4.	heute einen ... Auftrag° erfüllt°	wichtig	unwichtig
5.	ein ... Interview für eine Beförderung°	leicht	hart
6.	eine ... Sporthalle in der Firma	herrlich	furchtbar
7.	einen ... Tag gehabt	fantastisch	miserabel
8.	einen ... Computer bekommen	nagelneu	uralt
9.	eine ... Kantine in der Firma	preiswert	teuer
10.	mit einem ... Mitarbeiter gesprochen	sympathisch	unsympathisch

assignment / completed
promotion

FREIE KOMMUNIKATION **Rollenspiel: Ein gutes Auto.** Sie haben gerade eine Stelle bei einer Bank bekommen. Es ist Ihre erste Stelle seit dem Studium und Sie brauchen viele Sachen, z.B. neue Kleidung. Stellen Sie mit einem Partner/einer Partnerin eine Liste von zehn wichtigen Sachen zusammen, die Sie unbedingt brauchen. Seien Sie so genau wie möglich, wenn Sie Ihrem Partner/Ihrer Partnerin erzählen, was sie alles brauchen (z.B. **das Auto, die Schuhe, der Anzug, die Aktentasche**).

S1: Das ist ja toll, dass du eine neue Stelle bei der Bank hast.
S2: Ja, aber ich brauche viele neue Sachen. Ich brauche ein gutes Auto ...

III Describing people and things (II)

Adjective endings with definite articles

Adjectives preceded by a definite article: nominative, accusative, and dative case endings

Like adjectives that follow **ein**-words, adjectives that follow the definite article also take endings that change according to the gender, the number, and the case of the noun that follows. These are the nominative, accusative, and dative endings of adjectives that follow **der**-words.

All plural and dative endings are **-en.** All nominative singular endings are **-e.**

	Masculine	Neuter	Feminine	Plural
Nominative	der neu**e** Beruf	das neu**e** Büro	die neu**e** Stelle	die neu**en** Berufe/Büros/Stellen
Accusative	den neu**en** Beruf	das neu**e** Büro	die neu**e** Stelle	die neu**en** Berufe/Büros/Stellen
Dative	dem neu**en** Beruf	dem neu**en** Büro	der neu**en** Stelle	den neu**en** Berufen/Büros/Stellen

Speakers use these adjective endings with any of the **der**-words (e.g., **dieser, jeder,** and **welcher**).

Nominative: Dieser neu**e** Computer hat kein Kabel.
Accusative: Angelika findet jedes neu**e** Gesprächsthema langweilig.
Dative: Welchem jung**en** Mann haben Sie den Schlüssel gegeben?

If you compare the adjective endings that occur after **der/das/die** with the endings used after **ein**-words, you will note that adjectives following a **der**-word have only one of two endings: **-e** or **-en.** The ending in the plural is always **-en.**

	Masculine	Neuter	Feminine	Plural
Nominative	**ein** neu**er** Chef **der** neu**e** Chef	**ein** neu**es** Büro **das** neu**e** Büro	**eine** neu**e** Stelle **die** neu**e** Stelle	**meine** neu**en** Kollegen **die** neu**en** Kollegen
Accusative	**einen** neu**en** Chef **den** neu**en** Chef	**ein** neu**es** Büro **das** neu**e** Büro	**eine** neu**e** Stelle **die** neu**e** Stelle	**meine** neu**en** Kollegen **die** neu**en** Kollegen
Dative	**einem** neu**en** Chef **dem** neu**en** Chef	**einem** neu**en** Büro **dem** neu**en** Büro	**einer** neu**en** Stelle **der** neu**en** Stelle	**meinen** neu**en** Kollegen **den** neu**en** Kollegen

31 **Die neue Stelle.** Herr Günther hat eine neue Arbeitsstelle. Er beantwortet die Fragen, die sein Freund Herr Winter über die neue Stelle hat.

die Stelle / gut

S1 (HERR WINTER): Wie ist die neue Stelle?
S2 (HERR GÜNTHER): Ach, sie ist eine gute Stelle.

1. die Stelle / gut
2. der Chef / tolerant
3. das Büro / groß
4. die Mitarbeiterin / gründlich
5. die Sekretärin / gut organisiert
6. das Gehalt° / schön
7. der Dienstwagen / komfortabel
8. der Computer / schnell
9. das Arbeitsklima° in der Firma / kollegial

salary

die Arbeitsatmosphäre

32 **Wie kann Herr Günther das machen?** Verbinden Sie eine Person oder ein Bürogerät in der linken Spalte mit einer Funktion in der rechten Spalte.

1. Mit dem schnellen Computer
2. Mit dem komfortablen Dienstwagen
3. Mit dem toleranten Chef
4. Mit der gründlichen Mitarbeiterin
5. Mit der gut organisierten Sekretärin
6. Mit dem schönen Gehalt
7. In dem großen Büro

a. kann Herr Günther effektiv zusammen arbeiten.
b. kann Herr Günther schnell rechnen°.
c. kann Herr Günther einen großen Schreibtisch und ein komfortables Sofa haben.
d. kann Herr Günther Kunden° am Flughafen abholen.
e. kann Herr Günther seine Existenz verbessern.
f. kann Herr Günther über alles sprechen.
g. kann Herr Günther täglich sehr viel erledigen.

compute

customers, clients

33 **Was macht Herr Günther lieber?** Beantworten Sie die Fragen zusammen mit einem Partner/einer Partnerin.

▣ mit dem fleißigen/faulen Mitarbeiter arbeiten

▣ S1: Arbeitet Herr Günther lieber mit dem fleißigen oder mit dem faulen Mitarbeiter?
S2: Er arbeitet lieber mit dem fleißigen Mitarbeiter.
S1: Und du?
S2: Ich arbeite (auch) lieber mit einem fleißigen Mitarbeiter.

1. mit dem fleißigen/faulen Mitarbeiter arbeiten
2. den neuen/alten Wagen fahren
3. mit dem schnellen/langsamen Computer schreiben
4. mit der kollegialen/unfreundlichen Person zusammenarbeiten
5. das komplizierte/einfache Inserat lesen
6. den billigen/teuren Computer kaufen
7. in der großen/kleinen Firma arbeiten
8. den unfähigen°/begabten Mann anrufen *incompetent*

C. Endings on unpreceded adjectives

An adjective that is neither preceded by an **ein**-word nor a **der**-word, has the same ending as a **der**-word.

Unser Chef trinkt ungern kalt**en** Kaffee.	*Our boss doesn't like to drink cold coffee.*
Frisch**e** Luft macht den Arbeitsplatz angenehm.	*Fresh air makes the workplace pleasant.*
Wir haben schön**es** Wetter.	*We're having nice weather.*
Nett**e** Mitarbeiter sind wichtig.	*Nice co-workers are important.*

34 **Persönliches Profil.** Sie bewerben sich um eine Stelle in diesen Berufen. Sie machen ein Vorstellungsgespräch. Beantworten Sie diese Fragen für jeden von diesen Berufen in der Liste.

Künstler(in) • Geschäftsperson • Professor(in) • Verkäufer(in)

▣ S1: Was für Kleidung tragen Sie normalerweise am Arbeitsplatz?
S2 (GESCHÄFTSPERSON): Ich trage normalerweise formelle Kleidung.
S1 (VERKÄUFERIN): Ich trage normalerweise informelle Kleidung.

1. Was für Kleidung tragen Sie normalerweise am Arbeitsplatz? (formell / informell / schick / modisch)
2. Was für Essen bestellen Sie bei einem Geschäftstreffen°? (deutsch / chinesisch / französisch / exotisch / vegetarisch) *business meeting*
3. Was für Getränke trinken Sie auf einer Geschäftsparty? (alkoholfrei / gesund / exotisch / alkoholisch)
4. Was für Autos fahren Sie gern? (schnell / sicher / teuer / bequem / gebraucht)
5. Was für Computerkenntnisse haben Sie? (gut / mäßig / schlecht)
6. Was für Aufgaben machen Sie gern? (schriftlich / mündlich)
7. Mit was für Leuten arbeiten Sie gern? (tolerant / kreativ / intelligent / interessant)

IV ▣ Expressing the city of origin

Forming adjectives from city names

German speakers form adjectives from city names by adding the ending **-er.** Unlike other adjective forms that reflect the case, the number, and the gender, this adjective form never changes.

Die **Berliner** Mauer steht nicht mehr. — *The Berlin Wall does not exist anymore.*

Meine Tochter isst gern **Wiener** Schnitzel. — *My daughter likes to eat Wiener Schnitzel.*

Adjectives that derive from city names like **Dresden, Bremen, München,** and **Zürich,** drop the last internal **e, i,** or **en.**

München → Münchner: Das **Münchner** Oktoberfest ist ein berühmtes Volksfest.
Bremen → Bremer: Die **Bremer** Stadtmusikanten sind Tiere aus einem Märchen.
Dresden → Dresdner: Sie arbeitet in einer **Dresdner** Stadtteilbibliothek.
Zürich → Zürcher: Das **Zürcher** Schauspielhaus präsentiert …

35 **Ihre Urlaubsziele.** Beantworten Sie diese Fragen.

1. Was wollen Sie in Magdeburg sehen?
2. Was möchten Sie in Salzburg hören?
3. Welche Märkte gibt es im Dezember?
4. Was müssen Sie in München besuchen?
5. Was kann man in Erfurt besuchen?
6. Wohin gehen Sie in Kaltenberg?

V ■ Comparing people and things

Comparative and superlative forms of adjectives and adverbs

A. *Comparative forms*

1. Regular adjectives and adverbs

To compare two or more people, objects, animals or activities, German speakers use the comparative form **(der Komparativ)** of an adjective **(das Adjektiv)** or adverb **(das Adverb).**

Das klingt schon **besser.**	*That sounds better.*
Das Herz pocht etwas **stärker.**	*The heart beats a little faster.*

Most adjectives and adverbs with an **e** or **i** in the stem form the comparative by adding **-er.** To express inequality, speakers use a comparative form with **als.**

Adjective:	Ein VW ist **schnell.**	*A VW is fast.*
Comparative:	Ein BMW ist **schneller als** ein VW.	*A BMW is faster than a VW.*
Adverb:	Ein VW fährt **schnell.**	*A VW goes fast.*
Comparative:	Ein BMW fährt **schneller als** ein VW.	*A BMW goes faster than a VW.*

Most German adjectives and adverbs are identical in form, unlike English where many adverbs are identifiable by the ending *-ly* (e.g., *happy, happily*).

To express equality in a comparison, German speakers use the construction **so ... wie** (*as . . . as*).

Ein Porsche ist **so** teuer **wie** ein Mercedes.	*A Porsche is as expensive as a Mercedes.*

Here are the base and comparative forms of some regular adjectives and adverbs.

Base	Comparative	Base	Comparative
bekannt	**bekannter**	schlecht	**schlechter**
billig	**billiger**	schnell	**schneller**
intelligent	**intelligenter**	schön	**schöner**
interessant	**interessanter**	schwer	**schwerer**
neu	**neuer**	wenig	**weniger**

Adjectives that end in **-er** or **-el** drop the internal **e** in the comparative form.

teuer:	Das Benzin wird jedes Jahr **teurer.**	*Gasoline gets more expensive every year.*
flexibel:	Ihre Arbeitszeit ist **flexibler** als meine.	*Her work hours are more flexible than mine.*

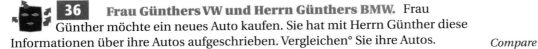

36 Frau Günthers VW und Herrn Günthers BMW. Frau Günther möchte ein neues Auto kaufen. Sie hat mit Herrn Günther diese Informationen über ihre Autos aufgeschrieben. Vergleichen° Sie ihre Autos.

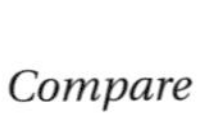

° Compare

■ billig sein

■ S1: Frau Günthers VW ist billiger als Herrn Günthers BMW.
S2: Herrn Günthers BMW ist ...

	Frau Günthers VW	*Herrn Günthers BMW*
billig (teuer) sein:	25.000 DM	70.000 DM
neu sein:	1998	2002
schnell fahren:	140 Km/h°	220 Km/h
schwer sein:	2,5 t°	3,1 t
schön sein:	_____	_____
Prestige haben:	_____	_____
Platz haben:	_____	_____
Benzin verbrauchen:	_____	_____

Stundenkilometer
Tonnen

2. Adjectives and adverbs that add an umlaut

Many one-syllable adjectives and adverbs with an **a, o,** or **u** in the stem add an umlaut in the comparative form.

Ich bin **älter** als mein Bruder. *I am older than my brother.*

Here are some adjectives and adverbs that add an umlaut in the comparative form.

	Base	Comparative		Base	Comparative
a > ä	alt	**älter**	**o > ö**	groß	**größer**
	hart	**härter**		oft	**öfter**
	kalt	**kälter**			
	lang	**länger**	**u > ü**	jung	**jünger**
	stark	**stärker**		kurz	**kürzer**
	warm	**wärmer**			

3. Irregular adjectives and adverbs

Some adjectives and adverbs are irregular in German. Note that **hoch** drops the **c** in the comparative.

Positive	Comparative	Examples	
gern	**lieber**	Ich gehe **lieber** ins Kino.	*I prefer to go to the movies.*
gut	**besser**	Siehst du jetzt **besser?**	*Do you see better now?*
hoch	**höher**	Dieses Gebäude ist **höher.**	*This building is taller.*
viel	**mehr**	Wir verdienen jetzt **mehr** Geld.	*We're earning more money now.*

37 **Freiburg ist kleiner als Berlin.** Stellen Sie Vergleiche an.

- Freiburg(–) / Berlin(+) / klein *Freiburg ist kleiner als Berlin.*
- Dresden(+) / Tübingen(+) / groß *Dresden ist so groß wie Tübingen.*

1. Freiburg(–) / Berlin(+) / klein
2. Dresden(+) / Tübingen(+) / groß
3. Die Uni in Tübingen(+) / die Uni in Bochum(–) / alt
4. Garmisch-Partenkirchen(+) / Stuttgart(–) / hoch liegen

5. Der Mercedes 500 SL(+) / der VW Golf(−) / teuer
6. Ein Motorrad(+) / ein Fahrrad(−) / schnell
7. Norddeutschland im Winter(−) / Süddeutschland im Winter(+) / Schnee haben
8. Der deutsche Weißwein(+) / der deutsche Rotwein(+) / gut
9. Bockbier(+) / Exportbier(−) / stark
10. Der Nürnberger Weihnachstmarkt(+) / der Bremer Weihnachstmarkt(−) / bekannt

38 **Interview.** Stellen Sie einem Partner/einer Partnerin die folgenden Fragen.

1. Wer ist kontaktfreudiger, dein Vater oder deine Mutter?
2. Ist deine Mutter älter oder jünger als dein Vater?
3. Verdient deine Mutter mehr als dein Vater?
4. Wer arbeitet länger, deine Mutter oder dein Vater?
5. Wer ist intelligenter, du oder deine Schwester (dein Bruder, dein Cousin)?
6. Bist du stärker als dein Bruder (deine Schwester, dein Cousin)?
7. Wer ist selbstständiger, du oder dein bester Freund / deine beste Freundin?
8. Wer ist sportlicher, du oder dein bester Freund / deine beste Freundin?
9. Wer studiert disziplinierter, du oder dein bester Freund / deine beste Freundin?
10. Wer ist zuverlässiger, du oder dein bester Freund / deine beste Freundin?

B. *Superlative forms*

1. Regular adjectives and adverbs

German speakers form the superlative by adding **-st** to the adjective or adverb stem and adding the appropriate adjective ending. Adjectives that follow the verb **sein** are in the predicate position and occur with the dative form **am** + *adjective* + **-sten** (e.g., **am schnellsten**). Adjectives that precede a noun are in the attributive position and must have an ending that reflects the gender and the number of the noun (e.g., **das schnellste Auto**).

Ein Porsche ist **am schnellsten.**	*A Porsche is the fastest (of all).*
Ein Porsche fährt **am schnellsten.**	*A Porsche goes the fastest (of all).*
Ein Porsche ist das **schnellste** Auto.	*A Porsche is the fastest car (of all).*

Stems that end in **-t** and **-z** form the superlative with **-est.** Many one-syllable adjectives and adverbs with an **-a, -o,** or **-u** in the stem add an umlaut in the superlative forms.

In dem großen Büro war es am **lautesten.**	*It was the loudest in the large office.*
Herr Müller ist unser **ältester** Mitarbeiter.	*Mr. Müller is our oldest co-worker.*

Here are the superlative forms of the regular adjectives and adverbs listed previously in this chapter.

Base	***Predicate superlative***	***Attributive superlative***
bekannt	**am bekanntesten**	das **bekannteste** Schloss in Deutschland
billig	**am billigsten**	der **billigste** Käse

dunkel	**am dunkelsten**	das **dunkelste** Blau
flexibel	**am flexibelsten**	die **flexibelsten** Arbeitszeiten
intelligent	**am intelligentesten**	die **intelligentesten** Studenten
interessant	**am interessantesten**	der **interessanteste** Kurs
miserabel	**am miserabelsten**	das **miserabelste** Wetter
neu	**am neuesten**	die **neuesten** Stellenangebote
schlecht	**am schlechtesten**	der **schlechteste** Tag
schnell	**am schnellsten**	die **schnellste** Mitarbeiterin
schön	**am schönsten**	das **schönste** Geschenk
schwer	**am schwersten**	die **schwersten** Fragen
teuer	**am teuersten**	die **teuersten** Autos
wenig	**am wenigsten**	die **wenigsten** Leute

2. Adjectives and adverbs with an umlaut

These are some adjectives and adverbs that add an umlaut in the superlative form. Stems that end in **-t** or **-z** also insert an **-e-** before the **-st.**

	Base	Superlative		Base	Superlative
a > ä	alt	**am ältesten**	**o > ö**	groß	**am größten**
	hart	**am härtesten**		oft	**am öftesten**
	kalt	**am kältesten**	**u > ü**	jung	**am jüngsten**
	lang	**am längsten**		kurz	**am kürzesten**
	stark	**am stärksten**			
	warm	**am wärmsten**			

3. Irregular adjectives and adverbs

Here are the superlative forms of the irregular adjectives and adverbs listed previously in this chapter.

Base	*Comparative*	*Superlative*	*Example*
gern	lieber	**am liebsten**	Er isst **am liebsten** Brot. *He likes to eat bread the most.*
gut	besser	**am besten**	**Der beste** Weißwein kommt aus Franken. *The best white wine is from Franken.*
hoch	höher	**am höchsten**	**Der höchste** Berg heißt Everest. *Mt. Everest is the tallest mountain.*
viel	mehr	**am meisten**	Wir verdienen viel Geld, aber er verdient **am meisten.** *We earn a lot of money, but he earns the most.*

German speakers frequently use the superlative forms with the definite articles **der, das,** and **die.**

Herr Hill ist **der beste** Chef.	*Mr. Hill is the best boss.*
Ich habe **das schönste** Büro.	*I have the nicest office.*

Er bewirbt sich um **die neueste** Stelle. *He is applying for the newest position.*
Die höchsten Gebäude stehen im Stadtzentrum. *The highest buildings are downtown.*

When German speakers use comparative and superlative forms of adjectives before nouns, they also add the correct ending for the gender, number, and case.

Wir haben **einen älteren Wagen** gekauft. *We bought an older car.*
Ich studiere an **der ältesten Universität** Deutschlands. *I'm studying at the oldest university in Germany.*

Some attributive adjectives form an independent expression by omitting the noun.

das Richtig**e**	*the right thing*	Er tut immer **das Richtige.** *He always does the right thing.*
das Best**e**	*the best thing*	Sie will nur **das Beste** kaufen. *She only wants to buy the best.*

39 **Studienzeiten.** Beantworten Sie diese Fragen mit Information aus der Tabelle.

1. Wo sind die Studenten am jüngsten, wenn sie mit dem Studium fertig sind?
2. Wo sind die Studenten am ältesten?
3. Sind Studenten in den USA jünger oder älter als Studenten in Frankreich?
4. In welchem Land sind die Studenten so alt wie in den Niederlanden?
5. In welchen zwei Ländern sind die Studenten fast° so alt wie in Deutschland? *almost*

40 **Fakten über Deutschland.** Sie arbeiten im Fremdenverkehrsamt in Frankfurt und müssen eine Tourismusbroschüre über Deutschland schreiben. Bilden Sie Aussagen im Superlativ.

Fakten ... Remember that any adjective following **der/das/die** must have the proper adjective ending **-e** or **-en.**

▣ die Gebäude / hoch = in Frankfurt
Die höchsten Gebäude sind in Frankfurt.

1. die Gebäude / hoch = in Frankfurt
2. der römische° Bau / bekannt = die Porta Nigra in Trier
3. der Fluss / lang = der Rhein
4. die Universität / alt = in Heidelberg
5. der Kirchturm° / hoch = in Ulm
6. die Bierbrauereien / viel = in Bayern
7. die Autos / schnell = Porsche und BMW
8. die Stadt / nördlich / in Deutschland = Flensburg
9. das Bundesland / klein = die Hansestadt Bremen

Roman

church steeple

■ FREIE ■ KOMMUNIKATION ■ **Verkäuferin gesucht.** Hier sind drei Personen, die sich für die Stelle bei Foto-Hirsch interessieren. Lesen Sie die Informationen über jede Person und besprechen Sie, wer für die Stelle besser (am besten) geeignet ist.

Junge(r), dynamische(r)
Verkäufer(in)
mit Führerschein für unsere Filiale in Seemarn
gesucht.
(Gewerbegebiet B 93).
Sie sollten selbstständig arbeiten können
und Spaß am Umgang mit Menschen
haben.
Bewerbungen mit Bild an
Foto-Kirsch
Arnoldstraße 13
09702 Seltz, Telefon 03941-14 79

	Fabian	Carlos	Jutta
Alter	20 Jahre	19 Jahre	18 Jahre
selbstständig	+++	+++	+++
dynamisch	+	++	++
kollegial	++	++	++
zuverlässig	+++	++	+
flexibel	+	+++	++
motiviert	++	+	+++

Schreibecke Ein Stellengesuch-Inserat schreiben. Sie suchen eine neue Stelle. Schreiben Sie ein Stellengesuch-Inserat. Sie dürfen maximal 50 Wörter verwenden°. Nennen Sie mindestens zwei Eigenschaften. Benutzen Sie die folgenden Inserate als Beispiele. *use*

> **Sekretärin (21)**
> zuverlässig und flexibel, sucht dringend neuen Wirkungskreis im Raum FG/BED, PC-Kenntnisse und Führerschein Klasse 3 vorhanden.

> **Einsatzfreudiger junger Mann,** 36 Jahre, sucht Tätigkeit als Kraftfahrer im Fern- oder Nahverkehr, FS Kl. 1 bis 5 vorhanden.

ZIELTEXT

Das Vorstellungsgespräch in der Bibliothek

Frau Müller hat ihr Vorstellungsgespräch mit Frau Schmidt von der Personalabteilung der Dresdner Stadtbibliothek. Frau Schmidt hat viele Fragen für Frau Müller: Fragen über ihre Berufserfahrung als Bibliothekarin und über ihre Bereitschaft° für diese Stelle. Am Ende vom Interview ist klar, dass Frau Müller einen positiven Eindruck auf Frau Schmidt gemacht hat. Spätestens Ende nächster Woche wird Frau Müller wissen, ob sie die Stelle bekommen wird oder nicht. *readiness*

Vorschau

41 Thematische Fragen. Beantworten Sie die folgenden Fragen auf Deutsch.

1. Was für Dokumente bringt man zum Vorstellungsgespräch?
   a. einen Lebenslauf (eine Biographie)
   b. ein Bewerbungsformular
   c. einen Bewerbungsbrief
   d. Aufsätze aus der Studienzeit
   e. Kontaktadressen von ehemaligen Arbeitgebern
   f. Informationen über das letzte monatliche Gehalt° *salary*
   g. Empfehlungen° von ehemaligen Arbeitgebern *recommendations*
   h. ein Testament° *will*
2. Was für Ratschläge geben Sie Frau Müller?

42 Was wird im Interview wohl passieren?

1. Welche Themen werden Frau Schmidt interessieren? Kreuzen Sie alle Möglichkeiten an.
   __ a. Frau Müllers Ausbildung (wo sie zur Schule gegangen ist)

— b. Frau Müllers Berufserfahrung (wo sie gearbeitet hat)
— c. Frau Müllers Familie
— d. Frau Müllers Gesundheit
— e. Frau Müllers Alter
— f. Frau Müllers früheres Gehalt
— g. Frau Müllers Hobbys

2. Welche Themen werden Frau Müller interessieren? Kreuzen Sie alle Möglichkeiten an.
— a. das Gehalt
— b. die Öffnungszeiten von der Stadtteilbibliothek
— c. die Zahl von Kollegen in der Stadtteilbibliothek
— d. Parkplätze
— e. Computerfragen
— f. der Urlaub° *vacation*
— g. Krankenurlaub° *sick days*

3. Wie kann Frau Müller im Vorstellungsgespräch Interesse zeigen? Kreuzen Sie alle Möglichkeiten an.
— a. Frau Müller stellt viele Fragen.
— b. Frau Müller spricht über ihre Religion.
— c. Frau Müller fragt nach Frau Schmidts Familie.
— d. Frau Müller lässt° Frau Schmidt alles fragen. *lets*
— e. Frau Müller dankt Frau Schmidt am Ende des Interviews.

43 Satzdetektiv. Welche Sätze bedeuten ungefähr das Gleiche?

1. Sie sind hier, um **sich vorzustellen** ... für die neue Stelle, die wir **ausgeschrieben** haben?
2. Ich hab' schon Ihre **Akte durchgeguckt.**
3. Was ich jetzt von Ihnen noch gern wissen wollte, ist ein bisschen **ausführlicher** ... zu Ihrem **beruflichen Werdegang.**
4. Haben Sie eine **bestimmte Abteilung** für sich da gehabt?

a. Ich möchte mehr Details über Ihre Ausbildung und Karriere hören.
b. Sie bewerben sich um die Stelle, die wir in der Zeitung annonciert haben?
c. Haben Sie da eine eigene Gruppe geleitet°? *directed*
d. Ich habe Ihre Dokumente schon durchgesehen.

---

5. Ich bin **mit** meinen Kollegen in der Stadtbibliothek immer **gut ausgekommen.**
6. Was sind Ihre **Gehaltsvorstellungen?**
7. Wie viel **Urlaub** hatten Sie da in der Stadtbibliothek?
8. Sie werden also spätestens dann Ende nächster Woche telefonisch von uns **Bescheid bekommen.**

e. Wir werden Sie nächste Woche per Telefon informieren.
f. Wie viel Mark im Monat möchten Sie verdienen?
g. Wie viele Wochen hatten Sie frei in der alten Stelle?
h. Meine Kollegen und ich waren immer kollegial miteinander.

ZIELTEXT

Das Vorstellungsgespräch in der Bibliothek

Hören Sie gut zu.

44 **Stimmt das?** Stimmen diese Aussagen zum Text oder nicht? Wenn nicht, was stimmt?

	Ja, das stimmt.	*Nein, das stimmt nicht.*	
1. Die Interviewerin sagt nie, was ihr Name ist. Frau Müller muss sie fragen, wie sie heißt.	___	___	
2. Frau Müller hat vor einem Jahr als Bibliothekarin gearbeitet.	___	___	
3. Frau Müller hat die Stelle in Chemnitz verloren, weil die Stadt Finanzen für die Bibliothek gekürzt° hat.	___	___	*cut back*
4. Frau Müller hat an der Universität studiert.	___	___	
5. Frau Müller hat in der Abteilung für Kinderliteratur gearbeitet.	___	___	
6. Nur zwei Personen werden in der Stadtbibliothek arbeiten; beide werden neue Mitarbeiter sein.	___	___	
7. Frau Müller hat ihre Mitarbeiter in Chemnitz immer problematisch gefunden.	___	___	
8. Frau Schmidt hat nur Gutes über Frau Müller gehört.	___	___	
9. Die Bibliothek kann Frau Müller sehr viel bezahlen.	___	___	
10. Frau Müller wird Ende nächster Woche hören, ob sie die Stelle bekommt oder nicht.	___	___	

45 **Was haben sie nicht diskutiert?** Welche Themen haben Frau Müller und Frau Schmidt im Vorstellungsgespräch nicht besprochen? Kreuzen Sie sie an.

___ 1. das Gehalt
___ 2. die Zahl von Mitarbeitern in der Stadtteilbibliothek
___ 3. die Öffnungszeiten von der Stadtteilbibliothek
___ 4. Frau Müllers Berufserfahrung
___ 5. Frau Müllers Ausbildung
___ 6. Frau Müllers Familienverhältnisse
___ 7. Frau Schmidts Familienverhältnisse
___ 8. Kommentare von früheren Chefs
___ 9. Frau Müllers Selbstständigkeit
___ 10. Urlaub
___ 11. Frau Müllers Abteilung
___ 12. Frau Müllers Geschmack in Kinderliteratur

46 **Ergänzen Sie: Diktat.** Ergänzen Sie diese Sätze mit Wörtern aus dem **Zieltext.**

1. Sie sind hier, um sich vorzustellen … für die neue Stelle, die wir ___ haben?
2. Ja, ich hab' schon Ihre ___ durchgeguckt.
3. Und was für Ressourcen hatten Sie da unter sich? Haben Sie eine bestimmte ___ für sich da gehabt?
4. Ja, das ist besonders wichtig für unsere ___.
5. So eine Bibliothek muss ja auch etwas tun, damit die Leute da nicht nur immer ___.
6. Ich bin mit meinen Kollegen in der Stadtbibliothek immer gut ___.
7. Mein altes ___ in der Stadtteilbibliothek lag bei 2.000 Mark im Monat.
8. Wir sind relativ ___ in dem Sinne, als wir eben unsre festen Tarife haben …
9. Sie werden also spätestens dann Ende nächster Woche telefonisch von uns ___ bekommen.
10. … und ich hab', wie gesagt, auch nur sehr ___ von Ihnen gehört …

47 **Kurz gefragt.** Beantworten Sie diese Fragen auf Deutsch.

1. Was hat Frau Schmidt von Frau Müllers Chef in Chemnitz gehört?
2. Was für eine Ausbildung hatte Frau Müller, bevor sie zur Chemnitzer Bibliothek gegangen ist?
3. Was war Frau Müllers Abteilung in der Chemnitzer Stadtbibliothek?
4. Warum sind diese Qualifikationen wichtig für die neue Stadtteilbibliothek?
5. Warum findet Frau Müller Literatur und Spiele wichtig für junge Leute?
6. Wie viele freie Stellen gibt es für die neue Stadtteilbibliothek?
7. Wie viele Kollegen werden in der neuen Stadtteilbibliothek arbeiten?
8. Hat Frau Müller viel Urlaub gehabt? Wie viel?
9. Wann wird Frau Müller wissen, ob sie diese Stelle bekommt oder nicht?
10. Wie sehen ihre Chancen aus? Was sagt Frau Schmidt in dieser Hinsicht°? *respect*

48 Eine Au-Pair Stelle. Sie und ein Partner/eine Partnerin sind Herr und Frau Langer, die Eltern von zwei Kindern: ein Kind ist fünf Jahre, das andere ist acht Jahre alt und geht zur Schule. Sie suchen eine Au-Pair Person, die sich um die Kinder kümmern soll. Eine Vermittlungsagentur zeigt Ihnen die Akten von zwei Kandidaten. Diskutieren und entscheiden Sie, wen Sie für die Stelle gut finden. Hier sind die Akten. Geben Sie drei Gründe für Ihre Entscheidung.

Junge Familie
sucht

AU-PAIR

für zwei Kinder (Willi, 5 und Julianna, 8) in Freiburg-Littenweiler.

Tätigkeiten: 2 Mahlzeiten kochen, mit den Kindern spielen, leichte Hausarbeit machen, den Kindern mit den Hausaufgaben helfen.

Bewerbungsbrief mit Foto an:
Frau Beate Langer
Schulweg 7a
78012 Freiburg

Anton Dunkel
18 Jahre alt
hat eine Schwester, die 8 Jahre alt ist
mag Kinder
ist ein durchschnittlicher Schüler
ist selbstständig und zuverlässig
kocht, aber nicht besonders gut
macht zu Hause nicht gern sauber
hat einen Führerschein
hat keine Erfahrung als Au-Pair

Amelie Eisner
21 Jahre alt
hat einen dreijährigen Bruder und eine vierzehnjährige Schwester
ist sehr kreativ und dynamisch
ist eine erfahrene Köchin
ist nicht immer pünktlich
studiert Kunst
wird manchmal ungeduldig

Schreibecke **Ein Brief von Frau Langer.** Schreiben Sie einen Brief an Anton Dunkel oder Amelie Eisner. Schreiben Sie, warum Sie ihm/ihr die Stelle (nicht) geben. Beginnen Sie Ihren Brief mit **Lieber Herr … / Liebe Frau …**

Mein Bewerbungsbrief. Schreiben Sie einen Bewerbungsbrief für eine Stelle als Buchhalter/Buchhalterin°. Sie können den Bewerbungsbrief von Andrea Wallner als Beispiel benutzen. Beantworten Sie in Ihrem Brief diese Fragen.

accountant

1. Wie und wo haben Sie von der Stelle gehört?
2. Welche Berufserfahrung haben Sie?
3. Wie beschreiben Sie Ihre Persönlichkeit?
4. Warum sind Sie für die Stelle gut qualifiziert?

Weinheim, den 21. April

Sehr geehrte Damen und Herren,

ich habe Ihre Anzeige für einen Chefbuchhalter/eine Chefbuchhalterin in der „Mannheimer-Post" gesehen. Ich habe mein Wirtschaftsstudium an der Universität Trier abgeschlossen. Ich habe drei Sommer als Praktikantin bei der Firma Müller gearbeitet. Ich habe die Buchhaltung in der Verkaufsabteilung° gemacht.

sales department

Ich bin freundlich und kollegial. Ich kann selbstständig arbeiten, und ich bin sehr zuverlässig und pünktlich. Weil ich Erfahrung als Buchhalterin und viel Interesse für Teamarbeit habe und immer zuverlässig bin, bin ich die richtige Kandidatin für diese Stelle. Ich hoffe, dass Sie sich für ein näheres Gespräch mit mir interessieren, und ich freue mich darauf, bald von Ihnen zu hören.

Hochachtungsvoll°

Respectfully

Andrea Wallner

Andrea Wallner

■ FREIE ■ KOMMUNIKATION ■ **Das Vorstellungsgespräch.** Geben Sie einem anderen Studenten/einer anderen Studentin Ihren Bewerbungsbrief. Er/Sie führt mit Ihnen ein Vorstellungsgespräch für diese Stelle. Werden Sie die Stelle bekommen? Besprechen Sie auch, wie viel Geld und wie viel Urlaub Sie bekommen werden.

■ Wortschatz ■

Arbeitssuche

die Arbeitsvermittlung *job placement agency*
die Aushilfe *temporary worker*
der Beruf, -e *occupation*
das Büro, -s *office*
der Fremdenführer, -/die Fremdenführerin, -nen *tour guide*
das Inserat, -e *newspaper advertisement*
das Interview, -s *interview*
der Job, -s *job*
  der Teilzeitjob *part-time job*

der Mitarbeiter, -/die Mitarbeiterin, -nen *co-worker*
die Stelle, -n *position, job*
die Suche, -n *search, hunt*
das Trinkgeld *tip, gratuity*
der Typ, -en *guy, fellow, person*
das Vorstellungsgespräch, -e *employment interview*
der Zweck, -e *purpose, point*

an·bieten (hat angeboten) *to offer*
sich aus·kennen (hat sich ausgekannt) mit + *dat.* *to know a lot about s.t.*
sich bewerben (bewirbt sich, hat sich beworben) um + *acc.* *to apply for s.t.*
drücken: die Daumen drücken (hat gedrückt) + *dat.* *to cross one's fingers for s.o.*
jobben (hat gejobbt) *to work a part-time job*
klingen (hat geklungen) *to sound*
Spaß machen (hat Spaß gemacht) + *dat.* *to be fun*
passieren (ist passiert) + *dat.* *to happen*
schaden (hat geschadet) + *dat.* *to harm, hurt*
suchen (hat gesucht) nach. + *dat.* *to search for, seek, look for*
verdienen (hat verdient) *to earn*
wünschen (hat gewünscht) *to wish*

erfahren *experienced*
spontan *spontaneous*
stinklangweilig *boring as heck*
unterbezahlt *underpaid*
ziemlich *rather, considerably*

Ausdrücke

alles Gute *all the best*
Das hat keinen Zweck. *That's pointless.*
Das kann nicht schaden. *That can't do any harm.*
genau das Richtige *just the right thing*
Ich drücke dir ganz fest die Daumen. *I'll cross my fingers for you.*
Melde dich, wenn sich etwas ergibt. *Call if something comes of it.*

Berufe

der Apotheker, -/die Apothekerin, -nen *pharmacist*
der Architekt, -/die Architektin, -nen *architect*
der Arzt, *pl.* **Ärzte/die Ärztin, -nen** *physician*
der Automechaniker, -/die Automechanikerin, -nen *car mechanic*
der Bäcker, -/die Bäckerin, -nen *baker*
der Beamte, [-n], -n/die Beamtin, -nen *civil servant*
der Berater, -/die Beraterin, -nen *counselor, advisor*
der Bibliothekar, -/die Bibliothekarin, -nen *librarian*
der Buchhalter, -/die Buchhalterin, -nen *accountant*
der Chef, -s/die Chefin, -nen *boss*
der Fleischer, -/die Fleischerin, -nen *butcher*
der Friseur, -/die Friseurin, -nen/die Friseuse *hairdresser*
der Geschäftsmann, ¨-er/ die Geschäftsfrau, -en *businessman, -woman*
der Ingenieur, -/die Ingenieurin, -nen *engineer*
der Kaufmann, ¨-er/die Kauffrau, -en *clerk*
der Kellner, -/die Kellnerin, -nen *waiter/waitress*
der Koch, ¨-e/die Köchin, -nen *cook*
der Krankenpfleger, -/die Krankenschwester, -n *orderly, nurse*
der Lehrer, -/die Lehrerin, -nen *teacher*
der Makler, -/die Maklerin, -nen *real estate agent*
der Metzger, -/die Metzgerin, -nen *butcher*
der Programmierer, -/die Programmiererin, -nen *programmer*
der Rechtsanwalt, ¨-e/die Rechtsanwältin, -nen *lawyer*
der Sekretär, -/die Sekretärin, -nen *secretary*
der Tellerwäscher, -/die Tellerwäscherin, -nen *dishwasher*
der Tierarzt, ¨-e/die Tierärztin, -nen *veterinarian*
der Verkäufer, -/die Verkäuferin, -nen *salesperson*
der Zahnarzt, ¨-e/die Zahnärztin, -nen *dentist*

Das Vorstellungsgespräch

der Abschluss *completion of program; degree*
das Arbeitsamt, ¨-er *(un)employment office*
die Aufregung *excitement, nervousness*
die Ausbildung, -en *education, job training*
der Ausbildungsleiter, - *head trainer, lead teacher*
die Beratung, -en *counseling*
der Betrieb, -e *business*
der Bewerber, -/ die Bewerberin, -nen *applicant*
der Eindruck, ¨-e *impression*
die Erwartung, -en *expectation*
die Firma, *pl.* **Firmen** *firm, company*
das Gefühl, -e *feeling*
der Grund, ¨-e *reason*
das Interesse, -n *interest*
der Personalchef, -s/die Personalchefin, -nen *head of the personnel deparment*
der Rat, *pl.* **Ratschläge** *advice*
das Verständnis *understanding, sympathy*
die Wahl, -en *selection, choice*

ab·bauen (hat abgebaut) *to reduce, decrease*
ein·fallen (fällt ein, ist eingefallen) + *dat.* *to think of something*

sich heraus·putzen (hat sich herausgeputzt) *to dress up, get decked out*
hinterlassen (hinterlässt, hat hinterlassen) *to leave behind*
sich informieren (hat sich informiert) über + *acc.* *to inform oneself, educate oneself about*
nach·fragen (hat nachgefragt) über + *acc.* *to ask, inquire about*
pochen (hat gepocht) *to pound, beat*
sich präsentieren (hat sich präsentiert) *to present oneself*
schaffen (hat geschafft) *to manage, to pass*
Fragen stellen (hat gestellt) *to ask questions*
sich unterhalten (unterhält sich, hat sich unterhalten) mit + *dat.* *to converse with, talk to*
sich verschließen (hat sich verschlossen) *to close oneself off, shut down*
versuchen (hat versucht) *to try, attempt*
sich vor·bereiten (bereitet sich vor, hat sich vorbereitet) auf + *acc.* *to prepare for*

abgetragen *worn-out*
aufgeregt *excited, tense, nervous*
daher *for that reason, that's why*
genügend *sufficient, enough*
hellwach *wide awake*
konfus *confused*
übermäßig *excessively*
vorher *ahead of time, beforehand*

Eigenschaften

analytisch *analytical*
begabt *talented*
diszipliniert *disciplined*
dynamisch *dynamic*
gründlich *thorough, careful*
kollegial *collegial*
kontaktfreudig *outgoing, sociable*
motiviert *motivated*
pünktlich *punctual*
qualifiziert *qualified*
selbstständig *independent, self-reliant*
zuverlässig *dependable*

Ausdrücke

am liebsten *most of all, the most*
bis dann! *see you later!*
eine halbe Stunde *a half an hour*
in guter Verfassung *in good shape*
mit Sicherheit *with certainty, for sure*
sonst niemand (-en, -em) *nobody else*
vor allem *above all*

Aus dem Zieltext

die Abteilung, -en *department*
die Akte, -n *file*
die Besprechung, -en *discussion*
das Bibliothekarswesen *library science*
der Fall, ¨-e *case*
die Finanzen *(pl.)* *finances*
das Gehalt, ¨-er *salary, wage*
die Gehaltsvorstellung, -en *salary expectation*
die Jugendliteratur *youth literature*
der Kandidat, [-en], -en/die Kandidatin, -nen *candidate*
das Kinderbuch, ¨-er *children's book*
der Kollege, [-n], -n/ die Kollegin, -nen *colleague, co-worker*
die Ressource, -n *resource*
die Richtung, -en *direction*
die Stadtteilbibliothek, -en *branch library*
der Tarif, -e *wage rate*
der Urlaub *vacation*
die Verantwortung, -en *responsibility*
der Werdegang *development; career*
die Zusammenarbeit, -en *collaboration, joint project*

aus·kommen (ist ausgekommen) mit + *dat.* *to get along with*
aus·schreiben (hat ausgeschrieben) *to advertise, announce*
Bescheid bekommen (hat Bescheid bekommen) *to get an answer, be notified*
benachrichtigen (hat benachrichtigt) *to inform*
durch·gucken (hat durchgeguckt) *to look through, look over*
ein·stellen (hat eingestellt) *to hire*
erarbeiten (hat erarbeitet) *to acquire, work out*
kombinieren (hat kombiniert) *to combine*
leiten (hat geleitet) *to lead, be in charge of*
übersehen (übersieht, hat übersehen) *to oversee*
vergrößern (hat vergrößert) *to enlarge, expand*

(sich) vor·stellen *to introduce (oneself)*
ausführlich *complete, in detail*
beeindruckend *impressive*
beruflich *professional*
bereit *ready*
leider *unfortunately*
spätestens *at the latest*
telefonisch *by telephone*
zufrieden *satisfied*

Ausdrücke

auf jeden Fall *at any rate, in any case*
Ende nächster Woche *end of next week*
in dem Sinne *in this sense*
wären Sie ... *would you be . . .*
zu zweit *two at a time, in a pair*

Deutsch im Beruf 3

Finding a job

Once you have identified your job interests and abilities (see **Deutsch im Beruf 2**), you need to concern yourself with the job market **(der Arbeitsmarkt, der Stellenmarkt).** Job counseling **(die Berufsberatung)** and the governmental employment service **(das Arbeitsamt)** are good ways to start. Furthermore, you can research the job market on your own by reading ads **(die Anzeige, die Annonce, das Inserat)** in the "Help Wanted" section of the newspaper **(Stellenangebote).** It takes special skills to gather information from these usually very concise ads. You need to interpret the information offered and guess at the meaning of what is only implied. Finally, you may opt to market your best qualities in an ad **(Stellengesuch)** to prospective employers.

IHRE ZUKUNFT

Berufsberatung
an der Uni!

Experten der Berufsberatung sind die richtigen Ansprechpartner für Sie zu Themen wie allgemeine Hochschulberatung, studienbegleitende Praktika, Auslandspraktika, Aufbaustudien, Bewerbungen, Einstieg in das Berufsleben, Verdienstmöglichkeiten und Trainee-Programme. Denken Sie frühzeitig über Chancen und Möglichkeiten Ihres zukünftigen Berufes nach!

Berufsberatung für Studenten,
Grindelallee 44, 20146 Hamburg,
Mo-Do 9.00-15.00 Uhr, Fr 10.00-14.00 Uhr,
Telefon: 0 40/24 85-23 13, -22 34.

Schauen Sie doch mal herein!

Arbeitsamt Hamburg
Kurt-Schumacher-Allee 16, 20097 Hamburg
Telefon: 0 40/24 85-23 13, -22 34

IHRE BERUFSBERATUNG

Infos über die Dienste und Leistungen des Arbeitsamtes finden Sie auch in BTX *69100#

1 **Ihre Zukunft – Ihre Berufsberatung.** Lesen Sie die Anzeige auf Seite 408. Sie vermittelt Informationen über die Berufsberatung am Hamburger Arbeitsamt. Kreuzen Sie an, für wen die Berufsberatung ist, und begründen° Sie Ihre Antwort mit einem Zitat aus dem Text. Mehrere Antworten können zutreffen.

justify

Diese Berufsberatung ist für ...	Im Text steht ...
1. ___ Verkäufer.	______________________
2. ___ Kellner.	______________________
3. ___ Studenten.	______________________
4. ___ Leute, die wissen wollen, wie viel sie in einem Beruf verdienen können.	______________________
5. ___ Leute, die praktische Erfahrung sammeln möchten.	______________________
6. ___ Leute, die kurz im Ausland arbeiten wollen.	______________________
7. ___ Leute, die auch nach dem Diplom weiterstudieren wollen.	______________________
8. ___ Leute, die am Ende ihrer Karriere stehen.	______________________
9. ___ Leute, die mitten in ihrer Karriere stehen.	______________________
10. ___ Leute, die am Anfang ihrer Karriere stehen, d.h. eine Karriere beginnen.	______________________

2 **Fragen an sich selbst.** Sie suchen eine Stelle. Welche drei Fragen stellen Sie sich? Fragen Sie dann einen Partner/eine Partnerin, was er/sie sich fragt.

S1: Welche drei Fragen stellst du dir?
S2: Zuerst frage ich mich, wie viel Geld ich verdienen kann, und dann frage ich mich, ob ich mit anderen zusammen oder alleine arbeite.
S1: Und was fragst du dich zuletzt?
S2: Zuletzt frage ich mich, was ich bei der Arbeit tue.

1. Was tue ich bei der Arbeit?
2. Ist die Arbeit monoton oder abwechslungsreich°?
3. Welche Belastungen° gibt es in dieser Arbeit: Stress, Lärm°, Geruch°?
4. Wie viel verdiene ich?
5. Mit welchen Maschinen, Materialien, Pflanzen oder Tieren gehe ich um°?
6. Arbeite ich mit Kollegen zusammen oder alleine?
7. Mit was für Menschentypen habe ich Kontakt?
8. Welche Ausbildung brauche ich für die Stelle?
9. Welche praktischen Erfahrungen kann ich in dieser Arbeit sammeln?
10. Ist die Arbeitszeit flexibel oder fix?
11. Ist die Arbeit ein Vollzeitjob, Teilzeitjob oder ein Nebenjob°?
12. Welche persönlichen Eigenschaften brauche ich für die Arbeit?
13. Gibt es die Möglichkeit für eine Beförderung°?

varied
burdens, strains / noise / smell
***gehe ... um:** to deal with*
moonlighting job
promotion

Für ein Großprojekt auf dem Gebiet des Klärwerkbaues in Berlin suchen wir eine/n erfahrene/n

Bauleiter/in

Wir bitten um Ihre Zuschrift.
Regierungsbaumeister Schlegel GmbH
Guntherstr. 29, 80639 München
Tel. 089/17902-123

Ohne Moos° nix los!

° slang for "money"

Gerade beim Studienbeginn werden Sie feststellen, wie schwierig Studium und Nebenjob unter einen (Doktor-)Hut zu bringen sind. Bei McDonald's kein Problem, denn **Studenten** finden hier als

Mit-arbeiter/in

Voll- oder Teilzeit

Arbeitszeit, die Sie selbst bestimmen können. Wir arbeiten Sie gründlich und individuell ein und die Zusammenarbeit in unseren Crews mit fröhlichen Kollegen/innen wird Ihnen sicher gefallen. Rufen Sie einen unserer Restaurantleiter an oder kommen Sie einfach einmal vorbei. Wir freuen uns auf Sie!

McDONALD'S RESTAURANTS

Theodor-Heuss-Platz/Dammt.
20354 Hamburg
040 / 44 92 29

Gerhart-Hauptmann-Platz 10
20095 Hamburg
040 / 33 50 04

Gänsemarkt 35
20354 Hamburg
040 / 34 20 07

Glockengießerwall 8-10
20095 Hamburg
040 / 32 69 34

Adenauerallee ZOB
20097 Hamburg
040 / 24 68 41

Das etwas andere Restaurant

Softwareentwickler/in

TPS Labs

Wir sind:

ein sehr engagiertes, international tätiges Unternehmen und sind im Bereich der Client Server-Entwicklung tätig. Wir befassen uns primär mit der Entwicklung von Informationssystemen für multinationale Konzerne.

Wir suchen:

Sie, nicht älter als 35, mit fundierten Kenntnissen im Bereich Client-Server unter Windows (SQL, Powerbuilder, Windows NT), mit mindestens 3 Jahren Erfahrung, Motivation und einem Hochschulabschluß.

Wir bieten:

selbständiges und dynamisches Arbeiten im Projekt, gute Aufstiegschancen, Weiterbildungsmöglichkeiten und die Umgebung eines professionellen Teams.

Ihre Bewerbungsunterlagen schicken Sie bitte an:

TPS Labs Gartner & Debbas GmbH
Kronstadter Straße 9, 81677 München

SÄCHSISCHES
STAATSMINISTERIUM
DER FINANZEN

Stellenausschreibung

Zu besetzen ist die Stelle eines/einer

Leiters/Leiterin der Sächsischen Schlösserverwaltung.

Gesucht wird eine dynamische Persönlichkeit, die der sächsischen Kunst- und Kulturgeschichte verbunden ist.

Es wird erwartet:

- ein abgeschlossenes Hochschulstudium einer geisteswissenschaftlichen Studienrichtung oder der Architektur
- ausgeprägte musische Interessen
- Verwaltungserfahrung in einem Wirtschaftsbetrieb oder der öffentlichen Verwaltung
- die Fähigkeit und Bereitschaft zu teamorientiertem Arbeiten.

Mit dieser Stelle ist zugleich die Leitung des Referats „Personal, Haushalt und Organisation" verbunden.
Die Stelle wird nach der Vergütungsgruppe Ia/IBAT-O bewertet.
Bewerbungen sind bis 19. April 1997 zu richten an

Sächsisches Staatsministerium der Finanzen
Abteilung IV • Carolaplatz 1 • 01097 Dresden

3 **Drei Anzeigen: Direkte und indirekte Information.** Sehen Sie sich die drei Anzeigen oben an. Welche von den 13 Fragen der vorhergehenden Aktivität **(Fragen an sich selbst)** beantworten diese Anzeigen direkt? Schreiben Sie diese Antworten in die Tabelle. Besprechen Sie mit einem Partner/einer Partnerin mögliche Antworten für die Information, die nicht in den Anzeigen ist.

Frage	McDonald's	TPS Labs	Schlösserverwaltung
1.	*steht nicht im Text*	*Software entwickeln°*	*ein Referat leiten*
2.			
3.			
4.			
5.			
6.			
7.			
8.			
9.			
10.			
11.			
12.			
13.			

°*develop*

4 **Meine Arbeit jetzt und mein zukünftiger Beruf.** Was für einen Job haben Sie zur Zeit oder zuletzt gehabt? Welchen Beruf werden Sie später einmal ausüben? Beantworten Sie die Fragen im Hinblick auf° die Stelle, die Sie jetzt haben (oder zuletzt hatten) und im Hinblick auf den Beruf, den Sie später ergreifen wollen.

***im ... auf:** with regard to*

▣ Ihre jetzige (oder letzte) Arbeit: Pizza-Ausfahrer
Ihr zukünftiger Beruf: Arzt

Frage	**Jetzige (letzte) Arbeit**	**Zukünftiger Beruf**
1. Was tue ich?	________	________
2. Ist die Arbeit monoton oder abwechslungsreich?	________	________
3. Welche Belastungen gibt es in dieser Arbeit: Stress, Lärm, Geruch?	________	________
4. Wie viel verdiene ich?	________	________
5. Mit welchen Maschinen, Materialien, Pflanzen oder Tieren gehe ich um?	________	________
6. Arbeite ich mit Kollegen zusammen oder alleine?	________	________
7. Mit was für Menschentypen habe ich Kontakt?	________	________
8. Welche Ausbildung brauche ich für die Stelle?	________	________
9. Welche praktischen Erfahrungen kann ich in dieser Arbeit sammeln?	________	________
10. Ist die Arbeitszeit flexibel oder fix?	________	________
11. Ist die Arbeit ein Vollzeitjob, Teilzeitjob oder ein Nebenjob?	________	________
12. Welche persönlichen Eigenschaften brauche ich für die Arbeit?	________	________
13. Gibt es die Möglichkeit für eine Beförderung?	________	________

5 **Der ideale Beruf.** Lesen Sie, wie Jeanne, Phil und Don ihren idealen Beruf beschreiben. Beschreiben Sie dann mit einem Partner/einer Partnerin die Eigenschaften dieser drei Leute und diskutieren Sie mögliche Berufe für sie. Sie können Ausdrücke aus den Listen benutzen.

S1: Was für eine Person ist Jeanne?
S2: Sie ist eine unkomplizierte Person.
S1: Warum?
S2: Weil (ihr vieles egal ist).

S1: Für welchen Job eignet sich Jeanne?
S2: Für einen Job als (Fließbandarbeiterin).
S1: Warum einen Job als (Fließbandarbeiterin)?
S2: Weil ...

Frage	Jeanne	Phil	Don
1. Was?	egal	Leuten helfen	etwas Technisches
2. Wie?	egal	abwechslungsreich	monoton ist O.K.
3. Belastungen?	egal	egal	keine Stressbelastung
4. Verdienst?	so viel wie möglich	durchschnittlich oder höher	durchschnittlich oder auch ein bisschen weniger
5. Maschinen usw.?	keine Maschinen	keine Maschinen	keine Pflanzen oder Tiere
6. Zusammen/alleine?	egal	mit Kollegen, aber auch alleine	lieber alleine
7. Menschentypen?	mit Leuten, die wenige Fragen stellen	mit Leuten, die Hilfe brauchen	mit keinen Leuten
8. Ausbildung?	Realschule	Universität	Berufsschule
9. Erfahrungen?	egal	mehr über Menschen und ihre Probleme	mehr über Technik und Maschinen
10. Arbeitszeit?	flexibel	flexibel	fix
11. Vollzeit-/Teilzeit-/Nebenjob?	Teilzeit- oder Nebenjob	Vollzeitjob	Vollzeitjob
12. Eigenschaften?	Geduld	Intelligenz, Mitgefühl	analytisches Denken, handwerkliches Geschick°
13. Beförderung?	möglich	sicher	wahrscheinlich

skill

Eigenschaften

dynamisch • hilfsbereit • analytisch • geduldig • intelligent • kontaktfreudig • einfallslos° • routineorientiert • unkompliziert • teamorientiert • selbstständig • flexibel • gebildet • kreativ • offen

unimaginative

Mögliche Berufe

Kellner/in • Gärtner/in • Computerprogrammierer/in • Sekretär/in • Arzt/Ärztin • Krankenpfleger/Krankenschwester • Mechaniker/in • Fließband°arbeiter/in • Zeitungsausträger/in • Lehrer/in • Tischler/in • Verkäufer/in • ?

assembly line

Schreibecke **Empfehlungsbrief°.** Beschreiben Sie Jeanne, Phil oder Don in einem Empfehlungsbrief. Betonen° Sie die guten Eigenschaften und verschweigen° Sie die schlechten.

letter of recommendation
emphasize / do not mention

In this chapter you will continue to learn how to relate events in the past. You will read and discuss fairy tales and compare holidays and vacation spots in Germany, Austria, and Switzerland.

Kommunikative Funktionen

- Narrating past events
- Talking about consecutive events in the past
- Talking about simultaneous events in the past
- Talking about events that occur repeatedly
- Telling when events occur
- Expressing possession

Strukturen

- The narrative past
- The past perfect
- Word order in sentences beginning with a subordinate clause
- The subordinating conjunctions **als, nachdem, ob, wann,** and **wenn**
- The genitive case

Vokabeln

- Märchen
- Die Schweiz: geographische Daten

Kulturelles

- Die Brüder Grimm: **Kinder- und Hausmärchen**
- Karneval, Fasching, Fastnacht
- Die Schweiz
- Fest- und Feiertage

Der Karneval in Mainz beginnt für diese Kinder am 11.11 um 11.11 Uhr.

KAPITEL ZEHN

Fest- und Feiertage

Go to the ***Vorsprung*** Website at
www.hmco.com/college

ANLAUFTEXT

Aschenputtel

(Ein Märchen nach den Brüdern Grimm)

Anna und ihre Freunde wollen zum Karneval ein langes Wochenende in Köln verbringen. Tagsüber gibt es viele kostümierte Narren° auf den Straßen und endlose Umzüge°. Und abends können sie auf einen Ball gehen, wo man bis spät in die Nacht tanzt und trinkt ... und sich vielleicht verliebt. Wer weiß? Vielleicht lernt Anna dort ihren Prinzen kennen, wie Aschenputtel° ...

fools
parades
Cinderella

Vorschau

Wissenswerte Vokabeln: Märchen

Talking about fairy tales

Did you enjoy reading fairy tales as a child? Why or why not? Which ones were your favorites?

„Es war einmal ein König ..."

der Königssohn / der Prinz, die Königin
der König, die Königstochter / die Prinzessin

die Stiefmutter

der Jäger

die Hexe

der Zwerg

die gute Fee

der Frosch

der Zauberer

der Spiegel

der Wald

ein giftiger Apfel

„... und wenn sie nicht gestorben sind, dann leben sie noch heute."

Was gibt die alte Frau Schneewittchen?

1 Schneewittchen. „Schneewittchen" ist ein sehr bekanntes° Märchen von den Brüdern Grimm. Lesen Sie die Sätze und setzen Sie die richtigen Wörter ein.

well-known

1. Eine böse _____ will ihre Stieftochter° Schneewittchen von einem _____ erschießen lassen°.

stepdaughter
***erschießen lassen:** have shot to death*

2. Er erschießt Schneewittchen nicht und sie läuft allein weg in den dunklen _____ hinein.
3. Schneewittchen wohnt bei sieben _____en.
4. Die Königin schaut jeden Tag in einen _____ und findet heraus, dass sie nicht die Schönste ist.
5. Die Königin verkleidet° sich als _____.
6. Die Königin gibt Schneewittchen einen giftigen _____ und Schneewittchen stirbt scheinbar°.
7. Die Zwerge legen Schneewittchen in einen Glassarg°. Ein _____ bekommt Schneewittchens Glassarg von den Zwergen und auf dem Heimweg fällt der Apfel aus ihrem Hals. Sie wird wieder lebendig.
8. Er heiratet Schneewittchen und so wird sie die neue _____.

disguises

apparently

glass coffin

W. Vok. Märchen are tales in which a hero/heroine survives an ordeal or injustice but is rewarded for perseverance, hope, and faith, where good triumphs over evil, and where there is often retribution for the evil-doer. Irrational forces play a significant role–animals talk, the forest hides witches and dwarves, and princes become enchanted frogs–but the hero/heroine, subjected to endless trial, learns to trust innate abilities and soon overcomes these powers to reach a happy ending. On the surface these are fantastic and antiquated tales, but **Märchen** speak to the unarticulated, unsophisticated fears of children with vivid imagery and a clear delineation between good and evil, helping them process their worries in a productive manner.

„Zum letzten Mal: Haut ab!° Ich bin nicht Eure Schneewittchen!"

Scram!

2 Thematische Fragen. Beantworten Sie die folgenden Fragen auf Deutsch.

1. Was passiert in der Version von „Aschenputtel", die wir in Nordamerika kennen? Lebt die Mutter noch? Lebt der Vater noch?
2. Wie ist das Leben für Aschenputtel? Was muss sie alles machen?
3. Wer hilft Aschenputtel, eine Fee oder ein Zauberer?
4. Hat Aschenputtel Stiefbrüder oder Stiefschwestern? Wie sind sie?
5. Wohin geht Aschenputtel?
6. Was verliert Aschenputtel auf dem Ball?

Thematische Fragen. The Disney animation *Cinderella* is based on Charles Perrault's French version of the tale.

3 **Zeitdetektiv.** Hier sind siebzehn Sätze im Präteritum°. Welche Sätze im Präsens bedeuten ungefähr das Gleiche?

1. Aschenputtels Mutter **starb.**
2. Eine schlimme Zeit **begann.**
3. Der König **lud** zu einem Fest **ein.**
4. Der Königssohn **hielt** Aschenputtel für eine fremde Königstochter.

a. Der Königssohn hält Aschenputtel für eine fremde Königstochter.
b. Der König lädt zu einem Fest ein.
c. Aschenputtels Mutter stirbt°.
d. Eine schlimme Zeit beginnt.

Aschenputtels Vater ...

5. ... **heiratete** eine neue Frau.
6. ... **sollte** für Aschenputtel einen Zweig zurückbringen.
7. ... **brachte** für Aschenputtel einen Haselzweig°.

Aschenputtels Vater ...

e. ... heiratet wieder.
f. ... bringt für Aschenputtel einen Haselzweig.
g. ... soll für Aschenputtel einen Haselzweig zurückbringen.

Aschenputtel ...

8. ... **sah** schmutzig **aus.**
9. ... **ging** jeden Tag zum Baum und **weinte.**
10. ... **zog** das Kleid **an.**
11. ... **rannte** schnell davon.
12. ... **verlor** auf der Treppe ihren linken Schuh.
13. ... **wollte** auch zum Tanz mitgehen.

Aschenputtel ...

h. ... rennt schnell davon.
i. ... will auch zum Tanz mitgehen.
j. ... zieht das Kleid an.
k. ... geht jeden Tag zum Baum und weint.
l. ... verliert auf der Treppe ihren linken Schuh.
m. ... sieht schmutzig aus.

Die Stiefschwestern ...

14. ... **nannten** sie Aschenputtel.
15. ... **riefen** Aschenputtel zu: „Wir gehen auf das Schloss des Königs."
16. ... **erkannten** Aschenputtel nicht.
17. ... **schnitten** sich die Zehe und die Ferse ab.

Die Stiefschwestern ...

n. ... erkennen Aschenputtel nicht.
o. ... nennen sie Aschenputtel.
p. ... schneiden sich die Zehe und die Ferse ab.
q. ... rufen Aschenputtel zu: „Wir gehen auf das Schloss des Königs."

narrative past

Zeitdetektiv. You will be learning about the narrative past **(Präteritum)** later in this chapter.

dies

hazelnut branch

4 **Wortfelder.** Welches Wort gehört zum gleichen Wortfeld wie das Wort in der linken Spalte? Unterstreichen Sie es.

▣	das Messer:	<u>schneiden</u>	schwer arbeiten	tanzen
1.	das Messer:	schneiden	schwer arbeiten	tanzen
2.	der Herd:	waschen	kochen	schlafen
3.	die Asche:	schön	weiß	schmutzig
4.	Edelsteine:	Diamanten	Kleid	Essen
5.	der Baum:	passen	bringen	pflanzen
6.	der liebe Gott:	beten	schwer arbeiten	studieren
7.	das Vögelchen:	fliegen	schwimmen	heiraten
8.	der Ball:	arbeiten	tanzen	studieren
9.	der Schuh:	weinen	anprobieren	trinken
10.	der Fuß:	das Haar	die Zehe	die Nase

Although long sometimes, **Märchen** generally contain many recurring expressions.

ANLAUFTEXT

Aschenputtel

Lesen Sie eine deutsche Version von „Aschenputtel".

Es war einmal ein hübsches Mädchen, dessen[1] Mutter krank wurde. Als die Frau fühlte, dass sie sterben musste, rief sie ihre Tochter zu sich: „Liebes Kind, bleib fromm und gut, so wird dir der liebe Gott immer helfen, und ich will vom Himmel auf dich herabblicken." Dann starb die Frau.

Nach einem Jahr heiratete der reiche Vater eine neue Frau, die zwei Töchter mit ins Haus brachte. Diese Schwestern waren schön von Gesicht aber böse von Herzen. Nun musste das Mädchen von morgens bis abends schwer arbeiten. Abends musste sie sich neben den Herd in die Asche legen. Und weil sie darum immer schmutzig aussah, nannten die Stiefschwestern sie Aschenputtel.

Eines Tages machte der Vater eine Reise. Er fragte, was er den Mädchen mitbringen sollte. „Schöne Kleider!", „Perlen und Edelsteine," sagten die Stiefschwestern. Aber Aschenputtel sagte: „Vater, bring mir einfach den ersten Zweig von einem Baum, den du auf dem Heimweg findest."

Der Vater brachte Kleider und Edelsteine für die Stiefschwestern und einen Haselzweig für Aschenputtel. Aschenputtel dankte ihm und pflanzte den Zweig auf dem Grab ihrer Mutter. Er wuchs zu einem schönen Haselnussbaum. Aschenputtel ging jeden Tag dreimal darunter, weinte und betete[2]. Jedes Mal kam ein weißes Vögelchen auf den Baum und gab dem Mädchen alles, was es sich wünschte.

Eines Tages lud der König alle Mädchen im Land zu einem Fest ein. Der Königssohn suchte eine Braut. Die zwei Stiefschwestern riefen Aschenputtel zu: „Wir gehen auf das Schloss des Königs." Aschenputtel wollte auch gern zum Tanz mitgehen. Die Stiefmutter aber erlaubte es nicht: „Du hast keine Kleider und Schuhe und willst tanzen? Du kommst nicht mit!" Darauf ging sie mit ihren beiden Töchtern fort.

---

[1] *whose*

[2] *prayed*

Aschenputtel ging zum Grab ihrer Mutter unter den Haselbaum und rief: „Bäumchen, rüttel° dich und schüttel° dich – wirf Gold und Silber über mich!“ Da warf ihr der Vogel ein Kleid aus Gold und Silber herunter. Aschenputtel zog das Kleid an und ging zum Fest. Ihre Schwestern und Stiefmutter erkannten sie nicht. Der Königssohn hielt sie für eine fremde Königstocher und tanzte nur mit ihr. Als Aschenputtel nach Hause gehen wollte, sprach der Königssohn: „Ich begleite° dich!“ Aber Aschenputtel lief schnell fort.

shake / shiver

accompany

Am zweiten Tag wiederholte sich alles. Am dritten Tag brachte das Vögelchen ein glänzendes Kleid und Schuhe aus Gold. Wieder tanzte der Königssohn nur mit ihr, wieder lief Aschenputtel schnell fort. Aber diesmal verlor sie auf der Treppe ihren linken Schuh.

Der Königssohn proklamierte: „Die Frau, deren° Fuß in diesen Schuh passt, soll meine Braut werden!“ Da freuten sich die Schwestern. Die älteste Stiefschwester nahm den Schuh mit in ihr Zimmer und probierte ihn an. Aber der Schuh war zu klein. Da sagte ihr die Mutter: „Schneid die Zehe ab! Wenn du Königin bist, so brauchst du nicht mehr zu Fuß zu gehen.“ Da schnitt die Schwester die Zehe ab.

whose

Der Königssohn nahm sie als seine Braut aufs Pferd. Als sie am Grab von Aschenputtels Mutter vorbeiritten°, riefen zwei Täubchen vom Haselbaum: „Rucke di guh, rucke di guh, Blut ist im Schuh. Der Schuh ist zu klein. Die rechte Braut sitzt noch daheim.“ Da sah der Königssohn das Blut und brachte sie zurück.

rode past

Da probierte die andere Schwester den Schuh an, aber die Ferse war zu groß. Da nahm sie ein Messer und schnitt die Ferse ab. Die Schwester und der Königssohn ritten am Grab vorbei und wieder riefen die Täubchen: „Rucke di guh, rucke di guh, Blut ist im Schuh …" Da brachte der Königssohn die falsche Braut wieder nach Hause zurück.

Er fragte den Vater: „Haben Sie noch eine andere Tochter?" „Nein", sagte der, „nur das schmutzige Aschenputtel. Sie kann nicht die Richtige sein." Der Königssohn wollte sie aber sehen. So probierte Aschenputtel den goldenen Schuh an, und er passte wie angegossen°. Dann nahm der Königssohn Aschenputtel aufs Pferd und ritt mit ihr fort. Diesmal riefen die Täubchen: „Rucke di guh, rucke di guh, kein Blut ist im Schuh. Der Schuh ist nicht zu klein, die rechte Braut, die führt er heim." Dann flogen die beiden Täubchen auf Aschenputtels Schultern, eines rechts, das andere links.

poured on

Rückblick

5 **Stimmt das?** Stimmen diese Aussagen zum Text oder nicht? Wenn nicht, was stimmt?

	Ja, das stimmt.	*Nein, das stimmt nicht.*
1. Aschenputtels Vater war krank und starb.	___	___
2. Aschenputtel musste in der Küche schwer arbeiten und in der Asche neben dem Herd schlafen.	___	___
3. Aschenputtels Vater brachte ihr Perlen und Edelsteine von seiner Reise zurück.	___	___
4. Der König lud alle Mädchen im Land zu einem Fest ein, weil sein Sohn eine Braut suchte.	___	___
5. Die Stiefmutter nahm Aschenputtel zum Ball mit.	___	___
6. Aschenputtel rannte zum Grab von ihrer Mutter und rief zum Haselbaum: „Rüttel dich und schüttel dich, wirf Gold und Silber über mich!“	___	___
7. Am dritten Abend brachte der Vogel Aschenputtel das schönste Kleid und Glasschuhe.	___	___
8. Aschenputtel verlor einen Schuh beim Tanzen.	___	___
9. Der Königssohn wollte die Frau heiraten, deren Fuß in den goldenen Schuh passte.	___	___
10. Aschenputtel musste sich die Ferse und die Zehe abschneiden, damit der Schuh passte.	___	___
11. Die Stiefmutter und die Stiefschwestern freuten sich, dass der Königssohn Aschenputtel als seine Braut erkannte.	___	___

6 **Ergänzen Sie.** Ergänzen Sie diese Sätze mit Wörtern aus dem **Anlauftext.**

1. Aschenputtels Mutter fühlte, dass sie ___ musste.
2. Die Mutter sagte Aschenputtel: „Bleib fromm und gut, und ich will vom ___ auf dich herabblicken.“
3. Weil das Mädchen immer so ___ aussah, nannten sie sie Aschenputtel.
4. Aschenputtels Vater brachte ihr einen ___ von einem Haselbaum.
5. Jeden Tag ging Aschenputtel dreimal zum Grab, ___ und betete.
6. Das Vögelchen am Grab gab dem Mädchen alles, was es sich ___.
7. Der Königssohn suchte eine ___.
8. Der Königssohn ___ nur mit Aschenputtel.
9. Die älteste Stiefschwester nahm den Schuh und ___ ihn an; der Schuh war zu klein.
10. Die Mutter gab ihr ein ___ und sagte: „Schneide die Zehe ab!“
11. Aschenputtel probierte den goldenen Schuh an, und er ___ wie angegossen.
12. Diesmal riefen die Vöglein: „Rucke di guh, rucke di guh, kein ___ ist im Schuh. Der Schuh ist nicht zu klein. Die rechte Braut, die führt er heim.“

7 **Kurz gefragt.** Beantworten Sie diese Fragen auf Deutsch.

Kurz gefragt. These questions are in the simple past.

1. Was sagte Aschenputtels Mutter zu ihrer Tochter, bevor sie starb?
2. Wie änderte sich Aschenputtels Leben, nachdem ihre Mutter starb?
3. Warum nannten die Stiefschwestern das Mädchen „Aschenputtel"?
4. Was für ein Andenken wünschte sich Aschenputtel von Vaters Reise und was machte sie damit?
5. Warum hielt der König ein Fest?
6. Warum wollten die Stiefschwestern (und auch Aschenputtel) zum Fest gehen?
7. Was machte das Vögelchen, als Aschenputtel zum Grab ging?
8. Wen nahm die Stiefmutter mit zum Fest?
9. Wie fand der Königssohn Aschenputtel wieder?
10. Wie wusste der Königssohn, dass Aschenputtel wirklich die richtige Braut war?

8 **Kurz interpretiert.** Beantworten Sie diese Fragen auf Deutsch.

1. In vielen Märchen hat die Zahl 3 eine symbolische Funktion. Zählen Sie alle Elemente in „Aschenputtel", die in Dreiergruppen passieren. Was symbolisieren sie wohl?
2. Aschenputtels Liebe zu ihrer Mutter ist sehr wichtig. Wie beweist° Aschenputtel diese Liebe? Hält die verstorbene Mutter ihr Versprechen ein und passt sie auf Aschenputtel auf? Wie?
3. Welche Zauberelemente oder unwahrscheinlichen Episoden gibt es in diesem Märchen? Was sind sie und warum sind sie wichtig?
4. In dieser Geschichte spielt Aschenputtels Vater praktisch keine Rolle. Warum ist die Figur des Vaters so neutral aber die Figuren der Stiefmutter und Stiefschwestern so böse und negativ?

prove

■ FREIE ■ KOMMUNIKATION ■ **Rollenspiel: Der Prinz und Aschenputtel.** S1 ist der Prinz und S2 ist die Königin. Sprechen Sie miteinander über Aschenputtel. Was haben Sie auf dem Fest gemacht? Wie war Aschenputtel? Was möchten Sie jetzt machen?

9 **Berühmte Märchensprüche.** Welches Zitat stammt aus welchem Märchen?

a. Rapunzel
b. Aschenputtel
c. Hänsel und Gretel
d. Rumpelstilzchen
e. Schneewittchen
f. Rotkäppchen
g. Die Bremer Stadtmusikanten

1. ___ „Ei, Großmutter, was hast du für ein entsetzlich großes Maul!" – „Dass ich dich besser fressen kann!"
2. ___ „Heute back ich, morgen brau ich, übermorgen hol ich der Königin ihr Kind; ach, wie gut, dass niemand weiß, dass ich _____ heiß!"
3. ___ „Zieh lieber mit uns fort, wir gehen nach Bremen; etwas Besseres als den Tod° findest du überall."
4. ___ „Rüttel dich und schüttel dich, wirf Gold und Silber über mich."

death

5. ___ „Rapunzel, Rapunzel, lass dein Haar herunter."
6. ___ „Knusper, knusper, kneischen, wer knuspert an meinem Häuschen?"
   – „Der Wind, der Wind, das himmlische Kind."
7. ___ „Spieglein, Spieglein an der Wand, wer ist die Schönste im ganzen Land?"

BRENNPUNKT KULTUR

Die Brüder Grimm und ihre Kinder- und Hausmärchen

There has been no single work of children's literature more important to Western culture than the **Kinder- und Hausmärchen,** an anthology of folk (fairy) tales **(Volksmärchen)** published by the Brothers Grimm, Jacob (1785–1863) and Wilhelm (1786–1859). The Brothers Grimm spent many years collecting these **Märchen,** which were, by tradition and practice, a form of oral literature. The texts existed only in the memory of the many people who told and retold them. Many of these tales were native to specific regions and were told in dialect; others were more universal and spread to other nations and languages, often developing interesting plot twists in travelling abroad. The Grimms did not write the fairy tales themselves, but instead sought out talented storytellers, recording and editing the tales they were told. The Brothers Grimm published the first volume of their anthology in 1812; a second volume, including contributions from other collectors of folk tales, was printed in 1814. They followed with an anthology of Germanic myths, **Deutsche Sagen,** in 1816–18. Because of their research and their fascination with the German language, the Grimm brothers are regarded as the founders of modern German studies **(Germanistik).** This reputation was enhanced by Jacob Grimm's **Deutsche Grammatik** and by their efforts to publish the first comprehensive **Deutsches Wörterbuch,** a project that lasted from 1852 to its completion in 1961.

Jakob und Wilhelm Grimm.

Jakob geb. d. 4. Jan. 1785 zu Hanau, gest. d. 26. Sept. 1863 zu Berlin.
Wilhelm geb. d. 24. Jan. 1786 zu Hanau, gest. d. 16. Dez. 1859 zu Berlin.

Zwei Brüder, durch Lebenslauf, Wirken und Sinnesart so eng verbunden, daß man des Einen nicht ohne den Andern gedenken mag. In deutscher Sprach-, Literatur- und Alterthumswissenschaft haben sie durch tiefe Forschung, schöpferischen Genius, sinnvolles Eingehn auf Gefühls- und Phantasieleben der Völker neue Gesichtskreise eröffnet und Anregungen geboten wie kaum ein Anderer. Mit eminenter Begabung des Geistes verbanden sie eine liebenswürdige Einfachheit des Gemüthes und der Art sich äußerlich zu geben. Unter den Gelehrten ihres Gleichen suchend, haben sie sich in der Kinderwelt dankbarste Herzen geschaffen durch ihre Märchen. Ihre männliche Charakterfestigkeit und Gewissenstreue aber hat sich an den Tag gelegt in ihrer Theilnahme an dem berühmten Professorenprotest gegen den hannover'schen Verfassungsumsturz von 1837.

10 **Märchenstruktur.** Was ist die normale Struktur in einem Märchen? In welcher Reihenfolge passieren diese Ereignisse°? Nummerieren Sie sie.

events

Die gute Person gewinnt dann doch den Konflikt. ___
Eine böse Person kommt in die Geschichte. ___
Der Leser/Die Leserin lernt eine gute Person kennen. 1
Es gibt einen Konflikt zwischen der guten Person und der bösen Person. ___
Man denkt, dass die böse Person den Konflikt gewinnen wird. ___
Die böse Person wird bestraft°. ___

wird bestraft: *is punished*

11 **Interview: Märchen.** Stellen Sie einem Partner/einer Partnerin die folgenden Fragen.

1. Hast du als Kind „Aschenputtel" gelesen? Was war damals deine Reaktion?
2. Was sollen Kinder von „Aschenputtel" lernen?
3. Welche Märchen machte das Disney-Studio als Zeichentrickfilme bekannt?
4. Welche Märchen findest du sexistisch? Warum?
5. Hast du als Kind gern Märchen gelesen? Hast du sie immer noch gern?
6. Welche sind deine Lieblingsmärchen? Beschreib' die Hauptfiguren in deinen Lieblingsmärchen.
7. Beschreib' den Feind° in deinen Lieblingsmärchen.
8. In den meisten Märchen passiert ein großes Unglück. Was war das Unglück in deinen Lieblingsmärchen?
9. Welche Zauberkräfte helfen der Hauptfigur in deinen Lieblingsmärchen?
10. Welche Märchen aus anderen Ländern, Kontinenten und Kulturen kennst du?

adversary

Strukturen und Vokabeln

I Narrating past events

The narrative past

In Chapter 5 you learned that the conversational past tense **(das Perfekt)** is used in informal contexts, in speaking, and in letter writing to talk about events in the past.

Tante Uschi **hat** als Kellnerin **gearbeitet.**

German speakers use the narrative past **(das Präteritum),** also called the simple past, to recount past events in written texts, such as novels, stories, news articles, and occasionally in speaking, especially when telling a long, uninterrupted story. Some of these forms look very much like the English simple past forms and should present few problems in reading.

Da **begann** eine schlimme Zeit.	*With that began a difficult time.*
Jedesmal **kam** ein weißes Vögelchen auf den Baum.	*A little white bird came to the tree every time.*

A. Narrative past: regular (weak) verbs

Regular (weak) verbs **(schwache Verben)** add a **-te** as a narrative past tense marker. All forms except the **ich-** and **er/sie/es-**forms add the same endings as in the present tense (e.g., **-st, -t,** or **-n**).

machen: *to do, make*				
Person	**Singular**		**Plural**	
1st	ich mach**te**	*I did, made*	wir mach**ten**	*we did, made*
2nd, informal	du mach**test**	*you did, made*	ihr mach**tet**	*you did, made*
2nd, formal	Sie mach**ten**	*you did, made*	Sie mach**ten**	*you did, made*
3rd	er/sie/es mach**te**	*he/she/it did, made*	sie mach**ten**	*they did, made*

The **ich**-form and the **er/sie/es**-forms of the narrative past are identical, as are the **wir-** and **sie/Sie**-forms.

ich er sie es	wein**te**	*I* *he* *she* *it*	*cried*	wir sie Sie	wein**ten**	*we* *they* *you*	*cried*

In general, weak or regular verbs in English form the past tense with **-ed.** However, the **-ed** sounds like **d** (e.g., **he cried, she prayed, it rained**), or **t** (e.g., **they walked, he skipped, we worked**).

Regular verbs with a stem ending in **-t** (e.g., **arbeiten, beten**), **-d** (e.g., **reden**), **-fn** (e.g., **öffnen**), or **-gn** (e.g., **regnen**), insert an additional **e** before the narrative past tense marker **-te** to facilitate pronunciation.

Aschenputtel weinte und bet**e**te. *Cinderella cried and prayed.*

These are the narrative past forms of **arbeiten.**

arbeiten: *to work*				
Person	**Singular**		**Plural**	
1st	ich arbeit**e**te	*I worked*	wir arbeit**e**ten	*we worked*
2nd, informal	du arbeit**e**test	*you worked*	ihr arbeit**e**tet	*you worked*
2nd, formal	Sie arbeit**e**ten	*you worked*	Sie arbeit**e**ten	*you worked*
3rd	er/sie/es arbeit**e**te	*he/she/it worked*	sie arbeit**e**ten	*they worked*

As in the present tense, regular verbs with separable prefixes place the prefix at the end of the sentence, leaving the conjugated narrative past form of the verb in the 2nd position.

anprobieren
Aschenputtel **probierte** den goldenen Schuh **an.** *Cinderella tried on the golden slipper.*

Remember that regular (weak) verbs have a letter **-t** in both the narrative past tense and the conversational past tense.

Infinitive	*Present*	*Narrative past*	*Conversational past*
sagen	ich sage	ich sag**te**	ich habe gesag**t**

12 **Meine eigene Verbtabelle.** Füllen Sie diese Verbtabelle mit den richtigen Verbformen aus.

Meine eigene Verbtabelle. These are all regular (weak) verbs. You may add other verbs to this list.

	Infinitiv	*Präteritum*	*Perfekt*
1.	lachen	______	______
2.	______	wohnte	______
3.	fragen	______	______
4.	legen	______	______
5.	______	______	hat getanzt
6.	feiern	______	______
7.	______	bedeutete	______
8.	______	______	hat gefühlt
9.	setzen	______	______
10.	______	______	hat sich gefreut
11.	______	______	ist marschiert
12.	______	küsste	______
13.	______	______	hat geregnet
14.	______	erzählte	______
15.	heiraten	______	______
16.	______	______	hat gemacht
17.	______	wartete	______
18.	kosten	______	______
19.	______	dauerte	______
20.	______	______	hat sich verliebt

13 **Hannelores Kindheit° in Deutschland.** Annas Mutter Hannelore erlebte° die 50er-Jahre in Deutschland. Erzählen Sie ihre Geschichte im Präteritum mit den angegebenen schwachen Verben.

childhood
experienced

Hannelore

1. in Weinheim leben
2. oft auf der Straße spielen
3. 1955 ihren fünften Geburtstag feiern
4. mit ihren Eltern im Wald Pilze° suchen
5. von amerikanischen Soldaten Englisch lernen

mushrooms

Oma Kunz

6. jeden Tag einkaufen
7. für die ganze Familie kochen
8. Opa heiraten
9. in der Stadt arbeiten
10. jeden Sonntag in der Kirche beten

Ihre Nachbarn

11. einen Tante-Emma-Laden° gründen° — *family-run shop*; *establish*
12. Brot, Käse und Wurst verkaufen
13. den Laden morgens um halb sieben aufmachen
14. den Laden abends um sechs zumachen
15. ein gutes Einkommen verdienen

14 Verliebt, verlobt, verheiratet. Erzählen Sie die Liebesgeschichte von Hannelore und Bob Adler mit den angegebenen schwachen Verben im Präteritum.

Hannelore

1. die Universität in Heidelberg wählen
2. zu Hause bei den Eltern wohnen und Geld sparen
3. mit dem Zug von Weinheim nach Heidelberg pendeln
4. Englisch und Volkswirtschaft studieren
5. mit Nachhilfestunden in Deutsch und Englisch Taschengeld verdienen
6. mit Schülern und mit amerikanischen Soldaten arbeiten
7. eines Tages einen Deutsch sprechenden GI namens Bob Adler kennen lernen

Bob

8. relativ gut Deutsch sprechen und Hannelore lustige Witze erzählen
9. einen guten Eindruck auf sie machen
10. als Ingenieur in der Armee dienen° — *serve*
11. sich auf die Wochenenden in Heidelberg freuen
12. die Studentin nach ihrer Telefonnummer fragen
13. sich schnell in die Hannelore verlieben
14. eine Weile warten und sich dann den Eltern in Weinheim vorstellen
15. sich nach einem romantischen Jahr in Heidelberg mit Hannelore verloben
16. im Juli 1972 die Hannelore heiraten

15 Der Karnevalsball. Der Narrenkönig in Köln hat Barbara auf einen Karnevalsball eingeladen. Dort hat sie Markus kennen gelernt. Erzählen Sie von diesem Abend. Benutzen Sie die schwachen Verben im Präteritum und entscheiden Sie, wer was machte.

▣ kennen lernen / auf dem Karnevalsball
Markus lernte Barbara auf dem Karnevalsball kennen.

1. kennen lernen / auf dem Karnevalsball
2. suchen / Tanzpartner(in)
3. tanzen / zu heißen Rhythmen
4. erzählen / dumme, aber lustige Witze
5. lachen / ein bisschen zu viel
6. sich setzen / an einen Tisch zusammen
7. bestellen / eine Flasche Weißwein
8. schütten° / ein Glas Wein auf den Tisch — *spill*
9. reichen° /ein Taschentuch und die Hand — *give*
10. danken / für das Taschentuch
11. küssen / zum ersten Mal
12. sich freuen / über den romantischen Abend

BRENNPUNKT KULTUR

Karneval, Fasching, Fastnacht

The "crazy" days (**Die tollen Tage**) of the **Karneval** season are some of the most popular holidays of the calendar in German-speaking countries. The name changes with location–**Karneval** in the Rhineland, **Fasching** in Bavaria and Austria, **Fastnacht** in Southwestern Germany, and **Fasnacht** in Switzerland–as do customs and actual dates, but it is generally regarded as the high point of the winter season. These are the days of revelry and merrymaking that precede the beginning of Lent **(die Fastenzeit)**, the period in which Catholics have been traditionally required to fast in preparation for Easter.

In the Rhineland, the **Karneval** season opens on November 11th at 11:11 A.M., **(am 11. 11., um 11 Uhr 11)**, while in the south the season traditionally begins on Epiphany, January 6 (**Dreikönigstag**). The season heats up on the last Thursday before Ash Wednesday (**Fetter Donnerstag**, or **Altweiberfastnacht**), when women customarily chase men with scissors and try to cut off a piece of their neckties. This marks the start of the six-day celebration: social taboos are relaxed, romances blossom, and the partying begins. Schools suspend classes while students hold costumed dance parties, and small towns and city neighborhoods put on their own parades. In and around the Rhineland, special "fools' guilds" (**Narrengesellschaften**) hold balls and "roasts" (**Kappensitzungen**) presided over by a **Narrenkönig** and **-königin.** On **Rosenmontag**, two days before Ash Wednesday, Cologne and Mainz host their famous **Umzüge:** huge parades with marching bands, costumed participants, dancing spectators, and decorated floats, some with humorous political themes, others from which candy and favors are tossed to the crowds. On **Karnevalsdienstag** final parades, parties, and costume balls signal the conclusion of the holiday season, which traditionally ends with a fish dinner and a ritualistic "funeral of the **Karneval**" on Ash Wednesday (**Aschermittwoch**).

Am Rosenmontag zieht der Narrenzug durch die Kölner Innenstadt.

B. Narrative past: irregular (strong) verbs

Strong verbs **(starke Verben)** show a vowel change from the infinitive to the narrative (simple) past. In English these verbs are referred to as *irregular verbs* (e.g., *see* > *saw, eat* > *ate*). You should learn to recognize these forms in German texts.

sehen > s**a**h
Da **sah** der Königssohn das Blut. *Then the king's son saw the blood.*

Some verbs change consonants as well as the vowel in the narrative past.

gehen > **ging**
Aschenputtel **ging** zum Grab ihrer Mutter. *Cinderella went to her mother's grave.*

Irregular verbs, like regular verbs, with separable prefixes position the prefix at the end of the sentence, leaving the conjugated narrative past form of the verb in the 2nd position.

an·z**ieh**en > z**o**g an
Aschenputtel **zog** das Kleid **an.** *Cinderella put the dress on.*
ab·schn**eid**en > schn**itt** ab
Da nahm sie ein Messer und **schnitt** die Ferse **ab.** *So she took a knife and cut off her heel.*

Irregular verbs have no ending in the **ich-** and the **er/sie/es-**forms like present tense modals, e.g., **muss.** The endings of all other forms are the same as the present tense endings.

		sehen: *to see*		
Person	**Singular**		**Plural**	
1st	ich sah	*I saw*	wir sah**en**	*we saw*
2nd, informal	du sah**st**	*you saw*	ihr sah**t**	*you saw*
2nd, formal	Sie sah**en**	*you saw*	Sie sah**en**	*you saw*
3rd	er/sie/es sah	*he/she/it saw*	sie sah**en**	*they saw*

Strong verbs with stems ending in **-t** or **-d** insert an additional **e** in the narrative past forms for **du** and **ihr** for easier pronunciation (e.g., **du schnittest, ihr schnittet**).

These are some of the most common strong verbs in the narrative and conversational past.

Infinitive	**Narrative past**	**Present perfect**	
	ich/er/sie/es	er/sie/es	
beg**i**nnen	beg**a**nn	hat begonnen	*began*
bek**o**mmen	bek**a**m	hat bekommen	*received*
b**i**tten	b**a**t	hat gebeten	*requested, asked for*
bl**ei**ben	bl**ie**b	ist geblieben	*stayed*
ein·l**a**den	l**u**d ein	hat eingeladen	*invited*
essen	**a**ß	hat gegessen	*ate*
f**a**hren	f**u**hr	ist gefahren	*drove*

Use your knowledge of English irregular verbs to aid you in remembering some of the German forms (e.g., *sing/sang, eat/ate, swim/swam*).

Infinitive	Narrative past	Present perfect	
fangen	fing	hat gefangen	*caught*
finden	fand	hat gefunden	*found*
fliegen	flog	ist geflogen	*flew*
geben	gab	hat gegeben	*gave*
gehen	ging	ist gegangen	*went*
halten	hielt	hat gehalten	*held*
helfen	half	hat geholfen	*helped*
kommen	kam	ist gekommen	*came*
laufen	lief	ist gelaufen	*ran*
lesen	las	hat gelesen	*read*
nehmen	nahm	hat genommen	*took*
reiten	ritt	ist geritten	*rode*
rufen	rief	hat gerufen	*called*
schlafen	schlief	hat geschlafen	*slept*
schneiden	schnitt	hat geschnitten	*cut*
schreiben	schrieb	hat geschrieben	*wrote*
schwimmen	schwamm	ist geschwommen	*swam*
sehen	sah	hat gesehen	*saw*
sitzen	saß	hat gesessen	*sat*
sprechen	sprach	hat gesprochen	*spoke*
stehen	stand	hat gestanden	*stood*
steigen	stieg	ist gestiegen	*climbed*
sterben	starb	ist gestorben	*died*
tragen	trug	hat getragen	*wore, carried*
treffen	traf	hat getroffen	*met*
trinken	trank	hat getrunken	*drank*
werfen	warf	hat geworfen	*threw, tossed*
ziehen	zog	hat gezogen	*pulled*

16 **Der gestiefelte Kater°.** Kennen Sie das Märchen vom gestiefelten Kater? Ein Müller° hatte drei Söhne. Der Müller starb, und der jüngste (und auch dümmste) Sohn bekam kein Geld, sondern nur einen Kater. Dieser Kater war aber sehr intelligent und half dem Sohn reich zu werden. Schreiben Sie das richtige Verb in die Lücke und erzählen Sie das Märchen vom gestiefelten Kater nach.

Puss in Boots
miller

aß • bat • begann • bekam • trug

Der jüngste Müllerssohn ______ nach dem Tod seines Vaters nichts als einen Kater. Doch plötzlich ______ dieser Kater zu sprechen und bat den Müllerssohn um ein Paar Stiefel. Bald ______ der Kater wunderbare rote Stiefel. Dann jagte° er Rebhühner°, brachte° sie zu dem König und sagte: „Die hat Ihnen mein Herr, der Graf°, geschickt!" Das freute den König sehr, weil er sehr gern Rebhühner ______, und er schenkte dem Kater einen Sack voll Gold. Der Müllerssohn war erstaunt, als ihm der Kater das Gold brachte und ihn ______: „Tu, was ich dir sage, und so wirst du reich!"

hunted
partridges / brought
count

fuhr • hörte • lief • lud ... ein • saß • schenkte • schwamm

Ein paar Tage später _____ der Müllerssohn im Fluss und der Kater versteckte° *hid*
seine Kleider. Als der König in seiner Kutsche° vorbei_____, rief der Kater: „Hilfe, *coach*
jemand hat meinem Herrn, dem Grafen, die Kleider gestohlen!!!" Der König _____
dem Müllerssohn schöne Kleider und _____ ihn _____ mitzufahren. In der
Kutsche _____ die schöne Tochter des Königs, die Prinzessin. Der Kater _____
voraus und befahl° den Leuten in den Feldern: „Gleich wird der König *ordered*
vorbeifahren. Wenn er fragt, so sagt, das ganze Land gehört dem Grafen!" Als der
König dies _____, meinte er, der Müllerssohn sei ein reicher Edelmann°. *nobleman*

ankam • fragte • fraß • bekam • kam • sprang

Bald _____ der Kater ins Schloss des großen Zauberers. Der Kater _____: „Also,
Zauberer, kannst du dich in jedes Tier verwandeln°?" „Ja, natürlich," sagte er! *transform*
Kaum hatte der Zauberer sich in eine Maus verwandelt, _____ der Kater auf und
_____ sie. So wurde der Müllerssohn der Besitzer des großen Schlosses. Als die
Kutsche am Schloss _____, begrüßte der Kater den König: „Willkommen im
Schloss meines Herrn!" Der arme Müllerssohn _____ die Prinzessin zur Frau und
wurde selbst König.

17 **Der Mann im Smoking°.** Helene Dornhuber ist in Tübingen *tuxedo*
auf einen Fastnachtsball gegangen, wie Barbara in Köln. Dort hat sie auch ihren „Prinzen" im Smoking getroffen. Leider hat ihr „Märchen" kein Happy-End. Ergänzen Sie die Geschichte mit der richtigen Präteritumform.

an·kommen	an·rufen	auf·schreiben	beginnen	essen	finden
sagen	sitzen	sprechen	tragen	treffen	trinken

Gestern Abend ging Helene auf einen Fastnachtsball in der Tübinger Stadthalle. Der Ball _____ um 20.00 Uhr, aber sie _____ erst um 21.00 Uhr an. Dort _____ sie einen jungen Mann. Er _____ einen eleganten Smoking. Sie _____ lange zusammen, _____ ein Glas Wein und tanzten. Sie _____ auch Pizza und Kuchen. Um 24.00 Uhr _____ sie, dass sie gehen musste. Er _____ ihre Adresse auf. Am nächsten Tag _____ er ihre Adresse nicht mehr und war sehr traurig darüber. Helene _____ den ganzen Tag in ihrem Zimmer und wartete auf den Mann im Smoking, aber er _____ sie nicht an.

C. *Narrative past:* sein, haben, *and the modal verbs*

German speakers frequently use the auxiliary verbs **haben** and **sein** in the narrative (simple) past—in speaking as well as in writing. These are their forms.

		sein: *to be*		
Person	**Singular**		**Plural**	
1st	ich **war**	*I was*	wir **waren**	*we were*
2nd, informal	du **warst**	*you were*	ihr **wart**	*you were*
2nd, formal	Sie **waren**	*you were*	Sie **waren**	*you were*
3rd	er/sie/es **war**	*he/she/it was*	sie **waren**	*they were*

		haben: *to have*		
Person	**Singular**		**Plural**	
1st	ich **hatte**	*I had*	wir **hatten**	*we had*
2nd, informal	du **hattest**	*you had*	ihr **hattet**	*you had*
2nd, formal	Sie **hatten**	*you had*	Sie **hatten**	*you had*
3rd	er/sie/es **hatte**	*he/she/it had*	sie **hatten**	*they had*

The modal verbs form their past tense like the regular (weak) verbs with the **-te** past tense marker. In the narrative past the umlaut is dropped. Although rarely used, the conversational past tense forms are also included in the chart below.

Infinitive	**Narrative past**	**Meaning**	**Conversational past**
dürfen	d**u**rfte	*was allowed to*	hat gedurft
können	k**o**nnte	*was able to, could*	hat gekonnt
mögen	m**o**chte	*liked*	hat gemocht
müssen	m**u**sste	*had to*	hat gemusst
sollen	so**ll**te	*was supposed to*	hat gesollt
wollen	wo**ll**te	*wanted to*	hat gewollt

Note that the **g** in **mögen** changes to **ch** in the narrative past.

18 **Als Kind durfte ich nicht rauchen.** Was durften (konnten usw.) Sie als Kind nicht machen? Beantworten Sie die Fragen auf Seite 434 mit einem Partner/einer Partnerin. Benutzen Sie das passende Modalverb im Präteritum.

▣ S1: Was durftest du als Kind nicht machen?
S2: Als Kind durfte ich nicht rauchen.

weit zur Schule fahren	mein Zimmer sauber machen	Sport treiben
Gemüse essen	schnell laufen	spät ins Kino gehen
früh aufstehen	(sich) baden	rauchen
Auto fahren	in die Schule gehen	Schlittschuh° laufen
Alkohol trinken	Deutsch sprechen	Klavier° üben°

ice skate
piano / practice

1. Was durftest du als Kind nicht machen?
2. Was konntest du als Kind nicht machen?
3. Was musstest du als Kind nicht machen?
4. Was wolltest du als Kind nicht machen?
5. Was solltest du als Kind zu Hause nicht machen?

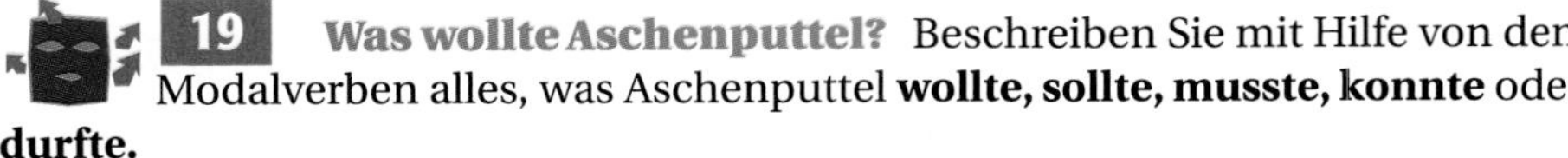

19 **Was wollte Aschenputtel?** Beschreiben Sie mit Hilfe von den Modalverben alles, was Aschenputtel **wollte, sollte, musste, konnte** oder **durfte.**

▣ fromm und gut bleiben *Aschenputtel sollte fromm und gut bleiben.*

1. fromm und gut bleiben
2. nicht mehr in einem Bett schlafen
3. neben dem Herd in der Asche schlafen
4. einen Zweig als Andenken von ihrem Vater bekommen
5. auch zum Fest des Königs mitgehen
6. ohne Kleid und Schuhe nicht zum Fest mitgehen
7. allein zu Hause bleiben
8. allein mit dem Königssohn tanzen
9. nur als letzte den Schuh anprobieren

D. Narrative past: mixed verbs

Mixed verbs **(gemischte Verben)** combine the past tense marker **-te** that is added to the stem of regular (weak) verbs with the vowel change of irregular (strong) verbs when forming the narrative (simple) past.

Infinitive: **denken**
Der Vater **dachte**: „Kann das Aschenputtel sein?" *The father thought: "Can that be Cinderella?"*

These are the most common mixed verbs.

	Infinitive	Narrative past	Conversational past	
e > a	br**e**nnen	br**a**nn**te**	hat gebrannt	*burned*
	d**e**nken	d**a**ch**te**	hat gedacht	*thought*
	erk**e**nnen	erk**a**nn**te**	hat erkannt	*recognized*
	k**e**nnen	k**a**nn**te**	hat gekannt	*knew (person or place)*
	n**e**nnen	n**a**nn**te**	hat genannt	*named*
	r**e**nnen	r**a**nn**te**	ist gerannt	*ran*
i > a	br**ing**en	br**ach**te	hat gebracht	*brought*
	verbr**ing**en	verbr**ach**te	hat verbracht	*spent time*

Similarly, the English verbs *bring/brought, think/thought* are mixed verb forms from an older form of English.

The consonants **nk** and **ng** in the infinitive change to **ch** in the narrative past.

Similarly, the verbs **wissen** and **werden** also mix both strong and weak verb narrative past tense markers. Note that **werden** has a **-d** instead of a **-t.**

Infinitive	Narrative past	Conversational past	
wissen	w**usste**	hat gewusst	*knew (a fact)*
werden	w**urde**	ist geworden	*became*

20 **Aus „Aschenputtel".** Ergänzen Sie diese Sätze aus „Aschenputtel" mit einer passenden Verbform aus der Liste.

nannten	wurde	brachte (3x)	erkannten
war	waren	hatte	rannte

1. Es war einmal ein hübsches Mädchen, dessen Mutter krank ______ und starb.
2. Nach einem Jahr nahm sich der Mann eine neue Frau, die zwei Töchter mit ins Haus ______.
3. Diese Schwestern ______ schön von Gesicht aber böse von Herzen.
4. Selbst ein Bett ______ das Mädchen nicht mehr, es musste neben dem Herd in der Asche liegen.
5. Und weil sie darum immer schmutzig aussah, ______ die Stiefschwestern sie „Aschenputtel".
6. Als der Vater zurückkam, ______ er Kleider und Edelsteine für die Stiefschwestern.
7. Ihre Schwestern und Stiefmutter ______ Aschenputtel nicht auf dem Fest.
8. Das Vögelchen ______ ihr ein noch viel schöneres Kleid.
9. Wieder ______ Aschenputtel schnell davon.
10. Da ging die andere Schwester in das Zimmer und probierte den Schuh an, aber die Ferse ______ zu groß.

FREIE KOMMUNIKATION

Ein tolles Fest! Erzählen Sie einem Partner/einer Partnerin im Präteritum von einem Fest. Geben Sie zehn Details an. Davon sind drei falsch. Der Partner/Die Partnerin bestimmt, welche drei Details falsch sind.

Das ist zu grausam°! Lesen Sie die folgende Schlussszene aus der Grimmschen Version von „Aschenputtel". Mehrere Eltern in der Schule halten diese Version für zu brutal für Kinder. Teilen Sie die Klasse in drei Gruppen auf: Pro, Kontra und Revisionisten. Die Kontra-Gruppe will diese Schlussszene verbieten°. Die Revisionisten finden die Schlussszene auch unakzeptabel und schlagen Änderungen vor. Die Pro-Gruppe argumentiert gegen eine Zensur°. Die Mitglieder von allen Gruppen erklären°, warum sie für oder gegen die Schlussszene sind. Ihr Dozent/Ihre Dozentin spielt den Schuldirektor/die Schuldirektorin und entscheidet wie das Märchen enden soll.

gruesome, cruel / *ban, prohibit* / *censorship* / *explain*

Als die Brautleute zur Kirche gingen, war die ältere Schwester zur rechten Seite und die jüngere zur linken Seite der Braut. Da pickten die Tauben° einer jeden° ein Auge aus. Danach, als sie aus der Kirche kamen, war die jüngere Schwester zur rechten Seite und die ältere zur linken Seite der Braut. Da pickten die Tauben einer jeden das andere Auge aus. So war Blindheit die Strafe° für ihre Bosheit° und Falschheit.

doves / ***einer jeden:*** *from each one* / *punishment* / *mean-spiritedness*

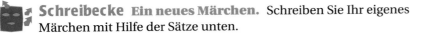

Schreibecke Ein neues Märchen. Schreiben Sie Ihr eigenes Märchen mit Hilfe der Sätze unten.

1. Es war einmal ...

   ein Prinz/eine Prinzessin • ein Student/eine Studentin • ein Zauberer/eine Hexe • ein Deutschlehrer/eine Deutschlehrerin • ...

2. Er/Sie war sehr ...

   schön/hässlich • intelligent/dumm • gut/böse • ...

3. Er/Sie lebte ...

   auf einem Schloss • in einem Studentenwohnheim • in einem Wald • an der Uni • ...

4. Dort hatte er/sie ...

   viele Freunde/Feinde • Bücher • wilde Tiere • giftige Äpfel • Edelsteine • ...

5. Er/Sie wollte ...
6. Da kam ein/eine ...
7. Der/Die war ...
8. Und wenn sie nicht gestorben sind, dann ...

FREIE KOMMUNIKATION **Ein erlebnisvoller° Abend.** Erzählen Sie einer Gruppe von drei bis vier Studenten von einem erlebnisvollen Abend auf einem Fest, einer Hochzeit oder einem anderen Tanzabend (z. B. *senior prom*). Was passierte dort? Was machten Sie? Beschreiben Sie fünf bis sechs Details im Präteritum (z.B. **Ich ging/aß/trank/tanzte** ...).

eventful

ABSPRUNGTEXT

Braunwald autofrei: Ein Wintermärchen ... hoch über dem Alltag

Anna und ihre Freunde haben im März Semesterferien und planen seit Wochen einen Skiurlaub. Sie haben Broschüren von bekannten Wintersportorten bestellt und jetzt diskutieren sie alle Möglichkeiten. Für Anna klingt Braunwald in der Schweiz wirklich ideal: viel Schnee und viele Pisten° zum Skilaufen in den Alpen und keine Autos! Die Gruppe muss sich entscheiden, ob sie sich einen Skiurlaub in der Schweiz leisten kann oder ob er einfach zu teuer ist.

ski runs

Vorschau

21 **Thematische Fragen.** Beantworten Sie die folgenden Fragen auf Deutsch.

1. Wann machen Sie lieber Urlaub: im Winter, Frühling, Sommer oder Herbst?
2. Wann haben Sie als Kind meistens mit der Familie Urlaub gemacht: im Winter, Frühling, Sommer oder Herbst?
3. Sind Sie als Kind weit gefahren oder sind Sie in der Nähe geblieben?
4. Was wollten Ihre Eltern damals im Urlaub erleben und was sind heute Ihre Ziele für den Urlaub? Kreuzen Sie die passenden Antworten an.

	Meine Eltern damals	***Ich heute***
a. viele Sehenswürdigkeiten sehen	___	___
b. Tiere und Natur erleben	___	___
c. Verwandte besuchen	___	___
d. Ruhe und Entspannung° haben	___	___
e. viel Aktivität haben	___	___
f. eine fremde Kultur und Sprache kennen lernen	___	___
g. so wenig Geld wie möglich ausgeben	___	___
h. viel Geld ausgeben und tolle Andenken kaufen	___	___
i. viel Zeit mit Freunden verbringen	___	___
j. gut essen und trinken	___	___

relaxation

5. Mit wem reisen Sie jetzt am liebsten, wenn Sie Urlaub machen? Oder fahren Sie lieber allein?
6. Was ist Ihr Traum-Urlaubsland? Warum? Was möchten Sie dort machen, sehen, hören, lernen? Wann wollen Sie dorthin reisen?

Sprache im Alltag: Urlaub versus Ferien

German has two separate words for vacation, **der Urlaub** and **die Ferien** *(pl).* **Ferien** are school-free vacation days that are scheduled into a school year and observed by students and teachers alike **(Schulferien, Semesterferien, Weihnachtsferien).** German university students have two long vacation breaks: **Winterferien** from mid-February to mid-April, and **Sommerferien** from mid-July to mid-October. **Urlaub,** on the other hand, is active vacation time taken to relax and recuperate from work, and in most instances, to travel. The average German employee gets 31 paid vacation days, or roughly six weeks.

22 Lesestrategien. Braunwald autofrei: Ein Wintermärchen.

Benutzen Sie die folgenden Strategien, um den Text „Braunwald autofrei" zu verstehen.

1. **Den Kontext verstehen.** Suchen Sie im Text die Information unten.
   a. Wie heißt der Ort?
   b. Welche Jahreszeit (Sommer, Herbst usw.) sieht man in der Broschüre dargestellt?
   c. Warum kommen Menschen dahin? Was kann man dort machen?
   d. Schauen Sie sich die Bilder an. Suchen Sie die Wörter *einen Schlitten, schlittelnde Kinder, Millionen von Menschen, die Autos.*

2. **Neue Wörter lernen.** Erraten Sie die Bedeutung von den Ausdrücken aus dem Kontext.
   a. „Glauben Sie, dass es die kleinen **Winterferienwunder** noch gibt?"
   Was sind die drei Wörter im Kompositum? Welche Stimmung° sieht man in den Bildern? Ist ein Wunder etwas Normales?

   Atmosphäre

   b. „Unten sind **gestresste Stadtmenschen** eingestiegen, oben steigen **gutgelaunte Ferienmenschen** aus."
   Welcher Kontrast zwischen Menschen sieht man hier im Satz? Können Sie den Unterschied° zwischen dem Alltagsleben in der Stadt und dem Leben in den Ferien erklären?

   difference

   c. „Gutgelaunte Spaziergänger in einer echten **Postkartenlandschaft.**"
   Die Landschaft bedeutet die Geographie des Landes. Wie ist die Landschaft in Braunwald? Was hat das mit einer Postkarte zu tun?

   d. „Ein Schlittelparadies, eine **Langlaufloipe** und eine Schweizer Skischule ... Pisten für Anfänger und Fortgeschrittene und auch Pisten zum gemütlichen Bergrestaurant."
   Es gibt zwei Arten von Skifahren – Alpin und Langlauf. Welche Art ist schneller? Für Alpin braucht man Pisten. Was braucht man für Langlauf?

   e. „Nach der Schussfahrt auf der Piste, Aufwärmen auf der **Sonnenterrasse** der **Bergwirtschaft** oder beim Kaffeefertig unten **im Dorf.**" In einer Wirtschaft kauft man etwas zu essen und trinken. Wo sind die zwei Wirtschaften in diesem Satz? Wo kann man sitzen, wenn man draußen im Freien etwas trinken will?

f. „Eine herzliche, unkomplizierte **Gastfreundschaft.** Ein gutes Gefühl, **Gast** in einem **gastlichen** Haus zu sein."
Ein Gast ist eine Person, die zu Besuch kommt und kurze Zeit bleibt. Gäste will man besonders nett und freundlich behandeln. Wie will man als Gastgeber seine Gäste behandeln? Was bietet man als Gastgeber dem Gast an? Wie verhalten sich gute Gäste? Schlechte Gäste?

g. „Abendliches Wintermärchen Braunwald: **Zauberstimmung.**"
Ein Zauberer ist ein Mann, der Magie macht. Wie ist die Stimmung am Abend in Braunwald? Was hat das mit Magie zu tun? Was ist die Verbindung zwischen Märchen, Zauber und Stimmung?

3. Strategien verwenden. Erraten Sie die fett gedruckten Wörter mit Hilfe der drei Strategien. Wählen Sie die korrekte Antwort.

Strategie 1: Weltwissen

a. Hier bringt der **Postbote** ... auf seinem Schlitten gerade die Morgenzeitung.
   - ☐ Der Briefträger bringt die Zeitung.
   - ☐ Ein Boot bringt die Zeitung.

b. **Gutgelaunt**e Spaziergänger in einer echten Postkartenlandschaft.
   - ☐ in schlechter Stimmung
   - ☐ in guter Stimmung

c. Was für ein Spass, im Pferdeschlitten durch das **verschneite** Wintermärchenland zu fahren!
□ eine Landschaft ohne Schnee □ eine Landschaft mit viel Schnee

d. Nach der Schussfahrt auf der **Piste ...**
□ Man fährt Ski auf einer Piste. □ Man fährt Auto auf einer Piste.

e. Pisten für Anfänger und **Fortgeschrittene ...**
□ für Leute, die schon sehr gut Ski laufen □ für Leute, die nicht gut Ski laufen

Note that in this Swiss text **ss** is used instead of standard German **ß** following long vowels, e.g., **Spaß-Spass, Fuß-Fuss, Straße-Strasse, Genießer-Geniesser.**

Strategie 2: Kontext

a. Es [das Bähnli] **rüttelt und schüttelt sich** und **klettert** durch den Schnee hinauf auf die Sonnenterrasse.
□ Es fährt sehr schnell. □ Es fährt langsam und mit Mühe hinauf.

b. Das Wunder des Wandels **findet** im Bähnli **statt ...** Unten sind gestresste Menschen eingestiegen, oben steigen gutgelaunte Ferienmenschen aus.
□ Etwas Wunderbares passiert im Bähnli. □ Man findet die Stadt im Bähnli.

c. Einfach keine Autos! Da **fehlt das Dröhnen** der Motoren.
□ Man hört keine Motoren. □ Man hört laute Motoren.

d. Eben Leute von heute. Gestresst, überarbeitet und **ferienreif.**
□ Leute, die Ferien brauchen □ Leute, die mehr Arbeit brauchen

e. Braunwald ist nichts für die Massen, sondern für **echte Geniesser.**
□ Menschen, die die Natur in Braunwald gut finden und verstehen.
□ Menschen, die die Natur in Braunwald uninteressant finden.

Strategie 3: Wortformen im „Schwyzerdüütsch" (Schweizerdeutsch-Dialekt)

a. **Wach' uf, liäbs Bruuwald.**
□ Wach auf, liebe Brunhilde. □ Wach auf, liebes Braunwald.

b. Das **Bähnli** führt in die Zukunft.
□ die kleine Eisenbahn° □ der Mann namens Bähnli

c. Man sagt **„Grüezi",** wenn man sich begegnet.
□ Grüß Sie! □ Gute Zeit!

liäbs Bruuwald refers to the place name, which is **das,** and not the forest **(der Wald).**

railroad

▣ Sprache im Alltag: Diminutives

The Swiss German dialects form diminutives by adding the suffix **-li** to nouns instead of the standard German **-chen** and **-lein.**

Standard	***Schweizerdeutsch***
das Bähnchen	das Bähnli
das Bähnlein	

These diminutives change the gender of the noun to **das,** and add an umlaut (e.g., **die Bahn > das Bähnli.**)

ABSPRUNGTEXT

Braunwald autofrei: Ein Wintermärchen ... hoch über dem Alltag

Lesen Sie jetzt den Text.

Wach' uf liäbs Bruuwald

Das Bähnliwunder im Wunderbähnli

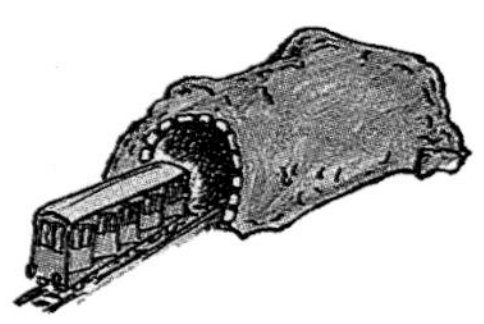

Glauben Sie, dass es die kleinen Winterferienwunder noch gibt? Wir aus Braunwald glauben daran, denn Winter für Winter erleben wir eine seltsame Geschichte ...

Nach Braunwald führt keine Strasse – nur ein Bähnli in die Zukunft. In dieses Bähnli steigen unten im Tal täglich Menschen aus dem Unterland. Müde vom Alltag, den grauen Wolken und langen Nebeltagen. Eben Leute von heute. Gestresst, überarbeitet und ferienreif.

Dann setzt sich das rote Bähnli in Bewegung°. Es rüttelt und schüttelt sich und klettert durch den Schnee hinauf auf die Sonnenterrasse.

° *motion*

Das Bähnli steigt und steigt. Jetzt noch der kleine Tunnel und schon ist das alltägliche Bähnliwunder von Braunwald perfekt.

Das Wunder des Wandels findet im Bähnli statt. Ob Millionär oder Tellerwäscher – am Bähnli kommt keiner vorbei. Unten sind gestresste Stadtmenschen eingestiegen, oben steigen gutgelaunte Ferienmenschen aus. Jeden Winter täglich neu: das kleine Bähnliwunder von Braunwald.

Guätä Morgä liäbs Bruuwald

Gut geschlafen, lieber Gast? Hier bringt der Postbote – den wir in Braunwald "Pöschtler" nennen – auf seinem Schlitten gerade die Morgenzeitung. Der "Pöschtler" geht zu Fuss, weil er kein Auto hat.

Das ist normal hier oben. Denn in Braunwald gibt es keine Autos. Braunwald ist autofrei. Zuerst ist es ein richtiger Schock. Einfach keine Autos! Da fehlt das Dröhnen der Motoren. An die saubere Luft muss man sich zuerst gewöhnen. Hier ist eben schon alles etwas anders als anderswo. Gast bedeutet nicht nur Gastfreundschaft. GAST heisst auch Gemeinschaft Autofreier Schweizer Tourismusorte.

Gutgelaunte Spaziergänger in einer echten Postkartenlandschaft. Schlittelnde Kinder, die keine Angst vor Autos haben.
Hier sagt man sich noch "Grüezi", wenn man sich begegnet.
Man kennt sich eben in Braunwald.

Guätä Tag liäbs Bruuwald

Der sanfte° Tourismus findet auch im Winter statt. Auch wer nicht Ski fährt, ist hier Erstklassgast. Was für ein Spass, im Pferdeschlitten durch das verschneite Wintermärchenland zu fahren!

Was den Winter attraktiv und sportlich macht, ist in Braunwald zu finden. Ein Schlittelparadies, eine Langlaufloipe und eine Schweizer Skischule.

Das Skifahren ist noch Spass und weniger aggressiv als anderswo. Pisten für Anfänger und Fortgeschrittene und auch Pisten zum gemütlichen Bergrestaurant. Sonnige Pisten auf der Südseite und Pulverschnee an den Nordhängen. Für die ehemaligen Skistars und die ewigen Anfänger, die gar nie Pistenraser° werden wollen.

Nach der Schussfahrt auf der Piste, Aufwärmen auf der Sonnenterrasse der Bergwirtschaft oder beim Kaffeefertig unten im Dorf. Eine ehrliche Gastronomie der kleinen Familienbetriebe.

Persönlichkeit ist alles –
Prestige ist gar nichts.
Eine herzliche, unkomplizierte
Gastfreundschaft. Ein gutes
Gefühl, Gast in einem gastlichen
Haus zu sein.

relaxing

speed demon

Guät Nacht liäbs Bruuwald

Abendliches Wintermärchen Braunwald: Zauberstimmung. Was ist schon Glück? Vielleicht die Stille eines Bergabends, eine nächtliche Schlittelfahrt, ein Kinoabend oder ein Schlummertrunk° an einer Hotelbar? "Hoch über dem Alltag" finden Sie noch Naturschönheit, Herzlichkeit und Lebensfreude. Millionen von Menschen kommen Gott sei Dank gar nie nach Braunwald.

Braunwald ist nichts für die Massen, sondern für echte Geniesser. Braunwald ist etwas ganz Besonderes. Die wesentlichen° Dinge sind in Braunwald sichtbar° – mit den Augen und dem Herzen.

essential
visible
nightcap

Rückblick

23 **Stimmt das?** Stimmen diese Aussagen zum Text oder nicht? Wenn nicht, was stimmt?

	Ja, das stimmt.	*Nein, das stimmt nicht.*
1. Nur mit dem „Bähnli" kommt man nach Braunwald, weil keine Straße dahin führt.	___	___
2. Es kann tagelang dauern, bis man in Braunwald gutgelaunt und in Ferienstimmung ist.	___	___
3. Im Winter bringt der Postbote die Post mit seinem Fahrrad.	___	___
4. Es ist ein Schock, dass man keine Motoren in Braunwald hört.	___	___
5. Die Leute in Braunwald sagen „Grüezi", wenn sie einander treffen.	___	___
6. Wer gern Ski läuft, kann hier Alpin und Langlauf machen, zur Skischule gehen und Pisten für Anfänger oder Fortgeschrittene finden.	___	___
7. Für die Nicht-Skifahrer gibt es in Braunwald nichts zu tun.	___	___
8. Essen kann man oben auf dem Berg in der Bergwirtschaft.	___	___
9. Abends gibt es wilde Après-Ski-Partys, laute Diskomusik und viel Bier.	___	___
10. Braunwald ist nicht für jedermann, sondern nur für echte Genießer.	___	___

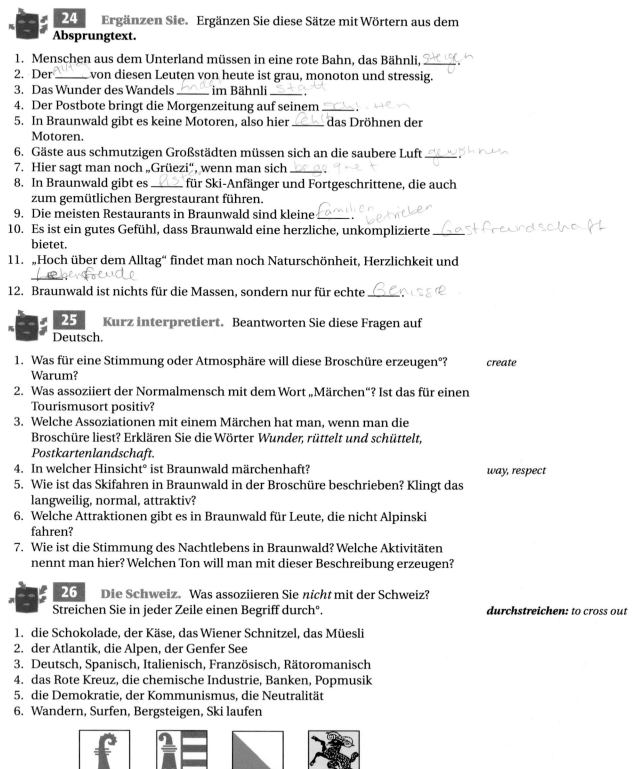

24 Ergänzen Sie. Ergänzen Sie diese Sätze mit Wörtern aus dem **Absprungtext.**

1. Menschen aus dem Unterland müssen in eine rote Bahn, das Bähnli, _____.
2. Der _____ von diesen Leuten von heute ist grau, monoton und stressig.
3. Das Wunder des Wandels _____ im Bähnli _____.
4. Der Postbote bringt die Morgenzeitung auf seinem _____.
5. In Braunwald gibt es keine Motoren, also hier _____ das Dröhnen der Motoren.
6. Gäste aus schmutzigen Großstädten müssen sich an die saubere Luft _____.
7. Hier sagt man noch „Grüezi", wenn man sich _____.
8. In Braunwald gibt es _____ für Ski-Anfänger und Fortgeschrittene, die auch zum gemütlichen Bergrestaurant führen.
9. Die meisten Restaurants in Braunwald sind kleine _____.
10. Es ist ein gutes Gefühl, dass Braunwald eine herzliche, unkomplizierte _____ bietet.
11. „Hoch über dem Alltag" findet man noch Naturschönheit, Herzlichkeit und _____.
12. Braunwald ist nichts für die Massen, sondern nur für echte _____.

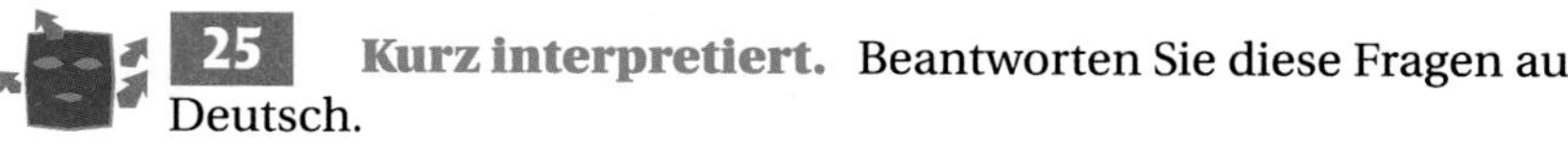

25 Kurz interpretiert. Beantworten Sie diese Fragen auf Deutsch.

1. Was für eine Stimmung oder Atmosphäre will diese Broschüre erzeugen°? Warum?
2. Was assoziiert der Normalmensch mit dem Wort „Märchen"? Ist das für einen Tourismusort positiv?
3. Welche Assoziationen mit einem Märchen hat man, wenn man die Broschüre liest? Erklären Sie die Wörter *Wunder, rüttelt und schüttelt, Postkartenlandschaft.*
4. In welcher Hinsicht° ist Braunwald märchenhaft?
5. Wie ist das Skifahren in Braunwald in der Broschüre beschrieben? Klingt das langweilig, normal, attraktiv?
6. Welche Attraktionen gibt es in Braunwald für Leute, die nicht Alpinski fahren?
7. Wie ist die Stimmung des Nachtlebens in Braunwald? Welche Aktivitäten nennt man hier? Welchen Ton will man mit dieser Beschreibung erzeugen?

create

way, respect

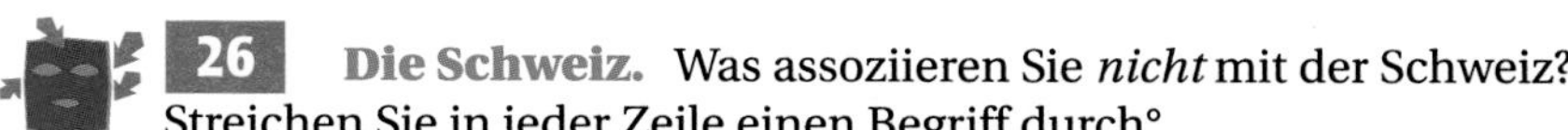

26 Die Schweiz. Was assoziieren Sie *nicht* mit der Schweiz? Streichen Sie in jeder Zeile einen Begriff durch°.

***durchstreichen:** to cross out*

1. die Schokolade, der Käse, das Wiener Schnitzel, das Müesli
2. der Atlantik, die Alpen, der Genfer See
3. Deutsch, Spanisch, Italienisch, Französisch, Rätoromanisch
4. das Rote Kreuz, die chemische Industrie, Banken, Popmusik
5. die Demokratie, der Kommunismus, die Neutralität
6. Wandern, Surfen, Bergsteigen, Ski laufen

Basel-Land

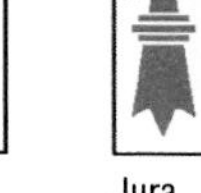
Jura

Zürich

Schaffhausen

BRENNPUNKT KULTUR

Die Schweiz

Switzerland (**die Schweiz,** officially **Confoederatio Helvetica**) is a small multilingual nation of over 7 million people located in the heart of central Europe. Bordered by Germany, France, Italy, Austria, and Liechtenstein, the country has four national languages: German, the native language of nearly two-thirds of all Swiss, French (spoken by 18% of the population), Italian (10%), and Rhaeto-Romanic (1%). Each of these languages is spoken in regional dialects. Important German-speaking cities are Bern, the capital of Switzerland; Zürich, the business and banking center; and Basel, the center of the Swiss chemical and pharmaceutical industry. Geneva (German: **Genf,** French: Genève), the chief French-speaking city, is headquarters for the International Red Cross and one of two European headquarters for the United Nations.

Switzerland is one of Europe's oldest democracies, dating from an alliance signed in 1291 by the cantons of Uri, Schwyz, and Unterwalden that guaranteed the traditional autonomy of the communes and their citizens. This loose confederation was later replaced with a federation of 26 individual Swiss states (**Kantone).** Since then, the Swiss have maintained a reputation of tolerance and respect for the rights and autonomy of individuals, although ironically, Swiss women did not acquire the right to vote until 1971. Switzerland has maintained a policy of diplomatic neutrality.

Although the country has relatively few natural resources and nearly 70% of its land mass is covered by the Alps and Jura Mountains, the Swiss economy is robust and its service industries are world-famous. In banking, insurance, and tourism, Switzerland has few peers. In addition, Swiss industries such as chemicals; pharmaceuticals; watchmaking; textiles; and metal-, machine-, and instrument-making have helped establish a per capita income that surpasses that of Germany, France, the U.S.A., Canada, and Sweden.

Bern: Die Hauptstadt der Schweiz

Wissenswerte Vokabeln: die Schweiz – geographische Daten

Talking about Switzerland

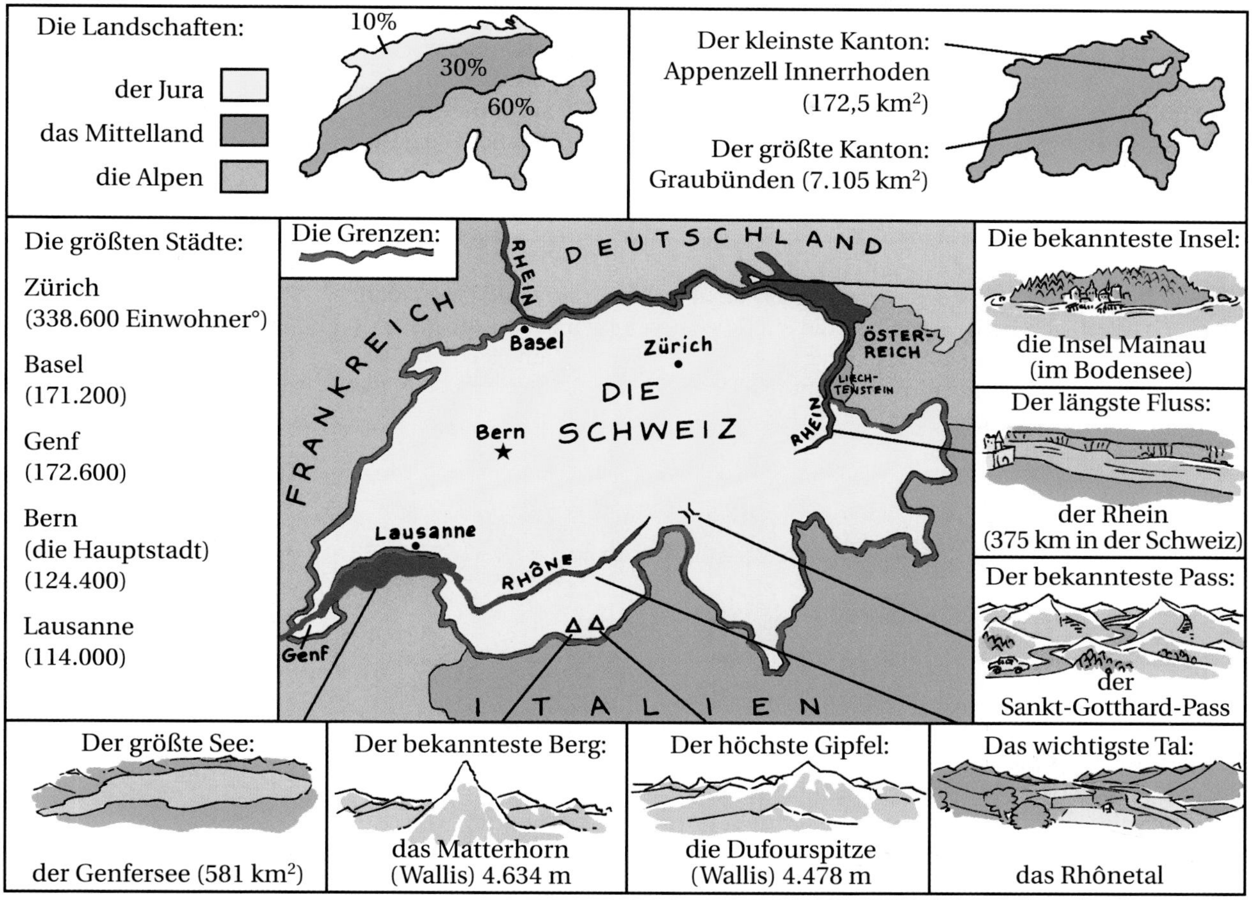

Die Landschaften:

der Jura
das Mittelland
die Alpen

10%
30%
60%

Der kleinste Kanton:
Appenzell Innerrhoden
(172,5 km²)

Der größte Kanton:
Graubünden (7.105 km²)

Die größten Städte:

Zürich
(338.600 Einwohner°)

Basel
(171.200)

Genf
(172.600)

Bern
(die Hauptstadt)
(124.400)

Lausanne
(114.000)

Die Grenzen:

DEUTSCHLAND
FRANKREICH
RHEIN
Basel
Zürich
ÖSTERREICH
LIECHTENSTEIN
DIE SCHWEIZ
Bern
RHEIN
Lausanne
RHÔNE
Genf
ITALIEN

Die bekannteste Insel:
die Insel Mainau
(im Bodensee)

Der längste Fluss:
der Rhein
(375 km in der Schweiz)

Der bekannteste Pass:
der Sankt-Gotthard-Pass

Der größte See:
der Genfersee (581 km²)

Der bekannteste Berg:
das Matterhorn
(Wallis) 4.634 m

Der höchste Gipfel:
die Dufourspitze
(Wallis) 4.478 m

Das wichtigste Tal:
das Rhônetal

Wie heißt der längste Fluss in der Schweiz?

***Einwohner:** inhabitants*

27 **Geographie-Jeopardy.** Sie wissen schon die Antwort, aber wie heißt die Frage? Fragen Sie nach Superlativen in der Schweiz.

S1: Zürich
S2: Was ist die größte Stadt in der Schweiz?

1. Zürich
2. Dufourspitze
3. Appenzell Innerrhoden
4. Graubünden
5. die Alpen
6. das Rhônetal
7. Mainau
8. der Sankt-Gotthard
9. der Rhein
10. der Genfersee

■ FREIE ■ KOMMUNIKATION ■ **Rollenspiel: Braunwald besuchen.** S1: Sie arbeiten im Reisebüro. Sie sind gerade vom Winterurlaub in Braunwald zurückgekommen und erzählen, was Sie alles dort gemacht haben und warum Braunwald Touristen so gut gefällt, oder was Touristen dort ärgert. Versuchen Sie den Kunden/die Kundin (S2) zu überzeugen, auch mal in Braunwald Urlaub zu machen, oder Braunwald fernzubleiben° und einen besseren Urlaubsort zu finden. S2: Sie planen eine Winterreise und suchen Informationen im Reisebüro. Sie fahren nicht so gern Ski, sind aber gern draußen im Winter, haben Massentourismus nicht so gern und sind etwas snobbistisch.

stay away from

Schreibecke **Reisetagebuch.** Sie haben in Braunwald eine Woche Urlaub gemacht. Schreiben Sie ein Reisetagebuch im Präteritum. Machen Sie für jeden Tag einen Eintrag°, in dem Sie beschreiben, was Sie machten und sahen. Vergessen Sie nicht das Datum: zuerst kommt der Tag, dann der Monat und zuletzt das Jahr.

15-29 Jan

entry

■ Strukturen und Vokabeln ■

II ■ Talking about consecutive and simultaneous events in the past

The past perfect

German speakers use the past perfect tense **(das Plusquamperfekt)** to refer to the earlier of two or more events that occurred in the past. It frequently occurs with the subordinating conjunction **nachdem** *(after)*. The past perfect consists of a form of **haben** or **sein** in the narrative past, and a past participle.

Nachdem Aschenputtels Vater ihr den Haselzweig **gebracht hatte,** pflanzte sie ihn auf dem Grab ihrer Mutter.	*After Cinderella's father had brought her the hazelnut branch, she planted it on her mother's grave.*

In colloquial speech Germans frequently prefer to use the conversational past instead of the past perfect. In these cases, the subordinating conjunction **nachdem** alone serves to signal the sequence of events.

Wohin bist du gegangen, nachdem wir uns **gesehen haben?**	*Where did you go after we saw each other?*

Word order in sentences beginning with a subordinate clause

The past perfect frequently occurs at the end of a subordinate clause. When a sentence begins with a subordinate clause, the subordinate clause fills the first position in the complete sentence. It is followed by the main clause, which begins with the verb and is followed by the subject. This results in two conjugated verbs appearing side by side. However, the subordinate clause is always separated from the main clause by a comma.

Nachdem Aschenputtel zum Grab ihrer Mutter **gegangen war, bekam** sie ein schönes Kleid von dem Vögelchen.

After Cinderella had gone to her mother's grave, she received a beautiful dress from the little bird.

28 Was passierte den Märchenfiguren nachher? Finden Sie für jeden Hauptsatz den Nebensatz, der erklärt, was im Märchen später passierte.

Nachdem Aschenputtel die kranke Mutter besucht hatte, starb die Mutter.

1. Nachdem Aschenputtel die kranke Mutter besucht hatte,
2. Nachdem der Wolf Rotkäppchen gefressen hatte,
3. Nachdem der gestiefelte Kater die Kleider seines Herrn genommen hatte,
4. Nachdem Schneewittchen in den vergifteten Apfel gebissen hatte,
5. Nachdem Schneewittchen eingeschlafen war,
6. Nachdem die böse Hexe Hänsel und Gretel ins Pfefferkuchenhaus eingeladen hatte,
7. Nachdem die Hexe ein Feuer im Ofen gemacht hatte,

a. ging er zum König und sagte, dass Diebe die Kleider gestohlen hatten.
b. schloss sie Hänsel in einen Käfig° ein. *cage*
c. schob Gretel die Hexe in den Ofen und sie verbrannte.
d. fiel sie tot um.
e. starb die Mutter.
f. legten die sieben Zwerge ihre Leiche° in einen Glassarg. *corpse*
g. kam der Jäger, schnitt dem Wolf den Bauch auf und rettete Rotkäppchen.

29 Was passierte zuerst? Bilden Sie Nebensätze im Plusquamperfekt und Hauptsätze im Präteritum, die die richtige Reihenfolge wiedergeben.

Aschenputtels Mutter: krank werden / sterben
Nachdem Aschenputtels Mutter krank geworden war, starb sie.

1. Aschenputtels Mutter: krank werden / sterben
2. Aschenputtels Vater: eine neue Frau heiraten / eine schlimme Zeit für Aschenputtel beginnen
3. Aschenputtel: schwer arbeiten / sich in die Asche legen müssen
4. Aschenputtels Vater: den Haselzweig für Aschenputtel bringen / Aschenputtel: jeden Tag zum Baum gehen
5. Aschenputtel: sich etwas wünschen / ihren Wunsch erfüllt bekommen
6. der Königssohn: alle schönen Jungfrauen zum Ball einladen / die Stiefschwestern: zum Ball gehen wollen
7. Aschenputtel: zum Grab laufen / der Vogel: Aschenputtel ein Kleid geben
8. Aschenputtel: nach Hause gehen / der Königssohn: ihren Schuh finden
9. die ältere Stiefschwester: den Schuh anprobieren / die Zehe abschneiden
10. der Königssohn: die Vögel am Grab hören / die falsche Braut zurückbringen
11. Aschenputtel: den Schuh anprobieren / der Königssohn: das Mädchen vom Fest erkennen
12. der Königssohn: Aschenputtel finden / sie heiraten

30 Meine Zeittafel°. Unten ist Annas Zeittafel. Schreiben Sie Ihre eigene Zeittafel. Stellen Sie sich dann mit einem Partner/einer Partnerin gegenseitig Fragen über Ihre Zeittafel. Beginnen Sie mit der Frage über die Schule.

time line

Meine Zeittafel. The most commonly used narrative past forms in speaking are **war, hatte, ging, kam,** and the modal verbs (**konnte, wollte, musste,** etc.).

S1: Was hast du gemacht, nachdem du die Schule angefangen hattest?
S2: Nachdem ich die Schule angefangen hatte, lernte ich schwimmen.

Anna Adler		*Ich:*
1982	in Fort Wayne geboren	_____
1987	die Schule anfangen	_____
1992	eine Reise nach Florida machen	_____
1994	nach Kanada fahren	_____
1996	im Softballtournier in San Diego spielen	_____
2000	die Uni in Michigan besuchen	_____
2002	nach Deutschland fliegen	_____

III Talking about simultaneous events in the past

Using the conjunction als

German speakers use the subordinating conjunction **als** *(when)* with the narrative (simple) past or the conversational past to talk about two or more past events that happened at the same time.

Als sie am Grab von Aschenputtels Mutter vorbeiritten, riefen zwei Täubchen vom Haselbaum.	*When they rode past the grave of Cinderella's mother, two doves called out from the hazelnut tree.*

31 Als Kind in Deutschland oder in den USA. Was machte Barbara in der Deutschen Demokratischen Republik als Anna in den USA Kind war? Stellen Sie einem Partner/einer Partnerin mit Hilfe der Tabellen Fragen.

S1: Was machte Anna, als Barbara Fußball spielte?
S2: Als Barbara Fußball spielte, spielte Anna Softball.

Tabelle A(S1):

Anna	Barbara
?	Fußball spielen
Orangensaft zum Frühstück trinken	?
jeden Sonntag in die Kirche gehen	?
bis spät nachmittags in der Schule bleiben	?
?	den Nachmittag frei haben
?	am Samstag die Schule besuchen
?	nach Italien fahren wollen
eine Reise durch Kanada machen	?

Tabelle B(S2):

Anna	**Barbara**
Softball spielen	?
?	Kaffee zum Frühstück trinken
?	jeden Sonntag spazieren gehen
?	um 13.00 Uhr nach Hause gehen
täglich nach der Schule Sport haben	?
am Samstag keine Schule haben	?
alle Länder besuchen können	?
?	eine Reise in die Sowjetunion machen

32 **Autogrammspiel: Als ich 5 Jahre alt war, ...** Bilden Sie Fragen im Präteritum. Finden Sie für jede Frage eine Person, die mit **Ja** antwortet. Bitten Sie dann die Person um ihre Unterschrift.

S1: Hattest du schon lange Haare, als du zehn Jahre alt warst?
S2: Ja.
S1: Unterschreib hier bitte. ____________________

1. 10 Jahre alt: lange Haare haben ____________________
2. 11 Jahre alt: groß sein ____________________
3. 12 Jahre alt: ein Instrument (z.B. Klavier) spielen können ____________________
4. 13 Jahre alt: Hausarbeit machen müssen ____________________
5. 14 Jahre alt: einen Computer haben ____________________
6. 15 Jahre alt: Deutsch sprechen können ____________________
7. 16 Jahre alt: Auto fahren dürfen ____________________
8. 17 Jahre alt: zur Uni gehen wollen ____________________

IV Telling when events occur

Using **wenn** vs. **wann** vs. **ob**

The subordinating conjunction **wenn** *(whenever, if)* points to an event that occurs repeatedly. It may be used either with the present tense or any past tense. German speakers often use it in the expression **immer wenn** *(always when, whenever)*.

Hier sagt man sich noch „Grüezi", **wenn** man sich begegnet.	*Here, people still greet each other with "Grüezi" whenever they meet.*
Immer wenn ich nachmittags nach Hause komme, habe ich Hunger.	*Whenever I come home in the afternoon, I'm always hungry.*

The interrogative pronoun **wann** *(when)* occurs in questions about when something happened or is happening. It establishes a specific point of time.

Wann ist der Ball? *When is the ball?*

Frequently, a question with **wann** is embedded into a sentence and the conjugated verb moves to the end of the subordinate clause.

Sie weiß nicht, **wann** der Ball stattfindet.	*She doesn't know when the ball is taking place.*

Wenn *(if)* also expresses a condition. The presence of **so** or **dann** in the second clause often signals that, e.g., **„... und *wenn* sie nicht gestorben sind, *dann* leben sie noch heute.** *("... and if they haven't died, then they are still living today.");* **Wenn du Königin bist, *so* brauchst du nicht mehr zu Fuß zu gehen.** *(If you are the queen, you do not need to go on foot anymore.)*

In complex sentences, embedded yes/no questions start with the subordinating conjunction **ob** *(if, whether)*.

Sie weiß nicht, **ob** der Ball stattfindet.	*She doesn't know if the ball will take place.*

You can always determine whether you should use **wenn**, **wann,** or **ob** by reconstructing the original question or statement.

Statement	***Question***
Der Ball findet um 20.00 Uhr statt.	**Wann** findet der Ball statt? *(correct)* [**Wenn** findet der Ball statt? *Incorrect*]
Question	***Statement***
Findet der Ball Sonnabend statt?	[Sie möchte wissen, **wenn** der Ball stattfindet. *Incorrect*] Sie möchte wissen, **wann** der Ball stattfindet. (*correct answer:* **um 20.00 Uhr**) Sie möchte wissen, **ob** der Ball Sonnabend stattfindet. (*correct answer:* **ja**)

 **33** **Als, wenn, wann oder ob?** Ergänzen Sie die Sätze mit **als, wenn, wann** oder **ob.**

1. ANNA: ______ kommst du morgen Abend vorbei? Um 19.00 Uhr?
   BARBARA: ______ ich Zeit habe, komme ich kurz vor 19.00 Uhr bei dir vorbei.

2. KARL: Weißt du, ______ der Film beginnt?
   STEFAN: Nein. Aber sag mir doch bitte, ______ du's herausfindest.
   KARL: Ich weiß nicht, ______ ich die Zeit dazu habe. Mal sehen.

3. ANNA: Immer ______ ich müde bin, bekomme ich Hunger.
   BARBARA: ______ ich Hunger habe, will ich schlafen.
   ANNA: ______ hast du zuletzt gegessen?
   BARBARA: ______ ich an der Uni war.

4. ANNA: ______ ist meine Mutter in die USA gegangen?
   OMA: ______ sie 23 Jahre alt war.
   OPA: Damals haben wir nicht gewusst, ______ wir die Hannelore je wiedersehen.
   OMA: Aber natürlich ist sie dann immer gekommen, ______ sie die Familie sehen wollte.
   ANNA: Und ______ kommt ihr endlich zum Besuch nach Fort Wayne?
   OPA: Ach, Anna! Vielleicht, ______ ich endlich Englisch verstehen kann.

5. KARL: ______ bist du heute Morgen zur Uni gegangen?
   INGE: Um halb acht. Warum? Hast du mich gehört?
   KARL: Ja, ______ die Tür zuknallte°, wachte ich auf. *slammed shut*
   INGE: Ich habe mich schon gefragt, ______ du das hörst. Ich werde vorsichtiger mit der Tür sein, ______ ich rausgehe.

6. STEFAN: Du, Anna, ______ macht die Mensa heute auf?
ANNA: Um halb elf, glaube ich. Willst du heute dort zu Mittag essen?
STEFAN: Nur, ______ es warmes vegetarisches Essen gibt.
ANNA: Gibt es. Das habe ich gelesen, ______ ich gestern in der Mensa war. Denn ich wollte herausfinden, ______ sie auch an Feiertagen geöffnet war.
STEFAN: Ja, Gott sei Dank. Denn du weißt ja, ich koche nur, ______ ich absolut muss.

BRENNPUNKT KULTUR

Fest- und Feiertage

Besides getting six weeks of paid vacation, Germans take off from work to celebrate numerous other holidays (**Fest- und Feiertage**) throughout the year. New Year's Eve (**Silvester**) is celebrated with parties, dances, and fireworks, and New Year's Day (**Neujahr**) is celebrated with a festive dinner. After the conclusion of the **Karneval** season, Christians observe the Lenten season (**Fastenzeit**) from Ash Wednesday (**Aschermittwoch**) to Good Friday (**Karfreitag**) and ending with Easter (**Ostern**). Children wait for a visit from the Easter bunny (**der Osterhase**), who hides chocolates and colored eggs. May 1 marks an ancient festival of spring that is now celebrated as International Labor Day (**Tag der Arbeit**), used by trade unions to organize public rallies and demonstrations for social or political reforms. During the rest of the spring, religious holidays, such as Ascension Day (**Christi Himmelfahrt**), Pentecost (**Pfingsten**), and Corpus Christi Day (**Fronleichnam**) are observed nationally.

Throughout the summer, towns throughout Germany stage local festivals, such as an annual fair (**Jahrmarkt/Kirmes/Kerb**) or the village marksmen's festival (**Schützenfest**), all of which feature local parades, rides, food and drink booths, contests, concerts, and dancing. Larger cities also have annual fairs: Hamburg stages its **Dom** several times a year, Dresden its **Vogelwiese**, Weimar the **Zwiebelmarkt**, and Stuttgart its **Cannstätter Wasen**. The most famous of all, Munich's sixteen-day **Oktoberfest**, features liter-and-a-half mugs of beer (**eine Maß Bier**) drunk in a local brewer's beer tent (**Bierzelt**) on the **Theresienwiese**.

Germans observe the Day of German Unity (**Tag der deutschen Einheit**) on October 3rd as their national holiday, commemorating the date in 1990 when the German Democratic Republic dissolved and was officially united with the Federal Republic of Germany.

While Jewish citizens look forward to Hanukkah, Christians prepare for the Christmas season (**Advent**). On December 6, St. Nicholas Day (**Sankt Nikolaustag**), children receive candy in their shoes from **Sankt Nikolaus**. Christmas presents are put under the tree on Christmas Eve (**der Heilige Abend**) by the Christ Child (**das Christkind**).

Open-air Christmas markets (**Weihnachtsmärkte**) are held in many cities, and families bake seasonal treats such as gingerbread (**der Lebkuchen**) and stollen (**der Christstollen**). On Christmas Eve, parents decorate the Christmas tree, often with real candles, and families exchange gifts. Christmas Day (**Weihnachten**) is generally spent quietly, visiting with relatives and friends. The day after Christmas (**zweiter Weihnachtstag**) is also an official holiday.

Sometimes **der Weihnachtsmann** comes in person with his assistant, **Knecht Ruprecht,** who punishes the bad children.

Der berühmte Christkindlmarkt in Nürnberg

34 **Interview: Fest- und Feiertage.** Stellen Sie einem Partner/einer Partnerin die folgenden Fragen.

1. Wie hat deine Familie Weihnachten (bzw. Hanukkah) gefeiert, als du Kind warst? Und jetzt?
2. Auf welchen Feiertag hast du dich am meisten gefreut, als du Kind warst? Warum? Und jetzt?
3. Kannst du dich an einen besonderen Feiertag aus deiner Kindheit erinnern?
4. Welche Feiertage feierst du, wenn du bei deiner Familie zu Hause bist?
5. Welche Feiertage feierst du mit Freunden?
6. Welche Feiertage feierst du gar nicht? Warum?
7. Wie feierst du deinen Geburtstag am liebsten?
8. Was hast du als Kind zu Halloween gemacht?
9. Welche deutschen Feiertage kennt man in Amerika und Kanada nicht?

V ▪ Expressing possession

The genitive case

The primary function of the genitive case **(der Genitiv)** is to show possession.

Wir gehen auf das Schloss **des Königs.** *We are going to the king's castle.*

The genitive is also used to express a relationship between things that is indicated by *of* in English.

Das Wunder **des Wandels** findet im Bähnli statt.	*The miracle of transformation takes place in the little train.*
Da fehlt das Dröhnen **der Motoren.**	*The roar of engines is missing.*
... die Stille **eines Bergabends**	*. . . the quiet calm of a mountain evening*

English speakers express possession by adding *'s* to the person who possesses the object or who is related to the person mentioned. *Of* can also be used.

Are you really **Cindy's** brother?
What's the name **of** that French restaurant?

The genitive case frequently occurs in answers to the question **wessen?** *(whose?)*

Question
Wessen Auto ist das? *Whose car is that?*

Answer
Das ist das Auto **der Studentin.** *That is the student's car (car of the student).*

Note the word order: In German, the person who possesses something follows the object being possessed. In English, the possessor precedes the item possessed.

das Auto **der Studentin** ***the student's*** *car*

A. Masculine and neuter nouns

Articles that precede masculine and neuter nouns in the genitive case end in **-es.** The masculine or neuter noun also adds an **-s** or **-es** ending in the genitive singular. Nouns of more than one syllable add **-s** (e.g., **meines Professors, dieses Märchens**). Most nouns of one syllable, and nouns ending in **-s, -ss, -ß, -tsch, -tz, -x, -z,** or **-zt** add **-es** (e.g., **eines Tages, des Buches**).

The genitive is used for indefinite time phrases, such as **eines Tages** *(one day)*, **eines Abends** *(one evening)*, **eines Morgens** *(one morning)*, and **eines Nachts** *(one night)*.

B. Feminine and plural nouns

Articles that precede all feminine and plural nouns in the genitive case end in **-er** (e.g., **meiner Mutter**). The feminine and plural nouns themselves have no special genitive endings like the **-(e)s** on masculine and neuter nouns.

C. Masculine N-nouns

Nouns like **der Student, der Herr, der Mensch** that add **-(e)n** in the accusative and dative singular also have the ending **-(e)n** instead of **-(e)s** in the genitive singular (e.g., **des Studenten, des Herrn, des Menschen**) and in the genitive plural.

D. Adjective endings

The ending on adjectives used with genitive nouns preceded by any article or possessive is always **-en.**

Eine ehrliche Gastronomie der klein**en** Familienbetriebe. *An honest catering trade of small family businesses.*

These are the genitive case forms.

Masculine	Neuter	Feminine	Plural
des König**s**	**des** Zimmer**s**	**der** Person	**der** Kinder
ein**es** Tag**es**	ein**es** Märchen**s**	ein**er** Frau	kein**er** Skiläufer
sein**es** Professor**s**	sein**es** Buch**es**	sein**er** Tochter	sein**er** Gäste
dies**es** Herr**n**	dies**es** Schloss**es**	dies**er** Stadt	dies**er** Hotels

E. Proper names

Proper names of people and countries simply add an **-s** without an apostrophe to show possession.

Er übernachtet in **Roberts** Ferienwohnung. — *He's staying overnight in Robert's vacation home.*

Die Schweiz liegt im Herzen **Mitteleuropas.** — *Switzerland is located in the heart of central Europe.*

However, when additional descriptive information is present, the genitive case is required.

Er übernachtet in der Ferienwohnung **meines Freundes Robert.** — *He's staying overnight in my friend Robert's vacation home.*

Although standard German does not add an apostrophe in the genitive, it is now widely used in the language.

F. The dative preposition von

As you learned in Chapter 6, German speakers frequently express possession with the preposition **von** + *dative*. The word **von** is increasingly replacing the genitive case in spoken German.

Was ist die Adresse **deines Hotels?**
Was ist die Adresse **von deinem Hotel?** — *What's the address of your hotel?*

Mich interessieren die Bücher **dieser italienischen Journalistin** sehr.
Mich interessieren die Bücher **von dieser italienischen Journalistin** sehr. — *I am very interested in the books by this Italian journalist.*

Genitive relative pronouns also designate possession. The genitive case relative pronouns are **dessen** (*m.* and *n.*) and **deren** (*f.* and all *pl.*), e.g., **Es war einmal ein hübsches Mädchen, *dessen* Mutter krank wurde.** *(Once upon a time there was a beautiful girl, **whose** mother became ill.)*

35 Wessen ist es? Ihre Freunde fragen dauernd°, wessen Sachen Sie benutzen. Antworten Sie mit den passenden Genitivformulierungen.

° *continuously*

S1: Wessen Wagen fährst du in der Schweiz? (mein Freund Tom)
S2: Ich fahre den Wagen meines Freundes Tom.

1. In wessen Haus hast du übernachtet? (meine Freunde Willi und Maria)
2. Wessen Skier hast du benutzt? (Willi)
3. Wessen Gastfreundschaft hast du genossen°? (mein guter Freund Willi)
4. Wessen Sonnenbrille hast du getragen? (meine gute Freundin Maria)
5. Wessen Anorak° hast du zum Skilaufen getragen? (Maria)
6. In wessen Sauna hast du den Nachmittag verbracht? (meine neue Bekannte Jutta)
7. Wessen Bier hast du getrunken? (mein lieber alter Freund Jörg)
8. Wessen Weingläser hast du eben kaputt gemacht? (meine lieben Freunde)

° *enjoy*
° *parka*

36 **Was ist der Preis?** Anna und ein Freund haben viele Informationen über einige Ferienorte in der Schweiz bekommen. Jetzt sollen sie für die ganze Gruppe eine preiswerte Unterkunft in Braunwald finden – die Schweiz ist ja° bekanntlich teuer. Was sollen sie nehmen: ein billiges Hotel, eine bewirtete° oder eine unbewirtete Gruppenunterkunft? Hauptsache, der Preis stimmt!

"as you know"
meals included

S1 (ANNA): Was ist der Preis von einem Doppelzimmer im Hotel Alpenblick?
S2 (FREUND): Der Preis eines Doppelzimmers liegt zwischen 104 und 135 Franken.

HOTELS **Hotelreservationen bitten wir Sie höflich, direkt beim Hotel zu tätigen**

Hoch über dem Alltag

Bellevue

*** -Hotel
Familie Lydia und Martin Vogel-Curty
Telefon 058 84 38 43, Fax 058 84 22 74
Telefon 055 643 30 30, Fax 055 643 10 00•
ec-direct

Preise (pro Person in Halbpension und Woche, inkl. MWSt.)	
Doppelzimmer mit Bad	950.–/1220.–/1360.–

Bekanntes Märchenhotel mit Märchenonkel, beim Eisfeld gelegen, 100 Betten, Direktwahltelefon, hoteleigenes Hallenbad, Sauna, Solarium, Whirlpool, Brandvollschultz, Spielzimmer mit Kindergärtnerin, Juniorenraum mit Spielcomputern, Luftschloss-Trampolin, Video-/TV-Raum, Bar mit Billard und Tischfussball, neue Veranda-Hotelhalle, Lesezimmer, 2 Lifte, Kiosk-Artikel, Tischtennis.–Seminarräumlichkeiten mit Einrichtung.–Restaurant.
Bankettsaal für 220 Personen.

Mitglied: Klub kinderfreundl. Schweizer Hotels

Alpenblick

*** -Hotel
Familie Gredinger
Telefon 058 84 15 44, Fax 058 84 19 75
Telefon 055 643 15 44, Fax 055 643 19 75•

Preise (pro Person in Halbpension pro Tag, inkl. MWSt.)	von	bis
Doppelzimmer mit Bad	104.–	135.–

100 Betten, Direktwahltelefon, Spezialitäten-Restaurant, Hotelbar, Kino, Taverne «Gade», TV-Raum, Kinderspielzimmer, Kinderspielplatz, Gartenbillard, Gratisbenützung des öffentlichen Hallenbades, Lift, Brandvollschutz, auf Wunsch TV im Zimmer mit Satellitenprogrammen, wöchentliches Familienprogramm.
Seminarräumlichkeiten mit kompletter Infrastruktur.
Restaurant mit Gartenterrasse.
Panorama-Saal für 200 Personen.
Vollwertkost.

Alpina

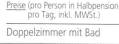

*** -Hotel
Familie Monika and Rolf Schweizer
Telefon 058 84 32 84, Fax 058 84 32 86
Telefon 055 643 32 84, Fax 055 643 32 86•

Preise (pro Person in Halbpension pro Tag, inkl. MWSt.)	von	bis
Doppelzimmer mit Dusche	101.–	124.–
Doppelzimmer mit fl. Wasser	87.–	100.–

55 Betten, Direktwahltelefon, grosse Sonnenterrassen, Aufenthaltsraum mit TV, Bibliothek. Gratisbenützung des öffentlichen Hallenbades. Restaurant und Stübli mit grossem Spezialitätenangebot und Tagesgerichten.
Seminarräumlichkeiten mit vollständiger, entsprechender Schulungseinrichtung
Bankettmöglichkeiten für 20 bis 80 Personen.

Gruppenunterkünfte

• ab 23. März 1996

Hoch über dem Alltag

Jugendherberge SJH

bewirtet

1400 m ü.M.

Familie Schneider-Berger
Telefon 058 84 13 56, Fax 058 84 24 35
Telefon 055 643 13 56, Fax 055 643 24 35•

Preise inkl. MWSt.	
pro Person Halbpension	*

* Erstübernachtung pro Person, Halbpension von Fr. 32.50 bis Fr. 42.–, jede weitere Übernachtung abzüglich Fr. 2.50; spezieller Rabatt für Schulen.

82 Schlafplätze, Zimmer mit 2, 4, 6 und 8 Betten (davon 7 Zimmer mit Lavabos), Waschräume mit Duschen, Tagesräume.
Baujahr 1981.

Berghaus Gumen

bewirtet

1904 m ü.M.

Telefon 058 84 13 24, oder 058 84 36 84*
Telefon 055 643 13 24, oder 055 643 36 84•*
*nur in der Zwischensaison

Preise inkl. MWSt.	
pro Person Halbpension	42.–

Bergstation Sesselbahn Gumen, Selbstbedienungsrestaurant, Aussichtsterrasse.
Unterkunft für 20 personen, Zimmer mit 2 und 3 Betten, Schlafsaal mit 10 Betten, fliessendes Wasser.
Restaurant 100 Plätze
Terrasse 100 Plätze

Skihaus Mattwald

unbewirtet

1600 m ü.M.

des Skiclubs Clariden
Kontaktadresse: Max Binder, Mädchenheim, 8777 Betschwanden
Telefon 058 84 27 48, 055 643 27 48•

Winterpreise inkl. MWSt.	
Erwachsene	18.–/Nacht
Kinder (6–16 Jahre)	13.–/Nacht
Pauschale ganzes Haus:	
Nacht von Samstag auf Sonntag	520.–
Eine Nacht werktags	470.–
Samstag bis Samstag	3070.–

Unterkunft für 45 Personen, Zimmer mit 4, 10, 13 und 18 Matratzen, Waschräume, Duschen, Kalt-/Warmwasser, Ess- und Aufenthaltsraum, modern eingerichtete Küche.

Pensionen und Restaurants

Hoch über dem Alltag

Haus Bergfrieden

1340 m ü.M.

Gästehaus der Diakonischen Schwesternschaft
Braunwald
Telefon 058 84 32 41, 055 643 32 41•

Preise (pro Pers. und Tag VP) inkl. MWSt.	von	bis
Südzimmer	61.–	69.–
Nordzimmer	53.–	57.–

für Kinder Spezialpreise

Christlich geführtes Haus (evang.-reformiert). 40 Betten. Lift. Aufenthaltsraum. Spielecke für Kinder. Zimmer mit fliessendem Warm- und Kaltwasser, Nasszellen in jedem Stockwerk.
Täglich Abendandachten.

1. ein Südzimmer im Haus Bergfrieden?
2. ein Nordzimmer im Haus Bergfrieden?
3. eine Übernachtung für Erwachsene im Skihaus Mattwald?
4. das ganze Haus (Skihaus Mattwald) pro Nacht am Wochenende? An Werktagen?
5. ein Doppelzimmer mit Bad im Märchenhotel Bellevue?
6. eine Übernachtung in der Jugendherberge SJH?
7. eine Übernachtung im Berghaus Gumen?
8. ein Doppelzimmer mit Dusche im Hotel Alpina?

Was ist der Preis? SJH is the acronym for **Schweizer Jugendherberge** *(Swiss Youth Hostel).*

37 **Allwissende° Anna.** Die Gruppe ist schon in Braunwald angekommen. Anna muss die Fragen ihrer Freunde mit Hilfe der Broschüre beantworten. Spielen Sie die Rollen von Anna und ihren Freunden. Anna benutzt den Genitiv und ihre Freunde benutzen **von.**

all-knowing

Wichtige Adressen und Öffnungszeiten

SAC Rettungsstation Braunwald: Alarm-Telefon-Nr. 058 84 30 76. Franz Jöhl, Obmann. Weitere Meldestellen: Kessler Sport, Telefon 058 84 22 22; H. Gredinger, Hotel Alpenblick, Telefon 058 84 15 44; Polizei, Telefon 117.

Verkehrsbüro (Telefon 058 84 11 08) **und Glarner Kantonalbank** (Telefon 058 84 21 25):
Im Dorfzentrum

Montag–Freitag	8:30–12.00/14.15–17.15 Uhr
Dienstag	15.15–18.15 Uhr
Samstag	8.30–11.30 Uhr

Post: Im Dorfzentrum, Telefon 058 84 16 05

Montag–Freitag	8:00–11.45/14.30–17.30 Uhr
Samstag	8.00–10.30 Uhr

Arzt: Dr. med. R. Schwab, Chefarzt Höhenklinik Braunwald, Telefon 058 85 51 51. Sprechstunden nach Vereinbarung (für Notfälle jederzeit).

Apotheke: Höhenklinik Braunwald, Praxis Dr. med. R. Schwab. Montag–Freitag 8.00–12.00/14.00–17.00 Uhr, Samstag 10.00–12.00 Uhr. Nur Medikamente, keine Drogerieartikel. Wegen kleinen Sortiments ist bei speziellen Medikamenten telefonische Anfrage empfohlen. Telefon 058 85 51 51.

Zahnarzt: Dr. med. dent. P. Eberle, Linthal, Telefon 058 84 18 55. Sprechstunden nach telefonischer Vereinbarung.

Transportunternehmen und Taxis: Pferdeschlittenfahrten, Elektrotaxis, Transporte aller Art.

Jakob Schuler	Telefon 058 84 11 34/84 11 47
Franz Schumacher	Telefon 058 84 32 35
Ahorn-Taxi Elektromobile	Telefon 058 84 15 37

Stromversorgung/Elektro
Elektrizitätswerk Linthal

Büro Linthal	Telefon 84 12 04
Filiale Braunwald	Fax/Telefon 84 37 74
Ortsmonteur Braunwald	priv. Telefon 84 21 17

Hallenbad Telefon 058 84 38 78

mit Sauna. Öffnungszeiten: Ab Mitte Dezember bis Saisonschluss.

		Sauna:
Montag	14.00–19.00 Uhr	Gemischt
Dienstag	14.00–21.30 Uhr	Gemischt
Mittwoch	14.00–19.00 Uhr	Gemischt
Donnerstag	14.00–21.30 Uhr	Damen
Freitag	16.30–18.00 Uhr	*Gemischt
Samstag	14.00–18.00 Uhr	Gemischt
Sonntag	geschlossen	

Für Benützer der Abendstunden: letzter Einlass spätestens 30 Minuten vor Schliessung. Wir danken für Ihr Verständnis!
Grössere Gruppen und Vereine auf Voranmeldung. Ab 14.00 Uhr Telefon besetzt: Telefon 058 84 38 78.
Bademeister: Michael Blöhs.
*Sauna schon ab 15.00 Uhr geöffnet!

die Telefonnummer / das Hallenbad

S1 (FREUND/FREUNDIN): Anna, was ist die Telefonnummer vom Hallenbad?

S2 (ANNA): Moment … Die Telefonnummer des Hallenbads ist 058 84 38 78.

1. die Telefonnummer / das Hallenbad
2. der Name / die einzige Bank in Braunwald

3. die Telefonnummer / die örtliche° Post
4. die Adresse / die Apotheke
5. der Name / der Arzt
6. die Telefonnummer / das Verkehrsbüro
7. die Öffnungszeiten / das Hallenbad / am Dienstag
8. die Alarm-Telefonnummer / die Rettungsstation Braunwald
9. die Öffnungszeiten / das Verkehrsbüro / am Wochenende
10. die Telefonnummer / das Transportunternehmen

local

38 **Interview: Das Leben eines Studenten.** Stellen Sie einem Partner/einer Partnerin die folgenden Fragen und beantworten Sie sie dann selber. Benutzen Sie den Genitiv.

S1: Mit wessen Geld finanzierst du dein Studium?
S2: Ich finanziere mein Studium mit dem Geld meiner Eltern.

1. Mit wessen Geld finanzierst du dein Studium?
2. In wessen Zimmer verbringst du mehr Zeit: in deinem eigenen Zimmer oder im Zimmer deiner Freundin (deines Freundes)?
3. Mit wessen Computer arbeitest du auf dem Campus? Zu Hause?
4. Was ist der Titel deines Lieblingskurses?
5. Wessen Kosmetik (Auto) leihst du dir für eine Verabredung?
6. Wessen Geld hast du mal genommen, ohne es zu sagen°?
7. Wessen Job möchtest du eines Tages haben? Warum?
8. An wessen Stelle möchtest du nie und nimmer sein? Warum?

***ohne ... sagen:** without telling*

FREIE KOMMUNIKATION **Rollenspiel: Italien oder Österreich?** Es ist März und Sie können zwei Wochen Urlaub machen. Fahren Sie lieber nach Italien oder nach Österreich? Besprechen Sie mit einem Partner/einer Partnerin die zwei Reisemöglichkeiten. Versuchen Sie, die andere Person mit Argumenten aus den folgenden Listen zu überzeugen°.

convince

S1 fährt gern im Auto, möchte in der Sonne liegen und etwas Exotisches erleben. S2 ist sehr aktiv, fährt gern mit dem Zug und hat Massentourismus nicht gern.

Italien	***Österreich***
in der Sonne liegen	Ski fahren
schwimmen gehen	eine Bergwanderung machen
relativ billig	relativ teuer
weit fahren	nicht so weit fahren
mit dem Auto fahren	mit dem Auto/Zug fahren
Italienisch hören	Deutsch sprechen
viele Touristen	wenige Touristen
viele Sehenswürdigkeiten besuchen	aktiv sein, Sport treiben
gutes Essen	gutes Bier

Schreibecke **Schönen Gruß aus der Schweiz!** Sie kommen gerade vom Skilaufen zurück und haben ein paar Minuten Zeit. Schreiben Sie Ihren Freunden/Freundinnen oder Ihrer Familie zu Hause, wie

Ihnen der Winterurlaub in der Schweiz gefällt. Erzählen Sie im Präteritum, was Sie schon alles gemacht haben. Dann adressieren Sie die Postkarte an den Empfänger/die Empfängerin. Die folgende Liste enthält° ein paar Ideen.

contains

> Ski laufen • Schlitten fahren • Gastfreundschaft • Spaß machen • autofrei • Postkartenlandschaft • märchenhafte Landschaft • Zauberstimmung • fehlen • gute Pisten • hoch über dem Alltag • Spaziergänger • Touristen • Grüezi!

ZIELTEXT

Stefans Puddingschlacht

An Urlaubserlebnisse erinnert man sich das ganze Leben lang – besonders, wenn sie lustig oder schlecht gewesen sind. Hier erzählt Stefan von seinen Erfahrungen in Frankreich als Reiseleiter einer deutschen Touristengruppe und was passieren kann, wenn erwachsene Menschen mit dem Essen herumspielen.

Vorschau

39 Thematische Fragen. Beantworten Sie die folgenden Fragen auf Deutsch.

1. Wohin fahren Sie am liebsten? Warum haben Sie es dort so gern?
2. Was missfällt° Ihnen am meisten, wenn Sie verreisen und unterwegs sind?
3. Was gefällt Ihnen am meisten am Reisen?
4. Wo übernachten Sie meistens, wenn Sie unterwegs sind: in Hotels? In Motels? In Pensionen? Bei Freunden? Im Zelt? In Gruppenunterkünften, wie Jugendherbergen°?
5. Haben Sie mal eine Gruppenreise gemacht? Wann? Wohin? Mit wem? Was hat Ihnen daran gefallen/nicht gefallen?
6. Wenn Sie im Ausland (oder im ausländischen Restaurant) sind, können Sie alles essen? Haben Sie besonders gute oder schlechte Erfahrungen mit der Küche gemacht?

displeases

youth hostels

40 Satzdetektiv. Welche Sätze passen zu welchem Bild? Schreiben Sie die passende Bildnummer neben jeden Satz.

Stefans Puddingschlacht

Bild Nr.

___ 1. Wirf doch mal den Pudding rüber ... Das kam zu einer richtigen Puddingschlacht im Speisesaal.
___ 2. Ich habe meine Ferien in Nordfrankreich verbracht.
___ 3. Es war mehr eine Kulturreise und Pudding gehört dann auch zur Kultur.
___ 4. Nein, es waren zwei Betreuer° und wir mussten dann ein Programm zusammenstellen für insgesamt zwei Wochen. *group guides*
___ 5. Aber das Aufräumen hat keinen Spaß gemacht.
___ 6. Aber sie waren alle in so einem Jugendhotel oder in einer Jugendherberge untergebracht.

ZIELTEXT

Stefans Puddingschlacht

Hören Sie gut zu und schauen Sie sich die Bilder auf Seiten 461–462 an.

Rückblick

41 **Stimmt das?** Stimmen diese Aussagen zum Text oder nicht? Wenn nicht, was stimmt?

	Ja, das stimmt.	*Nein, das stimmt nicht.*
1. Stefan ist allein nach Frankreich in Urlaub gefahren.	_____	_____
2. Stefan hat eine Gruppe von Schülern, Studenten, und auch älteren Leuten betreut°.	_____	_____
3. Es war keine Sprachreise, sondern mehr eine Kulturreise für die Touristen.	_____	_____
4. Sie waren im Luxushotel untergebracht.	_____	_____
5. Sie schliefen alle in Mehrbettzimmern und hatten nicht immer gutes Essen.	_____	_____
6. Eines Tages beim Mittagessen gab es zum Nachtisch einen schönen Schokoladenpudding.	_____	_____
7. Der Pudding hat allen gut geschmeckt und sie wollten immer mehr davon.	_____	_____
8. Einer aus der Gruppe rief zu einem Freund: „Wirf doch mal den Pudding 'rüber!"	_____	_____
9. Der Freund warf den Pudding, und so kam es zu einer richtigen Puddingschlacht im Speisesaal.	_____	_____
10. Als die Puddingschlacht begann, gab es nur zwei Möglichkeiten: sich unter dem Tisch verstecken oder mitmachen.	_____	_____
11. Das Aufräumen und Saubermachen nach der Puddingschlacht hat viel Spaß gemacht.	_____	_____
12. Stefan hatte mit einer zweiten Person zusammen die ganze Tour geplant – Anreise, Abreise, Kulturprogramm – und auch betreut.	_____	_____

°*took care of*

42 **Ergänzen Sie: Diktat.** Ergänzen Sie diese Sätze mit Wörtern aus dem **Zieltext.**

1. Ich habe mal die _____ in Frankreich verbracht, in Nordfrankreich …
2. Die waren dann so in einer Art _____ untergebracht.
3. Das waren also Schüler, Studenten, auch etwas ältere Leute, also durchaus _____.
4. Sie waren alle in so einem Jugendhotel oder in einer Jugendherberge _____, in Mehrbettzimmern.
5. Und _____ _____ kam es zu einem Zwischenfall beim Mittagessen.
6. Es gab zunächst französische _____ und im Anschluss dann einen Pudding.
7. Der hat den Pudding geworfen. Es kam zu einer richtigen _____ im Speisesaal.

8. Und da gab's nur zwei Möglichkeiten: entweder mitmachen oder sich unter dem Tisch _____.
9. Aber das _____ hat keinen Spaß gemacht.
10. Das war nicht so toll. Auch eine Katastrophe im _____.
11. Warst du da allein _____ als Reiseleiter oder?
12. Nein, es waren zwei Betreuer, und wir mussten dann ein Programm _____ für insgesamt zwei Wochen.

43 **Kurz gefragt.** Beantworten Sie diese Fragen auf Deutsch.

1. Warum war Stefan in Nordfrankreich?
2. Musste er dort allein arbeiten?
3. Wer gehörte zu der Gruppe?
4. Wo waren die Touristen untergebracht?
5. Wie fing die Puddingschlacht an?
6. Was waren die zwei Möglichkeiten, nachdem die Schlacht begonnen hatte?
7. Warum machte das Stefan keinen Spaß?
8. Was waren seine Aufgaben als Reiseleiter?
9. Was gehörte alles zu der Planung für die Reise?
10. Für wen arbeiteten die Betreuer eigentlich?

FREIE KOMMUNIKATION

Ein altes Märchen erzählen. Bilden Sie eine Gruppe von fünf Personen und erzählen Sie der Gruppe Ihr Lieblingsmärchen. Wenn Sie möchten, benutzen Sie beim Sprechen das Perfekt (z. B. **hat gewohnt, hat geheiratet**). Die anderen Studenten/Studentinnen müssen den Titel Ihres Märchens erraten. Geben Sie Ihrem Märchen einen typischen Anfang und ein typisches Ende.

SIE: Es war einmal ein(e) ...
...
... Und wenn sie nicht gestorben sind, dann leben sie noch heute.

Ein modernes Märchen erzählen. Bilden Sie eine Gruppe von drei bis vier Personen und erzählen Sie ein modernes Märchen aus Ihrem Leben. Geben Sie einige wahre° und ein paar erfundene° Details an. Die anderen Studenten/Studentinnen raten, was falsch ist.

true / made up

Ein Märchen gemeinsam erzählen. Bilden Sie eine Gruppe von sechs bis sieben Personen. Bilden Sie mit Ihren Stühlen einen Kreis. S1 beginnt die Erzählung mit einem Satz. Der nächste Student/Die nächste Studentin im Kreis erfindet den nächsten Satz usw., bis alle Personen einen Satz gesagt haben.

Schreibecke **Anekdoten aus dem Urlaub.** Jeder von uns hat komische oder traurige Erinnerungen an den Urlaub. Was ist Ihnen mal im Urlaub passiert, das Sie in einer kurzen Geschichte erzählen können? Schreiben Sie eine kleine Erzählung von mindestens zehn Sätzen im Präteritum.

Beschreiben Sie, wo Sie waren, mit wem Sie da waren, was Sie machen wollten und was dann passierte.

Ein Märchen schreiben. Schreiben Sie die Handlung Ihres Lieblingsmärchens nach. Es kann auch ein amerikanisches Märchen sein, wie z.B. „Paul Bunyan", „Pecos Bill", „Johnny Appleseed" usw. Vergessen Sie nicht, das Präteritum zu benutzen (z.B. **war, gab, kam, wohnte**). Hier sind einige bekannte Märchen zur Auswahl°.

° *choice*

Hänsel und Gretel	Dornröschen	Die kleine Meerjungfrau
Der Froschkönig	Schneewittchen	Der Wolf und die sieben jungen Geißlein
Das hässliche Entlein	Rotkäppchen	Des Kaisers neue Kleider
Die goldene Gans	Rumpelstilzchen	
Rapunzel		

Wortschatz

Aschenputtel

die Asche, -n *ash, cinder*
das Blut *blood*
die Braut *bride*
der Edelstein, -e *jewel*
die Ferse, -n *heel*
das Fest, -e *festival, feast*
die Freude, -n *joy*
das Gold *gold*
das Grab, ¨er *grave*
der Herd *hearth, fireplace*
der Himmel *heaven*
der Königssohn, ¨e *prince*
das Märchen, - *folk (fairy) tale*
das Messer, - *knife*
die Perle, -n *pearl*
das Pferd, -e *horse*
das Silber *silver*
die Stiefmutter, ¨ *stepmother*
die Stiefschwester, -n *stepsister*
das Täubchen, *pigeon, dove*
das Vögelchen, - *little bird*
der Zeh, -en *toe*
der Zweig, -e *branch*

ab·schneiden (schnitt ab, hat abgeschnitten) *to cut off*
an·probieren (hat anprobiert) *to try on*
begleiten (hat begleitet) *to accompany*
beten (hat gebetet) *to pray*
danken (hat gedankt) + *dat.* *to thank*
ein·laden (lädt ein, lud ein, hat eingeladen) *to invite*
erkennen (erkannte, hat erkannt) *to recognize*
erlauben (hat erlaubt) *to permit, allow*
fort·gehen (ging fort, ist fortgegangen) *to go away*
führen (hat geführt) *to lead*
halten (hält, hielt, hat gehalten) für + *acc.* *to think someone is something, believe someone to be*
herab·blicken (hat herabgeblickt) *to look down*
mit·bringen (brachte mit, hat mitgebracht) *to bring along, bring back*
nennen (nannte, hat genannt) *to name, call someone something*
passen (hat gepasst) *to fit*
pflanzen (hat gepflanzt) *to plant*
proklamieren (hat proklamiert) *to proclaim*
rennen (ist gerannt) *to run*
rufen (rief, hat gerufen) *to call*
rütteln (hat gerüttelt) *to shake*
schütteln (hat geschüttelt) *to shiver, shake*
sterben (stirbt, starb, ist gestorben) *to die*
suchen (hat gesucht) *to look for*
vorbei·reiten (ritt vorbei, ist vorbeigeritten) *to ride by, ride past (on horseback)*
wachsen (wächst, wuchs, ist gewachsen) *to grow*
weinen (hat geweint) *to cry*
werfen (wirft, warf, hat geworfen) *to throw, toss*
wiederholen (hat wiederholt) *to repeat*
wünschen (hat gewünscht) *to wish*
zurück·bringen (brachte zurück, hat zurückgebracht) *to bring back*

Andere Wörter

daheim *at home*
fromm *pious, religious*
glänzend *gleaming*

Ausdrücke

böse von Herzen *mean-hearted*
er passte wie angegossen *it fit as if it had been poured on*
nach einiger Zeit *awhile later*
schön im Gesicht *beautiful to look at*

Märchenfiguren

die Fee, -n *fairy*
der Frosch, ¨-e *frog*
die Hexe, -n *witch*
der Jäger, - *hunter*
der König, -e *king*
die Königin, -nen *queen*
die Königstochter, ¨- *princess*
der Prinz, -en *prince*
die Prinzessin, -nen *princess*
der Zauberer, - *magician, sorcerer*
der Zwerg, -e *dwarf*

Märchenelemente

ein giftiger Apfel *poisonous apple*
das Schloss, *(pl.)* **Schlösser** *castle*
der Spiegel, - *mirror*
das Tier, -e *animal*
der Wald, ¨-er *forest, woods*

Ausdrücke

Es war einmal ein ... *Once upon a time there was . . .*
Und wenn sie nicht gestorben sind, dann leben sie noch heute. *And they lived happily ever after.*

Braunwald: Ein Wintermärchen

der Alltag *everyday life*
der Anfänger, - *beginner*
das Bähnli, -s *little train*
die Bergwirtschaft, -en *mountain restaurant*
das Dorf, ¨-er *village*
der Familienbetrieb, -e *family-owned business*
der Ferienort, -e *resort town*
der/die Fortgeschrittene, -n *advanced student (adj. as noun)*
der Gast, ¨-e *guest*
die Gastfreundschaft *hospitality*
die Gemeinschaft, -en *association, group*
der Genießer, - *connoisseur*
das Glück *happiness, joy, luck*
die Herzlichkeit *warmth, heartiness, sincerity*
der Kinoabend, -e *night at the movies*
der Langlauf *cross-country skiing*
die Langlaufloipe, -n *cross-country ski run*
die Lebensfreude *joy of life*
die Masse, -n *mass, crowd*
der Millionär, -e *millionaire*
die Naturschönheit, -en *natural beauty*
das Paradies, -e *paradise*
die Persönlichkeit, -en *personality*
die Piste, -n *(downhill) ski run, track*
der Postbote, [-n], -n *mailman, letter carrier*
das Prestige *prestige*
der Pulverschnee *powder snow*
die Schlittelfahrt, -en *toboggan run; sleighride*
der Schlitten, - *sled, sleigh*
der Pferdeschlitten, - *horse-drawn sleigh*
der Schock, -s *shock*
die Schussfahrt, -en *schussing*
die Sonnenterrasse, -n *sunning deck*
der Spaziergänger, - *walker, stroller*
die Stille *quiet, silence*
der Tunnel, -s *tunnel*
der Wandel *change, transformation*
das Wunder, - *miracle, wonder*
die Zauberstimmung *magical mood*
die Zukunft *future*

Angst haben (hat, hatte, hat gehabt) vor + *dat.* *to be afraid of*
auf·wärmen (hat aufgewärmt) *to warm up*
aus·steigen (stieg aus, ist ausgestiegen) *to disembark, climb out*
begegnen (ist begegnet) + *dat.* *to meet, run into*
dröhnen (hat gedröhnt) *to drone*
ein·steigen (stieg ein, ist eingestiegen) *to board, climb in, on*
erleben (hat erlebt) *to experience*
fehlen (hat gefehlt) *to be missing, be lacking*
sich gewöhnen (hat sich gewöhnt) an + *acc.* *to get used to, get accustomed to*
glauben (hat geglaubt) an + *acc.* *to believe in*
klettern (ist geklettert) *to climb*
Ski laufen (läuft Ski, lief Ski, ist Ski gelaufen) *to ski*
statt·finden (fand statt, hat stattgefunden) *to occur, take place*
steigen (stieg, ist gestiegen) *to climb*

abendlich *evening time*
aggressiv *aggressive*
autofrei *car-free*
ehemalig *former(ly), previous(ly)*
ehrlich *honest*
ewig *eternal*
ferienreif *ready for a vacation*
gastlich *hospitable, friendly*
gestresst *stressed*
gutgelaunt *in a good mood*
herzlich *hearty, warm*
nächtlich *nighttime, nocturnal*
sanft *gentle, soft*
sauber *clean*
schlittelnd *sledding, by sled*
seltsam *strange, unusual*
sichtbar *visible, clear to the eye*
sonnig *sunny*
überarbeitet *overworked*
verrückt *crazy*
verschneit *snow covered*
wesentlich *essential*

anderswo *someplace else*
eben *just*
gar nicht *not at all*
gar nie *never at all*
Grüezi! *Hello! (Swiss German dialect)*
hoch über dem Alltag *far beyond the everyday*
nachdem *after (conjunction)*

Die Schweiz: geographische Daten

die Alpen *(pl.) the Alps*
der Berg, -e *mountain*
der Fluss, *(pl.)* **Flüsse** *river*
der Gipfel, - *mountain peak*
die Grenze, -n *border*
die Hauptstadt *capital city*
die Insel, -n *island*
der Jura *Jura Mountains*
der Kanton, -e *canton, state*
die Landschaft, -en *landscape, scenery*
das Mittelland *midlands, flatland*
der Pass, *(pl.)* **Pässe** *mountain pass*
der See, -n *lake*
das Tal, ¨er *valley*

Aus dem Zieltext

die Abreise *departure*
die Anreise *arrival*
der Betreuer, - *person in charge*
die Ferien *(pl.) school vacation*
die Jugendherberge, -n *youth hostel*
das Jugendhotel, -s *budget youth hotel*
die Katastrophe, -n *catastrophe*
die Küche, -n *kitchen; cuisine, food*
die Kultur, -en *culture*
das Mehrbettzimmer, - *room with multiple beds*
die Möglichkeit, -en *possibility*
die Planung, -en *planning*
das Programm, -e *program*
der Pudding, -s *pudding*
der Reiseleiter, - *group leader, tour guide*
das Reiseunternehmen, - *travel agency*
die Schlacht, -en *battle, fight*
der Speisesaal, *(pl.)* **Speisesäle** *hotel dining room*
die Sprachreise, -n *language study tour*
der Tourismus *tourism*
der Urlaub, -e *vacation*
die Versicherung, -en *insurance*
die Vorbereitung, -en *preparation*
der Zwischenfall, ¨e *incident*

auf·räumen (hat aufgeräumt) *to pick up, clean up*
bewerkstelligen (hat bewerkstelligt) *to manage, take care of*
mit·machen (hat mitgemacht) *to join in, participate*
mischen (hat gemischt) *to mix*
unter·bringen (brachte unter, hat untergebracht) *to house, put up overnight*
verstecken (hat versteckt) *to hide, conceal*
zusammen·stellen (hat zusammengestellt) *to put together, organize*

Adjektive und Adverbien

tätig *active, involved*
verantwortlich *responsible*
zunächst *first of all*

Andere Wörter

eines Tages *one day*
entweder ... oder *either . . . or*
hinten *way back*
im Anschluss *subsequently, afterwards*
im Auftrag von *commissioned by*
insgesamt *for a total of*
zum Teil *partially*

In this chapter you will learn to talk about activities that you might do, make polite suggestions and requests, describe actions as a process, and state what you could or should have done.

Kommunikative Funktionen

- Speculating about activities
- Making polite requests and suggestions
- Making role reversal statements *(If I were you, . . .)*
- Stating what one should have done (but did not do)
- Talking about actions as a process
- Expressing substitution, opposition, causality, duration, and position

Strukturen

- The subjunctive mood
- The passive voice
- Genitive prepositions

Vokabeln

- Sehenswürdigkeiten in Berlin
- Regierung und Politik
- Die Länder und Flüsse Deutschlands

Kulturelles

- Berlin nach dem Zweiten Weltkrieg
- Deutschland: von der Diktatur zur Demokratie
- Die Deutsche Demokratische Republik

Das Brandenburger Tor ist seit 1989 wieder das Zentrum der Stadt Berlin.

KAPITEL ELF

Geschichte und Geographie

Go to the *Vorsprung* Website at
www.hmco.com/college

ANLAUFTEXT

Was würdest du dann vorschlagen?

In den Ferien fährt Anna nach Berlin, wo sie ihren Onkel Werner besucht. Beim Abendessen erzählt Anna ihrem Onkel Werner von ihrem ersten Tag in Berlin. Anna wollte den Reichstag und die Mauer sehen. Aber der Reichstag war geschlossen und sie konnte die Mauer nicht finden. Anna und Onkel Werner machen Pläne für die nächsten Tage und besprechen, was Anna sehen möchte und was sie zusammen machen könnten. Heute Abend gehen sie ins Konzert, und nachher will Anna noch jemanden treffen.

Vorschau

1 **Thematische Fragen.** Beantworten Sie die folgenden Fragen auf Deutsch.

1. Wie lernen Sie am ersten Tag eine neue Stadt kennen?
   a. auf einer Stadtrundfahrt° — *city bus tour*
   b. auf einer Führung° — *walking tour*
   c. durch einen Ton-Dia-Vortrag° — *slide show*
   d. allein
   e. mit Freunden
   f. durch ein Video
2. Wo informieren Sie sich über eine neue Stadt?
   a. bei Freunden
   b. bei Verwandten
   c. bei jungen Leuten
   d. beim Verkehrsbüro
   e. beim Fremdenführer/bei der Fremdenführerin
   f. beim Telefondienst
   g. im World Wide Web
3. Was möchten Sie als Tourist/Touristin als erstes in Berlin erleben?
   a. die Museen
   b. die Clubszene
   c. die Architektur
   d. die tollen Parks und Seen
   e. die Musikszene
   f. die Kunstszene

Wissenswerte Vokabeln: Sehenswürdigkeiten in Berlin

Talking about sights in and around Berlin

der Kurfürstendamm

die Kaiser-Wilhelms-Gedächtniskirche

die Philharmonie

die Museumsinsel

das Nikolaiviertel

Unter den Linden

das Brandenburger Tor

der Alexanderplatz

das Schloss Charlottenburg

die Humboldt-Universität

Berlin-Mitte

der Reichstag

die Spree

die Mauer

Potsdam

der Prenzlauer Berg

Was würdest du in Berlin machen? *Ich würde die Mauer besichtigen°.*

visit, look at

2 Lernen Sie Berlin kennen. Wählen Sie die beste Beschreibung für jede Sehenswürdigkeit in **Wissenswerte Vokabeln.**

W. Vok. The **Nikolaiviertel,** the oldest part of Berlin, has been restored as a historic district in downtown **Berlin-Mitte.**

1. Hier spielt das berühmteste Orchester Deutschlands, die Berliner Philharmoniker.
2. Diese Kirche – im Krieg bombardiert – steht heute noch als Ruine.
3. Das ist ein großer Platz im östlichen Teil Berlins; hier steht der Fernsehturm°.
4. Lebendige Einkaufsstraße° im westlichen Teil Berlins.
5. Sitz des deutschen Bundestages ab 1999.
6. Südwestliche Nachbarstadt von Berlin; hier steht das Schloss Sanssouci.
7. Der Stadtteil, der bei jungen Leuten „in" ist, mit vielen Szene-Clubs und einem bunten multikulturellen Leben.
8. Diese Barriere stand als Symbol des Kalten Krieges zwischen Ost und West. Sie existiert nicht mehr als Ganzes.
9. Ein Sommerpalast mitten in Berlin, der für die Frau von König Friedrich I, Sophie Charlotte, gebaut wurde.
10. Das Wahrzeichen Berlins; steht am Anfang von Unter den Linden.
11. Elegante Hauptstraße im östlichen Teil Berlins.

TV tower

shopping street

Lernen Sie Berlin kennen. Sanssouci is the name of a palace and its surrounding park in Potsdam. **Friedrich der Große,** King of Prussia, had **Sanssouci** built in the spirit of Enlightenment and in the architectural style of French rococo.

12. Der berühmteste Fluss Berlins.
13. Hier gibt es fünf Museen: die Alte Nationalgalerie, das Bodemuseum, das Pergamonmuseum, das Alte Museum und das Neue Museum.
14. Der historische Mittelpunkt Berlins.
15. Historischer Stadtteil um die Nikolaikirche.
16. Die älteste Universität Berlins.

3 Würdest° du das machen? Was würden Sie als Tourist/Touristin in einer fremden Stadt machen? Kreuzen Sie die Aktivitäten an. Fragen Sie dann einen Partner/eine Partnerin, was er/sie machen würde.

would

Würdest du das machen? The **würde/könnte** *(would/could)* + infinitive constructions will be introduced later in this chapter.

S1: Würdest du in ein Konzert gehen?
S2: Ja, das würde ich machen. *(oder)*
Nein, das würde ich nicht machen.

	Ich		*Mein(e) Partner(in)*	
	Ja	*Nein*	*Ja*	*Nein*
1. in ein Konzert gehen	___	___	___	___
2. historische Denkmäler° anschauen	___	___	___	___
3. eine historische Kirche oder einen Dom° ansehen	___	___	___	___
4. einen Park oder einen Platz im Freien° besuchen	___	___	___	___
5. eine berühmte Sehenswürdigkeit anschauen	___	___	___	___
6. durch die Altstadt bummeln	___	___	___	___
7. ein Museum besuchen	___	___	___	___
8. die Clubszene ausprobieren	___	___	___	___
9. durch Geschäfte bummeln	___	___	___	___
10. eine berühmte Universität besichtigen	___	___	___	___

monuments
cathedral
outdoors

Determine which activities both of you find interesting and report to the class what you could do together (e.g., **Wir könnten zusammen in ein Konzert gehen.**).

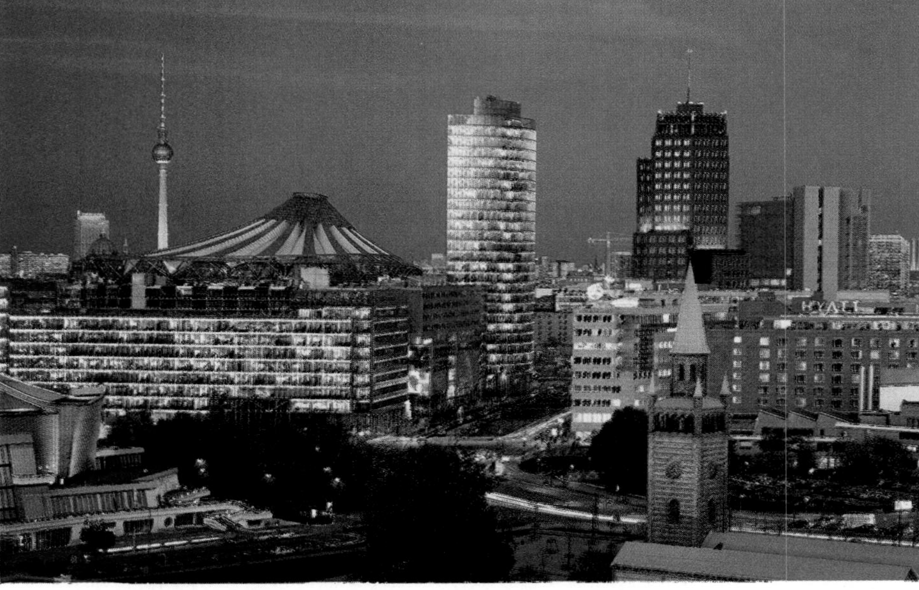

Seit der Vereinigung ist der Potsdamer Platz ein Symbol für das neue Berlin geworden.

 **ANLAUFTEXT**

 Hören Sie gut zu.

Was würdest du dann vorschlagen?

1
Grüß dich, Onkel Werner. Entschuldige die Verspätung.
Komm, erzähl mal von deinem ersten Tag in Berlin.

2
Haben wir Zeit?
Klar. Die Philharmonie fängt erst um 20 Uhr an. Wir essen erst eine Kleinigkeit.

3
Also, es war recht interessant, aber frustrierend. Ich wollte als erstes den Reichstag sehen. Aber der war geschlossen, wegen Umbauarbeiten.
Ja, der Reichstag wird momentan renoviert.
Und dann bin ich zum Brandenburger Tor gelaufen, weil ich die Mauer sehen wollte, aber da war nichts. Und ich hätte sie so gern gesehen!

4
Was? Es gibt doch Mauerreste direkt hinter dem Reichstag! Aber ich hätte dich warnen sollen. Wir könnten ja morgen oder übermorgen zur East Side Gallery, oder mal zum Mauerpark. Dort gibt es Mauerreste.
Gut. Das würde mich schon interessieren.

5
Abgemacht. Und was hast du für morgen vor?
Tja, ich würde gern Potsdam sehen. Vielleicht morgen Nachmittag …

6
Nee, nee pass mal auf. Allein für den Park Sanssouci braucht man einen ganzen Tag! Wir sollten damit bis Samstag warten. Dann habe ich mehr Zeit.

7
Klingt gut. Aber was würdest du dann für morgen vorschlagen?

An deiner Stelle würde ich am Vormittag einen Bummel auf dem Kurfürstendamm machen, die Gedächtniskirche besuchen und so. Und am Nachmittag könnten wir zusammen Unter den Linden hochlaufen und Berlin-Mitte sehen – die Humboldt-Universität, das Nikolaiviertel und die Museumsinsel.
8

Das wäre schön. Und ich würde gern sehen, wo das neue Regierungsviertel entsteht …
Ja, das könnten wir machen.
9

Fantastisch! Und, Onkel Werner, ich hätte noch einen Wunsch: Könnten wir nach der Philharmonie zum Prenzlauer Berg fahren?

Was willst du denn dort um diese Zeit?
BAR
10

Tja, ich habe heute jemanden kennen gelernt, der dort wohnt. Und der hat von der Clubszene am Prenzlauer Berg geschwärmt.
Am Wochenende wäre es aber lebendiger …
11

Aber ich bin für heute Abend verabredet!
Ah. *(für sich)* Das hätte ich gleich ahnen sollen!
12

Rückblick

4 **Gesprächspuzzle.** Welcher Dialogteil passt zu welchem Bild? Schreiben Sie über jeden Dialogteil die passende Bildnummer.

Bild ___

WERNER: Nee, nee, pass mal auf. Allein für den Park Sanssouci braucht man einen ganzen Tag! Wir sollten damit bis Samstag warten. Dann habe ich mehr Zeit.

Bild ___

ANNA: Aber ich bin für heute Abend verabredet!
WERNER: Aha. *(für sich)* Das hätte ich gleich ahnen sollen!

Bild ___

ANNA: Also, es war recht interessant, aber frustrierend. Ich wollte als erstes den Reichstag sehen. Aber der war geschlossen, wegen Umbauarbeiten.
WERNER: Ja, der Reichstag wird momentan renoviert.
ANNA: Und dann bin ich zum Brandenburger Tor gelaufen, weil ich die Mauer sehen wollte, aber da war nichts. Und ich hätte sie so gern gesehen!

Bild ___

ANNA: Das wäre schön. Und ich würde gern sehen, wo das neue Regierungsviertel entsteht …
WERNER: Ja, das könnten wir machen.

Bild ___

ANNA: Haben wir Zeit?
WERNER: Klar. Die Philharmonie fängt erst um 20 Uhr an. Wir essen erst eine Kleinigkeit.

Bild ___

ANNA: Fantastisch! Und, Onkel Werner, ich hätte noch einen Wunsch: Könnten wir nach der Philharmonie zum Prenzlauer Berg fahren?
WERNER: Was willst du denn dort um diese Zeit?

Bild ___

WERNER: Was? Es gibt doch Mauerreste direkt hinter dem Reichstag! Aber ich hätte dich warnen sollen. Wir könnten ja morgen oder übermorgen zur East Side Gallery oder mal zum Mauerpark. Dort gibt es Mauerreste.
ANNA: Gut. Das würde mich schon interessieren.

Bild ___

WERNER: An deiner Stelle würde ich am Vormittag einen Bummel auf dem Kurfürstendamm machen, die Gedächtniskirche besuchen und so. Und am Nachmittag könnten wir zusammen Unter den Linden hochlaufen und Berlin-Mitte sehen – die Humboldt-Universität, das Nikolaiviertel und die Museumsinsel.

Bild ___

ANNA: Grüß dich, Onkel Werner. Entschuldige die Verspätung.
WERNER: Komm, erzähl mal von deinem ersten Tag in Berlin.

Bild ___

WERNER: Abgemacht. Und was hast du für morgen vor?
ANNA: Tja, ich würde gern Potsdam sehen. Vielleicht morgen Nachmittag …

The **Kurfürstendamm,** West Berlin's main boulevard and shopping street, has its name because it was originally constructed by Berlin's electors **(Kurfürsten).**

The Humboldt-Universität was founded in 1809 by Wilhelm von Humboldt.

***Bild*___**

ANNA: Tja, ich habe heute jemanden kennen gelernt, der dort wohnt. Und der hat von der Clubszene am Prenzlauer Berg geschwärmt°.

to be wild about something

WERNER: Am Wochenende wäre es aber lebendiger …

***Bild*___**

ANNA: Klingt gut. Aber was würdest du dann für morgen vorschlagen?

5 Stimmt das? Stimmen diese Aussagen zum Text oder nicht? Wenn nicht, was stimmt?

	Ja, das stimmt.	*Nein, das stimmt nicht.*
1. Annas erster Tag in Berlin war frustrierend.	___	___
2. Der Reichstag war geschlossen.	___	___
3. Anna hat die Mauer gesehen, aber das Brandenburger Tor hat sie nicht finden können.	___	___
4. Für morgen hat Anna keine Pläne.	___	___
5. Werner meint, dass man für Potsdam und den Park Sanssouci nur ein paar Stunden braucht.	___	___
6. Werner schlägt Anna vor, dass sie am Vormittag den Kurfürstendamm allein besuchen soll.	___	___
7. Am Nachmittag könnten sie Berlin-Mitte besuchen.	___	___
8. Heute Abend gehen sie zusammen in ein Rockkonzert.	___	___
9. Nachher will Anna zum Prenzlauer Berg fahren.	___	___
10. Werner versteht endlich, dass Anna noch heute mit einem jungen Mann am Prenzlauer Berg verabredet ist.	___	___

6 Ergänzen Sie. Ergänzen Sie diese Sätze mit Wörtern aus dem **Anlauftext.**

1. Anna konnte den Reichstag nicht besuchen, denn er war heute ______.
2. Im Moment wird der Reichstag ______.
3. Anna wollte am Brandenburger Tor die ______ sehen.
4. Im Mauerpark oder bei der East Side Gallery kann man noch ______ finden.
5. Onkel Werner fragt Anna: „Was hast du für morgen ______?"
6. Nachdem Werner sagt, dass er am Samstag Zeit für Potsdam und Park Sanssouci hat, sagt Anna: „______ gut!"
7. Aber sie fragt ihn, was er dann für morgen ______ würde.
8. An Annas ______ würde Werner einen ______ auf dem Kurfürstendamm machen.
9. Am Nachmittag ______ sie zusammen Unter den Linden hochlaufen.
10. In Berlin-Mitte steht die Humboldt-Universität, das Nikolai______ und die Museums______.
11. Anna möchte auch sehen, wo das neue Regierungsviertel ______.
12. Heute Abend will Anna noch zum Prenzlauer Berg fahren, weil sie dort mit einem jungen Mann ______ ist.

Five museums in the heart of Berlin-Mitte form the nucleus of Berlin's art exhibition space: die Alte Nationalgalerie, with German art of the 19th and 20th centuries; das Bodemuseum, with collections ranging from Egyptian and Byzantine art to sculpture; das Pergamonmuseum with its famous Greek Pergamon altar and collections of Near Eastern and Islamic art; and das Alte Museum, with a program of special exhibits.

7 Kurz gesagt. Vervollständigen° Sie diese Sätze mit einem Nebensatz. Benutzen Sie Ihre eigenen Worte.

complete

1. Werner und Anna haben heute Abend Eile°, weil …
2. Anna soll noch eine Kleinigkeit essen, bevor …

***haben Eile:** are in a hurry*

3. Anna hat den Reichstag nicht gesehen, weil ...
4. Werner meint, er hätte Anna warnen sollen, dass ...
5. Werner schlägt Anna vor, morgen nicht nach Potsdam zu fahren, weil ...
6. Werner sagt, dass er an Annas Stelle morgen Vormittag ...
7. Anna möchte zum Prenzlauer Berg fahren, weil ...

Sprache im Alltag: Confirming what someone said

In informal conversation, German speakers often seek confirmation with **nicht wahr?** or **na?** Confirmation is given with the expressions **fantastisch, fein, klar** or the utterances **Das wäre schön, Das klingt gut!** or **Das hört sich gut an.** Sometimes **das** is abbreviated or dropped. **('S wäre schön. Klingt gut!) Ich bin ganz deiner Meinung** or **Du hast vollkommen recht** indicate agreement with an opinion. **Abgemacht!** indicates agreement with a proposal, and **Aha, Ach so,** or **Naja** express reluctance.

8 Was möchtest du in Berlin sehen? Sie verbringen ein paar Tage in Berlin. Was möchten Sie machen? Planen Sie mit einem Partner/einer Partnerin den ersten Tag. Benutzen Sie die Sehenswürdigkeiten in **Wissenswerte Vokabeln: Sehenswürdigkeiten in Berlin.**

S1: Was möchtest du in Berlin machen?
S2: Ich möchte gern das Nikolaiviertel sehen, und du?
S1: Ich möchte auch gern ... *(oder)*
Naja, ich möchte lieber zum Prenzlauer Berg gehen.
S2: (Das) Klingt gut!

Berlin nach dem Zweiten Weltkrieg

At the end of World War II, the Allies that had defeated Germany – the U.S., Great Britain, France, and the Soviet Union – divided the country and the capital of Berlin into four occupation zones **(Besatzungszonen).** Tensions immediately grew between the western Allies and the Soviets. In 1948, the Soviets attempted to gain control of Berlin and blockaded all roads to West Berlin. The Allies responded with a massive air transport of goods to West Berlin **(die Luftbrücke)** that lasted 11 months. It saved West Berlin and forced the Soviets to back down.

Two completely different economic and political systems evolved in the western and eastern halves of Germany: one a Western-oriented, free market economy in a democracy, the other a planned economy in a Marxist society. Following currency reforms in 1948 that introduced the use of different German marks in the west and east, the German nation split into two separate political states in 1949: the Federal Republic of Germany (**die Bundesrepublik Deutschland**) in the west, and the German Democratic Republic (**die Deutsche Demokratische Republik,** or **DDR**) in the east. Berlin remained divided as well, West Berlin becoming a de facto state of the Federal Republic, while East Berlin became the capital of the **DDR.** American, British, French, and Russian troops remained stationed in Germany and Berlin for the next 40 years.

Throughout the Cold War, the tensions between East and West were never more obvious than in Berlin. To guarantee West Berlin's viability, the West German government established federal agencies in Berlin, gave West Berliners significant tax breaks and subsidies, and encouraged international trade fairs, conferences, and new construction. Young people were drawn to West Berlin's progressive universities, **die Freie Universität Berlin** and **die Technische Universität,** and the city's liberal politics and attitudes. West Berlin became everything that East Berlin was not: affluent, colorful, free-spirited, and western.

BRENNPUNKT KULTUR

East Berlin, in contrast, turned somber as East Germany made its transition to a Marxist workers' state and socialist economy – changes that were not universally supported. In 1953, workers in East Berlin staged a spontaneous revolt against productivity quotas and price hikes, which was crushed by Soviet forces. As life in East Germany became more and more repressive and borders became harder to cross, many (20,000 per day by the late 1950s) attempted to flee to the West via Berlin, where movement between the different parts of the city was basically unrestricted. To end the drain on its workforce, the **DDR** began to construct a wall around West Berlin during the night of August 13, 1961. The **DDR** later justified this physical barrier as its "anti-fascist protective wall" **(der antifaschistische Schutzwall)**, but it became known to the rest of the world as "The Wall" **(die Mauer)**. Even though the Berlin Wall encircled West Berlin, it was the East Berliners and East Germans who were truly locked in. Soviet-style concrete apartment buildings went up, yet war rubble was left unmoved for decades, and quality consumer goods—everything from automobiles to bananas – were virtually impossible to obtain.

Even though the East German economy was the wealthiest of all Warsaw Pact nations, large-scale dissatisfaction with socialism kept spreading at grass-roots levels throughout the **DDR.** In 1989, the citizens of Leipzig bravely started weekly demonstrations against the state. That summer, East Germans vacationing in Czechoslovakia and Hungary stormed embassies and borders demanding access to the West, and won. On November 9, 1989, fearing another mass flight of refugees to the West, East German authorities opened borders to the West for the first time in 28 years. This was the beginning of the end for the **DDR:** within a year, the East German **Volkskammer** voted the Socialist state out of existence, and on October 3, 1990, the unification of Germany was completed with the admission of the German Democratic Republic to the Federal Republic of Germany. As stipulated by the German Constitution **(das Grundgesetz)**, the capital of unified Germany was henceforth Berlin.

Since unification the Federal Government has been relocating ministries and agencies to Berlin, and in 1999 the **Reichstag** was rededicated as the seat of the German Parliament **(der Bundestag)**.

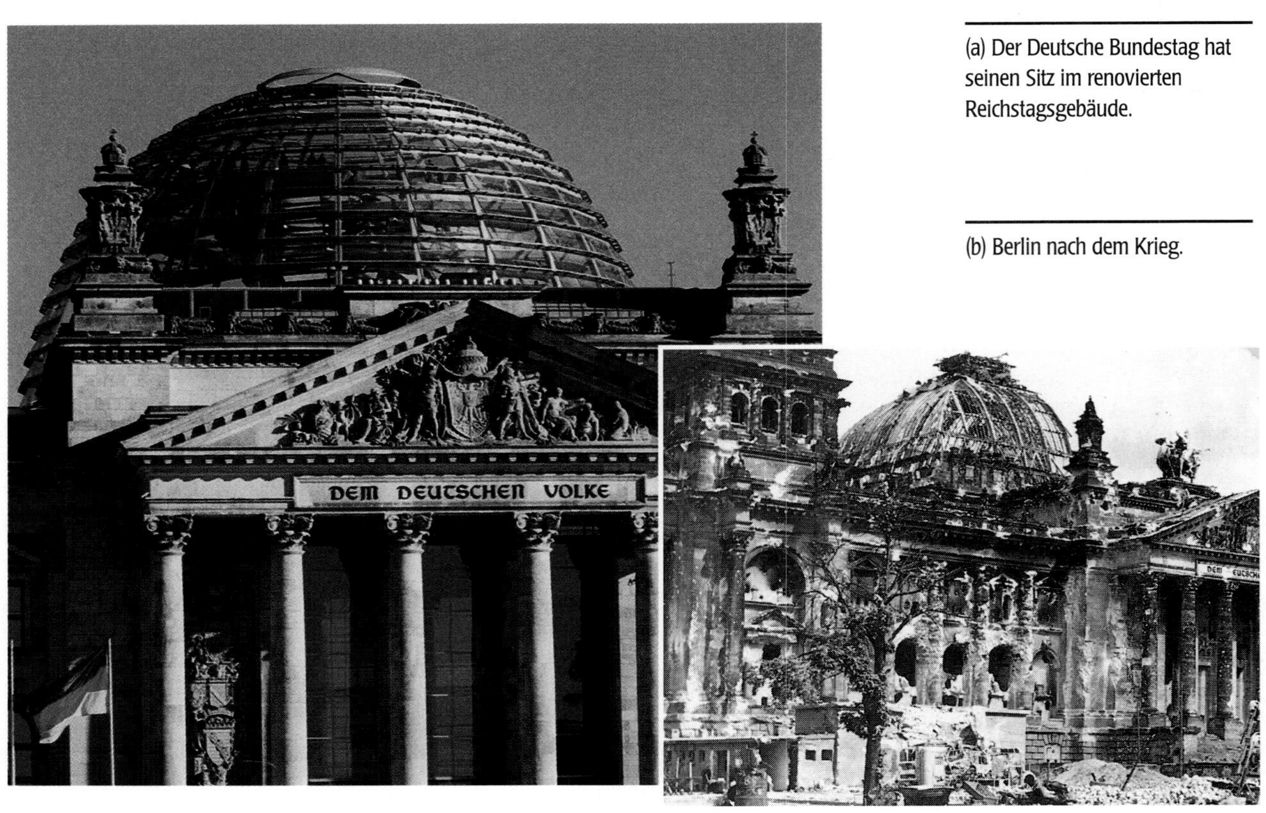

(a) Der Deutsche Bundestag hat seinen Sitz im renovierten Reichstagsgebäude.

(b) Berlin nach dem Krieg.

Strukturen und Vokabeln

I Speculating about activities, making suggestions

The subjunctive mood

The *mood* **(Modus)** of a verb expresses certainty, doubt, probability, impossibility, or the hypothetical nature of what the speaker is saying. Mood is reflected in the form of the verb. Factual statements use the indicative mood **(der Indikativ).**

Heute Morgen **können** wir **einkaufen gehen.**	*We can go shopping this morning.*
Morgen **sehen** wir uns Sanssouci **an.**	*Tomorrow we are going to see Sanssouci.*

To discuss hypothetical or contrary-to-fact matters or to make polite suggestions or requests, German speakers use the subjunctive mood **(der Konjunktiv).** In this chapter we will focus on the subjunctive in polite suggestions or requests and hypothetical statements.

The third mood is the imperative, which is used for commands: **Sei schnell!**

In Chapter 12 you will learn about the use of the special subjunctive in quotations.

Wir **könnten** ja morgen zur East Side Gallery (gehen).	*We could go to the East Side Gallery tomorrow.*
An deiner Stelle **würde** ich mir Sanssouci ansehen.	*If I were you, I would see Sanssouci.*

A. *The present subjunctive with* würde + *infinitive*

German speakers use the **würde-**construction (**würde** + infinitive) to make polite requests and suggestions. The infinitive appears at the end of the main clause.

Aber was **würdest** du dann für morgen **vorschlagen?**	*But what would you suggest then for tomorrow?*
An deiner Stelle **würde** ich einen Bummel auf dem Kurfürstendamm **machen.**	*If I were you, I'd go for a stroll on the Kurfürstendamm.*
Ich **würde** gern Potsdam **sehen.**	*I would like to see Potsdam.*
Das **würde** mich schon **interessieren.**	*That would sure interest me.*

Würde is the subjunctive form of the verb **werden.** It is formed from the narrative past form with the addition of an umlaut and is used with an infinitive at the end of the clause.

Infinitive	***Narrative past***	***Subjunctive***
werden	wurde	würde

The **würde**-construction is the most common way to form the present subjunctive in speaking. These are the forms of **würde.**

Person	Singular	Plural
	würde: *would*	
1st	ich **würde** sagen *I would say*	wir **würden** sagen *we would say*
2nd, informal	du **würdest** sagen *you would say*	ihr **würdet** sagen *you would say*
2nd, formal	Sie **würden** sagen *you would say*	Sie **würden** sagen *you would say*
3rd	er/sie/es **würde** sagen *he/she/it would say*	sie **würden** sagen *they would say*

9 **Anna würde gern alles sehen.** Anna hofft, alles in Berlin zu sehen. Onkel Werner möchte auch einige Sehenswürdigkeiten besuchen. Fragen Sie einen Partner/eine Partnerin, was Anna und ihr Onkel sehen möchten. Fragen Sie dann, was Ihr Partner/Ihre Partnerin gern sehen möchte.

S1: Was würde Anna gern machen?
S2: Sie würde gern die Mauer sehen.
S1: Würdest du gern die Mauer sehen?
S2: Ja (Nein), ich würde die Mauer (nicht) gern sehen.

Placing **nicht gern** towards the end of the sentence gives it special emphasis.

Tabelle A (S1):

	Anna	Onkel Werner	Partner(in)
die Mauer sehen	?	Ja	_____
die Mauerreste fotografieren	Ja	?	_____
den Reichstag besichtigen	Ja	?	_____
nach Potsdam fahren	Ja	?	_____
das Museum am Checkpoint Charlie besuchen	?	Nein	_____
in Kreuzberg türkisch essen	?	Ja	_____
einkaufen gehen	Ja	?	_____
ins Ägyptische Museum gehen	?	Ja	_____
ins Olympia-Stadion gehen	Nein	?	_____
die Gedächtniskirche anschauen	?	Nein	_____

Anna würde gern alles sehen. Checkpoint Charlie was the most famous border crossing from the American to the Soviet sector of Berlin and the site of heroic escape attempts and confrontations between American and Soviet diplomats and soldiers.

Kreuzberg, a district of Berlin, is known for its counter-cultural ambiance and its large Turkish population.

Tabelle B (S2):

	Anna	Onkel Werner	Partner(in)
die Mauer sehen	Ja	?	_____
die Mauerreste fotografieren	?	Nein	_____
den Reichstag besichtigen	?	Nein	_____
nach Potsdam fahren	?	Ja	_____
das Museum am Checkpoint Charlie besuchen	Nein	?	_____
in Kreuzberg türkisch essen	Nein	?	_____
einkaufen gehen	?	Nein	_____
ins Ägyptische Museum gehen	Ja	?	_____
ins Olympia-Stadion gehen	?	Nein	_____
die Gedächtniskirche anschauen	Ja	?	_____

10 **Autogrammspiel: Berlin.** Finden Sie für jede Frage eine Person, die mit **Ja** antwortet. Bitten Sie die Person um ihre Unterschrift.

S1: Würdest du gern in die Philharmonie gehen?
S2: Ja.
S1: Unterschreib hier bitte. ____________________

1. in die Philharmonie gehen ____________________
2. den Reichstag sehen ____________________
3. Mauerreste suchen ____________________
4. Potsdam sehen ____________________
5. einen Bummel auf dem Kurfürstendamm machen ____________________
6. die Humboldt-Universität anschauen ____________________
7. das Brandenburger Tor besuchen ____________________
8. die Szene am Prenzlauer Berg auschecken° ____________________
9. das neue Regierungsviertel sehen ____________________
10. die Museumsinsel besuchen ____________________
11. im Fernsehturm Kaffee trinken ____________________

° *check out*

Autogrammspiel. German slang often borrows liberally from English: **auschecken** *(to check out),* **cool, angetörnt** *(to be turned on).*

B. *The present subjunctive of* haben *and* sein

German speakers frequently use the present subjunctive forms of **haben** and **sein.** Like **würde,** which is derived from the narrative past of **werden, hätte** and **wäre** derive their present subjunctive forms from the narrative past tense with the addition of an umlaut. Note that **wäre** also adds an **-e** in the forms for **ich, du, er/sie/es,** and **ihr.** In conversation, many speakers glide over the **-e-** in the **du-** and **ihr-**forms, e.g., **du wärst, ihr wärt.**

Infinitive	*Narrative past*	*Subjunctive*
haben	hatte	h**ä**tte
sein	war	w**ä**re

Here are the present subjunctive forms of **haben.**

		hätte: *would have*		
Person	**Singular**		**Plural**	
1st	ich **hätte**	*I would have*	wir **hätten**	*we would have*
2nd, informal	du **hättest**	*you would have*	ihr **hättet**	*you would have*
2nd, formal	Sie **hätten**	*you would have*	Sie **hätten**	*you would have*
3rd	er/sie/es **hätte**	*he/she/it would have*	sie **hätten**	*they would have*

Wenn die berühmten Leute ihre Memoiren nicht erst im Alter, sondern schon viel früher schreiben würden, wären ihre Bücher bestimmt dünner und billiger.

Here are the present subjunctive forms of **sein.**

		wäre: *would be*		
Person	**Singular**		**Plural**	
1st	ich **wäre**	*I would be*	wir **wären**	*we would be*
2nd, informal	du **wärest**	*you would be*	ihr **wäret**	*you would be*
2nd, formal	Sie **wären**	*you would be*	Sie **wären**	*you would be*
3rd	er/sie/es **wäre**	*he/she/it would be*	sie **wären**	*they would be*

11 **Das wäre wirklich interessant!** Onkel Werner hat viele Vorschläge für einen Tag in Berlin. Reagieren Sie auf seine Vorschläge mit einer passenden Antwort aus der Liste.

S1 (ONKEL WERNER): Ich habe eine Idee: Gehen wir heute Abend ins Konzert!
S2 (SIE): Das wäre aber wirklich langweilig.

+	–
Das wäre …	Das wäre aber …
ganz toll!	wirklich langweilig.
prima!	zu gefährlich!
echt spitze!	viel zu teuer.
super gut!	Nein, aber ich hätte …
Ich hätte schon …	gar keine Lust dazu.
Lust dazu.	überhaupt kein Interesse daran.
Interesse daran.	

1. heute Abend ins Konzert gehen
2. einen Kaffee trinken
3. in die Nationalgalerie gehen
4. in die Disko gehen
5. die Punkerszene suchen
6. zum Konzentrationslager Sachsenhausen fahren
7. die Clubszene am Prenzlauer Berg erleben
8. das neue Regierungsviertel besuchen
9. mit der U-Bahn zum Olympiastadion fahren
10. die Neue Synagoge in der Oranienburger Straße besuchen

C. *The present subjunctive of* können *and the other modal verbs*

German speakers frequently use the present subjunctive of modal verbs, such as **können,** to express the possibility or the potential of an action. The infinitive appears at the end of the main clause.

Könnten wir nach der Philharmonie zum Prenzlauer Berg **fahren?**	*Could we go to Prenzlauer Berg after the concert in the Philharmonie?*
Ja, das **könnten** wir.	*Yes, we could.*

These are the present subjunctive forms of **können.**

könnte: *could*				
Person	**Singular**		**Plural**	
1st	ich **könnte**	*I could*	wir **könnten**	*we could*
2nd, informal	du **könntest**	*you could*	ihr **könntet**	*you could*
2nd, formal	Sie **könnten**	*you could*	Sie **könnten**	*you could*
3rd	er/sie/es **könnte**	*he/she/it could*	sie **könnten**	*they could*

The other modal verbs follow the same pattern in the present subjunctive as **können/könnte.** Only the modals with an umlaut in the infinitive add an umlaut in the subjunctive. The narrative past and the present subjunctive of **sollen (sollte)** and **wollen (wollte)** are identical.

Infinitive	**Subjunctive**	
mögen	ich **möchte**	*I would like to*
dürfen	ich **dürfte**	*I would be allowed to*
müssen	ich **müsste**	*I would have to*
sollen *(no umlaut)*	ich **sollte** *(no umlaut)*	*I should, ought to*
wollen *(no umlaut)*	ich **wollte** *(no umlaut)*	*I would want to*

12 Das könntest du machen! Anna hilft Onkel Werner eine Party zu planen. Was sagt Anna?

S1 (ONKEL WERNER): Tanja hat viele CDs.
S2 (ANNA): Sie könnte die Musik organisieren.

1. Tanja hat viele CDs.
2. Margit und Waltraud haben ein Auto.
3. Andreas kennt die Nachbarn relativ gut.
4. Ich habe heute Geld bekommen.
5. Wir haben morgen relativ viel Zeit.
6. Karl und ich kochen gern.
7. Claudia möchte helfen, aber sie hat vor der Party überhaupt keine Zeit.
8. Klaus-Peter arbeitet im Supermarkt.

a. zwei Kästen° Bier mitbringen
b. nachher abwaschen
c. die anderen anrufen
d. auch die Nachbarn einladen
e. alles bezahlen
f. die Musik organisieren
g. Brot und Käse mitbringen
h. Obstsalat machen

cases

Kästen = northern German; Kasten = southern German

13 Aber ich könnte das! Werner erklärt, dass er einfach nicht imstande° ist, alles zu machen. Anna antwortet mit Vorschlägen, wer Werner helfen könnte. Benutzen Sie den Konjunktiv von **können** in Annas Antwort.

capable

S1 (WERNER): Ich kann nicht mit dem Hund spazieren gehen. (die Nachbarin)
S2 (ANNA): Die Nachbarin könnte mit dem Hund spazieren gehen.

1. Ich kann nicht mit dem Hund spazieren gehen. (die Nachbarin)
2. Wir können heute nicht in die Neue Nationalgalerie. (wir / übermorgen)
3. Ich will morgen frische Brötchen vom Bäcker holen. (ich / noch heute)

4. Wir können keine Theaterkarten für Freitagabend kriegen. (du / zwei für Sonnabend am Telefon reservieren)
5. Wir können erst nächste Woche zu Erich und Veronika hinausfahren. (sie / zu uns kommen)
6. Du darfst nicht alleine in die Clubs gehen! (ich / mit dem Typ vom Prenzlauer Berg gehen)
7. Mein Chef möchte dich einladen. (er / morgen)
8. Ich soll dir das Konzentrationslager Sachsenhausen zeigen. (wir / mit dem Bus fahren)

D. Making polite requests and suggestions

To make polite requests and suggestions **(höfliche Bitten und Vorschläge),** German speakers often use the present subjunctive. The subjunctive makes a request or suggestion sound less explicit or demanding than the indicative or imperative. Compare the tone in the following statements.

Imperative	*Subjunctive*
Bringen Sie mir bitte die Speisekarte!	**Könnten (Würden)** Sie mir bitte die Speisekarte **bringen?**
Kauf nicht bei Müller ein!	Du **solltest** nicht bei Müller **einkaufen.**

Indicative	*Subjunctive*
Haben Sie einen Tisch frei?	**Hätten** Sie einen Tisch frei?
Ich **will** ein Bier trinken.	Ich **würde** gern ein Bier **trinken.**
Ich **will** bezahlen.	Ich **möchte bezahlen.**
Können Sie mir sagen, wo die U-Bahn-Haltestelle ist?	**Könnten** Sie mir sagen, wo die U-Bahn-Haltestelle ist?

14 **Annas zweite Reaktion.** Onkel Werner hat viele Vorschläge für Anna. Anna sagt nicht sofort, was sie denkt, denn sie will eine höfliche Antwort geben. Geben Sie den Buchstaben an, der Annas höfliche Antwort beschreibt.

▣ Werner sagt: Wir könnten ins Ägyptische Museum gehen.
Anna denkt: Das finde ich nicht so interessant.
Anna sagt: g (Das würde ich nicht so interessant finden.)

a. Das könnte sehr schön sein.
b. Darauf hätte ich schon Appetit!
c. Das wäre eine großartige Idee.
d. Das würde schon Spaß machen.
e. Die Idee würde mir schon gefallen.
f. Das könnte ich gut gebrauchen.
g. Das würde ich nicht so interessant finden.
h. Dazu hätte ich nicht so viel Lust.
i. Das wäre für mich nichts Neues.
j. Ich hätte wirklich kein Interesse daran.

1. Werner sagt: Wir könnten ins Ägyptische Museum gehen.
Anna denkt: Das finde ich nicht so interessant.
Anna sagt: ___

2. Werner sagt: Wir könnten ein Picknick an der Spree machen.
   Anna denkt: Die Idee gefällt mir schon.
   Anna sagt: ___
3. Werner sagt: Wir könnten Kaffee bei meinen Nachbarn trinken.
   Anna denkt: Dazu habe ich nicht so viel Lust.
   Anna sagt: ___
4. Werner sagt: Wir könnten einen ruhigen Abend im Biergarten verbringen.
   Anna denkt: Das kann ich gut gebrauchen.
   Anna sagt: ___
5. Werner sagt: Wir könnten Checkpoint Charlie besuchen.
   Anna denkt: Das ist eine großartige Idee.
   Anna sagt: ___
6. Werner sagt: Wir könnten die alternative Kunstszene aufsuchen.
   Anna denkt: Das macht schon Spaß.
   Anna sagt: ___
7. Werner sagt: Wir könnten einfach zu Hause fernsehen.
   Anna denkt: Ich habe wirklich kein Interesse daran.
   Anna sagt: ___
8. Werner sagt: Wir könnten ins Hard-Rock-Café gehen.
   Anna denkt: Das ist für mich nichts Neues.
   Anna sagt: ___
9. Werner sagt: Wir könnten einmal richtig berlinerisch essen gehen.
   Anna denkt: Darauf habe ich schon Appetit!
   Anna sagt: ___
10. Werner sagt: Wir könnten eine Stadtrundfahrt machen.
    Anna denkt: Das kann sehr schön sein.
    Anna sagt: ___

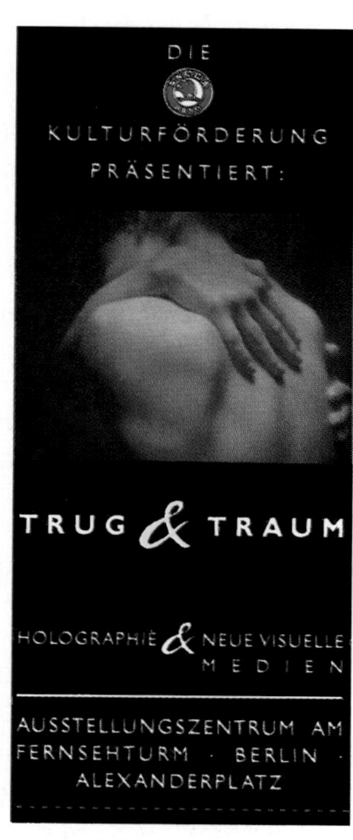

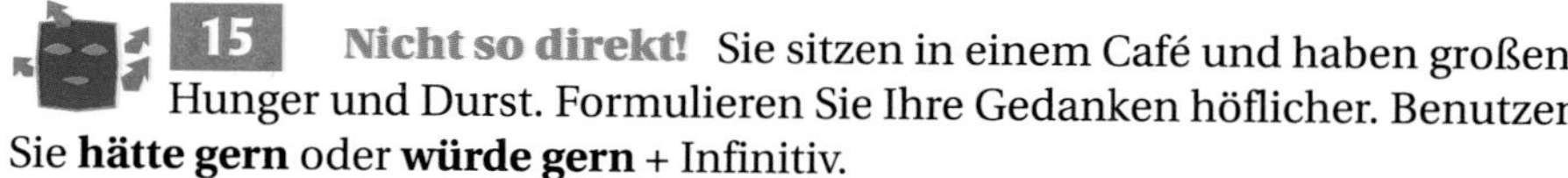

15 **Nicht so direkt!** Sie sitzen in einem Café und haben großen Hunger und Durst. Formulieren Sie Ihre Gedanken höflicher. Benutzen Sie **hätte gern** oder **würde gern** + Infinitiv.

- Ich will ein Bier haben. *Ich hätte gern ein Bier.*
- Wir wollen jetzt bestellen. *Wir würden jetzt gern bestellen.*

1. Ich will ein Bier haben.
2. Wir wollen jetzt bestellen.
3. Ich will die Speisekarte sehen.
4. Bringen Sie uns sofort die Vorspeisen!
5. Wir wollen eine Pizza mit Salami bestellen.
6. Wir wollen auch gleich zahlen.

E. *Making role-reversal statements with* an deiner (Ihrer, *etc.*) Stelle ... *and the present subjunctive*

A common expression to introduce a hypothetical suggestion in German is **An deiner** (**Ihrer**, etc.) **Stelle würde ich ...** *(If I were you, I'd . . ./In your position, I would . . .)*

16 **An deiner Stelle würde ich ...** Ihr Partner/Ihre Partnerin hat Probleme. Geben Sie ihm/ihr Rat.

S1: Du, ich habe ein Problem. Ich muss morgen mein Referat einreichen°, aber ich bin noch nicht fertig.
S2: An deiner Stelle würde ich mich konzentrieren und die Arbeit zu Ende schreiben.

hand in

1. Ich muss morgen mein Referat einreichen, aber ich bin noch nicht fertig.
2. Ich möchte morgen Abend ins Brecht-Theater gehen und „Die Dreigroschenoper" sehen.
3. Ich muss einen Brief per Express nach New York schicken.
4. Ich weiß nicht, was ich meiner Mutter zum Geburtstag schenken soll.
5. Ich habe meine Miete nicht bezahlt, und die Vermieterin will mich auf die Straße setzen.

a. die Theaterkasse anrufen und Karten bestellen
b. schnell die Miete zahlen und der Vermieterin Blumen bringen
c. einen Expressdienst anrufen und den Brief abholen lassen°
d. einfach fragen, was sie zum Geburtstag möchte
e. mich konzentrieren und die Arbeit zu Ende schreiben

abholen lassen: *have picked up*

17 **An seiner Stelle würde ich ...** Besprechen Sie mit einem Partner/einer Partnerin, was diese Personen in Annas Studentenwohnheim machen sollen. Was würden Sie an ihrer Stelle machen?

S1: Tina (Fabian) trinkt zu viel Kaffee und kann nachts nicht schlafen.
S2: An ihrer (seiner) Stelle würde ich nicht so viel Kaffee trinken.

1. Tina (Fabian) trinkt zu viel Kaffee und kann nachts nicht schlafen.
2. Jennifer fährt übers Wochenende nach Berlin. Was soll sie dort machen?
3. Johnny und Dagmar helfen ihren Kindern nicht mit den Hausaufgaben.
4. Katja ist mit ihrem Job nicht zufrieden.
5. Sascha hat Karten für die Philharmonie, aber er will nicht hingehen.
6. Ulf braucht einen neuen Computer, aber er hat nicht genug Geld.
7. Ingo hat einen Monat Urlaub und möchte wenig Geld ausgeben.
8. Karin hat neue Arbeitsangebote in München und in Basel bekommen.

F. The past-time subjunctive

The past-time subjunctive **(der Vergangenheitskonjunktiv)** expresses events that might have taken place in the past. The past-time subjunctive is formed with **hätte** or **wäre** + past participle.

Werner **hätte** das nicht **gemacht!**	*Werner wouldn't have done that!*
Ich **hätte** die Antwort **gewusst.**	*I would have known the answer.*
Wir **wären** nach Potsdam **gefahren.**	*We would have gone to Potsdam.*

The past-time subjunctive looks like the past perfect, except for the umlaut on **hätte** and **wäre** and the **-e** ending on **wäre.**

Infinitive	*Past perfect*	*Past-time subjunctive*
sehen	hatte gesehen	hätte gesehen
fahren	war gefahren	wäre gefahren

The past subjunctive is used for all three past tense forms used in the indicative.

Conversational past
Er **hat** das **gewusst.**
Er **ist** nach Hause **gefahren.**

Narrative past
Er **wusste** das.
Er **fuhr** nach Hause.

Past perfect
Er **hatte** das **gewusst.**
Er **war** nach Hause **gefahren.**

→ Er **hätte** das **gewusst.**
Er **wäre** nach Hause **gefahren.**

18 **Ich hätte es anders gemacht.** Ein reicher Freund/Eine reiche Freundin erzählt von einer luxuriösen Europareise. Sie haben nicht so viel Geld. Was hätten Sie anders gemacht? Benutzen Sie den Vergangenheitskonjunktiv.

S1 (FREUND/IN): Ich habe überall in Luxushotels gewohnt.
S2 (SIE): Ich hätte in Jugendherbergen übernachtet.

1. in Luxushotels gewohnt	a. in Jugendherbergen übernachtet
2. jeden Abend in die Oper gegangen	b. das Essen im Lebensmittelgeschäft gekauft
3. ein Auto gemietet°	c. an die Nordsee an den Strand gefahren
4. in den besten Restaurants gegessen	d. mit dem Zug gefahren
5. tagsüber in Museen und alte Kirchen gegangen	e. auf dem Land oder im Wald wandern gegangen
6. nach Baden-Baden in die Casinos gefahren	f. den Abend mit jungen Leuten in der Stadt verbracht

rented

G. *The double-infinitive construction*

Sometimes German speakers use a special construction called the *double infinitive* **(der Doppelinfinitiv)** to express the past-time subjunctive in statements with a modal verb. The term *double infinitive* refers to the presence of two infinitives at the end of the clause that present an alternate form of the past participle. **Hätten** (never **wäre**) is always used with a modal in the past subjunctive.

The double infinitive construction (in the subjunctive) can be used with any model verb, e.g., **hätte machen können (dürfen, müssen, sollen, wollen)** = *could have, would have been allowed to, would have had to, should have, would have wanted to.*

Ach, Anna, ich **hätte** dich **warnen sollen.**	*Oh, Anna, I should have warned you.*
Ich **hätte** es gleich **ahnen sollen.**	*I should have guessed it right away.*

In subordinate clauses following **weil, dass,** etc., **hätte** occurs before the double infinitive.

Onkel Werner hat gesagt, dass er es **hätte ahnen sollen.**

19 Wir hätten das machen sollen! Onkel Werner und Anna sprechen über ihren gemeinsamen Tag. Anna berichtet, was sie beide nicht gemacht haben, und Onkel Werner sagt, was sie (nicht) hätten machen sollen. Drücken Sie seine Gedanken im Vergangenheitskonjunktiv mit einem Doppelinfinitiv aus.

S1 (ANNA): Wir sind nicht ins Schloss Charlottenburg gegangen.
S2 (ONKEL WERNER): Wir hätten ins Schloss Charlottenburg gehen sollen.

1. Wir sind nicht ins Schloss Charlottenburg gegangen.
2. Ich habe das Käthe-Kollwitz-Museum vergessen.
3. Wir haben die Aufführung von Brechts „Dreigroschenoper" verpasst.
4. Wir sind einfach am Nikolaiviertel vorbeigelaufen.
5. Wir sind in Kreuzberg nicht türkisch essen gegangen.
6. Du hast deine Kamera vergessen.
7. Ich habe meinen Studentenausweis vergessen.
8. Wir sind nicht zum Wannsee gefahren.
9. Du hast mir die Babelsberger Filmstudios nicht gezeigt.

Wir hätten das machen sollen! Käthe Kollwitz (1867–1945) was a German painter, sculptor, and graphic artist who commented on the societal ills of her time in her art. Her most famous works depict children, mothers, and the poor.

Babelsberg was the home of the UFA film studios in the golden age of German cinema in the 1920s and during the Third Reich. Renamed DEFA studios by the GDR, it was also home to a famous film school. After unification it was privatized, remodeled, and is now open for tours as an **Erlebnispark** in Potsdam.

Works by Käthe Kollwitz can be seen at www.kaethe-kollwitz.de

FREIE KOMMUNIKATION

Rollenspiel: Besuch aus Deutschland. Sie haben einen Besucher/eine Besucherin aus Deutschland und Sie möchten ihm/ihr Ihre Stadt zeigen. Besprechen Sie, was Sie zusammen in Ihrer Stadt unternehmen können. Was würde diese Person interessieren? Stellen Sie Fragen und machen Sie Vorschläge.

S1 (SIE): Wir könnten zusammen in den Zoo gehen.
S2 (BESUCHER/IN): Das wäre OK, aber ich würde lieber schwimmen gehen.
S1: Schwimmen wäre auch möglich. Wie wäre es mit einem amerikanischen Footballspiel?
S2: Hm, …

zum Strand • wandern • ins Rockkonzert • zum Rodeo • amerikanisches Footballspiel • Sehenswürdigkeiten ansehen • klettern° • ins Museum

° *climbing*

Rollenspiel: Besuch in Deutschland. Sie sind bei einer Gastfamilie in Deutschland und sprechen mit einer Person aus der Familie. Sie möchten eine interessante Stadt besuchen. Sagen Sie, wohin Sie fahren möchten und warum. Sie können ein paar Tage in dieser Stadt verbringen.

S1 (SIE): Ich würde gern das Museum am Checkpoint Charlie in Berlin sehen.
S2: Ja, das könnten wir machen, aber ich würde lieber zum Prenzlauer Berg gehen.
S1: Oh, das wäre toll!
(oder)
S1: Ich würde gern nach München fahren.
S2: Warum würdest du gern nach München fahren? Das ist so weit weg.
S1: Wir könnten dort ins BMW-Museum gehen oder …

Schreibecke **Ein wunderbarer Urlaub.** Beschreiben Sie einen Urlaub, den Sie einmal gemacht haben. Beschreiben Sie Ihre Urlaubsaktivitäten und was Sie im Nachhinein° zusätzlich° hätten machen sollen.

retrospect / in addition

Ihre Sorgen. Mein Rat. Frau Maria Burg schreibt für eine Zeitung und beantwortet Fragen der Leser/Leserinnen. Sie bekommt viele Briefe von Frauen und Männern, die Antworten auf ihre Probleme suchen. Lesen Sie die Probleme der folgenden Personen und schreiben Sie Frau Burgs Antwortbrief(e). Benutzen Sie den Konjunktiv (z.B. **An Ihrer Stelle hätte ich ... ; Ich würde das ...**).

Ihre Sorgen
mein Rat
Haben Sie Schwierigkeiten in der Ehe?
Kummer mit den Kindern? Ärger im Beruf?
Ich helfe Ihnen gern. Schreiben Sie mir – mit
Altersangabe und Adresse:
DAS NEUE BLATT, Maria Burg, 20079 Hamburg
Maria Burg

Lutz F.:
Sucht eine Partnerin, bisher ohne Erfolg. Er schreibt, dass Frauen in seinem Alter (53) nur Sex und Geld suchen. Sein Hund ist sein bester Freund.

This is a summary of authentic letters seeking advice from Maria Burg.

Anna G.:
Ihre Tochter Peggy hat keinen Mann. Jetzt schreibt sie intensiv an ihrer Doktorarbeit. Die Chance, einen Mann zu finden, wird immer schlechter.

ABSPRUNGTEXT I
Die Geschichte Berlins

Vorschau

Berlin hat in der deutschen Geschichte eine wichtige Rolle gespielt. Zu verschiedenen Zeiten war Berlin Hauptstadt, Regierungssitz, Kulturzentrum und auch das Hauptquartier Adolf Hitlers. Später wurde Berlin Brennpunkt des Kalten Krieges und die Hauptstadt der Deutschen Demokratischen Republik, bevor es die Hauptstadt des vereinten Deutschlands wurde. In der Geschichte Berlins spiegelt sich die politische Geschichte Deutschlands wider°.

spiegelt wider: *is reflected*

Wissenswerte Vokabeln: Regierung und Politik

Discussing forms of government

Die Monarchie: 1871 bis 1918
König Wilhelm I. von Preußen wurde im Jahre 1871 der erste deutsche Kaiser. Sein Kanzler war Otto von Bismarck.

W. Vok. After defeating Denmark, Austria, and France in war and establishing the North German Union, Prussian Chancellor Bismarck negotiated with the south German states to create a unified Germany in 1871. This made Germany one of the last major European countries to become a unified nation.

Die Diktatur: 1933 bis 1945
Der Nazi-Terror dauerte zwölf Jahre.

Die Republik: 1918 bis 1933, die Demokratie: 1949 bis zur Gegenwart°
Die Bürger wählen Abgeordnete für Land und Bund°. Die Abgeordneten repräsentieren die Bürger.

present
federal government

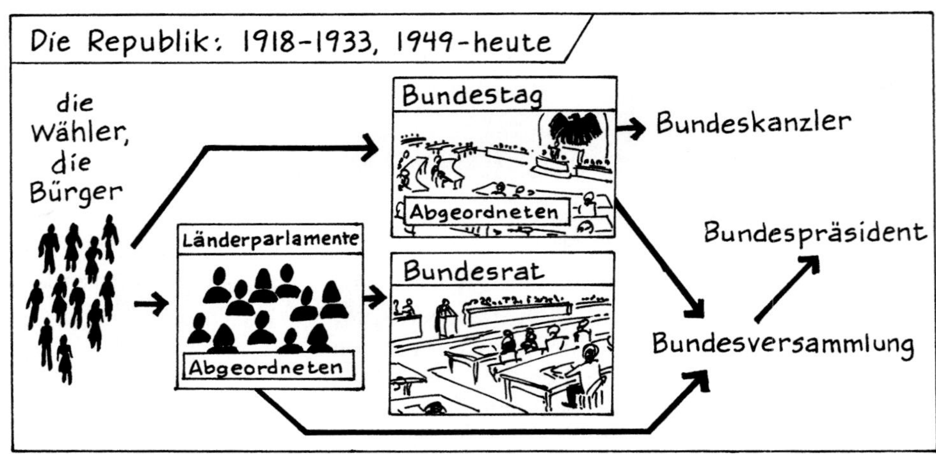

- Haben Sie einen Kanzler oder einen Präsidenten in Ihrem Land?

BRENNPUNKT KULTUR

Deutschland: von der Diktatur zur Demokratie

Germany's evolution to a peaceful democratic republic was slow and painful. It took Germany until 1871 to unify as a nation, ruled by an emperor (**Kaiser**), Kaiser Wilhelm I., and his chancellor, (**Kanzler**) Otto von Bismarck. After the defeat of the Germans in World War I (**der Erste Weltkrieg**) and the abdication of the **Kaiser**, Germany formed a democracy with the founding of the Weimar Republic (**Weimarer Republik**) in 1918. However, the republic was weakened by insufficient support for democratic government and radical forces on both the left and the right, most notably the Nazi party, officially known as **die Nationalsozialistische Deutsche Arbeiterpartei (NSDAP).** The stability of the government was undermined by immense war reparations to France, the post-war occupation of German territory by foreign troops, large-scale unemployment, astronomical inflation, and the stock market crash and world economic crisis of 1929. Social and economic misery made the German people susceptible to the "quick-fix" rhetoric of the Nazi party, which promised to create jobs, fix social chaos and economic misery, and eliminate the root causes of these problems, which the Nazis designated as world Jewry. By 1933, Adolf Hitler and the Nazi party had assumed power, established a one-party dictatorship, and were preparing to establish **das Dritte Reich.** In short order the Nazis broke up trade unions, repressed the freedom of the press, and abolished most human and civil rights, denying Jews and others of their German citizenship and basic protection under the law. Dissent was eliminated, and Jews and other minorities were forced into labor camps and concentration camps. The German populace was organized, observed, and controlled by Nazi party organizations while the German military set its sights on new territories throughout Europe and northern Africa. Hitler's 1939 attack on Poland signaled the beginning of World War II (**der Zweite Weltkrieg**), which would last over five years, engulf the continent in war, lead to the Holocaust, and claim an estimated 55 million lives.

The surrender of Nazi Germany on May 8/9, 1945, raised an immense political problem for the Allied forces. It was agreed that Germany should be disarmed, demilitarized, denazified, and divided into occupation zones controlled by the Allied powers – the United States, Great Britain, France, and the Soviet Union – but beyond that there was little consensus. The Soviets established Soviet hegemony and allowed formation of political parties in the Soviet zone in 1945. The Western Allies were more reluctant to encourage political activity in the three western zones and they became wary as the Soviets established a pro-Communist regime ruled by the Socialist Unity Party (**Sozialistische Einheitspartei, SED**) in their zone. Wanting to respond with strong Western political and economic systems and Western values, the Allies pursued the establishment of joint political and economic structure in the three West German zones. Germany was rapidly evolving (or dissolving) into two very different countries: one, a one-party Marxist state with a centrally planned economy supported by the Soviets in the east, and the other, an elective democracy and social market economy supported by the U.S., Great Britain, and France in the west. The currency reform of 1948, which introduced the new **Deutsche Mark** only to the three western zones, reinforced the political and economic drift and made the division of the German nation into two separate states inevitable. The Federal Republic of Germany (**die Bundesrepublik Deutschland**) drew up its constitution-like Basic Law (**das Grundgesetz**) establishing rule-of-law and welfare state principles in the territories of the three western zones in 1949. Shortly thereafter, the **SED** established a government in the Soviet zone, and the German Democratic Republic, or GDR (**die Deutsche Demokratische Republik, DDR**) came into being. From 1949 to 1989, the two separate German states were the focal point of the Cold War (**der Kalte Krieg**) between East and West that ended with the collapse of Soviet hegemony in eastern Europe and the dissolution of the German Democratic Republic.

Since unification (**die Vereinigung**) in 1990, the German federal system of government has been extended to the former states of East Germany. Elections to the **Bundestag** are usually held every four years. The **Bundestag** passes laws and selects the **Bundeskanzler** who forms a government (**die Bundesregierung**) with a cabinet of ministers (**das Bundeskabinett**). Together with the **Bundestag,** they propose legislation and guide it through the legislative process. The **Bundeskanzler** is officially nominated by the **Bundespräsident,** who is head of state and represents the Federal Government in international relations. In addition to passing laws and selecting the **Bundeskanzler,** the **Bundestag,** along with the **Bundesrat,** whose members represent the interests of the **Länder,** is responsible for electing judges to the Federal Constitutional Court (**das Bundesverfassungsgericht**).

Der Bundestag wird alle vier Jahre gewählt.

20 **Was ist das?** Finden Sie für jede Definition in der linken Spalte den passenden Begriff oder Namen in der rechten Spalte.

1. ___ das deutsche Parlament
2. ___ moderner deutscher Regierungschef (wie z.B. der Premierminister in Kanada)
3. ___ der Führer
4. ___ moderne Staatsform in Deutschland
5. ___ Repräsentant im deutschen Parlament
6. ___ der deutsche Monarch
7. ___ Oberhaupt° Deutschlands (wie z.B. die Königin in Großbritannien) — *head of state*
8. ___ die erste deutsche Republik (1918–1933)
9. ___ die Verfassung° der Bundesrepublik — *constitution*
10. ___ nationalsozialistische Diktatur

a. das Dritte Reich
b. der Bundestag
c. die Republik
d. das Grundgesetz
e. der Bundeskanzler
f. der Abgeordnete
g. Adolf Hitler
h. der Kaiser
i. die Weimarer Republik
j. der Bundespräsident

21 **Zeittafel: Was wissen Sie schon?** Welche Daten gehören zu welchen Ereignissen°? — *events*

	Daten		*Ereignisse*
1.	___ 1918	a.	Ex-DDR wird Teil der Bundesrepublik Deutschland.
2.	___ 1933	b.	Die DDR baut die Mauer um West-Berlin.
3.	___ 1945	c.	Der 1. Weltkrieg endet.
4.	___ 1961	d.	Der 2. Weltkrieg endet.
5.	___ 1989	e.	Die Berliner Mauer fällt. DDR-Bürger dürfen in den Westen.
6.	___ 1990	f.	Hitler und die Nazis kommen an die Macht.

22 **Thematische Fragen.** Beantworten Sie die folgenden Fragen auf Deutsch.

1. Berlin ist jetzt die Hauptstadt Deutschlands. Wie hieß die Hauptstadt der Bundesrepublik im Jahre 1989?
2. Was assoziieren Sie mit Berlin?
3. Warum spielt Berlin so eine wichtige Rolle in der Weltgeschichte?
4. Kennen Sie den Namen Bismarck? Warum ist er eine wichtige Persönlichkeit der deutschen Geschichte?

23 Lesestrategien: Die Geschichte Berlins. Benutzen Sie die folgenden Strategien, um den Text zu verstehen.

1. **Den Kontext herstellen.** Finden Sie in dem **Absprungtext I** Antworten auf die folgenden Fragen.
   a. Welche drei wichtigen Persönlichkeiten werden hier genannt?
   b. In welchem Jahr sind die folgenden Ereignisse passiert?

   - die nationalsozialistische Machtergreifung (das Dritte Reich):
   - die Gründung der Bundesrepublik Deutschland:
   - die Gründung der Weimarer Republik:
   - die Gründung des Zweiten Deutschen Reiches:
   - der Beitritt der DDR zur Bundesrepublik Deutschland:
   - die Gründung der Deutschen Demokratischen Republik:

2. **Strategien verwenden.** Können Sie diese neuen Wörter ungefähr verstehen? Versuchen Sie, die fett gedruckten Wörter zu erraten. Benutzen Sie die Strategien, die Sie gelernt haben.

Strategie 1: Weltwissen

a. **die Machtergreifung:** Hitler ist auf legale Weise Reichskanzler geworden. Der Kanzler hat die **Macht** zu regieren. Hitler hat dann sehr schnell auf illegale Weise mehr Macht genommen oder ergriffen. Spricht man in den USA von einer Machtergreifung bei der Präsidentenwahl? Hat Saddam Hussein die Macht im Irak bekommen oder ergriffen? Haben die Bolschewiken in Russland die Macht bekommen oder ergriffen?

b. **statt·finden:** Alle vier Jahre finden in den USA die Wahlen für die Präsidentschaft statt. Alle vier Jahre finden die Olympischen Spiele statt. Wie oft findet der Deutschkurs statt?

c. **besetzen:** Wenn man die Toilette nicht benutzen kann, weil jemand anders sie benutzt, sagt man: *Die Toilette ist besetzt.* Im militärischen Kontext ist ein Land besetzt, wenn ein ausländisches Militär die Macht hat. Welche Länder haben die Nazis im Krieg besetzt?

d. **Siegermächte:** Das sind die Mächte oder Länder, die einen Krieg gewinnen. Wer war im Jahr 1945 eine Siegermacht – die USA oder Nazi-Deutschland?

e. **verwalten:** Die Verwaltung ist der Staatsapparat oder die Bürokratie. Wer hat Deutschland nach dem Krieg verwaltet?

f. **das Abkommen:** Wenn zwei Staaten zu einem Verständnis kommen, ist das ein **Abkommen.** Haben die USA Abkommen mit Kanada oder Kuba?

Strategie 2: Kontext

a. **zerstören:** Wenn man etwas **zerstört,** macht man es kaputt. Die Nazis haben viele jüdische Geschäfte in der Kristallnacht zerstört. Welchen Teil eines Hauses oder eines Geschäftes kann man leicht mit einem Stock zerstören?

b. **vollenden:** Etwas ist nur dann **vollendet,** wenn man alle Ziele erreicht und vielleicht sogar perfektioniert hat. Dann hat man nicht nur das Ende erreicht, man hat etwas **vollendet.** Hat Hitler seine Pläne für ein Drittes Reich vollendet?

c. **bei·treten** (+ *dat.*) Wenn man Mitglied in einem Club, einer Organisation oder einer Partei wird, tritt man der Organisation bei. Was bedeutet wohl **beitreten?**

Strategie 3: Wortformen

a. **erobern:** Sowjetische Soldaten kamen als erste nach Berlin. Die Sowjets hatten die Kontrolle. Die Nazis kapitulierten, und die Sowjets hatten Berlin erobert. Welches Land hat Japan im Zweiten Weltkrieg erobert?

b. **die Arbeitsnorm:** Eine Norm ist ein Standard oder eine Quote. Was für Normen hat man am Arbeitsplatz?

c. **erhöhen:** Von welchem Adjektiv ist **höher** die Komparativform? Das Präfix **er-** findet man auch in **erhärten (hart werden)** und **erstarken (stark werden).** Was bedeutet wohl das Verb **erhöhen?**

d. **der Aufstand:** Von welchem Verb stammt dieses Nomen? Stellen Sie sich die Bewegung im Verb **auf·stehen** vor: ist sie aktiv oder passiv? Nun stellen Sie sich diese Aktion als politische Aktion vor: ist sie freundlich oder aggressiv? Was wäre ein gutes Synonym für das Wort **Aufstand?**

e. **der Widerstand:** Wenn man aktiv gegen eine politische Struktur kämpft, die man für unmenschlich hält, leistet man politischen **Widerstand.** Wogegen hat Dr. Martin Luther King Widerstand geleistet?

ABSPRUNGTEXT I

Die Geschichte Berlins

Lesen Sie jetzt den Text.

1740 Friedrich II. (Friedrich der Große) wird König von Preußen. Berlin gewinnt als Hauptstadt Preußens europäischen Rang°. *status*

1871 Gründung des Deutschen Reiches. Berlin wird Residenz des deutschen Kaisers und Reichshauptstadt.

1918 (9. November) Vom Balkon des Reichstages in Berlin ruft der Sozialdemokrat Philipp Scheidemann die „Deutsche Republik" aus°. Berlin ist Hauptstadt der Weimarer Republik. ***aus·rufen: proklamieren***

1933 Machtergreifung der Nationalsozialisten. Hitler wird Reichskanzler. Berlin wird Zentrum der nationalsozialistischen Diktatur, aber auch des Widerstandes.

1936 Die XI. Olympischen Sommerspiele finden in Berlin statt.

1938 (9. November) Reichspogromnacht („Kristallnacht"). Jüdische Geschäfte werden von den Nazis zerstört.

1945 Berlin wird durch die Rote Armee erobert. Berlin wird von den vier Siegermächten (USA, UdSSR, Großbritannien, Frankreich) besetzt und verwaltet.

1948/49 Die Blockade Berlins: Die Stadt wird politisch geteilt. Die westlichen Alliierten reagieren mit der „Luftbrücke", dem größten Lufttransportunternehmen der Geschichte.

1949 Aus den westdeutschen Besatzungszonen wird die Bundesrepublik Deutschland mit Hauptstadt Bonn gegründet. Aus der sowjetischen Besatzungszone entsteht die Deutsche Demokratische Republik mit Hauptstadt Berlin (Ost).

1953 (17. Juni) Die Arbeitsnormen und auch die Preise für Lebensmittel werden in Ost-Berlin erhöht. Es kommt zum Aufstand Ost-Berliner Arbeiter.

1961 (13. August) Die Stadt wird durch den Bau der Mauer geteilt.

1963 Berlin wird vom amerikanischen Präsidenten Kennedy besucht. („Ich bin ein Berliner.")

1972 Das Vier-Mächte-Abkommen regelt den Transit sowie Reisen und Besuche in die DDR.

1989 (9. November) Die Mauer fällt: Die Grenzen zu West-Berlin und zur Bundesrepublik Deutschland werden von der DDR geöffnet.

1990 (3. Oktober) Die DDR tritt der Bundesrepublik Deutschland nach Artikel 23 des Grundgesetzes bei. Die deutsche Einheit ist vollendet.

In his famous 1963 speech, President Kennedy expressed that Berlin was the focus of the free world by stating in German: **Ich bin ein Berliner.** Kennedy's visit to Berlin demonstrated the Allied resolve to keep West Berlin free.

Berlin wurde 1963 vom amerikanischen Präsidenten Kennedy besucht.

Rückblick

24 **Was wissen Sie jetzt von Berlin?** Wählen Sie die richtige Antwort.

1. Zur Zeit Friedrich des Großen war Berlin die Hauptstadt von ______.
   a. Preußen b. Weimar c. der Bundesrepublik Deutschland
2. Der Reichstag steht ______.
   a. in Weimar b. in Berlin c. in Bonn
3. Berlin war die Hauptstadt der ersten deutschen Republik von ______.
   a. 1871–1918 b. 1918–1933 c. 1933–1945
4. Von 1949 bis 1989 war Berlin (Ost) die Hauptstadt von ______.
   a. der Deutschen Demokratischen Republik
   b. der Bundesrepublik Deutschland
   c. dem Freistaat Bayern
5. Der schwarze Amerikaner Jesse Owens hat 1936 in Berlin an ______ teilgenommen.
   a. den Olympischen Spielen
   b. der Kristallnacht
   c. der Eroberung Berlins

6. Die Luftbrücke ____.
   a. ist eine Brücke über die Spree in Berlin-Mitte
   b. war der Transport von Gütern und Lebensmitteln für West-Berliner per Flugzeug
   c. war 1953 in Ost-Berlin
7. Präsident Kennedy hat in Berlin ____.
   a. Urlaub gemacht
   b. studiert
   c. eine sehr wichtige Rede während° des Kalten Krieges gehalten — *during*
8. 1961 baute die DDR eine Mauer ____.
   a. um West-Berlin
   b. durch die Mitte Ost-Berlins
   c. um Ost-Berlin
9. Während des Kalten Krieges waren in Berlin Truppen von ____ stationiert.
   a. den USA, Frankreich, Großbritannien und der UdSSR
   b. den USA und der UdSSR
   c. der UNO

25 **Ergänzen Sie.** Ergänzen Sie diese Sätze mit Wörtern aus dem **Absprungtext I.** Schreiben Sie alle Verben im Präsens.

1. Durch die ____ der Nationalsozialisten wird Adolf Hitler Reichskanzler.
2. 1933 wird Berlin zum Zentrum der nationalsozialistischen ____.
3. 1936 ____ in Berlin die Olympischen Spiele ____.
4. Am 9. November 1938 ____ die Nazis viele jüdische Geschäfte.
5. Die Rote Armee der Sowjetunion erreicht Berlin zuerst und ____ die Stadt.
6. Die vier ____ (USA, UdSSR, Großbritannien und Frankreich) besetzen und verwalten die Stadt gemeinsam.
7. Man ____ die Bundesrepublik Deutschland 1949 aus den drei westdeutschen Zonen.
8. Die Deutsche Demokratische Republik entsteht aus der sowjetischen ____.
9. 1953 reagieren Ost-Berliner Arbeiter gegen die Preiserhöhung mit einem ____.
10. 1961 ____ die Kommunisten die Stadt Berlin mit dem Bau der Mauer.
11. Das Vier-Mächte-Abkommen ____ den Transit und Besuche in die DDR.
12. Am 9. November 1989 fällt die Berliner ____, und die Grenzen zum Westen werden geöffnet.

26 **Kurz gefragt/kurz interpretiert.** Beantworten Sie diese Fragen auf Deutsch.

1. Schauen Sie sich eine Karte von Deutschland an. Wo liegt Berlin: im Nordwesten, im Nordosten oder im Südwesten von Deutschland?
2. Welchen Einfluss hat Berlins geographische Lage auf seine politische Rolle?
3. Für viele Ausländer ist Berlin das Symbol von Nazi-Deutschland. Ist dieses Image gerechtfertigt°? Was meinen Sie? — *justified*
4. Welche symbolische Rolle spielte Berlin zur Zeit des Kalten Krieges für die Siegermächte? Für die Ostdeutschen? Für die Westdeutschen?
5. Berlin hat eine negative und eine tragische Geschichte. Wie sehen Sie die Rolle Berlins in der Zukunft?

Strukturen und Vokabeln

II Talking about actions as a process

The passive voice

A. The passive voice: present tense

In most sentences the grammatical subject performs the action described by the verb. This subject is called the *agent,* and it is the focus of the sentence. The verb in these sentences uses the form of the active voice.

subject Philipp Scheidemann ruft die *direct object* „Deutsche Republik" aus.	*Philipp Scheidemann proclaims the "German Republic."*

Philipp Scheidemann is the grammatical subject as well as the agent in this sentence. Sometimes, however, it is important to focus on the process **(Vorgang)** and not on the agent. This may be because the agent or performer of the action is not known at all or may simply not be as important as the action itself. In these sentences the passive voice **(das Passiv)** is used. The present tense of the passive voice is formed with the verb **werden** and a past participle, which comes at the end of the clause.

Der Reichstag **wird** momentan **renoviert.**	*The Reichstag is currently being/getting renovated.*
Die „Deutsche Republik" **wird** von Philipp Scheidemann **ausgerufen.**	*The "German Republic" is being proclaimed by Philipp Scheidemann.*
Jüdische Geschäfte **werden** von den Nazis **zerstört.**	*Jewish businesses are being destroyed by the Nazis.*

In English, the present continuous verb form (e.g., *is being renovated*) conveys the meaning of a process in progress.

geliebt werden: *to be loved*				
Person	**Singular**		**Plural**	
1st	ich	**werde geliebt** *I am loved*	wir	**werden geliebt** *we are loved*
2nd, informal	du	**wirst geliebt** *you are loved*	ihr	**werdet geliebt** *you are loved*
2nd, formal	Sie	**werden geliebt** *you are loved*	Sie	**werden geliebt** *you are loved*
3rd	er/sie/es	**wird geliebt** *he/she/it is loved*	sie	**werden geliebt** *they are loved*

27 Was wird hier gemacht? Verbinden Sie eine Sehenswürdigkeit in Berlin mit einer passenden (Passiv)-Konstruktion.

▣ in der Bibliothek an der Humboldt-Universität

▣ S1: Was wird in der Bibliothek gemacht?
S2: Hier werden viele Bücher gelesen.

1. in der Bibliothek an der Humboldt-Universität
2. am Brandenburger Tor
3. auf dem Kurfürstendamm
4. in der Clubszene am Prenzlauer Berg
5. in den Cafés am Alexanderplatz
6. im Reichstag

a. Andenken von Berlin werden verkauft und gekauft
b. viele Bücher werden gelesen
c. Neue Gesetze° werden gemacht — *laws*
d. Musik wird gemacht
e. viele Fotos werden gemacht
f. Kaffee wird getrunken

28 Das geht leider nicht. Onkel Werner und Anna besprechen, was sie machen können, aber im Moment wird in Berlin sehr viel gebaut oder renoviert.

▣ S1 (ANNA): Wie wäre es mit dem Reichstag?
S2 (WERNER): Tja, das geht leider nicht. Der Reichstag wird momentan umgebaut°. — *renovated*

1. der Reichstag / momentan umbauen
2. die Philharmonie / wegen Regenschaden° reparieren — ***wegen Regenschaden:*** *because of rain damage*
3. das Schloss Charlottenburg / von oben bis unten putzen
4. die Gedächtniskirche / heute renovieren
5. das Museum für deutsche Geschichte / neu organisieren
6. das Neue Museum auf der Museumsinsel / wieder aufbauen° — *reconstruct*
7. die Kongresshalle / für die nächste Konferenz sauber machen
8. das Schloss Sanssouci / außen und innen reinigen° — *clean*

B. The passive voice: narrative and conversational past

1. Narrative past tense

The narrative past tense of the passive voice is formed with the narrative past tense forms of **werden** and a participle at the end of the clause.

Die Grenzen zu West-Berlin **wurden** 1989 geöffnet. — *The borders to West Berlin were opened in 1989.*

wurde angerufen: *was called*		
Person	**Singular**	**Plural**
1st	ich **wurde angerufen** *I was called*	wir **wurden angerufen** *we were called*
2nd, informal	du **wurdest angerufen** *you were called*	ihr **wurdet angerufen** *you were called*
2nd, formal	Sie **wurden angerufen** *you were called*	Sie **wurden angerufen** *you were called*
3rd	er/sie/es **wurde angerufen** *he/she/it was called*	sie **wurden angerufen** *they were called*

2. Conversational past and past perfect of the passive

The conversational past of the passive voice is formed with the participle of the main verb (i.e., the verb expressing the action) and the conversational past of the verb **werden.** The conversational past of the verb **werden** consists of a conjugated form of **sein** and the shortened past participle **worden.**

Ich **bin** vor einer Stunde **angerufen worden.** *I was/got called one hour ago.*

The past perfect is formed with a form of **war** instead of **sein.**

Ich **war** schon **angerufen worden.** *I had already been called.*

The conversational past and the past perfect always consist of three verbs:

1. a conjugated form of **sein** (e.g., **bin** in the conversational past) or **war** (for the past perfect)
2. the past participle of the verb expressing the action (e.g., **angerufen**)
3. **worden** (a shortened form of the past participle of **werden**)

angerufen worden: *was called*		
Person	**Singular**	
1st	ich **bin angerufen worden**	*I was/have been called*
2nd, informal	du **bist angerufen worden**	*you were/have been called*
2nd, formal	Sie **sind angerufen worden**	*you were/have been called*
3rd	er/sie/es **ist angerufen worden**	*he/she/it was/has been called*

Person	**Plural**	
1st	wir **sind angerufen worden**	*we were/have been called*
2nd, informal	ihr **seid angerufen worden**	*you were/have been called*
2nd, formal	Sie **sind angerufen worden**	*you were/have been called*
3rd	sie **sind angerufen worden**	*they were/have been called*

The passive is formed in informal English with the verb, *get,* e.g. *The car got hit by a bus.*

Here is a summary chart of tenses in the passive voice.

Present	Er **wird angerufen.**	*He is being called.*
Narrative past	Er **wurde angerufen.**	*He was called.*
Conversational past	Er **ist angerufen worden.**	*He was/has been called.*
Past perfect	Er **war angerufen worden.**	*He had been called.*

29 **Wann ist das gemacht worden?** Beschreiben Sie diese Ereignisse aus der deutschen Geschichte. Benutzen Sie das Passiv.

die Mauer / abreißen° — *tear down*

S1: Wann ist die Mauer abgerissen worden?
S2: Die Mauer ist 1990 abgerissen worden.

1871 1918 1938 1949 1953 1961 1972 1990 1995

1. die Mauer / abreißen
2. die Bundesrepublik Deutschland und die DDR / gründen
3. der Reichstag / von dem Künstler Christo verhüllen° — *to wrap*
4. die Mauer / bauen
5. die Arbeitsnormen in Ost-Berlin / erhöhen
6. die Weimarer Republik / ausrufen
7. jüdische Geschäfte / zerstören
8. der Transit zwischen Ost und West / regeln

30 **Eine Zeittafel für Ihre Heimatstadt.** Schreiben Sie eine Zeittafel für Ihre Heimatstadt mit mindestens fünf wichtigen Ereignissen. Die folgende Liste enthält einige Ideen.

das neue Schwimmbad *Das neue Schwimmbad ist 1994 gebaut worden.*

das neue Schwimmbad	ist	gegründet	worden
das neue Einkaufszentrum°		erweitert°	
die neue Schule		gebaut	
unser neues Haus		benannt	
die neue Autobahn		abgerissen	
das alte Autokino		zerstört	
die Innenstadt		renoviert	
das Sportstadion		geschlossen	
die Kirche		wieder aufgebaut	

mall / expanded

Die Geschichte meiner Heimatstadt _____:

	Jahr	*Ereignis*
1.	_____	_____
2.	_____	_____
3.	_____	_____
4.	_____	_____
5.	_____	_____

C. The agent in a passive voice sentence

The preposition **von** *(by)*, followed by the dative case denotes the agent of the action in a passive sentence.

Die Grenzen zu West-Berlin und zur Bundesrepublik Deutschland werden **von** der DDR geöffnet.	*The borders to West Berlin and the Federal Republic of Germany are being opened by the GDR.*

When the agent is an impersonal or inanimate force, speakers use the preposition **durch** *(through, by, by means of)* followed by the accusative case.

Berlin ist **durch** die Rote Armee erobert worden. — *Berlin was conquered by the Red Army.*

However, speakers use the preposition **von** more often than **durch** in passive sentences.

31 Das 20. Jahrhundert. Stellen Sie einem Partner/einer Partnerin die folgenden Fragen. Beantworten Sie die Fragen mit einem Passiv-Satz. Benutzen Sie **von.** Wechseln Sie ab.

die Deutsche Republik ausrufen

S1: Von wem ist die Deutsche Republik ausgerufen worden?
S2: Die Deutsche Republik ist von Philipp Scheidemann ausgerufen worden.

die DDR • Philipp Scheidemann • der deutsche König • die Siegermächte • die Alliierten • John F. Kennedy • die Nazis • Adolf Hitler

1. die Deutsche Republik ausrufen
2. jüdische Geschäfte und Synagogen zerstören
3. Deutschland nach dem Krieg besetzen
4. die Mauer bauen
5. die Macht ergreifen
6. Berlin im Jahre 1963 besuchen
7. die Luftbrücke organisieren
8. Preußen regieren

D. The impersonal passive

Both English and German allow passive sentences to be formed from an active sentence with a direct object.

Active

direct object	*direct object*
Die DDR hat **die Grenze** geöffnet.	*The GDR opened **the border.***

Passive

Die Grenze ist von der DDR geöffnet worden. — ***The border** was opened by the GDR.*

Unlike English, however, German has passive constructions with no corresponding direct object in the active sentence. These expressions have only approximate equivalents in English. There are two frequently occurring types of verbs which do not have a direct object.

1. Intransitive verbs (e.g., **schwimmen, singen, sprechen, tanzen**)

   Es wird getanzt. — *There is dancing going on.*
   Es wird laut gesungen. — *Loud singing is going on.*

2. Dative verbs (e.g., **helfen**, **danken**)

   Dem Mann ist nicht geholfen worden. — *The man was not being helped.*
   Der Frau wird gedankt. — *The woman is being thanked.*

Since intransitive verbs and dative verbs do not have direct objects in the active voice, they cannot have a subject in the passive voice and are therefore termed *impersonal passive* or *subjectless passive.* The subject is always in the third person singular, while the English equivalent may have a plural subject.

Den Männern **wird** geholfen. *The men **are** being helped.*

An impersonal passive construction frequently begins with **es.** This **es** is a placeholder, not the subject, and drops out whenever another element begins the sentence, such as an adverb of location (e.g., **hier**).

Hier wird getanzt. *Dancing is going on here.*

The corresponding active sentence uses **man.**

Man tanzt hier. *One dances here.*

Dependent clauses that begin with a subordinate conjunction, such as **weil, als, dass, wenn,** also omit the placeholder **es** in the passive.

Es wird heute gegrillt. *There's barbecuing going on today.*
Wir hören, **dass** heute gegrillt wird. *We hear that there's barbecuing today.*

32 Was wird hier gemacht? Beschreiben Sie, was an jedem Ort gemacht wird.

▣ in der Diskothek *Hier wird getanzt.*

1. in der Diskothek	a. arbeiten
2. in der Oper	b. auftanken
3. im Lesesaal	c. einkaufen
4. im Kaufhaus	d. lernen
5. im Büro	e. schwimmen
6. im Deutschkurs	f. singen
7. im Schwimmbad	g. Deutsch sprechen
8. an der Tankstelle	h. tanzen

Wissenswerte Vokabeln: Länder und Flüsse Deutschlands

Talking about geographic landmarks in Germany

Die 16 Bundesländer

Baden-Württemberg	
Hauptstadt:	Stuttgart
Fläche:	35 751 km²
Einwohner:	9,8 Millionen

Brandenburg	
Hauptstadt:	Potsdam
Fläche:	29 056 km²
Einwohner:	2,6 Millionen

Hessen	
Hauptstadt:	Wiesbaden
Fläche:	21 114 km²
Einwohner:	5,8 Millionen

Bayern	
Hauptstadt:	München
Fläche:	70 554 km²
Einwohner:	11,4 Millionen

Bremen	
Hauptstadt:	Bremen
Fläche:	404 km²
Einwohner:	0,68 Millionen

Mecklenburg-Vorpommern	
Hauptstadt:	Schwerin
Fläche:	23 559 km²
Einwohner:	1,9 Millionen

Berlin	
Hauptstadt:	Berlin
Fläche:	889 km²
Einwohner:	3,4 Millionen

Hamburg	
Hauptstadt:	Hamburg
Fläche:	755 km²
Einwohner:	1,7 Millionen

Niedersachsen	
Hauptstadt:	Hannover
Fläche:	47 351 km²
Einwohner:	7,4 Millionen

Nordrhein-Westfalen	
Hauptstadt:	Düsseldorf
Fläche:	34 070 km²
Einwohner:	17,3 Millionen

Sachsen	
Hauptstadt:	Dresden
Fläche:	18 341 km²
Einwohner:	4,8 Millionen

Thüringen	
Hauptstadt:	Erfurt
Fläche:	16 251 km²
Einwohner:	2,6 Millionen

Rheinland-Pfalz	
Hauptstadt:	Mainz
Fläche:	19 849 km²
Einwohner:	3,8 Millionen

Sachsen-Anhalt	
Hauptstadt:	Magdeburg
Fläche:	20 607 km²
Einwohner:	2,9 Millionen

Saarland	
Hauptstadt:	Saarbrücken
Fläche:	2570 km²
Einwohner:	1,1 Millionen

Schleswig-Holstein	
Hauptstadt:	Kiel
Fläche:	15 731 km²
Einwohner:	2,6 Millionen

Die Hauptflüsse

1. der Rhein
2. der Main
3. die Elbe
4. die Donau
5. die Mosel
6. die Weser
7. die Oder
8. die Neiße

Wie heißt das kleinste Bundesland?
Wie heißt der bekannteste Fluss?

33 **Land und Leute kennen lernen.** Beantworten Sie diese Fragen mit Hilfe der Länderkarte am Anfang des Buches und den Informationen aus **Wissenswerte Vokabeln.**

1. Welche drei Großstädte sind auch Bundesländer?
2. Welche drei Bundesländer haben die meisten Einwohner?
3. Welche drei Bundesländer haben die wenigsten Einwohner?
4. Welches Bundesland hat die größte Landfläche?
5. Welche drei Bundesländer grenzen an die Nord- und/oder Ostsee?
6. Welche drei Bundesländer grenzen an Frankreich?
7. Durch welche Bundesländer fließt der Rhein?
8. Für welche Bundesländer bilden die Oder und die Neiße eine Grenze mit Polen?
9. Durch welche Bundesländer fließt die Elbe?
10. Durch welche Bundesländer fließt die Weser?

Schreibecke **Am liebsten würde ich das Bundesland sehen ...** Schreiben Sie einen kurzen Aufsatz über das Bundesland, das Sie auf Ihrer nächsten Deutschlandreise am liebsten sehen würden. Erklären Sie, warum Sie dieses Bundesland so interessant finden würden und was Sie dort sehen, besuchen und machen könnten.

ABSPRUNGTEXT II

Maikäfer flieg!

(von Christine Nöstlinger)

In diesem Auszug aus ihrer Erzählung „Maikäfer° flieg!" beschreibt die Autorin Christine Nöstlinger ihre Kindheit am Ende des Zweiten Weltkrieges in Wien. Das Jahr ist 1945. Österreich kämpft auf der Seite von Nazi-Deutschland. Ihr Vater kommt als verwundeter° Soldat von der Front zurück und muss ins Krankenhaus. Die Rote Armee ist nicht mehr weit von Wien. Die Stadt wird bombardiert, und man sitzt mit den Nachbarn zehn Stunden lang im Luftschutzkeller. Es herrscht Angst, Panik und Wut. Das Haus wird zerstört, aber sie überleben.

June bug

wounded

Vorschau

34 **Thematische Fragen.** Beantworten Sie die folgenden Fragen auf Deutsch.

1. Haben Sie Verwandte, Freunde oder Bekannte, die als Soldaten im (Zweiten) Weltkrieg gedient haben? Was haben Sie von diesen Menschen über den Weltkrieg gehört? Erzählen sie gern vom Krieg, oder wollen sie lieber nicht darüber sprechen?
2. Würden Sie sich als Pazifist/Pazifistin bezeichnen? Wird es jemals eine Zeit ohne Krieg auf der Erde geben? Wie können wir Krieg verhindern?
3. Was ist Ihre persönliche Einstellung zum Militärdienst? Würden Sie sich freiwillig° als Soldat melden° oder nicht? Wie würden Sie von diesem Erlebnis profitieren?

volunteer / sign up

35 **Der Krieg und seine Folgen°.** Welche Folgen haben diese Ereignisse im Krieg? Tragen Sie den passenden Buchstaben ein.

consequences

Ereignis	***Folgen***
1. ___ Man spricht schlecht über einen Politiker/einen Diktator.	a. Man kommt in ein Lazarett°.
2. ___ Man wird als Soldat verletzt.	b. Man kann nicht mehr richtig gehen, sondern nur herumhumpeln.
3. ___ Tiefflieger und Bomber kommen.	c. Man hat nichts zum Heizen. Man muss frieren.
4. ___ Eine Granate trifft einen am Bein.	d. Sirenen warnen vor den Tieffliegern und Bombern.
5. ___ Man hört Warnsirenen.	e. Man geht in den Keller, um Schutz zu suchen.
6. ___ Eine Bombe trifft ein Haus.	f. Eine Person, die den Politiker/Diktator mag, wird sehr böse.
7. ___ Es ist kalt.	g. Das Haus wird zerstört. Manche Leute werden hysterisch.

Militärkrankenhaus

36 **Lesestrategien: Maikäfer flieg!** Benutzen Sie die folgenden Lesestrategien, um den Text „Maikäfer flieg!" zu verstehen.

1. **Den Kontext verstehen.** Finden Sie im Text Antworten auf die folgenden Fragen.
   a. Welches Jahr ist es? Welche Jahreszeit?
   b. Was ist die Situation?
   c. Welche Personen werden erwähnt°? Wie heißen sie?
   d. Wo sind sie? Welche Stadt wird erwähnt? Welche Länder werden erwähnt?
   e. Welche Wörter aus der deutschen Geschichte werden benutzt?

mentioned

2. **Neue Wörter lernen: Komposita.** Was bedeuten diese Wörter? Lesen Sie die Erklärungen, und beantworten Sie die Fragen.
   a. russische **Tiefflieger:** Ein Tiefflieger ist ein Flugzeug, das im Krieg nicht sehr hoch fliegt. Was wirft ein Tiefflieger im Krieg ab: Schokolade oder Bomben?
   b. **der Urlaubsschein = Urlaub + Schein**: **Urlaub** kommt von **erlauben,** und ein **Schein** ist ein Stück Papier, wie z.B. ein Geldschein. Was erlaubt ein **Urlaubsschein** im militärischen Kontext?
   c. **Führerhauptquartier:** Wo man lebt, ist sein Quartier. Der Führer Adolf Hitler lebte hauptsächlich in der deutschen Hauptstadt Berlin. Kann man heute noch das **Führerhauptquartier** in Berlin besichtigen?
   d. **der Bombenangriff:** Das Wort **Bombe** existiert auch im Englischen. **Angriff** stammt von dem Verb **angreifen** und bedeutet Attacke. Wenn Flugzeuge Bomben abwerfen, nennt man das einen **Bombenangriff.** Wird ein **Bombenangriff** von den Menschen auf der Erde begrüßt?
   e. **Kellerhocker: Hocken** bedeutet auf den eigenen Fersen sitzen, oder lange Zeit unaktiv an einem Ort sitzen. Wie sitzt man während eines Bombenangriffs im Keller? Ist das bequem? Fühlt man sich wohl?
   f. **der Schutthaufen:** In dieser Geschichte finden Sie das Wort **Schutt** dreimal: **der Schutt, der Schutthaufen, verschüttet. Schutt** ist das, was bleibt, wenn ein Gebäude zerstört wird. Ein kleiner Berg von **Schutt** ist ein **Schutthaufen.** Wenn in dieser Geschichte eine Bombe landet und eine Frau schreit: „Wir sind **verschüttet!** Wir sind lebendig begraben!", was fürchtet sie?

3. **Strategien verwenden.** Versuchen Sie die fett gedruckten Wörter zu erraten. Benutzen Sie die Strategien, die Sie gelernt haben.

Because this literary text was written before reforms in the German language were legislated, the ß has been retained in certain words, e.g. **daß, wüßte, Rußland.**

Strategie 1: Weltwissen

a. [Der Frühling kam] sehr früh. Das war gut, weil wir kein Holz und keine Kohlen mehr **zum Heizen** hatten.
   □ zu verbrennen □ zu verkaufen □ aufzuheben

b. Mein Vater lag nun in Wien in einem **Lazarett ...** Mein Vater hatte zerschossene Beine.
   □ Haus □ Krankenhaus □ Luxushotel

c. Daß mein Vater nun in Wien im Lazarett war, war weder **Zufall** noch° Glück.
   □ geplant und erwartet □ nicht geplant und nicht erwartet

***weder ... noch**: neither ... nor*

d. ... da **heulten** um fünf Uhr am Morgen die Luftschutzsirenen ...
   □ waren laut □ sind still geblieben, haben keinen Ton gemacht

Strategie 2: Kontext

a. Mein Vater hatte zerschossene Beine, und überall auf seinem Körper eiterten **Granatsplitter** aus dem Fleisch.
   - □ Teilchen von explodierten Granaten □ Ganze Granate

b. Doch er konnte mühselig **herumhumpeln** … und durfte zu uns nach Hause kommen und bis Abend bei uns bleiben.
   - □ langsam und hinkend laufen □ passiv herumsitzen

c. … Armbanduhren und Wecker und eine Küchenuhr. Der Großvater hatte sie wie einen **Schatz gehütet.**
   - □ teure kostbare Sachen geschützt □ alltägliche Sachen benutzt

d. Jeden zweiten Tag **fiel** die Schule **aus,** wegen der Bombenangriffe in der Nacht.
   - □ Es gab keinen Schulunterricht. □ Es gab Schulunterricht.

e. Niemand **wagte,** den Keller zu verlassen.
   - □ Niemand hatte Angst, aus dem Keller zu gehen.
   - □ Niemand hat es riskiert, aus dem Keller zu gehen.

f. Unsere Nachbarin **brüllte:** „Wir sind verschüttet! … Wir kommen da nie mehr heraus!"
   - □ sprach leise □ schrie laut

g. Unser Haus sah aus wie ein trauriges Puppenhaus. Die eine Hälfte war **eingestürzt,** und die andere Hälfte stand hilflos und sehr allein.
   - □ zusammengefallen □ schön und bunt

This literary text retains the old spelling of words like **daß, Rußland** and **wüßte.**

Strategie 3: Wortformen

a. Wenn die Russen kämen, würde die Frau Brenner sich selber … **vergiften.**
   - □ Gift nehmen und sterben □ Medikamente nehmen und leben

b. Die Frau Brenner **empörte sich** darüber und **jammerte** wieder einmal ihr „wenn-das-der-Führer-wüßte"…
   - □ ärgerte sich und heulte □ freute sich und sang

c. Als die Bombe in unser Haus **einschlug**…
   - □ vom Flugzeug abgeworfen wurde □ landete und explodierte

ABSPRUNGTEXT II

Maikäfer flieg!

Lesen Sie jetzt den Text.

1. Im Jahr neunzehnhundertfünfundvierzig kam der Frühling sehr früh. Das war gut, weil wir kein Holz und keine Kohlen mehr zum Heizen hatten. Viel besser war noch, daß im März mein Vater von der Front kam.

2. Mein Vater lag nun in Wien in einem Lazarett. Vorher war er in Deutschland in einem Lazarett gewesen und noch vorher in einem Lazarett in Polen. Und noch davor in Rußland in einem Eisenbahnzug, irgendwo auf den Schienen°, ohne Lokomotive. Mit dreißig anderen Soldaten in einem offenen Güterwaggon° und darüber russische Tiefflieger. Mein Vater hatte zerschossene Beine, und

tracks
freight car

überall auf seinem Körper eiterten° Granatsplitter aus dem Fleisch. Doch er konnte mühselig° herumhumpeln, und er bekam jeden Morgen im Spital einen Urlaubsschein und durfte zu uns nach Hause kommen und bis zum Abend bei uns bleiben.

festered
with difficulty

3. Daß mein Vater nun in Wien im Lazarett war, war weder Zufall noch Glück. Das hatte mein Onkel, der Bruder meiner Mutter, erreicht. Der war ein großer SS-Nazi, in Berlin im Führerhauptquartier. Und daß mein Vater jeden Tag einen Urlaubsschein bekam, war auch kein Zufall. Unter den Uhrenfurnituren vom Großvater, ganz unten in der letzten Lade vom Schrank, waren noch etliche Uhren gewesen, Armbanduhren und Wecker und eine Küchenuhr. Der Großvater hatte sie wie einen Schatz gehütet. Nun bekam sie der Unteroffizier in der Schreibstube vom Lazarett. Der schrieb dafür die vielen Urlaubsscheine aus.

4. Die Russen waren nicht mehr weit von Wien weg. Wo sie waren, wußte niemand genau. Jeden zweiten Tag fiel die Schule aus. Wegen der Bombenangriffe in der Nacht. Das war aber ganz gleich, weil wir sowieso nicht lernen konnten. In unserer Schule waren jetzt auch die Schüler von zwei anderen Volksschulen, die zerbombt worden waren.

5. Die Frau Brenner grüßte noch immer mit Heil Hitler, und die Frau Sula, die bei der Frau Brenner einmal in der Woche die Fenster putzte, sagte, daß sich die Frau Brenner eine Menge Gift besorgt° habe. Wenn die Russen kämen, würde die Frau Brenner sich selber und den Herrn Brenner und die Brenner-Hedi und den Brenner-Hund vergiften. Mir tat der Brenner-Hund leid.

acquired

6. Dann kam ein Tag, da heulten um fünf Uhr am Morgen die Luftschutzsirenen auf den Dächern. Um sieben heulten sie wieder, und um acht heulten sie auch. Zu Mittag konnte nur noch eine Sirene heulen. Die anderen Sirenen lagen auf den Schutthaufen unter Dachziegeln° und Mauerbrocken° und zerschlagenen Türen und zerbrochenen Fenstern und umgefallenen Schornsteinen°. Mein Vater sagte, daß wir trotzdem Glück haben, weil die Amerikaner keine Brandbomben° herunterwerfen.

roofing slates / chunks of walls / chimneys
fire bombs

7. Wir saßen seit zehn Stunden im Keller. Wir waren hungrig. Doch niemand getraute° sich, aus den Wohnungen Essen zu holen. Niemand wagte den Keller zu verlassen. Im Keller war kein Klo. Die Leute hockten sich in die Kellerwinkel°. Der Berger Schurli sang: „Drunt' in Stein am Anger steht ein Kampfverband, ein langer, rechts keine Jäger, links keine Flak, doch wir schießen alle ab!"

dared
corners of the cellar

8. Die Frau Brenner empörte sich° darüber und jammerte wieder einmal ihr „wenn-das-der-Führer-wüßte", und die Frau Berger, die Mutter vom Schurli, schaute die Frau Brenner an und sagte langsam: „Wissen Sie, was mich Ihr Führer kann? Ihr Führer kann mich am A---- lecken!°"

empörte sich: *became angry*
am A---- lecken: *kiss my a . . . !*

9. Die anderen Kellerhocker nickten° zustimmend.

nodded

10. Als die Bombe in unser Haus einschlug, sauste° und krachte° und wackelte° es auch nicht mehr als vor einer Stunde, als das Nachbarhaus kaputtgegangen war. Doch der ganze Keller war voll Mauerstaub, und der Verputz° fiel von den Wänden und ein paar Ziegelsteine° hinterher. Dem Herrn Benedikt fiel ein Ziegelstein auf den Kopf. Der Herr Benedikt bekam große Angst. Er wollte aus dem Keller. Er schlug wild um sich. Er boxte alle, die ihm im Weg waren, zur Seite. Er trat mich in den Bauch. Das tat weh.

whistled / crashed / wobbled
plaster
bricks

11. Unsere Nachbarin brüllte: „Wir sind verschüttet! Wir sind lebendig begraben! Wir kommen da nie mehr heraus!"

12. Das war aber nicht wahr. Wir waren nicht verschüttet. Die Kellertür war aus den Angeln gerissen° und lag zerbrochen auf der Kellertreppe, und darauf lagen

aus den Angeln gerissen: *torn off its hinges*

die gußeiserne° Bassena° und die Hausleiter und der Vogelkäfig der Hausmeisterin (ohne Vogel) und Ziegel und Schutt. Doch das war leicht wegzuräumen. *cast iron / wash basin*

13. Unser Haus sah aus wie ein trauriges Puppenhaus°. Die eine Hälfte war eingestürzt, und die andere Hälfte stand hilflos und sehr allein mit offenen, halben Zimmern. Das Stiegenhaus° war auch weg. *doll house* / *stairwell*

Rückblick

37 **Stimmt das?** Stimmen diese Aussagen zum **Absprungtext II** oder nicht? Wenn nicht, was stimmt?

	Ja, das stimmt.	*Nein, das stimmt nicht.*
1. 1945 freut man sich in Wien, dass der Frühling sehr früh kommt.	___	___
2. Der Vater ist immer noch an der Front.	___	___
3. Der Vater wohnt nicht zu Hause, sondern in einem Lazarett, aber er darf tagsüber nach Hause kommen.	___	___
4. Es ist nur Zufall, eine Glückssache, dass der Vater nach Wien ins Lazarett kommt.	___	___
5. Vaters Besuche zu Hause werden von einem Unteroffizier mit Uhren „gekauft".	___	___
6. Frau Brenner bleibt treue Nationalsozialistin und will sich und ihre Familie töten, wenn die Russen Wien erreichen.	___	___
7. An einem Morgen zwischen fünf Uhr und Mittag wird die Stadt Wien zerbombt.	___	___
8. Die Leute sitzen nur kurz im Keller, haben viel zu Essen und gehen in den Pausen zwischen Bombenangriffen auf die Straße.	___	___
9. Frau Berger spricht für alle außer Frau Brenner, wenn sie auf grobe° Weise sagt, sie hat genug vom Führer.	___	___
10. Bomben zerstören das Haus und das Nachbarhaus, aber kein Mensch in den zwei Häusern wird getötet.	___	___

coarse

38 **Ergänzen Sie.** Ergänzen Sie diese Sätze mit Wörtern aus dem **Absprungtext II.**

1. Der Vater kam im Frühling von der ______ zurück.
2. Als verwundeter Veteran musste der Vater in einem ______ bleiben.
3. Jeden Morgen bekam er einen ______ und durfte nach Hause kommen.
4. Es war weder ______ noch Glück, dass der Vater in Wien stationiert war.
5. Der Großvater hatte seine Uhren wie einen ______ gehütet.
6. Wegen der vielen ______ in der Nacht fiel die Schule oft aus.
7. Schüler von zwei anderen Schulen kamen jetzt in diese Schule, weil ihre Schulen ______ worden waren.
8. Frau Brenner wollte ihre Familie ______, wenn die Russen Wien eroberten.
9. Im Keller hatten alle Hunger, aber niemand ______ den Keller zu verlassen.

10. Im Keller gab es kein Klo, also mussten sich alle in die Kellerwinkel ____, wenn sie auf die Toilette mussten.
11. Die anderen Kellerhocker ____ in Zustimmung, als Frau Berger zu Frau Brenner sagte: „Wissen Sie, was mich Ihr Führer kann? ..."
12. Die Nachbarin ____: „Wir sind verschüttet! Wir sind lebendig ____!"

39 **Absatzthemen.** **Absprungtext II** hat 13 Absätze°. Einige Absätze sind nur einen Satz lang, aber die meisten sind länger. Jeder Absatz hat eine Aussage. Schreiben Sie vor jede Aussage die richtige Absatznummer.

paragraphs

Absatz-nummer ***Aussage***

3 a. Mit Beziehungen° und Bestechung° bekommt man im Krieg, was man braucht.

connections / bribes

__ b. Die anderen Leute im Keller denken dasselbe.
__ c. Eine Bombe trifft das Haus, und ein Mann gerät in Panik.
__ d. Im Krieg gibt es wenig Brennstoff. Wenn es kalt ist, friert man.
__ e. Nach einem Bombeneinschlag sieht das Haus traurig aus. Man kann nicht mehr darin wohnen.
__ f. Eine pessimistische Frau glaubt, dass alle Leute im Keller sterben werden.
__ g. Wegen der Bomben gibt es nur noch selten Schule.
__ h. Der Vater ist nun in Wien im Krankenhaus, aber tagsüber darf er nach Hause.
__ i. Während der Bombenangriffe geht man in den Keller. Im Keller ist es weder komfortabel noch hygienisch.
__ j. Frau Brenner streitet mit einem Mann, der von Adolf Hitler schlecht gesprochen hat.
__ k. Frau Brenner ist noch immer Hitler-treu.
__ l. An einem Tag gibt es besonders viele Bombenangriffe. Während des Tages werden immer mehr Häuser zerstört.
__ m. Obwohl das Haus zerstört wurde, haben alle Leute im Keller überlebt.

40 **Kurz gefragt/kurz interpretiert.** Beantworten Sie die folgenden Fragen auf Deutsch.

1. Diese Erzählung wird aus der Perspektive eines jungen Mädchens erzählt. Für Kinder sind Kriege besonders tragisch. Trotzdem merkt man einen gewissen Optimismus an dem Mädchen. Wo sind im Text Beispiele für diesen Optimismus?
2. Welche normalen Bedürfnisse° werden in der Erzählung erwähnt? *needs*
3. Ist Frau Brenners Angst vor den Russen angebracht°? *appropriate*
4. Die Erzählung hat viele Wörter, die nur im Krieg benutzt werden. Können Sie einige dieser Wörter finden und Kategorien dafür aufstellen?

41 **Zehn Stunden im Keller.** Die Autorin hat im Krieg viele Stunden im Keller verbracht. Was hätten Sie als Kind gemacht, wenn Sie zehn Stunden im Keller gewesen wären? Fragen Sie einen Partner/eine Partnerin.

S1: Hättest du im Keller Hausaufgaben gemacht?
S2: Nein, ich hätte keine Aufgaben gemacht.
S1: Warum nicht?
S2: Wir hätten keine Schule gehabt.

1. im Keller lernen
2. im Keller essen
3. den Keller verlassen°, um Essen zu holen
4. im Keller Angst haben
5. im Keller singen
6. im Keller mit jemandem streiten
7. im Keller gut schlafen
8. lebendig aus dem Keller kommen

leave

Strukturen und Vokabeln

III Expressing substitution, opposition, causality, duration, and position

Genitive prepositions

You learned in chapters 7 and 10 that the genitive case indicates possession. German speakers use the genitive case also with certain prepositions, whose English meanings frequently include *of.*

(an)statt	*instead of*
außerhalb	*outside of*
innerhalb	*inside of*
trotz	*in spite of*
während	*during*
wegen	*on account of, because of*

There are other genitive prepositions, but German speakers do not use them often. You may learn them in more advanced German courses.

Remember that masculine and neuter nouns end with an **-s** or an **-es** in the genitive singular.

Trotz **des** Krieg**es** sind wir immer noch in die Schule gegangen.	*In spite of the war we still went to school.*
Während **des** Krieg**es** hat man immer Angst gehabt.	*During the war, everyone was always afraid.*
Wegen **der** Bombenangriffe fiel die Schule aus.	*On account of the bombing raids there was no school.*

Sprache im Alltag: Replacing the genitive in spoken German

In written texts, German speakers prefer the genitive case. However, in spoken German, the genitive case often sounds formal and stilted. Therefore the dative case frequently replaces the genitive.

Written German
Trotz **des** Regen**s** sind wir zu Fuß hingegangen.

Spoken German
Trotz **dem** Regen sind wir zu Fuß hingegangen.

Despite the rain we walked there.

42 **Das Ende des Krieges.** Wählen Sie für jeden Satz die richtige Genitivpräposition.

trotz (an)statt während wegen innerhalb außerhalb

1. ______ des Frühlings kam das Ende des Krieges.
2. ______ der Bombenangriffe mussten wir in den Keller.
3. ______ des Kellers herrschte Hunger und Angst.
4. ______ unserer Angst sind wir nachher auf die Straße gegangen.
5. ______ des Krieges sind wir immer noch in die Schule gegangen.
6. Die Russen waren nicht weit von Wien, aber sie blieben noch ______ der Stadt.
7. ______ der Amerikaner kamen die Russen zuerst nach Wien.

FREIE ■ KOMMUNIKATION ■

Was hätte man gegen die Nazis machen können? Viele, aber nicht alle Deutsche waren Nazis. In den frühen Jahren war es noch möglich, gegen die Nazis zu protestieren. Nach 1933 wurde es lebensgefährlich°, denn die Nazis begannen, ihre Gegner° zu töten. In einer Gruppe von drei Personen diskutieren Sie, was man hätte machen können, um das Naziregime zu verhindern oder abzuschaffen°. Hier sind einige hilfreiche Ausdrücke.

lebensgefährlich: life-threatening / Gegner: opponents / abzuschaffen: abolish

1. während des Naziaufstiegs° (1930–1933)
2. während der Machtergreifung der Nazis (1933)
3. während der Machtkonsolidierung der Nazis (1934–1939)
4. während der Hauptkriegszeit (1939–1943)
5. während des Zusammenbruchs° des Regimes (1944–1945)

die Nazis nicht wählen°
Juden und Nazigegner verstecken°
emigrieren
gegen die Nazis protestieren
aktiven Widerstand leisten
ausländisches Radio hören
Zeitungsartikel schreiben
die Jugendorganisationen boykottieren
kein Parteimitglied° werden
Flugblätter verteilen°

the Nazis' rise to power / elect
hide
***Kollaps** / party member*
***Flugblätter verteilen:** distribute leaflets*

■ Während des Naziaufstiegs hätte man Zeitungsartikel gegen die Nazis schreiben können.

Schreibecke **Eine Seite aus dem Tagebuch.** Sie haben einen Wirbelsturm° in einem Keller überlebt°. Schreiben Sie in Ihr Tagebuch, was Sie während des Wirbelsturms erlebt haben. War es während des Tages oder der Nacht? Haben Sie die Sirenen gehört? Haben Sie Angst gehabt? Mit wem sind Sie in den Keller gegangen? Was ist im Keller passiert? Wie lange sind Sie im Keller gewesen? Wie sind Sie aus dem Keller gekommen? Wurde das Haus zerstört? Haben Sie alle Hausgegenstände gefunden? Was hätten Sie anders machen sollen? Würden Sie das nächste Mal etwas anders machen?

tornado / survived

ZIELTEXT
Ich habe mich nie wohl gefühlt

Anna unterhält sich mit ihrer Freundin Barbara, die in der sozialistischen DDR aufgewachsen ist. Sie diskutieren die Vereinigung Deutschlands. Barbara spricht von der Zeit vor der Wende°: von ihrer Einstellung° zur DDR, von ihrer Familiensituation und den Reisemöglichkeiten der damaligen DDR-Bürger.

change of events / attitude

Sprache im Alltag: Special meanings of Wende

The verb **wenden** means *to turn,* and the noun **die Wende** can refer to any significant turn of events or change. Today it almost always refers to the time in former East Germany just before unification since that has been the most profound change in post-war German history.

Vorschau

43 Was wissen Sie schon? Welche der folgenden Beschreibungen passen auf die ehemalige DDR? Welche passen auf die Bundesrepublik Deutschland *vor* oder auch *nach* der Vereinigung?

Was wissen Sie schon? If necessary, check the timeline in **Absprungtext I.**

Beschreibung	*DDR*	*Bundesrepublik vor der Vereinigung*	*Bundesrepublik nach der Vereinigung*
1. fast keine Arbeitslosigkeit°	___	___	___
2. totale Reisefreiheit°	___	___	___
3. hohe Kriminalität	___	___	___
4. die Mauer wird gebaut	___	___	___
5. viele Leute emigrieren	___	___	___
6. wichtiges Mitglied° der Nato	___	___	___
7. Planwirtschaft	___	___	___
8. sehr hoher Lebensstandard	___	___	___
9. Partner der USA	___	___	___
10. Partner der Sowjetunion	___	___	___

unemployment
freedom to travel
member

44 Der Tag nach der Maueröffnung. Nehmen wir an°, Sie wohnen in Ost-Berlin. Es ist der 9. November 1989, und die Mauer ist gerade „gefallen", d.h. die Grenzen zum Westen sind geöffnet worden. Was würden Sie zuerst machen? Was würden Sie danach machen? Fragen Sie dann Ihren Partner/Ihre Partnerin.

Nehmen ... an: *Let us assume*

S1: Würdest du Freunde oder Verwandte im Westen besuchen?
S2: Ja, das würde ich machen. *(oder)*
Nein, das würde ich nicht machen.
S1: Was würdest du zuerst machen? Und als Zweites?

1. Freunde oder Verwandte im Westen besuchen
2. im Westen einkaufen gehen
3. im Westen bummeln gehen
4. Freunde in der DDR anrufen und mit ihnen feiern
5. zu Hause bleiben und nichts Besonderes machen

6. an eine westdeutsche Uni schreiben: vielleicht dort studieren
7. eine große Reise ins Ausland planen
8. eine Übersiedlung° in die Bundesrepublik planen *move*
9. vielleicht ins Ausland ziehen
10. ganz laut und offen die politische Meinung ausdrücken
11. Souvenirs sammeln: ein Stück Mauer holen, eine Tageszeitung kaufen usw.
12. im Westen ins Kino gehen und West-Filme anschauen

45 **Thematische Fragen.** Beantworten Sie die Fragen auf Deutsch.

1. Haben Sie im November 1989 im Fernsehen die Berichte über die Öffnung der Berliner Mauer gesehen? Warum waren alle Menschen so euphorisch? Warum haben sich die DDR-Bürger so gefreut? Und auch die Westdeutschen?
2. Viele Deutsche sind in den 50er-Jahren ausgewandert° und wohnen jetzt in den USA und Kanada. Was waren wohl die Gründe für diese Leute, damals ihr Heimatland zu verlassen? *emigrated*
3. Wer wandert Ihrer Meinung nach wahrscheinlich mehr ins Ausland aus: junge oder alte Menschen? Warum?
4. Welche Bürger durften Ihrer Meinung nach in der sozialistischen DDR vor 1989 ins westliche Ausland reisen? Unter welchen Bedingungen? Was verlangte der Staat als Garantie, dass sie in die DDR zurückkehren würden?

ZIELTEXT

Ich habe mich nie wohl gefühlt

Hören Sie gut zu.

Rückblick

46 **Stimmt das?** Stimmen diese Aussagen zum Text oder nicht? Wenn nicht, was stimmt?

	Ja, das stimmt.	*Nein, das stimmt nicht.*
1. Als die Mauer geöffnet wurde, dachte Barbara, dass es schön war, in Deutschland zu wohnen.	—	—
2. Barbaras Familie war schon immer sehr patriotisch.	—	—

Stimmt das? Retired people were allowed to travel abroad. Since East Germans automatically received West German citizenship and West German benefits if they moved to the West, this allowed the GDR government to discontinue payment of their old-age benefits and save money.

3. Barbara hatte früh gelernt, Schule von Familie zu trennen und in der Schule nicht immer zu sagen, was sie dachte. ___ ___
4. Barbara und die Familie fühlten sich terrorisiert und schizophren, weil sie immer das ideologisch Richtige sagen mussten. ___ ___
5. Barbaras Verwandte sind in den 70er-Jahren ausgewandert. ___ ___
6. Durch Telefonanrufe hat Barbara den Kontakt mit dem Onkel in den USA aufrechterhalten. ___ ___
7. Dieser Onkel durfte nie wieder in die DDR reisen. ___ ___
8. Nachdem die Mauer gebaut wurde, durfte niemand mehr aus Barbaras Familie in den Westen. ___ ___
9. Zu DDR-Zeiten durften ältere Menschen in den Westen fahren. ___ ___
10. Die DDR hätte weiter Rente zahlen müssen, wenn ältere Leute nach Westdeutschland ausgewandert wären. ___ ___
11. „Einen alten Baum verpflanzt man nicht" bedeutet hier, dass alte Menschen ungern ihre Heimat verlassen°. ___ ___ *leave*
12. Die meisten alten DDR-Bürger, die in den Westen reisten, kamen zurück, weil ihre Familien im Osten waren. ___ ___

47 **Ergänzen Sie.** Ergänzen Sie diese Sätze mit Wörtern aus dem **Zieltext.**

1. Die ____ nach der Wende war am Anfang euphorisch.
2. Wegen ihrer Familiensituation hat Barbara sich nie mit dem Staat ____.
3. Barbara hat sich in der DDR nicht ____ gefühlt.
4. In der Schule hatte sie von früh an gelernt, mit zwei ____ zu sprechen.
5. Während der 50er-Jahre sind große Teile der ____ weggegangen.
6. Zu DDR-Zeiten hat Barbaras Familie durch Briefe den Kontakt ____.
7. Verwandte aus dem Westen haben die Familie in der DDR besucht, aber umgekehrt hat das nicht ____.
8. Der Großvater durfte vor der Wende in die Bundesrepublik fahren, weil er für das ____ nicht mehr wichtig war.
9. Wenn er in der Bundesrepublik geblieben wäre, hätte man ihm auch keine ____ mehr zahlen müssen.
10. Weil er nicht mehr gearbeitet hat, hat er nichts mehr für den Staat ____.
11. Einen alten Baum ____ man nicht.

Flagge der DDR

48 **Barbaras Familie.** Welche Familienmitglieder sind in der DDR geblieben? Hören Sie sich den **Zieltext** noch einmal an und kreuzen Sie an, was stimmt.

Familienmitglied	*in der DDR geblieben*	*ins Ausland (in den Westen) gegangen*
1. Barbara	___	___
2. Barbaras Eltern	___	___
3. Barbaras Großeltern	___	___
4. Barbaras Onkel und Tanten	___	___
5. Barbaras Kusinen	___	___

49 **Kurz gefragt.** Beantworten Sie diese Fragen auf Deutsch.

1. Warum durfte Barbaras Großvater in die Bundesrepublik fahren?
2. Warum war Barbara keine überzeugte° Kommunistin? *committed, convinced*
3. Wie störend war es für Barbara, die DDR-Außenwelt von der Familie zu trennen?
4. Wieso durften so viele Familienangehörige die DDR verlassen?
5. Wann sind Barbaras Verwandten in den Westen gegangen? Wohin?
6. Wo wohnt Barbaras Großvater jetzt?
7. Warum hätte der Großvater vor der Wende im Westen bleiben dürfen, wenn er es gewollt hätte?
8. Warum sind die meisten DDR-Rentner im Osten geblieben, obwohl sie in den Westen hätten ausreisen dürfen?

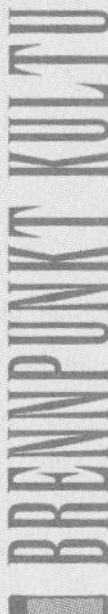

Die Deutsche Demokratische Republik

The German Democratic Republic (**die Deutsche Demokratische Republik** or **DDR**) was a socialist state founded in 1949 in the Soviet occupation zone in reaction to the establishment of the Federal Republic of Germany out of the western zones. From the outset, political power was held by the Socialist Unity Party (**die Sozialistische Einheitspartei Deutschlands** or **SED**), which was formed in 1946 from the Communist Party (**die Kommunistische Partei Deutschlands** or **KPD**) and the Social Democrats. For 40 years the **SED** exerted totalitarian rule in the people's parliament **(die Volkskammer).** Both Walter Ulbricht, the first Chairman and leader of the country, and his successor, Erich Honecker, who was responsible for erecting the Berlin Wall in 1961, showed unquestioning loyalty to the Soviets, who maintained a strong military presence in the **DDR.**

With only 16 million inhabitants, the **DDR** developed the strongest economy in the Warsaw Pact and one of the strongest economies in the world. As a so-called worker's state, where pro-communist, anti-fascist sentiment found a home, the **DDR** guaranteed full employment, inexpensive housing, universal health care, child care, and free education for all its citizens. The effectiveness of its sports programs was exemplified by its extraordinary success at the Olympic Games. As the Cold War intensified and the nuclear threat increased, the **DDR** promoted an official policy of world peace. At the same time, many East Germans fled to the West, gradually draining the country of its vital manpower. The construction of the Berlin Wall in August 1961 eliminated all but the most dangerous attempts at escape. With the opening of the Berlin Wall on Nov. 8/9, 1989, the eventual demise of the **DDR** had become inevitable.

Die deutsche Wiedervereinigung wird am Brandenburger Tor gefeiert.

■ FREIE ■ KOMMUNIKATION ■ Was hätten Sie gemacht, wenn Sie in der DDR aufgewachsen wären?

Stellen Sie sich vor, Sie wären in der DDR geboren. Wie hätten Sie in einer marxistisch-sozialistischen Gesellschaft gelebt: zufrieden oder frustriert? Hätten Sie sich dort frei gefühlt? Was hätten Sie in der Schule gemacht? Hätten Sie die Ideologie angenommen, oder hätten Sie Widerstand geleistet? Wären Sie in die Partei eingetreten? Was wäre Ihnen wohl passiert? Hätten Sie für oder gegen den Staat demonstriert, als der Zusammenbruch begann? Wären Sie sofort ausgewandert, als es möglich wurde?

Schreibecke Was ich in Mitteleuropa unbedingt sehen müsste.

Hier finden Sie eine Liste von wichtigen Städten, Flüssen und Sehenswürdigkeiten, die in ***Vorsprung*** erwähnt worden sind. Was würden Sie auf einer Europareise unbedingt sehen wollen? Schreiben Sie einen kurzen Aufsatz und erklären Sie, warum es für Sie wichtig wäre, diesen Ort zu besuchen.

- das Goethehaus in Frankfurt/Main
- der Reichstag
- die Universität in Tübingen
- Bad Krozingen
- der Dresdner Zwinger
- die Berliner Mauer
- Zürich in der Schweiz
- die Romantische Straße
- Wien
- St. Pauli in Hamburg
- ein Konzentrationslager
- der Kölner Dom
- das Brandenburger Tor
- Berlin-Mitte
- der Rhein
- Waldhäuser-Ost in Tübingen
- Bismarcks Grab
- Stuttgart
- das Heidelberger Schloss
- Braunwald in der Schweiz
- die Alster in Hamburg
- Weinheim
- die Nikolaikirche in Leipzig
- die Quadratenstadt Mannheim
- die Deutsche Bank in Frankfurt/Main
- das Schloss Sanssouci in Potsdam
- die Elbe

Wortschatz

Berlin

der Bummel, - *walk, leisurely stroll*
die Bundesrepublik Deutschland *Federal Republic of Germany*
die Deutsche Demokratische Republik (DDR) *German Democratic Republic (GDR)*
der Dom, -e *cathedral*
die (Kaiser-Wilhelm-) Gedächtniskirche *(Kaiser Wilhelm) Memorial Church*
die Kleinigkeit, -en *trifle, a little something; detail*
die Mauer, -n *(exterior) wall*
die Mitte, -n *middle*
das Parlament, -e *parliament*
die Philharmonie *(Berlin) Philharmonic Orchestra*
der Platz, ¨-e *plaza, square*
der Reichstag *German Parliament (1871–1933)*
die Republik, -en *republic*
der Rest, -e *rest, remainder*
die Szene, -n *scene; "in-crowd"*
der Teil, -e *part, portion*
das Tor, -e *gate*
das Brandenburger Tor *Brandenburg Gate*
die Umbauarbeit, -en *renovation work, remodeling*
die Verspätung *delay, late arrival, tardiness*
das Viertel, - *quarter, district, neighborhood*
der Wunsch, ¨-e *wish, request*
das Zentrum, *pl.* **Zentren** *center*

ab·reißen (riss ab, hat abgerissen) *to tear down, demolish*
ahnen (hat geahnt) *to guess, suspect, sense*
an·fangen (fängt an, fing an, hat angefangen) *to begin, start*
entschuldigen (hat entschuldigt) *to excuse, pardon*
entstehen (entstand, ist entstanden) *to originate; to be built*
hoch·laufen (läuft hoch, lief hoch, ist hochgelaufen) *to walk up (a street)*
klingen (klang, hat geklungen) *to sound*
renovieren (hat renoviert) *to renovate, remodel*
schwärmen (hat geschwärmt) von + *dat.* *to rave about, be wild about*
sich verabreden (hat sich verabredet) mit + *dat.* *to make a date with*
vor·haben (hat vor, hatte vor, hat vorgehabt) *to plan, have planned*
vor·schlagen (schlägt vor, schlug vor, hat vorgeschlagen) *to suggest*

fantastisch *fantastic*
frustrierend *frustrating*
gedeckt *set*
geschlossen *closed*
lebendig *lively, alive*
übermorgen *the day after tomorrow*
verabredet *commited; have a date*

Ausdrücke

abgemacht! *deal! agreed!*
an deiner Stelle ... *if I were you . . .*
Ich hätte das gleich ahnen sollen. *I should have guessed it right off.*
Ich hätte dich warnen sollen. *I should have warned you.*
Ich hätte (sie) gern gesehen! *I would have liked seeing (it)!*
Pass mal auf! *Look here! Now listen up!*
... und so *. . . and stuff like that*
zum größten Teil *for the most part*

Regierung und Politik

der / die Abgeordnete, -n *(adjective as noun) representative*
der Bund *alliance; federal government*
der Bundespräsident [-en] / die Bundespräsidentin *Federal President*
der Bundesrat *Federal Council*
die Bundesregierung *Federal Government*
der Bundestag *Federal Parliament*
der Bürger, - *citizen*
der Bürgermeister, - / die Bürgermeisterin, -nen *mayor*
der Diktator, -en *dictator*
die Diktatur, -en *dictatorship*
der Führer, - *leader (of Nazi Party)*
das Grundgesetz *basic law, constitution*
der Kaiser, - / die Kaiserin, -nen *emperor, empress*
der Kanzler, - / die Kanzlerin, -nen *chancellor*
das Königtum, ¨-er *kingdom*
die Monarchie, -n *monarchy*
das Reich, -e *empire; realm*
die Republik, -en *republic*
der Wähler, - / die Wählerin, -nen *voter*
der Widerstand *resistance*

Zeittafel für Berlin

das Abkommen, - *treaty*
die Alliierten *(pl.) the Allies*
die Arbeitsnorm, -en *work quota/standard*
die (Rote) Armee, -n *(Red) army*
der Aufstand, ¨-e *revolt, uprising*
die Besatzungszone, -n *occupation zone*
die Blockade, -n *blockade*
die Einheit, -en *unity*
die Führung, -en *leadership*
die Grenze, -n *border*
die Gründung, -en *founding*
die Hauptstadt, ¨-e *capital city*
die Luftbrücke, -n *airlift*
die Machtergreifung *Nazi seizure of power*
der Nationalsozialist, [-en], -en *National Socialist, Nazi*
der Rang, ¨-e *rank, standing*
der Regierungsantritt, -e *taking office, rise to power*
die Siegermacht, ¨-e *victor, victorious foreign power*
die Sowjetunion (UdSSR) *Soviet Union (USSR)*
der Transit *transit*
das Unternehmen, - *undertaking, project, operation*
die Vereinigung, -en *union, unification*
der Weltkrieg, -e *world war*

aus·rufen (rief aus, hat ausgerufen) *to proclaim, announce*
bei·treten (tritt bei, trat bei, ist beigetreten) + *dat. to join, become a member*
besetzen (hat besetzt) *to occupy*
erhöhen (hat erhöht) *to raise, increase*
erobern (hat erobert) *to conquer, capture*
öffnen (hat geöffnet) *to open*
reagieren (hat reagiert) *to react*
regeln (hat geregelt) *to regulate*
spalten (hat gespaltet) *to separate*
statt·finden (fand statt, hat stattgefunden) *to take place, occur*
teilen (hat geteilt) *to divide*
verwalten (hat verwaltet) *to administrate*
zerstören (hat zerstört) *to destroy*

gemeinsam *in partnership, together*
überraschend *surprising(ly)*
vollendet *completed*

Die deutschen Bundesländer

Baden-Württemberg *Baden-Württemberg*
Bayern *Bavaria*
Berlin *Berlin*
Brandenburg *Brandenburg*
Bremen *Bremen*
Hamburg *Hamburg*
Hessen *Hesse*
Mecklenburg-Vorpommern *Mecklenburg-Western Pomerania*
Niedersachsen *Lower Saxony*
Nordrhein-Westfalen *North Rhine-Westphalia*
Rheinland-Pfalz *Rhineland-Palatinate*
Saarland *Saarland*
Sachsen *Saxony*
Sachsen-Anhalt *Saxony-Anhalt*
Schleswig-Holstein *Schleswig-Holstein*
Thüringen *Thuringia*

Die Hauptflüsse Deutschlands

die Donau *Danube River*
die Elbe *Elbe River*
der Main *Main River*
die Mosel *Moselle River*
die Neiße *Neisse River*
die Oder *Oder River*
der Rhein *Rhine River*
die Weser *Weser River*

„Maikäfer flieg!"

die Armbanduhr, -en *wrist watch*
der Bombenangriff, -e *bombardment, bombing attack*
der Eisenbahnzug, ¨-e *train*
die Flak (Flugabwehrkanone) *flak, anti-aircraft weapon*
der Granatsplitter, - *grenade shell, shrapnel*
das Gift, -e *poison*
der Güterwaggon, -s *freight car*
der Haufen, - *heap, pile*
die Hausleiter, -n *fire escape*
das Holz, ¨-er *wood*
der Kampfverband, ¨-e *fighting unit*
der Kellerhocker, - *person staying in an air-raid shelter*
der Kellerwinkel, - *corner of the cellar*
die Kohle, -n *coal*
die Lade, -n (Schublade) *drawer*
das Lazarett, -e *military hospital*
der Luftschutzkeller, - *air-raid cellar*
die Luftschutzsirene, -n *air-raid siren*
die Menge, -n *here: a bunch of; crowd*
der Schatz, ¨-e *treasure*
die Schiene, -n *train track*
die Schreibstube, -n *office*
der Schutt *rubble*
der Tiefflieger, - *low-flying (fighter) plane*
der Unteroffizier *non-commissioned officer*
der Urlaubsschein, -e *pass for leave*
der Ziegelstein, -e *brick*
der Zufall, ¨-e *coincidence*

ab·schießen (schoss ab, hat abgeschossen) *to shoot down*
aus·fallen (fällt aus, fiel aus, ist ausgefallen) *to be canceled*
brüllen (hat gebrüllt) *to yell*
ein·schlagen (schlägt ein, schlug ein, ist eingeschlagen) *to strike, impact*
ein·stürzen (ist eingestürzt) *to collapse*
sich empören (hat sich empört) *to become indignant*
heizen (hat geheizt) *to heat*
herum·humpeln (ist herumgehumpelt) *to hobble around*
heulen (hat geheult) *to howl*
hüten (hat gehütet) *to guard, protect*
jammern (hat gejammert) *to whine; to lament*
nicken (hat genickt) *to nod*
treten (tritt, trat, hat getreten) *to kick*
vergiften (hat vergiftet) *to poison*

verlassen (verlässt, verließ, hat verlassen) *to leave a place*
wagen (hat gewagt) *to dare, risk*
weg·räumen (hat weggeräumt) *to clear away*
zu·stimmen (hat zugestimmt) + *dat. to agree with someone*

begraben *buried*
drunt' (darunter) *down below*
verschüttet sein *to be blocked in*
zerbombt *bombed out*
zerbrochen *broken to pieces*
zerschlagen *all beat up*
zerschossen *all shot up*

Genitivpräpositionen

(an)statt *instead of*
außerhalb *outside of*
innerhalb *inside of*
trotz *in spite of*
während *during*
wegen *because of*

Aus dem Zieltext

das Bruttosozialprodukt, -e *gross national product (GNP)*
der Einfluss, *(pl.)* **Einflüsse** *influence*
der Fall, ¨-e *case*
der/die Familienangehörige,-n *family member*
der Kontakt, -e *contact, communication*
die Rente, -n *pension*
die Schizophrenie *schizophrenia*
der Staat, -en *state, government*
die Stimmung, -en *atmosphere, mood*
die Verwandtschaft *relatives*
die Wende *turning point; here: time before unification*
die Zunge, -n *tongue*
aufrecht·erhalten (erhält aufrecht, erhielt aufrecht, hat aufrecht erhalten) *to maintain, preserve*
aus·wandern (ist ausgewandert) *to emigrate*
sich identifizieren (hat identifiziert) mit + *dat. to identify with something*
klappen (hat geklappt) *to work out all right*
leisten (hat geleistet) *to achieve, accomplish*

Adjektive und Adverbien

euphorisch *euphoric*
umgekehrt *the other way around, vice versa*
verschieden *different*

Ausdrücke

im Gegenteil *in opposition, contrary to*
mit zwei Zungen sprechen *to talk out of both sides of one's mouth*
sonst wo (sonst irgendwo) *somewhere else*
von früh an *from early on, from a young age*

In this chapter you will learn to speculate about situations and talk about environmental concerns. You will read and talk about the European Union and Austria, which joined the EU in 1995. You will also have an opportunity to review the people you have met in *Vorsprung.*

Kommunikative Funktionen

- Talking about unreal situations
- Expressing the purpose of an action
- Expressing how actions are to be done
- Describing a state or condition

Strukturen

- Subjunctive II
- The conjunctions **um … zu, ohne … zu**
- Modal verbs with the passive voice
- The statal passive

Vokabeln

- Mitgliedschaft in der Europäischen Union
- Österreichische Leute und Länder
- Die Umwelt

Kulturelles

- Die Europäische Union und die Zukunft Europas
- Österreichs Geschichte
- Österreichs kulturelles Leben

Deutschland spielt eine zentrale Rolle in der Europäischen Union.

KAPITEL ZWÖLF

Das neue Europa

Go to the ***Vorsprung*** Website at **www.hmco.com/college**

ANLAUFTEXT

Stefan und Anna sprechen über ihre Zukunft

Seit Anna den Betriebswirtschaftsstudenten Stefan im Studentenwohnheim kennen gelernt hat, verbringt sie viel Zeit mit ihm. Annas Aufenthalt in Deutschland geht bald zu Ende, aber Anna und Stefan wollen den Kontakt auch nach Annas Rückkehr in die USA aufrechterhalten. Stefan hofft, dass er später einmal eine Stelle bei einer internationalen Organisation findet und dass er im Ausland – vielleicht in den USA – arbeiten kann. Deswegen hat er sich für ein Praktikum bei der UNO in Wien beworben. Stefan bekommt die folgende Antwort: Er kann nächstes Jahr bei der UNO in Wien als Praktikant° arbeiten. Anna wird sich für das Bundestag-Internship-Programm bewerben, damit sie wieder nach Deutschland zurückkommen kann. Sie spricht mit Stefan vor seinem Postfach im Wohnheim.

intern

Deutscher Bundestag Internationale Parlaments - Praktika (IPP) Internship Programm provides an opportunity for young Americans interested in politics to learn about the German political system. The program is financed by the German **Bundestag** and is conducted with the cooperation of the **Humboldt Universität zu Berlin**. Applicants serve as interns in the German **Bundestag** and attend courses at the university. Applicants must be American citizens with a B.A. degree who speak good German.

Vorschau

1 Thematische Fragen. Beantworten Sie die folgenden Fragen auf Deutsch.

1. Was sind Ihre Pläne für die nächsten Semester?
2. Was möchten Sie am liebsten nach dem Studium machen? Ins Ausland fahren? Eine feste Arbeitsstelle finden? Eine Familie gründen?
3. Welche Möglichkeiten haben Sie, neben dem Studium Berufserfahrung zu sammeln°: ein Praktikum machen, eine Assistentenstelle suchen, an einem Projekt arbeiten?
4. Haben Sie durch Ihre Universität Gelegenheit, im Ausland zu arbeiten?

obtain

5. Was ist Ihrer Meinung nach wichtiger – viel Geld verdienen oder anderen Menschen helfen? Warum?
6. Können Sie sich eine internationale Karriere vorstellen: im politischen Bereich (UNO, World Court, EU), im sozialen Bereich (Internationales Rotes Kreuz, Amnesty International, UNICEF, CARE), im Handel (IBM, BMW, BASF, DaimlerChrysler, Citibank)?

2 **Satzdetektiv.** Welche Sätze bedeuten ungefähr das Gleiche?

1. Stefan sagt: Ich bin bei der UNO als Praktikant angenommen worden.
   a. Stefan darf in einem EU-Land studieren.
   b. Stefan ist jetzt bei der UNO Manager.
   c. Die UNO hat Stefan ein Praktikum angeboten.
2. Stefan sagt: … ein Praktikum bei der UNO wäre eine ideale Gelegenheit, internationale Erfahrungen zu sammeln.
   a. In einem Praktikum bei den Vereinten Nationen würde Stefan viel Theoretisches lernen.
   b. In einem Praktikum bei den Vereinten Nationen würde Stefan Wichtiges für den späteren Beruf lernen.
   c. Ein Praktikum bei den Vereinten Nationen würde viel Geld kosten.
3. Stefan sagt: Und die USA klingen immer attraktiver, seitdem mir eine gewisse Amerikanerin bekannt ist …
   a. Stefan hält nicht viel von einem Aufenthalt in den USA, seitdem er Anna kennt.
   b. Stefan hält viel von einem Aufenthalt in den USA, seitdem er Anna kennt.
   c. Stefan hält nicht viel von einem Aufenthalt in den USA, seitdem er Amerika kennt.

Die USA is always used with a plural verb in German.

4. Stefan sagt: Ach, du wolltest dich ja für dieses Bundestag-Programm bewerben.
   a. Anna möchte das Bundestag-Programm organisieren.
   b. Anna möchte eine Stelle im Bundestag-Programm bekommen.
   c. Anna möchte Abgeordnete im Bundestag werden.
5. Anna sagt: Sogar mein Vater hat gesagt, es wäre Wahnsinn, auf eine solche Gelegenheit zu verzichten.
   a. Anna würde einen Fehler machen, wenn sie sich nicht für das Programm bewerben würde.
   b. Annas Vater sagt, sie ist verrückt.
   c. Es wäre blöd°, wenn Anna als Assistentin arbeiten würde.

dumm

6. Stefan sagt: Kannst du vielleicht deine Eltern bitten, dir die Unterlagen zu schicken?
   a. Anna kann ihren Eltern sagen, sie sollten ihr die Papiere für die Bewerbung schicken.
   b. Anna kann ihren Eltern ihre Papiere schicken.
   c. Anna kann ihre Eltern bitten, einen Flugschein zu schicken.
7. Anna sagt: Ich wünschte, ich wüsste das genau.
   a. Anna möchte das genau wissen.
   b. Anna möchte das gar nicht wissen.
   c. Anna weiß es schon.

ANLAUFTEXT

Hören Sie gut zu.

Stefan und Anna sprechen über ihre Zukunft

Rückblick

3 **Stimmt das?** Stimmen diese Aussagen zum Text oder nicht? Wenn nicht, was stimmt?

Anlauftext. The German **Bundestag** was relocated from Bonn to Berlin in 1999.

	Ja, das stimmt.	*Nein, das stimmt nicht.*
1. Stefan ist als Praktikant bei der UNO akzeptiert worden.	___	___
2. Im Frühling geht Stefan zur UNO nach Genf.	___	___
3. Dr. Osswald meinte, ein Praktikum bei der UNO wäre der ideale Start für Stefans internationale Karriere.	___	___
4. Dr. Osswald meinte auch, mit dieser Erfahrung hätte Stefan bessere Chancen, eine feste Stelle bei der UNO in Genf oder New York zu bekommen.	___	___
5. Stefan findet eine Stelle in den USA attraktiv.	___	___
6. Es könnte passieren°, dass Anna zur gleichen Zeit als Assistentin im Bundestag nach Deutschland zurückkehren° würde.	___	___

happen

return

	Ja, das stimmt.	*Nein, das stimmt nicht.*
7. Annas Vater ist dagegen. Bob Adler meint, es wäre Wahnsinn, wenn Anna nach Deutschland zurückgehen würde.	___	___
8. Anna hat alle Unterlagen für das Programm und weiß über alles Bescheid.	___	___
9. Annas Eltern wollen ihr die Unterlagen fürs Bundestag-Programm nicht schicken.	___	___
10. Stefan und Anna wollen nicht so weit voneinander entfernt° sein.	___	___

far apart

4 Ergänzen Sie. Ergänzen Sie diese Sätze mit Wörtern aus dem **Anlauftext.**

1. Stefan hat gute Nachrichten von der UNO ____.
2. Stefan ist als ____ bei der UNO in Wien angenommen worden.
3. Die Situation ist für Stefan wirklich ____.
4. Ein Praktikum bei der UNO ist die ideale ____, internationale Erfahrungen zu ____.
5. Später hat er dann gute Chancen, eine feste ____ bei der UNO zu finden.
6. Die USA ____ für Stefan immer attraktiver, seitdem er Anna kennt.
7. Anna fragt Stefan, was ____ würde, wenn sie zu der Zeit nach Deutschland zurückkäme.
8. Anna will sich für das Bundestag-Programm ____.
9. Sogar Annas Vater meint, es wäre Wahnsinn, auf diese Gelegenheit zu ____.
10. Anna glaubt, die Bewerbung muss im Herbst ____ werden, aber sie weiß es nicht genau.
11. Stefan meint, die Adlers können Anna die ____ aus Amerika zuschicken.
12. Aber wenn sie das tun, muss Anna ihnen erklären, warum sie sich für internationale ____ interessiert.

5 Kurz gefragt: Vorbereitungen auf den Beruf. Beantworten Sie diese Fragen auf Deutsch.

Kurz gefragt. Review reflexive verbs (Chapter 8).

1. Was hat Stefan gerade erfahren?
2. Wo wird er denn nächstes Jahr sein?
3. Was sagt Dr. Osswald über Stefans Stelle?
4. Was ist der persönliche Grund, warum Stefan in den USA arbeiten möchte?
5. Was will Anna im kommenden Jahr machen?
6. Wann muss sich Anna für das Programm bewerben?

6 Autogrammspiel: Karrieren. Finden Sie für jede Frage eine Person, die mit **Ja** antwortet. Bitten Sie die Person um ihre Unterschrift.

S1: Hättest du Interesse an einer Praktikantenstelle?
S2: Ja.
S1: Unterschreib hier bitte. ____________

1. Hättest du Interesse an einer Praktikantenstelle? ____________
2. Hast du schon einmal ein Praktikum gemacht? ____________

3. Hast du vor, eine Praktikantenstelle zu suchen? ________________
4. Würdest du dich für eine internationale Karriere interessieren? ________________
5. Würdest du ohne Bezahlung arbeiten, wenn du in einer Stelle viele Erfahrungen sammeln könntest? ________________
6. Würdest du eine Zeit lang für wenig Geld für eine karitative° Organisation arbeiten? ________________
7. Würdest du eine Stelle annehmen, von der deine Eltern wenig oder nichts halten? ________________
8. Würdest du eine neue Sprache lernen, damit du eine neue Stelle bekommen könntest? ________________
9. Würdest du eine Stelle annehmen, damit du bei Freunden/deiner Familie wohnen könntest? ________________

Twelve other countries have applied for membership to the European Union: Bulgaria, Cyprus, the Czech Republic, Estonia, Hungary, Latvia, Lithuania, Malta, Poland, Romania, Slovakia and Slovenia.

charity

The economic force of the EU has prompted other efforts at economic unity, most notably the North American Free Trade Agreement (NAFTA) between the U.S.A., Canada, and Mexico in 1994.

BRENNPUNKT KULTUR

Die Europäische Union und die Zukunft Europas

Efforts to unify Europe economically and politically continue under the structure of the European Union **(die Europäische Union).** Beginning with a series of economic agreements in the early 50s that established the European (Economic) Community **(die Europäische Wirtschaftsgemeinschaft),** European countries have gradually moved toward greater unification. In the process each country has had to relinquish more control of its national laws in exchange for international uniformity. An agreement enacted on November 1, 1993, changed the name of the community to the **Europäische Union,** and extended the areas of cooperation beyond economic issues to foreign and defense policy **(die Außen- und Sicherheitspolitik)** and judicial and internal security policy **(die Justiz- und Innenpolitik).** As of 1996, 15 European countries belonged to the European Union, while several additional countries had applied for membership. While retaining their own national parliaments, each country also sends representatives to **das Europäische Parlament,** located in Strasbourg, France. European unity allows the almost unrestricted movement of goods, people, and services across national borders. The greatest single unifier of all, a common currency called **der Euro,** may indeed prove to be the biggest hurdle to complete unity. Introduced in 1999, the Euro has steadily lost value and popularity among Europeans (such as the British and the Danes) who oppose elimination of their national currencies in 2002.

Daten zur Europäischen Union

Land	A Österreich	B Belgien	D Deutschland	DK Dänemark	E Spanien	F Frankreich	GB Groß-brit.	GR Griechenland	I Italien	IRL Irland	L Luxemburg	NL Niederlande	P Portugal	S Schweden	SF Finnland	EU15
Fläche in 1000qkm	83,9	30,5	356,9	43,1	504,8	544,0	244,1	132,0	301,3	70,3	2,6	41,2	92,4	450,0	337,1	3 234,2
Bevölkerung in Mio. 1993	7,9	10,1	80,6	5,2	39,1	57,5	58,0	10,3	56,9	3,6	0,4	15,2	9,9	8,7	5,1	368,5
Bruttoinlandsprodukt je Einwohner in Tsd. ECU 1993	19,5	17,8	20,1	22,3	10,4	18,6	13,9	7,4	14,6	11,3	26,9	17,3	7,3	18,3	14,1	16,0
Sitze im Europäischen Parlament	21	25	99	16	64	87	87	25	87	15	6	31	25	22	16	626
Stimmen im Rat bei qualifizierter Mehrheit	4	5	10	3	8	10	10	5	10	3	2	5	5	4	3	87

Quelle: eurostat

7 **Fakten über die EU.** Beantworten Sie mit Hilfe der Tabellen die Fragen über die EU.

1. Welches Land hat die meisten Einwohner?
2. Welche westeuropäischen Länder sind nicht in der EU?
3. Gehören Polen, Ungarn oder Russland zur EU?
4. Ist die EU größer oder kleiner als die USA?
5. Wo wohnen mehr Menschen – in der EU oder in den USA?

Die EU im Vergleich

	EU 15[1]	USA	Japan
Fläche in 1000 qkm	3 234	9 373	378
Bevölkerung in Mio. 1993	368,5	258,8	125,5
BIP/Kopf in Tsd. ECU 1993	16,2	19,6	25,5
Export 1993 in Mio. ECU	621,5	397,1	308,3
Import 1993 in Mio. ECU	583,4	634,5	205,8

1)Für Daten vor 1995: 12 EU-Staaten und Finnland, Österreich, Schweden; Export und Import: nur Drittländer, ohne Intra-Handel der Staaten untereinander

Strukturen und Vokabeln

I Talking about unreal situations

Subjunctive

You learned in Chapter 11 how to use the auxiliary verb **würde** + infinitive to talk about a hypothetical situation in the present tense and how to use the auxiliary verbs **hätte** and **wäre** + a past participle to talk about hypothetical situations in the past tense.

An deiner Stelle **würde** ich einen Bummel auf dem Ku'damm machen.
If I were you, I would go for a stroll on the Ku'damm.
Ich **hätte** die Mauer so gern **gesehen.**
I would have really liked to see the wall.
Das **wäre** schön **gewesen.**
That would have been nice.

This subjunctive form is called the subjunctive II **(Konjunktiv zwei)** to distinguish it from the subjunctive I **(Konjunktiv eins),** which will not be practiced in this book. An explanation of the formation of the subjunctive II is discussed below in section B.

A. *Expressing unreal conditions:* Wenn-*clauses*

A conditional sentence **(der Konditionalsatz)** consists of two parts: the condition expressed in the **wenn**-clause and the conclusion. When a conditional sentence expresses a fact, the indicative form of the verb is used.

Wenn es **regnet, gehen** wir nicht spazieren.	*If it rains, we won't go for a walk.*
Wenn er sein Geld **findet, kann** er das kaufen.	*If he finds his money, he will be able to buy it.*

A conditional sentence may also express a hypothetical, unreal, or contrary-to-fact situation **(irrealer Konditionalsatz).** In this case the subjunctive II is always used.

Anna **würde** mehr machen, wenn sie mehr Zeit **hätte.**	*Anna would do more if she had more time. (But she has no time, so she can't do more.)*
Was **würde** passieren, wenn ich zu der Zeit nach Deutschland **zurückkäme?**	*What would happen if I came back to Germany at that time? (I'm not sure I will return to Germany.)*

The **wenn**-clause with the conjugated verb in final position frequently introduces the conditional sentence. The main clause with the conjugated verb in the first position follows the **wenn**-clause. This results in two conjugated verbs occurring side by side.

Wenn er netter **wäre, würde** ich ihn öfter anrufen.	*If he were nicer, I would call him more often. (But he's not nice, so I won't call him.)*

Informal, spoken German allows the use of **würde** in **wenn**-clauses while more formal, written German requires the single subjunctive II verb form.

Formal writing: Das wäre natürlich ganz toll, wenn du nach Amerika **kämest.** *Informal speech:* Das wäre natürlich ganz toll, wenn du nach Amerika **kommen würdest.**	*That would of course be just great if you came (would come) to America.*

In formal English, too, it is considered improper to use **would** in an **if**-clause, but it is very common in speech (e.g., If she would come to Austria . . .)

To express hypothetical past tense events, German speakers use the past tense of the subjunctive II.

Wenn Anna nicht nach Tübingen **gekommen wäre, hätte** sie Stefan nicht **kennen gelernt.**
If Anna had not come to Tübingen, she would not have met Stefan. (But she came to Tübingen and she met him.)

B. *Subjunctive II forms of regular, irregular, and mixed verbs*

Each verb bases its subjunctive II form on the narrative past tense form of the verb. The narrative past form is usually the second form listed in traditional verb charts.

German has another subjunctive form, the subjunctive I **(Konjunktiv I).** Speakers use it primarily for indirect speech, but since the subjunctive II frequently replaces the subjunctive I in indirect speech, it is not discussed in this book. The most common form is **sei** (< **sein).**

Infinitive	Narrative past	Subjunctive II
haben	hatte	hätte
sein	war	wäre
werden	wurde	würde

In speech, German speakers mostly use **würde** when expressing hypothetical situations in the present tense.

Due to the similarity of the subjunctive II and the narrative past indicative of weak verbs and to the fact that native speakers do not often use these forms, only the **würde**-form will be practiced for production.

1. Regular (weak) verbs

Regular (weak) verbs are identical in the past tense and in the subjunctive II, adding **-te** and the endings **st, -n,** or **-t** to the stem. These are the subjunctive II forms of **machen.**

Person	Singular	**machen:** *to do; to make*	Plural	
1st	ich mach**te**	*(if) I did*	wir mach**ten**	*(if) we did*
2nd, informal	du mach**test**	*(if) you did*	ihr mach**tet**	*(if) you did*
2nd, formal	Sie mach**ten**	*(if) you did*	Sie mach**ten**	*(if) you did*
3rd	er/sie/es mach**te**	*(if) he/she/it did*	sie mach**ten**	*(if) they did*

Because of the similarity between the narrative past and the subjunctive II of regular verbs, German speakers prefer to use **würde** + infinitive in the subjunctive II.

> Wenn ich Zeit **hätte, machte** ich einen Bummel auf dem Kurfürstendamm.
> Wenn ich Zeit **hätte, würde** ich einen Bummel auf dem Kurfürstendamm **machen.**
> *If I had time, I would go for a stroll on the Kurfürstendamm.*

8 **Was würde Stefan (Anna) machen, wenn ...?** Fragen Sie einen Partner/eine Partnerin, was Anna oder Stefan in den folgenden Situationen machen würde. Fragen Sie dann, was Ihr Partner/Ihre Partnerin machen würde. Benutzen Sie **würde** + Infinitiv.

Was würde Stefan (Anna) machen, wenn ... You should recognize the verbs in both **Tabellen** as the subjunctive II forms of common weak verbs.

S1: Was würde Stefan machen, wenn er mehr Geld hätte?
S2: Wenn Stefan mehr Geld hätte, würde er eine Reise machen.
S1: Was würdest du machen, wenn du mehr Geld hättest?
S2: Ich würde (ins Ausland reisen).

Tabelle A (S1):

Wenn er/sie ...	Stefan	Anna	Partner(in)
mehr Geld hätte	?	kaufte sie ein neues Auto	_____
mehr Zeit hätte	besuchte er seine Eltern	?	_____
Lust hätte	schickte er Anna Blumen	?	_____
Freunde in Berlin hätte	?	wohnte sie ein Jahr lang dort	_____
die Unterlagen hätte	schickte er sie ein	?	_____
mit dem Studium fertig wäre	?	bezahlte sie nichts mehr dafür	_____

Tabelle B (S2):

Wenn er/sie …	Stefan	Anna	Partner(in)
mehr Geld hätte	machte er eine Reise	?	______
mehr Zeit hätte	?	besuchte sie die Günthers	______
Lust hätte	?	lernte sie Spanisch	______
Freunde in Berlin hätte	hörte er auf, in Tübingen zu studieren	?	______
die Unterlagen hätte	?	reichte sie sie ein	
mit dem Studium fertig wäre	arbeitete er im Ausland	?	______

2. Irregular (strong) verbs

The subjunctive II forms of irregular (strong) verbs add the endings **-e, -est, -en,** or **-et** to the stem of the narrative past verb **(Präteritum).** Stems with **a, o,** and **u** also add an umlaut.

Infinitive	*Narrative past*	*Subjunctive II*	*Meaning*
kommen	er kam	er **käme**	*if he came/would come*

These are the subjunctive II forms of **kommen.**

	kommen: *to come*			
Person	**Singular**		**Plural**	
1st	ich **käme**	*(if) I came*	wir **kämen**	*(if) we came*
2nd, informal	du **kämest**	*(if) you came*	ihr **kämet**	*(if) you came*
2nd, formal	Sie **kämen**	*(if) you came*	Sie **kämen**	*(if) you came*
3rd	er/sie/es **käme**	*(if) he/she/it came*	sie **kämen**	*(if) they came*

The following chart lists the most frequently used irregular (strong) verbs in the subjunctive II. There are many other subjunctive II forms that German speakers generally avoid in speech because they are archaic, (e.g., **hülfe**), or because they sound like non-subjunctive forms (e.g., **nähme** vs. **nehme**).

Infinitive	Subjunctive II	Infinitive	Subjunctive II
bleiben	**bliebe**	kommen	**käme**
fahren	**führe**	nehmen	**nähme**
finden	**fände**	sprechen	**spräche**
geben	**gäbe**	stehen	**stünde**
gehen	**ginge**	tun	**täte**

Wenn es etwas zu Essen **gäbe, bliebe** ich hier. — *If there were something to eat, I would stay here.*

Es **ginge** mir besser, wenn wir nicht so weit **führen.** — *I would feel better if we wouldn't drive so far.*

3. Mixed verbs

Mixed verbs add **-te** to the stem like regular verbs. Some have a vowel change like irregular verbs in the subjunctive II, and others do not. The only mixed verb that is used with any frequency is **wüsste.** The others almost always occur with **würde,** e.g., **würde bringen, würde denken.**

Infinitive	Subjunctive II
bringen	br**ä**chte
denken	d**ä**chte
kennen	kennte
nennen	nennte
rennen	rennte
wissen	w**ü**sste

9 **Es wäre schön, wenn ...** Stefan und Anna spekulieren über eine gemeinsame Zukunft, besonders über die Stelle in New York bei der UNO.

> **Es wäre schön, wenn ...** Use the **würde**-construction in **wenn**-clauses since this is what most native speakers do, except when the verb is **hätte** or **wäre.**
>
> The verb **gehen** is used here to mean *to go* or *move permanently* or *to go for a longer period of time.*

S1 (ANNA): Es wäre schön, wenn die Stelle in New York wäre.
S2 (STEFAN): Ja. Wenn die Stelle in New York wäre, würde ich bei Freunden in Manhattan wohnen.

1. wenn die Stelle in New York wäre,
2. wenn du in die USA gehen würdest,
3. wenn dir die UNO in New York die Stelle anbieten würde,
4. wenn das Formular bald ankäme,
5. wenn es eine Möglichkeit gäbe,

a. ich würde mich dafür bewerben
b. wir würden uns öfter sehen
c. ich würde bei Freunden in Manhattan wohnen
d. ich würde es sofort ausfüllen
e. ich würde die Gelegenheit wahrnehmen°

°*take advantage of*

Wissenswerte Vokabeln: Mitgliedschaft in der Europäischen Union

Talking about citizenship and regulations in the European Union

> Turkey has not yet become a member of the EU.
>
> All Germans carry a **Personalausweis.**
>
> Every worker must apply for a **Lohnsteuerkarte** *(income tax card).* Taxes on earnings are automatically deducted from one's wages.

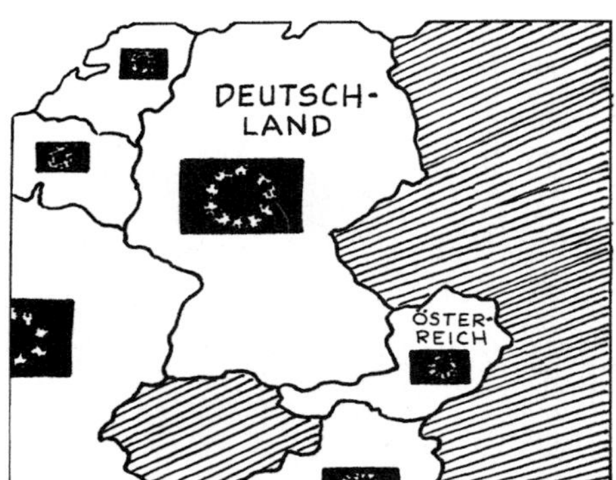

Österreich (seit 1. Jan. 1995) und Deutschland sind Mitgliedstaaten der Europäischen Union.

Kazim kommt aus der Türkei. Er ist türkischer Staatsbürger.

Weil Kazim eine Arbeitsstelle bei Ford in Köln bekommt, braucht er als Arbeitnehmer eine Arbeitserlaubnis für Deutschland.

Auf der Ausländerbehörde bekommt er einen Stempel in seinen Pass.

W. Vok. According to German law, citizenship is based on one's heritage (*ius sanguinis* — the right of blood) and not on the location of birth (*ius soli* — the law of one's birthplace, as in the U.S.). Ethnic Germans whose families have lived for centuries in Russia have returned to Germany since the collapse of communism to reclaim German citizenship, while Turks and others who were born and have been raised in Germany are not automatically entitled to German citizenship.

Auf dem Finanzamt beantragt er eine Lohnsteuerkarte. Die Steuer wird regelmäßig von seinem Gehalt abgezogen.

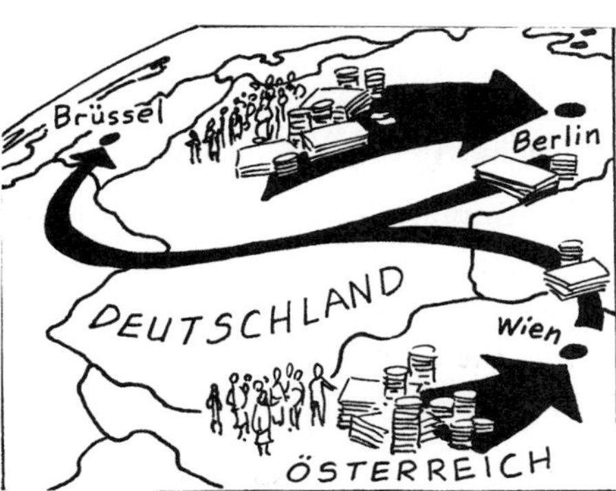

Die Einwohner Deutschlands und Österreichs zahlen Steuern an den Staat. Der Staat schickt eine Abgabe° an die EU.

tax, duty

Wenn die Türkei Mitglied der EU wäre, würde Kazim keine Arbeitserlaubnis für Deutschland brauchen.

Auch wenn Kazim in Deutschland geboren wäre, wäre er vor dem 1. Januar 2000 nicht automatisch deutscher Staatsangehöriger.

Since Jan. 1, 2000 children of foreign-born workers born in Germany automatically become German citizens.

Warum braucht Kazim eine Arbeitserlaubnis?

10 **Staatsbürgerliche Verantwortungen.** Ergänzen Sie die Sätze mit den Wörtern aus der Liste.

Jahresabgaben • Ausländerbehörde • Staatsbürger • Lohnsteuerkarte • Mitgliedstaat • Personalausweis • Stempel

1. Frankreich ist ein _____ der EU.
2. Die Günthers und die Müllers sind alle _____ Deutschlands.
3. Weil Anna Adler Ausländerin ist, muss sie zur _____ gehen und einen _____ in ihren Reisepass bekommen.
4. In Deutschland hat jeder Einwohner einen _____.
5. Alle Arbeitnehmer brauchen eine _____ und eine Nummer, damit die Steuern abgezogen werden können.
6. Die EU-_____ der reichsten EU-Staaten helfen den anderen Mitgliedstaaten.

11 **Kandidatin für eine Arbeitsstelle in der EU.** Die internationale Möbelfirma Lagler & Co. in Klagenfurt sucht Mitarbeiter/Mitarbeiterinnen für ihre Niederlassung° in England. Man erwägt° Tina McMurray, eine Kandidatin aus Kanada, die zur Zeit in Österreich wohnt. Doch leider gibt es einige Hindernisse°. In der zweiten Spalte sind Informationen über Frau McMurray. Benutzen Sie **wenn**-Sätze im Konjunktiv.

branch / considers

obstacles

Kandidatin für eine Arbeitsstelle ... Remember that the subjunctive II forms of the modal verbs are **dürfte, könnte, möchte, müsste, sollte,** and **wollte.**

▣ Wenn Frau McMurray die EU-Bürgerschaft hätte, würde sie keine Arbeitserlaubnis brauchen.

1.	EU-Bürgerschaft:	hat nicht	sie braucht eine Arbeitserlaubnis
2.	Deutschkenntnisse:	nicht gut	wir können uns den Deutschkurs nicht sparen
3.	Arbeitserlaubnis:	hat keine für England	sie ist keine gute Kandidatin
4.	Stempel:	braucht einen für GB	sie kann nicht sofort beginnen
5.	Lohnsteuerkarte:	braucht keine neue	wir machen das nicht für sie
6.	Steuern:	hat letztes Jahr keine bezahlt	sie muss jetzt zum Finanzamt gehen

12 **Interview: Was würdest du gern machen?** Stellen Sie einem Partner/einer Partnerin die folgenden Fragen.

1. Was würdest du gern machen, wenn du als Praktikant arbeiten könntest?
2. Wo würdest du gern wohnen, wenn du die Gelegenheit hättest, im Ausland zu arbeiten?
3. Für welche Stelle würdest du dich bewerben, wenn es Stellen in Berlin, Paris und Tokio gäbe? Warum?
4. Was würdest du gern machen, wenn du fließend° Deutsch sprechen könntest?
5. Wie könntest du dein Deutsch verbessern, wenn du nach dem Studium eine Stelle in Österreich bekommen würdest?
6. Wie viele Jahre würdest du gern im Ausland arbeiten, wenn du die Gelegenheit hättest?
7. Welche Vorteile würde ein Auslandsaufenthalt bieten?

fluently

■ FREIE ■ KOMMUNIKATION ■ **Einerseits° ... anderseits° ...** Suchen Sie zwei andere Studenten/Studentinnen, die das gleiche oder ein ähnliches Hauptfach° wie Sie haben, und bilden Sie eine Gruppe. Besprechen Sie die folgenden Fragen:

On the one hand / on the other hand

major

1. Welche Vorteile könnte ein Praktikum im Ausland in Ihrem Hauptfach haben?
2. Welche Nachteile könnte es haben?
3. Was wäre die beste Gelegenheit?
4. Warum würden Sie gern ein Praktikum im Ausland machen?

C. *Expressing contrary-to-fact wishes: ich wünschte; es wäre nett, wenn*

German speakers express a wish with the subjunctive II. The subjunctive II indicates that an event did not or in all likelihood will not occur. Contrary-to-fact wishes always represent the opposite of the factual indicative statement. Here are three ways to express a wish.

1. **ich wünschte** or **ich wollte**

   Ich wünschte, ich wüsste das genau. *I wish I knew that for sure. (But I don't.)*

2. a **wenn**-clause that usually includes **(doch) nur**

   Ach Stefan, wenn du **nur** nach Amerika kommen könntest! *Oh, Stefan, if only you could come to America. (But you probably can't.)*

3. **es wäre nett/schön/gut, wenn ...**

   Es wäre nett, wenn er kommen würde. *It would be nice, if he would come. (But he won't.)*

To express a wish in the past tense, speakers use the past subjunctive.

Wenn es nur nicht **geregnet hätte!** *If it only hadn't rained! (But it did rain!)*
Ich wünschte, sie **wäre geflogen.** *I wish she had flown. (But she didn't.)*

13 **Wie alles anders sein könnte.** Anna denkt an ihren Freund Stefan. Welche Wünsche hat sie? Benutzen Sie eine der drei Konstruktionen.

Wie alles anders sein könnte. Alternate with a partner in formulating the responses.

■ Die USA und Deutschland sind so weit auseinander.
Wenn die USA und Deutschland nur nicht so weit auseinander wären! (oder)
Ich wünschte, die USA und Deutschland wären nicht so weit auseinander!

1. Die USA und Deutschland sind so weit auseinander.
2. Er wohnt so weit weg.
3. Stefan spricht nicht gut Englisch.
4. Mein Deutsch ist nicht perfekt.
5. Ich muss bald wieder nach Amerika.
6. Es gibt keine Gelegenheit, seine Eltern kennen zu lernen.
7. Ich habe ihn so spät im Jahr näher kennen gelernt.
8. Wir haben wenig Zeit miteinander gehabt.
9. Wir sehen uns nicht oft.
10. Ich weiß nicht, ob wir uns wieder sehen werden.

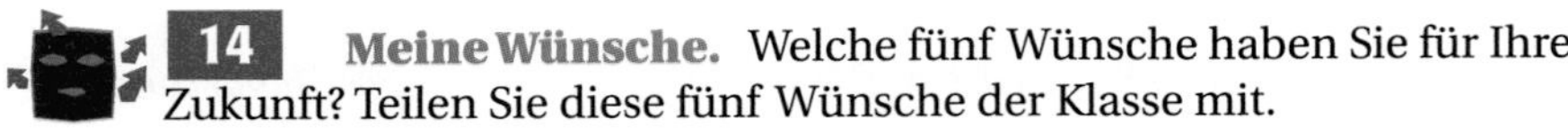

14 **Meine Wünsche.** Welche fünf Wünsche haben Sie für Ihre Zukunft? Teilen Sie diese fünf Wünsche der Klasse mit.

Wenn ich nur mehr Geld hätte!
Ich wünschte, ich würde besser Deutsch sprechen!

1. mehr Geld / Zeit / Freunde haben
2. mehr schlafen/reisen/ausgehen können
3. öfter ins Kino/in die Oper/ins Stadion gehen können
4. besser Deutsch/besser Spanisch/besser Japanisch sprechen/schreiben/verstehen
5. Physik/Mathematik/Philosophie leichter finden
6. meine Familie/meine Freundin/meinen Freund öfter sehen
7. viele Partys/Professoren/Kurse besuchen

15 **Was wäre passiert, wenn ich nicht Deutsch gelernt hätte?** Denken Sie an das letzte Jahr zurück und kreuzen Sie die Aussagen an, die das Jahr beschreiben. Überlegen Sie sich dann, was passiert wäre, wenn Sie etwas *nicht* gemacht hätten.

viele nette Leute kennen gelernt
Wenn ich nicht viele nette Leute kennen gelernt hätte, hätte ich große Schwierigkeiten gehabt.

Ich habe	___ viele nette Leute kennen gelernt.	Wenn ich nicht …
	___ viel Deutsch gelernt.	
	___ einen sympathischen Dozenten/eine sympathische Dozentin gehabt.	
	___ freundliche Professoren/Professorinnen gehabt.	
	___ Heimweh gehabt.	
	___ kein Auto gehabt.	
	___ ein Fahrrad gefunden.	
	___ Lotto gespielt.	
	___ ?	
Ich bin	___ nicht oft krank gewesen.	Wenn ich …
	___ nie zu meinen Professoren/Professorinnen gegangen.	
	___ nicht oft auf Partys gegangen.	
	___ nie ins Theater gegangen.	
	___ ?	

FREIE KOMMUNIKATION

Rollenspiel: Das schief gegangene° Treffen°. Sie haben einen Traumabend – ein Treffen mit einem berühmten Filmstar – gewonnen. Wer war es? Leider ist alles schief gegangen. Sie haben dummes Zeug° erzählt und sich total falsch benommen°. Besprechen Sie mit einem Freund/einer Freundin, was Sie besser anders gemacht hätten.

gone wrong / meeting

***dummes Zeug:** nonsense*
***falsch benommen:** behaved improperly*

Schreibecke **Was hätten Sie im Studium anders gemacht?** Ihr jüngerer Bruder/Ihre jüngere Schwester möchte nächstes Jahr an Ihrer Universität/Ihrem College beginnen und braucht ein paar Tipps. Was hätten Sie in Ihrem Studium anders gemacht? Was hätten Sie vielleicht gar nicht gemacht? Schreiben Sie eine E-Mail an Ihren jüngeren Bruder/Ihre jüngere Schwester.

Eine kleine Katastrophe. Denken Sie an eine kleine Katastrophe. Beschreiben Sie die Katastrophe und schreiben Sie dann, wie Sie sie hätten vermeiden° können.

avoid

ABSPRUNGTEXT

EU zieht neue Grenze: Das ändert sich beim Zoll

Seit Januar 1995 ist Österreich Mitglied der Europäischen Union. Das hat jetzt noch verschiedene Folgen°, besonders in Kärnten. Weil die Grenzen zu den anderen EU-Nachbarländern weniger kontrolliert werden, verlieren viele österreichische Grenzbeamte, die an der italienischen Grenze arbeiten, ihre Stelle. An der Grenze zu Slowenien, einem Nicht-EU-Land, steigt der legale aber auch der illegale Transitverkehr. Darum machen sich jetzt die österreichischen Beamten große Sorgen.

consequences

Kärnten *(Carinthia)* is one of 9 **Bundesländer** in Austria. Its capital is Klagenfurt. The others are: **Niederösterreich** *(Lower Austria)*—St. Pölten; **Oberösterreich** *(Upper Austria)*—Linz; **Salzburg**—Salzburg; **Tirol** *(The Tyrol)*—Innsbruck; **Vorarlberg**—Bregenz; **die Steiermark** *(Styria)*—Graz; **das Burgenland**—Eisenstadt; **Wien** *(Vienna)*—Wien.

Vorschau

16 **Thematische Fragen.** Beantworten Sie die folgenden Fragen auf Deutsch.

1. Welche Länder, die an Österreich grenzen, sind Mitglied der Europäischen Union? Welche sind nicht Mitglied der EU?
2. Welche Vorteile bringt die Mitgliedschaft in der EU in Bezug° auf Grenzkontrollen°?
3. Was ist in den frühen 90er-Jahren im ehemaligen Jugoslawien passiert? Welche Probleme hat(te) das für Österreich und die EU zur Folge?
4. Welche Produkte muss man bei der Einreise in ein fremdes Land beim Zoll deklarieren?

in Bezug auf: *regarding*
border controls

17 **Lesestrategien: EU zieht neue Grenze.** Benutzen Sie die Lesestrategien aus Kapitel 7, um den Text zu verstehen.

1. **Den Kontext verstehen.** Finden Sie im Text Antworten auf die folgenden Fragen.
   a. Welche Länder werden im Artikel erwähnt°?
   b. Welche Leute werden im Artikel erwähnt? Welche sind kriminell und welche nicht?
   c. Welche drei Synonyme werden für Zöllner verwendet?
   d. Welches Problem wird im Artikel beschrieben?
   e. Woher kommt dieser Artikel? Wo kann man einen solchen Artikel finden?
2. **Neue Wörter lernen.** Was bedeuten diese Wörter? Lesen Sie die Erklärungen und wählen Sie eine Antwort.

mentioned

a. „Sie [Reisende] müssen an der Grenze zu Slowenien in Zukunft **mit verschärften Kontrollen rechnen!**“
- □ Reisende werden an der Grenze öfter durchsucht.
- □ Reisende werden an der Grenze weniger durchsucht.

b. „Die wenigen Beamten, die hier noch **Passkontrollen durchführen,** sollen in spätestens zwei Jahren abgezogen werden.“
- □ Wenige Beamte fahren über den Pass.
- □ Die Beamten sehen sich die Reisepässe an.

c. „Viele Kollegen werden bald wohl stundenlange Anreisen zu ihren neuen Dienststellen **in Kauf nehmen** müssen.“
- □ akzeptieren und einplanen
- □ einkaufen gehen

3. Neue Wörter lernen: drei Strategien. Erraten Sie die fett gedruckten Wörter mit Hilfe der drei folgenden Strategien.

Strategie 1: Weltwissen

a. Sie müssen an der **Grenze** zu Slowenien …
- □ Die national-politische Barriere zwischen Österreich und Slowenien.
- □ Die Kooperation mit Slowenien.

b. Die 170 km lange EU-Außengrenze wird durch Patrouillen° rund um die Uhr **hermetisch abgeriegelt.** *patrols*
- □ Die Grenze wird dicht geschlossen.
- □ Die Grenze wird weit geöffnet.

Strategie 2: Kontext

a. „Sie werden verstärkt im Kampf gegen **Schlepper,** Drogendealer und Waffenschieber eingesetzt.“
- □ Personen, die legal Menschen ins Land einführen.
- □ Personen, die illegal Menschen ins Land einführen.

b. Zusätzlich geplant sind fünf mobile Einsatzgruppen für **stichprobenartige** Kontrollen im Landesinnern.
- □ Polizisten werden mitten im Land ab und zu einige Autos kontrollieren.
- □ Polizisten werden mitten im Land alle Autos kontrollieren.

c. Er verlangt daher von den Politikern klare **Vorgaben.**
- □ Er will einen klaren Plan sehen.
- □ Er will mehr Geld verdienen.

Strategie 3: Wortformen

a. Kärntens **Zöllner**
- □ Menschen, die beim Zoll arbeiten
- □ Menschen, die arbeiten sollen

b. **Grenzwächter**
- □ Menschen, die an der Grenze auf illegale Aktivitäten achten° *watch for*
- □ Menschen, die an der Grenze aufwachen

c. „Doch Kärntens Zöllner sind **verunsichert.**“
- □ Die Situation macht die Zöllner ruhig und sicher.
- □ Die Situation macht die Zöllner unruhig und unsicher.

d. **Sondereinsatzgruppen**
- □ Polizisten, die besonders eingesetzt oder benutzt werden
- □ Gruppen von Kriminellen

ABSPRUNGTEXT

EU zieht neue Grenze: Das ändert sich beim Zoll

Lesen Sie jetzt den Text.

EU zieht neue Grenze: Das ändert sich beim Zoll

Neue Aufgaben für „Grenzwächter" in Kärnten

- *Reisende erwarten offene Schlagbalken°, aber auch schärfere Kontrollen*

barriers

VON JOHANN PALMISANO

Nach dem Beitritt Österreichs zur EU warten auf Kärntens Zöllner neue Aufgaben: Sie werden verstärkt° im Kampf gegen Schlepper, Drogendealer und Waffenschieber eingesetzt. Aber auch für Reisende wird sich einiges ändern: Sie müssen an der Grenze zu Slowenien in Zukunft mit verschärften Kontrollen rechnen!

reinforced

Durch die Öffnung der Grenze zu Italien wurden viele „Grenzwächter" über Nacht arbeitslos. Und auch die wenigen Beamten, die hier noch Passkontrollen durchführen, sollen in spätestens zwei Jahren abgezogen werden. Für die rund 570 Zöllner in Kärnten wurde deshalb ein neuer Einsatzplan erstellt. Und so sieht das Konzept im Detail aus:

- Verstärkte Kontrollen an den Zollämtern zu Slowenien. Die 170 km lange EU-Außengrenze wird durch Patrouillen rund um die Uhr hermetisch abgeriegelt.
- Unterstützt° wird der Grenzdienst im Kampf gegen Schlepper, Drogen- und Waffenschmuggler durch zwei Sondereinsatzgruppen beim Zollamt Karawankentunnel und auf dem Flughafen Klagenfurt.
- Zusätzlich geplant sind fünf mobile Einsatzgruppen für stichprobenartige Kontrollen im Landesinnern.

supported

Doch Kärntens Zöllner sind verunsichert. Zollgewerkschafter° Max Klemenjak: „Es ist noch völlig unklar, wie viele Beamte wohin versetzt° werden. Viele Kollegen werden bald wohl stundenlange Anreisen zu ihren neuen Dienststellen in Kauf nehmen müssen." Er verlangt daher von den Politikern klare Vorgaben: „Die Beamten müssen sich ja endlich entscheiden können, ob sie in den Grenzdienst oder aber zur Gendarmerie wechseln sollen!"

member of the trade union for customs agents / transferred

Und das erwartet die Reisenden: Der 1000-S-Freibetrag° für Slowenien wird noch genauer kontrolliert. Hingegen bleibt der Grenzbalken zu Italien noch offen. Doch das will nichts heißen°. Denn in Zukunft können Zöllner auch im Landesinnern den Kofferraum öffnen lassen …

1,000 Schilling duty-free limit

Doch … heißen: *That does not mean you can get away with everything*

Rückblick

18 **Stimmt das?** Stimmen diese Aussagen zum Text oder nicht? Wenn nicht, was stimmt?

	Ja, das stimmt.	*Nein, das stimmt nicht.*
1. Nach dem Beitritt Österreichs zur EU haben die Zöllner an der slowenischen Grenze weniger zu tun.	___	___
2. Kärntens Zöllner werden stärker gegen illegale internationale Kriminelle wie Schlepper, Drogendealer und Waffenschieber arbeiten müssen.	___	___
3. Mit dem Beitritt Österreichs zur EU haben *alle* Grenzwächter an der italienischen Grenze automatisch ihre Stellen verloren.	___	___
4. Die Kontrollen an der EU-Außengrenze werden strenger.	___	___
5. Man will die Grenze zu Slowenien weniger als vorher kontrollieren.	___	___
6. Man will den Kampf gegen Schlepper, Drogen- und Waffenschmuggler mit zwei neuen Sondereinsatzgruppen am Karawankentunnel und am Flughafen Klagenfurt unterstützen.	___	___
7. Die Durchsuchung von *allen* Autos im Landesinnern ist geplant.	___	___
8. Fünf mobile Einsatzgruppen werden auch im Ausland Österreicher kontrollieren können.	___	___
9. Wegen der neuen Einsatzpläne haben Kärntens Zöllner keine Angst mehr um ihre Arbeitsstellen.	___	___
10. Max Klemenjak ist Politiker.	___	___
11. Die Grenzbeamten haben eine unsichere Zukunft.	___	___
12. Jeder Reisende darf Waren im Wert von 1000 Schilling über die Grenze nach Hause bringen.	___	___

19 **Ergänzen Sie.** Ergänzen Sie diese Sätze mit Wörtern aus dem **Absprungtext.**

1. Nach Österreichs _____ zur EU gibt es neue Aufgaben für Kärntens _____.
2. Sie werden stärker als vorher im Kampf gegen Schlepper, Drogendealer und Waffenschieber _____.
3. Touristen müssen mit verschärften Kontrollen an der slowenischen Grenze _____.
4. Viele Zöllner, auch _____ genannt, wurden aber über Nacht arbeitslos.
5. Und die Beamten, die noch Passkontrollen _____, sollen bald _____ werden.
6. Für die 570 Zöllner Kärntens hat man einen neuen _____ erstellt.
7. Im Kampf gegen Schlepper, Drogen- und _____ wird der Grenzdienst durch zwei neue Sondereinsatzgruppen _____.
8. Fünf mobile Einsatzgruppen können auch im _____ stichprobenartige Kontrollen machen.
9. Trotz der neuen Einsatzpläne sind Kärntens Zöllner _____.
10. „Viele Kollegen werden bald wohl stundenlange Anreisen zu ihren neuen Dienststellen in _____ nehmen müssen.“

Ergänzen Sie. You used your knowledge of the world to understand the word **Grenze.** Try to understand words with **Grenz-** in their prefix from the context.

11. Klemenjak ____ von den Politikern klare Vorgaben für die Zöllner.
12. Die Zöllner sollen sich endlich entscheiden können, ob sie im Grenzdienst bleiben oder zur Gendarmerie ____ sollen.

20 **Kurz gefragt.** Beantworten Sie diese Fragen auf Deutsch.

1. Welche neuen Aufgaben werden die Zöllner Kärntens haben?
2. Welche Probleme erwarten Reisende an der Grenze nach Slowenien?
3. Warum werden die Beamten an der Grenze zu Italien bald arbeitslos sein?
4. Was müssen die Grenzbeamten, die an die slowenische Grenze versetzt werden, in Kauf nehmen?
5. Welche Entscheidung werden manche Grenzbeamten endlich treffen müssen?
6. Wozu werden die zwei Sondereinsatzgruppen in Kärnten eingesetzt?
7. Warum müssen sich Österreicher trotz Freibetrag und offener Grenze zu Italien an die Zollbestimmungen halten?

21 **Kurz interpretiert.** Beantworten Sie diese Fragen auf Deutsch.

1. Warum werden erst jetzt mehr Zöllner im Kampf gegen Schlepper, Drogen- und Waffenschmuggler eingesetzt?
2. Warum wurden so viele Grenzwächter an der österreichisch-italienischen Grenze sozusagen „über Nacht" arbeitslos?
3. Warum will man die Kontrollen an der slowenischen Grenze verschärfen?
4. Ist es möglich, eine 170 km lange Grenze durch Patrouillen rund um die Uhr hermetisch abzuriegeln? Kennen Sie andere Beispiele dafür?
5. Was scheint das größte Problem zu sein, wenn Zöllner an neue Dienststellen versetzt werden? Warum widerspricht° das der europäischen Mentalität? *contradicts*
6. Wie würden Sie auf diese Situation reagieren, wenn Sie Zöllner wären? Würden Sie sich eine neue Arbeit suchen?

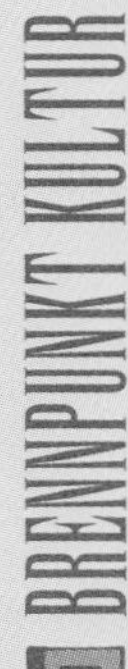

Österreichs Geschichte

Austria (**Österreich**) is a true multicultural and cosmopolitan society today because of its rich history and geographic location in Europe. Vienna (**Wien**), which was made the capital in 1156, was twice besieged by invading Turks from the East. Later it was twice occupied by Napoleon. The Congress of Vienna, which met from 1814 to 1815 to divide up Europe after Napoleon was defeated, exemplifies Vienna's current status as a city of mediation. Vienna has traditionally regarded itself as a bridgehead between the East and the West. As headquarters of the United Nations and OPEC, Vienna is closely associated with numerous international conventions and summits.

At the beginning of the twentieth century, the Austrian monarchy encompassed portions of present-day Hungary (**Ungarn**), Italy (**Italien**), the former Yugoslavia (**Jugoslawien**), and the former Czechoslovakia (**die Tschechoslowakei**) and was known as the Austro-Hungarian Empire (**Österreich-Ungarn**).

BRENNPUNKT KULTUR

World War I **(der Erste Weltkrieg)** was ignited by the assassination of Archduke Franz Ferdinand, the heir to the Austrian throne, in Sarajevo in 1914. Austria remained a monarchy until **Karl der Erste** resigned on November 11, 1918, at the close of World War I, when Austria became for the first time a parliamentary democracy **(die Erste Republik)** which lasted until 1938. In 1938, in the midst of the Third Reich, Nazi Germany and its Austrian-born leader, Adolf Hitler, annexed Austria **(der Anschluss).** The state of Austria ceased to exist; all Austrians became German citizens subject to German law.

After the defeat of Germany in World War II, Austrian territory was divided, like Germany itself, into four **Besatzungszonen** by the Allied militaries, with Vienna being occupied by all four Allied powers. 1945 saw the reestablishment of a functioning democracy, the signing of a declaration of independence, and free elections. By committing itself to permanent neutrality, Austria convinced the Soviet Union to sign a peace treaty, which in turn allowed for the enactment of the Austrian Constitution **(das Bundesverfassungsgesetz)** on October 26, 1955.

On January 1, 1995, Austria joined the European Union, thereby becoming the second German-speaking country after Germany to do so.

Austrian culture has accommodated many influences from its former East European territories, along with their languages, customs and cuisines, making Austria one of the earliest multi-ethnic, multicultural societies in Europe.

Following the annexation of Austria by the Nazis, all able-bodied Austrian males were drafted into the German military, and the extension of the Nuremberg Laws to Austrian territory decimated Austria's Jewish population.

Wissenswerte Vokabeln: Österreichs Leute und Länder

Talking about Austria

Austria is comparable in size to Iowa.

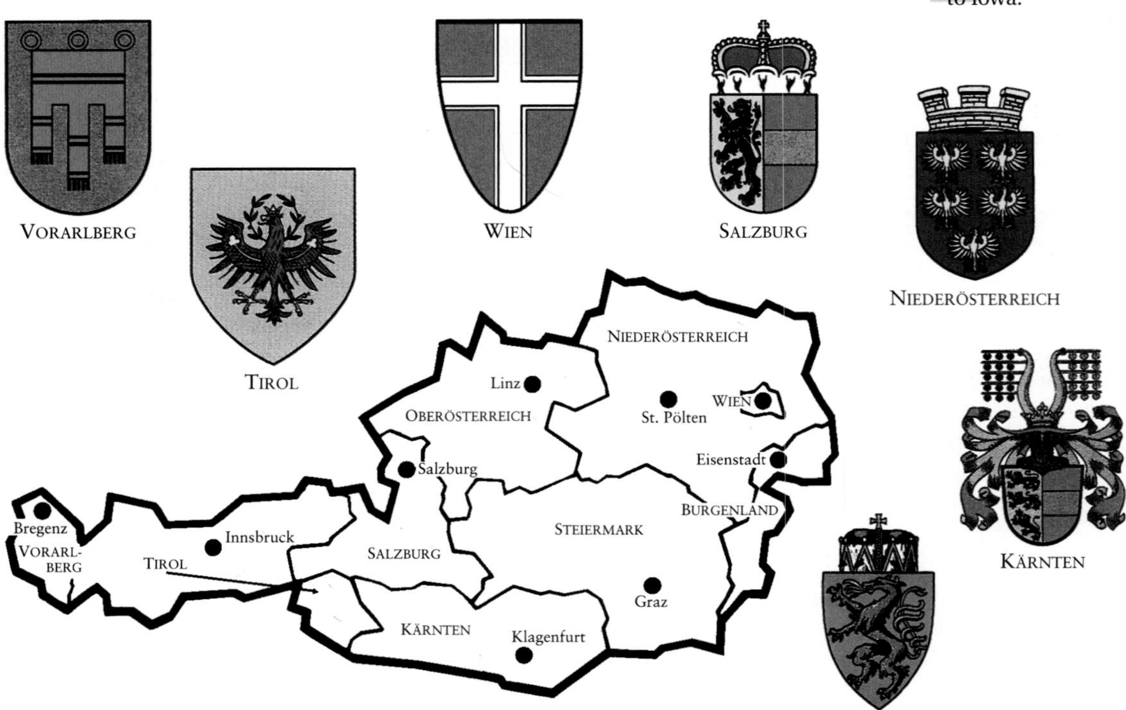

■ Wie heißt die Hauptstadt von Österreich?

Fläche	Bevölkerung	Hauptstadt
83 855 km²	rund 8,07 Millionen	Wien
Sprachzugehörigkeit 98% deutsch *andere:* slowenisch, kroatisch, ungarisch, tschechisch		
Religionszugehörigkeit 78% römisch-katholisch, 5% protestantisch, 4,5% andere, 9% konfessionslos, 3,5% ohne Angaben		
Arbeitnehmer (Österreicher) 3 055 800 (1992)		
Männer 1 766 900		**Frauen** 1 288 900

BURGENLAND

OBERÖSTERREICH

Welche Sprachen hört man in Österreich?

22 **Fragen über Österreich.** Stellen Sie einem Partner/einer Partnerin die folgenden Fragen über Österreich.

1. Wie viele Bundesländer hat Österreich?
2. Hat Österreich mehr oder weniger Einwohner als Deutschland?
3. Findet man mehr Priester oder Pastoren in Österreich? Warum?
4. Welches Bundesland ist gleichzeitig die Hauptstadt des Bundeslandes?
5. Was unterscheidet Oberösterreich von Niederösterreich? Was meinst du?
6. Welches Bundesland möchtest du am liebsten besuchen? Warum?

23 **Informationen über Österreich.** Vervollständigen Sie diese Sätze mit Informationen aus **Brennpunkt Kultur.** Es kann mehrere richtige Antworten geben.

1. Österreich ist …
   a. eine Monarchie. b. eine Demokratie. c. eine Diktatur.
2. In Österreich gibt es …
   a. keine internationalen Organisationen. b. die UNO und die OPEC. c. die NATO.
3. Österreich ist Mitglied …
   a. in der NATO. b. in der EU. c. im Ostblock. d. in der UNO.
4. Österreich grenzt …
   a. an ehemalige Ostblockstaaten.
   b. nur an EU-Staaten.
   c. an drei andere deutschsprachige Staaten.
   d. an Staaten des ehemaligen Jugoslawiens.
   e. an zwei EU-Staaten.

24 **Fragen über Europa.** Schauen Sie sich die Liste mit den Ländernamen und eine Landkarte von Europa am Ende des Buches an und beantworten Sie dann diese Fragen.

Kroatien • Frankreich • Deutschland • die Tschechische Republik • Italien • Ungarn • Schweden • Slowenien • Liechtenstein • die Slowakische Republik • die Schweiz • Polen • Großbritannien • Norwegen • Spanien • Portugal • Irland • Dänemark • Island • Finnland • die Niederlande • Belgien • Griechenland • Luxemburg • die Ukraine

1. Welche Länder grenzen an Österreich?
2. Welche Länder sind Mitglied der EU?
3. Welche Länder gehörten zum ehemaligen Jugoslawien?
4. Welche Länder gehörten zum Ostblock?
5. Welche Länder sind Mitglied der NATO?
6. Welche Länder sind Monarchien?
7. Welches Nachbarland von Österreich ist wirtschaftlich am ärmsten?
8. Die Grenze zu welchem Nachbarland wird wahrscheinlich am schärfsten kontrolliert? Warum?

25 **An der Grenze.** Was wissen Sie im Allgemeinen über Grenzverkehr? Wählen Sie die besten Antworten.

1. Grenzbeamte (Zöllner) achten besonders auf das Schmuggeln von …
   a. Schokolade. c. Alkohol. e. Waffen. g. Drogen.
   b. Kleidung. d. Menschen. f. Tabak. h. Büchern.

2. Offene Grenzen existieren zwischen …
   a. armen und reichen Ländern.
   b. EU-Ländern.
   c. EU- und nicht-EU-Ländern.

3. An offenen Grenzen kontrollieren Zöllner …
   a. nur stichprobenartig.
   b. alle Autos.
   c. keine Autos.

4. Zöllner kontrollieren …
   a. nur an der Grenze.
   b. nur im Landesinneren.
   c. an der Grenze und im Landesinneren.

5. Was muss man an der Grenze *nicht* vorzeigen?
   a. Den Reisepass.
   b. Die Autoversicherung (die grüne Karte).
   c. Eine Bankkarte.

26 **Interview: Grenzerlebnisse.** Stellen Sie einem Partner/einer Partnerin die folgenden Fragen.

1. Bist du jemals nach Mexiko oder Kanada gefahren?
2. Wurdest du an der Grenze kontrolliert?
3. Hast du etwas eingeführt? War es etwas Legales?
4. Hast du jemals versucht, etwas über die Grenze zu schmuggeln?

5. Was ist deiner Meinung nach schlimmer: Tabak und Alkohol über die Grenze schmuggeln oder exotische Tiere und Pflanzen?
6. An den US-Grenzen werden viele illegale Drogen eingeschmuggelt. Bist du dafür oder dagegen, dass alle Reisenden kontrolliert werden sollen? Warum? Warum nicht?
7. Illegale Immigration ist ein Problem in den USA. Wie kann man dieses Problem am besten bewältigen°?

resolve

BRENNPUNKT KULTUR

Österreichs kulturelles Leben

Austria has a proud cultural history that links it to some of the world's greatest music, literature, and art. Salzburg, the birthplace of **Wolfgang Amadeus Mozart** (1756–1791), is home to the world famous conservatory, **das Mozarteum,** and the annual **Salzburger Festspiele. Joseph Haydn** (1739–1809) served for years in Prince Esterházy's court in Eisenstadt, and the composer **Anton Bruckner** served as organist for **Stift St. Florian** near Linz.

As the capital of the Austro-Hungarian Empire, Vienna **(Wien)** created a reputation for itself as the musical center of Europe, serving at different times as the home of **Mozart, Ludwig van Beethoven, Franz Schubert,** and **Johannes Brahms. Johann Strauß Sohn** made both the Viennese Waltz **(der Walzer)** and operettas such as **Die Fledermaus** popular in the nineteenth century.

Vienna is also internationally known for having one of the best German-language theaters in Europe **(das Burgtheater).** It is also home to the Lippizaner stallions of the Spanish riding school **(die Spanische Reitschule)** and the most famous boy's choir in the world, the Vienna Boys Choir **(die Wiener Sängerknaben).** Viennese culture flourished at the turn of the century and has made household names of the founder of psychoanalysis **Sigmund Freud,** the artist **Gustav Klimt,** and the composers **Gustav Mahler, Franz Lehár,** and **Arnold Schönberg.** The modern art of cinema (including Hollywood) has also been enriched by the contributions of Austrian filmmakers like **Otto Preminger** and **Billy Wilder,** and the actors **Klaus Maria Brandauer** and **Arnold Schwarzenegger.**

In literature, Vienna is associated with the playwrights **Arthur Schnitzler** and **Hugo von Hofmannsthal,** and the novelist **Robert Musil,** while the German-speaking community of Austro-Hungarian Prague produced such literary luminaries as **Franz Werfel, Rainer Maria Rilke,** and **Franz Kafka.** Many other twentieth-century Austrian authors are not as well known to North Americans but are very popular with European readers and include such names as the author **Ingeborg Bachmann,** the playwrights **Ödön von Horváth** and **Thomas Bernhard,** the feminist novelist **Elfriede Jelinek,** the widely read author **Peter Handke,** and the Nobel Prize-winning playwright and autobiographer **Elias Canetti.**

In the visual arts, the contemporary painter and artist **Friedensreich Hundertwasser** has produced graphics, paintings, and architecture that consistently delight the public.

Finally, anybody who has ever ordered a Café Vienna in a coffee shop and read a newspaper or played chess is enjoying a pastime that the Viennese themselves cherish in their many **Kaffeehäuser.**

Die Spanische Reitschule

For moviegoers from around the world the beauty and charm of Salzburg and the surrounding countryside have been forever immortalized in the film *The Sound of Music.*

Mozart (1756–1791)

Architektur der Gegenwart in Wien: Hundertwassers Wohnbau

Strukturen und Vokabeln

II Expressing the purpose of an action

The conjunction **um ... zu**

To express the purpose of an action, German speakers use the subordinating conjunction **um ... zu** *(in order to).* The subject of both the main clause and the implied subject of the subordinate clause must be identical. The construction is usually set off by commas.

> Stefan arbeitet als Praktikant, **um** Berufserfahrungen **zu** sammeln.
> *Stefan is working as an intern (in order) to gain professional experience.*

In separable-prefix verbs, **zu** separates the prefix from the rest of the infinitive.

> Barbara geht nach Hause, **um** ihre Mutter an**zu**rufen.
> *Barbara is going home (in order) to call her mother.*

When the infinitival clause includes a modal verb, the modal verb occurs at the end of the clause, and is immediately preceded by **zu.**

> Anna braucht die Unterlagen, **um** sich bewerben **zu** können.
> *Anna needs the forms (in order) to be able to apply.*

27 **Wieso macht man das?** Anna hat viele Leute in Deutschland kennen gelernt. Im Gespräch mit ihnen erfährt Anna, warum die Personen die folgenden Sachen machen. Bilden Sie Sätze mit Elementen aus beiden Spalten. Benutzen Sie **um ... zu.**

▣ Barbara studiert Betriebswirtschaft, um Kauffrau zu werden.

1. Barbara studiert Betriebswirtschaft.
2. Sia studiert Medizin.
3. Stefan akzeptiert eine Praktikantenstelle.
4. Stefan geht für ein Jahr nach Amerika.
5. Karen arbeitet als Aushilfskellnerin.
6. Annas Freunde fahren mit dem Fahrrad statt mit dem Auto.
7. Julian geht zur Telefonzelle.
8. Die Günthers haben einen Komposthaufen°.

a. Sie wird Kauffrau.
b. Sie wird Ärztin.
c. Er ruft seine Eltern an.
d. Sie kommen billiger zur Uni.
e. Sie recyclen alles aus dem Garten.
f. Sie spart Geld für ein Semester in Paris.
g. Er verbessert sein Englisch.
h. Er hat später bessere Berufschancen.

Wieso macht man das? German speakers have slightly different ways of asking *why?* You have already learned **warum,** as well as the other main question words **wer, wie, wann, wo, was,** and the **wo-**compounds, but German speakers use **wozu** to ask *to what end?,* or **wieso** to ask *just how does it happen that . . .?* or *for what reason . . .?*

° *compost pile*

28 **Interview.** Stellen Sie einem Partner/einer Partnerin die folgenden Fragen. Benutzen Sie **um ... zu.**

1. Lernst du Deutsch, um später mal in Deutschland zu arbeiten? Wenn nicht, warum?
2. Studierst du an dieser Uni, um diese Stadt kennen zu lernen? Wenn nicht, warum?
3. Was studierst du? Studierst du das, um viel Geld zu verdienen? Wenn nicht, warum?
4. Wo wohnst du? Wohnst du da, um Geld zu sparen? Wenn nicht, warum?
5. Gehst du gern ins Café, um Kaffee zu trinken? Wenn nicht, warum?
6. Möchtest du nach dem Studium eine Reise machen? Warum?

The conjunction *ohne ... zu*

To express that one action occurs while another action does not, German speakers use the **ohne ... zu** construction. It corresponds to the English construction *without . . . ing.* The **ohne ... zu** construction follows the same rules for position and punctuation as the **um ... zu** construction.

Das Paar ging aus dem Restaurant, **ohne zu** zahlen.	*The couple left the restaurant without paying.*
Stefan ist gestern vorbeigekommen, **ohne** vorher an**zu**rufen.	*Stefan came by yesterday without calling beforehand.*

29 **Was hat Stefan alles nicht gemacht?** Bilden Sie Sätze mit **ohne ... zu.**

▣ Stefan ist gestern zu Anna gekommen. Er hat vorher nicht angerufen.
Stefan ist gestern zu Anna gekommen, ohne vorher anzurufen.

1. Stefan ist gestern zu Anna gekommen. Er hat vorher nicht angerufen.
2. Stefan ist fürs Wochenende weggefahren. Vorher packte er seinen Koffer nicht.

3. Er ist nach Wien gefahren. Er hat sich gar nicht über die Stadt informiert.
4. Er ging einfach zum Bahnhof. Er hat keinen Platz reserviert.
5. Gestern Abend war er bei Anna und Barbara. Er hat kein Wort über seine Reise gesagt.

Wissenswerte Vokabeln: die Umwelt

Talking about the environment

Die Umwelt ist ein wichtiges Problem für die Zukunft in der EU. Viele Menschen glauben, die Umwelt muss geschützt werden.

Die Wegwerf-Gesellschaft macht das Leben einfach, aber sie hat viel Müll verursacht. Die Umwelt darf nicht verschmutzt werden.

Um die Müll-Lawine zu stoppen, werden Verpackungen sortiert und zur Sammelstelle gebracht.

Die modernen Gesellschaften der EU verbrauchen viel Energie. Erdöl ist eine begrenzte Energiequelle. In kurzer Zeit ist diese Energiequelle verbraucht.

The high gas prices in 2000 prompted consumer protests in France, Germany, and Great Britain.

Man erforscht umweltfreundliche Energiequellen, wie zum Beispiel Windenergie und Sonnenenergie.

Der Treibhauseffekt: Abgase von Autos und Industrie verschmutzen die Luft und machen das Klima wärmer.

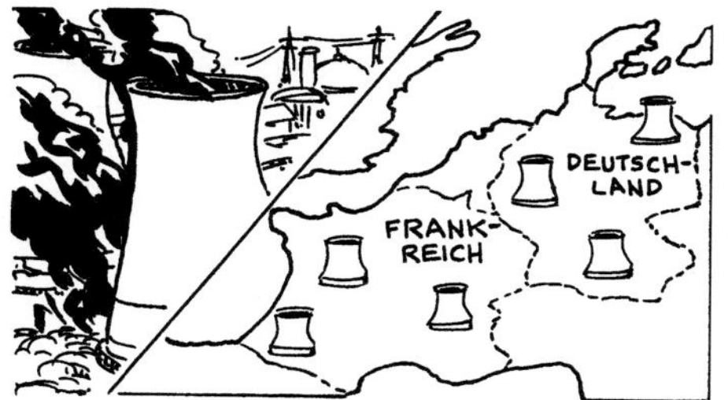

Obwohl es 1986 in Tschernobyl einen schweren atomaren Unfall gab, ist Atomenergie (Kernkraft) in Europa noch sehr verbreitet.

Weil Spraydosen mit FCKWs° der Ozonschicht schaden, sind sie jetzt in Deutschland und Österreich verboten.

chlorofluorocarbons

▣ Was hat die Wegwerf-Gesellschaft verursacht?

The government of Gerhard Schröder is committed to phasing out all nuclear reactors.

III ▣ Expressing how actions are to be done

Modal verbs with the passive voice

A modal verb with a passive infinitive expresses what can be **(kann),** may not be **(darf nicht),** has to be **(muss),** or ought to be done **(soll).** To express what will be done, German speakers use a form of **werden.** The passive infinitive consists of a past participle and **werden** (e.g., **gemacht werden**). When a modal verb is present, **werden** follows the participle at the end of the clause.

Die Verpackungen **können sortiert werden.**	*Packaging can be sorted.*
Die Umwelt **darf** nicht **verschmutzt werden.**	*The environment may not be polluted.*
Die Umwelt **muss geschützt werden.**	*The environment has to be protected.*
Benzin **soll gespart werden.**	*Gas should be conserved.*
In der Zukunft **wird** noch viel Energie **verbraucht werden.**	*Lots of energy will still be consumed in the future.*

30 **Was muss für die Umwelt gemacht werden?** Was muss/soll/kann Ihrer Meinung nach gemacht werden, um die Umwelt zu schützen?

▣ weniger Energie verbrauchen *Weniger Energie soll verbraucht werden.*

1. weniger Energie verbrauchen
2. Wasser sparen° — *to conserve*
3. Altglas zum Recycling bringen
4. Verpackungen umweltfreundlicher machen
5. Dosen°, Flaschen und Papier zum Recycling bringen — *cans*
6. Papier sortieren
7. umweltfreundliche Energiequellen finden
8. bleifreies° Benzin° benutzen — *unleaded / gasoline*

 **31** **Die Müll-Macher.** Analysieren Sie das folgende Schaubild.

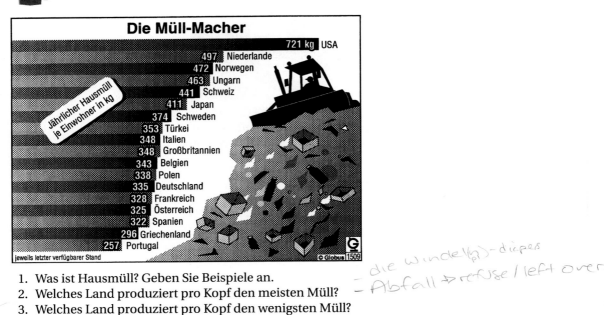

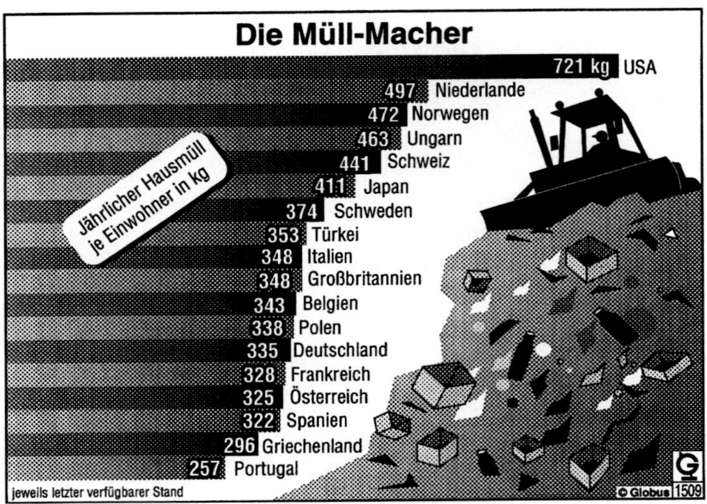

1. Was ist Hausmüll? Geben Sie Beispiele an.
2. Welches Land produziert pro Kopf den meisten Müll?
3. Welches Land produziert pro Kopf den wenigsten Müll?
4. Sind diese Länder relativ arm oder reich?
5. Was haben die reichen Länder gemeinsam°?
6. Welcher Faktor ist für die pro-Kopf-Müllmenge wichtiger: pro-Kopf-Einkommen oder umweltfreundliches Denken?

in common

32 **Unser Müllberg.** Wenn man zu viel wegwirft, dann verschwendet man Material, Energie und Geld. Sparen ist das Gegenteil von Verschwenden. Was kann man alles sparen, um die Umwelt zu schützen? Strom (Elektrizität)? Wasser? Was noch? Besprechen Sie mit Ihrem Partner/Ihrer Partnerin, was für die Umwelt gemacht werden kann.

IV ▣ Describing a state or condition

The statal passive

To describe a state of being rather than an action, German speakers use the past participle of the action verb with **sein.** This construction is called the *statal passive* **(das Zustandspassiv)** and is similar to the predicate adjective construction.

The statal passive is similar to the regular English passive formation, e.g., *Chlorofluorocarbons are banned in the U.S.A.*

Statal passive

Spraydosen mit FCKWs **sind verboten.**	*Spray cans are prohibited.*
Atomenergie **ist** sehr **verbreitet** in Europa.	*Nuclear energy is very widespread in Europe.*

Predicate adjective

Spraydosen sind **umweltunfreundlich.**	*Spray cans are hazardous to the environment.*

The statal passive is often used for posting regulations.

Parken ist hier verboten. *No parking here.*

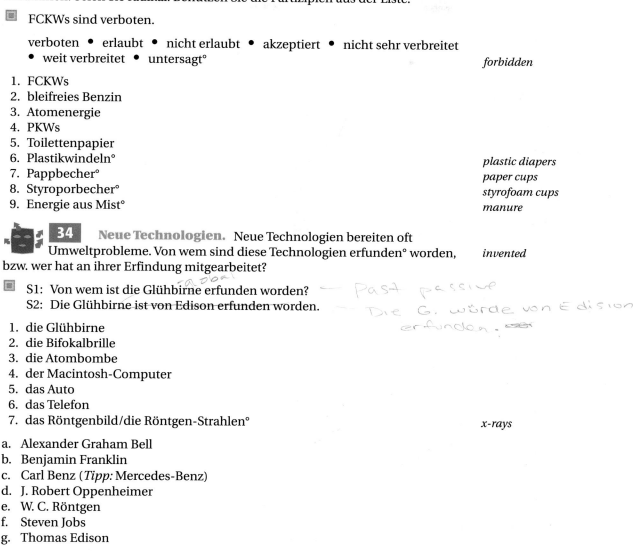

33 Umweltregelungen in der Zukunft. Stellen Sie mit einem Partner/einer Partnerin eine Liste von Umweltregelungen für die Zukunft zusammen. Seien Sie radikal! Benutzen Sie die Partizipien aus der Liste.

FCKWs sind verboten.

verboten • erlaubt • nicht erlaubt • akzeptiert • nicht sehr verbreitet • weit verbreitet • untersagt° *forbidden*

1. FCKWs
2. bleifreies Benzin
3. Atomenergie
4. PKWs
5. Toilettenpapier
6. Plastikwindeln° *plastic diapers*
7. Pappbecher° *paper cups*
8. Styroporbecher° *styrofoam cups*
9. Energie aus Mist° *manure*

34 Neue Technologien. Neue Technologien bereiten oft Umweltprobleme. Von wem sind diese Technologien erfunden° worden, bzw. wer hat an ihrer Erfindung mitgearbeitet? *invented*

S1: Von wem ist die Glühbirne erfunden worden?
S2: Die Glühbirne ist von Edison erfunden worden.

1. die Glühbirne
2. die Bifokalbrille
3. die Atombombe
4. der Macintosh-Computer
5. das Auto
6. das Telefon
7. das Röntgenbild/die Röntgen-Strahlen° *x-rays*

a. Alexander Graham Bell
b. Benjamin Franklin
c. Carl Benz (*Tipp:* Mercedes-Benz)
d. J. Robert Oppenheimer
e. W. C. Röntgen
f. Steven Jobs
g. Thomas Edison

FREIE KOMMUNIKATION

Die Zukunft. In den letzten 50 Jahren hat man Fernsehen, Personalcomputer, Handys, Videocassettenrecorder und andere neue Technologien entwickelt°. Stellen Sie mit einem Partner/einer Partnerin eine Liste von Erfindungen oder Entdeckungen zusammen, die in Ihrem Leben entwickelt und verbreitet sein werden. Beenden Sie den Satz unten. Sie haben maximal drei Minuten. *developed*

In meinem Leben wird (werden) … entdeckt (erfunden) werden.

ZIELTEXT

Studenten besprechen die EU

Die Europäische Union bringt viele Änderungen für die Staaten und die Menschen Europas. Auf der einen Seite gibt es klare Vorteile, aber auf der anderen Seite sind viele Leute noch sehr skeptisch. In diesem letzten **Zieltext** spricht Anna mit ihren Freunden Karl, Inge und Stefan über eventuelle Probleme in der Europäischen Union der Zukunft.

Vorschau

35 Thematische Fragen. Beantworten Sie die folgenden Fragen auf Deutsch.

1. Wenn man über eine Grenze fährt, muss man vieles machen, z.B. den Pass vorzeigen, Waren deklarieren und Geld wechseln. Was muss man innerhalb der USA nicht machen, wenn man in einen anderen Staat fährt?
2. Welche Vorteile bringt der gemeinsame Markt° den Staaten der USA?
3. In Europa hat man Angst, dass die Europäische Union die Identität der einzelnen Länder zerstören wird. Sehen Sie im gemeinsamen Markt Europas Nachteile? Welche?
4. Halten Sie die Europäische Union für eine gute Idee? Warum? Warum nicht?

common market

36 Satzdetektiv. Welche Wörter und Ausdrücke bedeuten ungefähr das Gleiche?

1. Also, wir müssen **uns** da wahrscheinlich **kräftig umstellen ...**
2. Ich habe gehört, dass für die **Bestimmungen** für Karamelbonbons 35.000 Seiten gedruckt wurden.
3. ... wenn man sich **die Organe** mal anguckt in der Europäischen Union ...
4. ... und das würde dann also alle, die **die Umwelt belasten,** höher **besteuern.**
5. ... mit einer **gemeinsamen Währung°,** mit dem Euro ...
6. Na, aber wie soll das [Belasten der Umwelt°] **gemessen** werden?

currency

***Belasten ... Umwelt:** strain on the environment*

a. Wie kann man statistisch feststellen, wie sehr die Umwelt verschmutzt ist?
b. Man muss lernen, völlig anders zu denken.
c. Um die Produktion von Bonbons in Europa zu vereinheitlichen, hat man ein sehr langes Dokument mit vielen kleinen Details geschrieben.
d. Es gibt viele Organisationen oder Strukturen innerhalb der EU, zum Beispiel den Europäischen Gerichtshof (die Judikative), den Ministerrat (die Legislative) und das Europa-Parlament (die Legislative und Kontrolle der Exekutive).
e. Wer die Umwelt verschmutzt, zahlt mehr Steuern.
f. Das einheitliche Geld für ganz Europa heißt der „Euro".

ZIELTEXT

Studenten besprechen die EU

Hören Sie gut zu.

Rückblick

37 **Stimmt das?** Stimmen diese Aussagen zum Text oder nicht? Wenn nicht, was stimmt?

	Ja, das stimmt.	*Nein, das stimmt nicht.*	
1. Stefan, Karl, und Inge sind alle sehr begeistert° von der EU.	___	___	*enthusiastic*
2. Inge findet einige EU-Regelungen dumm.	___	___	
3. Die Gruppe diskutiert den Umweltschutz innerhalb der EU.	___	___	
4. Stefan meint, um die Gefahren für die Umwelt zu beseitigen°, muss man privat was machen.	___	___	*eliminate*
5. Stefan hat gehört, dass die Grünen einen umweltfreundlichen Steuerplan haben.	___	___	
6. Stefan meint, kulturelle Unterschiede müssen überwunden° werden.	___	___	*overcome*
7. Die europäische Währungseinheit heißt *Eurodollar.*	___	___	
8. Inge hat Hoffnung auf die nächste Generation.	___	___	

38 **Ergänzen Sie: Diktat.** Ergänzen Sie diese Sätze mit Wörtern aus dem **Zieltext.**

1. Was ____ ihr eigentlich von der Europäischen Union?
2. Also wir müssen uns da wahrscheinlich kräftig umstellen, in der ____.
3. … wenn man sich die ____ mal anguckt in der Europäischen Union …
4. Da gibt's den Europäischen Gerichtshof, den Ministerrat, den Gesetzgeber, … und das europäische ____, das wir seit 1979 wählen …
5. Ich habe gehört, dass einer von den ____ Politikern ein ökologisches Steuersystem vorschlägt.

6. Ja, und dann gibt es auch noch die kulturellen _____ in Europa.
7. Ja, alles wird eben _____.
8. … dass die weniger Schwierigkeiten haben als unsere _____.

39 **Kurz gefragt.** Beantworten Sie diese Fragen auf Deutsch.

1. Welches extreme Beispiel für die Probleme der EU-Bürokratie bringt Inge?
2. Welche Probleme können durch die EU entstehen? Nennen Sie drei.
3. Wie heißt die gemeinsame europäische Währung? Welche Vorteile bringt eine gemeinsame Währung?
4. Wo ist der Sitz des Europäischen Parlaments?

40 **Der Grüne Punkt: das duale System.** Das *Duale System Deutschland (DSD)* ist ein detailliertes Umweltprogramm. Lesen Sie die folgenden Informationen und beantworten Sie dann die Fragen.

DER GRÜNE PUNKT UND DAS DUALE SYSTEM: WARUM IST DER GRÜNE PUNKT WICHTIG:

Bei Verpackungen, die den Grünen Punkt tragen, sind die Kosten für deren Sammlung und Sortierung sowie bei Kunststoffverpackungen die Verwertung über das Duale System bezahlt.

Bitte sortieren Sie zu Hause die geleerten Verpackungen, und werfen Sie diese dann in die entsprechenden Sammelbehälter. Ganz wichtig: Glas kommt, nach Farben getrennt, in die Glascontainer in Ihrer Nähe. Papier-, Karton- und Pappverpackungen gehören in Papiercontainer oder Papiertonnen oder können zur Papiersammlung gegeben werden. Die Leichtverpackungen mit dem grünen Punkt aus Metallen, Kunststoffen und Verbundstoffen gehören in den Wertstoffcontainer, in die Wertstofftonne oder in den Wertstoffsack. Diese Behältnisse werden regional unterschiedlich eingesetzt und haben in vielen Regionen die Farbe Gelb. Bekannt sind sie in der Regel als Gelbe Tonne oder Gelber Sack.

DER GRÜNE PUNKT
EIN GUTES ZEICHEN FÜR DIE UMWELT

1. Wer beim dualen System mitmachen will, soll 1) Produkte mit dem grünen Punkt kaufen und 2)
   a. Glasflaschen benutzen.
   b. Glas, Papier- und Pappeverpackungen° wegwerfen. *cardboard packaging*
   c. Glas, Papier- und Pappeverpackungen richtig sortieren.
2. Die Produkte mit dem Grünen Punkt
   a. kommen aus den Tropen°. *tropical country*
   b. sind gelb.
   c. finanzieren das Umweltprogramm.
3. Der Grüne Punkt ist ein Symbol für
   a. umweltfreundliche Produkte.
   b. EU-Produkte.
   c. Produkte aus dem Regenwald°. *rain forest*
4. Das Sortieren von Glas, Papier und Pappeverpackungen kann
   a. kompliziert sein.
   b. man zu Hause machen.
   c. gefährlich sein.
5. Man soll das Glas vorher
   a. kaputt schlagen.
   b. waschen.
   c. nach Farbe trennen.
6. Man soll das Material … werfen.
   a. in gelbe Container oder Behältnisse
   b. in den Müll
   c. in Plastiktaschen

41 Autogrammspiel: Der Umweltschutz. Finden Sie für jede Frage eine Person, die mit **ja** antwortet. Bitten Sie die Person um ihre Unterschrift.

S1: Sparst du Wasser?
S2: Ja, ich spare Wasser.
S1: Unterschreib hier, bitte. ____________________

1. wenig Müll produzieren ____________________
2. selten Auto fahren ____________________
3. mit dem Fahrrad fahren ____________________
4. einen Komposthaufen anlegen ____________________
5. umweltfreundliche Produkte kaufen ____________________
6. keine Produkte aus dem Regenwald kaufen ____________________
7. die Klimaanlage° im Auto und zu Hause nicht benutzen ____________________ *air conditioner*
8. Pfandflaschen° benutzen ____________________ *refundable bottles*

42 Alle zusammen für die Umwelt. Lesen Sie die Liste der Umwelt-Aufgaben und entscheiden Sie, ob das besser privat, vom Staat oder von der Wirtschaft° gemacht werden soll. Stellen Sie dann mit einem Partner/einer Partnerin die fünf besten Aktivitäten für die Umwelt zusammen. *business*

S1: Wer soll Autos mit kleineren Motoren produzieren?
S2: Die Wirtschaft soll Autos mit kleineren Motoren produzieren.

	Ich	*Staat*	*Wirtschaft*
1. Autos mit kleineren Motoren produzieren	—	—	—
2. benzinsparende bzw. elektrische Autos benutzen	—	—	—
3. weniger Verpackungsmaterial verwenden	—	—	—
4. umweltfreundliche Produkte produzieren	—	—	—
5. Steuervorteile° für umweltfreundliche Produkte erlassen°	—	—	—
6. alternative Energien entwickeln	—	—	—
7. Produkte verbieten, die der Umwelt schaden	—	—	—
8. elektrische Autos verlangen	—	—	—
9. die Eisenbahn subventionieren	—	—	—
10. Produkte aus dem Regenwald boykottieren	—	—	—

tax breaks
pass

▪ FREIE ▪ KOMMUNIKATION ▪

Rollenspiel: eine politische Diskussion. Im **Zieltext** sagt Stefan, dass die politischen Institutionen nicht alle Probleme lösen können. Welche Probleme werden besser privat gelöst und welche werden besser kooperativ gelöst? Entscheiden Sie in einer Gruppe von vier Personen, welche Themen Sie besprechen werden. Muss man in der Tat im Privaten anfangen? Ist das genug? Was kann man im Privaten nicht erreichen? Zwei Personen befürworten private Lösungsversuche und zwei andere vertreten staatliche Lösungsversuche.

Rollenspiel: Eine Wahrheit – viele Versionen. Anna spricht mit ihren Freunden, ihrem Deutschprofessor/ihrer Deutschprofessorin und ihrer Familie über ihren Aufenthalt in Deutschland. Je nachdem mit wem sie spricht, sind bestimmte Themen wichtiger als andere. S1 spielt Anna. S2 spielt eine dieser Rollen: Mutter, Vater, Freund/Freundin, Deutschprofessor/Deutschprofessorin. Dies sind die Themen.

1. Gespräch mit den Eltern: Wie war es, die deutschen Verwandten kennen zu lernen oder wieder zu sehen? Wie sehen die Verwandten jetzt aus? Wie sind sie? Wollen sie einmal zu Besuch in die USA kommen?
2. Gespräch mit Freunden: Wen hat Anna kennen gelernt? Wie hat Anna Stefan kennen gelernt? Wie ist Stefan? Hat die Beziehung mit Stefan Chancen?
3. Gespräch mit dem Professor/der Professorin: Hat sich Anna in den ersten Wochen verständigen können? Hat sie ihre Sprachfähigkeit verbessert? Hat sie mehr über die Geographie und Geschichte der deutschsprachigen Länder gelernt? Was genau? Wie waren die deutsche Universität und das Studentenwohnheim nun wirklich?

Schreibecke

Zurück in den USA. Anna ist wieder in den Vereinigten Staaten und schreibt ihren ersten Brief an Stefan in Deutschland. Je nach ihrer Stimmung° klingt der Brief optimistisch oder pessimistisch. Wählen Sie ein Thema und schreiben Sie Annas Brief. Hier sind die Themen.

mood

1. Anna, in optimistischer Stimmung, beschreibt, wie sehr sich ihre Familie und Freunde über ihre Rückkehr gefreut haben und dass alle Stefan bald kennen lernen wollen. Anna beschreibt auch Pläne für Stefans baldigen Besuch in den USA.

2. Anna, etwas melancholisch, fasst ihren Aufenthalt in Deutschland zusammen. Sie beschreibt auch, welche Rolle Stefan für sie gespielt hat. Aber insgesamt spricht sie mehr über die Vergangenheit als über die Zukunft.
3. Anna, in ziemlich deprimierter Stimmung, schreibt Stefan ganz klar, dass die Lage hoffnungslos ist. Unter anderen Umständen könnten sie vielleicht zusammenbleiben, aber so wie es ist, scheint eine Beziehung unmöglich zu sein.

Zurück in den USA. 1. A typical sentence might read: **Und wenn wir einen tollen Sonnenuntergang** *(sunset)* **sehen wollen, könnten wir zum Grand Canyon fahren.** 2. A typical sentence might read: **Und wenn immer ich etwas traurig oder unsicher war, warst du für mich da.** 3. Typical sentences might read: **Wenn wir eine feste Stelle hätten und mehr Geld verdienten, könnten wir einander öfter sehen. Aber weil wir erst unser Studium fertigmachen müssen ...**

Ein Umweltwettbewerb°: Stadtenergie. Die Stadtenergie in Ihrer Stadt hat einen Wettbewerb ausgeschrieben. Um einen Preis von 10.000 DM und Sonnenkollektoren für ein Haus zu gewinnen, sollen Sie ein Essay über das Thema **Wie kann der einzelne die Energiequellen der Gegenwart für die Zukunft besser konservieren** schreiben. Beschreiben Sie, wie jeder Einzelne Energie sparen und die Umwelt schützen kann und was alles vom Staat gemacht werden kann.

°*environmental contest*

Wortschatz

Vorbereitung auf die Zukunft

der Aufenthalt, -e *a stay, time spent in a place*
die Bewerbung, -en *application*
die Erfahrung, -en *experience*
die Gelegenheit, -en *opportunity*
die Nachricht, -en *news, message*
das Praktikum, *pl.* **Praktika** *internship*
der Praktikant, -en/die Praktikantin, -nen *intern, trainee*
die Rückkehr *return*
die Unterlage, -n *form, document*

an·nehmen (nimmt an, nahm an, hat angenommen) *to accept; to assume*
sich bewerben (bewirbt, bewarb, hat beworben) um/für + *acc.* *to apply for*
ein·schicken (hat eingeschickt) *to send in*
erhalten (erhält, erhielt, hat erhalten) *to get or receive*
sich interessieren (hat interessiert) für + *acc.* *to be interested in*
sammeln (hat gesammelt) *to collect, gather*
verzichten (hat verzichtet) auf + *acc.* *to forego, pass up*
ziehen (zog, hat gezogen) *to move (one's residence)*

eventuell *perhaps, possibly; possible*
gewiss *certain*
seitdem *ever since*

Ausdrücke

Erfahrung sammeln (hat gesammelt) *to gain experience*

Mitgliedschaft in der Europäischen Union

die Abgabe, -n *tax, duty*
der Arbeitnehmer, - *employee*
die Arbeitserlaubnis, -se *work permit*
die Ausländerbehörde, -n *foreigner's registration office*
die Lohnsteuerkarte, -n *income tax card*
die Mitgliedschaft *membership*
der/die Staatsangehörige, -n *(adjective used as noun) citizen*
der Staatsbürger, - *citizen*
der Stempel, - *stamp*
die Steuer, -n *tax*
das Finanzamt, ⸚er *tax office*

ab·ziehen (zog ab, hat abgezogen) *to deduct*
beantragen (hat beantragt) *to apply for*
zahlen (hat gezahlt) *to pay*

Österreich und die Europäische Union

die Anreise, -n *here: the commute to work*
die Aufgabe, -n *task, job*
die Außengrenze, -n *external border (of the EU)*
der Beamte, -n/die Beamtin, -nen *official, civil servant*
der Beitritt, -e *joining*
der Einsatz, ⸚e *deployment*
die Folge, -n *consequence*
die Gendarmerie *(state) police*
die Gewerkschaft, -en *trade union*
der Gewerkschafter, -/die Gewerkschafterin, -nen *trade union member*
der Grenzbalken, - *border crossing (lit. beam, rafter)*
der Grenzwächter, - *border guard*
die Kontrolle, -n *search*
das Landesinnere *the interior (of a country)*
das Mitglied, -er *member*
die Öffnung, -en *opening*
die Passkontrolle, -n *passport check*
der Schlepper, - *person who smuggles illegal immigrants into a country*
der Transitverkehr *transit traffic, transit trade*
der Waffenschieber, - *weapons dealer*
die Zollgewerkschaft, -en *customs officials' trade union*
der Zöllner, -/die Zöllnerin, -nen *customs agent*

ab·riegeln (hat abgeriegelt) *to lock up, seal*
ab·ziehen (zog ab, hat abgezogen) *to withdraw*
durch·führen (hat durchgeführt) *to carry out*
ein·setzen (hat eingesetzt) *to deploy, use, implement*
erwarten (hat erwartet) *to expect*
kontrollieren (hat kontrolliert) *to check*
versetzen (hat versetzt) *to transfer (someone)*
verstärken (hat verstärkt) *to strengthen, reinforce*
verunsichern (hat verunsichert) *to make uncertain*
wechseln (hat gewechselt) *to change*

hermetisch *hermetically, air-tight*
stichprobenartig *at random, randomly*
völlig *completely*

Ausdrücke

doch das will nicht heißen ... *however, that is not supposed to mean ...*
hingegen *on the other hand, in contrast to*
in Kauf nehmen (nahm, hat genommen) *to accept*
mit etwas rechnen (hat gerechnet) *to count on, expect*

Die Bundesländer Österreichs

das Burgenland *Burgenland*
Kärnten *Carinthia*
Niederösterreich *Lower Austria*
Oberösterreich *Upper Austria*
Salzburg *Salzburg*
die Steiermark *Styria*
Tirol *the Tyrol*
Vorarlberg *Vorarlberg*
Wien *Vienna*

Die Umwelt

das Abgas, -e *exhaust fumes*
die Atomenergie *nuclear energy*
die Dose, -n *can*
die Energiequelle, -n *source of energy*
das Erdöl *(petroleum) oil*
die Gesellschaft, -en *society*
die Kernkraft *nuclear energy*
das Klima, -s *climate*
die Luft, ⸚e *air*
der Müll *garbage*
die Müll-Lawine, -n *garbage avalanche*
die Ozonschicht, -en *ozone layer*
das Recycling *recycling*
die Sammelstelle, -n *collection site*
der Treibhauseffekt *greenhouse effect*
der Unfall, ⸚e *accident*
die Verpackung, -en *packaging*

die Wegwerf-Gesellschaft, -en *disposable society*
die Zukunft *future*

erforschen (hat erforscht) *to research*
schaden (hat geschadet) + *dat.* *to damage*
schützen (hat geschützt) *to protect*
sortieren (hat sortiert) *to sort*
verbrauchen (hat verbraucht) *to use (up), consume*
verschmutzen (hat verschmutzt) *to pollute*
verschwenden (verschwendet) *to waste*
verursachen (hat verursacht) *to cause*

verboten *prohibited*
verbreitet *distributed*

Aus dem Zieltext

die Bestimmung, -en *stipulation*
die Einrichtung, -en *institution, establishment*
die Einstellung, -en *attitude, outlook*
der Gerichtshof, ¨-e *court*
der Gesetzgeber, - *law maker*
das/der Karamelbonbon, -s *caramel candy*
der Ministerrat, ¨-e *council of ministers*
das Organ, -e *power, branch of government*
die Währung, -en *currency*

an·gucken *(coll.)* **(hat angeguckt)** *to take a look at*
belasten (hat belastet) *to burden*
besteuern (hat besteuert) *to tax*
drucken (hat gedruckt) *to print; to press*
erziehen (erzog, hat erzogen) *to raise children*
heraus·finden (fand heraus, hat herausgefunden) *to find out, discover*
messen (misst, maß, hat gemessen) *to measure*
überwinden (überwand, hat überwunden) *to overcome*
um·stellen (hat umgestellt) *to adjust, adapt*

eher *(comparative of* **bald***) here: sooner*
einheitlich *uniform*
gemeinsam *common, joint, unified*
ökologisch *ecological*

Ausdrücke

Tritt fassen (hat gefasst) *to get in step*
von oben her *from above*

Deutsch im Beruf 4

Money earned—money spent

After graduating from college you will need to get a job to earn a living. This means that a good portion of your salary **(das Gehalt, der Lohn)** or income **(das Einkommen)** will be consumed by everyday expenses **(die Lebenshaltungskosten)** and that you will need to consider questions of affordability and budgeting.

1 **Meine finanzielle Zukunft.** Besprechen Sie die folgenden Fragen über Ihre finanzielle Zukunft mit einem Partner/einer Partnerin.

1. In welcher Stadt möchten Sie später gern wohnen? Welche Stadt können Sie sich wahrscheinlich leisten°?
2. Möchten Sie später in einem Haus, in einer Eigentumswohnung° oder in einer Mietwohnung° wohnen? Was können Sie sich leisten?
3. Wie viel Geld werden Sie für ein Auto, für die Freizeit ausgeben?
4. Wie viel Geld müssen Sie für Unkosten° ausgeben: für die Heizung°, die Klimaanlage°, den Strom°, die Wasserrechnung° und die Telefonrechnung?
5. Wie viel Steuern werden Sie zahlen?
6. Wie viel Geld werden Sie brauchen, um Schulden° abzuzahlen°? Bankkredite? Kreditkarten?
7. Wie viel werden Sie wahrscheinlich sparen?
8. Was wird für Ihre Lebensqualität oder Ihren Lebensstandard besonders wichtig sein?

sich ... leisten: *to afford*
condominium
apartment
utilities / heating
air conditioning / electricity / water bill
debts / to pay off / ***Kredite:*** *loans*

2 **Wirtschaftliche Lebensqualität.** Personen, die die Staatsbürgerschaft in einem Mitgliedstaat der EU besitzen, können in jedem anderen Land der EU wohnen. Welche wirtschaftlichen Kriterien wären für Sie in der Wahl eines Landes wichtig? Ordnen Sie die folgenden Kriterien nach ihrer Wichtigkeit.

___ Durchschnittseinkommen° pro Person
___ Ladenöffnungszeiten°
___ Kaufkraft°
___ Inflation
___ Ersparnisse pro Person
___ Schulden pro Person
___ Feiertage pro Jahr

average income
store hours
buying power

Kaufkraft	
Italien	157
Portugal	157
Griechenland	145
Spanien	144
Großbritannien	136
Österreich	100
EU-Schnitt	117

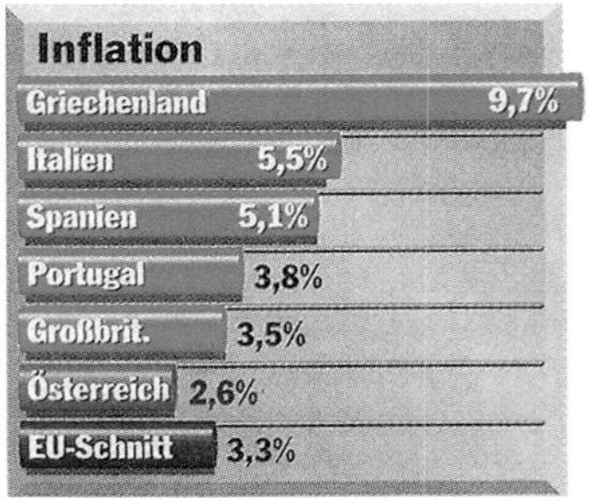

Inflation	
Griechenland	9,7%
Italien	5,5%
Spanien	5,1%
Portugal	3,8%
Großbrit.	3,5%
Österreich	2,6%
EU-Schnitt	3,3%

The **Kaufkraft** chart shows how much value the consumer can buy for 100 Austrian schillings ($10) in the other EU countries mentioned.

Einkommen

Deutschland	303.000 öS
Dänemark	296.000 öS
Luxemburg	255.000 öS
Belgien	255.000 öS
Österreich	233.00 öS
EU-Schnitt	170.000 öS

Feiertage

Portugal	19
Deutschland	18
Österreich	15
Großbritannien	14
Frankreich	13
Italien	12
EU-Schnitt	12

The incomes given in the **Einkommen** chart are Austrian schillings per person per year (14 schillings = approximately $1.00). The numbers in **Ersparnisse** and **Schulden** represent thousands of schillings. The **Feiertage** chart shows holidays per year and **Ladenöffnungszeiten** records business hours per week for stores.

3 **Europäische Länder im Vergleich.** Sehen Sie sich die statistischen Tabellen an und beantworten Sie diese Fragen.

1. In welchen Ländern könnte ein Österreicher mehr kaufen als in Österreich?
2. Ist die Inflationsrate in Österreich höher oder niedriger als im EU-Durchschnitt?
3. In welchen Teilen Europas ist die Inflationsrate besonders hoch?
4. In welchem EU-Land verdienen die Leute am meisten?
5. In welchen EU-Ländern verdienen die Leute mehr als im EU-Durchschnitt?
6. In welchen EU-Ländern sparen die Leute mehr als im EU-Durchschnitt? In welchem Land sparen die Leute am meisten?
7. In welchem EU-Land haben die Leute die höchsten Schulden? In welchen Ländern haben die Leute höhere Schulden als im EU-Durchschnitt?
8. Wie viele arbeitsfreie Feiertage gibt es in den USA? An welcher Stelle stehen Deutschland und Österreich?
9. In welchem EU-Land sind die Geschäfte am längsten geöffnet? Wie lange sind sie geöffnet? Liegt Österreich über oder unter dem EU-Durchschnitt? Ist der EU-Durchschnitt im Vergleich zu den USA hoch oder niedrig?

4 **Mein liebstes EU-Land.** In welchem EU-Land würden Sie am liebsten leben? Vergleichen Sie Ihre Antworten in der Aktivität **Wirtschaftliche Lebensqualität** mit den Informationen in den statistischen Tabellen. Fragen Sie dann drei andere Personen im Kurs: In welchem EU-Land möchten die meisten Personen, in welchem die wenigsten Leute in Ihrem Kurs wohnen? Warum?

S1: In welchem EU-Land möchtest du am liebsten leben?
S2: In Griechenland.
S1: Und warum?
S2: Weil dort die Läden lange geöffnet sind.

5 **Währungen.** Verbinden Sie diese Währungen mit dem Land, aus dem sie kommen.

Währung	*Land*
1. der Franken	a. China
2. der Yen	b. Großbritannien
3. der Schilling	c. Deutschland
4. der Yuan	d. die Tschechische Republik
5. die Mark	e. die Schweiz
6. das Pfund	f. Polen
7. die Tschechen-Krone	g. Österreich
8. der Peso	h. Japan
9. der Zloty	i. Mexiko
10. der Rubel	j. Russland

Der „Big Mac"-Währungsindex zeigt:

Der US-Dollar ist kraß unterbewertet!

Seit vielen Jahren veröffentlicht der britische „Economist" den kuriosen „Big Mac"-Index, dessen Aussagekraft aber immer mehr Anerkennung findet. Worum es dabei geht? Nun, es wird der Preis für einen „Hamburger" in den USA als Bezugsbasis hergenommen und ein weltweiter Index erstellt, der die unterschiedliche Kaufkraft in den einzelnen Ländern berücksichtigt. Daraus ergibt sich, welche Währungen über- und welche unterbewertet sind. Gewiß, kein wissenschaftlich strenges Verfahren, aber, mampf, ein unkonventionelles Beurteilungsmodell, das so seine Vorzüge hat (zumindest für die „Test-Esser" ...)

Und das sind die neuesten Ergebnisse beim „Big Mac"-Index: Der Schweizer Franken ist gegenüber dem US-Dollar um 124 Prozent überbewertet, der japanische Yen um 100 Prozent, der österreichische Schilling um 73 Prozent und die DM um 50 Prozent. Als unterbewertet gegenüber dem Dollar gelten nach dem „Hamburger Standard" der chinesische Yuan (–55 Prozent), der Hongkong-Dollar (–47), der polnische Zloty (–37), der Austral-Dollar (–22), die Tschechen-Krone (–18) und neuerdings der mexikanische Peso (–26 Prozent, nachdem er ein Jahr zuvor noch als „überbewertet" eingestuft worden war, was sich auf den „echten" Währungsmärkten inzwischen ja tatsächlich als zutreffend herausgestellt hat).

Sie sind skeptisch? Na, dann machen Sie doch selbst den „Big Mac"-Test! Sie brauchen dazu bloß ein bißchen Zeit (immerhin wird er in 79 Ländern durchgeführt) und, wie böse Zungen behaupten, einen starken Magen ...

6 **Hamburger Index.** Überfliegen° Sie den Text über den „Big Mac"-Währungsindex. Vervollständigen Sie dann mit einem Partner/einer Partnerin die Sätze und beantworten Sie die Fragen. *skim*

1. Der Hamburger Index bezieht° sich auf ... *relates*
   a. den Preis eines Big Mac-Hamburgers in den USA.
   b. den Preis eines Big Mac-Hamburgers in Russland.
   c. den Preis eines Big Mac-Hamburgers in Deutschland.
2. Der Index vergleicht diesen Preis mit ...
   a. dem Preis eines Hühnchens im gleichen Land.
   b. dem Preis eines Hühnchens in der ganzen Welt.
   c. dem Preis des gleichen Hamburgers in der ganzen Welt.

3. Dieser Vergleich demonstriert ...
   a. die Kaufkraft in verschiedenen Ländern.
   b. die Ersparnisse in verschiedenen Ländern.
   c. die Ladenöffnungszeiten in verschiedenen Ländern.
4. Je mehr dieses Produkt in einem Land kostet, ...
   a. desto° mehr ist die Währung dieses Landes unterbewertet°.
   b. desto mehr ist die Währung dieses Landes überbewertet.
   c. desto mehr essen die Leute in diesem Land.

Je ... desto ...: *The . . . the* / *undervalued*

5. In wie vielen Ländern wird der Big Mac-Test gemacht?
   a. In 97 Ländern.
   b. In 79 Ländern.
   c. In 790 Ländern.
6. Ordnen Sie diese Länder nach ihrer Kaufkraft im Vergleich mit der Kaufkraft der USA. Die USA liegen an siebter Stelle. Welches Land liegt mit der höchsten Kaufkraft an erster Stelle? Welches Land liegt mit der geringsten Kaufkraft an letzter Stelle?

   Mexiko • die Schweiz • Hongkong • die Tschechische Republik • China • Australien • Japan • Polen • Deutschland • Österreich

   1. ______
   2. ______
   3. ______
   4. ______
   5. ______
   6. ______
   7. die USA
   8. ______
   9. ______
   10. ______
   11. ______

7. Um wie viel Prozent ist ein Big Mac in diesen deutschsprachigen Ländern teurer als in den USA? Verbinden Sie jedes Land mit der richtigen Antwort.

   Deutschland — um 50 Prozent
   die Schweiz — um 124 Prozent
   Österreich — um 73 Prozent

Fischmac®

Big Mac®

Hamburger Royal mit Käse

7 **Grundstückspreise° in Wien.** Sehen Sie sich die Tabelle an und beantworten Sie dann die Fragen mit einem Partner/einer Partnerin.

das Grundstück: real estate

Grundstückspreise in Wien	Preis gute Lage		Preis schlechte Lage		Trend
	von	bis	von	bis	
10. Bezirk, Favoriten	3.500,–	4.500,–	3.000,–	4.000,–	=
11. Bezirk, Simmering	3.500,–	4.500,–	3.000,–	4.000,–	+
12. Bezirk, Meidling	5.000,–	6.000,–	3.500,–	5.000,–	+
13. Bezirk, Hietzing	7.000,–	9.000,–	5.000,–	6.000,–	=
14. Bezirk, Penzing	3.500,–	5.000,–			=
16. Bezirk, Ottakring	6.000,–	8.000,–			=
17. Bezirk, Hernals	6.000,–	8.000,–			=
18. Bezirk, Währing	9.000,–	12.000,–	7.000,–	9.000,–	=
19. Bezirk, Döbling	9.000,–	12.000,–	8.000,–	9.500,–	=
21. Bezirk, Floridsdorf	3.000,–	4.000,–			=
22. Bezirk, Donaustadt	2.500,–	3.500,–			=
23. Bezirk, Liesing	5.000,–	7.000,–	3.500,–	4.000,–	=

These prices given are per square meter, roughly equivalent to a square yard or 9 square feet.

Vienna consists of 23 different administrative districts called **Bezirke.**

1. In welchen Bezirken wohnen wahrscheinlich viele Diplomaten?
2. Welche Bezirke sind vielleicht Arbeiterbezirke?
3. In welchen Bezirken kosten Grundstücke in schlechter Lage° nicht viel weniger als in guter Lage?
4. In welchen Bezirken sind Grundstücke eine gute Investition?
5. Rechnen Sie aus, wie viel ein typisches amerikanisches Vorstadtgrundstück° (12,000 square foot) im billigsten Wiener Bezirk kosten würde.

location

die Vorstadt: suburb

8 **Mein monatliches Budget.** Schreiben Sie auf, wie viel Prozent Ihres monatlichen Einkommens Sie für diese Dinge ausgeben. Vergleichen Sie Ihre Zahlen mit den Prozentzahlen von mindestens drei anderen Leuten und beantworten Sie dann die Fragen weiter unten.

	Ausgabe	*Mein Budget*	*Person 1*	*Person 2*	*Person 3*
1.	Miete oder Hauskredit	______%	______%	______%	______%
2.	Essen	______%	______%	______%	______%
3.	Strom, Gas, Wasser	______%	______%	______%	______%
4.	Kleidung	______%	______%	______%	______%
5.	Telefon	______%	______%	______%	______%
6.	Kreditrückzahlung: Auto, Universität usw.	______%	______%	______%	______%
7.	Kreditkarten	______%	______%	______%	______%
8.	Versicherung°	______%	______%	______%	______%
9.	Freizeit (Film, Unterhaltung, Sport usw.)	______%	______%	______%	______%
10.	Transport				
11.	Sparen	______%	______%	______%	______%
12.	Diverses	______%	______%	______%	______%
	Gesamtsumme	100%	100%	100%	100%

insurance

1. Wofür geben Sie prozentuell das meiste aus?
2. Wofür geben Sie prozentuell das wenigste aus?
3. Wer gibt das meiste für Miete (oder Essen, Freizeit usw.) aus?
4. Wer gibt das wenigste für Miete (oder Essen, Freizeit usw.) aus?
5. Wer hat nach Meinung der ganzen Gruppe das vernünftigste Budget?

9 **Mein jetziges Budget – mein zukünftiges Budget.** Tragen Sie die Prozentzahlen Ihres jetzigen Budgets in die folgende Liste ein. Schreiben Sie daneben, wie viel Prozent Ihres Einkommens Sie für diese Kostenpunkte° ausgeben wollen, wenn Sie mit der Uni fertig sind und Ihren ersten „richtigen Job" haben. Besprechen Sie dann mit einem Partner/einer Partnerin, ob Sie ein gutes Budget haben oder was Sie besser machen können. Wechseln Sie Ihre Rollen.

° expense items

S1: Warum gibst du so viel für (Kleidung) aus?
S2: Weil ich (mich in meinem Beruf gut anziehen muss).
S1: Aber (Kleidung) ist wirklich keine gute Investition. Zahl lieber deine Kreditkarten ab.

	Ausgabe	***Jetziges Budget***	***Zukünftiges Budget***
1.	Miete oder Hauskredit	___%	___%
2.	Essen	___%	___%
3.	Strom, Gas, Wasser	___%	___%
4.	Kleidung	___%	___%
5.	Telefon	___%	___%
6.	Kreditrückzahlung: Auto, Universität usw.	___%	___%
7.	Kreditkarten	___%	___%
8.	Versicherung	___%	___%
9.	Freizeit (Film, Unterhaltung, Sport usw.)	___%	___%
10.	Transport		
11.	Sparen	___%	___%
12.	Diverses	___%	___%
	Gesamtsumme	100%	100%

Schreibecke **Finanzielle Neujahrsvorsätze°.** Es ist Neujahr und Sie beginnen ein neues Budget. Dieses Jahr wollen Sie es besser machen. Werden Sie mehr sparen? Weniger Schulden machen? Wofür werden Sie mehr und wofür werden Sie weniger Geld ausgeben? Schreiben Sie auf, was Sie anders machen werden.

° New Year's resolutions

▪ Principal Parts ▪

Principal parts of irregular (strong) and mixed verbs

The following list contains most of the high-frequency irregular (strong) verbs and mixed verbs encountered in ***Vorsprung***. Other verbs with separable and inseparable prefixes follow the pattern of the corresponding verbs found here and are not included in the list. A few high-frequency verbs with separable prefixes, whose meaning differ from the base verb, have been included, however. Most past participles listed here take **haben**; verbs that take **sein** are marked with the third-person form **ist**.

Infinitive	Present	Narrative Past	Past Participle	Meaning
an·fangen	fängt an	fing an	angefangen	*to begin*
an·rufen	ruft an	rief an	angerufen	*to telephone*
sich an·ziehen	zieht an	zog an	angezogen	*to get dressed*
sich aus·ziehen	zieht aus	zog aus	ausgezogen	*to get undressed*
befehlen	befiehlt	befahl	befohlen	*to command*
beginnen	beginnt	begann	begonnen	*to begin*
biegen	biegt	bog	gebogen	*to bend; to turn*
bieten	bietet	bot	geboten	*to offer*
bitten	bittet	bat	gebeten	*to request*
bleiben	bleibt	blieb	ist geblieben	*to stay*
brechen	bricht	brach	gebrochen	*to break*
brennen	brennt	brannte	gebrannt	*to burn*
bringen	bringt	brachte	gebracht	*to bring*
denken	denkt	dachte	gedacht	*to think*
dürfen	darf	durfte	gedurft	*to be allowed; may*
ein·laden	lädt ein	lud ein	eingeladen	*to invite*
empfehlen	empfiehlt	empfahl	empfohlen	*to recommend*
sich entscheiden	entscheidet	entschied	entschieden	*to decide*
essen	isst	aß	gegessen	*to eat*
fahren	fährt	fuhr	ist gefahren	*to drive*
fallen	fällt	fiel	ist gefallen	*to fall*
finden	findet	fand	gefunden	*to find*
fliegen	fliegt	flog	ist geflogen	*to fly*
fließen	fließt	floss	ist geflossen	*to flow*
geben	gibt	gab	gegeben	*to give*
gefallen	gefällt	gefiel	gefallen	*to please*
gehen	geht	ging	ist gegangen	*to go*
genießen	genießt	genoss	genossen	*to enjoy*
gewinnen	gewinnt	gewann	gewonnen	*to win*
haben	hat	hatte	gehabt	*to have*
halten	hält	hielt	gehalten	*to stop; to hold*
hängen	hängt	hing	hat/ist gehangen	*to be hanging*
heben	hebt	hob	gehoben	*to lift*
heißen	heißt	hieß	geheißen	*to be named*
helfen	hilft	half	geholfen	*to help*
kennen	kennt	kannte	gekannt	*to know*
klingen	klingt	klang	geklungen	*to sound*
kommen	kommt	kam	ist gekommen	*to come*
können	kann	konnte	gekonnt	*to be able; can*

Infinitive	Present	Narrative Past	Past Participle	Meaning
lassen	lässt	ließ	gelassen	*to let; to allow*
laufen	läuft	lief	ist gelaufen	*to run*
leihen	leiht	lieh	geliehen	*to lend*
lesen	liest	las	gelesen	*to read*
liegen	liegt	lag	gelegen	*to lie*
messen	misst	maß	gemessen	*to measure*
mögen	mag	mochte	gemocht	*to like*
müssen	muss	musste	gemusst	*to have to; must*
nehmen	nimmt	nahm	genommen	*to take*
nennen	nennt	nannte	genannt	*to name*
reißen	reißt	riss	gerissen	*to rip*
reiten	reitet	ritt	ist geritten	*to ride*
rennen	rennt	rannte	ist gerannt	*to run, race*
riechen	riecht	roch	gerochen	*to smell*
rufen	ruft	rief	gerufen	*to call*
scheinen	scheint	schien	geschienen	*to shine; to seem*
schlafen	schläft	schlief	geschlafen	*to sleep*
schließen	schließt	schloss	geschlossen	*to close*
schneiden	schneidet	schnitt	geschnitten	*to cut*
schreiben	schreibt	schrieb	geschrieben	*to write*
schwimmen	schwimmt	schwamm	ist geschwommen	*to swim*
sehen	sieht	sah	gesehen	*to see*
sein	ist	war	ist gewesen	*to be*
sitzen	sitzt	saß	gesessen	*to sit*
sollen	soll	sollte	gesollt	*to be supposed to; should*
sprechen	spricht	sprach	gesprochen	*to speak*
springen	springt	sprang	ist gesprungen	*to jump*
stehen	steht	stand	gestanden	*to stand*
steigen	steigt	stieg	ist gestiegen	*to climb*
sterben	stirbt	starb	ist gestorben	*to die*
stinken	stinkt	stank	gestunken	*to stink*
sich streiten	streitet	stritt	gestritten	*to argue*
tragen	trägt	trug	getragen	*to wear; to carry*
treffen	trifft	traf	getroffen	*to meet*
treiben	treibt	trieb	getrieben	*to engage in*
treten	tritt	trat	getreten	*to step*
trinken	trinkt	trank	getrunken	*to drink*
tun	tut	tat	getan	*to do*
vergessen	vergisst	vergaß	vergessen	*to forget*
verlieren	verliert	verlor	verloren	*to lose*
wachsen	wächst	wuchs	gewachsen	*to grow*
waschen	wäscht	wusch	gewaschen	*to wash*
werden	wird	wurde	ist geworden	*to become*
werfen	wirft	warf	geworfen	*to throw; to toss*
wissen	weiß	wusste	gewusst	*to know*
wollen	will	wollte	gewollt	*to want to*
ziehen	zieht	zog	gezogen	*to pull; to wear*
zwingen	zwingt	zwang	gezwungen	*to compel*

German-English Vocabulary

This German-English vocabulary is a comprehensive compilation of all active and passive vocabulary used in ***Vorsprung.*** The information in brackets indicates the chapter in which the word was first used for recognition, e.g., [K. 7] or the text section in which the word was presented as active vocabulary, e.g., [ZT 5]. The abbreviations used in brackets are: **AL-Anlauftext, AB-Absprungtext, ZT-Zieltext, WV-Wissenswerte Vokabeln, G-Grammatik, SiA-Sprache im Alltag.** The symbol ~ represents the key word within an entry.

Nouns are preceded by the definite articles; the plural endings follow after a comma. Weak masculine nouns have the accusative, dative and genitive endings in brackets before the plural ending, e.g., **[-en], -en.** Entries for professions give both male and female variations with appropriate plural endings. If the plural form of a noun is rarely or never used, no plural ending is indicated.

Regular (weak) verbs are listed with conversational past tense forms only in parentheses, e.g., **spielen (hat gespielt).** Irregular (strong or mixed) verbs generally are listed with both the narrative and conversational past tense forms in parentheses, e.g., **ziehen (zog, hat gezogen);** if there is a present tense vowel change, the present tense will be listed before the other tenses, e.g., **geben (gibt, gab, hat gegeben).** Separable prefixes are indicated with a raised dot, e.g., **zurück·bringen.** Reflexive verbs are preceded by the reflexive pronoun **sich.**

The glossary uses the following abbreviations:

acc. accusative
adj. adjective
adv. adverb
colloq. colloquial
conj. conjunction
dat. dative
fam. familiar
gen. genitive
pl. plural
sing. singular

ab und zu occasionally [K. 7]
ab·bauen (hat abgebaut) to reduce, decrease [AB 9]
ab·biegen (bog ab, ist abgebogen) to turn [AL 7/G]
die Abbildung, -en illustration [K. 7]
ab·drehen (hat abgedreht) to turn off [K. 6]
der Abend, -e evening [K. 3]; **Guten ~!** Good Evening! [AB 1/BK] **der Heilige ~** Christmas Eve [K. 10]
das Abendbrot evening meal, supper [AL 3/BK]
das Abendessen evening meal, supper [AL 3/BK]
abendlich evening time [AB 10]
abends in the evening [AB 2/WV]
der Abenteuerfilm, -e adventure film [AB 7/WV]
aber but [AL 1]
das Abgas, -e exhaust fumes [AB 12/WV]
ab·geben (gibt ab, gab ab, hat abgegeben) to turn in (a paper) [K. 8]
Abgemacht! Deal! Agreed! [AL 11]
der/die Abgeordnete, -n representative [AB 11/I WV]
abgetragen worn out [AB 9]
ab·hauen (ist abgehauen) to take off, scram [K. 10]
ab·heben (hob ab, hat abgehoben) to withdraw money [AL 7]
ab·holen (hat abgeholt) to pick up [K. 4]
das Abitur high school graduation exam [K. 8]
das Abkommen, - treaty [AB 11/I]
ab·lenken (hat abgelenkt) to divert [K. 5]
abnormal abnormal, unusual [AL 8/WV]
die Abrechnung, -en reckoning, accounting [AL 7]
die Abreise, -n departure [K. 8; ZT 10]
ab·reißen (riss ab, hat abgerissen) to tear down, demolish [AL 11]
ab·riegeln (hat abgeriegelt) to lock up, seal [AB 12]
der Absatz, ¨-e paragraph [K. 11]
ab·schaffen (hat abgeschafft) to abolish [K. 11]
die Abschiedsparty, -s bon voyage party [K. 4]
ab·schießen (schoss ab, hat abgeschossen) to shoot down [AB 11/II]
ab·schließen (schließt ab, schloss ab, hat abgeschlossen) to lock [K. 6]
der Abschluss, *pl.* **Abschlüsse** completion of program, degree [K. 8; AB 9]
ab·schneiden (schnitt ab, hat abgeschnitten) to cut off [AL 10]
die Abstammung origin [K. 6]
der Abstellraum, ¨-e storage room [AL 6/WV]
das Abteil, -e compartment [K. 6]
die Abteilung, -en department [ZT 9]
ab·trocknen (hat abgetrocknet) to dry off [AL 8/WV]
abwechselnd alternatingly [K. 9]
ab·ziehen (zog ab, hat abgezogen) to deduct [AL 12/WV]
Ach so! Oh! I see! I get it! [K. 1]
acht eight [AB 1/WV]
achten (hat geachtet) auf + *acc.* to pay attention to, watch for [K. 12]
achtzehn eighteen [AB 1/WV]
achtzig eighty [AB 1/WV]
das Adjektiv, -e adjective [AL 1]
das Adressbuch, ¨-er address book [AL 4/WV]
der Advent Advent [K. 10]
das Adverb, -(i)en adverb [AL 1]
afrikanisch African [K. 6]
die AG: die Aktiengesellschaft, -en corporation [K. 9]
aggressiv aggressive [AB 10]
ahnen (hat geahnt) to guess, suspect, sense [AL 11]
ähnlich similar, resembling [K. 4]
die Akte, -n file [ZT 9]

die Aktiengesellschaft, -en corporation [K. 9]
die Aktivität, -en activity [AB 2/WV]
aktuell current, up-to-date [AB 7]
akzeptabel acceptable [K. 8]
der Alarm alarm [K. 10]
der Albtraum, ⸚e nightmare [K. 1]
der Alexanderplatz Alexander Square *(in Berlin)* [K. 11]
der Alkohol alcohol [K. 4]
alkoholfrei non-alcoholic [K. 8]
alle all, everybody [AL 1]; **aller Art** all kinds of [AB 4]; **alles Gute** all the best [AL 9]; **Alles klar!** OK!, Great! [AL 6]; **alles, was du brauchst** everything you need [AL 6]; **vor allem** above all [AB 9]
allein alone [AB 2]
allerdings nonetheless [AB 8]
die Alliierten *(pl.)* the Allies [AB 11/I]
der Alltag everyday life, routine [AB 2/WV]; **hoch über dem ~** far beyond the everyday [AB 10]
allwissend all-knowing [K. 10]
die Alpen *(pl.)* the Alps [AB 10/WV]
als as, when [AB 5]; when [AB 10/G]
also well, alright, OK *(conversation starter)* [ZT 4]; well . . . , so . . . *(for stalling)* [AL 6]
alt old [AB 1/VW]
der Altar, ⸚e altar [K. 7]
das Alter age [K. 2; AB 5]
das Altglas used glass [K. 12]
die Altstadt historic part of town [AB 3]
am (17. August) on the (17th of August) [AB 2]; **~ liebsten** most of all, the most [AB 9]
Amerika America [AB 1/WV]
der Amerikaner, -/die Amerikanerin, -nen American [AB 1]
amerikanisch American
die Ampel, -n traffic light [AL 7/G]
an along, by [AL 5]
analytisch analytical [AB 9/WV]
an·bieten (bot an, hat angeboten) to offer [AL 9]
das Andenken, - souvenir [AL 4]
andererseits on the other hand [K. 12]
anderswo someplace else [AB 10]
die Anekdote, -n anecdote [K. 10]
der Anfang, ⸚e beginning [K. 6]
an·fangen (fängt an, fing an, hat angefangen) to start, begin [AB 5]
der Anfänger, - beginner [AB 10]
der Anführer, - ringleader [AB 7]
angebracht appropriate [K. 11]
angeln to fish [AB 3]
angenehm pleasant [AB 1]; **Sehr ~!** Pleased to meet you! [AB 1]
der Anglist, -en/die Anglistin, -nen English major [K. 8]
die Anglistik English language and literature [AB 8]
die Angst, ⸚e fear, anxiety
Angst haben (hat, hatte, hat gehabt) vor + *dat.* to be afraid of [K. 2; AB 10]
an·gucken (hat angeguckt) to take a look at [ZT 12]
an·halten (hält an, hielt an, hat angehalten) to stop [AL 6]
an·kommen (kam an, ist angekommen) to arrive [AB 2]
an·kreuzen (hat angekreuzt) to check (off) [K. 4]
die Ankunft, ⸚e arrival [ZT 4]
an·melden (hat angemeldet) to announce, register [AL 8]
an·nehmen (nimmt an, nahm an, hat angenommen) to accept; to assume [AL 12]
die Annonce, -n want ad [K. 4]
der Anorak, -s parka [K. 10]
an·probieren (hat anprobiert) to try on [AL 10]
an·reden (hat angeredet) to address [K. 4]
die Anreise arrival [ZT 10]; commute to work [AB 12]
an·rufen (rief an, hat angerufen) to phone, call up [AB 2/WV]
an·schauen (hat angeschaut) to (take a) look at [AB 6]
der Anschluss *pl.* **Anschlüsse** (train) connection [K. 10]; annexation [K. 12]
die Ansichtskarte, -n picture postcard [K. 4]
an·sprechen (spricht an, sprach an, hat angesprochen) to initiate a conversation [AL 5]
anspruchsvoll demanding; sophisticated [K. 6]
an·starren (hat angestarrt) to stare at [K. 5]
anstatt instead of [AB 11/II G]
der Ansturm, ⸚e onslaught, rush [AB 8]
die Antwort, -en answer [AB 6]
antworten (hat geantwortet) to answer [AB 1]
die Anweisung, -en direction [K. 7]
an·zeigen (hat angezeigt) to indicate, show [K. 4]
sich an·ziehen (zog sich an, hat sich angezogen) to put on clothes, get dressed [AL 8/WV]
der Apfel, ⸚ apple [AL 3/WV]
die Apfelsine, -n orange [AL 3/WV]
die Apotheke, -n pharmacy, drug store [K. 3]
der Apotheker, -/die Apothekerin, -nen pharmacist [K. 5; AL 9/WV]
Appetit: Guten~! Bon appetit!, Enjoy your meal! [ZT 6]
der April April [AB 2/WV]
das Äquivalent, -e equivalent [K. 2]
die Arbeit, -en work [AB 2/WV]
arbeiten (hat gearbeitet) to work [AL 5]
der Arbeiter, -/die Arbeiterin, -nen worker [AB 7]
der Arbeitnehmer -/die Arbeitnehmerin, -nen employee [AT 12/WV]
das Arbeitsamt, ⸚er (un)employment agency [AB 9]
das Arbeitsbuch ⸚er workbook [AB 1/WV]
die Arbeitserfahrung, -en work experience [K. 9]
die Arbeitserlaubnis, -se work permit [AT 12/WV]
die Arbeitsgruppe, -n study group [AL 8]
das Arbeitsklima work environment [K. 9]
arbeitslos unemployed [K. 9]
die Arbeitsnorm, -en work quota/standard [AB 11/I]
der Arbeitsplatz, ⸚e job; place of work [K. 6]
die Arbeitsvermittlung, -en job placement agency [AL 9]
das Arbeitszimmer, - work room; study [AL 6/WV]
der Architekt, -en/die Architektin, -nen architect [AL 9/WV]
sich ärgern (hat sich geärgert) über + *acc.* to be angry about [AB 8/G]
der Arm, -e arm [AB 6/WV]
die Armbanduhr, -en wrist watch [AB 11/II]
die Armee, -n army [AB 11/I]; **die Rote ~** Red Army
der Arzt, *pl.* **⸚e/die Ärztin, -nen** physician [K. 5; AL 9/WV]
die Asche, -n ash, cinder [AL 10]; **Aschenputtel** Cinderella [AL 10]; **der Aschermittwoch** Ash Wednesday [K. 10]
asiatisch Asian [K. 6]
das Aspirin aspirin [K. 6]
der Assistent, [-en], -en/die Assistentin, -nen assistant [K. 8]
die Astronomie astronomy [K. 7]

die Atomenergie nuclear energy, atomic energy [AB 12/WV]
attraktiv attractive [AB 1/WV]
auch also [AL 2]
auf on, onto [K. 4;AL 7/G]; **auf dem Dachboden** in the attic [AL 6/WV]
auf•bleiben (blieb auf, ist aufgeblieben) to stay up [K. 6]
der Aufenthalt, -e stay, time spent in a place [AL 12]
die Aufgabe, -n assignment, task [K. 5]; task, job [AB 12]
auf•geben (gibt auf, gab auf, hat aufgegeben) to drop off, post; to give up [AL 7/WV]
aufgeregt excited; tense, nervous [K. 4; AB 9]
aufgrund on the basis of [K. 8]
auf•hängen (hat aufgehängt) to hang up [K. 6]
auf•hören (hat aufgehört) to stop [AL 2/WV]
auf•kriegen (hat aufgekriegt) to get open *(colloq.)* [AL 6]
auf•machen (hat aufgemacht) to open [AL 1/WV]
auf•passen (hat aufgepasst) auf + *acc.* to watch out for, pay attention to [K. 4]
auf•räumen (hat aufgeräumt) to pick up, clean up [K. 4; ZT 10]
aufrecht•erhalten (erhält aufrecht, erhielt aufrecht, hat aufrecht erhalten) to maintain, preserve [ZT 11]
sich auf•regen (hat sich aufgeregt) to get upset, nervous; to get excited [K. 9]
die Aufregung -en excitement; nervousness [AB 9]
auf•schauen (hat aufgeschaut) to look up [AB 6]
auf•schließen (hat aufgeschlossen) to unlock [AL 6]
der Aufschnitt cold cuts [K. 3]
auf•schreiben (schrieb auf, hat aufgeschrieben) to write down [K. 4; AL 6]
der Aufstand, ¨-e revolt, uprising [AB 11/I]
auf•stehen (steht auf, stand auf, ist aufgestanden) to get up, get out of bed [AL 1/WV]
der Auftrag, ¨-e assignment [K. 9]
auf•wachen (ist aufgewacht) to wake up [AL 1]
auf•wachsen (wächst auf, wuchs auf, ist aufgewachsen) to grow up [AB 6]
auf•wärmen (hat aufgewärmt) to warm up [AB 10]
das Auge, -n eye [AB 1/WV]
die Augenbraue, -n eyebrow [AB 6]
der August August [AB 2/WV]
aus + *dat.* from [AB 1]
die Ausbildung, -en education, job training [AB 9]
der Ausbildungsleiter, -/die Ausbildungsleiterin, -nen head trainer, lead teacher [AB 9]
aus•checken (hat ausgecheckt) to check out *(slang)* [K. 11]
der Ausdruck, ¨-e expression [AL 1]
aus•fahren (fährt aus, fuhr aus, ist ausgefahren) to deliver [K. 5]
aus•fallen (fällt aus, fiel aus, ist ausgefallen) to be canceled [AB 11/II]
aus•füllen (hat ausgefüllt) to fill out [K. 4]
aus•geben (gibt aus, gab aus, hat ausgegeben) to spend money [AL 4]
aus•gehen (ging aus, ist ausgegangen) to go out [AL 5]
ausgesprochen decidedly [AB 8]
ausgezeichnet excellent [K. 4]
die Aushilfe, -n temporary, part-time worker [AB 8]
sich aus•kennen, (hat sich ausgekannt) mit + *dat.* to know a lot about [AL 9]
aus•kommen (kam aus, ist ausgekommen) mit + *dat.* to get along with [ZT 9]
das Ausland abroad; foreign country [K. 4]
der Ausländer, -/die Ausländerin, -nen foreigner [ZT 6]
die Ausländerbehörde, -n foreigner's registration office [AT 12/WV]
der Auslandsaufenthalt, -e stay abroad [K. 12]
aus•liegen (lag aus, hat ausgelegen) to be displayed [ZT 7]
die Ausnahme, -n exception [AB 4]
ausnahmsweise as an exception, just this once [K. 4]
die Ausrede, -n excuse [K. 8]; **Ausreden machen (hat gemacht)** to make excuses [K. 8]
aus•rufen (rief aus, hat ausgerufen) to proclaim, announce [AB 11/I]
sich aus•ruhen (hat sich ausgeruht) to relax [AL 8/WV]
aus•schreiben (schrieb aus, hat ausgeschrieben) to advertise, announce [ZT 9]
die Aussage, -n statement [K. 11]
das Aussehen appearance [AB 1/WV]
aus•sehen (sieht aus, sah aus, hat ausgesehen) to appear, look (like) [ZT 2]
die Außengrenze, -n external border of the EU [AB 12]
die Außenpolitik foreign policy [K. 12]
außer + *dat.* except for [AB 6/G]
außerdem besides, by the way [AB 5]
außerhalb + *gen.* outside of [K. 8; AB 11/II G]
die Aussicht, -en view [ZT 3]; prospect
aus•steigen (stieg aus, ist ausgestiegen) to get out of, disembark [AL 7/G; AB 10]
der Ausstieg, -e stepping down, resignation [AL 7]
der Austausch exchange [K. 2]; **der Austauschstudent, [-en], -en/die Austauschstudentin, -nen** exchange student [K. 2]
aus•tragen (trägt aus, trug aus, hat ausgetragen) to deliver [K. 5]
(das) Australien Australia [K. 2]
der Austritt, -e withdrawal, resignation [AL 7]
[einen Beruf] aus•üben (hat ausgeübt) to practice, pursue [a profession] [K. 9]
die Auswahl selection [K. 7]
aus•wählen (hat ausgewählt) to pick out, select [ZT 8]
aus•wandern (ist ausgewandert) to emigrate [ZT 11]
auswendig by heart, memorized [K. 4]
die Auszeichnung award, recognition [K. 8]
sich aus•ziehen (zog sich aus, hat sich ausgezogen) to get undressed [AL 8/WV]
der/die Auszubildende, -n apprentice [K. 8]
authentisch authentic [AB 7]
das Auto, -s automobile, car [ZT 4]; **fahren** to drive a car [K. 6]
die Autobahn, -en autobahn, superhighway [AB 4]
die Autobiographie, -n autobiography [AB 7/WV]
autofrei car-free [AB 10]
das Autogrammspiel, -e autograph game [K. 2]
der Automat, [-en], -en vending machine [AL 6]
der Automechaniker, -/die Automechanikerin, -nen car mechanic [AL 9/WV]

der Autor, -en/die Autorin, -nen author [AB 6]
der Autoschlüssel, - car key [K. 3]
der/die Azubi, -s apprentice [K. 8]

babysitten (hat gebabysittet) to babysit [K. 5]
der Babysitter, -/die Babysitterin, -nen babysitter [K. 4]
der Bäcker, -/die Bäckerin, -nen baker [AL 9/WV]
die Bäckerei, -en bakery [K. 3; AL 7/WV]
sich baden (hat sich gebadet) to bathe [AL 8/WV]
das Badetuch, ¨-er bath towel [AL 8/WV]
die Badewanne, -n bathtub [AL 8/WV]
das Badezimmer, - bathroom [AL 6]
das BAföG federal tuition assistance, financial aid [AB 8]
die Bahn, -en railroad, train [K. 4; AB 7/WV]
die Bahncard "bahncard," discount rail pass [K. 4]
der Bahnhof, ¨-e train station [AL 3]; **~ verstehen** to not speak much German [AL 3]
das Bähnli, -s little train *(Swiss dialect)* [AB 10]
bald soon [AB 2]
baldig coming, soon-to-be [K. 12]
der Balkon, -s (-e) balcony [AL 6/WV]
der Ballungsraum, ¨-e population center [AB 8]
die Banane, -n banana [AL 3/WV]
die Bank, -en bank [AL 7]
der Bankkredit, -e bank loan [K. 10]
das Barock Baroque [K. 3]
die Barriere, -n barrier [K. 11]
die Bassena wash basin [K. 11]
der Bauch, ¨-e stomach [AB 6/WV]
bauen (hat gebaut) to construct, build [AB 8]
beachten (hat beachtet) to observe, pay attention to [AB 4]
der Beamte, [-en] -n/die Beamtin, -nen civil servant, official [AL 9/WV]
beantragen (hat beantragt) to apply for [AT 12/WV]
der Becher, - cup [AL 8/WV]
bedeckt overcast [AL 5/WV]
bedeuten (hat bedeutet) to mean [K. 4; AL 5]
das Bedürfnis, -se need [K. 11]
sich beeilen (hat sich beeilt) to hurry [AL 8/WV]
beeindruckend impressive [ZT 9]
beenden (hat beendet) to finish, complete [K. 12]
der Befehl, -e command [K. 4]
befehlen (befiehlt, befahl, hat befohlen) to command [K. 10]
die Beförderung, -en advancement, promotion [K. 9]
befürworten (hat befürwortet) to approve [K. 12]
begabt talented [AB 9/WV]
begegnen (ist begegnet) + *dat.* to meet, run into [AB 10]
begeistert enthusiastic, excited [K. 5]
beginnen (begann, hat begonnen) to begin [AB 2]
begleiten (hat begleitet) to accompany [AL 10]
begraben to bury; buried [AB 11/II]
begrenzt limited [AB 8]
Beispiel: zum~ for example [AL 2]
behalten (behält, behielt, hat behalten) to keep [K. 5]
behaupten (hat behauptet) to claim, maintain [K. 8]
beheizt heated [K. 3]
bei + *dat.* at, by, near, with [K. 4; AB 6/G]
beige beige [AB 1/WV]
das Bein, -e leg [K. 4; AB 6/WV]
bei·treten (tritt bei, trat bei, ist beigetreten) + *dat.* to join, become a member [AB 11/I]
der Beitritt, -e joining [AB 12]
bekannt familiar, well-known [ZT 8]
der/die Bekannte, -n *(adj. as noun)* acquaintance [K. 5]
bekannt geben (gibt bekannt, gab bekannt, hat bekannt gegeben) to announce [AB 7]
die Bekanntschaft, -en acquaintanceship [K. 5]
bekommen (bekam, hat bekommen) to get, receive [K. 3; AL 6]
belasten (hat belastet) to burden [ZT 12]
belegen (hat belegt) to enroll in [K. 8]
(das) Belgien Belgium [K. 12]
beliebt popular [AB 4]
benachrichtigen (hat benachrichtigt) to inform [ZT 9]
das Benehmen behavior [K. 8]
sich benehmen (benimmt sich, benahm sich, hat sich benommen) to behave [K. 12]
benötigen (hat benötigt) to require, need [K. 4]
benutzen (hat benutzt) to use [K. 4]
das Benzin gasoline [AB 4]
der Berater, -/die Beraterin, -nen counselor, advisor [K. 8; AL 9/WV]
die Beratung counseling [K. 8; AB 9]
bereit ready [AB 7]
die Bereitschaft readiness [K. 9]
der Berg, -e mountain [AB 10/WV]
bergsteigen (ist berggestiegen) to go mountainclimbing [K. 10]
die Bergwirtschaft, -en mountain restaurant [AB 10]
der Bericht, -e report [AB 7]
der Beruf, -e profession, job, occupation [K. 2; AL 9]
die Berufsschule, -n technical-vocational high school [K. 9]
berühmt famous [K. 8]
die Besatzungszone, -n occupation zone [AB 11/I]
Bescheid bekommen (hat Bescheid bekommen) to get an answer, be notified [ZT 9]
beschreiben (beschrieb, hat beschrieben) to describe [K. 4; AB 7]
beseitigen (hat beseitigt) to eliminate [K. 12]
der Besessene, [-n], -n obsessed person [K. 7]
besetzen (hat besetzt) to occupy [AB 11/I]
der Besitzer, - owner [K. 6]
besonders especially [AB 4]
besorgen (hat besorgt) to acquire, get [AL 7]
besprechen (bespricht, besprach, hat besprochen) to discuss [K. 4]
die Besprechung, -en discussion [ZT 9]
besser better [AB 2]
Besserung: Gute ~! Speedy recovery! [AL 8/WV]
das Beste the best (thing) [K. 9]
die Bestechung, -en bribe, bribery [AB 7/K. 11]
bestellen (hat bestellt) to order [K. 5; AB 7]
besteuern (hat besteuert) to tax [ZT 12]
bestimmt undoubtedly [AL 3]
die Bestimmung, -en stipulation [ZT 12]
bestrafen (hat bestraft) to punish [K. 10]
der Bestseller, -s bestseller [K. 7]
besuchen (hat besucht) to visit [ZT 2]
beten (hat gebetet) to pray [AL 10]
der Betreuer, - person in charge [ZT 10]
der Betrieb, -e business [AB 9]

die Betriebswirtschaft business administration [AL 2/WV]
das Bett, -en bed [AB 3]
bevor before [ZT 2]
bewältigen (hat bewältigt) to resolve [K. 12]
beweisen (bewies, hat bewiesen) to prove [K. 10]
sich bewerben (bewirbt sich, bewarb sich, hat sich beworben) an to apply to [K. 8]; ~ **um/für** + *acc.* to apply for [AL 9/AL 12]
der Bewerber, -/ die Bewerberin, -nen applicant [AB 9]
die Bewerbung, -en application [AL 12]
der Bewerbungsbrief, -e letter of application [K. 9]
das Bewerbungsformular, -e application form [K. 9]
bewerkstelligen (hat bewerkstelligt) to manage, take care of [ZT 10]
bewerten (hat bewertet) to evaluate [K. 8]
bewirtet meals included [K. 10]
bewölkt cloudy, overcast [K. 5]
bezahlbar payable [AB 8]
bezahlen (hat bezahlt) to pay [ZT 4]
bezeichnen (hat bezeichnet) als to characterize/designate as [AB 7]
beziehen (bezog, hat bezogen) to move in [AB 8]
die Beziehung, -en contact, relationship [K. 5; AB 7]; **internationale Beziehungen** *(pl.)* international relations [AL 2/WV]
Bezug: in ~ auf in regard to [K. 12]
das Bezugswort, ¨-er antecedent [AL 9/G]
die Bibliothek, -en library [AB 3]
der Bibliothekar, -/die Bibliothekarin, -nen librarian [AL 9/WV]
das Bibliothekarswesen library science [ZT 9]
das Bier beer [K. 2; AL 3]
die Bierbrauerei, -en brewery [K. 9]
das Bierzelt, -e beer tent [K. 10]
das Bild, -er picture [AL 6/WV]
bilden (hat gebildet) to construct, form [K. 4]
billig cheap, inexpensive [K. 4]
die Biographie, -n biography [AB 7/WV]
der Bioladen, ¨ health food store [AL 7/WV]
die Biologie biology [AL 2/WV]
bis until [AL 8]; ~ **gleich!** See you soon! [AL 6]
bisschen: ein ~ a little [AB 2]

bitte please [AL 1/WV], you're welcome; ~ **schön!** There you are! [K. 7]
die Bitte, -n request [K. 11]
bitten (bat, hat gebeten) um + *acc.* to ask for, request [AB 8/G]
das Blatt, ¨-er page, sheet [AB 6]
blättern (hat geblättert) in + *dat.* to leaf through [AB 6]
blau blue [AB 1/WV]
bleiben (blieb, ist geblieben) to stay, remain [K. 2; AL 3]
bleifrei unleaded [K. 12]
blitzen (hat geblitzt) to have lightning [AL 5/WV]
das Blitzlicht, -er flash (for a camera) [AL 4/WV]
die Blockade, -n blockade [AB 11/I]
blond blond [AB 1/VW]
die Blume, -n flower [ZT 4]
die Bluse, -n blouse [AL 4/WV]
das Blut blood [AL 10]
der Bombenangriff, -e bombardment, bombing attack [AB 11/II]
die Bordkarte, -n boarding pass [AL 4/WV]
die Börse stock market [K. 4]
böse sein (war, ist gewesen) auf + *acc.* to be upset with, mad at [AL 7/G]
die Bosheit, -en meanspiritedness [K. 10]
der Boss *pl.* **Bosse** boss [K. 7]
boxen (hat geboxt) to box, hit [K. 11]
die Brandbombe, -n fire bomb [K. 11]
Brandenburg Brandenburg [AB 11/I WV]
das Brandenburger Tor Brandenburg Gate (in Berlin) [K. 11]
die Bratwurst, ¨-e bratwurst, fried sausage [K. 3]
brauchen (hat gebraucht) to need [AB 4]
braun brown [AB 1/WV]
die Braut, ¨-e bride [AL 10]
sich etwas brechen (bricht sich, brach sich, hat sich gebrochen) to break [AL 8]
brennen (brannte, hat gebrannt) to burn [K. 10]
Brett: das schwarze ~ bulletin board [AL 6]
die Bretzel, -n pretzel [AL 7/WV]
der Brief, -e letter [K. 2]
die Briefmarke, -n stamp [AL 7/WV]
die Brokkoli *(pl.)* broccoli [K. 4]
die Broschüre, -n brochure [K. 4]
das Brot, -e bread [AL 3/WV]
das Brötchen, - hard roll [AL 3/WV]

die Brücke, -n bridge [AB 3]
der Bruder, ¨ brother [AL 2/WV]
die Brüderschaft brotherhood, fraternity [K. 5]
brüllen (hat gebrüllt) to yell, scream [AB 11/II]
die Brust, ¨-e breast, chest [AB 6/WV]
das Bruttosozialprodukt, -e gross national product (GNP) [ZT 11]
das Buch, ¨-er book, textbook [AL 1/WV]
das Bücherregal, -e book case [AL 6/WV]
der Buchhalter, -/die Buchhalterin, -nen accountant [AL 9/WV]
die Buchhandlung, -en bookstore [AL 7]
buchstabieren (hat buchstabiert) to spell [AL 5/G]
die Bude, -n student room (*colloq.*) [AL 6]
der Bummel, - walk, leisurely stroll [AL 11]
der Bund alliance; Federal Government [AB 11/I WV]
der Bundeskanzler Federal Chancellor [K. 6]
das Bundesland, ¨-er state, province [AB 1/I WV]
der Bundespräsident, [-en], -en/die Bundespräsidentin, -nen Federal President [AB 11/I WV]
der Bundesrat Federal Council [AB 11/I WV]
die Bundesregierung Federal Government [AB 11/I WV]
die Bundesrepublik Deutschland (BRD) Federal Republic of Germany [AL 11]
der Bundestag Federal Parliament [AB 11/I WV]
der Bürger, - citizen [AB 11/I WV]
der Bürgermeister, -/die Bürgermeisterin, -nen mayor [AB 11/I WV]
das Büro, -s office [AL 9]
die Bürste, -n (hair)brush [AL 8/WV]
sich die Haare bürsten (hat sich gebürstet) to brush one's hair [AL 8/WV]
der Bus, -se bus [AB 7/WV]
die Bushaltestelle, -n bus stop [AL 7]
die Butter butter [AL 3/WV]

das Café, -s café [ZT 3]
der Campingplatz, ¨-e camp ground [AB 3]
der Campus campus [AB 8]
die CD, -s compact disc [AL 4/WV]

der CD-Player, - CD player [AL 4/WV]
Celsius Centigrade [AL 5/WV]
chaotisch chaotic [K. 8]
der Chef, -s/die Chefin, -nen boss [K. 3; AL 9/WV]
die Chemie chemistry [AL 2/WV]
chinesisch Chinese [K. 5]
der Chor, ¨-e chorus, choir [K. 9]
das Christentum Christianity [AB 6]
Christi Himmelfahrt Ascension Day [K. 10]
das Christkind Christ child [K. 10]
die Christlich-Demokratische Union (CDU) Christian Democratic Union [K. 7]
die Christlich-Soziale Union (CSU) Christian Social Union [K. 7]
die Clique, -n clique, circle of friends [AB 5]
der Club, -s club [K. 6]
die Cola, -s cola [AL 3]
der Computer, - computer [AL 6/WV]
Confoederatio Helvetica Switzerland [K. 10]
die Couch, -es (-en) couch [AL 6/WV]
der Cousin, -s male cousin [AL 2/WV]

da there [ZT 4]
der Dachboden, ¨ attic [AL 6/WV]
der Dachziegel, - roofing slate [K. 11]
dagegen against it [K. 5]
daheim at home [AL 10]
daher for that reason, that's why [AB 9]
damals back then [ZT 5]
damit so that [AB 7/G]
danach afterwards [K. 3; AL 5]
(das) Dänemark Denmark [K. 12]
danke thanks, thank you [AB 1]; **~ schön!** Thanks a lot! [K. 1]
danken (hat gedankt) + *dat.* to thank [AL 6]; **~ für** + *acc.* to thank for [AB 8/G]
dann then [K. 1]
darf may, be permitted [AB 2]
dass that *(conj.)* [ZT 2]
dauern (hat gedauert) to last [ZT 4]
dazu·kommen (kam dazu, ist dazugekommen) to get to; to arrive at [K. 5]
der Deckel, - lid, top [AB 6]
dein your *(fam. sing.)* [AB 2]
der Dekan, -e dean [K. 8]
deklarieren (hat deklariert) to declare [K. 12]
die Demokratie, -n democracy [K. 10]
denken (dachte, hat gedacht) an + *acc.* to think of [AL 4]
das Denkmal, ¨-er monument [K. 11]
denn for, because, then [K. 1]
das Deospray, -s deodorant spray [AL 4/WV]
deprimiert depressed [K. 12]
deren whose [K. 10]
deshalb that's (the reason) why [AL 5]
dessen whose [K. 10]
deswegen that's why, for that reason [ZT 6]
das Detail, -s detail [K. 4]
(Das) Deutsch the German language [K. 1; AL 2/WV]; **auf Deutsch** in German
die Deutsche Demokratische Republik, (DDR) German Democratic Republic (GDR) [AL 11]
der/die Deutsche, -n *(adj. as noun)* German [AB 1/WV]
der Deutschkurs, -e German language course [AB 2]
(das) Deutschland Germany [AB 1/WV]
der Dezember December [AB 2/WV]
dich you *(informal sing., acc.)* [AB 3/G]
die Diele, -n entrance hallway [AL 6/WV]
dienen (hat gedient) to serve [K. 10]
der Dienstag, -e Tuesday [AB 2/WV]
dieser, diese, dieses this, that [AB 6/G]
der Diktator, -en dictator [AB 11/I WV]
die Diktatur, -en dictatorship [AB 11/I WV]
das Ding, -e object, thing [K. 4]
der Dinosaurier, - dinosaur [K. 6]
das Diplom, -e diploma [K. 8]
die Diskothek, -en discotheque [ZT 3]
der Diskurs, -e discourse [AB 6]
die Diskussion, -en discussion [AL 7]
diskutieren (hat diskutiert) über + *acc.* to discuss [AL 5]
diszipliniert disciplined [AB 9/WV]
doch go ahead and . . . *(persuasive particle)* [K. 2; AL 4/G]; Oh, yes it is! *(response to negative statement)* [ZT 3]
der Doktortitel,- doctorate, Ph.D. [K. 8]
der Dokumentarfilm, -e documentary film [AB 7/WV]
der Dom, -e cathedral [K. 4; AL 11]
die Donau Danube River [AB 11/I WV]
donnern (hat gedonnert) to thunder [AL 5/WV]
der Donnerstag, -e Thursday [AB 2/WV]
das Doppelbett, -en double bed [K. 6]
der Doppelinfinitiv, -e double infinitive [K. 11]
das Dorf, ¨-er village [AB 10]
dort there; **~ drüben** over there [ZT 5]
die Dose, -n can [AB 12/WV]
der Dozent, [-en], -en/die Dozentin, -nen assistant professor, instructor [AL 8]
drahtlos cordless [K. 12]
das Drama, *pl.* **Dramen** drama , play [AB 7/WV]
drehen (hat gedreht): einen Film ~ über + *acc.* to make a movie about [AB 7]
dringend urgent [K. 6]
dringlich urgent, pressing [AB 7]
die Droge, -n drug [K. 4; AL 7]
dröhnen (hat gedröhnt) to drone [AB 10]
der Druck pressure [AB 8]
drucken (hat gedruckt) to print; to press [ZT 12]
die Daumen drücken (hat gedrückt) + *dat.* to cross one's finger for [AL 9]
der Drucker, - printer [AL 6/WV]
drunt' (darunter) down below [AB 11/II]
du you *(informal sing.)* [AB 1/G]; Hey . . . *(used to introduce an utterance)*
dumm dumb, stupid [AB 4/WV]
dunkel dark [AB 1/WV]
durch + *acc.* through [ZT 4]; **~ dick und dünn** through thick and thin [AB 5]
der Durchfall diarrhea [AL 8/WV]
durch·führen (hat durchgeführt) to carry out [AB 12]
durch·gucken (hat durchgeguckt) to look through, look over [ZT 9]
durch·machen (hat durchgemacht) to stay up, get through [AL 5]
dürfen (darf, durfte, hat gedurft) may; to be allowed to, permitted to [AL 4]
die Dusche, -n shower [AL 6]
(sich) duschen (hat sich geduscht) to shower [K. 6; AL 8/WV]
der Duschraum, ¨-e shower room [AL 6]
dynamisch dynamic [AB 9/WV]

eben just [K. 5; AB 10]
echt authentic, genuine; real(ly) [AL 6]
die Ecke, -n corner; **an der ~** at the corner [AL 7/G]
der Edelmann, ⸚er nobleman [K. 10]
der Edelstein, -e jewel, precious stone [AL 10]
ehemalig former(ly), previous(ly) [AB 10]
eher rather [AB 8]; sooner [ZT 12]
ehrlich honest [K. 5; AB 10]
das Ei, -er egg [K. 3]; **weichgekochtes ~** softboiled egg
eifersüchtig jealous [K. 5]
eigen own [AL 6]
die Eigenschaft, -en personal trait, quality, characteristic [AB 4/WV]
eigentlich actually [ZT 5; AB 6]
der Eilzug, ⸚e fast train [K. 6]
einander one another [AL 5/WV]
die Einbahnstraße, -n one-way street [AB 4]
der Eindruck, ⸚e impression [AB 9]
einerseits on the one hand [K. 12]
einfach simple, simply [AB 3]
die Einfahrt, -en entry [K. 4]
ein·fallen (fällt ein, fiel ein, ist eingefallen) + *dat.* to think of something, get an idea, occur to [AB 9]
einfallslos uncreative [AB 4/WV]
das Einfamilienhaus, ⸚er single-family house [AL 6/WV]
der Einfluss, *pl.* **Einflüsse** influence [ZT 11]
der Eingang, ⸚e entrance, front door [AL 6/WV]
eingestellt: ~ sein auf to be geared for, ready for [AB 8]
die Einheit, -en unity [AB 11/I]
einheitlich standard, uniform [ZT 12]
einige a few, several [AB 4]
ein·kaufen (hat eingekauft) to shop [AL 5/G]
Einkaufs... *(in compounds)* shopping; **der Einkaufsbummel, -** shopping trip [K. 5]; **der Einkaufskorb, ⸚e** shopping basket [K. 7]; **die Einkaufstasche, -n** shopping bag [K. 7]; **die Einkaufstüte, -n** shopping bag [K. 7]
ein·laden (lädt ein, lud ein, hat eingeladen) to invite; to take out [AL 5]
die Einreise, -n arrival [K. 12]
ein·richten (hat eingerichtet) to set up, institute [K. 6]
die Einrichtung, -en institution, establishment [ZT 12]
eins one [AB 1/WV]
der Einsatz, ⸚e deployment [AB 12]
ein·schicken (hat eingeschickt) to send in [AL 12]
ein·schlafen (schläft ein, schlief ein, ist eingeschlafen) to fall asleep [AL 5/G]
ein·schlagen (schlägt ein, schlug ein, ist eingeschlagen) to strike, impact [AB 11/II]
ein·setzen (hat eingesetzt) to start [K. 6]; to deploy, use, implement [AB 12]
ein·steigen (stieg ein, ist eingestiegen) to get into a vehicle, board, climb in [AL 7/G]
ein·stellen (hat eingestellt) to hire [ZT 9]
die Einstellung, -en attitude, outlook [K. 11; ZT 12]
ein·stürzen (ist eingestürzt) to collapse [AB 11/II]
der Eintopf, ⸚e stew [K. 3]
der Eintrag, ⸚e entry [K. 10]
der Einwohner, -/die Einwohnerin, -nen inhabitant [AB 3]
das Einzelzimmer, - single room [K. 6]
ein·ziehen (zog ein, ist eingezogen) to move in [AB 5/WV]; to deposit [AL 7/WV]
einzig single [AB 4]
einzigartig unique, singular [K. 8]
der Einzug moving into a house/an apartment [AL 6]
das Eis ice; ice cream [K. 3]
der Eisenbahnzug, ⸚e train [AB 11/II]
der Eiskunstlauf figure skating [K. 10]
das Eisstadion, *pl.* **Stadien** skating rink [K. 3]
eitern (hat geeitert) to fester [K. 11]
die Elbe Elbe River [K. 5; AB 11/I WV]
elegant elegant [K. 4]
der Ellenbogen, - elbow [AB 6/WV]
die Eltern *(pl.)* parents [AL 2/WV]
empfehlen (empfiehlt, empfahl, hat empfohlen) to recommend [AL 7]
die Empfehlung, -en recommendation [K. 9]
sich empören (hat sich empört) to become indignant [AB 11/II]
das Ende, -n end [AL 6]
endlich finally [AB 2]
die „Endlösung" "final solution" [K. 7]
die Energiequelle, -n source of energy [AB 12/WV]
(das) England England [AB 1/WV]
der Engländer, -/die Engländerin, -nen Englishman/Englishwoman [AB 1/WV]
(das) Englisch the English language [AL 2/WV]
der Enkel, -/die Enkelin, -innen grandson/granddaughter [AL 2/WV]
das Enkelkind, -er grandchild [AL 2/WV]
entdecken (hat entdeckt) to discover [K. 3]
die Entdeckung, -en discovery [K. 12]
entfernt distant [K. 12]
enthalten (enthält, enthielt, hat enthalten) to contain [K. 10]
sich entscheiden (entschied sich, hat sich entschieden) für/gegen + *acc.* to decide on/against [K. 4; AB 6]
die Entscheidung, -en decision [ZT 5]
entschuldigen (hat entschuldigt) to excuse, pardon [K. 5; AL 11]
die Entschuldigung, -en excuse [K. 8]; **Entschuldigung!** Pardon! Excuse me! [AL 1]
die Entspannung relaxation [K. 10]
entstehen (entstand, ist entstanden) to originate; to be built [AL 11]
enttäuscht disappointed [AB 5]
entweder ... oder either . . . or [ZT 10]
entwickeln (hat entwickelt) to develop [K. 5]
er he, it [AB 1/G]
erarbeiten (hat erarbeitet) to acquire, work out [ZT 9]
die Erbse, -n pea [AL 3/WV]
das Erdgeschoss, *pl.* **Geschosse** ground floor [AL 6]; **im ~** on the ground floor [AL 6]
die Erdkunde geography [K. 2]
das Erdöl petroleum oil [AB 12/WV]
erfahren experienced [AL 9]
die Erfahrung, -en experience [AB 5]
erfinden (erfand, hat erfunden) to invent [K. 5]
die Erfindung, -en invention [K. 12]
erforschen (hat erforscht) to research [AB 12/WV]
erfüllen (hat erfüllt) to fulfill, complete [K. 9]
erfunden made-up, invented [K. 10]
sich ergeben (ergibt sich, ergab sich, hat sich ergeben) to materialize, result [K. 9]
erhalten (erhält, erhielt, hat erhalten) to get, receive [AL 12]

erhöhen (hat erhöht) to raise, increase [AB 11/I]
sich erholen (hat sich erholt) to recuperate [AL 8/WV]
sich erinnern (hat sich erinnert) an + *acc.* to remember [K. 5; AL 8/G]
sich erkälten (hat sich erkältet) to catch cold [AL 8]
die Erkältung, -en common cold [AL 5]
erkennen (erkannte, hat erkannt) to recognize [ZT 4; AB 6]
erklären (hat erklärt) to explain [ZT 6]
erklären (hat erklärt) für + *acc.* to declare; to describe [AB 7]
erlassen (erlässt, erließ, hat erlassen) to pass a law [K. 12]
erlauben (hat erlaubt) to permit, allow [AL 10]
erlaubt allowed, permitted [K. 4]
erläutern (hat erläutert) to explain [K. 10]
erleben (hat erlebt) to experience [AB 10]
erledigen (hat erledigt) to take care of, deal with [AL 7]
ernst serious [AB 4/WV]
erobern (hat erobert) to conquer, capture [AB 11/I]
eröffnen (hat eröffnet) to open [AL 7]
erraten (errät, erriet, hat erraten) to guess [K. 6]
erschießen (erschoss, hat erschossen) to shoot to death [K. 10]
erst not until; first [AB 2]; **erst seit** just since [AB 5/G]; **zum ersten Mal** for the first time [AL 5]
erstaunt astonished [AB 6]
erträglich tolerable, manageable [AB 8]
erwägen (hat erwägt) to consider [K. 12]
erwähnen (hat erwähnt) to mention [K. 5]
erwarten (hat erwartet) to expect [AB 12]
die Erwartung, -en expectation [AB 9]
erweitern (hat erweitert) to expand [K. 11]
erwünscht desired, sought [K. 8]
erzählen (hat erzählt) von + *dat.* to talk/tell a story about [AB 8/G]
die Erzählung, -en story [AB 7/WV]
erzeugen (hat erzeugt) to create [K. 10]
erziehen (erzog, hat erzogen) to raise children [ZT 12]
es it [AB 1/G]
essen (isst, aß, hat gegessen) to eat [AL 3]
das Essen food [AL 3/WV]
die Etage, -n floor [AL 6/WV]; **die erste (zweite) ~** second (third) floor [AL 6]
etwas some, somewhat [AB 2/G]; **~ anderes** something else [AL 4]
euch you *(informal pl. acc. dat.)* [AB 3/G]
euer your *(pl., familiar)* [AL 3/G]
euphorisch euphoric [ZT 11]
der Euro, -s Euro *(European currency unit)* [K. 12]
(das) Europa Europe [K. 12]
europäisch European [K. 4]
die Europäische Union European Union [AL 8]
der Euroscheck, -s Euro check [K. 7]
eventuell perhaps, possibly; eventually [K. 8; AL 12]
ewig eternal [AB 10]
der Exot, -en/die Exotin, -nen exoticum, "rare bird" [K. 8]
exotisch exotic [AB 8]
der Experte, [-n], -n/die Expertin, -nen expert [K. 4]

das Fach, ⸚er academic subject; compartment [ZT 6]
der Fachbereich, -e academic department [AB 6]
die Fachhochschule, -n college [K. 8]
die Fachoberschule, -n technical college [K. 8]
die Fachschule, -n special school, technical college [K. 8]
das Fachwerk half-timbered architecture [K. 6]
die Fachzeitschrift, -en professional journal [K. 7]
fahren (fährt, fuhr, ist gefahren) to drive, ride [AL 4]; **per Anhalter ~** to hitch-hike [AL 4]
der Fahrplan, ⸚e schedule of transportation [K. 7]
die Fahrprüfung, -en driving test [K. 4]
das Fahrrad, ⸚er bicycle [AB 3]
der Fahrschein, -e public transportation ticket
die Fahrschule, -n driving school, driver's education [K. 4]
die Fahrt, -en trip, journey [AB 3]
das Fahrzeug, -e vehicle [AB 4]
der Faktor, -en factor [K. 8]
der Fall, ⸚e case, situation [K. 4] [ZT 9]; **auf jeden ~** at any rate, in any case [ZT 9]; **in diesem Fall(e)** in this case [AB 4]
fallen (fällt, fiel, ist gefallen) to fall [K. 6; AL 7/G]
die Familie, -n family [AL 2/WV]
der/die Familienangehörige, -n family member [ZT 11]
der Familienbetrieb, -e family-owned business [AB 10]
der Familienstammbaum, ⸚e family tree [K. 5]
das Familienverhältnis, -se family affair [K. 9]
der Fan, -s fan [K. 6]
die Fantasie, -n fantasy [K. 6]
fantastisch fantastic [AL 11]
die Farbe, -n color [AB 1/WV]; **Welche Farbe hat ...?** What color is . . . ? [AB 1/WV]
der Fasching Carnival, Fasching [K. 10]
das Fass, *pl.* **Fässer** barrel [AB 3]
Tritt fassen (hat gefasst) to get in step [ZT 12]
fast almost, practically [AB 5]
die Fastenzeit Lent [K. 10]
die Fastnacht Carnival, Fasching [K. 10]
faul lazy [AB 4/WV]
das Fax fax [AB 2]
faxen (hat gefaxt) to fax [K. 5]
die FCKS *(pl.)* chlorofluorocarbons
der Februar February [AB 2/WV]
die Fee, -n fairy [AL 10/WV]
fehlen (hat gefehlt) to be missing, be lacking [K. 6; AB 10]
fein fine [AL 6]
der Feind, -e enemy, adversary [K. 10]
das Feldhockey field hockey [K. 2]
das Fenster - window [AB 1/WV]
die Ferien *(pl.)* (school) vacation [ZT 10]
der Ferienort, -e resort town [AB 10]
ferienreif ready for a vacation [AB 10]
die Ferienwohnung, -en vacation home [AB 10/G]
fern·bleiben (blieb fern, ist ferngeblieben) + *dat.* to stay away from [K. 10]
fern·sehen (sieht fern, sah fern, hat ferngesehen) to watch television [AL 2]
der Fernseher, - television set [AB 1/WV]
der Fernsehturm, ⸚e television tower [K. 11]
die Ferse, -n heel [AL 10]

fertig werden (wird, wurde, ist geworden) mit + *dat.* to come to grips with, accept [ZT 5]
fest permanent [K. 12]
das Fest, -e festival, feast [AL 10]
das Festspiel, -e festival [K. 12]
fest·stellen (hat festgestellt) to determine [K. 6]
die Fete, -n party; **auf eine ~ gehen**; to go to a party [AL 7/WV]
die Feuerwache, -n fire station [K. 3]
das Fieber fever, temperature [AL 8/WV]
die Figur, -en figure; (story) character [K. 4]
die Filiale, -n branch office [AL 7]
der Film, -e movie, film [K. 4; AB 7/WV]
der Filmemacher, -/die Filmemacherin, -nen filmmaker [AB 7]
das Finanzamt, ¨er tax office (equivalent to the IRS) [AL 12/WV]
die Finanzen *(pl.)* finances [ZT 9]
finden (fand, hat gefunden) to find [AL 1]
der Finger, - finger [AB 6/WV]
der Fingernagel, ¨ fingernail [K. 8]
(das) Finnisch the Finnish language [K. 2]
(das) Finnland Finland [K. 12]
die Firma, *pl.* **Firmen** firm, company [AB 9]
der Fisch, -e fish [AL 3/WV]
der Fischmarkt, ¨e fish market [AL 5]
das Fitnessstudio, -s health club [AL 7/WV]
die Fläche, -n surface area [K. 4]
die Flak (Flugabwehrkanone) flak, anti-aircraft weapon [AB 11/II]
die Flasche, -n bottle
das Fleisch meat [AL 3/WV]
der Fleischer, -/die Fleischerin, -nen butcher [AL 9/WV]
die Fleischerei, -en butcher shop [AL 7/WV]
fleißig industrious, busy [AB 4/WV]
flexibel flexible [K. 9]
fliegen (flog, ist geflogen) to fly [AL 2]
fließen (floss, ist geflossen) to flow [K. 11]
fließend fluent(ly) [K. 12]
flirten (hat geflirtet) to flirt [AB 5/WV]
die Flötenmusik flute music [K. 5]
der Flug, ¨e flight [ZT 4]
der Flughafen, ¨ airport [K. 4]
der Flugschein, -e plane ticket [AL 4/WV]
das Flugticket, -s plane ticket [K. 6]
das Flugzeug, -e airplane [K. 4; ZT 5]
der Flur, -e hall, corridor [AL 6/WV]
der Fluss, *pl.* **Flüsse** river [K. 3; AB 10/WV]
die Folge, -n consequence [AB 12]
folgend following [K. 4]
die Folie, -n overhead transparency [AL 8]
der Föhn, -e blow dryer [AL 8/WV]
sich die Haare föhnen (hat sich geföhnt) to blow-dry one's hair [AL 8/WV]
die Fontäne, -n fountain [K. 3]
die Forschung, -en research [K. 8]
der/die Fortgeschrittene, -n *(adj. as noun)* advanced student [AB 10]
fort·gehen (ging fort, ist fortgegangen) to go away [AL 10]
das Fotoalbum, *pl.* **Alben** photo album
der Fotograf, [-en], -en/die Fotografin, -nen photographer [K. 3]
der Fotoapparat, -e photo camera [AL 4/WV]
die Frage, -n question [AB 2]; **Fragen stellen (hat gestellt)** to ask questions [AB 9]
fragen (hat gefragt) to ask [AL 1]; **~ nach** + *dat.* to ask about [AB 8/G]
das Fragewort, ¨er question word, interrogative [AB 1/G]
(das) Frankreich France [AB 1/WV]
der Franzose, [-n], -n/die Französin, -nen French man/woman [AB 1/WV]
(das) Französisch the French language [AL 2/WV]
die Frau, -en woman; Mrs., Ms. [AB 1]; wife, wives [AL 2/WV]
die Frauenzeitschrift, -en women's magazine [K. 7]
das Fräulein, - Miss [AB 1/BK]
frei free, open; allowed [AB 4]; **im Freien** outdoors [K. 11]
der Freibetrag, ¨e duty-free limit [K. 12]
die Freie Demokratische Partei (FDP) Free Democratic Party [K. 7]
das Frei(schwimm)bad, ¨er outdoor swimming pool [K. 3]
der Freitag, -e Friday [AB 2/WV]
freiwillig voluntarily [K. 11]
die Freizeit free time, leisure time [AB 3]
der/die Fremde, -n *(adj. as noun)* foreigner [K. 4]
der Fremdenführer, -/die Fremdenführerin, -nen tour guide [AL 9]
der Fremdenhass xenophobia [K. 4]
fressen (frisst, fraß, hat gefressen to eat *(said of animals)*
die Freude, -n joy [AL 10]
sich freuen (hat sich gefreut) to be happy; **~auf** + *acc.* to look forward to [K. 2; AL 8]; **~über** + *acc.* to be happy about [K. 2; AB 8/G]
der Freund, -e/die Freundin, -nen friend, boy/girlfriend [AL 2]; **die Freunde** *(pl.)* a group of friends [AL 2]
freundlich friendly [AB 1]
die Freundschaft, -en friendship [AB 5/WV]
der Friseur, -e/die Friseurin, -nen/die Friseuse, -n hair dresser [AL 9/WV]
froh happy [ZT 5]
fromm pious, religious [AL 10]
der Fronleichnam, -e Corpus Christi Day [K. 10]
der Frosch, ¨e frog [AL 10/WV]
der Frühling spring [AL 5/WV]
das Frühstück breakfast [AL 3/BK]
frustrierend frustrating [AL 11]
sich fühlen (hat sich gefühlt) to feel [K. 4; AB 6]; **sich krank ~** to feel sick [AL 8/WV]; **sich wohl ~** to feel good [AB 9]
führen (hat geführt) to lead [K. 3; AL 10]
der Führer, - leader (used to refer to Adolf Hitler) [AB 11/I WV]
der Führerschein, -e driver's license [K. 4]
die Führung, -en leadership [AB 11/I]; tour [K. 11]
für + *acc.* for [AB 4]
das Fürstentum, ¨er principality, kingdom [K. 10]
der Fuß, ¨e foot [AB 6/WV]; **zu ~** on foot [AB 7/WV]
der Fußball soccer [AL 3]
der Fußgänger, -/die Fußgängerin, -nen pedestrian [AB 4]
der Fußgängerbereich, -e pedestrian zone [AB 4]
die Fußgängerzone, -n pedestrian zone [ZT 3]
der Fußweg, -e walkway [K. 4]
füttern (hat gefüttert) to feed [K. 4]

die Gabel, -n fork [K. 6]
der Gang, ¨e hall, hallway, corridor [AL 6]
ganz all, entirely [AB 2]; entirely, totally [K. 4]; **~ schlimm** really bad [AL 5]
gar nicht not at all [ZT 3]
die Garage, -n garage [AL 6/WV]
die Gardine, -n curtain(s) [AL 6/WV]

der Garten, ¨ garden [AL 6/WV]
die Gaskammer, -n gas chamber [AL 7]
der Gast, ¨e guest [K. 7; AB 10]
das Gästezimmer, - guest room [AL 6/WV]
die Gastfreundschaft hospitality [AB 10]
der Gastgeber, -/die Gastgeberin, -nen host [K. 7]
der Gasthof, ¨e inn [AB 3]
gastlich hospitable, friendly [AB 10]
das Gebäck pastry [AL 7/WV]
geben (gibt, gab, hat gegeben) to give [AL 3]; **es gibt (gab, hat gegeben)** there is, there are [AL 3]
das Gebiet, -e district, area [K. 8]
geboren to be born [K. 5]
gebraucht used [K. 6]
gebunden hard-bound [K. 7]
das Geburtshaus, ¨er birth place [K. 4]
der Geburtstag, -e birthday [K. 6]
die Gedächtniskirche (Kaiser Wilhelm) Memorial Church [AL 11]
der Gedanke [-n], -n thought [K. 5]; **auf andere Gedanken kommen** to get one's mind off something [K. 5]
gedeckt set [AL 11]
das Gedicht, -e poem [AL 5]
die Geduld patience [AB 8]
gefährlich dangerous [K. 4]
gefallen (gefällt, gefiel, hat gefallen) + *dat.* to please; to like [AL 5;AB 6/G]
das Geflügel poultry, fowl [AL 3/WV]
der Gefrierpunkt freezing point [AL 5/WV]
das Gefühl, -e feeling [AB 9]
gegen + *acc.* against; around *(time)* [AB 4/G]
gegenseitig each other, reciprocal(ly) [K. 10]
der Gegenstand, ¨e object [K. 8]
Gegenteil: im ~ in opposition, contrary to [ZT 11]
gegenüber + *dat.* in regard to [K. 6]; **~ (von)** + *dat.* across from [AL 7]
der Gegner, -/die Gegnerin, -nen opponent [K. 11]
das Gehalt, ¨er salary, wage [ZT 9]
die Gehaltsvorstellung, -en salary expectation [ZT 9]
gehen (ging, ist gegangen) to go [AL 1]; **unter die Dusche ~** to take a shower [AL 8/WV]
gehören (hat gehört) + *dat.* to belong to [AB 6/G]
geil way cool *(slang)* [K. 11]
gelb yellow [AB 1/WV]
das Geld money [AL 4]
die Gelegenheit, -en opportunity [AL 12]
gemeinsam common, shared, in partnership [K. 4; AB 11/I]
die Gemeinschaft, -en association, group [AB 10]
das Gemeinschaftsbad, ¨er shared bathroom, floor bathroom [AL 6]
die Gemeinschaftsküche, -n shared kitchen [ZT 6]
gemischt mixed [K. 6]
das Gemüse, - vegetable, vegetables [AL 3/WV]
genau exactly [ZT 4]
die Gendarmerie (state) police [AB 12]
genießen (genoss, hat genossen) to enjoy [K. 10]
der Genießer, -/die Genießerin, -nen connoisseur [AB 10]
der Genitiv -e genitive case [AB 10/G]
genug enough, sufficient [AL 4]
genügend sufficient, enough [AB 9]
das Gepäck luggage [AL 3]
gerade just [K. 8]
geradeaus straight ahead [AL 7/G]
der Gerichtshof, ¨e court [ZT 12]
gering low, small, limited [AB 4]
die Germanistik German studies [K. 10]
gern + *verb* to like to . . . [AL 2]; **~ geschehen!** Glad to help!, My pleasure! [ZT 6]; **~ haben** to like [AL 2/G]
die Gesamtschule, -n comprehensive secondary school [K. 8]
das Geschäft, -e store, business [K. 5]
der Geschäftsmann, ¨er/die Geschäftsfrau, -en businessman/ -woman [K. 7; AL 9/WV]
die Geschäftsreise, -n business trip [K. 5]
das Geschenk, -e gift, present [AL 4/WV]
die Geschichte, -n history [AL 2/WV]; story [AL 5]
geschieden divorced [AL 2/WV]
die Geschirrspülmaschine, -n dishwasher [K. 6]
geschlossen closed [AL 11]
der Geschmack, ¨e(r) taste [K. 9]
gesellig gregarious, sociable [AB 4/WV]
die Gesellschaft, -en society [AB 12/WV]
das Gesetz, -e law [K. 11]
der Gesetzgeber, - law maker [ZT 12]
das Gesicht, -er face [AB 6/WV]
gespannt excited [K. 4]; **~ sein auf** + *acc.* to be excited about [AB 8/G]
das Gespräch, -e conversation [AB 5]; **ins ~ kommen** to strike up a conversation [K. 6]
gestern yesterday [AL 5/G]
gestresst stressed [AB 10]
gesund healthy [AB 4]
das Getränk, -e beverage, drink [AL 3/WV]
sich getrauen (hat sich getraut) to venture, dare [K. 11]
getrennt separate [K. 4]
die Gewalt violence [ZT 5]
die Gewerkschaft, -en trade union [AB 12]
der Gewerkschafter, -/die Gerwerkschafterin, -nen trade union member [AB 12]
gewinnen (gewann, hat gewonnen) to win [K. 4]
gewiss certain [K. 7; AL 12]
das Gewitter thunderstorm [AL 5/WV]
sich gewöhnen (hat sich gewöhnt) an + *acc.* to get used to, get accustomed to [AB 10]
gezielt specifically [K. 9]
das Ghetto, -s ghetto [K. 6]
das Gift, -e poison [AB 11/II]
giftig poisonous [AL 10/WV]
der Gipfel, - mountain peak [AB 10/WV]
der Gips, -e cast [AL 8/WV]
glänzend gleaming [AL 10]
der Glassarg, ¨e glass coffin [K. 10]
glatt smooth, straight [AB 1/WV]
glauben (hat geglaubt) to believe, think [ZT 4]; **~ an** + *acc.* to believe in [AB 8/G]
glaubhaft plausible, believable [K. 8]
gleich just, right away [K. 1; AB 2]; **~ um die Ecke** right around the corner [AL 7/G]
gleichzeitig simultaneously, at the same time [K. 8]
das Glück good luck, fortune [K. 6; AB 8]
glücklich lucky, happy [K. 3]
die Glühbirne, -n light bulb [K. 12]
das Gold gold [AL 10]
der Golf golf [K. 2]
der Golfschläger, - golf club [K. 6]
der Gott, ¨er God [AL 1]; **~ sei Dank!** Thank God! [AL 1]
das Grab, ¨er grave [AL 10]
der Grad degree [AL 5/WV]
der Graf, [-en], -en count [K. 10]
das Gramm gram [AL 3/BK]

die Grammatik grammar [K. 4]
der Granatsplitter, - grenade shell, shrapnel [AB 11/II]
die Graphik, -en graphics [K. 8]
grau gray [AL 1]; **dunkelgrau** dark gray [AB 1/WV]; **hellgrau** light gray [AB 1/WV]
grausam gruesome, cruel [K. 10]
der Grenzbalken, - border crossing (lit. beam, rafter) [AB 12]
die Grenze, -n border [AB 10/WV]
grenzen (hat gegrenzt) an + *dat.* to border on [K. 11]
der Grenzwächter, - border guard [AB 12]
(das) Griechenland Greece [K. 12]
grillen (hat gegrillt) to grill, barbeque [K. 11]
der Groschen, - **10-Pfennig** coin [AB 6]
groß large, big, tall [AL 1]
die Größe, -n size [K. 6]
die Großeltern *(pl.)* grandparents [AL 2/WV]
die Großmutter, ¨ grandmother [AL 2/WV]
die Großstadt, *pl.* **Großstädte** big city [ZT 5]
der Großvater, ¨ grandfather [AL 2/WV]
großzügig generous [AB 8]
Grüezi! Hello! *(in Switzerland)* [AB 1/BK]
grün green [AB 1/WV]
der Grund, ¨e reason [K. 4; K. 6 AB 9]
gründen (hat gegründet) to establish [K. 10]
das Grundgesetz Basic Law (Germany's constitution) [AB 11/I WV]
gründlich thorough, careful [AB 9/WV]
die Grundschule, -n elementary school [K. 8]
die Gründung, -en founding
die Grünen the Green Party [K. 7]
die Gruppe, -n group [K. 5]
der Gruppenleiter, -/die Gruppenleiterin, -nen group leader [K. 6]
das Gruppenreferat, -e group research paper [K. 8]
die Gruppenunterkunft, ¨e group lodging [K. 10]
der Gruß, ¨e greeting [AL 1]; **Herzliche Grüße** Sincerely yours *(to close a letter)* [AB 2]
grüßen: Grüßt euch! Grüß dich! Hi, you (guys)! [ZT 6]; **Grüß Gott!** Hello! *(in southern Germany)* [AB 1/BK]
gucken (hat geguckt) to look [AL 6]
gusseisern cast iron [K. 11]
gut good [AB 1]
der Güterwaggon, -s freight car [AB 11/II]
gut gelaunt in a good mood [AB 10]
der Gymnasiast, [-en], -en/die Gymnasiastin, -nen college track high school student [K. 8]
das Gymnasium, *pl.* **Gymnasien** college track high school [K. 8]

das Haar, -e hair [AB 1/WV]
das Haarwaschmittel, - shampoo [AL 8/WV]
haben (hat, hatte, hat gehabt) to have [AL 2/G]
das Hackfleisch hamburger, chopped meat [K. 3]
der Hafen, ¨ harbor [AB 3]
das Hähnchen, - chicken [AL 3/WV]
der Haken, - hook [AL 8/WV]
halb half; **halb [zwei]** half past [one] [AB 2/WV]
das Hallenbad, ¨er indoor swimming pool [K. 3]
Hallo! Hello! [AB 1/BK]
der Hals, ¨e throat [AB 6/WV]
Halsschmerzen *pl.* sore throat [AL 8/WV]
halt just [ZT 8]
halten (hält, hielt, hat gehalten) to stop [K. 4]; ~ **für** + *acc.* to believe someone to be [AL 10]; ~ **von** + *dat.* to think of [AL 3]
der Hamburger, - hamburger [AL 3]; **~/die Hamburgerin** resident of Hamburg
die Hand, ¨e hand [AB 6/WV]
das Hand-out, -s hand out [AL 8]
handeln (hat gehandelt) von + *dat.* to be about [ZT 7]
die Handlung, -en dramatic action, plot [K. 5]
der Handschuh, -e glove, mitten [AL 4]
die Handtasche, -n handbag, purse [AL 4/WV]
hängen (hat gehängt) to hang up [AL 7/G]
hängen (hing, hat gehangen) to be hanging [AL 7/G]
hässlich ugly [K. 3]
der Haufen, - heap, pile [AB 11/II]
häufig frequent [K. 8]
Haupt... *(in compounds)* main; **das Hauptfach, ¨er** main subject, major [K. 12]; **das Hauptgericht, -e** main course [AL 3/BK]; **die Hauptstraße, -n** main street [ZT 3]
die Hauptschule, -n equivalent to junior high school, technical-vocational school [K. 8]
der Hauptschüler, -/die Hauptschülerin, -nen technical-vocational student [K. 8]
das Hauptseminar, -e advanced seminar [K. 8]
die Hauptstadt, ¨e capital city [AB 10/WV]
das Haus, ¨er house [AL 6/WV]; **nach Hause** go home; **zu Hause** at home
die Hausaufgabe -n homework, assignment [K. 2]
der Hauskamerad, [-en], -en/die Hauskameradin, -nen housemate [K. 8]
die Hausleiter, -n fire escape [AB 11/II]
der Hausmeister, -/die Hausmeisterin, -nen custodian, superintendent [K. 6]
der Hauswart, -e custodian [ZT 6]
heben (hob, hat gehoben) to lift, raise [AB 6]
das Heftpflaster, - Band-Aid [AL 8/WV]
der Heilig-Geist Holy Ghost [K. 3]
die Heimat home, hometown [K. 5]
die Heimatstadt, ¨e home town [K. 3]
das Heimweh homesickness [K. 5]
heiraten (hat geheiratet) to get married [AL 5]
heiß hot [AL 5/WV]
heißen (hieß, hat geheißen) to be called [AL 1]
heiter funny, cheerful [AB 4/WV]; sunny, clear [AL 5/WV]
heizen (hat geheizt) to heat [AB 11/II]
die Heizung, -en heating system; heat [K. 6]
die Hektik frenzy, fast pace [ZT 5]
helfen (hilft, half, hat geholfen) + *dat.* to help [AB 4]; **auf die Sprünge ~** to give a boost to [K. 8]
hell light [AB 1/WV]
hellwach wide awake [AB 9]
(das) Helvetia Switzerland *(Latin)* [K. 10]
das Hemd, -en shirt [K. 4]
her here *(from point of origin)* [AL 7/G]
herab·blicken (hat herabgeblickt) to look down [AL 10]

heraus·finden (fand heraus, hat herausgefunden) to find out, discover [ZT 12]
sich heraus·putzen (hat sich herausgeputzt) to dress up, get decked out [AB 9]
der Herbst autumn, fall [AL 5/WV]
der Herd, -e cooking stove [AL 10]
Herein, bitte! Please come in! [AL 8]
das Herkunftsland, ¨-er country of origin, home country [AB 6]
hermetisch hermetically, air-tight [AB 12]
der Herr, [-n], -en (gentle)man; Mr. [AB 1/BK]
herum·humpeln (ist herumgehumpelt) to hobble around [AB 11/II]
das Herz, -en heart; **im Herzen** in the heart [AB 3]
herzlich heartfelt, warm [AB 10]; **~ willkommen in ... !** Welcome to . . . ! [ZT 4]
die Herzlichkeit warmth, heartfeltness, sincerity
Hessen Hesse [K. 4; AB 11/I WV]
heulen (hat geheult) to cry; to howl [AB 11/II]
heute today [AB 2/WV]; **~ Abend** this evening [AB 8/G]; **~ Morgen** this morning [AB 8/G]; **~ Nachmittag** this afternoon [AB 8/G]
die Hexe, -n witch [AL 10/WV]
hier here [AL 1]
die Hilfe, -n help, aid [AL 6]
der Himmel heaven, sky [AL 10]
hin there *(point of destination)* [AL 7/G]; **~ und wieder** now and then [AL 4]
das Hindernis, -se obstacle [K. 12]
hinein inside [K. 1]
hingegen on the other hand, in contrast to [AB 12]
sich hin·legen (hat sich hingelegt) to lie down [AL 8]
die Hinsicht respect, regard [K. 4]
hinten behind, in back [K. 4; AB 5]
hinter behind, in back of [AL 7/G]
hinterlassen (hinterlässt, hinterließ, hat hinterlassen) to leave behind [AB 9]
der Hintermann, ¨-er backer, contact [AL 7]
der Hintern, - rear [AB 6/WV]
historisch historic [AB 1]
hitlertreu loyal to Hitler [K. 11]
die Hiwi-Stelle, -n research assistant position [AB 8]
der Hobbygärtner, -/die Hobbygärtnerin, -nen amateur gardener [K. 6]
der Hobbyraum, ¨-e hobby room [AL 6/WV]
hoch high, up [AB 6]
hochachtungsvoll respectfully [K. 9]
hochaktuell very current, very timely [ZT 7]
hoch·laufen (läuft hoch, lief hoch, ist hochgelaufen) to walk up (a street) [AL 11]
hoffen (hat gehofft) auf + *acc.* to hope for [ZT 6]
holen (hat geholt) to go get, fetch [ZT 4]
das Holz, ¨-er wood [AB 11/II]
der/die Homosexuelle, -n *(adj. as noun)* homosexual [K. 7]
der Honig honey [K. 3]
hören (hat gehört) to hear, listen to [AL 2]
das Horoskop, -e horoscope [K. 7]
der Hörsaal, *pl.* **Hörsäle** lecture hall [AL 1]
die Hose, -n pants [AL 4/WV]
das Hotel, -s hotel [AB 3]
der Hoteleingang, ¨-e hotel entrance [AL 7/G]
hübsch pretty [AB 1/VW]
der Humor humor, sense of humor [K. 5]
humorvoll humorous [K. 5]
hundemüde dog-tired [AL 6]
der Hunger hunger; **~ haben** to be hungry [K. 6]
hüten (hat gehütet) vor + *dat.* to guard, protect from [AB 11/II]
der Hypochonder, - hypochondriac [K. 6]
hypochondrisch hyprochondriac(al) [K. 6]

ich I [AB 1]
die Idee, -n idea [ZT 3]
sich identifizieren (hat sich identifiziert) mit + *dat.* to identify with [ZT 11]
identisch identical [K. 4]
ihn him *(acc.)* [AB 3/G]
ihr her; their [AL 3/G]; you *(fam. pl.)* [AB 1/G]
Ihr your *(formal)* [K. 1]
immer always [AL 3]; **immer [beliebter]** more and more [popular] [AB 4]
imstande sein to be capable of [K. 11]
in in [AB 1]; into [AL 7/G]
indes meantime, meanwhile [K. 8]
indianisch Native American [K. 6]
der Indikativ indicative mood [K. 11]
die Industrie, -n industry [K. 5; AL 8]
die Info, -s information [AB 4]
die Informatik computer science [AL 2/WV]
die Information, -en information [AB 3]
sich informieren (hat sich informiert) über + *acc.* to inform oneself, educate oneself about [AB 9]
der Ingenieur, -e/die Ingenieurin, -nen engineer [AL 9/WV]
das Ingenieurwesen engineering [AL 2/WV]
der Inhalt, -e content [ZT 8]
inklusive including [K. 6]
die Innenpolitik domestic policy, internal security policy [K. 12]
innerhalb + *gen.* inside of [AB 11/II G]
die Insel, -n island [AB 10/WV]
das Inserat, -e newspaper advertisement [AL 9]
insgesamt for a total of [ZT 10]
das Institut, -e institute [K. 6]
integriert integrated [K. 6]
intelligent intelligent [AB 4/WV]
interessant interesting [AB 4/WV]
das Interesse, -n interest [AB 2/WV]
interpretieren (hat interpretiert) to interpret [K. 4]
das Interview, -s interview [K. 3; AL 9]
inzwischen in the meantime [K. 4]
irgendwas something, anything [K. 8]
(das) Irland Ireland [K. 12]
ironisch ironic [K. 6]
irritieren (hat irritiert) to irritate [AL 5/G]
irritierend irritating [K. 8]
der Islam Islam [AB 6]
(das) Island Iceland [K. 12]
(das) Italien Italy [K. 3]
italienisch Italian [K. 5]

ja yes [AB 1/G]
die Jacke, -n jacket [K. 4]
der Jäger, -/die Jägerin, -nen hunter [AL 10/WV]
das Jahr, -e year [AL 2]; **schon seit Jahren** for years [AB 5]
die Jahreszeit, -en season [AL 5/WV]
der Jahrmarkt, ¨-e fair [K. 10]
jammern (hat gejammert) to whine, cry, lament [AB 11/II]
der Januar January [AB 2/WV]; **im ~** in January
(das) Japan Japan [AB 1/WV]

der Japaner, -/die Japanerin, -nen Japanese [AB 1/WV]
der Jazzkeller, - jazz club [AL 7/WV]
jedenfalls anyway, at any rate [AL 8]
jeder, jedes, jede each; every [AB 6/G]
jederzeit anytime [ZT 6]
jemand someone, somebody [K. 3; AB 6/SiA]; **irgend ~** somebody, anybody [K. 5]
jetzt now [AL 2]
das Jiddisch Yiddish [K. 4]
der Job, -s job [AB 8]
jobben (hat gejobbt) to work part-time [K. 8; AL 9]
das Jubiläum, *pl.* **Jubiläen** anniversary [K. 5]
der Jude, [-n], -n/die Jüdin, -nen Jew [AB 7]
jüdisch Jewish [AB 7]
die Jugendherberge, -n youth hostel [AB 3]
das Jugendhotel, -s budget youth hotel [ZT 10]
die Jugendliteratur youth literature [ZT 9]
Jugendstil Art Nouveau [K. 3]
(das) Jugoslawien Yugoslavia [K. 12]
der Juli July [AB 2/WV]
jung young [AB 1/WV]
der Junge, [en], -n *(adj. as noun)* boy
der Juni June [AB 2/WV]
der Jura Jura Mountains [AB 10/WV]
die Justizpolitik judicial policy [K. 12]

der Kaffee coffee [AL 3/WV]
das Kaffeehaus, ¨-er coffee house [K. 12]
die Kaffeemaschine, -n coffee maker [K. 6]
der Kaiser, -/die Kaiserin, -nen emperor, empress [AB 11/I WV]
Kalifornien California [K. 2]
kalt cold [K. 3; AL 5/WV]
der Kamin, -e fireplace [K. 7]
der Kamm, ¨-e comb [AL 8/WV]
sich die Haare kämmen (hat sich gekämmt) to comb one's hair [AL 8/WV]
der Kampfverband, ¨-e fighting unit [AB 11/II]
(das) Kanada Canada [AB 1/WV]
der Kanadier, -/die Kanadierin, -nen Canadian [AB 1/WV]
der Kandidat, [-en], -en/die Kandidatin, -nen candidate [ZT 9]
die Kantine, -n cafeteria, cantine [K. 9]
der Kanton, -e canton, state *(in Switzerland)* [AB 10/WV]
der Kantor, -en choirmaster [K. 9]
der Kanzler, -/die Kanzlerin, -nen chancellor [AB 11/I WV]
die Kappensitzung, -en Carnival guild party, "roast" [K. 10]
das/der Karamelbonbon, -s caramel candy [ZT 12]
der Karfreitag, -e Good Friday [K. 10]
karitativ charitable, charity [K. 12]
der Karneval Carnival [K. 10]
Kärnten Carinthia [AB 12/WV]
die Karotte, -n carrot [AL 3/WV]
die Karriere, -n career [K. 8]
die Kartoffel, -n potato [AL 3/WV]
der Käse cheese [AL 3/WV]
die Kasse, -n check-out counter, cash register [ZT 7]
der Kasten, -, (¨-) case [K. 11]
der Katalog, -e catalogue [ZT 7]
die Katastrophe, -n catastrophe [ZT 10]
Kater: der gestiefelte ~ Puss in Boots [K. 10]
die Katze, -n cat [K. 4]
kauen (hat gekaut) to chew [K. 4]
kaufen (hat gekauft) to buy, purchase [AL 4]
der Kaufmann, ¨-er/die Kauffrau, -en clerk [AL 9/WV]
der Kaugummi, -s chewing gum [AL 3]
kaum hardly [AB 5]
kein no, none [AB 1/G]; **~ ... mehr** no more [AB 5]
der Keller, - basement, cellar [AL 6]
der Kellerhocker, - person staying in an air-raid shelter [AB 11/II]
der Kellerwinkel, - corner of the celler [AB 11/II]
der Kellner, -/die Kellnerin, -nen waiter/waitress [AL 5;AL 9/WV]
kennen (kannte, hat gekannt) to know (a city, person) [AB 3/G]
kennen lernen (hat kennen gelernt) to meet, get to know [AB 2]
die Kerb fair [K. 10]
das Kilogramm kilogram [AL 3/BK]
das Kind, -er child, children [AL 2/WV]
das Kinderbuch, ¨-er children's book [ZT 9]
der Kindergarten, ¨- kindergarten [K. 8]
das Kindergeld child raising subsidy [K. 9]
das Kinderzimmer, - children's room, nursery [AL 6/WV]
das Kinn -e chin [AB 6/WV]
das Kino, -s movie theater, cinema [K. 5; AL 7/WV]; **ins ~ gehen** to go to the movies [AB 3/WV]
der Kinoabend, -e night at the movies [AB 10]
der Kiosk, -s kiosk, stand [AL 7]
die Kirche, -n church [AB 3]
der Kirchturm, ¨-e church tower, steeple [K. 9]
die Kirmes fair [K. 10]
die Kirsche, -n cherry [AL 3/WV]
die Klamotten *(pl.)* clothes, duds [AL 6/WV]
klappen (hat geklappt) to work out all right [ZT 11]
klar clear; **Klar!** Sure! All clear! [ZT 6]
die Klassengröße, -n class size [K. 8]
das Klassenzimmer, - classroom [AB 1/WV]
das Klavier, -e piano [K. 3]
das Kleid, -er dress [AL 4/WV]
der Kleiderschrank, ¨-e armoire, wardrobe [AL 6/WV]
die Kleidung, -en clothing, clothes [AL 4]
klein short [AB 1/VW]
das Kleingeld pocket change [AB 8]
das Kleingolf mini-golf [K. 3]
die Kleinigkeit, -en trifle, a little something; detail [AL 11]
klettern (ist geklettert) to climb [AB 10]
das Klima, *pl.* **Klimen** climate [AB 12/WV]
die Klimaanlage, -n air conditioner [K. 12]
klingen (klang, hat geklungen) to sound [ZT 8]
das Klo, -s (das Klosett, -e) toilet *(colloq.)* [AL 6]
klopfen (hat geklopft) to knock [K. 8]
klug smart, intelligent [AL 2]
knapp just barely, almost [AB 8]
die Kneipe, -n bar, pub [AL 5]
das Knie, - knee [AB 6/WV]
der Koch, ¨-e/die Köchin, -nen cook, chef [AL 9/WV]
kochen (hat gekocht) to cook [AB 3/WV]
der Koffer, - suitcase [AL 4/WV]
der Kofferraum trunk of a car [ZT 4]
der Kognat -e cognate [K. 3]
die Kohle, -n coal [AB 11/II]
der Kollege, [-n], -n/die Kollegin, -nen colleague, co-worker [K. 5; ZT 9]
kollegial collegial [AB 9/WV]
kombinieren (hat kombiniert) to combine [ZT 9]

kommen (kam, ist gekommen) aus + *dat.* to come, be from [AB 1]
der Kommilitone, [-n], -n/die Kommilitonin, -nen fellow student [AB 8]
die Kommode, -n chest of drawers [AL 6/WV]
der Kommunismus communism [K. 10]
der Kommunist, [-en], -en/die Kommunistin, -nen communist [K. 7]
kompliziert complicated [ZT 6]
das Kompositum *pl.* **Komposita** composite word [K. 9]
der Komposthaufen, - compost pile [K. 12]
der Konditionalsatz, ⸚e conditional sentence [K. 12]
die Konditorei, -en pastry shop [AL 7/WV]
der Konflikt, -e conflict [K. 8]
konfus confused [AB 9]
die Kongresshalle, -n convention center [K. 11]
das Kongresszentrum, *pl.* **-zentren** convention center [AB 3]
der König, -e/die Königin, -nen king/queen [AL 10/WV]
der Königssohn, ⸚e prince [AL 10]
die Königstochter, ⸚ princess [AL 10/WV]
das Königtum, ⸚er kingdom [AB 11/I WV]
die Konjunktion, -en conjunction [K. 5]
der Konjunktiv subjunctive mood [K. 11]
konkret concrete [K. 6]
können (kann, konnte, hat gekonnt) to be able to; can [K3; AL 4]
könnte could [ZT 8]
konstruieren (hat konstruiert) to construct [K. 8]
der Kontakt, -e contact, communication [K. 6; AB 8]
kontaktfreudig outgoing, sociable [AB 9/WV]
der Kontext, -e context [K. 8]
das Konto, *pl.* **Konten** bank account [AL 7]
der Kontrast, -e contrast [K. 4]
die Kontrolle, -n search [AB 12]
kontrollieren (hat kontrolliert) to check [K. 6; AB 12]
kontrovers controversial [K. 7]
die Konversation, -en conversation [K. 5]
sich konzentrieren (hat sich konzentriert) auf + *acc.* to concentrate on [AL 8]
das Konzept, -e concept [K. 12]
der Konzern, -e company [K. 5]
das Konzert, -e concert [AL 7/WV]
der Kopf, ⸚e head [K. 7; AB 6/WV]
die Kopfschmerzen *(pl.)* headache [AL 8/WV]
kopieren (hat kopiert) to copy [AL 8]
der Kopierer, - photocopier [AB 6]
der Kopierladen, ⸚ copy shop [K. 6]
der Körper, - body [K. 4]
der Körperteil, -e body part [AB 6/WV]
der Korridor, -e hall, corridor [AL 6]
die Kost food [AL 7/G]
die Kosten *(pl.)* expenses, costs [AB 4]
kotzen (hat gekotzt) to throw up *(slang)* [K. 8]
der Krach argument, quarrel, noise [AB 5]
krachen (hat gekracht) to crash [K. 11]
die Kraftfahrstraße, -n road for motorized vehicles [K. 4]
krank sick, ill [K. 4]
das Krankenhaus, ⸚er hospital [K. 5]
der Krankenpfleger, -/die Krankenschwester, -n orderly, nurse [AL 9/WV]
der Krankenurlaub sick leave, sick days [K. 9]
die Krankenversicherung, -en health insurance [K. 9]
kraus tightly curled [AB 1/WV]
die Krawatte, -n necktie [K. 4]
kreativ creative [AB 4/WV]
die Kreditkarte, -n credit card [AL 4/WV]
die Kreide chalk [AB 1/WV]
die Kreuzung, -en intersection, crossing [AL 7/G]; **bis zur ~** up to the intersection [AL 7/G]
der Krieg, -e war; **der Kalte ~** Cold War [K.11]
kriegswichtig essential for the war effort [AB 7]
der Krimi, -s detective story [AB 7/WV]
die Kriminalität crime, criminal activity [K. 4]
der Kriminalroman, -e (der Krimi, -s) detective story [AB 7/WV]
der/die Kriminelle, -n *(adj. as noun)* criminal [K. 12]
die Kristallnacht "Kristallnacht" (Nov. 9, 1938, night of anti-Semitic violence) [K. 11]
die Kriterien *(pl.)* criteria [K. 8]
kritisieren (hat kritisiert) to criticize [K. 6]
(das) Kroatien Croatia [K. 12]
die Küche, -n kitchen [AL 6]; cuisine, food [ZT 10]
der Kuchen, - cake [K. 3]
kühl cool [AL 5/WV]
der Kühlschrank, ⸚e refrigerator [ZT 6]
die Kultur, -en culture; civilization [ZT 10]
der Kulturbeutel, - shaving kit/cosmetic kit [AL 4/WV]
das Kulturzentrum, *pl.* **Zentren** arts center, cultural center [AB 3]
das Kultusministerium, *pl.* **Ministerien** Ministry of Culture and Education [K. 8]
der Kunde, [-n], -n/die Kundin, -nen customer, client [K. 9]
die Kunst art [AL 2/WV]
die Kunsthalle, -n art museum [AB 3]
die Kunsthochschule, -n art and design school [K. 8]
der Künstler, -/die Künstlerin, -nen artist [K. 9]
der Kunstverein, -e art association [AB 3]
kurfürstlich electoral [K. 3]
die Kurpfalz Palatinate [K. 3]
kurpfälzisch Palatine [K. 3]
der Kurs, -e course [ZT 8]
kurz short [AB 1/WV]
kürzen (hat gekürzt) to cut back, shorten [K. 9]
die Kurzgeschichte, -n short story [AB 7/WV]
die Kusine, -n female cousin [AL 2/WV]
küssen (hat geküsst) to kiss [AL 5]
die Kutsche, -n coach, carriage [K. 10]

lächeln (hat gelächelt) to smile [AL 3]
lachen (hat gelacht) to laugh [AL 1/WV]; **~ über** + *acc.* to laugh about, at
die Lade, -n drawer [AB 11/II]
die Lage, -n position, situation [K. 8]
der Lagerarbeiter, -/die Lagerarbeiterin, -nen warehouse worker [K. 9]
lahm weak, boring, lame [ZT 8]
die Lampe, -n lamp, light, light fixture [AB 1/WV]
das Land, ⸚er country [AB 1/WV]
landen (ist gelandet) to land [K. 4]
die Landeshauptstadt, ⸚e state capital [AL 7/BK]

das Landesinnere the interior of a country [AB 12]
die Landfläche, -n land mass [K. 11]
die Landkarte, -n map [AB 1/WV]
die Landschaft, -en landscape, scenery [AB 10]
lang *(adj.)* long; tall [AB 1/WV]
lange *(adv.)* for a long time [AL 3]
die Länge, -n length [K. 7]
der Langlauf cross-country skiing [AB 10]
die Langlaufloipe, -n cross-country ski run *(Swiss dialect)* [AB 10]
langsam slow(ly) [K. 4]
langweilig boring [ZT 3]
lassen (lässt, ließ, hat gelassen) to let, allow; to leave [K. 9]
laufen (läuft, lief, ist gelaufen) to run; to walk [AL 1; AL 5/G]
laut loud [AB 4/WV]
das Lazarett, -e military hospital [AB 11/II]
das Leben, - life [K. 5]
lebendig alive, lively [K. 4; AL 11]
die Lebensfreude joy of life [AB 10]
lebensgefährlich life-threatening
die Lebensmittel *(pl.)* groceries [AL 3/WV]
die Leberwurst, ¨-e liverwurst, liver sausage [K. 3]
der Lebkuchen, - gingerbread [K. 10]
lecker delicious [AB 8]
die Lederhose, -n lederhosen [K. 3]
ledig single [AL 2/WV]
leer empty [K. 6]
legen (hat gelegt) to lay down, put down [AL 7/G]
das Lehrangebot, -e course offering [K. 8]
der Lehrassistent, [-en], -en/die Lehrassistentin, -nen teaching assistant [K. 8]
die Lehre, -n apprenticeship [K. 9]
der Lehrer, -/die Lehrerin, -nen teacher [K. 3; AL 9/WV]
der Lehrling, -e apprentice [K. 8]
leicht easy [K. 4; AB 5]; light
Leid tun (tat Leid, hat Leid getan) + *dat.* to feel sorry for [AL 5]
leidenschaftlich passionately [AL 5]
leider unfortunately [ZT 9]
leihen (lieh, hat geliehen) to lend; to borrow [K. 3; AL 6]
das Leihhaus, ¨-er pawn shop [K. 6]
die Leinwand, ¨-e projection screen [AB 1/WV]
leisten (hat geleistet) to achieve, accomplish [ZT 11]; **sich ~ (hat sich geleistet)** to afford [K. 10]
leiten (hat geleitet) to lead, be in charge of [ZT 9]
lernen (hat gelernt) to learn; to study [AL 2]
lesbisch lesbian [K. 5]
lesen (liest, las, hat gelesen) to read [AL 1]
die Lesestrategie, -n reading strategy [K. 7]
die Leute *(pl.)* people [AB 2]
lieb dear; **Liebe .../Lieber ...** Dear . . . *(used to begin a letter)* [AB 2]
die Liebe love [K. 4; AB 5/WV]
lieben (hat geliebt) to love [K. 3]
lieber (*comparative of* **gern**) preferably, rather; **~ als** rather than [K. 3]; ~ + *verb* preferably; [I would] rather . . . [AL 3/G; ZT 3]
das Liebesgedicht, -e love poem [AB 5]
der Liebeskummer lovesickness [AB 5/WV]
der Liebesroman, -e romance novel [K. 7; AB 7/WV]
Liechtenstein principality of Liechtenstein [K. 10]
liegen (lag, hat gelegen) to lie, be located [K. 3; AL 7/G]; **es liegt daran, dass ...** that's because . . . [K. 5]
lila purple [AB 1/WV]
links left, on the left [ZT 4]
die Lippe, -n lip [AB 6/WV]
der Lippenstift, -e lipstick [AL 4/WV]
der Lippizaner, - Lippizaner horse [K. 4]
die List cunning [AB 7]
die Liste, -n list [AL 7]
der Liter, - liter [AL 3/BK]
die Literatur literature [AB 7/WV]
locken (hat gelockt) to entice, attract [K. 8]
locker relaxed, cool *(colloq.)* [AB 4/WV]
der Löffel, - spoon [K. 6]
die Lohnsteuerkarte, -n income tax card [AT 12/WV]
das Lokal, -e pub [AB 3]
die Lokalzeitung, -en local newspaper [K. 7]
der Lokalzug, ¨-e local commuter train [K. 6]
Los! Let's go! [K. 4]
lösen (hat gelöst) to solve [K. 12]
los·fahren (fährt los, fuhr los, ist losgefahren) to take off, leave, drive away [ZT 4]
die Lösung, -en solution [K. 6]
die Luft, ¨-e air [AB 12/WV]
die Luftbrücke, -n airlift [AB 11/I]
der Luftschutzkeller, - air-raid cellar [AB 11/II]
die Luftschutzsirene, -n air-raid siren [AB 11/II]
(die) Lust haben to want, wish, have desire [ZT 8]
lustig funny, jovial, comical [AB 4/WV]
(das) Luxemburg Luxembourg [K. 12]
die Luxusbude, -n "luxury" student room *(colloq.)* [AL 6]

machen (hat gemacht) to make, do [AL 1]
die Machtergreifung (Nazi) seizure of power [AB 11/I]
das Mädchen, - girl [AB 5]
das Magazin, -e magazine [K. 5]
der Magister, - Master of Arts [K. 8]
Mahlzeit! Good day! *(at lunchtime)*, Have a nice lunch! [AB 1/BK]
der Mai May [AB 2/WV]
der Makler, -/die Maklerin, -nen real estate agent [AL 9/WV]
mal once *(emphatic particle)* [AL 4/G]
man (einen, einem) a person, anybody; you *(impersonal)*, one [AB 6/SiA]
der Manager, -/die Managerin, -nen manager [K. 12]
manch many a [K. 4]
der Mann, ¨-er man; husband [AL 2/WV]
der Mantel, ¨ coat [K. 4]
das Märchen, - folk/fairy tale [AB 7/WV]
das Märchenelement, -e fairy tale element [AL 10/WV]
die Märchenfigur, -en fairy tale character [AL 10/WV]
markieren (hat markiert) to mark [K. 4]
der Markt, ¨-e farmers' market [AL 7/WV]
die Markthalle, -n market hall, indoor market [AL 7/BK]
der Marktplatz, ¨-e market square [AB 3]
die Marmelade, -n marmelade, preserves [AL 3/WV]
der März March [AB 2/WV]
der Maschinenbau mechanical engineering [AB 8]
die Masern *(pl.)* measles [K. 5]
die Maß, -en one and a half liters [K. 10]; **die ~ Bier** one and a half liters of beer
die Massage, -n massage [K. 8]

die Masse, -n mass, crowd [AB 10]; **die Massen-Uni, -s** mega-university [AB 8]
das Material, -ien material [K. 8]
die Mathematik mathematics [AL 2/WV]
die Matura high school graduation exam *(in Austria)* [K. 8]
die Mauer, -n exterior wall [AL 11]
der Mauerbrocken, - chunk of wall [K. 11]
maximal maximally [K. 4; AL 8]
die Medizin medicine [AL 2/WV]
das Meer, -e sea [K. 8]
mehr more [K. 3]
das Mehrbettzimmer, - room with multiple beds [ZT 10]
mein my [AL 2]
meinen (hat gemeint) to think, have an opinion [AL 2]
die Meinung, -en opinion [K. 5]
meistens usually, mostly [AL 5]
melancholisch melancholic [K. 12]
sich melden (hat sich gemeldet) to report, show up; to get in touch [AL 8]
die Menge, -n a bunch of, a lot of; crowd [AB 11/II]
die Mensa, *pl.* **Mensen** student dining hall [K. 5; AB 8]
das Mensa-Essen food in student dining hall [K. 8]
der Mensch, [-en], -en person, human being [ZT 3]; **Mensch!** Man! [K. 4]
messen (misst, maß, hat gemessen) to measure [ZT 12]
das Messer, - knife [K. 6; AL 10]
der Meter, - meter [AL 3/BK]
der Metzger, -/die Metzgerin, -nen butcher [AL 9/WV]
die Metzgerei, -en butcher shop [AL 7/WV]
der Mexikaner, -/die Mexikanerin, -nen Mexican [AB 1/WV]
(das) Mexiko Mexico [AB 1/WV]
mich me *(acc.)* [AB 3/G]
mies rotten, lousy [AL 5/WV]
die Miete, -n rent [AB 8]
der Mikrowellenherd, -e microwave oven [K. 6]
die Milch milk [AL 3/WV]
die Million, -en million [K. 4]
mindestens at least [AL 4]
das Mineralwasser, - mineral water [AL 3/WV]
der Ministerrat, ⸚e council of ministers [ZT 12]
mir me *(dat.)* [AL 6/G]
mischen (hat gemischt) to mix [ZT 10]
miserabel miserable [K. 8]
missfallen (missfällt, missfiel, hat missfallen) + *dat.* to displease [K. 10]
das Missverständnis, -se misunderstanding [K. 4]
der Mist manure [K. 12]
mit + *dat.* with [AB 6/G]
der Mitarbeiter, -/die Mitarbeiterin, -nen co-worker [AL 9]
mit·bringen (brachte mit, hat mitgebracht) to bring along, bring back [AL 3; AL 10]
miteinander with one another [K. 4; AL 5]
das Mitglied, -er member [AB 12]
die Mitgliedschaft, -en membership [AT 12/WV]
mit·machen (hat mitgemacht) to join in, participate [K. 6; ZT 10]
mit·nehmen (nimmt mit, nahm mit, hat mitgenommen) to take along [AL 4]
das Mittagessen, - lunch [AL 3/BK]
die Mitte, -n middle [AL 11]
(das) Mitteleuropa Central Europe [K. 10]
das Mittelland midlands, flatlands [AB 10/WV]
der Mittelpunkt midpoint, center [K. 11]
die Mittlere Reife 10th grade high school exam [K. 8]
mittlerweile meantime, meanwhile [K. 8]
der Mittwoch, -e Wednesday [AB 2/WV]
die Möbel *(pl.)* furniture [AL 6/WV]
möchte would like to [AL 2; AL 4/G]
der Modus, *pl.* **Modi** mood [K. 11]
mögen (ich/er mag, mochte, hat gemocht) to like [AL 4]
die Möglichkeit, -en possibility [K. 3; ZT 10]
der Mokka mocca coffee [K. 4]
mollig chubby, plump [AB 1/WV]
Moment: ~ mal! Wait a minute! [ZT 2]
momentan at the moment, momentarily [K. 5; ZT 7]
die Monarchie, -n monarchy [AB 11/I WV]
der Monat, -e month [AB 2/WV]
der Montag, -e Monday [AB 2/WV]
montags on Mondays [AB 2/WV]
der Morgen morning; **Guten ~!** Good morning! [AB 1]
morgen tomorrow [AB 8/G]; **~ Abend (früh, Nachmittag)** tomorrow evening (morning, afternoon) [AB 8/G]
morgens in the morning [AB 2/WV]
die Moschee, -n mosque [AL 7/WV]
das Motiv, -e motive [AB 7]
motiviert motivated [AB 9/WV]
das Motorrad, ⸚er motorcycle [AB 7/WV]
das Müesli müesli, whole grain cereal [K. 3]
mühselig with difficulty [K. 11]
der Müll garbage [AB 12/WV]
die Müll-Lawine, -n garbage avalanche [AB 12/WV]
der Multikulturalismus multiculturalism [K. 8]
multikulturell multicultural [K. 11]
der Mund, ⸚er mouth [AL 3]
das Museum, *pl.* **Museen** museum [AB 3]
die Museumsinsel "Museum Island" *(in Berlin)* [K. 11]
die Musik music [AL 2]
musikalisch musical [K. 3; AB 4/WV]
der Musikant, [-en], -en/die Musikantin, -nen musician [K. 9]
die Musikhochschule, -n music conservatory [K. 8]
der Muskelkater, - sore muscle [AL 8/WV]
müssen (muss, musste, hat gemusst) to have to, must; to be required to [ZT 3; AL 4]
mutig brave, courageous [AL 5]
die Mutter, ⸚ mother [AL 2/WV]
die Mutti, -s mom, ma, mommy [ZT 2]
die Mütze, -n cap, hat [K. 4]

na ... well . . . *(stalling mechanism)* [K. 4; AL 5]; **~, wie auch immer ...** yeah, whatever . . . [AL 5]
nach + *dat.* to *(countries, cities)* [AL 2]; past, after [AB 2/WV]
nachdem *(conj.)* after [ZT 5; AB 10]
nachher *(adv.)* afterwards [K. 4; AL 5]
die Nachhilfestunde, -n tutoring lesson [K. 5]
die Nachricht, -en news, message [AL 12]
das Nachrichtenmagazin, -e news magazine [K. 7]
die Nachspeise, -n dessert [AL 3/BK]
nächst: nächste Woche next week [AB 8/G]
die Nacht, ⸚e night [AL 5]; **Gute ~!** Good night! [AB 1/BK]
der Nachteil, -e disadvantage [K. 8]

der Nachtisch, -e dessert [AL 3/BK]
nächtlich nighttime, nocturnal [AB 10]
nackt naked [K. 8]
nagelneu brand-new [K. 9]
nah near [K. 8]
die Nähe vicinity [AB 8]; **in der ~ von** in the vicinity of, near [AB 3/KG]
naja ... well . . . *(as a hesitation marker)* [AL 2]
der Name, [-n], -n name [AL 1]
namens by the name of [K. 7]
nämlich namely, that is [AL 5]
der Narr, [-en], -en fool [K. 10]
die Narrengesellschaft, -en fools' guild [K. 10]
die Nase, -n nose [AB 6/WV]
nass wet, damp [AL 5/WV]
der Nationalsozialist, [-en], -en/die Nationalsozialistin, -nen National Socialist, Nazi [AB 11/I]
die Natur, -en nature [K. 5]
die Naturschönheit, -en natural beauty [AB 10]
die Nazigröße, -n Nazi V.I.P. [AB 7]
der Nebel, - fog [K. 4; AL 5/WV]
neben next to, beside [K. 4; AL 6]
nebenan next door [K. 6]
nebendran adjacent, next to [AB 6]
nee nope, naw [K. 4]
der Neffe, [-n], -n nephew [AL 2/WV]
nehmen (nimmt, nahm, hat genommen) to take [AB 1]; **in Kauf ~** to accept [AB 12]; **Platz ~** to have a seat [AB 1]
nein no [AB 1/G]
nennen (nannte, hat genannt) to name, call someone something [AL 10]
der Neo-Nazi, -s Neo-Nazi [K. 7]
nervös nervous; irritable [AB 4/WV]
nett nice [AL 6]
die Neuauflage, -n reprint [K. 7]
der Neubau, -ten new building [AB 8]
neugierig curious, nosy [K. 6]
das Neujahr New Year's Day [K. 10]
die Neutralität neutrality [K. 10]
nicht not [AL 1]; **~ sehr** not very [K. 2]; **~ so** not so [K. 2]; **gar ~** not at all [ZT 3]
die Nichte, -n niece [AL 2/WV]
nichts nothing [K. 1]
nicken (hat genickt) to nod [AB 11/II]
nie never [AL 4]; **gar ~** never at all [AB 10]
nieder·brennen (brannte nieder, hat niedergebrannt) to burn down [K. 11]
die Niederlande *(pl.)* the Netherlands [K. 12]
die Niederlassung, -en branch office [K. 12]
niemand (niemanden, niemandem) no one, nobody [AB 6/SiA]
der Nikolaustag St. Nicholas Day [K. 10]
das Niveau, -s level [K. 6]
noch still [AL 5]
(das) Nordamerika North America [K. 4]
der Nordosten northeast [K. 11]
der Nordwesten northwest [K. 11]
normalerweise normally, usually [K. 6]
(das) Norwegen Norway [K. 12]
der Notarzt, ¨-e emergency room physician [K. 8]
die Notiz, -en note [K. 4]
notwendig necessary [K. 8]
das Notwendigste bare necessities [ZT 6]
der November November [AB 2/WV]
der Numerus clausus restricted enrollment [K. 8]
nur only, just [K1; AL 3]

ob whether, if [AB 5/G]
das Obst fruit, fruits [AL 3/WV]
oder or [K1; AL 3/G]
offen open [AB 4/WV]
öffentlich public(ly) [AB 7]
öffnen (hat geöffnet) to open [AL 1]
die Öffnung, -en opening [AB 12]
oft often [K. 3]
ohne + *acc.* without [AB 4/G]; **ohne ... zu** without . . . ing [K. 12]
das Ohr, -en ear [AB 6/WV]
Oje! Geez! Oh boy! [AL 5]
ökologisch ecological [ZT 12]
der Oktober October [AB 2/WV]
das Öl, -e oil [AB 4]
das Olympia-Stadion Olympic Stadium in Berlin [K. 11]
die Olympiade, -n Olympic Games [K. 10]
die Oma, -s grandma [AL 2/WV]
der Onkel, - uncle [AL 2/WV]
der Opa, -s grandpa [AL 2/WV]
die Oper, -n opera; opera house [K. 5; AL 7/WV]
die Opposition, -en opposition [K. 7]
optimistisch optimistic [K. 3]
orange orange [AB 1/WV]
die Orange, -n orange [AL 3/WV]
ordnen (hat geordnet) to put in order, organize [K. 4]
das Organ, -e organ; power, branch of government [ZT 12]
die Organisation, -en organization [AL 7]
organisieren (hat organisiert) to organize [K. 4]
die Orientierung, -en orientation [K. 4]
die Orientierungsstufe orientation stage (5th and 6th grades) [K. 8]
örtlich local [K. 10]
ostdeutsch East German [AB 7]
der Osterhase, [-n], -n Easter bunny [K. 10]
Ostern Easter [K. 10]
(das) Österreich Austria [AB 1/WV]
(das) Österreich-Ungarn Austro-Hungarian Empire [K. 12]
der Österreicher, -/die Österreicherin, -nen Austrian [AB 1/WV]
der Overheadprojektor, -en overhead projector [AB 1/WV]
die Ozonschicht, -en ozone layer [AB 12/WV]

paar: ein ~ a few, some [AB 2/G]
packen (hat gepackt) to pack [AL 4/WV]
die Pädagogik pedagogy, education [AL 2/WV]
das Paket, -e package [AL 7/WV]
die Panik panic [K. 4]
der Papa, -s papa, dad [K. 3]
der Papierkorb, ¨-e wastepaper basket [AB 1/WV]
der Pappbecher, - paper cup [K. 12]
die Pappverpackung, -en cardboard packaging [K. 12]
das Paradies, -e paradise [AB 10]
parken (hat geparkt) to park [K. 4]
die Parkgebühr, -en parking fee [ZT 4]
das Parkhaus, ¨-er parking garage [ZT 4]
der Parkplatz, ¨-e parking space, parking lot [AB 8]
der Parkschein, -e parking stub, ticket [ZT 4]
das Parlament, -e parliament [AL 11]
die Partei des demokratischen Sozialismus (PDS) Party of Democratic Socialism [K. 7]
die Party, -s party [AL 7/WV]; **auf eine ~ gehen** to go to a party [AL 7/WV]
der Pass, *pl.* **Pässe** passport [AL 4/WV]; mountain/ski pass [AB 10/WV]
passen (hat gepasst) zu + *dat.* to suit, fit [ZT 8]
passieren (ist passiert) + *dat.* to happen [K. 5; AL 9]
die Passkontrolle, -n passport check [AB 12]
der Pastor, -en pastor [K. 3]

der Patient, [-en], -en/die Patientin, -nen patient [K. 6]
die Patrouille, -n patrol [K. 12]
die Pause, -n break, recess [K. 2]
der Pazifist, [-en], -en/die Pazifistin, -nen pacifist [K. 11]
Pech haben (hat Pech gehabt) to have bad luck [AL 8]
der Pendler, -/Pendlerin, -nen commuter [AB 8]
die Pension, -en guest-house [AB 3]
peppig peppy [ZT 8]
perfekt perfect [K. 2]
die Perle, -n pearl, bead [AL 10]
die Person, -en person
die Personalabteilung, -en personnel department [K. 9]
der Personalchef, -s/die Personalchefin, -nen head of the personnel department [AB 9]
der Personenkraftwagen, - car [K. 4]
die Persönlichkeit, -en personality [AB 10]
pessimistisch pessimistic [K. 6]
die Pfandflasche, -n returnable bottle, deposit bottle [K. 12]
die Pfanne, -n pan [K. 6]
der Pfeffer pepper [K. 6]
der Pfennig, -e pfennig (1/100 of a mark) [K. 3]
das Pferd, -e horse [AL 10]
der Pferdeschlitten, - horse-drawn sleigh [AB 10]
(das) Pfingsten Pentecost [K. 10]
die Pflanze, -n plant [AL 6/WV]
pflanzen (hat gepflanzt) to plant [AL 10]
pflegen (hat gepflegt) to maintain, keep up [K. 4]
der Pfleger, - orderly, male nurse [K. 8]
der Pflichtkurs, -e required course [K. 8]
das Pfund, -e pound [AL 3/BK]
die Pharmazie pharmaceutics [AL 5]
die Philharmonie (Berlin) Philharmonic Orchestra [AL 11]
die Philosophie, -n philosophy [AL 2/WV]
die Physik physics [AL 2/WV]
der Pilz, -e mushroom [K. 10]
die Piste, -n (downhill) ski run, track [AB 10]
der Pistenraser, - speed demon [K. 10]
der Pizzazusteller, -/die Pizzazustellerin, -nen pizza deliverer [K. 9]
der PKW, -s (Personenkraftwagen) car [AB 7/WV]
der Plan, ⸚e plan [K. 4]
das Planetarium, *pl.* **Planetarien** planetarium [AL 7/BK]
die Planung, -en plan [AL 7]; planning [ZT 10]
die Plastikwindel, -n disposable diaper [K. 12]
das Plattengeschäft, -e record store [ZT 3]
der Platz, ⸚e plaza, square [AB 3]; space, room; seat [AB 4]
plaudern (hat geplaudert) to chat [ZT 8]
der Pluspunkt, -e advantage, plus [AB 8]
pochen (hat gepocht) to pound, beat [AB 9]
(das) Polen Poland [K. 12]
die Politik politics [AL 2/WV]
die Politikwissenschaft political science [AL 2/WV]
die Popmusik popular music [AL 3]
populär popular [K. 4]
das Portmonee, -s wallet [AL 4/WV]
die Portion, -en portion [AB 8]
(das) Portugal Portugal [K. 12]
das Porzellan porcelain, china [K. 9]
positiv positive [AB 6]
die Post post office [AL 7]
der Postbote, [-n], -n/die Postbotin, -nen mailman, letter carrier [AB 10]
das Poster, - poster [AL 6/WV]
das Postfach, ⸚er mailbox, P.O. box [AL 6]
die Postkarte, -n postcard [K. 2]
der Praktikant, [-en], -en /die Praktikantin, -nen intern, trainee [AL 12]
die Praktikantenstelle, -n internship position [K. 8]
das Praktikum, *pl.* **Praktika** internship [AL 12]
praktizieren (hat praktiziert) to practice (a profession) [K. 6]
sich präsentieren (hat sich präsentiert) to present oneself [AB 9]
der Preis, -e price [AL 7]; prize
das Prestige prestige [K. 9; AB 10]
(das) Preußen Prussia [K. 11]
der Prinz, [-en], -en/die Prinzessin, -nen prince/princess [AL 10/WV]
prinzesshaft princess-like [AB 6]
das Privatbad, ⸚er private bath [AL 6]
die Privatstunde, -n private lesson [K. 5]
pro per [AB 8]
probieren (hat probiert) to try [ZT 8]
das Problem, -e problem [AB 5]
problemlos without a problem, hassle-free [AB 8]
der Professor, -en/die Professorin, -nen professor [AB 1]
das Programm, -e program [ZT 10]
der Programmierer, -/die Programmiererin, -nen programmer [AL 9/WV]
das Projekt, -e project [K. 5]
proklamieren (hat proklamiert) to proclaim [AL 10]
das Proseminar, -e introductory seminar [K. 8]
die Prüfung, -en test, examination [K. 4]
die Psychiatrie psychiatry; psychiatric ward [K. 8]
die Psychologie psychology [AL 2/WV]
der Pudding, -s pudding [ZT 10]
der Pullover, - pullover sweater [K. 2; AL 4/WV]
der Pulverschnee powder snow [AB 10]
pünktlich punctual, on time [AB 9/WV]
das Puppenhaus, ⸚er doll house [K. 11]
die Pute, -n turkey [AL 3/WV]
putzen (hat sich geputzt): sich die Zähne ~ to brush one's teeth [AL 8/WV]

das Quadrat, -e square [K. 3]
qualifiziert qualified [AB 9/WV]
quer diagonal, across [K. 7]
die Quittung, -en receipt [ZT 7]

das Rad, ⸚er bicycle [AL 7]; **Rad fahren (fährt Rad, fuhr Rad, ist Rad gefahren)** to bicycle [AB 3/WV]
das Radfahren bicycle riding [K. 3]
der Radfahrer, -/die Radfahrerin, -nen cyclist, bicycle rider [AB 4]; **~ frei** open to cyclists, bicycles allowed [K. 4]
das Radio, -s radio [AL 6/WV]
der Radweg, -e bicycle path [K. 4]
der Rang, ⸚e rank, standing [AB 11/I]
rar rare [AB 8]
der Rasierapparat, -e electric razor, shaver [K. 6; AL 8/WV]
sich rasieren (hat sich rasiert) to shave [AL 8/WV]
der Rat, *(pl.)* **Ratschläge** advice [K. 4; AB 9]
das Ratespiel, -e guessing game [K. 6]

das Rathaus, *pl.* **Rathäuser** city hall [AB 3]
(das) Rätoromanisch the Romansh language [K. 10]
der Ratschlag, ¨-e advice, suggestion [K. 4]
das Rätsel, - puzzle, riddle [K. 5]
der Ratskeller, - ratskeller, town hall basement restaurant [K. 4]
rauchen (hat geraucht) to smoke [K. 4]
raus out [K. 6]
raus·kommen (kam raus, ist rausgekommen) to come out [ZT 4]
reagieren (hat reagiert) to react [K. 6; AB 11/I]
die Reaktion, -en reaction [K. 6]
realistisch realistic [K. 4]
die Realität, -en reality [K. 5]
die Realschule, -n non-college track high school [K. 8]
der Realschüler, -/die Realschülerin, -nen high school student [K. 8]
das Rebhuhn, ¨-er partridge [K. 10]
rechnen (hat gerechnet) mit + *dat.* to count on, reckon with, expect [AB 8]
der Rechtsanwalt, ¨-e/die Rechtsanwältin, -nen lawyer [AL 9/WV]
Recht haben (hat Recht gehabt) to be right [ZT 3]
recht sein (ist, war, ist gewesen) + *dat.* to be all right with someone [AL 6]; **wenn es dir recht ist** if it's all right with you [AL 6]
rechtfertigen (hat gerechtfertigt) to justify [K. 11]
rechts right, on the right [ZT 4]
rechtsextremistisch right-wing extremist [AB 7]
der/die Rechtsradikale, -n *(adj. as noun)* right-wing extremist [K. 6]
der Rechtsradikalismus right-wing extremism [AB 7]
das Recycling recycling [AB 12/WV]
reden (hat geredet) über + *acc.* to talk about [AB 5]
reduzieren (hat reduziert) to lower, drop, reduce [K 8]
das Referat, -e seminar paper, presentation [AL 8]; **ein ~ halten** to make an oral presentation [AL 8]
das Reformhaus, ¨-er health food store [AL 7/WV]
das Regal, -e shelf, shelving [AL 6/WV]
die Regel, -n rule, regulation [AB 4]
regeln (hat geregelt) to regulate [AB 11/I]
der Regen rain [AL 5/WV]
der Regenmantel, ¨- raincoat [K. 4]
der Regenschirm, -e umbrella [K. 3]
der Regenwald, ¨-er rain forest [K. 12]
der Regierungsantritt, -e taking office [AB 11/I]
das Regierungsviertel, - area of federal government buildings [K. 11]
regnen (hat geregnet) to rain [K. 3; AL 5/WV]
das Reich, -e empire; realm [AB 11/I WV]
reichen (hat gereicht) to be enough, suffice, last [AB 6]; to hand, give [K. 10]
der Reichstag German Parliament 1871–1933 [AL 11]; building in Berlin
die Reifeprüfung, -en high school exam *(Switzerland)* [K. 8]
die Reihenfolge, -n order, sequence [K. 4; AL 6]
die Reinemachefrau, -en cleaning lady [K. 6]
rein·stellen (hat reingestellt) to put in [ZT 6]
der Reis rice [ZT 6]
die Reise, -n trip, journey, travel [AL 4]
der Reisekoffer, - suitcase [K. 6]
der Reiseleiter, -/die Reiseleiterin, -nen tour guide, courier, group leader [ZT 10]
der Reiseplan, ¨-e travel itinerary [K. 6]
der Reisescheck, -s traveller's check [AL 4/WV]
das Reisetagebuch, ¨-er travel log, diary [K. 5]
das Reiseunternehmen, - travel agency [ZT 10]
die Reiseverbindung, -en travel connection [K. 4]
reißen (hat gerissen): aus den Angeln ~ to tear off its hinges [K. 11]
reiten (ritt, ist geritten) to ride horseback [AB 3]
die Spanische Reitschule the Spanish Riding School in Vienna [K. 4]
rekonstruieren (hat rekonstruiert) to reconstruct [K. 5]
das Relativpronomen, - relative pronoun [AL 9/G]
der Relativsatz, ¨-e relative clause [AL 9/G]
die Religion, -en religion [K. 2]
rennen (ist gerannt) to run, race [AL 10]
renovieren (hat renoviert) to renovate, remodel [AL 11]
die Rente, -n pension [ZT 11]
die Rentenversicherung, -en pension insurance, social security [K. 9]
die Republik, -en republic [AL 11]; **die Weimarer ~** Weimar Republic [K. 11]
der Republikaner, -/die Republikanerin, -nen member of the Republican Party [K. 7]
respektieren (hat respektiert) to respect [K. 5]
die Ressource, -n resource [ZT 9]
der Rest, -e rest, remainder [AL 11]
das Restaurant, -s restaurant [K. 2; ZT 3]
das Resultat, -e result [K. 3]
retten (hat gerettet) vor + *dat.* to rescue, save from [AB 7]
die Rettungsaktion, -en rescue mission [AB 7]
der Revisionist, -en/die Revisionistin, -nen revisionist [K. 10]
die Revolution, -en revolution [K. 4]
richtig right [AL 1]; authentic, really [AL 6]
das Richtige the right thing [K. 9]
die Richtung, -en direction [AB 4]
das Rindfleisch beef [AL 3/WV]
riskant risky [K. 7]
riskieren (hat riskiert) to risk [AB 7]
der Rock, ¨-e skirt [AL 4/WV]
rodeln (ist gerodelt) to sled [K. 10]
der Rolladen, ¨- roll-top shutters [AL 6/WV]
die Rolle, -n role, part [K. 6]
die Rollerblades *(pl.)* in-line skates [AB 7/WV]
der Rollschuh, -e roller-skates
der Roman, -e novel [K. 3; AB 7/WV]
romantisch romantic [AB 1]
römisch Roman [K. 9]
rosa pink [AB 1/WV]
die Rose, -n rose [K. 6]
rot red [AB 1/WV]
die Routine, -n routine [K. 5; AL 8/WV]
der Rücken, - back [AB 6/WV]
die Rückkehr return [AL 12]
der Rucksack, ¨-e backpack [AL 4/WV]
rufen (rief, hat gerufen) to call [AL 10]
ruhig quiet, peaceful [AB 4/WV]
rund approximately, roughly [AB 4]
rund um all around [AB 8]
die Runde, -n round [K. 4]
runzeln (hat gerunzelt): die Stirn ~ to wrinkle one's forehead [K. 6]
(das) Russisch the Russian language [AL 2/WV]

rütteln (hat gerüttelt) to shake [AL 10]

die Sache, -n thing, object, item [K. 4]
die Sachertorte, -n Sacher chocolate layer cake [K. 4]
der Saft, ¨-e juice [AL 3/WV]
die Sage, -n myth, legend [K. 10]
sagen (hat gesagt) to say [AB 1]
die Saison, -s (travel) season [K. 7]
der/das Sakko, -s sport coat [K. 4]
der Salat, -e salad; lettuce [AL 3/WV]
das Salz salt [K. 6]
sammeln (hat gesammelt) to collect, gather [AL 12]; **Erfahrung ~** to gain experience [AL 12]
die Sammelstelle, -n collection site [AB 12/WV]
der Samstag, -e Saturday (in Southern Germany) [AB 2/WV]
die Sandale, -n sandal [K. 3]
sanft gentle, soft [AB 10]
der Sängerknabe, [-n], -en choir boy; **die Wiener Sängerknaben** Vienna Boys' Choir [K. 4]
der Satz, ¨-e sentence [K. 4]
sauber clean [K. 6; AB 10]
sauber machen (hat sauber gemacht) to clean [K. 6]
die Sauna, -s sauna [K. 10]
sausen (hat gesaust) to whistle [K. 11]
schaden (hat geschadet) + *dat.* to harm, hurt [AL 9]
schaffen (hat geschafft) to manage, get done; to "make it" [AL 8]
der Schal, -s scarf, shawl [K. 5]
der Schatz, ¨-e treasure [AB 11/II]
schauen (hat geschaut) to look [ZT 2; AB 6]; **Schau mal!** Look! [ZT 2]
der Schauer, - shower; shivers [AL 5/WV]
das Schauspielhaus, ¨-er theater [K. 9]
der Schein, -e paper money, bill [AB 6]; course credit certificate [K. 8]
scheinbar apparently, seemingly [K. 10]
scheinen (schien, hat geschienen) to shine; to appear to be [AL 5/WV; AB 6]
schenken (hat geschenkt) to give a gift [K. 6]
schicken (hat geschickt) to send [AB 2]
schief gehen (ging schief, ist schief gegangen) to fail, go wrong
die Schiene, -n train track [AB 11/II]
das Schiff, -e boat [AB 7/WV]
die Schifffahrt, -en boat trip [AB 3]
das Schild, -er sign [AB 4]
schildern (hat geschildert) to portray, describe (an action) [ZT 7]
der Schirm, -e umbrella [K. 4]
die Schizophrenie schizophrenia [ZT 11]
die Schlacht, -en battle, fight [ZT 10]
schlafen (schläft, schlief, hat geschlafen) to sleep [K. 2; AL 6]
schlafen gehen (ging schlafen, ist schlafen gegangen) to go to sleep [AB 2/WV]
das Schlafzimmer, - bedroom [AL 6/WV]
der Schlager, - popular song, hit [K. 2]
die Schlange, -n waiting line; snake [ZT 8]; **[in der] ~ stehen** to stand/wait in line [ZT 8]
schlank slim, slender [AB 1/WV]
der Schleier, - veil [K. 6]
der Schlepper, - person smuggling illegal immigrants [AB 12]
schließlich finally [K. 5]
schlimm bad, nasty [AL 5]
die Schlittelfahrt, -en toboggan run, sleighride *(Swiss dialect)* [AB 10]
schlittelnd sledding, by sled *(Swiss dialect)* [AB 10]
der Schlitten, - sled, sleigh [AB 10]
Schlittschuh laufen (läuft, lief, ist gelaufen) to skate [K. 10]
das Schlittschuhlaufen skating [K. 10]
das Schloss, *pl.* **Schlösser** castle [AB 3]
der Schlossgarten, ¨ palace grounds, castle garden [AL 7/BK]
der Schlossplatz, ¨-e castle square [AL 7/BK]
der Schlummertrunk, -e bedtime drink, nightcap [K. 10]
der Schluss, *pl.* **Schlüsse** conclusion, finish, end [K. 5]
der Schlüssel, - key [AL 6]
schmecken (hat geschmeckt) + *dat.* to taste good [AB 6/G]
der Schmerz, -en pain [AL 8/WV]
die Schmerztablette, -n pain killer [AL 8/WV]
sich schminken (hat sich geschminkt) to put on make-up [AL 8/WV]
schmuggeln (hat geschmuggelt) to smuggle [K. 12]
schmusen (hat geschmust) to cuddle [AB 5/WV]
schmutzig dirty [K. 8]
der Schnee snow [AL 5/WV]
das Schneewittchen Snow White [K. 10]
die Schneidemaschine, -n slicer [K. 6]
sich schneiden (schnitt sich, hat sich geschnitten) in + *acc.* to cut oneself in [AL 8/WV]
schneien (hat geschneit) to snow [AL 5/WV]
schnell fast, quickly [AL 1]
der Schnupfen head cold; **einen ~ haben** to have a head cold [AL 8/WV]
der Schock, -s shock [AB 10]
die Schokolade, -n chocolate [K. 3]
schon already [K1]
schonen (hat geschont) to save, preserve [K. 4]
schön pretty, beautiful [AB 1]
die Schönheit, -en beauty [K. 3]
der Schornstein, -e chimney [K. 11]
der Schrank, ¨-e closet, wardrobe [AL 6/WV]
schreiben (schrieb, hat geschrieben) to write [AL 1]; **~ an** + *acc.* to write to
die Schreibstube, -n office [AB 11/II]
der Schreibtisch, -e desk [AB 1/WV]
die Schublade, -n drawer [AB 11/II]
schüchtern shy, bashful [AB 4/WV]
der Schuh, -e shoe [AL 4/WV]
das Schuhgeschäft, -e shoe store [K. 3]
der Schulbereich, -e school district [K. 4]
der Schülerausweis, -e high school student ID [K. 7]
die Schulpflicht mandatory education [K. 8]
die Schulter, -n shoulder [AB 6]
die Schulzeit, -en school days [AB 5]
die Schussfahrt, -en schussing *(Swiss dialect)* [AB 10]
der Schutt rubble [AB 11/II]
schütteln (hat geschüttelt) to shiver, shake [AL 10]
schütten (hat geschüttet) to spill [K. 10]
schützen (hat geschützt) to protect [AB 12/WV]
das Schützenfest, -e marksmen festival [K. 10]
der Schutzumschlag, ¨-e dust cover [K. 7]
Schwaben Swabia [AL 7/BK]
schwach weak [AL 3/G]
schwärmen (hat geschwärmt) von + *dat.* to rave about, be wild about [AL 11]
schwarz black [AB 1/WV]

schwätzen (hat geschwätzt) to talk, blab *(southern German dialect)* [ZT 5]
(das) Schweden Sweden [K. 12]
Schwein haben (hat Schwein gehabt) to be lucky [AL 6]
das Schweinefleisch pork [AL 3/WV]
die Schweiz Switzerland [AB 1/WV]
der Schweizer, -/die Schweizerin, -nen Swiss [AB 1/WV]
schwer difficult [ZT 4]; heavy
schwerhörig hard-of-hearing [K. 6]
die Schwester, -n sister [AL 2/WV]
das Schwimmbad, ¨-er swimming pool [AB 3]
schwimmen (schwamm, ist geschwommen) to swim [AL 5/G]
schwul gay, homosexual *(colloq.)* [K. 5]
schwül humid [AL 5/WV]
der See, -n lake [AB 10/WV]
die See, -n sea [AB 11/WV]
segeln (ist gesegelt) to sail [AB 3]
sehen (sieht, sah, hat gesehen) to see [AL 2]
die Sehenswürdigkeit, -en sight-seeing attraction [AB 3]
sehr very [AB 1]
die Seife, -n soap [AL 8/WV]
die Seifenoper, -n soap opera [K. 5]
sein his, its [AL 3/G]
sein (ist, war, ist gewesen) to be [AL 1]
seit + *dat.* since, for *(+ time phrase)* [AL 5]
seitdem ever since [AL 12]
die Seite, -n page; side [K. 7]
der Sekretär, -e/die Sekretärin, -nen secretary [AL 9/WV]
die Sekunde, -n second [K. 4]
selber self; oneself, myself, etc. [AL 6]
selbst self; (by) oneself, myself, etc. [AB 4]
selbstständig independent, self-reliant [AB 9/WV]
selbstsicher self-assured, self-confident [AB 4/WV]
die Selbstunterdrückung self-oppression, self-repression [K. 6]
seltsam strange, unusual [AB 10]
das Semester, - semester [AL 2]
die Semesterkarte, -n semester bus pass [AL 7]
das Seminar, -e seminar; academic department [K. 6; AB 8]
die Seminararbeit, -en seminar paper [K. 8]
der Seminarraum, ¨-e seminar room [AL 8]
die Semmel, -n hard roll *(in southern Germany)* [AL 3/BK]
senden (hat gesendet) to send [K. 2]
die Sendepause, -n non-broadcast time [K. 5]
der September September [AB 2/WV]
die Serenade, -n serenade [K. 9]
Servus! Hello! *(in Austria)* [AB 1/BK]
der Sessel, - armchair [AL 6/WV]
setzen (hat gesetzt) to set down, put down [AL 7/G]; **sich ~ (hat sich gesetzt)** to sit (oneself) down [AL 1/WV]
das Shampoo, -s shampoo [AL 8/WV]
sicher certain(ly), sure(ly) [AL 3]
die Sicherheit, -en safety, security [AB 4]
die Sicherheitspolitik defense policy [K. 12]
sichtbar visible, clear to the eye [AB 10]
sie she, it; they [AB 1/G]; her, it, them (*acc.*) [AB 3/G]
Sie you *(formal)* [AL 1], *(formal nom. + acc.)* [AB 3/G]
die Siegermacht, ¨-e victor, victorious foreign power [AB 11/I]
das Silber silver [AL 10]
das Silvester New Year's Eve [K. 10]
sitzen (saß, hat gesessen) to be sitting, sit [AL 7/G]
der Skandal, -e scandal [K. 8]
Ski laufen (läuft Ski, lief Ski, ist Ski gelaufen) to ski [K. 3; AB 10]
der Skianorak, -s ski parka [K. 6]
die Skihütte, -n ski chalet [K. 6]
der Skistiefel, - ski boot [K. 6]
die Skizze, -n sketch [K. 6]
das Skript, -en lecture notes [K. 8]
die Slowakei Slovakia [K. 12]
(das) Slowenien Slovenia [K. 12]
der Smoking, -s tuxedo [K. 10]
so so [AL 2]; **~ war das** that's the way it was [ZT 5]
sobald as soon as [K. 4]
die Socke, -n sock [K. 4]
das Sofa, -s sofa [AL 6/WV]
der Sohn, ¨-e son [AL 2/WV]
solange as long as [K. 4]
sollen (soll, sollte, hat gesollt) should, ought to; to be supposed to [AL 4]
der Sommer, - summer [AL 5/WV]
der Sommerpalast, ¨-e summer palace [K. 11]
die Sonderausgabe, -n special edition [K. 8]
die Sondereinsatzgruppe, -n special services [K. 12]
sondern but, rather [AL 3/G]
der Sonnabend, -e Saturday *(in northern Germany)* [AB 2/WV]
die Sonne, -n sun [K. 4; AL 5/WV]
die Sonnenterrasse, -n sunning deck [AB 10]
sonnig sunny [AL 5/WV]
der Sonntag, -e Sunday [AB 2/WV]
sonst otherwise [ZT 6]; **~ noch etwas?** Anything else? [K. 3]
Sonstiges other things [K. 7]
sonst wo (sonst irgendwo) somewhere else [ZT 11]
die Sorge, -n worry, concern [K. 4]; **sich Sorgen machen** to worry [AL 4]
sortieren (hat sortiert) to sort [AB 6]
die Sowjetunion (UdSSR) Soviet Union (USSR) [K. 10; AB 11/I]
die Soziologie sociology [AL 2/WV]
die Spalte, -n column [K. 5]
spalten (hat gespaltet) to separate [AB 11/I]
(das) Spanien Spain [K. 12]
das Spanisch the Spanish language [AL 2/WV]
spannend exciting [AB 7/WV]
sparen (hat gespart) to save [AL 7/WV]
die Sparkasse, -n savings bank [AL 7]
der Spaß, ¨-e fun [K. 4]; **~ machen** + *dat.* to be fun [K. 6; AL 9]
spät late [K. 3]; **später** later [AL 5]; **spätestens** at the latest [ZT 9]
spazieren gehen (ging spazieren, ist spazieren gegangen) to go for a walk [AB 2/WV]
der Spaziergang, ¨-e walk, stroll [K. 3; AL 5]
der Spaziergänger, -/die Spaziergängerin, -nen walker, stroller [AB 10]
der Speisesaal, *pl.* **Säle** hotel dining room [ZT 10]
der Spiegel, - mirror [AL 6/WV]
spielen (hat gespielt) to play [AL 2]
der Spielkamerad, [-en] -en/die Spielkameradin, -nen playmate [K. 5]
der Spielplatz, ¨-e playground [K. 7]
das Spielzeug, -e toy [K. 5]
das Spital, ¨-er hospital *(in Austria)* [K. 11]
die Spitze, -n peak, summit [K. 10]
spontan spontaneous [AB 5]
der Sport sports, athletics [K. 2]
der Sportler, - /die Sportlerin, -nen athlete [K. 3]

sportlich athletic [AL 2]
die Sportstätte, -n training field [K. 3]
die Sprache, -n language [K. 2; AL 4]
das Sprachlabor, -s, (-e) language lab [K. 8]
die Sprachreise, -n language study tour [ZT 10]
die Spraydose, -n aerosol container [K. 12]
sprechen (spricht, sprach, hat gesprochen) to speak [AB 1]; **~ für** + *acc.* to speak for, speak well of; to indicate [AB 4]; **~ über** + *acc.* to talk about [K. 5; AL 7/G]
die Sprechstunde, -n office hour [AL 8]
das Sprichwort, ¨-er proverb [K. 6]
springen (sprang, ist gesprungen) to jump [AL 7/G]
das Spülbecken, - kitchen sink [K. 6]
der Staat, -en state, government [ZT 11]
staatlich governmental, state- [K. 12]
der/die Staatsangehörige, -n *(adj. as noun)* citizen [AT 12/WV]
der Staatsbürger, -/die Staatsbürgerin, -nen citizen [AT 12/WV]
das Staatsexamen, - state exam; teacher's degree [K. 8]
die Staatsgalerie, -n state gallery [AL 7/BK]
das Stadion, *pl.* **Stadien** stadium [AL 7/WV]
die Stadt, ¨-e city [AB 3]
der Stadtplan, ¨-e city map [K. 6]
der Stadtrand, ¨-er outskirts of the city [AB 8]
die Stadtrundfahrt, -en city bus tour [K. 11]
der Stadtteil, -e city district [K. 11]
die Stadtteilbibliothek, -en library branch [ZT 9]
stark strong [AL 3/G]
statistisch statistically [K. 12]
statt + *gen.* instead of [AB 11/II G]
statt·finden (fand statt, hat stattgefunden) to take place, occur [AB 10]
staub·saugen (hat staubgesaugt) to vacuum [K. 4]
die Steckdose, -n electric socket [AB 1/WV]
stecken (hat gesteckt) to stick [AB 6]
stehen (stand, hat gestanden) to stand [AL 1/WV; AL 7/G]
steif stiff, ill-at-ease [AB 4/WV]
steigen (stieg, ist gestiegen) to climb; to rise [AB 10]

die Stelle, -n position, job [AB 8]; **an deiner ~** if I were you [AL 11]
stellen (hat gestellt) to put standing [AL 7/G]
der Stempel, - stamp [AT 12/WV]
sterben (stirbt, starb, ist gestorben) to die [AL 5/G]
die Stereoanlage, -n stereo set [AL 6/WV]
die Steuer, -n tax, duty [AL 12/WV]
der Steuervorteil, -e tax break [K. 12]
stichprobenartig at random, randomly [AB 12]
der Stiefbruder, ¨- step-brother [AL 2/WV]
der Stiefel, - boot [AL 4/WV]
die Stiefmutter, ¨- step-mother [AL 10]
die Stiefschwester, -n step-sister [AL 10]
das Stiegenhaus, ¨-er stairwell [AB 11/II]
der Stift, -e pen or pencil [AL 6]
still still, quiet [K. 1]
die Stille quiet, silence [AB 10]
stimmen (hat gestimmt) to be correct [AL 1]
die Stimmung, -en atmosphere, mood [K. 10; ZT 11]
stinken (stank, hat gestunken) to stink [K. 4]
stinklangweilig boring as heck [AL 9]
das Stipendium, *pl.* **Stipendien** scholarship, stipend [K. 8]
die Stirn, -en forehead [AB 6]
der Stock, *pl.* **Stockwerke** floor, story [AL 6]; **der erste ~** second floor [AL 6]; **auf/in dem zweiten ~** on the third floor [AL 6]; **einen ~ höher** one floor up [AL 6]; **einen ~ tiefer** one floor down [AL 6]
stolpern (ist gestolpert) to stumble [K. 9]
stolz proud [K. 5]
stören (hat gestört) to disturb [ZT 7]
die Strafe, -n punishment [K. 10]
der Strand, ¨-e beach [K. 5]
die Straße, -n street [AB 4]; **die ~ entlang** down the street [AL 7/G]
die Straßenbahn, -en streetcar [AB 7/WV]
sich streiten (streitet, stritt, hat gestritten) to argue, quarrel [K. 5]
stressen (hat gestresst) to stress [K. 4]
die Struktur, -en structure [AB 7]
die Strumpfhose, -n panty hose, tights [K. 4]
das Stück, -e piece [AL 3]
der Student, [-en], -en/die Studentin, -nen student [AL 1]

das Studenten(wohn)heim, -e dormitory [AL 6]
der Studentenausweis, -e student ID [K. 7]
die Studentenermäßigung, -en student discount [K. 7]
die Studentenkneipe, -n student bar, pub [AL 5]
das Studentenleben student life [AB 8]
der Studentenpass, *pl.* **Pässe** semester (bus) pass [K. 7]
das Studentenzimmer, - student room [AL 6/WV]
das Studienbuch, ¨-er ledger of completed courses [K. 8]
das Studienfach, ¨-er academic subject [AL 2/WV]
der Studienplatz, ¨-e place; university admission [K. 8]
studieren (hat studiert) to study [AL 2]
das Studium, *pl.* **Studien** studies, college education [AL 5]
der Stuhl, ¨-e chair [AB 1/WV]
die Stunde, -n hour [ZT 5]
der Stundenplan, ¨-e schedule [K. 2]
der Styroporbecher, - styrofoam cup [K. 12]
subventionieren (hat subventioniert) to subsidize [K. 12]
die Suche, -n search, hunt [AL 9]
suchen (hat gesucht) to look for [AL 1]; **~ nach** + *dat.* to search for, seek, look for [AL 9]
südamerikanisch South American [K. 5]
der Südwesten southwest [K. 11]
südwestlich southwestern [K. 11]
der Supermarkt, ¨-e supermarket [K. 3; AL 7/WV]
die Suppe, -n soup [AL 3/BK]
surfen (hat gesurft) to surf [K. 10]
sympathisch likeable, pleasant, nice [AB 4/WV]
das Symptom, -e symptom [K. 6]
die Synagoge, -n synagogue [AL 7/WV]
systematisch systematically [K. 7]
die Szene, -n scene [AL 7]; "in-crowd" [AL 11]

die Tabelle, -n table, chart [K. 4]
die Tafel, -n blackboard [AL 1]
der Tag, -e day [AL 2]; **~ der deutschen Einheit** Day of German Unity [K. 10]; **eines Tages** one day [AL 5]; **Guten ~!** Good day!, Hello! [AB 1]; **jeden ~** every day [AB 8/G]

der Tagesablauf plan for the day, day's schedule [K. 6]
täglich daily [K. 5]
das Tal, ¨-er valley [AB 10]
die Tankstelle, -n gas station [K. 7]
der Tankwart, -e/die Tankwartin, -nen gas station attendant [K. 7]
die Tante, -n aunt [AL 2/WV]
tanzen (hat getanzt) to dance [K. 2; AB 3/WV]
der Tarif, -e wage rate [ZT 9]
das Taschengeld pocket money, allowance [K. 6]
das Taschentuch, ¨-er tissue [K. 8]
tätig active, involved [ZT 10]
das Täubchen, - pigeon, dove
das Taxi, -s taxi cab [K. 5; AB 7/WV]
der Tee, -s tea [AL 3/WV]; **~ kochen** to make tea [ZT 6]
der Teil, -e part, portion [AL 11]
teilen (hat geteilt) to divide [AB 11/I]; **sich ~ (hat sich geteilt)** to share; to divide, split (up) [K. 5; ZT 6]
der Teilzeitjob, -s part-time job [AL 9]
das Telefon, -e telephone [AB 3]
telefonisch by telephone [ZT 9]
die Telefonzelle, -n telephone booth [AL 6]
der Tellerwäscher, -/die Tellerwäscherin, -nen dish washer [K. 9]
die Temperatur, -en temperature [AL 5/WV]; **Die ~ liegt um 15 Grad.** The temperature is around 15 degrees. [AL 5/WV]
das Tennis tennis [K. 2]
der Tennisball, ¨-e tennis ball [K. 4]
der Tennisschläger, - tennis racket [K. 4]
der Teppich, -e carpet, rug [AL 6/WV]
der Termin, -e appointment, date [K. 6]
der Terrorismus terrorism [K. 4]
teuer expensive [AB 2]
das Theater, - theater [AB 3]
das Theaterstück, -e play [AB 7/WV]
das Thema, *pl.* **Themen** topic, theme [AB 5]
der Tiefflieger, - low-flying (fighter) plane [AB 11/II]
das Tier, -e animal [AL 10/WV]
der Tierarzt, ¨-e/die Tierärztin, -nen veterinarian [AL 9/WV]
der Tierpark, -s zoo [K. 9]
die Tochter, ¨ daughter [AL 2/WV]
der Tod death [K. 10]
todmüde dead-tired [ZT 4]
die Toilette, -n toilet; bathroom [AL 6/WV]
der Toilettenartikel, - toiletry [AL 4/WV]
tolerant tolerant [K. 5]
toleriert tolerated [K. 6]
toll great, neat, cool [ZT 2]
die Tomate, -n tomato [AL 3/WV]
die Ton-Dia-Vorstellung, -en slide show with sound track [K. 11]
die Tonne, -n ton [K. 9]
der Topf, ¨-e pot [ZT 6]
das Tor, -e gate [AL 11]
die Torte, -n layer cake [AL 7/WV]
tot dead [K. 4]; **tote Hose** completely dead, totally boring [K. 8]
töten (hat getötet) to kill [K. 7]
der Tourismus tourism [ZT 10]
tragen (trägt, trug, hat getragen) to wear [AL 4/WV]
der Transit transit [AB 11/I]
der Transitverkehr transit traffic, transit trade [AB 12]
das Transportunternehmen, - transportation company [K. 10]
die Tratschzeitschrift, -en gossip magazine
die Traube, -n grape [AL 3/WV]
der Traum, ¨-e dream [K. 1]
der Traumpartner, - dream partner [K. 5]
treffen (trifft, traf, hat getroffen) to meet, run into [K. 6; AL 7/WV]
treiben (trieb, hat getrieben) to do, play [K. 2]
der Treibhauseffekt greenhouse effect [AB 12/WV]
sich trennen (hat sich getrennt) von + *dat.* to break up with, separate from [AB 8/G]
die Treppe, -n stairs, stairway [AL 6/WV]
das Treppenhaus, ¨-er stairway [AL 6/WV]
treten (tritt, trat, hat getreten) to kick, step [AB 11/II]
treu faithful, loyal, true [K. 5]
der Trimm-dich-Pfad, -e exercise course [AB 3]
trinken (trank, hat getrunken) to drink [K. 2; AL 3]
das Trinkgeld, -er tip, gratuity [AL 5]
trivial trivial [K. 9]
trocken dry [AL 5/WV]
die Tropen *(pl.)* tropics [K. 12]
trotz + *gen.* in spite of, despite [AB 11/II G]
trotzdem nevertheless [AL 5]
(das) Tschechien, die Tschechische Republik Czech Republic [K. 12]
die Tschechoslowakei Czechoslovakia [K. 12]
Tschüss! Bye! [AL 6]
die Tulpe, -n tulip [K. 6]
tun (tat, hat getan) to do; put [ZT 4]
der Tunnel, -s, (-) tunnel [AB 10]
die Tür, -en door [AL 1]
der Türke, [-n], -n/die Türkin, -nen Turk [AB 6]
die Türkei Turkey [AB 6]
der Turm, ¨-e tower [K. 6]
das Turnier, -e tournament [K. 5]
die Tüte, -n sack, bag [ZT 7]
der Tutor, -en/die Tutorin, -nen tutor [K. 8]
der Typ, -en type; guy, fellow *(colloq.)* [AL 9]
typisch typical [K. 3]

die U-Bahn, -en subway [AB 7/WV]
die USA *(pl.)* U.S.A. [AB 1]
üben (hat geübt) to practice, rehearse [K. 10]
über above, over [K. 3; AL 7/G]
überarbeitet over-worked [AB 10]
überfüllt overfilled, oversubscribed [ZT 8]
sich übergeben (übergibt sich, übergab sich, hat sich übergeben) to vomit [AL 8/WV]
überhaupt at all [K. 4]; **~ kein** none at all [AL 2/SiA]
überholen (hat überholt) to pass (a vehicle) [K. 4]
überlegen (hat überlegt) to consider, think about [AB 6]; **sich ~ (überlegt sich, hat sich überlegt)** to think over, consider [AL 8]
übermäßig excessively [AB 9]
übermorgen the day after tomorrow [AB 8/G]
überprüfen (hat überprüft) to check [K. 7]
überraschend surprising(ly) [AB 11/I]
übersehen (übersieht, übersah, hat übersehen) to oversee, supervise [ZT 9]
der Übersetzer, -/die Übersetzerin, -nen translator, interpreter [K. 9]
übertreiben (übertrieb, hat übertrieben) to exaggerate [K. 6]
die Übertreibung, -en exaggeration [K. 5]
überwinden (überwand, hat überwunden) to overcome [ZT 12]
üblich usual, common [AB 8]
die Übung, -en practice; exercise; discussion section [K. 8]
die Uhr, -en clock, watch [AB 1/WV]
die Ukraine Ukraine [K. 12]

um + *acc.* around; at *(time)* [AB 2/WV; AB 4/G]
umarmen (hat umarmt) to embrace [AB 5/WV]
die Umbauarbeit, -en renovation work, remodeling [AL 11]
um·bauen (hat umgebaut) to renovate [K. 11]
sich um·drehen (hat sich umgedreht) to turn (self) around [AL 1]
die Umgebung, -en surroundings, area [AL 4]
umgekehrt the other way around, vice versa [ZT 11]
um·stellen (hat umgestellt) to adjust, adapt [ZT 12]
die Umwelt environment [AB 12/WV]
umweltfreundlich environmentally friendly [AB 4]
der Umweltschutz environmental protection [K. 12]
der Umzug, ¨-e parade [K. 10]
um ... zu in order to [K. 12]
unattraktiv unattractive [AB 1/WV]
unbedingt absolutely, really [AL 2]
und and [AL 1]; **... ~ so** . . . and stuff like that [AL 11]; **~ so weiter (usw.)** etcetera (etc.) [AL 5]
undenkbar unthinkable [K. 8]
der Unfall, ¨-e accident [AB 12/WV]
unfreundlich unfriendly [AB 4/WV]
(das) Ungarn Hungary [K. 12]
ungeduldig impatient [AB 6]
die Uni, -s university [K. 4]
die Universität, -en university [AL 1]; **an der ~** at college, at the university [AB 2]
unmusikalisch unmusical [AB 4/WV]
die UNO United Nations Organization (UN) [K. 12]
unpersönlich impersonal [AL 1]
uns us *(acc., dat.)* [AB 3/G]
unser our [AL 3/G]
unsicher unsure, insecure [AB 4/WV]
unsportlich unathletic [AB 4/WV]
unsympathisch unlikeable, disagreeable [AB 4/WV]
unten downstairs [AL 6]
unter under, underneath [AL 7/G]; **~ sich** among themselves [K. 6]; **~ Verschluss halten** to keep under lock and key [ZT 6]
unterbezahlt underpaid [AL 9]
unter·bringen (brachte unter, hat untergebracht) to house, put up overnight [ZT 10]
unterdrücken (hat unterdrückt) to oppress, repress [AB 6]
die Unterdrückung oppression, repression [AB 6]
sich unterhalten (unterhält sich, unterhielt sich, hat sich unterhalten) mit + *dat.* to converse with, talk to [K. 5; AB 9]
unterhaltend entertaining [AB 7/WV]
unter·kommen (ist untergekommen) to find lodging [AB 8]
die Unterlage, -n form, document [AL 12]
das Unternehmen, - business, company; undertaking, project [K. 7; AB 11/I]
der Unternehmer, -/die Unternehmerin, -nen entrepreneur, venture capitalist [K. 7]
unternehmungslustig active, eager to participate [K. 5]
der Unteroffizier, -e non-commissioned officer [AB 11/II]
der Unterricht instruction, lesson, class [K. 4]
unterrichten (hat unterrichtet) to instruct, teach [K. 8]
untersagt forbidden, prohibited [K. 12]
der Unterschied, -e difference [K. 8]
unterstützen (hat unterstützt) to support [K. 12]
der Untertitel, - subtitle [K. 7]
die Unterwäsche underwear [AL 4/WV]
unterwegs enroute, underway [ZT 4]
der Urlaub, -e vacation [ZT 9]
der Urlaubsschein, -e leave permit, pass [AB 11/II]
die Ursache, -n cause [K. 6]
ursprünglich originally [K. 7]

der Vater, ¨ father [AL 2/WV]
der Vati, -s dad [ZT 3]
vegetarisch vegetarian [K. 3]
sich verabreden (hat sich verabredet) mit + *dat.* to make a date with [AL 11]
verabredet commited; have a date [AL 11]
die Verabredung, -en date [K. 5]
verantwortlich responsible [ZT 10]
die Verantwortung, -en responsibility [ZT 9]
verbessern (hat verbessert) to improve [AL 2]
verblüfft stunned [AB 6]
das Verbot, -e ban, prohibition [AB 4]; **~ der Einfahrt** no entry [K. 4]; **~ für Fahrzeuge aller Art** closed to all vehicles [K. 4]; **~ für Radfahrer** no bicycles allowed [K. 4]
verboten forbidden, prohibited [K. 6; AB 12/WV]
verbrauchen (hat verbraucht) to consume, use [AB 4]
verbreitet distributed [AB 12/WV]; spread
[Zeit] verbringen (verbrachte, hat verbracht) to spend [time] [AL 2]
verdienen (hat verdient) to earn [AL 5]
sich verdoppeln (hat sich verdoppelt) to double [K. 8]
der Verein, -e association, organization, club [AB 3]
vereinheitlichen (hat vereinheitlicht) to standardize [K. 12]
die Vereinigten Staaten *(pl.)* the United States (of America) [K. 6]
die Vereinigung, -en union, unification [AB 11/I]
vergessen (vergisst, vergaß, hat vergessen) to forget [AL 3/G]
vergiften (hat vergiftet) to poison [AB 11/II]
vergleichen (verglich, hat verglichen) to compare [K. 5]
vergleichsweise comparatively [K. 4]
vergrößern (hat vergrößert) to enlarge, expand [ZT 9]
verheiratet married [AL 2/WV]
verhüllen (hat verhüllt) to wrap, conceal [K. 11]
der Verkäufer, -/die Verkäuferin, -nen salesperson [ZT 7; AL 9/WV]
die Verkaufsabteilung, -en sales department [K. 9]
der Verkehr traffic [AB 4]
der Verkehrsbetrieb, -e transportation company [K. 7]
das Verkehrsmittel, - means of transportation [K. 8]
die Verkehrsregel, -n rule of the road, traffic regulation [K. 4]
das Verkehrsschild, -er traffic sign [K. 4]
der Verkehrsverein, -e tourist office [AB 3]
das Verkehrszeichen, - traffic sign [AB 4]
verkleiden (hat verkleidet) to disguise [K. 10]
verlangen (hat verlangt) to demand, require [K. 9]
verlassen (verlässt, verließ, hat verlassen) to leave [AB 11/II]
der Verleih, -e rental company [K. 3]

sich verletzen (hat sich verletzt) to hurt oneself, injure oneself [K. 6]
sich verlieben (hat sich verliebt) in + *acc.* to fall in love with [AB 5/WV]
verliebt sein (ist verliebt gewesen) in + *acc.* to be in love with [AL 5]; **bis über beide Ohren verliebt in** + *acc.* head over heels in love with [AL 5]
sich verloben (hat sich verlobt) mit + *dat.* to get engaged to [AL 5]
vermeiden (vermied, hat vermieden) to avoid [K. 12]
vermissen (hat vermisst) to miss [K. 5]
die Vermittlungsagentur, -en placement agency [K. 9]
die Vernetzung, -en network, connection [ZT 7]
vernünftig reasonable, logical [AB 5]
die Verpackung, -en packaging [AB 12/WV]
die Verpflegung food, board [K. 8]
der Verputz plaster [K. 11]
verreisen (ist verreist) to go on a trip [K. 4]
verrückt crazy [AB 10]
verschieden different [ZT 8]
verschlafen (verschläft, verschlief, hat verschlafen) to oversleep [K. 8]
sich verschließen (hat sich verschlossen) to close oneself off [AB 9]
der Verschluss, *pl.* **Verschlüsse** lock, clasp [ZT 6]
verschmutzen (hat verschmutzt) to pollute [AB 12/WV]; to soil
verschneit snow-covered [AB 10]
verschüttet blocked in [AB 11/II]
verschwenden (hat verschwendet) to waste [AB 12/WV]
versetzen (hat versetzt) to transfer [AB 12]
die Versicherung, -en insurance [ZT 10]
die Version, -en version [K. 4]
sich versöhnen (hat sich versöhnt) mit + *dat.* to make up, reconcile with [AB 5/WV]
die Verspätung, -en delay, late arrival, tardiness [K. 8; AL 11]
versprechen (verspricht, versprach, hat versprochen) to promise [K. 8]
die Versprechung, -en promise [K. 8]
der Verstand reason, logic [AB 7]
das Verständnis understanding, sympathy [AB 9]
verstärken (hat verstärkt) to strengthen, reinforce [AB 12]
verstecken (hat versteckt) to hide, conceal [ZT 10]
verstehen (verstand, hat verstanden) to understand, comprehend [AL 1]; **~ von** + *dat.* to know something (anything) about [AL 3]
versuchen (hat versucht) to try, attempt [AB 9]
das Vertrauen trust [AB 5]
verunsichern (hat verunsichert) to make uncertain [AB 12]
verursachen (hat verursacht) to cause [AB 12/WV]
vervollständigen (hat vervollständigt) to complete [K. 11]
verwalten (hat verwaltet) to administrate [AB 11/I]
verwandeln (hat verwandelt) to transform [K. 10]
der/die Verwandte, -n *(adj. as noun)* relative [AL 2/WV]
die Verwandtschaft, -en relatives [ZT 11]
verwenden (hat verwendet) to apply, use [K. 4]
verwunden (hat verwundet) to wound [K. 11]
verwundert amazed [AB 6]
verzichten (hat verzichtet) auf + *acc.* to forgo, pass up [AL 12]
der Vetter, - male cousin [AL 2/WV]
der Videofilm, -e movie on video cassette [K. 7]
der Videoverleih, -e video store [K. 7]
viel a lot, much [AB 2/G]; **viele** many [AB 2]; **Vielen Dank!** Thanks a lot! [AL 6]
vielleicht perhaps, maybe [ZT 2]
das Vier-Mächte-Abkommen Quadropartite Treaty [K. 11]
das Viertel, - quarter; district, neighborhood [AL 11]; **~ nach** quarter past [AB 2/WV]; **~ zwei** quarter past two [AB 2/WV]; **drei viertel zwei** quarter of two, quarter to two [AB 2/WV]
der Vogel, ¨ bird; **Er hat einen ~** He's crazy. He's nuts. [AL 6/SiA]; **das Vögelchen, -** little bird [AL 10]
der Vogelkäfig, -e bird cage [K. 11]
die Volkskammer People's Chamber of the GDR Parliament [K. 11]
die Volkswirtschaft, -en economics [AL 2/WV]
der Volkswagen, - Volkswagen [K. 3]
vollendet completed [AB 11/I]
völlig completely [AB 12]
von + *dat.* from, by [K. 2; AB 6/G]; **~ da an** from that point on [AL 5]; **~ oben her** from above [ZT 12]; **~ wem?** from whom? [ZT 2]; **~ ... bis** from . . . until [AB 2/WV]
vor to, of [K. 2]; in front of [AL 7/G]; ago [AL 6]
vorbei·reiten (ritt vorbei, ist vorbeigeritten) to ride by, ride past on horseback [AL 10]
vor·bereiten (hat vorbereitet) to prepare [AL 8]; **sich ~ (hat sich vorbereitet) auf** + *acc.* to prepare for, get ready for [AL 8/WV]
die Vorbereitung, -en preparation [ZT 10]
vorbildlich exemplary [AB 8]
die Vorgabe, -n intention [K. 12]
vorgeschrieben prescribed [K. 4]
vor·haben (hat vor, hatte vor, hat vorgehabt) to plan, have planned [AL 11]
vorher before, previously [K. 4; AB 9]
vor·kommen (ist vorgekommen) + *dat.* to appear to be [ZT 8]
vor·lesen (liest vor, las vor, hat vorgelesen) to read aloud; lecture [K. 5]
die Vorlesung, -en lecture [AL 6]
das Vorlesungsverzeichnis, -se course catalogue [ZT 7]
vor·machen (macht vor, hat vorgemacht) to fool, kid, delude [K. 8]
vormittags in the morning, A.M. [K. 2]
vorne up front [AB 1]; **da~** over there [AL 1]
der Vorschlag, ¨e suggestion [K. 5]
vor·schlagen (schlägt vor, schlug vor, hat vorgeschlagen) to suggest [AL 11]
die Vorschrift, -en regulation [K. 12]
vorsichtig careful, cautious [AL 4]
die Vorspeise, -n appetizer [AL 3/BK]
sich vor·stellen (hat sich vorgestellt) to imagine; to introduce oneself [AL 2/K. 8]
das Vorstellungsgespräch, -e job interview [AB 9]
der Vorteil, -e advantage [K. 8]
das Vorurteil, -e prejudice [K. 6]
vor·zeigen (hat vorgezeigt) to present, show [K. 12]
vor·ziehen (zog vor, hat vorgezogen) + *dat.* to prefer to [K. 8]
der VW, -s VW, Volkswagen [K. 3]

wachsen (wächst, wuchs, ist gewachsen) to grow [AB 8; AL 10]
wackeln (hat gewackelt) to wobble [K. 11]
der Waffenschieber, - weapons dealer [AB 12]
wagen (hat gewagt) to dare, risk [AB 11/II]

der Wagen, - car [K. 4; AB 7/WV]
waghalsig daredevil, foolhardy [K. 7]
die Wahl, -en selection, choice; election [AB 9]
wählen (hat gewählt) to choose, select; elect [K. 8]
der Wähler, -/die Wählerin, -nen voter [AB 11/I WV]
der Wahnsinn insanity [K. 12]
wahr real, true [K. 10]
während + *gen.* during [K. 9]
wahrscheinlich probably [AL 3]
die Währung, -en currency [ZT 12]
die Währungseinheit, -en currency unit [K. 12]
das Wahrzeichen, - emblem, symbol [AB 3]
wahr·nehmen (nimmt wahr, nahm wahr, hat wahrgenommen) to perceive; to take advantage of [K. 12]
der Wald, ⸚er forest, woods [AL 10/WV]
die Wand, ⸚e interior wall [AB 1/WV]
der Wandel, - change, transformation [AB 10]
wandern (ist gewandert) to hike, go hiking [AL 2]
die Wanderung, -en hike [K. 4]
wann when [AB 1/G]
warm warm [K. 3; AL 4]
warten (hat gewartet) to wait [ZT 3]; to service [K. 4]; **~ auf** + *acc.* to wait for [AL 7/G]
die Wartezeit, -en waiting period [AB 8]
warum why [AB 1/G]
was what [AB 1/G]; **Was gibt's?** What's up? [AL 3/G]; **Was tut dir weh?** Where do you hurt? [AB 6/WV]
das Waschbecken, - sink [AL 6/WV]
sich waschen (wäscht sich, wusch sich, hat sich gewaschen) to wash; **sich die Haare ~** to shampoo [AL 8/WV]
die Waschküche, -n laundry room [AL 6/WV]
die Waschmaschine, -n washing machine [K. 6]
Wasserski fahren (fährt, fuhr, ist gefahren) to waterski [K. 3]
das Wasserspiel, -e trick fountains [K. 3]
der Wassersport water sports [K. 3]
der Wasserturm, ⸚e water tower [AB 3]
das WC, -s toilet [AL 6/WV]
wechseln (hat gewechselt) to change money [AB 6]; to change [AB 12]
der Wecker, - alarm clock [AL 6/WV]
weg away [K. 5]
der Weg, -e path [AB 4]; **auf dem ~** on the way [K. 7]
wegen + *gen.* because of [K. 4; AB 11/II G]
weg·räumen (hat weggeräumt) to clear away [AB 11/II]
die Wegwerf-Gesellschaft, -en disposable society [AB 12/WV]
weh tun, (tat weh, hat weh getan) + *dat.* to hurt (someone) [AL 8/WV]
der Weihnachstmarkt, ⸚e Christmas market [K. 9]
das Weihnachten Christmas [K. 10]
weil + *dat.* because [AL 5]
die Weile awhile [ZT 8]
der Wein, -e wine [AL 3/WV]
der Weinachtsmann, ⸚er Santa Claus [K. 10]
der Weinberg, -e vineyard [K. 7]
weinen (hat geweint) to cry [AL 10]
der Weisheitszahn, ⸚e wisdom tooth [K. 8]
weiß white [AB 1/WV]
weit far [K. 5]; **~ weg** far away [ZT 5]
weiter·gehen (geht weiter, ging weiter, ist weitergegangen) to continue [AB 5]
welch (-er, -es, -e) which [AB 6/G]
wellig wavy [AB 1/VW]
die Welt, -en world [AB 6]
der Weltkrieg, -e world war [AB 11/I]
wem whom *(dat.)* [AL 6/G]
wen whom *(acc.)* [AL 2/G]
die Wende turning point; time in East Germany before unification [ZT 11]
wenig little [AB 2/G]; **wenige** a few [AB 2/G]; **weniger** fewer, less [K. 3]
wenigstens at least [AL 5]
wenn if, when [K. 4;AB 6/G]
wer who *(nom.)* [AB 1/G]
die Werbeagentur, -en advertising agency [K. 6]
die Werbebroschüre, -n advertising brochure [K. 6]
der Werdegang, ⸚e development; career [ZT 9]
werden (wird, wurde, ist geworden) to become [AL 3/G]; will, shall *(future tense)* [AB 8/G]
werfen (wirft, warf, hat geworfen) to throw, toss [AL 10]
das Werk, -e (creative) work [K. 7]
wertvoll valuable [K. 8]
wesentlich essential [AB 10]
wessen whose [AB 10/G]
das Wetter weather [K. 4; AL 5/WV]
der Wetterbericht, -e weather report [K. 5]
wichtig important [AB 4]
die Wichtigkeit, -en importance [K. 4]
das Wichtigste the most important thing [AL 8]
widersprüchlich contradictory [AB 7]
der Widerstand, ⸚e resistance [AB 11/I WV]
wie how; what [AL 1]; **~ alt?** how old? [K. 2]; **~ bitte?** Please repeat that. [AB 1/G]; **~ heißen Sie?** What's your name? [AL 1]; **~ viele** how many [AB 1/G]
wieder·aufbauen (hat wiederaufgebaut) to reconstruct [K. 11]
wiederholen (hat wiederholt) to repeat [AB 6]
wieder·kommen (ist wiedergekommen) to come back, return [ZT 8]
Wiedersehen: Auf ~! Good bye! [K. 3]
Wien Vienna [AB 12/WV]
die Wiese, -n meadow [AB 8]
wie viel how much [AB 1/G]; **~ Uhr ist es?** What time is it? [AB 2/WV]
das Willkommen, - welcome [AB 1]; **Herzlich willkommen in ...** Welcome to . . . [ZT 4]
windig windy [AL 5/WV]
die Windpocken *(pl.)* chicken-pox [K. 5]
der Winter, - winter [AL 5/WV]
wir we [AB 1/G]
der Wirbelsturm, ⸚e tornado [K. 11]
wirken (hat gewirkt) to effect, have an effect, impact [AL 7]
wirklich really [ZT 4]
die Wirkung, -en effect [K. 6]
die Wirtschaftszeitung, -en business/economics newspaper [K. 7]
wissen (weiß, wusste, hat gewusst) to know (a fact) [AL 3/G]; **~ von** + *dat.* to know about [AB 8/G]
der Witz, -e joke, wit [K. 4]
wo where [AL 1]
die Woche, -n week [K. 5]; **vor einer ~** a week ago [AL 6]
das Wochenende, -n weekend [AB 2/WV]
der Wochentag, -e day of the week [AB 2/WV]
woher from where [AB 1]
wohin where to [AB 1/G]
wohl in all likelihood, no doubt, probably [AL 3/G]; well [AB 8/G]
wohlbehütet well-protected, sheltered [AB 6]
wohnen (hat gewohnt) to live [AL 2; AL 6]; **in Untermiete ~** to live in a sublet room [K. 6]

die Wohngemeinschaft, -en shared apartment, cooperative living [K. 6]
die Wohnung, -en apartment [K. 6]
der Wohnungsmarkt, ¨-e real estate market [AB 8]
das Wohnzimmer, - living room [AL 6/WV]
die Wolke, -n cloud [AL 5/WV]
wolkig cloudy [AL 5/WV]
wollen (will, wollte, hat gewollt) to want to [AL 4]
womit with what [K. 8]
das Wort, ¨-er word [AL 5]
das Wörterbuch, ¨-er dictionary [AL 4/WV]
wortwörtlich literally [K. 8]
das Wunder, - miracle, wonder [K. 8; AB 10]
wunderbar wonderful [AB 2]
der Wunsch, ¨-e wish, request [AL 11]
wünschen (hat gewünscht) to wish [AL 9]
die Wurst, ¨-e sausage [AL 3/WV]
die Wut rage [K. 11]

x-mal umpteen times [AL 7/G]

die Zahl, -en number [AB 1/WV]
zahlen (hat gezahlt) to pay [AT 12/WV]
zahllos innumerable [AB 8]
zahlreich multiple, many [K. 3]
der Zahn, ¨-e tooth [AB 6/WV]
der Zahnarzt, ¨-e/die Zahnärztin, -nen dentist [K. 6; AL 9/WV]
die Zahnbürste, -n toothbrush [AL 4/WV]
die Zahnpasta, *pl.* **Pasten** toothpaste [AL 4/WV]
die Zahnschmerzen *(pl.)* toothache [AL 8/WV]
der Zauberer, - magician, sorcerer [AL 10/WV]
die Zauberstimmung magical mood [AB 10]
der Zeh, -en toe [AB 6/WV]
das Zeichen, - sign, marker [AB 4]
der Zeichenblock, ¨-e sketch pad [K. 4]
der Zeichentrickfilm, -e animated movie, cartoon [AB 7/WV]
zeichnen (hat gezeichnet) to draw, sketch [K. 4]
die Zeichnung, -en drawing, sketch [K. 4]
zeigen (hat gezeigt) to show, point [AB 1/G]
die Zeile, -n line [K. 5]
die Zeit, -en time [AB 2]; **die ganze ~** the whole time [AL 5]
die Zeitschrift, -en magazine [AL 7/WV]
die Zeittafel, -n time table, time line [K. 5]
die Zeitung, -en newspaper [K. 3]
der Zeitungskiosk, -e newspaper stand [AL 7/WV]
der Zeitungsstand, ¨-e newspaper stand [AL 7/WV]
das Zelt, -e tent [AB 8]
die Zensur, -en censorship [K. 10]
das Zentrum, *pl.* **Zentren** center [AL 11]
zerbombt bombed out [AB 11/II]
zerbrechlich fragile, breakable [AB 6]
zerbrochen broken to pieces [AB 11/II]
zerreißen (zerriss, hat zerrissen) to rip up, tear up [K. 5]
zerschlagen all beat up [AB 11/II]
zerschossen shot up, riddled with bullet holes [AB 11/II]
zerstören (hat zerstört) to destroy [AB 11/I]
der Zettel, - note, scrap of paper [K. 6]
das Zeug stuff, things [ZT 6]; **Dummes ~!** Nonsense! [K. 12]
der Ziegelstein, -e brick [AB 11/II]
ziehen (zog, hat gezogen) to pull, raise [AB 6]
ziemlich rather, pretty . . . [K. 4; AL 6]
der Zigeuner, -/die Zigeunerin, -nen gypsy [K. 7]
zigmal umpteen times [AB 7/G]
das Zimmer, - room [AB 3]; **~ und Verpflegung** room and board [K. 8]; **die ~- und Wohungsvermittlung, -en** housing placement service [K. 6]
der Zimmerkamerad, [-en], -en/die Zimmerkameradin, -nen roommate [K. 3]
die Zimmernummer, -n room number [AL 6]
der Zoll, ¨-e customs [ZT 4]; **durch den ~** through customs [ZT 4]
die Zollgewerkschaft, -en customs officials' trade union [AB 12]
der Zöllner, -/die Zöllnerin, -nen customs agent [AB 12]
der Zoo, -s zoo [AB 3]
zu + *dat.* to [AB 6/G]; **~ Hause** at home [K. 6]
zuerst first of all [ZT 3]
der Zufall, ¨-e coincidence [AB 11/II]
zufrieden satisfied, content [AB 6]
der Zug, ¨-e train [AB 7/WV]
zu·geben (gibt zu, gab zu, hat zugegeben) to admit [K. 9]
zu·hören (hat zugehört) + *dat.* to listen [ZT 8]
der Zuhörer, -/die Zuhörerin, -nen listener [K. 6]
zu·knallen (hat zugeknallt) to slam shut [AL 1]
die Zukunft future [K. 5; AB 10]
zuletzt finally [K. 3]
zum to (the) [K. 4]; for; **~ ersten Mal** for the first time [AL 5]; **~ Spaß** for fun [K. 7]
zu·machen (hat zugemacht) to close [AL 1/WV]
zunächst first of all [ZT 10]
der Zündstoff, -e explosive material [AB 7]
die Zunge, -n tongue [ZT 11]
zu·reden (hat zugeredet) + *dat.* to talk to [ZT 5]
zurück·bringen (brachte zurück, hat zurückgebracht) to bring back, return [AL 10]
zurück·geben (gibt zurück, gab zurück, hat zurückgegeben) to give back, return [K. 6]
zurück·gehen (ging zurück, ist zurückgegangen) to go back [AL 7/WV]
zurück·kehren (ist zurückgekehrt) to return [K. 12]
zurück·kommen (kam zurück, ist zurückgekommen) to come back, return, get back [AB 2/WV]
zusammen together [AL 5]
die Zusammenarbeit, -en collaboration, joint project [ZT 9]
der Zusammenbruch, ¨-e collapse [K. 11]
zusammen·leben (hat zusammengelebt) to live together, cohabitate [AB 5/WV]
zusammen·stellen (hat zusammengestellt) to put together, organize [ZT 10]
zusätzlich additionally [AL 8]
zu·stimmen (hat zugestimmt) + *dat.* to agree with someone [AB 11/II]
zuverlässig dependable [AB 9/WV]
zu viel(e) too much, too many [ZT 3]
zwar actually, in fact [AL 6]
der Zweck, -e purpose, point [AL 9]
der Zweig, -e branch [AL 10]
zweit second; by two [K. 3]; **zu ~** as a couple [AL 5]; two at a time, in a pair [ZT 9]
der Zwerg, -e dwarf [AL 10/WV]
zwischen between [AL 7/G]
der Zwischenfall, ¨-e incident [ZT 10]

■ English-German Vocabulary ■

The English-German vocabulary focuses on key words (highest frequency words) from the core texts and the **Wissenswerte Vokabeln** sections of the chapters. Definite articles and plural forms are given for all nouns. Verbs are listed with their participles. Separable-prefix verbs are marked with a raised dot: **mit·bringen.** For the principal parts of irregular (strong) verbs, refer to pages R-1 and R-2.

absolutely unbedingt
accident der Unfall, ¨-e
achieve leisten (hat geleistet)
accompany begleiten (hat begleitet)
accomplish leisten (hat geleistet)
account: on ~ of wegen + *gen.*
acquaintance der/die Bekannte, -n *(noun decl. like adj.)*
active tätig; aktiv
activity die Aktivität, -en
actually eigentlich; zwar
additionally zusätzlich
address book das Adressbuch, ¨-er
adjust um·stellen (hat umgestellt)
administer verwalten (hat verwaltet)
admit zu·geben (hat zugegeben)
advanced student der/die Fortgeschrittene, -n *(noun decl. like adj.)*
advantage der Pluspunkt, -e; der Vorteil, -e; der Vorsprung
advertisement die Annonce, -n; das Inserat, -e; die Anzeige, -n
advice der Rat, *pl.* Ratschläge
after nach + *dat. (prep.);* nachdem *(conj.)*
afternoon der Nachmittag, -e; **this ~** heute Nachmittag
afternoons nachmittags
afterwards nachher
afraid: to be ~ of Angst haben (hat gehabt) vor + *dat.*
African afrikanisch
again wieder; noch einmal
against gegen + *acc.*
ago vor + *dat.*
agree zu·stimmen (hat zugestimmt) + *dat.*
air die Luft
airline ticket der Flugschein, -e; das Flugticket, -s
airplane das Flugzeug, -e
airport der Flughafen, ¨
alarm clock der Wecker, -
alcohol der Alkohol
alcoholic alkoholisch; **non-~** alkoholfrei
all alle; **at ~** überhaupt; **~ day** den ganzen Tag
Allies die Alliierten *(pl.)*
allow erlauben (hat erlaubt)
allowed: to be ~ dürfen (hat gedurft)
almost fast; beinahe
alone allein
Alps die Alpen *(pl.)*
already schon
also auch
although obwohl
always immer
America (das) Amerika; **United States of ~** die Vereinigten Staaten von Amerika
American amerikanisch *(adj.);* der Amerikaner, -/die Amerikanerin, -nen
among unter + *dat.;* **~ themselves** unter sich
and und; **~ so on** und so weiter
angry böse; **to be ~** sich ärgern (hat sich geärgert) über + *acc.*
animal das Tier, -e
animation der Zeichentrickfilm, -e
announce aus·rufen (hat ausgerufen); bekannt geben (hat bekannt gegeben); aus·schreiben (hat ausgeschrieben)
answer die Antwort, -en; **to ~** antworten + *dat.;* beantworten + *acc.*
any einige; etwas
anything irgendetwas, irgendwas; **~ else?** Sonst noch etwas?
anytime jederzeit
anyway jedenfalls
apartment die Wohnung, -en
appear scheinen (hat geschienen), erscheinen (ist erschienen); aus·sehen (hat ausgesehen); **to ~ to be** vor·kommen (ist vorgekommen) + *dat.*
appearance das Aussehen
appetizer die Vorspeise, -n
apple der Apfel, ¨; **~ juice** der Apfelsaft
application die Bewerbung, -en; **~ form** das Bewerbungsformular, -e
apply beantragen (hat beantragt); sich bewerben (hat sich beworben) für/um + *acc.*
appointment der Termin, -e
apprentice der Lehrling, -e; der/die Auszubildende, -n *(noun decl. like adj.);* der/die Azubi, -s
approximately ungefähr
April der April
architect der Architekt [-en], -en/die Architektin, -nen
area die Umgebung; **in the ~** in der Nähe; in der Umgebung
area code die Vorwahl, -en
argue sich streiten (hat sich gestritten) mit + *dat.*
argument der Krach
arm der Arm, -e
around um + *acc.;* **~ [time]** gegen + *acc.*
arrival die Ankunft, ¨-e; die Anreise, -n
arrive an·kommen (ist angekommen)
art die Kunst; **~ association** der Kunstverein, -e; **~ museum** die Kunsthalle; **~ school** die Kunsthochschule, -n
artist der Künstler, -/die Künstlerin, -nen
article der Artikel, -
as als; wie; **~... ~** so . . . wie; **~ always** wie immer
Asian asiatisch
ask: to ~ about fragen (hat gefragt) nach + *dat.;* **~ for** bitten (hat gebeten) um + *acc.;* **to ~ a question** eine Frage stellen (hat gestellt); **to ~ about** fragen (hat gefragt) nach + *dat.*
aspirin das Aspirin
assignment die Aufgabe, -n
association der Verein, -e; die Gemeinschaft, -en
astonished erstaunt
at an; auf; in; **~ (someone's house)** bei + *dat.;* **~ [time]** um + *acc.*
at all überhaupt
athlete der Sportler, -/die Sportlerin, -nen

athletic sportlich
atmosphere die Stimmung, -en
atomic energy die Atomkraft; die Kernkraft
attempt versuchen (hat versucht)
attic der Dachboden, ¨-
August der August
aunt die Tante, -n
Austria (das) Österreich
Austrian österreichisch *(adj.);* der Österreicher, -/die Österreicherin, -nen
Austro-Hungarian empire Österreich-Ungarn
authentic echt; authentisch
author der Autor, -en/die Autorin, -nen
automobile das Auto, -s; der Wagen, -
autumn der Herbst, -e
away weg; ab; fort; **far ~** weit weg
awhile eine Weile

back der Rücken, -; *(adv.)* zurück
backpack der Rucksack, ¨-e
bad schlecht; schlimm; böse; **not ~** ganz gut, nicht schlecht; **too ~** schade
bag die Tüte, -n
baggage das Gepäck
baker der Bäcker, -/die Bäckerin, -nen
bakery die Bäckerei, -en; **at the ~** beim Bäcker; **to the ~** zum Bäcker
balcony der Balkon, -s
ballpoint pen der Kugelschreiber, -, der Kuli, -s *(colloq.)*
ban das Verbot, -e
banana die Banane, -n
band die Band, -s
Band-Aid das Heftpflaster, -
bank die Bank, -en; die Sparkasse, -n; **~ account** das Konto, *pl.* Konten
bar die Bar, -s; die Kneipe, -n; das Lokal, -e
barrel das Fass, *pl.* Fässer
basement der Keller, -
basketball der Basketball
bath das Bad, ¨-er; **~towel** das Badetuch, ¨-er; **~tub** die Badewanne, -n
bathe baden (hat gebadet)
bathing suit der Badeanzug, ¨-e
bathroom das Badezimmer, -; **to go to the ~** auf die Toilette (aufs Klo, *colloq.*) gehen
be: to ~ sein (ist gewesen); **to ~ about** handeln (hat gehandelt) von + *dat.;* **to ~ in charge** leiten (hat geleitet); **to ~ all right with someone** recht sein (ist gewesen) + *dat.;* **to ~ enough** reichen (hat gereicht)
beautiful schön
because weil; denn *(conj.)*
because of wegen *(prep.)* + *gen.*
become werden (ist geworden)
bed das Bett, -en; **~room** das Schlafzimmer, -
beef das Rindfleisch
beer das Bier
before vor + *dat.;* vorher *(adv.);* bevor *(conj.)*
begin an·fangen (hat angefangen); beginnen (hat begonnen)
beginner der Anfänger, -/die Anfängerin, -en
beginning der Anfang, ¨-e
behind hinter + *acc./dat.*
believe glauben (hat geglaubt); **to ~ in** glauben an + *acc.*
believable glaubhaft
belong to gehören (hat gehört) + *dat.*
beside bei + *dat.;* neben *acc./dat.*
besides außerdem; außer + *dat.*
best best; **~ of all** am besten
better besser
between zwischen + *acc./dat.*
beverage das Getränk, -e
bicycle das Fahrrad, ¨-er; das Rad, ¨-er; **to ~** Rad fahren (ist Rad gefahren); **to ride a ~** mit dem Fahrrad fahren
bicycle path der Radweg, -e
bicycle rider der Radfahrer, -/die Radfahrerin, -nen
big groß; **~ city** die Großstadt, ¨-e
bike das Rad, ¨-er
biology die Biologie
bird der Vogel, ¨-; **little ~** das Vögelchen, -
birdcage der Vogelkäfig, -e
birthday der Geburtstag, -e; **When is your ~ ?** Wann hast du Geburtstag?; **for one's ~** zum Geburtstag
black schwarz
blackboard die Tafel, -n
blood das Blut
blond blond
blouse die Bluse, -n
blow-dry föhnen (hat geföhnt)
blow dryer der Föhn, -e
blue blau
body der Körper, -; **~ part** der Körperteil, -e
bombed out zerbombt
book das Buch, ¨-er
bookcase das Bücherregal, -e
bookkeeper der Buchhalter, -/die Buchhalterin, -nen
bookstore die Buchhandlung, -en
boot der Stiefel, -
border die Grenze, -n; **~ crossing** der Grenzbalken, -; **~ guard** der Grenzwächter, -
border on grenzen (hat gegrenzt) an + *acc.*
boring langweilig; **~ as heck** stinklangweilig
born geboren
borrow leihen (hat geliehen)
boss der Chef, -s/die Chefin, -nen
both beide; beides
bother stören (hat gestört)
bottle die Flasche, -n
boy der Junge [-n], -n; **~friend** der Freund, -e
branch der Zweig, -e; **~ office** die Filiale, -n
brave mutig
bread das Brot, -e
break brechen (hat gebrochen); **to ~ up with** sich trennen (hat getrennt) von + *dat.*
breakable zerbrechlich
breakfast das Frühstück; **for ~** zum Frühstück
brewery die Bierbrauerei, -en
brick der Ziegelstein, -e
bribe die Bestechung, -en
bride die Braut, ¨-e
bridge die Brücke, -n
bright hell
bring bringen (hat gebracht); **~ along** mit·bringen (hat mitgebracht)
broken kaputt; **~ to pieces** zerbrochen
brother der Bruder, ¨-; **brothers and sisters** die Geschwister *(pl.)*
brown braun
brush die Bürste, -n; **hairbrush** die Haarbürste, -n; **tooth~** die Zahnbürste, -n; **to ~ one's hair** sich die Haare bürsten (hat sich gebürstet); **to ~ one's teeth** sich die Zähne putzen (hat sich geputzt)
build bauen (hat gebaut); konstruieren (hat konstruiert)
bulletin board das schwarze Brett, -er
bus der Bus, -se; **~ stop** die Bushaltestelle, -n
business das Geschäft, -e; der Betrieb, -e; **~ trip** die Geschäftsreise, -n
business administration die Betriebswirtschaft
businessman/businesswoman der Geschäftsmann, ¨-er/die Geschäftsfrau, -en
but aber; sondern
butcher der Metzger, -/die Metzgerin, -nen; der Fleischer, -/die Fleischerin,

-nen; **~ shop** die Metzgerei, -en; die Fleischerei, -en
butter die Butter
buy kaufen (hat gekauft)
by bei + *dat.*, an + *dat.*, von + *dat.*; **~ [car]** mit [dem Auto]

café das Café, -s
cafeteria die Mensa, *pl.* Mensen
cake der Kuchen, -; **layer ~** die Torte, -n
call rufen (hat gerufen); an·rufen (hat angerufen), telefonieren (hat telefoniert); **to ~ someone something** nennen (hat genannt)
called: to be ~ heißen (hat geheißen)
calm ruhig
camera still ~ der Fotoapparat, -e; **movie ~** die Kamera, -s
campground der Campingplatz, ⸚e
campus der Campus
can können (hat gekonnt)
can die Dose, -n
Canada (das) Kanada
Canadian kanadisch *(adj.)*; der Kanadier, -/die Kanadierin, -nen
candidate der Kandidat, [-en], -en/die Kandidatin, -nen
cancelled to be ~ aus·fallen (ist ausgefallen)
canton der Kanton, -e
cap die Mütze, -n
capital die Hauptstadt, ⸚e
car das Auto, -s; der Wagen, -
card die Karte, -n; **to play cards** Karten spielen (hat Karten gespielt)
cardboard die Pappe
care die Sorge, -n; **to take ~ of something** erledigen (hat erledigt)
careful vorsichtig
carpet der Teppich, -e
carrot die Karotte, -n
carry tragen (hat getragen); **to ~ out** durch·führen (hat durchgeführt)
case der Fall, ⸚e
cash register die Kasse, -n
cassette die Kassette, -n
cast der Gips
castle das Schloss, *pl.* Schlösser; **~ garden** der Schlossgarten, ⸚; **~ square** der Schlossplatz, ⸚e
cat die Katze, -n
catalogue der Katalog, -e
catastrophe die Katastrophe, -n
cathedral der Dom, -e
cause die Ursache, -n; der Grund, ⸚e; **to ~** verursachen (hat verursacht)
CD player der CD-Player, -; der CD-Spieler, -
celebration die Feier, -n; das Fest, -e
cellar der Keller, -
center die Mitte, -n; das Zentrum, *pl.* Zentren
century das Jahrhundert, -e
certain bestimmt; gewiss; sicher
chair der Stuhl, ⸚e; **easy ~** der Sessel, -
chalk die Kreide
chancellor der Kanzler, -/die Kanzlerin, -nen
change der Wandel; **to ~** wechseln (hat gewechselt); **pocket ~** das Kleingeld
characteristic die Eigenschaft, -en
chat plaudern (hat geplaudert)
cheap billig
check der Scheck, -s; **traveller's ~** der Reisescheck, -s
check kontrollieren (hat kontrolliert)
cheerful heiter
cheese der Käse
chemistry die Chemie
chest: ~ of drawers die Kommode, -n; **clothes ~** der Kleiderschrank, ⸚e
chew kauen (hat gekaut)
chewing gum der Kaugummi, -s
chicken das Hähnchen, -
child das Kind, -er; **~ care subsidy** das Kindergeld
children's book das Kinderbuch, ⸚er
children's room das Kinderzimmer, -
chin das Kinn
chocolate die Schokolade, -n
choose wählen (hat gewählt)
choice die Wahl, -en
Christianity das Christentum
Christmas das Weihnachten; **Merry ~!** Fröhliche Weihnachten!
chubby mollig
church die Kirche, -n
cigarette die Zigarette, -n
circle der Kreis, -e
citizen der Bürger, -; der Staatsbürger, -; der/die Staatsangehörige, -n
city die Stadt, ⸚e; **old part of the ~** die Altstadt; **~ hall** das Rathaus, ⸚er; **~ district** der Stadtteil, -e; das Stadtviertel; **~ map** der Stadtplan, ⸚e; **~ outskirts** der Stadtrand, ⸚er; **~ bus tour** die Stadtrundfahrt, -en
civil servant der Beamte, -n/ die Beamtin, -nen
class die Klasse, -n; der Unterricht; **~room** das Klassenzimmer, -; **~ size** die Klassengröße, -n
classical klassisch
clean sauber; **to ~** sauber machen (hat sauber gemacht); **to ~ up** auf·räumen (hat aufgeräumt)
cleaning lady die Reinemachefrau, -en
clear klar; heiter; **to ~ away** weg·räumen (hat weggeräumt)
climate das Klima
climb klettern (ist geklettert); **to ~ into a train, car, etc.** ein·steigen (ist eingestiegen); **to ~ out** aus·steigen (ist ausgestiegen)
clique die Clique, -n
clock die Uhr, -en; **alarm ~** der Wecker, -
close eng; nah(e); **~ to** in der Nähe von + *dat.*
close schließen (hat geschlossen), zu·machen (hat zugemacht)
clothing die Kleidung; die Klamotten *(pl.)*
cloud die Wolke, -n
cloudy wolkig
club der Verein, -e; der Klub, -s
coal die Kohle, -n
coat der Mantel, ⸚; **rain ~** der Regenmantel, ⸚; **sport ~** der/das Sakko, -s
coffee der Kaffee; **~house** das Kaffeehaus, ⸚er; **~maker** die Kaffeemaschine, -n
coincidence der Zufall, ⸚e
cola die Cola, -s
cold kalt *(adj.)*; **~ war** der Kalte Krieg; **~** *(noun)* die Erkältung, -en; der Schnupfen, -; **to catch a ~** sich erkälten (hat sich erkältet)
collaboration die Zusammenarbeit, -en
collapse der Zusammenbruch; **to ~** ein·stürzen (ist eingestürzt)
collegial kollegial
colleague der Kollege [-n] -n/die Kollegin, -nen
collect sammeln (hat gesammelt)
college die Universität, -en; **to go to ~** studieren (hat studiert), an die Universität gehen
color die Farbe, -n; **What ~ is ... ?** Welche Farbe hat . . . ?
comb der Kamm, ⸚e; **to ~ one's hair** sich die Haare kämmen (hat sich gekämmt)
combine kombinieren (hat kombiniert)
come kommen (ist gekommen); **to ~ along** mit·kommen (ist mitgekommen); **to ~ by** vorbei·kommen (ist vorbeigekommen); **to ~ out** raus·kommen (ist rausgekommen)
command befehlen (hat befohlen) + *dat.*

common gemeinsam; **~ bathroom** das Gemeinschaftsbad, ¨-er
communism der Kommunismus
communist der Kommunist, [-en], -en
commuter der Pendler, -
compact disc die Compact Disc, -s; die CD, -s
company die Gesellschaft, -en; die Firma, *pl.* Firmen; der Konzern, -e
compare vergleichen (hat verglichen)
compartment das Fach, ¨-er
complete ganz; voll; völlig; **to ~** vervollständigen (hat vervollständigt); ergänzen (hat ergänzt)
completed vollendet
complicated kompliziert
compost pile der Komposthaufen, -
compromise der Kompromiss, *pl.* Kompromisse
computer der Computer, -; **~ science** die Informatik
concentrate sich konzentrieren (hat sich konzentriert) auf + *acc.*
concert das Konzert, -e; **to go to a ~** ins Konzert gehen
connoisseur der Genießer, -/die Genießerin, -nen
conquer erobern (hat erobert)
consequence die Folge, -n
consider sich überlegen (hat sich überlegt)
constitution die Verfassung, -en; **German ~** das Grundgesetz
consume verbrauchen (hat verbraucht)
contact der Kontakt, -e
contain enthalten (hat enthalten)
content der Inhalt, -e
continue fort·fahren (ist fortgefahren); **~ walking** weiter·gehen (ist weitergegangen)
contradictory widersprüchlich
contrary: on the ~ sondern; doch
controversial kontrovers
conversation das Gespräch, -e; die Unterhaltung, -en
converse with sich unterhalten (hat sich unterhalten) mit + *dat.*
cook der Koch, ¨-e/die Köchin, -nen; **to ~** kochen (hat gekocht)
cool kühl; cool; locker
copy die Kopie, -n; **to ~** kopieren (hat kopiert); **~ shop** der Kopierladen, ¨-; das Kopiergeschäft, -e
corner die Ecke, -n
correct richtig; **that's ~!** das stimmt!
corridor der Flur, -e; der Gang, ¨-e; der Korridor, -e
cost kosten (hat gekostet)
couch die Couch, -es/-en
could könnte
counsel beraten (hat beraten)
counseling die Beratung, -en
counselor der Berater, -/die Beraterin, -nen
count zählen (hat gezählt); **to ~ on** rechnen (hat gerechnet) mit + *dat.*
country das Land, ¨-er; der Staat, -en; **in the ~** auf dem Land(e)
courageous mutig
course der Kurs, -e; **~ catalogue** das Vorlesungsverzeichnis, -se; **of ~** natürlich; klar; selbstverständlich
court (of law) der Gerichtshof, ¨-e
courtyard der Hof, ¨-e
cousin (female) **~** die Kusine, -n; (male) **~** der Vetter, -n; der Cousin, -s
co-worker der Mitarbeiter, -/die Mitarbeiterin, -nen
cozy gemütlich
cramp der Muskelkater, -
crazy verrückt
create schaffen (hat geschaffen)
credit card die Kreditkarte, -n
crime die Kriminalität
criminal der Kriminelle [-n], -n
criteria die Kriterien *(pl.)*
criticise kritisieren (hat kritisiert)
cross-country skiing der Langlauf; **~ trail** die Langlaufloipe, -n
crossing die Kreuzung, -en
crowd die Masse, -n; die Menge, -n
cruel grausam
cry weinen (hat geweint)
cucumber die Gurke, -n
cuddle schmusen (hat geschmust)
cuisine die Küche, -n
culture die Kultur, -en
cultural kulturell; **~ center** das Kulturzentrum, *pl.* Kulturzentren
cunning die List
curious neugierig; gespannt
currency die Währung, -en; **~ unit** die Währungseinheit, -en
current aktuell
custodian der Hauswart, -e
customer der Kunde, [-n], -n/die Kundin, -nen
customs der Zoll; **~ agent** der Zöllner, -/die Zöllnerin, -nen; der Zollbeamte, [-n], -n/die Zollbeamtin, -nen
cut schneiden (hat geschnitten); **to ~ oneself** sich schneiden in + *acc.;* **to ~ back** kürzen (hat gekürzt); **to ~ off** ab·schneiden (hat abgeschnitten)
cyclist der Radfahrer, -/die Radfahrerin, -nen

dad der Vati, -s; **grand~** der Opa, -s
daily täglich
damp nass, feucht
dance tanzen (hat getanzt)
dangerous gefährlich
dare wagen (hat gewagt); riskieren (hat riskiert)
dark dunkel
darling der Liebling, -e
data die Tatsachen, die Daten *(pl.)*
date das Datum, *pl.* Daten; die Verabredung, -en; **to make a ~** sich verabreden (hat sich verabredet) mit + *dat.*
daughter die Tochter, ¨-
day der Tag, -e; **one ~** eines Tages; **all ~** den ganzen Tag; **~'s schedule** der Tagesablauf
day of the week der Wochentag, -e
dead tot; **~ tired** todmüde
dear lieb (-er, -e, -es)
December der Dezember
decide sich entscheiden (hat sich entschieden); **to ~ on/against** sich entscheiden für/gegen + *acc.*
decidedly ausgesprochen
decision die Entscheidung, -en
declare deklarieren (hat deklariert); bekannt geben (hat bekannt gegeben); erklären (hat erklärt) für + *acc.*
deduct ab·ziehen (hat abgezogen)
degree der Abschluss, *pl.* Abschlüsse; (temperature) der Grad
delicious lecker
dentist der Zahnarzt, ¨-e/die Zahnärztin, -nen
depart ab·fahren (ist abgefahren)
departure die Abreise, -n; die Abfahrt, -en; der Abflug, ¨-e
department die Abteilung, -en; **academic ~** der Fachbereich, -e
department store das Kaufhaus, ¨-er
describe beschreiben (hat beschrieben)
desk der Schreibtisch, -e
dessert die Nachspeise, -n; der Nachtisch, -e
destroy zerstören (hat zerstört)
detail die Kleinigkeit, -en; das Detail, -s
detective story der Kriminalroman, -e; der Krimi, -s
dependable zuverlässig
develop entwickeln (hat entwickelt)
development die Entwicklung, -en; der Werdegang

dialect der Dialekt, -e
diarrhea der Durchfall
dictator der Diktator, -en
dictatorship die Diktatur, -en
dictionary das Wörterbuch, ¨-er
die sterben (ist gestorben)
difference der Unterschied, -e
different verschieden; anders; **something ~** etwas anderes
difficult schwer; schwierig
dining hall die Mensa, *pl.* Mensen
dining room das Esszimmer, -; **hotel ~** der Speisesaal, *pl.* Speisesäle
dinner das Abendessen, -; **for ~** zum Abendessen
diploma das Diplom, -e
direction die Richtung, -en
disappointed enttäuscht
disciplined diszipliniert
discotheque die Diskothek, -en
discover entdecken (hat entdeckt)
discuss diskutieren (hat diskutiert) über + *acc.*; besprechen (hat besprochen); sich unterhalten (hat sich unterhalten) über + *acc.*
discussion die Diskussion, -en; die Besprechung, -en
dishes das Geschirr
dishwasher der Tellerwäscher, -; **electric ~** die Geschirrspülmaschine, -n
diskette die Diskette, -n
distributed verbreitet
district das Viertel, -; **city ~** das Stadtviertel, -
disturb stören (hat gestört)
divide teilen; auf·teilen (hat aufgeteilt) in + *acc.*
divorced geschieden
do machen (hat gemacht); tun (hat getan); **to ~ homework** Hausaufgaben machen
doctor der Arzt, ¨-e/die Ärztin, -nen
dog der Hund, -e
done fertig, erledigt
door die Tür, -en
dormitory das Studentenwohnheim, -e
dove das Täubchen, -
downstairs unten; **to go ~** die Treppe hinunter·gehen (ist hinuntergegangen)
drama das Drama, *pl.* Dramen
drawer die Schublade, -n
dream der Traum, ¨-e; **to ~ of** träumen (hat geträumt) von + *dat.*
dress das Kleid, -er; **to ~, get dressed** sich an·ziehen (hat sich angezogen)
drink das Getränk, -e; **to ~** trinken (hat getrunken)
drive fahren (ist gefahren); **to ~ away** weg·fahren (ist weggefahren)
driver der Fahrer, -/die Fahrerin, -nen
driver's license der Führerschein, -e
drug die Droge, -n
dry trocken; **to ~ off** ab·trocknen (hat abgetrocknet); **to ~ hair** föhnen (hat geföhnt)
dumb dumm; doof; **something ~** etwas Dummes
during während + *gen.*
dwarf der Zwerg, -e
dynamic dynamisch

each jed- (-er, -es, -e); **~ other** einander
ear das Ohr, -en
early früh
earn verdienen (hat verdient)
east der Osten; **~ German** ostdeutsch
Easter Ostern
easy einfach; leicht
eat essen (hat gegessen); **to ~** *(said of animals)* fressen (hat gefressen)
ecological ökologisch
economics die Volkswirtschaft
economy die Wirtschaft
educate aus·bilden (hat ausgebildet)
education die Erziehung; die Ausbildung; die Pädagogik
effect die Wirkung, -en; **to ~** wirken (hat gewirkt)
egg das Ei, -er
either . . . or entweder ... oder
elbow der Ellenbogen, -
election die Wahl, -en
else: what ~ ? was noch?; **something ~?** sonst noch etwas?
emblem das Wahrzeichen, -
embrace umarmen (hat umarmt)
emperor der Kaiser, -
empire das Reich, -e
employed berufstätig
employee der Arbeitnehmer, -/die Arbeitnehmerin, -nen; der Mitarbeiter, -/die Mitarbeiterin, -nen
employer der Arbeitgeber, -/die Arbeitgeberin, -nen
empty leer
end das Ende, -n; **in/at the ~** am Ende
energy die Energie; **source of ~** die Energiequelle, -n
engaged verlobt; **to get ~** sich verloben (hat sich verlobt) mit + *dat.*
engineer der Ingenieur, -e/die Ingenieurin, -nen
engineering das Ingenieurwesen; **mechanical ~** der Maschinenbau
England (das) England
English englisch *(adj.)*; **~ language** (das) Englisch
enjoy genießen (hat genossen)
enjoyment die Lust; das Vergnügen; der Spaß
enlarge vergrößern (hat vergrößert)
enough genug; genügend
entertaining unterhaltend
entrance der Eingang, ¨-e; **~ hall** die Diele, -n; der Flur, -e
environment die Umwelt
environmental protection der Umweltschutz
environmentally friendly umweltfreundlich
especially besonders
etcetera (etc.) und so weiter (usw.)
eternal ewig
Euro (currency unit) der Euro, -s
Europe (das) Europa
European europäisch; **~ Union** die Europäische Union
even sogar; **~ if** auch wenn
evening der Abend, -e; **good ~** Guten Abend; **this ~** heute Abend
evenings abends
eventually schließlich, endlich
every jed- (-er, -es, -e)
everyone jeder; alle
everything alles
exactly genau
examination die Prüfung, -en; das Examen, -; **high school graduation ~** das Abitur
examine überprüfen (hat überprüft)
example das Beispiel, -e; **for ~** zum Beispiel (z.B.)
excellent ausgezeichnet
except außer + *dat.*
exciting spannend
excited: to be ~ about gespannt sein auf + *acc.*
excitement die Aufregung, -en
excuse die Ausrede, -n; die Entschuldigung, -en; **~ me!** Entschuldigung!; **to ~** entschuldigen (hat entschuldigt)
expand erweitern (hat erweitert)
expect erwarten (hat erwartet)
expectation die Erwartung, -en
expensive teuer
experience die Erfahrung, -en; **to ~** erleben (hat erlebt); **to gain ~** Erfahrung sammeln (hat gesammelt)
explain erklären (hat erklärt)
explanation die Erklärung, -en
explosives der Zündstoff, -e
expression der Ausdruck, ¨-e
expressway die Autobahn, -en

eye das Auge, -n

face das Gesicht, -er
fairly ganz; ziemlich
fairy die Fee, -n; **~tale** das Märchen, -; **~tale figure** die Märchenfigur, -en
fall der Herbst; **to ~** fallen (ist gefallen); **to ~ asleep** ein·schlafen (ist eingeschlafen); **to ~ in love** sich verlieben (hat sich verliebt) in + *acc.*
false falsch
familiar bekannt
family die Familie, -n; **~ member** der/die Familienangehörige, -n; **~-owned business** der Familienbetrieb, -e; **~ tree** der Familienstammbaum, ⸚e
famous bekannt; berühmt
fantastic phantastisch; toll; prima
far weit; **~ away** weit weg
fast schnell
fat dick; mollig
father der Vater, ⸚; **grand~** der Großvater, ⸚
fax das Fax; **to ~** faxen (hat gefaxt)
fear die Angst, ⸚e; **to ~** Angst haben (hat gehabt) vor + *dat.*
feast das Fest, -e
February der Februar
Federal Republic of Germany die Bundesrepublik Deutschland
feel sich fühlen (hat sich gefühlt); **to ~ like** Lust haben
feeling das Gefühl, -e
fetch holen (hat geholt)
fever das Fieber
few wenig(e); **a ~** ein paar
fight sich streiten (hat sich gestritten)
film der Film, -e; **~maker** der Filmemacher, -
finally endlich, schließlich
finances die Finanzen *(pl.)*
find finden (hat gefunden); **to ~ out** heraus·finden (hat herausgefunden)
fine fein; gut; **I'm ~.** Es geht mir gut.
finger der Finger, -
finished fertig; zu Ende
fireplace der Kamin, -e
firm die Firma, *pl.* Firmen
first erst; **~ of all** zuerst; zunächst
first name der Vorname [-n], -n
fish der Fisch, -e; **~ market** der Fischmarkt, ⸚e
fit passen (hat gepasst) zu + *dat.*
flash das Blitzlicht, -er
flexible flexibel
flight der Flug, ⸚e
flirt flirten (hat geflirtet)
floor der Stock, *pl.* Stockwerke; die Etage, -n; **first ~** das Erdgeschoss; **one ~ down** einen Stock tiefer
flow fließen (ist geflossen)
flower die Blume, -n
fluent fließend
fly fliegen (ist geflogen)
fog der Nebel
food das Essen; die Lebensmittel *(pl.)*; die Kost
foot der Fuß, ⸚e; **to go on ~** zu Fuß gehen (ist gegangen); laufen (ist gelaufen)
for für + *acc.*; denn *(conj.)*; (time) seit/schon seit + *dat.*; **~ years** seit Jahren
forbidden verboten
foreign fremd
foreigner der Ausländer, -/die Ausländerin, -nen; der/die Fremde, -n *(noun decl. like adj.)*; **~ registration office** die Ausländerbehörde
forest der Wald, ⸚er
forever ewig
forget vergessen (hat vergessen)
forehead die Stirn, -en
fork die Gabel, -n
form die Unterlage, -n; das Formular, -e
former ehemalig
formerly früher
fragile zerbrechlich
France (das) Frankreich
free frei; **~ time** die Freizeit
frequent häufig; oft
freeway die Autobahn, -en
French französisch *(adj.)*; **~ (language)** (das) Französisch
Frenchman der Franzose, [-n], -n; **Frenchwoman** die Französin, -nen
Friday der Freitag
friend der Freund, -e/die Freundin, -nen
friendliness die Freundlichkeit
friendly freundlich
friendship die Freundschaft, -en
frog der Frosch, ⸚e
from von + *dat.*; **~ (native of)** aus + *dat.*
front up ~ da vorne
fruit das Obst
frustrating frustierend
full voll
fun der Spaß; **That's ~.** Das macht Spaß. (hat gemacht)
funny lustig
furniture die Möbel *(pl.)*
further weiter
future die Zukunft
game das Spiel, -e
garage die Garage, -n
garbage der Müll
garden der Garten, ⸚
gasoline das Benzin
gate das Tor, -e
generous großzügig
gentle sanft
gentleman der Herr [-n], -en
genuine echt, authentisch
German deutsch *(adj.)*; **~ (person)** der/die Deutsche *(noun decl. like adj.)*; **~ (language)** (das) Deutsch; **~ Mark** die D-Mark; **~ studies** die Germanistik; **~ Democratic Republic** die Deutsche Demokratische Republik (DDR)
Germany (das) Deutschland; die Bundesrepublik Deutschland
get bekommen (hat bekommen); kriegen (hat gekriegt); erhalten (hat erhalten; besorgen (hat besorgt); **to go ~** holen (hat geholt); **to ~ through** durch·machen (hat durchgemacht); **to ~ up** auf·stehen (ist aufgestanden); **to ~ used to** sich gewöhnen (hat sich gewöhnt) an + *acc.*; **to ~ to know** kennen lernen (hat kennen gelernt); **to ~ in touch** sich melden (hat sich gemeldet)
girl das Mädchen, -
girlfriend die Freundin, -nen
give geben (hat gegeben); **to ~ (as a gift)** schenken (hat geschenkt); **to ~ up** auf·geben (hat aufgegeben)
glad froh; **to be ~** sich freuen (hat sich gefreut)
gladly gern
glove der Handschuh, -e
go gehen (ist gegangen); **to ~ along** mit·gehen (ist mitgegangen); **to ~ by [train]** mit [dem Zug] fahren (ist gefahren); **to ~ away** fort·gehen; weg·gehen; **to ~ on foot** zu Fuß gehen
God der Gott, ⸚er
gold das Gold
golf: ~ club der Golfschläger, -
gone weg
good gut
good-bye auf Wiedersehen; tschüss *(colloq.)*
got to müssen (hat gemusst)
government die Regierung, -en; der Staat, -en; **~ district** das Regierungsviertel; **taking ~ office** der Regierungsantritt, -e
grade die Note, -n; **[seventh] ~** [die siebte] Klasse
gram das Gramm

grammar die Grammatik
grand groß; großartig
grandchild das Enkelkind, -er
granddaughter die Enkelin,-nen
grandfather der Großvater, ¨; der Opa, -s
grandmother die Großmutter, ¨; die Oma, -s
grandparents die Großeltern *(pl.)*
grandson der Enkel, -
grape die Traube, -n
grave das Grab, ¨er
gray grau
great toll, ausgezeichnet, prima
Greece (das) Griechenland
green grün
greeting der Gruß, ¨e
groceries die Lebensmittel (*pl.*)
ground der Boden, ¨; **~ floor** das Erdgeschoss
group die Gruppe, -n; **~ leader** der Gruppenleiter; der Betreuer; **~ project** das Gruppenprojekt, -e; **~ research paper** das Gruppenreferat, -e; **study ~** die Arbeitsgruppe, -n
grow wachsen (ist gewachsen); **to ~ up** auf·wachsen (ist aufgewachsen)
gruesome grausam
guest der Gast, ¨e; der Besucher, -/die Besucherin, -nen; **~ room** das Gästezimmer, -; **~ house** die Pension, -en; das Gasthaus, ¨er; der Gasthof, ¨e
guard hüten (hat gehütet) vor + *dat.*
guitar die Gitarre, -n
guy der Typ, -en; **a really nice ~** ein ganz netter Typ

hair das Haar, -e
hairdresser der Friseur, -e/die Friseurin, -nen/die Friseuse, -n
hall der Flur, -e; der Gang, ¨e; der Korridor, -e
hand die Hand, ¨e
handbag die Handtasche, -n
handout das Handout, -s
hang: to ~ up hängen (hat gehängt)
hanging hängen (hat gehangen)
happen passieren (ist passiert); **What happened to you?** Was ist dir passiert?
happy froh, glücklich
harbor der Hafen, ¨
hard hart; schwer
hardly kaum
hard-working fleißig
harm schaden (hat geschadet) + *dat.*
hatred der Hass; **~ of foreigners** der Ausländerhass
have haben (hat gehabt); **to ~ to** müssen (hat gemusst)
head der Kopf, ¨e; **~ cold** der Schnupfen
headache die Kopfschmerzen *(pl.)*
health die Gesundheit; **~ club** das Fitnessstudio, -s; **~ food store** der Bioladen,¨; das Reformhaus, ¨er
heap der Haufen, -
hear hören (hat gehört)
hearth der Herd, -e
heaven der Himmel, -
heavy schwer
hello Guten Morgen/Tag/Abend; Grüß dich.; Hallo.
help die Hilfe, -n; **to ~** helfen (hat geholfen) + *dat.*
her (*possessive*) ihr; *(pronoun)* sie *(acc.)*; ihr *(dat.)*
here hier, da; ~ [toward the speaker] her; **~ you are** bitte sehr
hey! du!; he!; Hallo!
hi! Tag! Grüß dich! Servus!
hide verstecken (hat versteckt)
high hoch
hike die Wanderung, -en; **to ~** wandern (ist gewandert)
him ihn *(acc.)*; ihm *(dat.)*
hire ein·stellen (hat eingestellt)
his *(possessive)* sein
history die Geschichte
hitchhike per Anhalter fahren (ist gefahren)
hobby das Hobby, -s; **~ room** der Hobbyraum, ¨e
hold halten (hat gehalten)
holiday der Feiertag, -e
home: at ~ zu Hause; daheim; **to go ~** nach Hause gehen (ist gegangen)
homeland die Heimat; das Herkunftsland, ¨er
homesickness das Heimweh
hometown die Heimatstadt, ¨e
homework die Hausaufgaben *(pl.)*; **to do ~** die Hausaufgaben machen
homosexual der/die Homosexuelle, -n *(noun decl. like adj.)*; schwul
honest ehrlich
hook der Haken, -
hope hoffen (hat gehofft) ; **to ~ for** hoffen auf + *acc.*
hopefully hoffentlich
horrible furchtbar; fürchterlich; schrecklich
horse das Pferd, -e; **~-drawn sleigh** der Pferdeschlitten, -
hospital das Krankenhaus, ¨er; [Austrian] ~ das Spital, ¨er
hospitality die Gastfreundschaft
host der Gastgeber, -/die Gastgeberin, -nen
hot heiß
hour die Stunde, -n
house das Haus, ¨er
how wie; **~ are you?** Wie geht es Ihnen?/Wie geht's?
human being der Mensch, [-en], -en
humid schwül
hunger der Hunger
hungry hungrig; **to be ~** Hunger haben (hat gehabt)
hunter der Jäger, -
hurry sich beeilen (hat sich beeilt)
hurt weh tun (hat weh getan) + *dat.*
husband der Mann, ¨er

ice das Eis; **~ cream** das Eis
idea die Idee, -n; der Einfall, ¨e
if wenn; ob; **even ~** wenn auch
identify: to ~ with sich identifizieren (hat sich identifiziert) mit + *dat.*
ill krank
illness die Krankheit, -en
image das Bild, -er
imagine sich vor·stellen (hat sich vorgestellt) + *dat.*; **~ that!** Stell dir mal vor!
immediately gleich
impatient ungeduldig
important wichtig; **the most ~ thing** das Wichtigste
impression der Eindruck, ¨e
impressive beeindruckend
improve verbessern (hat verbessert)
inn der Gasthof, ¨e
in in + *dat.*; **into** in + *dat.*; hinein
increase erhöhen (hat erhöht)
industrious fleißig
industry die Industrie, -n
influence der Einfluss, *pl.* Einflüsse; **to ~** beeinflussen (hat beeinflusst)
inhabitant der Einwohner, -/die Einwohnerin, -nen
injure verletzen (hat verletzt)
innumerable zahllos
in order to um ... zu
inquire fragen (hat gefragt) nach + *dat.*
insecure unsicher
inside innerhalb + *gen.*
in spite of trotz + *gen.*
instead of (an)statt + *gen.*
institution die Einrichtung, -en
instrument das Instrument, -e
insurance die Versicherung, -en
intelligent intelligent, klug
intend to vor·haben (hat vorgehabt)
interest das Interesse, -n

interested: to be ~ed in (sich) interessieren für+ *acc.*
interesting interessant
intern der Praktikant [-en], -en/die Praktikantin, -nen
internship das Praktikum, *pl.* Praktika; die Praktikantenstelle, -n
international international; **~ relations** internationale Beziehungen *(pl.)*
intersection die Kreuzung, -en
interview das Interview, -s; das Vorstellungsgespräch, -e
into in + *acc.;* hinein
introduce vor·stellen (hat vorgestellt)
invite ein·laden (hat eingeladen)
irritate irritieren (hat irritiert)
Islam der Islam
is ist; **isn't it?** nicht?; nicht wahr? *(tag question)*
Italian italienisch *(adj.);* (das) Italienisch

jacket die Jacke, -n
January der Januar
Japanese (das) Japanisch; der Japaner, -/die Japanerin, -nen
jazz die Jazzmusik; **~ club** der Jazzkeller, -
jeans die Jeans *(pl.)*
Jew der Jude [-n], -n /die Jüdin, -nen.
Jewish jüdisch
job der Job, -s; die Stelle, -n; **to have a part-time ~** jobben
join bei·treten (ist beigetreten) + *dat.;* **to ~ in** mit·machen (hat mitgemacht)
joy die Freude, -n
juice der Saft, ¨-e
July der Juli
jump springen (ist gesprungen)
June der Juni
just eben; erst; gerade; halt

key der Schlüssel, -
kick treten (hat getreten)
kilogram das Kilo(gramm), -
kilometer der Kilometer, -
kind gut; nett; **what ~ of . . . ?** was für ein ...?
kindergarten der Kindergarten
king der König, -e
kingdom das Königtum, ¨-er
kiss der Kuss, *pl.* Küsse; **to ~** küssen (hat geküßt)
kitchen die Küche, -n
knee das Knie, -
knife das Messer, -
know: to ~(a fact) wissen (hat gewusst); **to ~ (be acquainted)** kennen (hat gekannt); **to ~ something about** etwas verstehen (hat verstanden) von + *dat.;* **to get to ~** kennen lernen (hat kennen gelernt)

lack fehlen (hat gefehlt)
lake der See, -n
lame lahm
lamp die Lampe, -n
land das Land, ¨-er
landscape die Landschaft, -en
language die Sprache, -n; **~ lab** das Sprachlabor, -s
large groß
last letzt; **~ night** gestern Abend; **to ~** dauern (hat gedauert)
late spät
later später; **until ~** bis später, tschüss, bis dann, bis bald
latest: at the ~ spätestens
laugh lachen (hat gelacht); **to ~ about** lachen über + *acc.*
laundry room die Waschküche, -n
law das Gesetz, -e; **~ (field of study)** Jura *(no article);* **~ maker** der Gesetzgeber, -; **Basic ~** *(German Constitution)* das Grundgesetz
lawyer der Rechtsanwalt, ¨-e/die Rechtsanwältin, -nen
lay legen (hat gelegt)
lazy faul
lead führen (hat geführt); leiten (hat geleitet)
leader der Führer, -
learn lernen (hat gelernt)
least: at ~ wenigstens; mindestens
leave lassen (hat gelassen); verlassen (hat verlassen); weg·fahren (ist weggefahren); ab·fahren (ist abgefahren)
lecture die Vorlesung, -en; **~ hall** der Hörsaal, *pl.* Hörsäle; **~ notes** das Skript, -en
left: on/to the ~ links
leg das Bein, -e
lend leihen (hat geliehen)
lesson der Unterricht; die Stunde, -n
let lassen (hat gelassen)
letter der Brief, -e
lettuce der Salat, -e
librarian der Bibliothekar, -e/die Bibliothekarin, -nen
library die Bibliothek, -en; **branch ~** die Stadtteilbibliothek, -en
lie liegen (hat gelegen); **to ~ down** (sich) hin·legen (hat sich hingelegt); **to tell a ~** lügen (hat gelogen)
life das Leben, -; **life-threatening** lebensgefährlich
light das Licht, -er; **traffic ~** die Ampel, -n; *(adj.)* leicht ; **~** *(color)* hell
like gern haben (hat gern gehabt); mögen (hat gemocht) ; gefallen (hat gefallen) + *dat.;* **I ~ to swim.** Ich schwimme gern.
likable sympathisch
limited begrenzt
line: waiting ~ die Schlange, -n; **to stand in ~** [in der] Schlange stehen (hat gestanden)
lip die Lippe, -n
lipstick der Lippenstift, -e
list die Liste, -n
listen zu·hören (hat zugehört) + *dat.;* **to ~ to music** Musik hören (hat gehört)
literature die Literatur, -en
little klein; wenig; **a ~** ein bisschen, ein wenig
live leben (hat gelebt); wohnen (hat gewohnt); **to ~ together** zusammen·leben (hat zusammengelebt)
lively lebendig
living room das Wohnzimmer, -
located: to be ~ liegen (hat gelegen)
lock das Schloss, *pl.* Schlösser; **to un~** auf·schließen (hat aufgeschlossen)
lodgings: to find ~ unterkommen (ist untergekommen)
logical vernünftig
long lang; lange; **for a ~ time** lange
longer: no ~ nicht mehr
look: to ~ at sich an·schauen (hat angeschaut); **to ~ like** aus·sehen (hat ausgesehen) wie; **to ~ down** herab·blicken (hat herabgeblickt); **to ~ for** suchen (hat gesucht); **to ~ forward to** sich freuen (hat sich gefreut) auf + *acc.;* **to ~ through** durch·gucken (hat durchgeguckt)
lose verlieren (hat verloren)
lot: a ~ viel
loud laut
lousy mies
love die Liebe, -n; **~ poem** das Liebesgedicht, -e; **to ~** lieben; **to be in ~ with** verliebt sein in + *dat.;* **to fall in ~** sich verlieben in + *acc.*
lovesickness der Liebeskummer
low gering; niedrig
luck das Glück; **to have bad ~** Pech haben
lucky: to be ~ Glück haben (hat gehabt); Schwein haben *(colloq.)*
lunch das Mittagessen; **for ~** zum Mittagessen; **to have ~** zu Mittag essen

machine die Maschine, -n
magazine die Zeitschrift, -en
magician der Zauberer, -
major subject das Hauptfach, ¨-er
mail die Post; **~ box** das Postfach, ¨-er
mail carrier der Briefträger, -/die Briefträgerin, -nen; der Postbote, [-n], -n/die Postbotin, -nen
main Haupt- ; **~ course** das Hauptgericht, -e; **~ street** die Hauptstraße, -n; **~ train station** der Hauptbahnhof, ¨-e
major: college ~ das Hauptfach, ¨-er
make machen (hat gemacht); **to ~ up with** sich versöhnen (hat sich versöhnt) mit + *dat.*
man der Mann, ¨-er; **Man!** Mensch! Mann!
manage schaffen (hat geschafft); bewerkstelligen (hat bewerkstelligt)
manner die Art
many viele; **how ~** wie viele; **too ~** zu viele
map die Landkarte, -n
March der März
market der Markt, ¨-e; **indoor ~** die Markthalle, -n
marketplace der Marktplatz, ¨-e
marmalade die Marmelade, -n
marriage die Heirat, -en;
married verheiratet
marry: to ~, get married heiraten (hat geheiratet)
mass die Masse, -n
math die Mathematik; die Mathe
May der Mai
may dürfen (hat gedurft); **that ~ well be** das mag wohl sein
maybe vielleicht
maximal maximal
me mich *(acc.)*; mir *(dat.)*; **~ too!** ich auch!
meadow die Wiese, -n
meal das Essen, -
mean böse; **to ~** meinen; bedeuten; **What does that ~?** Was bedeutet das?
meaning die Bedeutung, -en
meanwhile inzwischen
measure messen (hat gemessen)
message die Nachricht, -en
meat das Fleisch
medicine die Medizin; das Medikament, -e
meet treffen (hat getroffen); kennen lernen (hat kennen gelernt)
member das Mitglied, -er
membership die Mitgliedschaft
merchant der Kaufmann, ¨-er/die Kauffrau, -en; *(pl.)* die Kaufleute
merry lustig
meter der Meter, -
Mexican mexikanisch; der Mexikaner, -/die Mexikanerin, -nen
microwave oven der Mikrowellenherd, -e
middle die Mitte, -n
milk die Milch
million die Million, -en
mineral water das Mineralwasser
minor subject das Nebenfach, ¨-er
minute die Minute, -n; **Just a ~ please!** Einen Moment, bitte!
miracle das Wunder, -
mirror der Spiegel, -
Miss das Fräulein, -
missing: to be ~ fehlen (hat gefehlt)
mix mischen (hat gemischt)
modern modern
mom die Mutti, -s
moment der Moment, -e; **at the ~** momentan; im Moment; zur Zeit
Monday der Montag
money das Geld
month der Monat, -e
mood die Stimmung, -en; **magical ~** die Zauberstimmung
more mehr; **no ~** kein ... mehr; **~ and ~** immer mehr; **~ or less** mehr oder weniger
morning der Morgen; **Good ~.** Guten Morgen.; **this ~** heute Morgen
mornings morgens
mosque die Moschee, -n
most of the time meistens
mother die Mutter, ¨-
motivated motiviert
motive das Motiv, -e
motorcycle das Motorrad, ¨-er
mountain der Berg, -e; **~ climbing** das Bergsteigen; **~ peak** der Gipfel, -
mouth der Mund, ¨-er
move ziehen (ist gezogen) nach; um·ziehen (ist umgezogen)
movie der Film, -e; **movie star** der Filmstar, -s; **~ theater** das Kino, -s; **to make a ~** einen Film drehen (hat gedreht)
movies: to go to the ~ ins Kino gehen
Mr. (der) Herr
Mrs. (die) Frau
Ms. (die) Frau
much viel; **how ~** wie viel; **too ~** zu viel
multicultural multikulturell
multiculturalism der Multikulturalismus
museum das Museum, *pl.* Museen
music die Musik; **~ conservatory** die Musikhochschule, -n
musical das Musical, -s
musical instrument das Musikinstrument, -e
musician der Musiker, -/die Musikerin, -nen; der Musikant [-en], -en
must müssen (hat gemusst)
mystery story der Krimi, -s

name der Name, [-n], -n; **by the ~ of** namens; **first ~** der Vorname, -ns, -n; **last ~** der Nachname, [-n], -n; **What is your ~?** Wie heißen Sie?; **to ~** nennen (hat genannt)
namely nämlich
narrow eng
naturally klar; natürlich; selbstverständlich
nature die Natur, -en
Nazi der Nazi, -s; der Nationalsozialist [-en], -en; **~ V.I.P.** die Nazigröße, -n; **neo-~** der Neo-Nazi, -s
near bei + *dat.*
nearby in der Nähe, nah(e)
necessary notwendig
neck der Hals, ¨-e
need brauchen (hat gebraucht)
nephew der Neffe [-n], -n
nervous nervös
network die Vernetzung, -en
never nie
nevertheless trotzdem
new neu; **What's ~?** Was gibt's Neues?; **~ building** der Neubau, -ten
news die Nachricht, -en
newspaper die Zeitung, -en
next nächst
nice nett; schön
niece die Nichte, -n
night die Nacht, ¨-e; **last ~** gestern Abend; **~mare** der Albtraum, ¨-e
nighttime nächtlich *(adj.)*
no nein; kein; nicht; **~ longer** nicht mehr; **~ more . . .** kein ... mehr
none kein; **~ at all** überhaupt kein
no one niemand
nod nicken (hat genickt)
north der Norden
nose die Nase, -n
not nicht; **isn't that so?** nicht?; nicht wahr?; **~ at all** gar nicht; **~ any** kein; **~ only . . . but also . . .** nicht nur ... sondern auch ...
note die Notiz, -en

notes: lecture ~ das Skript, -en
notebook das Heft, -e
nothing nichts; **~ special** nichts Besonderes
notice bemerken (hat bemerkt), merken (hat gemerkt)
novel der Roman, -e
November der November
now jetzt; nun; **~ and then** ab und zu; hin und wieder
number die Zahl, -en
nurse der Krankenpfleger, -/die Krankenschwester, -n
nursery school der Kindergarten, ¨

obtain bekommen (hat bekommen); kriegen (hat gekriegt); erhalten (hat erhalten)
occupied: to be ~ beschäftigt sein
occupy besetzen (hat besetzt)
occur statt·finden (hat stattgefunden)
ocean der Ozean, -e; die See, -n
October der Oktober
of von + *dat.*
offer an·bieten (hat angeboten)
office das Büro, -s; (military) die Schreibstube, -n; **~ hours** die Sprechstunde, -n
often oft
oh ach, ah; **~ I see** ach so; **~ my** o je; **~ well** naja
O.K. O.K.; okay; ganz gut; **It's (not) ~.** Es geht (nicht).
old alt; **~ town** die Altstadt, ¨e
Olympic Games die Olympiade, -n
on an; auf + *acc./dat.*; **~ account of** wegen + *gen.*; **~ foot** zu Fuß
once einmal; mal; **~ more** noch einmal
one *(pronoun)* man; **~ another** einander
oneself selbst, selber
only nur; erst
open offen, geöffnet; **to ~** auf·machen (hat aufgemacht); auf·schließen (hat aufgeschlossen); öffnen (hat geöffnet)
opening die Öffnung, -en; **~ time** die Öffnungszeit, -en
opera die Oper, -n
opinion die Meinung, -en; **to have an ~** meinen (hat gemeint); **What's your ~?** Was hältst du davon?
oppress unterdrücken (hat unterdrückt)
oppression die Unterdrückung, -en
or oder
orange die Apfelsine, -n; Orange, -n; **~ juice** der Orangensaft
orchestra das Orchester, -
order die Ordnung; die Reihenfolge, -n; **in ~** in Ordnung; **to ~** bestellen (hat bestellt); **to put in ~** ordnen (hat geordnet)
orderly der Krankenpfleger, -; ordentlich
organization die Organisation, -en
organize organisieren (hat organisiert)
originate entstehen (ist entstanden)
other ander- (-er, -es, -e); **the ~ way around** umgekehrt
otherwise sonst
our unser
out of aus + *dat.*
outgoing gesellig, kontaktfreudig
outside draußen
over *(time)* vorbei; **~** *(position)* über + *acc./dat.*; **~-filled** überfüllt; **~-worked** überarbeitet
overcome überwinden (hat überwunden)
overhead: ~ projector der Overheadprojektor, -s; **~ transparency** die Folie, -n
oversee übersehen (hat übersehen)
own *(adj.)* eigen; **to ~** besitzen (hat besessen)
ozone layer die Ozonschicht, -en

pack packen (hat gepackt); ein·packen (hat eingepackt)
package das Paket, -e
packaging die Verpackung, -en
page die Seite, -n; das Blatt, ¨er
pain der Schmerz, -en
painkiller die Schmerztablette, -n
palace das Schloss, *pl.* Schlösser
pale blass
pants die Hose, -n
pantyhose die Strumpfhose, -n
paper das Papier; **~ (theme, essay)** die Arbeit, -en; das Referat, -e
paperback das Taschenbuch, ¨er
paradise das Paradies, -e
pardon! Entschuldigung!; **I beg your ~?** Wie bitte?
parents die Eltern *(pl.)*
park der Park, -s; **to ~** parken (hat geparkt)
parking: ~ fee die Parkgebühr, -en; **~ garage** das Parkhaus, ¨er; **~ space, lot** der Parkplatz, ¨e; **~ stub** der Parkschein, -e
parliament das Parlament
part der Teil, -e; **in ~** zum Teil
participate (in) mit·machen (hat mitgemacht) bei + *dat.*; teil·nehmen (hat teilgenommen) an + *dat.*
particular besonder-
particularly besonders
party die Party, -s; das Fest, -e; die Fete, -n; **political ~** die Partei, -en; **to give a ~** ein Fest geben; **to go to a ~** auf eine Party (Fete) gehen (ist gegangen)
passenger der Passagier, -e; **~ vehicle** der Personenkraftwagen, -; der PKW, -s
passionate leidenschaftlich
passive passiv
pass der Pass, *pl.* Pässe
passport der Pass, *pl.* Pässe; **~ check, control** die Passkontrolle, -n
pastry das Gebäck; **~ shop** die Konditorei, -en
path der Weg, -e
patience die Geduld
pay zahlen (hat gezahlt); **to ~ for** bezahlen (hat bezahlt)
peak der Gipfel, -
pearl die Perle, -n
pedestrian der Fußgänger, -/die Fußgängerin, -nen; **~ zone** die Fußgängerzone, -n; der Fußgängerbereich, -e
pen der Kugelschreiber, -; der Kuli, -s; der Stift, -e
pencil der Bleistift, -e
pension die Rente, -n
pensioner der Rentner, -/die Rentnerin, -nen
people die Leute *(pl.)*; die Menschen *(pl.)*; man
per pro
percent das Prozent, -e
perhaps vielleicht; eventuell
period der Punkt, -e
permit erlauben (hat erlaubt); lassen (hat gelassen)
permitted erlaubt; **to be ~** dürfen (hat gedurft)
person der Mensch [-en], -en; die Person, -en
personality die Persönlichkeit, -en
personnel: ~ department die Personalabteilung, -en; **head of ~** der Personalchef, -s/die Personalchefin, -nen
pharmaceutics die Pharmazie
pharmacy die Apotheke, -n
philosophy die Philosophie
photograph das Bild, das Foto; **to ~** fotografieren (hat fotografiert)
photographer der Photograph, [-en], -en/die Photographin, -nen
physics die Physik
piano das Klavier, -e; **~ lesson** die Klavierstunde, -n

pick: to ~ out aus·suchen (hat ausgesucht); aus·wählen (hat ausgewählt); **to ~ up** ab·holen (hat abgeholt); **(mess)** auf·räumen (hat aufgeräumt)
picture das Bild, -er
piece das Stück, -e
pink rosa
pity: what a ~ schade
place der Platz, ¨-e; die Stelle, -n; der Ort, -e; **to my ~** zu mir; **at my ~** bei mir
plan der Plan, ¨-e; die Planung, -en; **to ~** vor·haben (hat vorgehabt); planen (hat geplant)
planetarium das Planetarium, *pl.* Planeterien
plant die Pflanze, -n; **to ~** pflanzen (hat gepflanzt)
plastic das Plastik
play das Theaterstück, -e; das Drama, *pl.* Dramen; **to ~** spielen (hat gespielt)
plaza der Platz, ¨-e
please bitte; **to ~** gefallen (gefällt, hat gefallen) + *dat.*
pleased: to be ~ (about) sich freuen (hat sich gefreut) über + *acc.*
pleasure die Freude, -n; die Lust; das Vergnügen
plump mollig
pocket die Tasche, -n
point der Punkt, -e; der Zweck, -e
pointless: it's ~ Das hat keinen Zweck.
poison das Gift, -e
poisonous giftig
police die Polizei; **state ~ (Austrian)** die Gendarmerie
political politisch; **~ science** die Politikwissenschaft, -en
politician der Politiker, -/die Politikerin, -nen
politics die Politik, -en
pollute verschmutzen (hat verschmutzt)
popular populär; beliebt; **~ music** die Popmusik
portion der Teil, -e; die Portion, -en
portray schildern (hat geschildert)
position die Stelle, -n; der Job, -s
possible möglich; **It's (not) ~.** Es geht (nicht).
possibility die Möglichkeit, -en
post office die Post; **to go to the ~** auf die Post gehen
postal code die Postleitzahl, -en
postcard die Postkarte, -n
poster das Poster, -
post office box das Postfach, ¨-er
positive positiv
pot der Topf, ¨-e
potato die Kartoffel, -n
poultry das Geflügel
pound das Pfund, -e; **to ~** pochen (hat gepocht)
power die Macht, ¨-e; **political ~** das Organ, -e
practice üben (hat geübt); **to ~ a profession** einen Beruf aus·üben (hat ausgeübt); praktizieren (hat praktiziert)
practical praktisch
pray beten (hat gebetet)
prefer: I ~ to work. Ich arbeite lieber.
preparation die Vorbereitung, -en
prepare (for) (sich) vor·bereiten (hat sich vorbereitet) auf + *acc.*
present das Geschenk, -e; **to ~ oneself** sich präsentieren (hat sich präsentiert)
presentation das Referat, -e; **to make a ~** ein Referat halten (hat gehalten)
president der Präsident [-en], -en/die Präsidentin, -nen
pressure der Druck
prestige das Prestige
pretty schön; **~ pale** ganz schön blass
price der Preis, -e
prince der Prinz [-en], -en; der Königssohn, ¨-e
princess die Prinzessin, -nen; die Königstochter, ¨-; **princess-like** prinzesshaft
print drucken (hat gedruckt)
printer der Drucker, -
private privat; **~ bath** das Privatbad, ¨-er; **~ lesson** die Privatstunde, -n
probably wahrscheinlich; wohl
problem das Problem, -e; **without a ~** problemlos
proclaim proklamieren (hat proklamiert)
produce her·stellen (hat hergestellt), produzieren (hat produziert)
product das Produkt, -e
profession der Beruf, -e
professor der Professor, -en/die Professorin, -nen
program das Programm, -e; **TV or radio ~** die Sendung, -en
programmer der Programmierer, -/die Programmiererin, -nen
project das Projekt, -e; das Unternehmen, -
promise die Versprechung, -en; **to ~** versprechen (hat versprochen)
protect schützen (hat geschützt)
proud stolz
Prussia (das) Preußen
psychiatry die Psychiatrie
psychology die Psychologie
pub die Kneipe, -n; die Gaststätte, -n; die Bar, -s; **student ~** die Studentenkneipe, -n
public öffentlich
pudding der Pudding, -s
pull ziehen (hat gezogen)
pullover der Pulli, -s; der Pullover, -
punctual pünktlich
pure rein
purple lila
purpose der Zweck, -e
purse die Handtasche, -n
put (horizontal) legen (hat gelegt); **(vertical)** stellen (hat gestellt); **(seated)** setzen (hat gesetzt); **(hanging)** hängen (hat gehängt); **(inserted)** stecken (hat gesteckt); **(general)** tun (hat getan); **to ~ up overnight** unterbringen (hat untergebracht); **to ~ together** zusammen·stellen (hat zusammengestellt)

qualified qualifiziert
quality die Qualität, -en
quarrel der Krach; der Streit; **to ~** sich streiten (hat sich gestritten) mit + *dat.*
quarter das Viertel, -
queen die Königin, -nen
question die Frage, -n; **~ word** das Fragewort, ¨-er; **to ~** fragen (hat gefragt); **to ask a ~** eine Frage stellen (hat gestellt)
questionable fraglich
quick schnell
quiet die Ruhe; die Stille; ruhig; still
quite ziemlich

race rennen (ist gerannt)
racism der Rassismus
radio das Radio, -s
railroad die Bahn, -en
rain der Regen; **to ~** regnen (hat geregnet)
raincoat der Regenmantel, ¨-
raise: to ~ heben (hat gehoben); **to ~ children** erziehen (hat erzogen)
random stichprobenartig
range (kitchen) der Herd, -e
rank der Rang, ¨-e
rare selten, rar
rather ziemlich; **~ than** lieber als
rave: to ~ about schwärmen (hat geschwärmt) von + *dat.*
raw material der Rohstoff, -e
razor: electric ~ der Rasierapparat, -e
reach erreichen (hat erreicht)

react reagieren (hat reagiert)
reaction die Reaktion, -en
read lesen (hat gelesen)
ready bereit; fertig
real echt; richtig
real estate agent der Makler, -/die Maklerin, -nen
reality die Wirklichkeit
really wirklich; richtig; ganz; echt *(slang)*; **~ neat** echt toll; ganz toll
rear der Hintern
reason der Grund, ⸚e; **for that ~** deshalb; deswegen; aus diesem Grund
reasonable vernünftig; (price) günstig
receipt die Quittung, -en
receive bekommen (hat bekommen); erhalten (hat erhalten)
recently vor kurzem; neulich
reckon with rechnen (hat gerechnet) mit + *dat.*
recognize erkennen (hat erkannt)
recommend empfehlen (hat empfohlen)
recommendation die Empfehlung, -en
record die Platte, -n; **~ store** das Plattengeschäft, -e
record player der Plattenspieler, -
recover (from) sich erholen (hat sich erholt) von + *dat.*
recuperate sich erholen (hat sich erholt) von + *dat.*
recycling das Recycling
red rot
refrigerator der Kühlschrank, ⸚e
regulate regeln (hat geregelt)
rehearsal die Probe, -n
reinforce verstärken (hat verstärkt)
related verwandt
relative der/die Verwandte *(noun decl. like adj.)*
relatives die Verwandtschaft
relax sich aus·ruhen (hat sich ausgeruht)
relaxed locker
religious fromm; religiös
remain bleiben (ist geblieben)
remaining übrig
remember sich erinnern (hat sich erinnert) an + *acc.*
renovate renovieren (hat renoviert)
rent die Miete, -n; **to ~** mieten (hat gemietet); **to ~ out** vermieten (hat vermietet)
repair reparieren (hat repariert); **~ person** der Mechaniker, -/die Mechanikerin, -nen
repeat wiederholen (hat wiederholt)
report der Bericht, -e; das Referat, -e; **to ~** berichten (hat berichtet); sich melden (hat sich gemeldet)
reporter der Reporter, -/die Reporterin, -nen
representative der/die Abgeordnete, -n
republic die Republik, -en
request bitten (hat gebeten) um + *acc.*
rescue retten (hat gerettet) vor + *dat.*; **~ mission** die Rettungsaktion, -en
resistance der Widerstand
resort der Ferienort, -e
resource die Ressource, -n
responsibility die Verantwortung, -en
responsible verantwortlich
rest der Rest, -e; **to ~** sich aus·ruhen (hat sich ausgeruht)
restaurant das Restaurant, -s; die Gaststätte, -n; **town hall ~** der Ratskeller, -
result das Resultat, -e
return die Rückkehr; **to ~** zurück·fahren (ist zurückgefahren); zurück·gehen (ist zurückgegangen); zurück·kommen (ist zurückgekommen); wieder·kommen (ist wiedergekommen); zurück·kehren (ist zurückgekehrt); **to ~ something** (etwas) zurück·geben (hat zurückgegeben); zurück·nehmen (hat zurückgenommen)
reunification die Wiedervereinigung; die Union
rice der Reis
rich reich
ride die Fahrt, -en; **to ~ a bike** mit dem Fahrrad fahren, Rad fahren (ist Rad gefahren); **to ~ horseback** reiten (ist geritten)
right das Recht, -e; **Is it all ~ with you?** Ist es dir recht?; **to be ~** Recht haben; **that's ~** genau; richtig; **on/to the ~** rechts; **~ around the corner** gleich um die Ecke
right-wing extremism der Rechtsradikalismus
ring der Ring, -e: **to ~** klingeln (hat geklingelt)
rinse spülen (hat gespült)
risk riskieren (hat riskiert)
risky riskant
river der Fluss, *pl.* Flüsse
rock music die Rockmusik
rock musician der Rockmusiker, -/die Rockmusikerin, -nen
role die Rolle, -n
roll das Brötchen, -; die Semmel, -n
Roman römisch
romance novel der Liebesroman, -e
romantic romantisch
room das Zimmer,-; **bathroom** das Badezimmer, -; **bedroom** das Schlafzimmer, -; **classroom** das Klassenzimmer, -; **living ~** das Wohnzimmer,-; **~ number** die Zimmernummer, -n
round rund; die Runde, -n
routine die Routine, -n; der Alltag
rubble der Schutt
rug der Teppich, -e
rule die Regel, -n
run laufen (ist gelaufen); rennen (ist gerannt)
running das Jogging
Russia (das) Russland
Russian russisch; (das) Russisch; der Russe [-n], -n/die Russin, -nen

sad traurig
safe sicher
safety die Sicherheit, -en
sail segeln (ist gesegelt)
salad der Salat, -e
salary das Gehalt, ⸚er; **~ expectation** die Gehaltsvorstellung, -en
sales person der Verkäufer, -/die Verkäuferin, -nen
same (der/das/die)selbe, gleich; **It's all the ~ to me.** Das ist mir egal.; **at the ~ time** gleichzeitig
sandwich das Brot, -e; das Butterbrot, -e; das belegte Brot
satisfied zufrieden
Saturday der Samstag; der Sonnabend
Saturdays samstags; sonnabends
sausage die Wurst, ⸚e
save sparen (hat gespart)
savings bank die Sparkasse, -n
say sagen (hat gesagt); erzählen (hat erzählt)
scene die Szene, -n
scenery die Landschaft, -en
schedule der Stundenplan, ⸚e
schizophrenia die Schizophrenie
school die Schule, -n; **elementary ~** die Grundschule, -n; **high ~ (non-college)** die Realschule, -n; **college prep. high ~** das Gymnasium, *pl.* Gymnasien; **technical-vocational ~** die Hauptschule, -n; **~ days** die Schulzeit, -en
schussing die Schussfahrt, -en
science die Wissenschaft, -en; die Naturwissenschaft, -en
scientist der Wissenschaftler, -/die Wissenschaftlerin, -nen
screen die Leinwand, ⸚e
sea die See, -n

search die Suche, -n; die Kontrolle, -n; **to ~ for** suchen (hat gesucht) nach + *dat.*
season die Jahreszeit, -en; **(sports) ~** die Saison, -s
seat der Platz, ¨-e; **Is this ~ taken?** Ist hier frei?; **to ~ oneself** sich setzen (hat sich gesetzt)
secretary der Sekretär, -e/die Sekretärin, -nen
see sehen (hat gesehen)
seem scheinen (hat geschienen)
seldom selten
select wählen (hat gewählt)
selection die Wahl; die Auswahl
self (oneself, myself, itself, etc.) selbst, selber; sich; **~-reliant** selbstständig; **~-assured** selbstsicher; **~-repression** die Selbstunterdrückung
sell verkaufen (hat verkauft)
semester das Semester, -; **~ bus pass** die Semesterkarte, -n
seminar das Seminar, -e; **~ room** der Seminarraum, ¨-e; **~ report** die Seminararbeit, -en
send schicken (hat geschickt); senden (hat gesendet)
sentence der Satz, ¨-e
separate trennen (hat getrennt); spalten (hat gespaltet)
September der September
sequence die Reihenfolge, -n
serious ernst; **Are you ~?** Ist das dein Ernst?
serve dienen (hat gedient)
set setzen (hat gesetzt); **to ~ the table** den Tisch decken (hat gedeckt)
several einige; mehrere
shake rütteln (hat gerüttelt); schütteln (hat geschüttelt); **to ~ hands** die Hand schütteln; die Hand geben (hat gegeben)
shampoo das Shampoo, -s; das Haarwaschmittel, -; **to ~** (sich) die Haare waschen (hat sich gewaschen)
share sich teilen (hat sich geteilt)
shared: ~ bathroom das Gemeinschaftsbad, ¨-er; **~ kitchen** die Gemeinschaftsküche, -n
shave (sich) rasieren (hat sich rasiert)
shaver (electric) der Rasierapparat, -e
shelf das Regal, -e
shine scheinen (hat geschienen)
ship das Boot, -e; das Schiff, -e
shirt das Hemd, -en
shock der Schock, -s
shoe der Schuh, -e
shop das Geschäft, -e; der Laden, ¨-; **to ~** ein·kaufen (hat eingekauft)
shopping: to go ~ ein·kaufen gehen (ist einkaufen gegangen); **~ bag** die Einkaufstasche, -n; die Einkaufstüte, -n; die Tragetasche, -n; **~ basket** der Einkaufskorb, ¨-e; **~ center** das Einkaufszentrum, *pl.* Einkaufszentren; **~ trip** der Einkaufsbummel
short kurz; **~ (people)** klein; **~ story** die Kurzgeschichte, -n
shorts die Shorts *(pl.)*
shoulder die Schulter, -n
show zeigen (hat gezeigt)
shower die Dusche, -n; **~ room** der Duschraum, ¨-e; **to ~** (sich) duschen (hat sich geduscht); unter die Dusche gehen (ist gegangen); **rain ~** der Schauer, -
shy schüchtern
sick krank
side die Seite, -n
sight-seeing attraction die Sehenswürdigkeit, -en
sign das Schild, -er; das Zeichen, -
silence die Stille
silver das Silber
similar ähnlich
simple einfach
simply einfach; bloß
simultaneous gleichzeitig
since seit *(prep.)*; seitdem, da *(conj)*; **~ when** seit wann
singer der Sänger, -/die Sängerin, -nen
single ledig; einzeln
single-family home das Einfamilienhaus, ¨-er
sink das Waschbecken, -
sister die Schwester, -n
sit sitzen (hat gesessen); **to ~ down** sich setzen (hat sich gesetzt)
situated: to be ~ liegen (hat gelegen)
situation die Lage, -n; die Situation, -en
skate: roller ~ der Rollschuh, -e; **ice ~** der Schlittschuh, -e; **in-line ~** der Rollerblade, -s; **to ice ~** Schlittschuh laufen (ist gelaufen); **to roller ~** Rollschuh laufen (ist gelaufen)
ski der Ski, -er; **to ~** Ski laufen (ist Ski gelaufen); **~ boot** der Skistiefel, -; **~ chalet** die Skihütte, -n; **~ parka** der Skianorak, -s; **~ run, track** die Piste, -n
skirt der Rock, ¨-e
slam shut zu·knallen (hat zugeknallt)
sled der Schlitten, -
sleep schlafen (hat geschlafen); **to go to ~** schlafen gehen (ist schlafen gegangen)
sleigh der Schlitten, -; **~ ride** die Schlittelfahrt, -en
slender schlank
slow langsam
small klein
smart intelligent; klug
smell riechen (hat gerochen); stinken (hat gestunken)
smile lächeln (hat gelächelt)
smoke der Rauch; **to ~** rauchen (hat geraucht)
smooth glatt
smuggle schmuggeln (hat geschmuggelt)
smuggler der Schlepper, - der Schmuggler, -;
snow der Schnee; **powder ~** der Pulverschnee; **to ~** schneien (hat geschneit); **~-covered** verschneit
so so; also; **Isn't that ~?** Nicht?; **~ that** damit; **~ long.** Tschüss.; **I believe ~.** Ich glaube schon/ja.
soap die Seife, -n; **~ opera** die Seifenoper, -n
soccer der Fußball
sociable gesellig; kontaktfreudig
society die Gesellschaft, -en
sock die Socke, -n
socket: electric ~ die Steckdose, -n
sofa das Sofa, -s
soft drink die Limonade, -n
software die Software
soldier der Soldat [-en], -en/die Soldatin, -nen
solution die Lösung, -en
solve lösen (hat gelöst)
some etwas; einige; manch (-er, -es, -e); **at ~ point** irgendwann
someone jemand; irgendjemand
something etwas, was; irgendetwas; **~ like that** so was
sometime irgendwann
sometimes manchmal
somewhat etwas
son der Sohn, ¨-e
song das Lied, -er
soon bald; **as ~ as** sobald
sort sortieren (hat sortiert); die Art, -en; die Sorte, -n
sorry: to be ~ Leid tun + *dat.* (hat Leid getan); **I'm ~** es tut mir Leid
sound klingen (hat geklungen)
soup die Suppe, -n
south der Süden; südlich; **South American** südamerikanisch
southwestern südwestlich
souvenir das Andenken, -
space der Platz, ¨-e
spaghetti die Spaghetti *(pl.)*
Spain (das) Spanien
Spanish spanisch; (das) Spanisch

Spaniard der Spanier, -/die Spanierin, -nen
speak reden (hat geredet); sprechen (hat gesprochen)
speechless sprachlos
spell buchstabieren (hat buchstabiert); **How do you ~ that?** Wie schreibt man das?
spend (money) aus·geben (hat ausgegeben); **to ~ (time)** verbringen (hat verbracht)
spite: in ~ of trotz + *gen.*
splendid großartig
spontaneous spontan
spoon der Löffel, -
sport der Sport; **to engage in sports** Sport treiben (hat getrieben); **~ coat** der/das Sakko, -s; die Jacke, -n
spring der Frühling, -e
stadium das Stadion, *pl.* Stadien
stair die Treppe, -n
stairwell das Treppenhaus, ¨-er; das Stiegenhaus, ¨-er
stamp: postage ~ die Briefmarke, -n; **rubber ~** der Stempel, -
stand der Kiosk, -s; der Stand, ¨-e; **to ~** stehen (hat gestanden); **to ~ up** auf·stehen (ist aufgestanden); **to ~/put upright** stellen (hat gestellt)
standing der Rang, ¨-e
standard German (das) Hochdeutsch
stare an·starren (hat angestarrt)
start an·fangen (hat angefangen); beginnen (hat begonnen); **to ~ a conversation** an·sprechen (hat angesprochen)
state (in Germany) das Land, ¨-er; das Bundesland, ¨-er; **~ (in the U.S.A.)** der Staat, -en; **~ exam** das Staatsexamen, -
state-owned staatlich
stay der Aufenthalt, -e; **~ abroad** der Auslandsaufenthalt, -e; **to ~** bleiben (ist geblieben)
step treten (ist getreten)
stepbrother der Stiefbruder, ¨-
stepfather der Stiefvater, ¨-
stepmother die Stiefmutter, ¨-
stepsister die Stiefschwester, -n
steps die Treppe, -n
stereo system die Stereoanlage, -n
stick stecken (hat gesteckt)
stiff steif
still still; die Stille; noch; immer noch; noch immer
stomach der Bauch, ¨-e
stomachache die Bauchschmerzen *(pl.)*
stop an·halten (hat angehalten); auf·hören (hat aufgehört); halten (hat gehalten); stehen·bleiben (ist stehengeblieben)
store das Geschäft, -e; der Laden, ¨-
story die Geschichte, -n
straight gerade
straighten up auf·räumen (hat aufgeräumt)
strange seltsam
street die Straße, -n
streetcar die Straßenbahn, -en
strengthen verstärken (hat verstärkt)
stress stressen (hat gestresst); der Stress; **stressful** stressig
strict streng
stroll spazieren gehen (ist spazieren gegangen); der Spaziergang, ¨-e
structure die Struktur, -en
strong stark
student der Student [-en], -en/die Studentin, -nen; **fellow ~** der Kommilitone, [-n], -n/die Kommilitonin, -nen; **~ ID** der Studentenausweis, -e; **~ room** das Studentenzimmer, -; die Studentenbude, -n; **~ life** das Studentenleben
studies das Studium, *pl.* Studien
study studieren (hat studiert); lernen (hat gelernt)
stuff das Zeug
stunned verblüfft
stupid dumm, doof
subject (academic) das Fach, ¨-er; **major ~** das Hauptfach, ¨-er; **minor ~** das Nebenfach, ¨-er
subway die U-Bahn, -en
such solch (-er, -es, -e); **~ a** so ein
suddenly plötzlich
suggest vor·schlagen (hat vorgeschlagen)
suggestion der Vorschlag, ¨-e
suit (man's) der Anzug, ¨-e; **(woman's) ~** das Kostüm, -e; **to ~** passen (hat gepasst) + *dat.*; stehen (hat gestanden) + *dat.*
suitcase der Koffer, -
summer der Sommer, -
sun die Sonne, -n
Sunday der Sonntag
Sundays sonntags
sunglasses die Sonnenbrille, -n
sunny sonnig
supermarket der Supermarkt, ¨-e
supper das Abendessen; **for ~** zum Abendessen; **to have ~** zu Abend essen
supposed: to be ~ to sollen (hat gesollt)
sure sicher; bestimmt; **(agreement) ~!** Natürlich!
surf surfen (hat gesurft)
surprise überraschen (hat überrascht)
surprisingly überraschend
suspense: to be in ~ gespannt sein
sweater der Pulli, -s; der Pullover, -
swim schwimmen (ist geschwommen); baden (hat gebadet)
swimming pool: indoor ~ das Hallenbad, ¨-er; **outdoor ~** das Frei(schwimm)bad, ¨-er
swimming trunks die Badehose, -n
swim suit der Badeanzug, ¨-e
Swiss *(adj.)* Schweizer; **~ (person)** der Schweizer, -/die Schweizerin, -nen
switch (to change) wechseln (hat gewechselt)
Switzerland die Schweiz
symbol das Wahrzeichen, -; das Symbol, -e
synagogue die Synagoge, -n

table der Tisch, -e
take nehmen (hat genommen); **to ~ along** mit·nehmen (hat mitgenommen); **to ~ care of** erledigen (hat erledigt); bewerkstelligen (hat bewerkstelligt); **to ~ off** aus·ziehen (hat ausgezogen); **to ~ place, occur** statt·finden (hat stattgefunden)
talented begabt; talentiert
talk sprechen (hat gesprochen); reden (hat geredet); diskutieren (hat diskutiert); *(dialect)* schwätzen (hat geschwätzt); **~ about** reden/sprechen/diskutieren über + *acc.*; **to ~ to** sprechen (etc.) mit + *dat.*; **~ over** besprechen (hat besprochen)
tall groß; hoch
tardiness die Verspätung, -en
task die Aufgabe, -n
taste der Geschmack; **to ~** schmecken (hat geschmeckt)
tasty lecker
tax die Steuer, -n; **income ~ card** die Lohnsteuerkarte, -n; **~ office** das Finanzamt, ¨-er; **to ~** besteuern (hat besteuert)
taxi das Taxi, -s
tea der Tee, -s
teach unterrichten (hat unterrichtet); lehren (hat gelehrt)
teacher der Lehrer, -/die Lehrerin, -nen; **~'s degree** das Staatsexamen, -

telephone das Telefon, -e; **to ~** telefonieren (hat telefoniert); an·rufen (hat angerufen); **~ booth** die Telefonzelle, -n; **by ~** telefonisch; **~ number** die Telefonnummer, -n
television das Fernsehen; **~ set** der Fernseher, -; **color ~** der Farbfernseher; **~ program** die Fernsehsendung, -en; **to watch ~** fern·sehen (hat ferngesehen)
tell sagen (hat gesagt); **to ~ about** erzählen (hat erzählt) von + *dat.*
temperature die Temperatur, -en
tennis das Tennis; **~ ball** der Tennisball, ¨-e; **~ racket** der Tennisschläger, -; **~ shoe** der Tennisschuh, -e
tent das Zelt, -e
terrace die Terrasse, -n
terrible schlimm; furchtbar; schrecklich
test die Prüfung, -en; **to ~** prüfen (hat geprüft); überprüfen (hat überprüft); **to take a ~** eine Prüfung schreiben (hat geschrieben)
than als
thank danken (hat gedankt) + *dat.*
thanks danke; **~ a lot!** danke schön; vielen Dank
that dass; jen- (-er, -es, -e); **~'s why** deshalb; deswegen
theater das Theater, -; das Schauspielhaus, ¨-er; **to go to the ~** ins Theater gehen; **~ play** das Theaterstück, -e
them sie *(acc.)*; ihnen *(dat.)*
theme das Thema, *pl.* Themen
then dann; da
there da; dort; dahin; **over ~** dort drüben; **~ is/are** es gibt (hat gegeben)
therefore also; deshalb; daher; darum; deswegen
these diese
they sie
thick dick
thin dünn, schlank
thing das Ding, -e; die Sache, -n
think denken (hat gedacht); meinen (hat gemeint); glauben (hat geglaubt); **to ~ of** denken an + *acc.*; halten (hat gehalten) von + *dat.*/für + *acc.*; **to ~ over** sich überlegen (hat sich überlegt); **What do you ~?** Was meinst du?
third das Drittel, -; dritt-
thirsty durstig; **to be ~** Durst haben
this dies (-er, -es, -e); **~ morning** heute Morgen; **~ afternoon** heute Nachmittag; **~ evening** heute Abend
throat der Hals, ¨-e; **to have a sore ~** Halsschmerzen haben (hat gehabt)
throw werfen (hat geworfen); **to ~ away** weg·werfen (hat wegeworfen)
thunder donnern (hat gedonnert)
Thursday der Donnerstag
thus also
ticket die Karte, -n; **airline ~** der Flugschein, -e; das Flugticket, -s
tie (necktie) die Krawatte, -n
time die Zeit, -en; das Mal, -e; **at that ~** damals; **at the same ~** zur gleichen Zeit; **for a long ~** lange; **What ~ is it?** Wie viel Uhr ist es?/Wie spät ist es?; **At what ~?** Um wie viel Uhr?; **~ line** die Zeittafel, -n
times mal; **[three] ~** [drei]mal
tip das Trinkgeld, -er
tired müde; **dead~** todmüde
to an; auf, in; nach; zu
today heute; **What day is it ~?** Welcher Tag ist heute?
toe der Zeh, -en
together zusammen
toilet die Toilette, -n; das WC, -s; das Klo, -s *(colloq.)*; **to go to the ~** auf die Toilette/aufs Klo gehen
toiletry der Toilettenartikel, -
tolerable erträglich
tolerant tolerant
tomato die Tomate, -n
tomorrow morgen; **~ morning** morgen früh; **~ afternoon** morgen Nachmittag; **~ evening** morgen Abend; **day after ~** übermorgen
tonight heute Abend
tongue die Zunge, -n
too zu; **me ~** ich auch; **~ little** zu wenig; **~ much** zu viel
tooth der Zahn, ¨-e
toothache die Zahnschmerzen *(pl.)*
toothbrush die Zahnbürste, -n
toothpaste die Zahnpasta
topic das Thema, *pl.* Themen
tour die Tour, -en; **~ guide** der Fremdenführer, -/die Fremdenführerin, -nen
tourism der Tourismus
tourist der Tourist [-en], -en/die Touristin, -nen; **~ office** das Fremdenverkehrsbüro, -s; der Verkehrsverein, -e
tower der Turm, ¨-e
town hall das Rathaus, ¨-er; **~ restaurant** der Ratskeller, -
traffic der Verkehr; **~ regulation** die Verkehrsregel, -n; **~ sign** das Verkehrsschild, -er; das Verkehrszeichen,-
train der Zug, ¨-e; die Bahn -en; **~ station** der Bahnhof, ¨-e; **main ~ station** der Hauptbahnhof, ¨-e; **~ track** die Schiene, -n; das Gleis, -e
transfer versetzen (hat versetzt); überweisen (hat überwiesen)
transformation der Wandel
translate übersetzen (hat übersetzt)
translator der Übersetzer, -/die Übersetzerin, -nen
transportation der Verkehr; **means of ~** das Verkehrsmittel, -
travel fahren (ist gefahren); reisen (ist gereist); **~ agency** das Reisebüro, -s; das Reiseunternehmen, -; **~ group leader** der Reiseleiter, -/die Reiseleiterin, -nen
traveller's check der Reisescheck, -s
treasure der Schatz, ¨-e
tree der Baum, ¨-e
treaty das Abkommen, -
trip die Reise, -n; die Fahrt, -en; die Tour, -en; **bike ~** die Radtour, -en
truck der Lastwagen, -; der LKW, -s
trunk der Kofferraum, ¨-e
true wahr; **that's (not) ~** das stimmt (nicht)
trust das Vertrauen
try versuchen (hat versucht); probieren (hat probiert); **to ~ on** an·probieren (hat anprobiert)
T-shirt das T-Shirt, -s
Tuesday der Dienstag
tunnel der Tunnel, -s
Turk der Türke [-n], -n/die Türkin, -nen
Turkish türkisch
Turkey die Türkei
turkey die Pute, -n
turn ab·biegen (ist abgebogen); **to ~ around** (sich) um·drehen (hat sich umgedreht); **to ~ in (a paper)** ab·geben (hat abgegeben); **to ~ on** an·drehen (hat angedreht); **to ~ off** aus·machen (hat ausgemacht)
TV das Fernsehen; **~ set** der Fernseher, -; **~ program** die Fernsehsendung, -en

umbrella der Regenschirm, -e; der Schirm, -e
unbelievable unglaublich
uncle der Onkel, -
under unter; **to keep ~ lock and key** unter Verschluss halten (hat gehalten)
underpaid unterbezahlt
understand verstehen (hat verstanden)

understanding das Verständnis
underway unterwegs
underwear die Unterwäsche
undress (sich) aus·ziehen (hat ausgezogen)
unemployed arbeitslos
unfortunately leider
unification die Vereinigung
unified vereinigt; vereint
union die Gewerkschaft, -en; **~ member** der Gewerkschafter, -/die Gewerkschafterin, -nen
university die Universität, -en; die Uni, -s; die Hochschule, -n; **to attend a ~** an/auf die Universität gehen; **at the ~** an/auf der Universität
unlikable unsympathisch
unlock auf·schließen (hat aufgeschlossen)
unsure unsicher
until bis; **~ now** bisher; **~ later** bis später; tschüss; bis dann; bis bald
up: ~ to bis zu; **~ front** da vorne
uprising der Aufstand, ¨-e
urgent dringend; dringlich
U.S.A. die USA *(pl.)*; die Vereinigten Staaten von Amerika; **from the ~** aus den USA
us uns *(acc. & dat.)*
use benutzen (hat benutzt); gebrauchen (hat gebraucht); **to ~ up** verbrauchen (hat verbraucht)
usual üblich
usually meistens; gewöhnlich
utensil das Gerät, -e

vacation der Urlaub; die Ferien *(pl.)*; **~ trip** die Ferienreise, -n; **on/during ~** in Urlaub/in den Ferien; **to go on ~** in Urlaub/in die Ferien fahren (ist gefahren); Urlaub nehmen (hat genommen); **~ home** die Ferienwohnung, -en; **ready for a ~** ferienreif
vacuum der Staubsauger, -; **to ~** staub·saugen (hat staubgesaugt)
valley das Tal, ¨-er
vegetable das Gemüse, -
vending machine der Automat [-en], -en
very sehr; ganz
veterinarian der Tierarzt, ¨-e/die Tierärztin, -nen
vice versa umgekehrt
vicinity die Nähe; **in the ~** in der Nähe
victor die Siegermacht, ¨-e
video das Video, -s; **~ camera** die Videokamera, -s; **~ game** das Videospiel, -e; **~ recorder** der Videorecorder, -; **~ store** der Videoverleih, -e
view die Aussicht, -en
village das Dorf, ¨-er
violence die Gewalt
visible sichtbar
visit der Besuch, -e; **to ~** besuchen (hat besucht)
volleyball der Volleyball
vomit sich übergeben (hat sich übergeben); kotzen (hat gekotzt) *(colloq.)*
vote die Wahl, -en; **to ~** wählen (hat gewählt)
voter der Wähler, -/die Wählerin, -nen

wage rate der Tarif, -e
wait die Wartezeit, -en; **to ~** warten (hat gewartet); **to ~ for** warten (hat gewartet) auf + *acc.*
waiting period die Wartezeit, -en
waiter/waitress der Kellner, -/die Kellnerin, -nen; **Oh,~!** Herr Ober! Fräulein! Frau Ober!
walk der Spaziergang, ¨-e; **to ~** laufen (ist gelaufen); **to take a ~** einen Spaziergang machen; **to go for a ~** spazieren gehen (ist spazieren gegangen)
wall die Wand, ¨-e; die Mauer, -n
wallet das Portmonee, -s
want (to) wollen (hat gewollt); Lust haben (hat gehaht)
war der Krieg, -e; **world ~** der Weltkrieg, -e; **cold ~** der Kalte Krieg
wardrobe der Kleiderschrank, ¨-e
warm warm
wash die Wäsche; **to ~** (sich) waschen (hat gewaschen); **to ~ dishes** ab·waschen (hat abgewaschen); Geschirr spülen (hat gespült)
washer: dish ~ der Tellerwäscher, -/die Tellwäscherin, -nen
washing machine die Waschmaschine, -n
waste verschwenden (hat verschwendet)
wastepaper basket der Papierkorb, ¨-e
watch die Armbanduhr, -en; **to ~** an·sehen (hat angesehen); schauen (hat geschaut); **to ~ TV** fern·sehen (hat ferngesehen); **to ~ out** auf·passen (hat aufgepasst)
water das Wasser; **~ sports** der Wassersport; **~ tower** der Wasserturm, ¨-e; **mineral ~** das Mineralwasser; **to ~ ski** Wasserski fahren (ist gefahren)
wavy wellig
way der Weg, -e; die Art; **on the ~** auf dem Weg; **this ~** so; auf diese Weise
weak schwach
wear tragen (hat getragen)
weather das Wetter; **~ map** die Wetterkarte, -n; **~ report** der Wetterbericht, -e
Wednesday der Mittwoch
week die Woche, -n
weekday der Wochentag, -e
weekend das Wochenende; **on the ~** am Wochenende
weightlifting das Gewichtheben
welcome das Willkommen; **you're ~** bitte (sehr)
well gut; wohl; **I'm not ~.** Ich fühle mich nicht wohl; ~ *(interjection)* na!; nun!; **~ now, oh ~** na
well-known bekannt
well-protected wohlbehütet
west der Westen
wet nass
what was; **~ kind (of), ~ a** was für (ein)
when wann; wenn; als
where wo; **~ (to)** wohin; **~ do you come from?** Woher kommst du?
whether ob
which welch(-er, -es, -e)
while die Weile, -n; **in a ~** in einer Weile; während
white weiß
who wer
whole ganz
whom wen *(acc.)*; wem *(dat.)*
whose wessen
why warum, wieso, weshalb; **that's ~** daher; deswegen; deshalb
wind der Wind
windy windig
window das Fenster, -
wine der Wein, -e
winter der Winter, -; **~ sports** der Wintersport
wish der Wunsch, ¨-e; **to ~** wünschen (hat gewünscht); **I ~ I had . . .** Ich wünschte/wollte, ich hätte ...
witch die Hexe, -n
with mit; **~ it** damit; **to live ~ a family** bei einer Familie wohnen
withdraw (money) ab·heben (hat abgehoben)
woman die Frau, -en
wonder das Wunder,-
wonderful wunderbar
woods der Wald, ¨-er
word das Wort, ¨-er

work die Arbeit, -en; **to ~** arbeiten (hat gearbeitet); **to ~ part time** jobben (hat gejobbt); **It doesn't ~.** Es geht nicht, Es funktioniert nicht; **to ~ out all right** klappen (hat geklappt); **~ experience** die Arbeitserfahrung, -en; **~ environment** das Arbeitsklima; **~ permit** die Arbeitserlaubnis; **~ place** der Arbeitsplatz, ¨-e; **~ quota** die Arbeitsnorm, -en
workbook das Arbeitsbuch, ¨-er
worker der Arbeiter, -/die Arbeiterin, -nen; der Arbeitnehmer, -/die Arbeitnehmerin, -nen
workroom das Arbeitszimmer, -
world die Welt, -en; **~ war** der Weltkrieg, -e
worry die Sorge, -n; **to ~ about** sich Sorgen machen (hat gemacht) um + *acc.*
worth der Wert; wert
worthwhile wert; **to be ~ it** sich lohnen (hat sich gelohnt)
would würde; **~ like** möchte
wound verwunden (hat verwundet)
wow Mensch!
write schreiben (hat geschrieben); **to ~ to** schreiben (hat geschrieben) an + *acc.;* **to ~ down** auf·schreiben (hat aufgeschrieben)
writer der Schriftsteller, -/die Schriftstellerin, -nen; der Autor, -en/die Autorin, -nen
wrong falsch; **What's ~?** Was ist los?; **What is ~ with you?** Was hast du?

xenophobia der Fremdenhass

year das Jahr, -e
yearly jährlich
yellow gelb
yes ja
yesterday gestern
yet noch; schon; **not ~** noch nicht
Yiddish das Jiddisch
you *(informal sing.)* du *(nom.);* dich *(acc.);* dir *(dat.); (formal sing. & pl.)* Sie *(nom. & acc.);* Ihnen *(dat.);* **~ guys** *(informal pl.)* ihr *(nom.);* euch *(acc. & dat.)*
young jung
your *(informal sing.)* dein; *(formal sing. & pl.)* Ihr; *(informal pl.)* euer
youth die Jugend; der/die Jugendliche *(noun decl. like adj.);* **~ hostel** die Jugendherberge, -n; **budget ~ hotel** das Jugendhotel, -s; **~ literature** die Jugendliteratur

zero die Null, -en
zip code die Postleitzahl, -en

Index

This index includes grammar topics, topics from the **Wissenswerte Vokabeln, Sprache im Alltag, Brennpunkt Kultur, Deutsch im Beruf,** and common communicative functions. References to student annotations are indicated as [SA].

Permissions and Credits

The authors and editors of ***Vorsprung*** would like to thank the following for their generous permission to use copyrighted material.

Texts

Deutsch im Beruf 1: p. 120: San Diego Convention and Visitors Bureau, for "San Diego: Auskunft über die Stadt auf Deutsch."

Kapitel 4: p. 148: Auszüge aus Broschüre "Sicherheitsinfo Nr. 8: Fahrrad fahren," herausgegeben im Auftrag des Bundesministeriums für Verkehr von der Bundesanstalt für Straßenwesen, October 1, 1990.

Kapitel 5: pp. 196–197: "Ein Freund, ein guter Freund ... das ist das Schönste, was es gibt," originally in *JUMA – Das Jugendmagazin* 4/91, pp. 22–23.

Kapitel 6: pp. 234–235: Birsen Kahraman, Hamburg, for "Am Kopierer," originally in *Hamburger Unizeitung*, April 15, 1993, p. 21.

Deutsch im Beruf 2: p. 260: Bundesanstalt für Arbeit (Hrsg.): *mach's richtig*. MEDIALOG, Gesellschaft für Medientechnik mbH + Co. KG Kommunikationssysteme, Mannheim, 1995, for "Berufswahl-Steckbrief: Was ist wichtig?"

Kapitel 7: p. 293: Dr. Bert Hentschel, Bertelsmann Club GmbH, for catalogue copy on *Schindlers Liste* and *Die Abrechnung*, originally in *Bertelsmann Club*, Spring 1994, p. 11.

Kapitel 8: pp. 335–336: *Der Spiegel* and Peter Ohm, Werner Bendix, and Lutz Harder, for "Welche Uni ist die Beste?" originally in *Spiegel Spezial* 3/1993, p. 38, p. 54 and p. 84.

Kapitel 9: p. 381: IZ – Informationszeitung der Berufsberatung, 4/93, Herausgeber: Bundesanstalt für Arbeit, for "Richtig bewerben: Vorstellungsgespräch," p.8.

Deutsch im Beruf 3: p. 408: Arbeitsamt, Hamburg, for Ihre Zukunft: Berufsberatung an der Uni, originally in *Studienführer: Informationen zum Studium in Hamburg*, © 1993; p. 410: MacDonald's, Hamburg, for "Ohne Moos, nichts los," originally in *Studienführer: Informationen zum Studium in Hamburg*, © 1993; p. 410: TPS Labs, München, & Schlösserverwaltung/Sachsen for want ads.

Kapitel 10: pp. 431–432: Text und Bild von Anny Hoffmann, aus "Der gestiefelte Kater" nach den Gebrüdern Grimm, © 1989. Pestalozzi-Verlag, Germany. ISBN 3-614-20810-9; pp. 437, 439, 441–444, 457–459: Kur- und Verkehrsverein Braunwald for "Braunwald: Ein Wintermärchen ... hoch über dem Alltag," and "Braunwald: Info Winter 1994/95."

Kapitel 11: pp. 494–495: Zeitbild-Verlag GmbH, Bonn & München, for the model time line "Unterrichtsprojekt Metropole Berlin," December 1990; pp. 506–508: Christine Nöstlinger, "Maikäfer flieg!" 1973: Weinheim and Basel, Beltz Verlag, Programm Beltz & Gelberg, Weinheim.

Kapitel 12: p. 539: *Neue Kronen Zeitung*, St. Peter-Straße 5, 9020 Klagenfurt, for "EU zieht neue Grenze: Das ändert sich beim Zoll," by Johann Palmisano, originally in *Neue Kronen Zeitung*, January 4, 1995, p. 14–15.

Deutsch im Beruf 4: p. 552: *Gewinn-Magazin*, 5/1995, Wailand & Waldstein GmbH, 1070 Wien, for "Big-Mac-Währungsindex", p. 14.

Photos

Kapitel 1: p. 1: Stuart Cohen; pp. 14 & 17: David R. Frazier Photolibrary; p. 20: Stuart Cohen; pp. 21 & 23 (top): David R. Frazier Photolibrary; p. 23 (bottom): Ulrike Welsch; p. 32 (both) dpa/ipol.

Kapitel 2: p. 39: David R. Frazier Photolibrary; p. 45: UPI/Bettmann.

Kapitel 3: p. 79: Stuart Cohen; p. 85: Ulrike Welsch; p. 96: David R. Frazier Photolibrary; p. 117 (left): Kathy Squires, (right): David R. Frazier Photolibrary.

Kapitel 4: p. 125: Stuart Cohen; pp. 140 & 150: David R. Frazier Photolibrary; p. 157: Stuart Cohen; p. 168: Ulrike Welsch.

Kapitel 5: p. 173: Ulrike Welsch; p. 180: Ulrike Welsch; p. 190: David R. Frazier Photolibrary; p. 191 (top): Kathy Squires; p. 191 (bottom) & p. 192: Ulrike Welsch; p. 199: David R. Frazier Photolibrary.

Kapitel 6: p. 215: H. Mark Weidman; p. 230 (left): Kathy Squires (right): Tom Lovik; pp. 237 & 253: Ulrike Welsch.

Kapitel 7: p. 265: David R. Frazier Photolibrary; p. 289: James/Sygma; p. 291: Sygma; p. 292: James/Sygma.

Kapitel 8: p. 313: David R. Frazier Photolibrary.

Kapitel 9: p. 361: David R. Frazier Photolibrary; p. 368: Kevin Galvin; p. 369: The Stock Market/ZEFA/Rossenbach; p. 377: Kevin Galvin; p. 383: Ulrike Welsch.

Kapitel 10: p. 415: dpa/ipol; p. 429: The Image Bank/Peter Ginter; p. 446: Kevin Galvin; p. 454: The Stock Market/ZEFA/Damm.

Kapitel 11: p. 469: The Image Works/Visum/Christian Thomas; p. 472: The Image Works/Visum/Rudi Meisel; p. 478 (left): dpa/ipol, (right): AP/Wide World; Stuart Cohen; p. 492: dpa/Photoreporters; p. 495: AP/Wide World; p. 515: Bisson/Sygma.

Kapitel 12: p. 521:dpa/ipol; p. 545: Deloche/Sygma; p. 546 (left): Erich Lessing/Art Resource/Gesellschaft der Musikfreunde, Wien, (right): The Stock Market/Bilderberg/Ernsting.

Illustrations

All illustrations by Tim Jones except pp. 57 (bottom) & 323 by Anna Veltfort.

Realia

Kapitel 1: p. 6: © 1996 KFS/Distr. Bull's; p. 8: *Quick*, 14 Mai 1992, Karl-Heinz Brecheis.

Kapitel 2: p. 46 top row left: Missouri Dept. of Natural Resources, Division of State Parks, (center): Vorarlberger Landesmuseum Bregen, (right): Historic Emigration Office, Tourismus-Zentrale Hamburg GmbH, (center row left): European Delicatessen & Restaurant, 402 N. Dixie Hwy., Lake Worth, FL 33460, (center): German-Texan Heritage Society, Austin, (right): courtesy Germanfest Committe, Fort Wayne, IN, (bottom row left): courtesy German-American Steuben Parade Committee, (center): courtesy Peter Buhrmann Productions, P.O. Box 31152, San Francisco, CA 94131, (right): courtesy New Glarus Wilhem Tell Festival Committee; p. 48: Brillenmacher Preiß GmbH, Bremen, Germany; p. 49: *Beim Analytiker* © Manfred von Papen, Fackelträger, Hannover; p. 66: Unicum Verlag, Bochum, Germany; p. 74: courtesy ActiLingua, Wien.

Kapitel 3: p. 80: Tourist-Service Mannheim; p. 97: INTERSPAR/SPAR Handels-AG; p. 98: Tourist Service Mannheim; p. 99 & 100: Fremdenverkehrsverband Neckarland-Schwaben; p. 99 (margin): Verlag *Heidelberg diese Woche*, Czernyring 30–32, D 69115 Heidelberg; p. 102(I): *Heidelberg City Revue '96;* p. 103: Verlag *Heidelberg diese Woche*, and Zum Seppl, Hauptstr.

213, 69117 Heidelberg, Rest. Kurpf. Museum, Tischer, unholtz, Schnitzelbank, Edm König & Bierkrug, Hauptstr. 147, Heidelberg; p. 104: Touristikverband Neckarland-Schwaben; p. 114: Verkehrsverein Heidelberg.

Deutsch im Beruf 1: p. 120: courtesy San Diego Convention & Visitors Bureau; p. 122 (top): Patentanwälte Abitz und Partner, München, (center): HERLITZ Internationale und Überseetransporte, München, (bottom): VOSSIUS & PARTNER, Patentanwälte, München; p. 123: courtesy VW, ADAC, Deutsche Bahn and BMW.

Kapitel 4: p. 126: Lauche & Maas, Alte Allee 28, D81245 München; p. 131: Goethe Institute & DAAD; p. 138: Deutsche Bundespost; p. 140: courtesy SFB, Berlin; p. 146: © *Rolling Stone;* German Edition; p. 147: Stadt Auto Bremen Car Sharing GmbH, Feldstrasse 13b, D28203 Bremen; pp. 148, 151 & 153: Bundesminister für Verkehr/Bundesanstalt für Straßenwesen; p. 156: Verkehrsamt Frankfurt am Main; p. 158: Deutsche Bahn; 167: Flughafen Frankfurt/Main AG; p. 171: Stiftung Automuseum Wolfsburg.

Kapitel 5: p. 175 (left): Tourismus-Zentrale Hamburg; p. 175 (right) & p. 181: Universität Hamburg; p. 187: Tourismus Zentrale Hamburg; p. 192: *Frankfurter Allgemeine Zeitung;* p. 196–197: courtesy *JUMA.*

Kapitel 6: p. 222: Eberhard-Karls-Universität Tübingen; p. 223: *Dschungelbuch,* Studentenwerk Uni Tübingen, Zeichnung Sepp Buchegger, Tübingen; pp. 229 & 231: *Tübingen hat viele Seiten,* Handel- und Gewerbeverein Tübingen; p. 242: © E. Rauschenbach, Berlin; p. 255: Touristikverband Winklern-Mörschach.

Deutsch im Beruf 2: p. 262: courtesy McDonald's, Germany.

Kapitel 7: p. 266: courtesy Commerzbank Tübingen, pp. 269 & 270: Tübinger Stadtbus; p. 275: cartoon by Fritz Wolf, courtesy *Schöner Wohnen;* p. 278 (left): Breisach-Info, (right): Tourist-Kongress und Saalbau GmbH Neustadt/Weinstraße; p. 281: Ihr Platz, Osnabrück; p. 282 (left): Mercedes-Benz Museum, (center): Carl-Zeiss-Planetarium, (right): Amt für Touristik, Stuttgart; p. 283: Abdruck der Karte mit Genehmigung des Stadtmessungsamts Stuttgart Nr. H.35; pp. 293 & 294: Bertelsmann Club GmbH; p. 298: Tourismus-Zentrale Hamburg; 309: courtesy Osiandersche Buchhandlung, Tübingen.

Kapitel 8: p. 319: Eberhard-Karls-Universität Tübingen Namens- und Vorlesungsverzeichnis Wintersemester 1993/4; p. 320: courtesy Lätta; pp. 335, 336 & 339: courtesy *Der Spiegel;* originally in *Spiegel Spezial* 3/1993; p. 345: Tranparente Landeskunde, 5th edition, by Friedrich Bubner, Bonn-Bad Godesberg: Inter Nationes, 1990. p. 347: Anzeige mit Titel Young Miss 3/93, BRIGITTE, Gruner & Jahr, Hamburg; p. 349: Eberhard-Karls-Universität Tübingen; p. 350: courtesy Schwartau Mövenpick.

Kapitel 9: p. 362: courtesy Karstadt AG, Hamburg; p. 375 (top): courtesy Esso, (bottom): Deutsche Bahn; p. 376: Toshiba Europe GmbH; p. 378: taz, *die tageszeitung* (Berlin); p. 381: Illustration von Thomas Marutschke; p. 388: Michael Gösler, Hamburg; p. 393: Kaltenberger Ritterturnier, Tierpark Hellabrunn, Salzburger Mozart-Serenaden, Verkehrverein Bremen, Thüringer Zoopark Erfurt, Bremer Freimarkt-Ausschuß, Landeshauptstadt Stuttgart, Magdeburger Rathaus; p. 394: © Grundig; p. 396: courtesy Pro7; p. 398: *Deutschland – Zeitschrift für Politik. Kultur, Wirtschaft und Wissenschaft,* Nr. 3, 12/93.

Deutsch im Beruf 3: p. 410 (top): courtesy McDonald's, Germany.

Kapitel 10: p. 417: Ekko Busch/Süddeutsche Zeitung; p. 419–421 & p. 449: courtesy Margret Rettich, Vordorf, for illustrations originally published in WUNDER-Buch Nr. 69, *Aschenputtel* (Rechte beim Illustrator); p. 424: from *Zweihundert Bildnisse und Lebensabrisse berühmter deutscher Männer,* Leipzig, Verlag von Georg Wigand, 1870; p. 432: Bild von Anny Hoffmann, aus "Der gestiefelte Kater" nach den Gebrüdern Grimm, © 1989, Pestalozzi-Verlag, Deutschland; p. 433: Kur- und Verkehrsverein Braunwald; p. 436: Stadt Köln; pp. 437, 439, 441–4, 457–9: Kur- und Verkehrsverein Braunwald.

Kapitel 11: p. 470: courtesy Berolina; p. 481: © E. Rauschenbach, Berlin; p. 489: courtesy Maria Burg, originally in *Das neue Blatt,* Nr. 21, 18. Mai 1994; pp. 502–3: Presse- und Informationsamt der Bundesregierung, Bonn; p. 514: Volkskammer der DDR – Sekretariat, 1987; p. 516 (left): Touristikverband Neckarland-Schwaben, (center): Arbeitsgemeinschaft der Fremdenverkehrsverbände am Rhein, Bonn, (right): Wiener Fremdenverkehrsverband.

Kapitel 12: p. 522: Deutscher Bundestag/Universität Bonn; p. 529: Presse- und Informationsamt der Bundesregierung; p. 539: © "Kärntner Krone"/ Uta Rosjek-Wiedergut; pp. 542–3: Bundeskanzleramt, Bundespressedienst, Wien; p. 550: Globus Kartendienst GmbH.

Deutsch im Beruf 4: pp. 560–561: NEWS-Magazin, 10. Aug. 1995, Nr. 32, p. 94; p. 563: courtesy McDonald's, Germany; p. 564: Gewinn-Magazin, 5/95, Weiland & Waldstein GmbH, 1070 Wien.

HMK

- Story 506-8
- Geschichte Berlins 494-5
- QUIZ on Stories + words
- exc. 37-40 (pattern)